BASIC WRITINGS OF
NIETZSCHE

Basic Writings of
Nietzsche

Introduction by Peter Gay

Translated and Edited
by Walter Kaufmann

THE MODERN LIBRARY

NEW YORK

2000 Modern Library Edition

Grateful acknowledgment is made to the following for permission
to reprint previously published material:
Columbia University Press and The Athlone Press Limited: Excerpt from *Nietzsche and
Philosophy,* by Gilles Deleuze. Copyright © 1983 by Columbia University Press. Rights
outside of the United States are controlled by The Athlone Press Limited, London.
Reprinted by permission of Columbia University Press and The Athlone Press Limited.
HarperCollins Publishers, Inc.: Excerpt from *Nietzsche, Volume IV: Nihilism,* by Martin
Heidegger, translated by Frank A. Capuzzi. English translation copyright © 1982 by
Harper & Row, Publishers, Inc. Notes and analysis copyright © 1982 by David Farrell
Krell. Reprinted by permission of HarperCollins Publishers, Inc.
Alfred A. Knopf, a division of Random House, Inc.: Excerpt from *The Rebel,* by Albert
Camus, translated by Anthony Bower. Copyright © 1956 by Alfred A. Knopf, Inc.
Reprinted by permission of Alfred A. Knopf, a division of Random House, Inc.

Library of Congress Cataloging-in-Publication Data
Nietzsche, Friedrich Wilhelm, 1844–1900.
[Selections. English. 2000]
Basic writings of Nietzsche / introduction by Peter Gay ;
translated and edited by Walter Kaufmann.
p.   cm.
Includes index.
ISBN 0-679-78339-3
1. Philosophy. I. Kaufmann, Walter Arnold. II. Title.
B3312.E5 K3 2000
193—dc21   00-064578

Modern Library website address: www.modernlibrary.com

Printed in the United States of America

FRIEDRICH NIETZSCHE

Friedrich Nietzsche was born in 1844 in Röcken (Saxony), Germany. He studied philology at the universities of Bonn and Leipzig, and in 1869 was appointed to the chair of classical philology at the University of Basel, Switzerland. Ill health led him to resign his professorship ten years later. His works include *The Birth of Tragedy, Thus Spoke Zarathustra, Beyond Good and Evil, On the Genealogy of Morals, The Case of Wagner, Twilight of the Idols, The Antichrist, Nietzsche contra Wagner,* and *Ecce Homo.* He died in 1900. *The Will to Power,* a selection from his notebooks, was published posthumously.

WALTER KAUFMANN

Walter Kaufmann was born in Freiburg, Germany, in 1921, came to the United States in 1939, and studied at Williams College and Harvard University. In 1947 he joined the faculty of Princeton University, where he became a professor of philosophy. He held many visiting professorships, including Fulbright grants at Heidelberg and Jerusalem. His books include *Critique of Religion and Philosophy, From Shakespeare to Existentialism, The Faith of a Heretic, Cain and Other Poems, Hegel, Tragedy and Philosophy,* and *Nietzsche: Philosopher, Psychologist, Antichrist,* as well as verse translations of Goethe's *Faust* and *Twenty German Poets.* He translated all of the books by Nietzsche listed in the biographical note above. He died in 1980.

Contents

INTRODUCTION BY PETER GAY   ix

A NOTE ON THIS EDITION   xvii

INTRODUCTION BY THE EDITOR   xix

ACKNOWLEDGMENTS   xxv

BASIC WRITINGS OF NIETZSCHE

     THE BIRTH OF TRAGEDY   1

     Seventy-Five Aphorisms from Five Volumes   145

     BEYOND GOOD AND EVIL   179

     ON THE GENEALOGY OF MORALS   437

     THE CASE OF WAGNER   601

     ECCE HOMO   655

INDICES   803

COMMENTARY   847

READING GROUP GUIDE   861

Introduction

PETER GAY

Ever since Nietzsche went insane, and silent, in 1889, as his fame was beginning to spread, his ideas have been most things to most men. Literally—for on the subject of women, interpretations of his views can hardly differ very much: he was an incurable misogynist. Nor could devout Christians derive any comfort from his writings, which are centrally preoccupied with a destructive analysis of Christianity, its birth, its triumph, its unfortunate longevity. As for principled democrats, they too cannot find much to please them in his work: whatever conclusion one may reach in the end about Nietzsche's political thinking, it calls for the distinct separation of an elite and the masses.

But existentialists and nihilists, chauvinists and cosmopolitans, anti-Semites and philo-Semites, Francophiles and professional Teutons, Wagnerites and Brahmsians, nature worshipers and pragmatists, followers of Freud and his critics, have been struggling over his legacy for a century and more. They cannot all be right; in fact, most of them are wrong, dining off a few scraps that Nietzsche had thrown them in a careless mood. But this has not stopped them from arguing.

Yet even in the less than angrily controversial domains, Nietzsche's work has been at the mercy of ideologists of all stripes. What is Nietzsche's evidence for women's presumed inferiority? What is the reason for his anti-Christian bent? What kind of elite is he calling for? Beyond that, when it comes to the theory of knowledge, is he an absolute skeptic? Do his generalizations about nations support racism? Why does he do his utmost to distance himself from the Germany of his time? And what of Wagner, first his friend and then his enemy? The questions pile up and there are all too many answers canceling each other out.

There is of course nothing new or unexpected concerning battles about the meaning of a thinker's work. One recalls Plato, Machiavelli, Hobbes, Rousseau, Hegel, and the debates that their "real" message has generated across the centuries. But Nietzsche's thought has been particularly susceptible to often envenomed controversies, generating incompatible claims about the influence of that thought not only on recent philosophy, but also, and more portentously, on recent politics.

Why? As readers of this volume can readily discover for themselves, Nietzsche was a superb stylist. Writing as trenchantly as he did, he was the antithesis of the traditional German professor, with his heavy vocabulary, serpentine sentences, and convoluted reasoning. But, paradoxical as it may sound, Nietzsche wrote too well for his own good. He coined memorable aphorisms and seductive locutions that have been used against him—by and large unfairly. Even if (indeed, especially if) we do not know much about Nietzsche, we are likely to remember his terms: "the blond beast," which can easily be taken as a sample of Aryan megalomania, or the "Übermensch," usually translated as "Superman," thus awakening images of Clark Kent donning his cape. And what of his heartless, condescending observation, "Everything about woman has a solution: it is called pregnancy"? Though such Nietzschean views leave an unpleasant aftertaste, most can be satisfactorily clarified by the context and the dominant style of thinking that pervades his thought. But this means that one can judge Nietzsche only after reading him, not before.

The fact is that many philosophers in many countries now read him, and with care; in all probability, Nietzsche is the most studied German thinker in English-, French-, and Italian-speaking cultures. His ability to turn accepted moral certitudes on their head, his skeptical questioning of confident realists who see the outside world as easily accessible to the investigator, and his astonishing psychological insights that have made it tempting to see Freud as his disciple (which he was not)—all this, as we have seen, makes him appealing to minds attached to the most varied systems. In some quarters, indeed, among some literary critics, he has become something of a fad. Postmodernists intent on showing that there is no stable world out there, and that everything is a "social construct," have taken comfort from a remark of Nietzsche's, "Truths are a useless fiction." Well, of course one can easily find statements in Nietzsche that uphold the opposite, or generate doubts about this statement. A faithful (but not slavish) reader of Nietzsche must acknowledge that one reason why there is so much debate about Nietzsche's meaning is that he occasionally contradicts himself. Hence the way to defend a certain position on Nietzsche is not to rely on a single aphorism, but to penetrate to the central significance of the texts in which the passage is embedded.

There is another, a historical, reason why Nietzsche has aroused so much rancor across the twentieth century, especially after the outbreak of the First World War: his presumed advocacy of a brutal Teutonic philosophy of life that explained the alleged conduct of the German armies during the war.

After January 30, 1933, this reproach grew even fiercer. On that day, Hitler was appointed chancellor of Germany, and with that, the charge that Nietzsche had inspired much of the Nazis' murderous ideology became widespread and seemed utterly plausible. In Germany itself, after that fateful date, servile commentators, knowing what would please Joseph Goebbels, did their utmost to claim Nietzsche for Hitler's "movement." This was not so easily done; it necessitated explaining away the passages in Nietzsche that could not possibly be reconciled with Hitlerian dogma, but which were present, the authors had to admit, in Nietzsche's works. One way of dealing with this dilemma was to falsify his texts, or to take some of Nietzsche's comments out of context. Thus, his infrequent anti-Jewish remarks, normally surrounded by declarations of admiration for the Jews, could be stripped of this praise, so that they could misdescribe Nietzsche's philo-Semitism as anti-Semitism. The fact is that it was particularly the German anti-Semites of his own time that Nietzsche most despised. In the United States, a not dissimilar view—Nietzsche the prophet of the Third Reich—though of course less infected with propaganda, carried the day. The one or two more responsible interpreters who knew their Nietzsche better than this were swamped in the hostile consensus.

One influential interpretation, which declared Nietzsche to be half a Nazi, was Crane Brinton's *Nietzsche,* published in 1941. A highly respected historian at Harvard University, Brinton was an accessible essayist whose weighty opinions seemed to confirm what more casual writers and readers had long held against Nietzsche. Then, nine years after, a philosopher at Princeton University, Walter A. Kaufmann, published *Nietzsche: Philosopher, Psychologist, Antichrist,* and Nietzsche scholarship was never the same again.

Polemics about philosophers rarely reach a wider audience, but the academic world and to some extent even the interested general public read Kaufmann's intellectual biography with admiration and shame— admiration for the author's powerful defense of Nietzsche and his effective work of demolishing legends about him; shame for their own hasty and ill-informed verdicts on a thinker who apparently deserved their close and sympathetic attention far more than they had believed possible. It is safe to say that in the course of the twentieth century no American academic study has had a wider, and more fully deserved, impact than Kaufmann's *Nietzsche.*

Kaufmann was nothing if not thorough. He exposed in detail the machinations of Nietzsche's sister Elisabeth to manipulate her brother's texts, and to enlist him in the very causes that he had consistently denounced. Her crude prejudices, including a heavy dose of anti-Semitism, had nothing in common with her brother's philosophy. Since she controlled his papers, she could publish from his vast pile of notes what she chose, and carpenter together materials that did not belong together or that he had discarded. For eleven years, until Nietzsche's death in 1900, and for years thereafter, she held a virtual monopoly on interpreting her brother to the world, and other commentators on Nietzsche's thought more or less helplessly followed her deceptive lead. What Kaufmann calls "the Nietzsche legend" owes more to her than to any other commentator.

Her work as her brother's editor, then, made the "real" Nietzsche virtually disappear from view. Readers in the English-speaking world who had no German faced an additional obstacle: the translations. In *Nietzsche,* Kaufmann spends no time giving the gruesome details, but he left no doubt that all the translations in the book were his in part because, he writes in the preface, "[t]he purpose of the quotations was often to establish new interpretations . . ." (p. ix). And he faced the consequences of his critical view toward existing translations: in order to enable English-speaking readers to confront Nietzsche as authentically as any translation can make it, Kaufmann, after publishing *Nietzsche* (a book that went into several editions), set about rendering Nietzsche's main writings into English. The reader of *Basic Writings of Nietzsche* is the beneficiary of Kaufmann's diligence: he has translated every text in this volume.

Friedrich Nietzsche's life was a dramatic one, but all his drama was interior. He was born in 1844, the son of a Lutheran pastor and a devout hausfrau, and proved a prodigy. After studying at the universities of

Bonn and Leipzig, in 1869 he was appointed, at the ripe age of twenty-four, to the chair of classical philology at Basel. Among his acquaintances was the great scholar Jakob Burckhardt, the historian who put the Italian Renaissance on the map. It was there that he wrote his first book, *The Birth of Tragedy* (1872), an original, highly suggestive analysis of tragedy and of ancient Greek culture as a tense struggle between liberated Dionysian impulses (whose prestige Nietzsche was intent on restoring) and controlled Apollonian reason. In its later chapters, the book threw a bridge between antiquity and his own times by extravagantly praising Richard Wagner, whose friend he had become. His next widely read work, *Untimely Meditations* (1873–76), a collection of four lengthy essays dealing with such subjects as Schopenhauer, Wagner, and the writing of history, displayed Nietzsche's interest in current affairs and his delight in polemics. The "Untimely" in the title of this collection must be read to mean only that its author stood ready to confront his times with some unconventional views.

Plainly, the philologist and lover of music was turning into a cultural commentator, an unrelenting critic of the modern bourgeoisie, of religion and moral philosophy as then practiced, and of the German Empire, founded in 1871, the unremitting target of his sarcasm and contempt. He took pride in calling himself a good European. His admiration for Wagner, that all-too-German composer and virulent anti-Semite, waned until his animosity became marked, principled, and public. Readers of this volume can get a good account of the grounds for this hostility in "The Case of Wagner" and in Walter Kaufmann's introduction (which, like all his other introductions in this volume, is outspoken and authoritative).

In 1879, intermittently troubled by ill health including almost intolerable headaches, Nietzsche resigned his professorship and sought relief in the Swiss mountains (the little village of Sils Maria) and Italian cities like Turin—in vain. It was by and large a lonely life, his solitude broken only by occasional visits by a few—a very few—loyal disciples. But for a decade, he produced his most enduring books in this hermitlike existence. Two among these crucial texts appear in this volume, in full: *Beyond Good and Evil* (1886) and *The Genealogy of Morals* (1887), and repay the closest attention.

For the most part his writings are cast in chains of brilliant aphorisms or connected essays. He pursued his quarrel with Christianity and conventional morality, his analysis of the aristocrats of life and the crowd man, his thoughts on human knowledge and human destiny. He did not complete a philosophical system; he had intended to write a synthesis of his thinking and diligently took notes for what he wanted to call "The Will to Power." But he never did, and what his sister brought out after his death under this title had neither the form, nor the intellectual argument, he had wanted to give it. Still, the enterprise he managed to stamp with his unique way of thinking was one of stupendous daring and unending interest even for the reader who in the end disagrees with Nietzsche. In 1888, the great Danish critic Georg Brandes gave Nietzsche his first general recognition in a series of lectures. And then, in January 1889, Nietzsche went mad and could no longer defend himself against the distortions by his sister and like-minded ideologues.

Yet now, thanks in considerable part to the expositions and the translations by Walter Kaufmann, of which generous samples appear in this volume, and to the work he inspired over the years, it is possible to see Nietzsche plain. As he put it a little pathetically in the intellectual autobiography he wrote shortly before his breakdown, *Ecce Homo,* a book eminently worth reading: *"Hear me! For I am such and such a person. Above all, do not mistake me for someone else."*

———————

PETER GAY is Sterling Professor Emeritus of History at Yale University and the director of the Center for Writers and Scholars at the New York Public Library. His works include *The Enlightenment* and, most recently, *Mozart* (Penguin Lives).

A Note on This Edition

This volume contains five of Nietzsche's major works, complete, as well as seventy-five aphorisms from his five aphoristic books, selections from his correspondence about *The Case of Wagner,* and variants from Nietzsche's drafts for *Ecce Homo.* I have also furnished footnote commentaries on all of this material, and have contributed introductions and indices.

All footnotes are mine, except three in *The Case of Wagner,* which are clearly identified: these are the only footnotes Nietzsche himself included in any of his books.

The translations were made especially for this volume. I have used Clifton Fadiman's early translation of *The Birth of Tragedy,* done when he was a graduate student, as a basis for some parts of my new version. But even where I did not start from scratch, I have compared every sentence with the original, and my revisions are so extensive that the new version is probably more different from his than most Nietzsche translations—including Fadiman's—are from those that preceded them. And in large part I did work from scratch. I have made extensive use of a draft translation of *On the Genealogy of Morals,* furnished me by R. J. Hollingdale; but I alone bear the responsibility for the final version. The other translations, as well as the commentaries, involved no collaboration.

In the original German, almost every numbered section constitutes a single paragraph. Nietzsche used dashes and three dots to indicate breaks. I have largely dispensed with these devices and begun new paragraphs wherever that seemed helpful.

W.K.

Introduction by the Editor

Nietzsche is one of the few philosophers since Plato whom large numbers of intelligent people read for pleasure. Philosophers of that sort are mostly French and rarely taken very seriously by twentieth-century philosophy professors. The only French philosopher whom professional philosophers generally accord highest honors is Descartes. Montaigne and Pascal, Voltaire and Rousseau, Bergson and Sartre do not enjoy their greatest vogue among philosophers, and of these only Rousseau has had any considerable influence on the history of philosophy (through Kant and Hegel). One may actually be led to wonder whether in philosophy there is an inverse proportion between profundity and importance on the one hand, and clarity and excellence of style on the other. If Plato seems to prove that this need not be so, many twentieth-century philosophers would be quick to counter that, *philosophically,* Plato's early and more literary dialogues are less important than his later dialogues, especially where they stump even professionals. And in Kant's case it is plain that his worst-written book, the *Critique of Pure Reason,* is his greatest work.

Where does this leave Nietzsche? At first glance it would seem in the company of Montaigne, Pascal, and Voltaire. But there is much more philosophy in his writings than in theirs, and his influence—also on philosophy professors—far exceeds theirs. A surprising number of German professors of philosophy have written books on him ever since he died in 1900, and hardly any German philosopher of note since that time has escaped the impact of Nietzsche's thought. To single out at least a few of them: Hans Vaihinger and Georg Simmel, Nicolai Hartmann and Karl Jaspers. Indeed, the only outstanding exception was Edmund Husserl; and his most renowned followers—Max Scheler and Martin Heidegger—changed their orientation drastically after coming under Nietzsche's influence. This is also true of Jean-Paul Sartre. Indeed, one of Sartre's best-known literary works can be shown to embody Nietzsche's ideas: the ethic of *The Flies* differs sharply from Sartre's own *Being and Nothingness,* finished at the same time, and from his famous lecture,

Existentialism Is a Humanism, but contains dozens of echoes of Nietzsche's writings, and the central motifs of the play are Nietzschean.[1]

Perhaps Nietzsche's influence on *literature* is even more striking than his impact on twentieth-century philosophy. Besides Sartre, one may think of Camus, Gide, and Malraux; of Thomas Mann and Hermann Hesse; and among German poets, of Rilke and Stefan George, Christian Morgenstern and Gottfried Benn.[2] His influence on Shaw, Yeats, and Joyce, and on Eugene O'Neill and other major American writers deserves more study than it has yet received.

Nietzsche's anticipations of and influence on various psychological theories are no less remarkable. In section 142 of *The Dawn* he anticipated the so-called James-Lange theory of the emotions; again and again he pioneered what Jaspers later called, in the title of his first major philosophical work, *Psychologie der Weltanschauungen* (psychology of world views); and Sigmund Freud remarked in an autobiographical sketch that Nietzsche's "premonitions and insights often agree in the most amazing manner with the laborious results of psychoanalysis."[3] Alfred Adler's modification of Freud's theories, which in turn profoundly influenced Sartre,[4] is even closer to Nietzsche's psychology of the will to power than Freudianism.

Freud also "several times said of Nietzsche that he had a more penetrating knowledge of himself than any other man who ever lived or was ever likely to live."[5] This is surely an extraordinary compliment from the founder of psychoanalysis whose life's work it had been to develop techniques to advance man's knowledge of himself. It may well

---

[1]See Walter Kaufmann, "Nietzsche Between Homer and Sartre: Five Treatments of the Orestes Story," in *Revue Internationale de Philosophie,* Numéro 67 (1964), pp. 50–73, esp. pp. 65 ff.; also Kaufmann, *Tragedy and Philosophy* (1968), section 51.

[2]See R. A. Nicholls, *Nietzsche in the Early Work of Thomas Mann* (1955). For the poets, see *Twenty German Poets,* ed. Walter Kaufmann, The Modern Library (1963); also Chapters 12 and 13 in Kaufmann, *From Shakespeare to Existentialism* (1959).

[3]*Selbstdarstellung; Gesammelte Werke,* XIV, 86.

[4]See, e.g., P. Rom and H. L. Ansbacher, "An Adlerian Case or a Character by Sartre," *Journal of Individual Psychology,* XXI (May 1965).

[5]Ernest Jones, *The Life and Work of Sigmund Freud,* II (1955), 344.

have been too generous. But it contrasts pleasantly with the occasional condescension of would-be psychologists who claim to have figured out the inner workings of "poor" Nietzsche's mind. And Freud was certainly right in suggesting that Nietzsche is of extraordinary interest not only as a philosopher and writer but also as a psychologist and a human being.

His influence extends much further than suggested so far. In the preface to *The Decline of the West*, Spengler said that he owed "everything" to Goethe and Nietzsche. Paul Tillich has frequently paid tribute to Nietzsche's influence on his own thought, actually hailing Marx, Nietzsche, and Freud as the greatest modern "Protestants." Martin Buber was eighty-five when he revealed in print that at age seventeen—that is, in 1895—he was "so taken by" *Thus Spoke Zarathustra* "that I decided to translate it into Polish and had even translated the first part. I had just gone to the second part when I received the letter of a known Polish author who likewise had translated several sections of the book and proposed to me that we do the work in common. I preferred renouncing in his favor."[6]

The full story of Nietzsche's influence has never been told and cannot be told yet. Buber's remark was not published until 1963; a letter in which Freud said of Nietzsche, "In my youth he signified a nobility which I could not attain," was published posthumously.[7] No doubt, many relevant documents will appear in years to come. What is called for in this introduction is merely an attempt to forestall snap judgments about Nietzsche.

Shallow judgments frequently take one of three forms. Either one knows all about Nietzsche: he was the man who said, or claimed, or believed this or that. Or one knows how to label Nietzsche as, say, an irrationalist metaphysician, or an evolutionist in ethics, or an existentialist. Worst of all, people who have never read a single one of his books from beginning to end "knew" at one time that he was the mind that had

---

[6] *The Philosophy of Martin Buber,* eds. Paul Arthur Schilpp and Maurice Friedman (1967), p. 13. In Buber's "Autobiographical Fragments" only one brief section (#8) is devoted to "Philosophers," and Buber singles out only two men: Kant and Nietzsche. (The German edition of *Martin Buber* appeared in 1963.)

[7] Jones, *op. cit.,* III, 460.

caused World War I, and a generation later that he was a Nazi philosopher. Regarding this last notion, suffice it here to say that all serious interpreters of Nietzsche, no matter how much they may disagree on other
points, agree that this absurdity can be supported only by either rank ignorance of his works (common at one time in the English-speaking
world) or an incredible lack of intellectual integrity (common to a few
Nazi hacks). In fact, no other philosopher since Plato and Aristotle, with
the exception of Kant and Hegel, has influenced so many widely different thinkers and writers so profoundly.

There are no signs that interest in Nietzsche is flagging. He is more
widely read and studied than ever; only the perspectives keep changing.
Once it was the fashion to link him with Darwin and evolutionary
thought, but his reputation did not pass with this fashion, and it actually
gained when more and more writers came to realize the inadequacy of
such an interpretation. The same goes for later vogues. What gradually
becomes more and more obvious is the unexampled richness of Nietzsche's thought.

Nietzsche was not a one-book man. Nor are there two or three books
that are obviously his best and most important. Born in 1844, Nietzsche
published his first book, *The Birth of Tragedy,* in 1872.[8] He followed it
with four shorter essays which he called "Untimely Meditations"; in the
English translation they were called *Thoughts Out of Season*—as if they
were collections of aphorisms, which they are not, not even in appearance. Nietzsche here became a critic of his time—the period after the
Franco-Prussian War of 1870–71, the rise of the new German Empire, the
age of Bismarck. Instead of joining in the growing self-satisfaction of his
people, Nietzsche developed into their severest critic.

Then came the break with Richard Wagner, the resignation from
the University of Basel, where he had been a professor of classical
philology from 1869 to 1879, and the publication of the three volumes of
Human, All-Too-Human, followed by *The Dawn* and *The Gay Science.*[9]
In these books Nietzsche turned against the romanticism of his first pe-

---

[8]The book is included in the present volume, complete, and discussed in the editor's Introduction to the translation.

[9]All are represented in this volume by selected aphorisms.

riod, consciously imitated the French aphorists of the Enlightenment, and became, in his own phrase, a Good European.

Had Nietzsche died then, at thirty-seven, he would be remembered as one of the greatest masters of German prose and a thinker comparable to Montaigne and Pascal. He would still be cited as proof that the German language can be used to write lucidly, penetratingly, wittily, and beautifully about topics on which German professors, from Kant down to Heidegger, have written without a trace of wit or beauty. But he would not be a world-historical figure; his influence would be nothing like what it has been—it would be as if Shakespeare had died at thirty-seven, in 1601. The author of *Romeo and Juliet, Richard II* and *III, The Merchant of Venice, Midsummer Night's Dream,* and *Henry IV* would be certain of a place of honor, but without his ten greatest works, all written during the next ten years, he would not have been what Shakespeare has been to millions since.

Nietzsche came into his own during the last six years of his creative life. Between the winter of 1882–83 and the end of 1888 he completed eight books. None of these are merely collections of aphorisms that can easily be represented by excerpts; all eight should be read in their entirety, with a regard for context and nuances. Four of these books were made available in a single volume, in entirely new translations, in 1954;[10] the other four are offered in the present volume, together with *The Birth of Tragedy* and some supplementary material. Thus all of Nietzsche's books are now available in two volumes, with the exception of the four meditations (of interest mainly as early works of the man who wrote the works included in these two volumes) and the aphoristic books (represented by sample in both volumes). Overlap has been avoided deliberately in order to make readily accessible as much as possible of Nietzsche's work.

The arrangement of the material in this volume is chronological, except for the Preface to *The Birth of Tragedy,* which was added by Nietzsche to the new edition of 1886 and is representative of his later style. All of the translations were made especially for the present volume

---

[10]*The Portable Nietzsche,* selected and translated, with an introduction, prefaces, and notes, by Walter Kaufmann.

and published for the first time in 1966–67. The editor has contributed a separate introduction for each of the five books included, as well as a detailed footnote commentary; and there are indices.

In sum, this edition is designed for serious study as well as enjoyment. Any dichotomy of these two would have been anathema to Nietzsche; and once the dichotomy is rejected, both "enjoyment" and "serious study" become infelicitous expressions. Nietzsche clearly wanted to be read with a delighted awareness of nuances of style and thought. He wanted readers whose sense of his exceptional versatility does not keep them from feeling that their own convictions and values are at stake and must be reconsidered in the light of what he says. There is no work of Nietzsche's that does not say to us, like Rilke's "Archaic Torso of Apollo":

"You must change your life."

Acknowledgments

But for Jason Epstein I should never have translated another Nietzsche book after 1954. He persevered; he left the choice of books and all particulars entirely up to me; and eventually I consented to go over some of the old versions to eliminate outright errors. This proved to be a thankless, endless, and all but impossible undertaking. Hence I gave up and made some more new translations. The commentaries, not anticipated, took form as the translations progressed.

Berenice Hoffman's editorial queries and suggestions have been unfailingly expert and gracious, and she deserves the readers' thanks as well as mine for her unstinting devotion to an often extremely difficult task.

Stephen Watson helped me with the indices, and Sonia Volochova made valuable additions to them. Mr. Watson, as a University Scholar at Princeton University, also called to my attention many points on which he thought students needed help, especially in *Beyond Good and Evil,* and aided me by reading proofs.

George Brakas read the page proofs of *Genealogy* and *Ecce Homo* and called to my attention many points that were not as clear as, I hope, they are now.

My wife, Hazel, kept up my spirits.

W.K.

The
BIRTH
of
TRAGEDY

FOR
My Apollinian Grandfather
Arnold Seligsohn (1854–1939)

AND

My Dionysian Grandmother
Julie Kaufmann (1857–1940)

CONTENTS

TRANSLATOR'S INTRODUCTION *3*
The Birth of Tragedy *15*

INDEX TO *The Birth of Tragedy* *803*

Translator's Introduction

This was Nietzsche's first book. It is far from being his best book, but the "Attempt at a Self-Criticism" that Nietzsche placed at the beginning of the "new edition" of 1886 is among the finest things he ever wrote. Perhaps no other great writer has written a comparable preface to one of his own works. Certainly this self-criticism is far superior to most of the criticisms others have directed against *The Birth of Tragedy*.

Before considering briefly the most famous critique of the book, it may be well to suggest something of its importance. Apart from the fact that this essay has been widely admired and is generally taken for one of Nietzsche's major works, its significance may be said to be threefold.

First of all, *The Birth of Tragedy* is, for all its faults, one of the most suggestive and influential studies of tragedy ever written. Perhaps only Aristotle's *Poetics* excels it. What other study of tragedy could one place beside it? Only Hegel's scattered remarks on the subject—many of them to be found only in posthumously published, and very badly edited, lectures. It is arguable that all three philosophers were wrong about the fourteen extant plays of Aeschylus and Sophocles and the nineteen of Euripides. But there is no denying that Aristotle, Hegel, and Nietzsche have vastly enriched the discussion of tragedy—probably more so than anyone else.

Secondly, *The Birth of Tragedy* does not deal only with tragedy—nor only with tragedy and with Wagner: it also deals with the relation of art to science, with the whole phenomenon of Greek civilization, and with the modern age. On all these subjects Nietzsche has much to say that is interesting, and a good deal that is exceptionally brilliant and penetrating.

Finally, some of the distressing faults of the essay are inseparable from its third claim to importance. Nietzsche was probably Germany's greatest prose stylist as well as one of the most profound and influential modern philosophers. But much of *The Birth of Tragedy* is badly overwritten and murky, as Nietzsche himself pointed out in section 3 of his "Attempt at a Self-Criticism"; and

occasionally a more extreme contrast to his later style—both literary and philosophical—would be difficult to imagine. To appreciate fully his later accomplishment, one should know his beginnings.
Indeed, it is one of Nietzsche's central points in the book that we
cannot do justice to the achievement of the Greeks and the triumph
of those powers of restraint that he calls Apollinian unless we first
behold the unrestrained Dionysian energies that the Greeks managed to harness. Similarly, his own later style, so remarkable for its
lucidity and aphoristic brevity, seems doubly impressive when we
compare it with the prose he himself found so embarrassing by
1886—prose that at times, particularly in the last ten sections,
reads like a parody of Wagner.

It is partly, though not only, on account of this third point
that the book should not be read by itself, without knowledge of
Nietzsche's later writings. And no other essay forms as perfect a
pair with it as the exceedingly brief and malicious *Case of Wagner,*
here offered in the same volume.

One corollary of what has just been said must be noted expressly. Confronted with the occasionally hyperromantic and turgid
prose of *The Birth of Tragedy,* it is tempting for the translator to
tone down what offends his own taste and to make the style leaner
and drier. But I have made a point of resisting this temptation. To
the extent to which one gives in to it, one makes nonsense of parts
of Nietzsche's brilliant "Attempt at a Self-Criticism," and one deprives those interested in Nietzsche's development of the opportunity to see for themselves to what extent Nietzsche changed. A
faithful translator should strive to let Rilke sound like Rilke, Heidegger like Heidegger, *The Case of Wagner* like *Der Fall Wagner*
—and *The Birth of Tragedy* like *Die Geburt der Tragödie.*

2

The first edition of *The Birth of Tragedy* was published in
1872, when Nietzsche was twenty-seven. It was immediately attacked by a young philologist, Ulrich Wilamowitz-Moellendorff, in
an unbridled polemical pamphlet entitled *Zukunftsphilologie!* [1]
Wagner's music was then called "music of the future," and Wilam-

---

[1] Berlin, Gebrüder Bornträger, 1872.

owitz tried to expose Nietzsche's "philology of the future"—a philology devoid of Greek quotations and footnotes.

Actually, there was much more to the attack than this. Nietzsche had been called to a chair at the University of Basel in Switzerland in 1869, and promoted to a full professorship of classical philology the following year—at the age of twenty-five. His doctoral degree had been conferred by the University of Leipzig without his having written a dissertation, on the basis of the call to Basel. That call, in turn, had been based on a superlative recommendation by Professor Ritschl, who had published articles by Nietzsche in the philological journal he edited and who had informed Basel that Nietzsche "is the first from whom I have ever accepted any contribution at all while he was still a student." The tenor of Ritschl's estimate of Nietzsche is perhaps best summed up in his sentence: "He will simply be able to do anything he wants to do." [2] Nietzsche's appointment to a chair at twenty-four was a sensation in professional circles, and it was to be expected that in his first book he would try to show the world of classical philology that his meteoric rise had been justified. Instead—he published *The Birth of Tragedy,* the kind of volume that could not be expected to appeal to the guild at any time, least of all to German professors in the new Empire, founded the year before.

Wilamowitz (1848–1931) was four years Nietzsche's junior, had just received his doctorate but not yet the title of professor—and the attack on Nietzsche was *his* first "book." He *did* try to establish the range and solidity of his scholarship by cataloguing Nietzsche's faults—and he saw nothing good at all in *The Birth.* His attack culminated in a charge of "ignorance and lack of love of truth" (p. 32).

Nietzsche's friend Erwin Rohde replied, still in 1872, in a pamphlet he called *Afterphilologie*[3] to signify a perversion of philology. Luther had liked the prefix *After,* which refers literally to the human posterior; Kant, too, had used it in his book on religion (1793); and Schopenhauer had spoken of *Afterphilosophie* when he attacked the philosophy of the universities. Rohde tried to show

---

[2] For Ritschl's letter, see *The Portable Nietzsche* (ed. and tr. by Walter Kaufmann), pp. 7–8.
[3] Leipzig, E. W. Fritzsch, 1872.

how many of the mistakes Wilamowitz claimed to have found in *The Birth* involved errors on *his* part. But Rohde also called Wilamowitz repeatedly "our Dr. phil." (our Ph.D.)—Rohde himself had just received the title of professor, though he was not yet a full professor—and "the pasquinader"; [4] and the level of his polemic was no higher than that of the attack he sought to meet. Two quotations may show this:

"I have emphasized this example because it may serve you as a sample at the outset of the manner in which throughout this pasquinade ignorance, the art of eager slander, and speculative reliance on the blind prejudices of the general reader are woven together into an attractive whole" (p. 10).

". . . really no more similar than an ape is to Heracles—indeed, even less; about as similar as our Dr. phil. von Wilamowitz is to the type of the 'Socratic man' whom our friend [Nietzsche] designates as the 'noblest opponent' of an artistic culture, although our Dr. phil. rather amusingly supposes that the designation fits him and the likes of him" (p. 12).

This last passage is important because it also illustrates Nietzsche's high esteem of the "Socratic man." *Afterphilologie,* to be sure, was written by Rohde, not Nietzsche; but the two men were very close friends at that time, and the point of Rohde's pamphlet was to expose misinterpretations of *The Birth of Tragedy*.

In 1873 Wilamowitz replied once more with a sequel to his *Zukunftsphilologie*.[5] The tenor of his reply may be gleaned from a remark near the end: "I should waste my time and energy on the inanities and wretchednesses of a couple of rotted brains?" (p. 23). Later, both Wilamowitz and Rohde made great reputations as classical philologists and never reprinted these early essays—presumably because they felt embarrassed by them.

Rohde, incidentally, had published a review of *The Birth of Tragedy* in the *Norddeutsche allgemeine Zeitung,* Sunday, May 26, 1872, before Wilamowitz's pamphlet appeared. And in 1882 he published a very critical and hostile review of Wilamowitz's *Antigonos von Karystos* (1881) in the *Litterarische Centralblatt.*

---

[4] Libeler.
[5] *Zukunftsphilologie: Zweites Stück* (Berlin, Gebrüder Bornträger, 1873).

Both of these reviews were reprinted in his *Kleine Schriften* (2 vols., 1901).

Nietzsche never referred to Wilamowitz in any of his works and went his own way without letting resentment eat into his soul. There are a few references to Wilamowitz in Nietzsche's letters of 1872 and 1873; but the most revealing passage is found in a letter to Rohde, March 19, 1874:

"To refute Dräseke's[6] contribution to the question of Wagner, of belly-shaking memory, Herr Bruno Meier[7] has written a lengthy and weighty treatise in which I am solemnly denounced as an 'enemy of our culture,' besides being represented as a wily deceiver among those who are deceived. He sent me his treatise personally, even furnishing his home address; I will send him the two essays of Wilamops. That's surely Christian beneficence toward one's enemies. For the delight of this dear Meier over Wilamops will surpass all words."

To explain Nietzsche's nickname for Wilamowitz: *Mops* is the German word for a pug, but the term was actually used to refer to a person with a disgruntled facial expression before it was transferred to the dog; it designates the quintessence of the comic, stupid, coarse, unfriendly, and inelegant. *Mopsig* means "boring"; *sich mopsen,* "to be bored." *Mops* seems to be related etymologically to the English "mope."

Nietzsche took Wilamowitz's attack very lightly; yet it has been claimed that Wilamowitz finished Nietzsche as a philologist, and even that Nietzsche retired in 1879, after only ten years as a professor, because the students stayed away as a result of Wilamowitz's polemics. In fact, the size of enrollments had nothing to do with Nietzsche's decision.

It may be of some interest to indicate what he taught and to note how few students he had all along. During his first year he gave the following courses (the number of students is indicated in

---

[6] Johannes Dräseke, "Beiträge zur Wagner-Frage" (contributions to the problem of Wagner), in *Musikalisches Wochenblatt,* IV (1873).

[7] Bruno Meyer (Nietzsche wrote "Meier"), "Beiträge zur Wagner-Frage: In eigener Sache" (in my cause), in *Deutsche Warte,* V, 641–73. Dräseke replied in *Musikalisches Wochenblatt,* V (1874), 403–05, 418–20, and 438–442, condemning Meyer's attack on Nietzsche.

each case in parentheses): Aeschylus' *Choephori* (6), Greek Lyric Poets (7), Latin Grammar (8). The next year: Sophocles' *Oedipus Rex* (11), Metrics (5), Hesiod's *Erga* (11). The third year: Introduction to the Study of Philology (9), Introduction to the Study of Plato's Dialogues (6), Introduction to Latin Epigraphy (9). In the summer of 1872, after the publication of *The Birth*, Nietzsche lectured on Pre-Platonic Philosophers (10) and Aeschylus *Choephori* (7); but that winter he had only two students in his Greek and Roman Rhetoric, and neither was a philologist. This drop in the number of students was surely due to Wilamowitz's first polemic. By the next summer, however, his lectures on the Pre-Platonic Philosophers drew eleven students; in 1876 the same course drew ten, and his lectures On Plato's Life and Doctrines nineteen. In 1878, finally, just before his retirement, he had more students than ever, though certainly not many: Hesiod's *Works and Days* (13), Plato's *Apology of Socrates* (6), Greek Lyrical Poets (13), Introduction to the Study of Plato (8). These data may give some idea of Nietzsche's career as a professor of classical philology, which was not exhausted by *The Birth of Tragedy*.

About the book opinions still differ, as they do about all of Nietzsche's works. F. M. Cornford, one of the leading British classicists of the first half of the twentieth century, known to generations of students for his translations of many Platonic dialogues and his remarkable commentaries, said in *From Religion to Philosophy* (1912) that *The Birth* was "a work of profound imaginative insight, which left the scholarship of a generation toiling in the rear."

For all that, Wilamowitz had a point, though he was completely blind to Nietzsche's merits. Some of the "philology" of the future aped the manifest defects of Nietzsche's book without partaking of his genius—and, by a remarkable irony of fate, Nietzsche himself was to suffer a great deal, posthumously, from pseudo-scholars who substituted effusive prose for precision and correctness.

On the whole, however, the general estimate of posterity has been much closer to Cornford's view, and he himself and Jane Harrison have done a good deal to sustain Nietzsche's central intuitions.

In 1965 Professor Gerald F. Else followed up his monumental analysis of *Aristotle's Poetics* (1957) with a short study of *The Origin and Early Form of Greek Tragedy*[8] in which he argues that Aristotle, Nietzsche, Gilbert Murray, and the Cambridge school have all been importantly wrong about the origin of tragedy. He shows his usual mastery of the whole literature, and in his notes at the end of the volume he gives abundant references to recent literature on the subject. Those wondering about the current status of some of the problems raised by Nietzsche may be referred to Else's work. But it is noteworthy that, in spite of his radical disagreement with Nietzsche, Else should say, *"The Birth of Tragedy* is a great book, by whatever standard one cares to measure it" (p. 10). And he adds: *"The Birth of Tragedy* has cast a spell on almost everybody who has dealt with the subject since 1871."

3

What is of lasting importance is not the contrast of the Apollinian[9] and Dionysian as such: that smacks of Schopenhauer's contrast of the world as representation and the world as will; and playing off two concepts against each other like that is rarely very fruitful, though it has been a popular pastime among German scholars.

When *The Birth* appeared, the prevalent conception of the Greeks was still that pioneered by Johann Joachim Winckelmann (1717–1768) and adopted by Goethe (1749–1832): *edle Einfalt, stille Grösse,* "noble simplicity, calm grandeur." Matthew Arnold (1822–1888), utterly unable as a critic to maintain the level of his poem "Dover Beach," had only recently led this view to the absurd with his famous formulation: "sweetness and light." [10] Nietzsche used Apollo as a symbol for this aspect of Greek culture which found superb expression in classical Greek temples and sculptures: the genius of restraint, measure, and harmony. Far from depreciating what he called "the Apollinian," he argued that one could not

---

[8] Cambridge, Mass., Harvard University Press, 1965.

[9] *Apollinisch* has often been rendered by "Apollonian"; but I follow Brinton, Morgan, and the translator of Spengler's *Decline of the West* in preferring "Apollinian": after all, Nietzsche did not say *Apollonisch.*

[10] This is the title of the first chapter of Arnold's *Culture and Anarchy* (1869). The text itself was originally presented as Arnold's last Oxford lecture, June 15, 1867, under the title "Culture and Its Enemies."

appreciate it sufficiently until one became aware of another side of Greek culture that was barbarous by comparison and found expression in the Dionysian festivals. Surely, *The Bacchae* of Euripides shows us passions that are worlds removed from the Greece of Winckelmann, Goethe, and Arnold; and Nietzsche claimed that the same boundless and cruel longing to exceed all norms is also occasionally encountered in the *Iliad* [11] and in subsequent Greek poetry —and "the birth of tragedy" cannot be understood apart from it.

A careful reading of *The Birth* shows that Nietzsche, far from glorifying "the Dionysian," argues that the achievements of the Greeks generally, and their tragedies in particular, cannot be understood adequately so long as we do not realize what potentially destructive forces had to be harnessed to make them possible. On this central point Nietzsche was surely right. If one wants a single well-written book which abounds in quotations and references that document this "dark" side of ancient Greece, there is probably none better than E. R. Dodds's superb study of *The Greeks and the Irrational*,[12] which also abounds in references to other recent literature on this subject.

The Birth of Tragedy reaches its first great climax in section 7, which is of interest also in connection with French existentialism. Then the book moves on to suggestions about the death of tragedy. For over forty years the ridiculous claims of Richard Oehler, in *Friedrich Nietzsche und die Vorsokratiker* (1904),[13] were repeated by one interpreter after another—even after Oehler had thoroughly discredited himself with one of the most unscrupulous books ever to have come from a writer with some scholarly pretensions, *Friedrich Nietzsche und die Deutsche Zukunft* (1935),[14] an attempt to identify Nietzsche with the aspirations of the Nazis, who had come to power in 1933. In the interim, Oehler had compiled two huge indices for the two most complete editions of Nietzsche's works, the latter index (for the so-called Musarion edition) comprising two and a half volumes. This did not prevent

---

[11] Compare also Nietzsche's early fragment "Homer's Contest" (pp. 32–39 in *Portable Nietzsche*).

[12] Berkeley, University of California Press, 1951; Boston, Beacon Press paperback, 1951.

[13] Leipzig, Dürr, 1904.

[14] Leipzig, Armanen, 1935.

him—on the contrary, it enabled him to stud his book of 1935 with utterly misleading quotations that seem to say the opposite of what Nietzsche actually says on the pages from which they are taken. At best the earlier volume shows that Oehler's stunning lack of intellectual integrity was fused with a limited intelligence and an appalling inability to understand Nietzsche. But this man was one of the pillars of the Nietzsche Archive, established by the philosopher's sister, and one of the editors of the works.[15]

Neither Oehler nor his early book would deserve mention here if that book had not been used and echoed uncritically by A. H. J. Knight in the only English full-length study of Nietzsche's relation to the Greeks,[16] and if Knight had not been relied on uncritically by Ernest Newman, Crane Brinton, and Erich Podach.[17] To catalogue Oehler's mistakes here would be pointless; but two of them have been repeated so often that it seems necessary to repudiate them specifically.

First, the young Oehler claimed that the early Nietzsche "was completely under the influence of Schopenhauer," and a pessimist (p. 28). In fact, however, Nietzsche's very first book, *The Birth,* constitutes a declaration of independence from Schopenhauer: while Nietzsche admires him for honestly facing up to the terrors of existence, Nietzsche himself celebrates Greek tragedy as a superior alternative to Schopenhauer's "Buddhistic negation of the will." From tragedy Nietzsche learns that one can affirm life as sublime, beautiful, and joyous in spite of all suffering and cruelty.

Second, Oehler understood *The Birth* as a manifesto against Socrates and Socratism. In fact, Nietzsche is no more against (or for) Socrates than he is against (or for) Apollo or Dionysus. His

---

[15] Cf. *Beyond Good and Evil,* section 251, note 27, on page 378 below; also Kaufmann's *Nietzsche,* check the references to Richard Oehler in the Index.

[16] Knight's *Some Aspects of the Life and Work of Nietzsche and particularly of His Connection with Greek Literature and Thought* (Cambridge, England: Cambridge University Press, 1933) is generally unreliable, and some of the many errors in the book are pointed out in Kaufmann's *Nietzsche.* In other words, the two monographs devoted to Nietzsche and the Greeks (Oehler's and Knight's) are both quite unhelpful.

[17] Erich Podach, *Nietzsches Werke des Zusammenbruchs* (Heidelberg, Wolfgang Rothe Verlag, 1961), p. 407. Cf. Kaufmann, "Nietzsche in the Light of His Suppressed Manuscripts," *Journal of the History of Philosophy* (1964), p. 216, note 13.

whole way of thinking is far removed from such crudities. And Nietzsche was as right as most of his interpreters, following Oehler, have been wrong when he said in 1888, in *Ecce Homo,* in the first section of his own analysis of *The Birth:* "It smells offensively Hegelian, and the cadaverous perfume of Schopenhauer sticks only to a few formulas."

Socrates is introduced in *The Birth* with the reverence befitting a god, the equal of Apollo and Dionysus. Of course, Nietzsche's critical powers do not spare even gods, and he finds Socrates deeply problematic. He always approached Socrates in this manner, stressing now his admiration, now his objections, and sometimes, as here, both at once.[18] Indeed, the two sections (14 and 15) in which the discussion of the death of tragedy reaches its climax— the second great highpoint of the book—suggest that but for Socrates Greek culture might have perished altogether; also that "the influence of Socrates necessitates ever again the regeneration of art"; and finally even that we need an "artistic Socrates."

Apollo and Dionysus reached a synthesis in tragedy; this synthesis was negated by Socrates; and now another synthesis is wanted, an artistic Socrates. Could Plato be meant? On the contrary. Those who feel that Nietzsche is unfair to Socrates and that Socratism is *not* opposed to tragedy should reconsider Plato's resolve, in the *Republic,* to tolerate no tragic poets in his ideal city, as well as the older Plato's remarks on tragedy in *The Laws.* The "artistic Socrates" is Nietzsche himself. He looks forward to a philosophy that admits the tragic aspect of life, as the Greek poets did, but does not sacrifice the critical intellect; a philosophy that denies Socrates' optimistic faith that knowledge and virtue and happiness are, as it were, Siamese triplets; a philosophy as sharply critical as Socrates' but able and willing to avail itself of the visions and resources of art.

For all that, one need not accept Nietzsche's view of the death of tragedy, though it has been served up to us again and again in the twentieth century. This is not the place to offer sustained criticisms of his theses; but to stimulate reflection I suggest that Nietzsche is blatantly unfair not to Socrates but to Euripides—and that

---

[18] All the relevant passages are considered in Chapter 13 of Kaufmann's *Nietzsche.*

the death of tragedy was far better explained by Goethe, when he said to Eckermann, May 1, 1825:

"Man is simple. And however rich, manifold, and unfathomable he may be, yet the circle of his states is soon run through. If the circumstances had been like those among us poor Germans where Lessing wrote two or three, I myself three or four, and Schiller five or six passable plays, there would have been room for a fourth, fifth, and sixth tragic poet. But among the Greeks with their abundant production, where each of the three great ones had written over one hundred, or close to one hundred, plays, and the tragic subjects of Homer and the heroic tradition had in some cases been treated three or four times—in view of such an abundance, I say, one may suppose that subject matter and contents had gradually been exhausted and poets writing after the three great ones did not really know what next. And when you stop to think about it, why should they? Wasn't it really enough for a while? . . . After all, these few grandiose views that have come down to us are of such dimension and significance that we poor Europeans have been occupying ourselves with them for centuries and will yet have food and work enough for a few more centuries."

Unfortunately, *The Birth of Tragedy* does not end with Section 15, as an early draft did and as the book clearly ought to. Another ten sections follow that weaken the whole book immeasurably.

Sections 1 through 6 are introductory and inferior stylistically. The heart of the book is found in Sections 7 through 15, which deal with the birth and death of tragedy. This is by far the best part of the book and can probably be understood fairly well by itself. Sections 16–25 are less worthy of Nietzsche than anything else of comparable length he ever published—and he himself soon felt this. The book as a whole, though it has a touch of genius, is marred by the faults Nietzsche enumerates in his "Attempt at a Self-Criticism." This "Attempt," however, shows us not only a brilliant writer who has grown far beyond the level of his first performance, but a great human being.

W. K.

The
BIRTH OF TRAGEDY

Or:

Hellenism And Pessimism

———◆◇◆———

by

FRIEDRICH NIETZSCHE

———◆◇◆———

New Edition

With an Attempt at a Self-Criticism[1]

---

[1] In the first edition of 1872 the title was *The Birth of Tragedy out of the Spirit of Music*. A second edition with very slight textual changes was printed in 1874 and appeared in 1878. In 1886, the same year that saw the publication of *Beyond Good and Evil*, the remaining copies of *both* editions were reissued with the new title page, above. The original title page was also retained but it now followed the "Attempt at a Self-Criticism."

Attempt at a Self-Criticism

Whatever may be at the bottom of this questionable book, it must have been an exceptionally significant and fascinating question, and deeply personal at that: the time in which it was written, in *spite* of which it was written, bears witness to that—the exciting time of the Franco-Prussian War of 1870/71. As the thunder of the battle of Wörth was rolling over Europe, the muser and riddle-friend who was to be the father of this book sat somewhere in an Alpine nook, very bemused and beriddled, hence very concerned and yet unconcerned, and wrote down his thoughts about the *Greeks*—the core of the strange and almost inaccessible book to which this belated preface (or postscript) shall now be added. A few weeks later—and he himself was to be found under the walls of Metz, still wedded to the question marks that he had placed after the alleged "cheerfulness" of the Greeks and of Greek art. Eventually, in that month of profoundest suspense when the peace treaty was being debated at Versailles, he, too, attained peace with himself and, slowly convalescing from an illness contracted at the front, completed the final draft of *The Birth of Tragedy out of the Spirit of Music*.— Out of music? Music and tragedy? Greeks and the music of tragedy? Greeks and the art form of pessimism? The best turned out, most beautiful, most envied type of humanity to date, those most apt to seduce us to life, the Greeks—how now? They of all people should have *needed* tragedy? Even more—art? For what—Greek art?

You will guess where the big question mark concerning the value of existence had thus been raised. Is pessimism *necessarily* a sign of decline, decay, degeneration, weary and weak instincts—as it once was in India and now is, to all appearances, among us, "modern" men and Europeans? Is there a pessimism of *strength?* An intellectual predilection for the hard, gruesome, evil, problematic aspect of existence, prompted by well-being, by overflowing health, by the *fullness* of existence? Is it perhaps possible to suffer precisely from overfullness? The sharp-eyed courage that tempts and attempts, that *craves* the frightful as the enemy, the worthy enemy, against whom one can test one's strength? From whom one can learn what it means "to be frightened"? What is the significance of the *tragic* myth among the Greeks of the best, the strongest, the most courageous period? And the tremendous phenomenon of the Dionysian—and, born from it, tragedy—what might they signify?— And again: that of which tragedy died, the Socratism of morality, the dialectics, frugality, and cheerfulness of the theoretical man—how now? might not this very Socratism be a sign of decline, of weariness, of infection, of the anarchical dissolution of the instincts? And the "Greek cheerfulness" of the later Greeks— merely the afterglow of the sunset? The Epicureans' resolve *against* pessimism—a mere precaution of the afflicted? And science itself, our science—indeed, what is the significance of all science, viewed as a symptom of life? For what—worse yet, *whence*—all science? How now? Is the resolve to be so scientific about everything perhaps a kind of fear of, an escape from, pessimism? A subtle last resort against—*truth*? And, morally speaking, a sort of cowardice and falseness? Amorally speaking, a ruse? O Socrates, Socrates, was that perhaps *your* secret? O enigmatic ironist, was that perhaps your—irony?

2

What I then got hold of, something frightful and dangerous, a problem with horns but not necessarily a bull, in any case a *new* problem—today I should say that it was *the problem of science itself*, science considered for the first time as problematic, as questionable. But the book in which my youthful courage and suspicion found an outlet—what an *impossible* book had to result from a task so uncongenial to youth! Constructed from a lot of immature, overgreen personal experiences, all of them close to the limits of communication, presented in the context of *art*—for the problem of science cannot be recognized in the context of science—a book perhaps for artists who also have an analytic and retrospective penchant (in other words, an exceptional type of artist for whom one might have to look far and wide and really would not care to look); a book full of psychological innovations and artists' secrets, with an artists' metaphysics in the background; a youthful work full of the intrepid mood of youth, the moodiness of youth, independent,

defiantly self-reliant even where it seems to bow before an authority and personal reverence; in sum, a first book, also in every bad
sense of that label. In spite of the problem which seems congenial
to old age, the book is marked by every defect of youth, with its
"length in excess" and its "storm and stress." On the other hand,
considering its success (especially with the great artist to whom it
addressed itself as in a dialogue, Richard Wagner), it is a *proven*
book, I mean one that in any case satisfied "the best minds of the
time." [1] In view of that, it really ought to be treated with some
consideration and taciturnity. Still, I do not want to suppress entirely how disagreeable it now seems to me, how strange it appears
now, after sixteen years—before a much older, a hundred times
more demanding, but by no means colder eye which has not become a stranger to the task which this audacious book dared to
tackle for the first time: *to look at science in the perspective of the
artist, but at art in that of life.*

3

To say it once more: today I find it an impossible book: I
consider it badly written, ponderous, embarrassing, image-mad and
image-confused, sentimental, in places saccharine to the point of
effeminacy, uneven in tempo, without the will to logical cleanliness,
very convinced and therefore disdainful of proof, mistrustful even
of the *propriety* of proof, a book for initiates, "music" for those
dedicated to music, those who are closely related to begin with on
the basis of common and rare aesthetic experiences, "music"
meant as a sign of recognition for close relatives *in artibus*[2]—an
arrogant and rhapsodic book that sought to exclude right from the
beginning the *profanum vulgus*[3] of "the educated" even more than
"the mass" or "folk." Still, the effect of the book proved and proves
that it had a knack for seeking out fellow-rhapsodizers and for luring them on to new secret paths and dancing places. What found
expression here was anyway—this was admitted with as much cu-

---

[1] An allusion to Schiller's lines in *Wallensteins Lager:* "He that has satisfied
the best minds of the time has lived for all times."

[2] In the arts.

[3] The profane crowd.

riosity as antipathy—a *strange* voice, the disciple of a still "un-known God," one who concealed himself for the time being under the scholar's hood, under the gravity and dialectical ill humor of the German, even under the bad manners of the Wagnerian. Here was a spirit with strange, still nameless needs, a memory bursting with questions, experiences, concealed things after which the name of Dionysus was added as one more question mark. What spoke here—as was admitted, not without suspicion—was something like a mystical, almost maenadic soul that stammered with difficulty, a feat of the will, as in a strange tongue, almost undecided whether it should communicate or conceal itself. It should have *sung*, this "new soul"—and not spoken! [4] What I had to say then—too bad that I did not dare say it as a poet: perhaps I had the ability. Or at least as a philologist: after all, even today practically everything in this field remains to be discovered and dug up by philologists! Above all, the problem that there *is* a problem here—and that the Greeks, as long as we lack an answer to the question "what is Dionysian?" remain as totally uncomprehended and unimaginable as ever. [5]

4

Indeed, what is Dionysian?— This book contains an answer: one "who knows" is talking, the initiate and disciple of his god. *Now* I should perhaps speak more cautiously and less eloquently about such a difficult psychological question as that concerning the

---

[4] When Nietzsche died in 1900, Stefan George, the most remarkable German poet of his generation, after Rilke, wrote a poem on "Nietzsche" that ends: "it should have sung, not spoken, this new soul." For George's whole poem, see *Twenty German Poets: A Bilingual Collection* (New York, The Modern Library, 1963).

[5] The conception of the Dionysian in *The Birth* differs from Nietzsche's later conception of the Dionysian. He originally introduced the term to symbolize the tendencies that found expression in the festivals of Dionysus, and contrasted the Dionysian with the Apollinian; but in his later thought the Dionysian stands for the creative employment of the passions and the affirmation of life in spite of suffering—as it were, for the synthesis of the Dionysian, as originally conceived, with the Apollinian—and it is contrasted with the Christian negation of life and extirpation of the passions. In the *Twilight of the Idols,* written in 1888, the outlook of the old Goethe can thus be called Dionysian (section 49).

origin of tragedy among the Greeks. The question of the Greek's relation to pain, his degree of sensitivity, is basic: did this relation remain constant? Or did it change radically? The question is whether his ever stronger *craving for beauty,* for festivals, pleasures, new cults was rooted in some deficiency, privation, melancholy, pain? Supposing that this were true—and Pericles (or Thucydides) suggests as much in the great funeral oration—how should we then have to explain the origin of the opposite craving, which developed earlier in time, the *craving for the ugly;* the good, severe will of the older Greeks to pessimism, to the tragic myth, to the image of everything underlying existence that is frightful, evil, a riddle, destructive, fatal? What, then, would be the origin of tragedy? Perhaps *joy,* strength, overflowing health, overgreat fullness? And what, then, is the significance, physiologically speaking, of that madness out of which tragic and comic art developed—the Dionysian madness? How now? Is madness perhaps not necessarily the symptom of degeneration, decline, and the final stage of culture? Are there perhaps—a question for psychiatrists—neuroses of *health?* of the youth and youthfulness of a people? Where does that synthesis of god and billy goat in the satyr point? What experience of himself, what urge compelled the Greek to conceive the Dionysian enthusiast and primeval man as a satyr? And regarding the origin of the tragic chorus: did those centuries when the Greek body flourished and the Greek soul foamed over with health perhaps know endemic ecstasies? Visions and hallucinations shared by entire communities or assemblies at a cult? How now? Should the Greeks, precisely in the abundance of their youth, have had the will to the tragic and have been pessimists? Should it have been madness, to use one of Plato's phrases, that brought the greatest blessings upon Greece? On the other hand, conversely, could it be that the Greeks became more and more optimistic, superficial, and histrionic precisely in the period of dissolution and weakness—more and more ardent for logic and logicizing the world and thus more "cheerful" and "scientific"? How now? Could it be possible that, in spite of all "modern ideas" and the prejudices of a democratic taste, the triumph of *optimism,* the gradual prevalence of *rationality,* practical and theoretical *utilitarianism,* no less than democracy itself which developed at the same time, might all have been symptoms of a decline of strength, of impending old age, and of physio-

logical weariness? These, and not pessimism? Was Epicurus an optimist—precisely because he was *afflicted?*

It is apparent that it was a whole cluster of grave questions
with which this book burdened itself. Let us add the gravest question of all. What, seen in the perspective of *life,* is the significance
of morality?

5

Already in the preface addressed to Richard Wagner, art,
and *not* morality, is presented as the truly *metaphysical* activity of
man. In the book itself the suggestive sentence is repeated several
times, that the existence of the world is *justified* only as an aesthetic phenomenon. Indeed, the whole book knows only an artistic
meaning and crypto-meaning behind all events—a "god," if you
please, but certainly only an entirely reckless and amoral artist-god
who wants to experience, whether he is building or destroying, in
the good and in the bad, his own joy and glory—one who, creating
worlds, frees himself from the *distress* of fullness and *overfullness*
and from the *affliction* of the contradictions compressed in his
soul.[6] The world—at every moment the *attained* salvation of God,
as the eternally changing, eternally new vision of the most deeply
afflicted, discordant, and contradictory being who can find salvation
only in *appearance:* you can call this whole artists' metaphysics
arbitrary, idle, fantastic; what matters is that it betrays a spirit who
will one day fight at any risk whatever the *moral* interpretation and
significance of existence. Here, perhaps for the first time, a pessimism "beyond good and evil" [7] is suggested. Here that "perversity
of mind" gains speech and formulation against which Schopenhauer never wearied of hurling in advance his most irate curses and
thunderbolts: a philosophy that dares to move, to demote, morality
into the realm of appearance—and not merely among "appearances" or phenomena (in the sense assigned to these words by

---

[6] Cf. the words which Heine, in his *Schöpfungslieder,* attributes to God:
"Disease was the most basic ground/of my creative urge and stress;/creating,
I could convalesce,/creating, I again grew sound."

[7] The book with that title was published in 1886, the same year that the new
edition of *The Birth of Tragedy* appeared, with this preface.

Idealistic philosophers), but among "deceptions," as semblance, delusion, error, interpretation, contrivance, art.

Perhaps the depth of this *antimoral* propensity is best inferred from the careful and hostile silence with which Christianity is treated throughout the whole book—Christianity as the most prodigal elaboration of the moral theme to which humanity has ever been subjected. In truth, nothing could be more opposed to the purely aesthetic interpretation and justification of the world which are taught in this book than the Christian teaching, which is, and wants to be, *only* moral and which relegates art, *every* art, to the realm of *lies;* with its absolute standards, beginning with the truthfulness of God, it negates, judges, and damns art. Behind this mode of thought and valuation, which must be hostile to art if it is at all genuine, I never failed to sense a *hostility to life*—a furious, vengeful antipathy to life itself: for all of life is based on semblance, art, deception, points of view, and the necessity of perspectives and error. Christianity was from the beginning, essentially and fundamentally, life's nausea and disgust with life, merely concealed behind, masked by, dressed up as, faith in "another" or "better" life. Hatred of "the world," condemnations of the passions, fear of beauty and sensuality, a beyond invented the better to slander this life, at bottom a craving for the nothing, for the end, for respite, for "the sabbath of sabbaths"—all this always struck me, no less than the unconditional will of Christianity to recognize *only* moral values, as the most dangerous and uncanny form of all possible forms of a "will to decline" [8]—at the very least a sign of abysmal sickness, weariness, discouragement, exhaustion, and the impoverishment of life. For, confronted with morality (especially Christian, or unconditional, morality), life *must* continually and inevitably be in the wrong, because life *is* something essentially amoral—and eventually, crushed by the weight of contempt and the eternal No, life *must* then be felt to be unworthy of desire and altogether worthless. Morality itself—how now? might not morality be "a will to negate life," a secret instinct of annihilation, a principle of decay, diminution, and slander—the beginning of the end? Hence, the danger of dangers?

---

[8] *Untergang*, as in the title of Spengler's *Decline of the West*, which was influenced decisively by this discussion. Spengler himself says in his preface that he owes "everything" to Goethe and to Nietzsche.

It was *against* morality that my instinct turned with this questionable book, long ago; it was an instinct that aligned itself with life and that discovered for itself a fundamentally opposite doctrine and valuation of life—purely artistic and *anti-Christian*. What to call it? As a philologist and man of words I baptized it, not without taking some liberty—for who could claim to know the rightful name of the Antichrist?—in the name of a Greek god: I called it Dionysian.

6

It is clear what task I first dared to touch with this book? How I regret now that in those days I still lacked the courage (or immodesty?) to permit myself in every way an individual language of my own for such individual views and hazards—and that instead I tried laboriously to express by means of Schopenhauerian and Kantian formulas strange and new valuations which were basically at odds with Kant's and Schopenhauer's spirit and taste! What, after all, did Schopenhauer think of tragedy?

"That which bestows on everything tragic its peculiar elevating force"—he says in *The World as Will and Representation*,[9] volume II, p. 495—"is the discovery that the world, that life, can never give real satisfaction and hence is *not worthy* of our affection: this constitutes the tragic spirit—it leads to *resignation*."

How differently Dionysus spoke to me! How far removed I was from all this resignationism!—[10] But there is something far worse in this book, something I now regret still more than that I obscured and spoiled Dionysian premonitions with Schopenhauerian formulations: namely, that I *spoiled* the grandiose *Greek problem,* as it had arisen before my eyes, by introducing the most modern problems! That I appended hopes where there was no ground for hope, where everything pointed all too plainly to an end! That on the basis of the latest German music I began to rave about "the German spirit" as if that were in the process even then of discover-

---

9 *Welt als Wille und Vorstellung,* ed. Julius Frauenstädt (Leipzig, F. A. Brockhaus, 1873). Translated by R. B. Haldane and J. Kemp as *World as Will and Idea* (London, Kegan Paul, 1907).

10 Nietzsche's coinage.

ing and finding itself again—at a time when the German spirit, which not long before had still had the will to dominate Europe and the strength to lead Europe,[11] was just making its testament and *abdicating* forever, making its transition, under the pompous pretense of founding a *Reich,* to a leveling mediocrity, democracy, and "modern ideas"!

Indeed, meanwhile I have learned to consider this "German spirit" with a sufficient lack of hope or mercy; also, contemporary *German music,* which is romanticism through and through and most un-Greek of all possible art forms—moreover, a first-rate poison for the nerves, doubly dangerous among a people who love drink and who honor lack of clarity as a virtue, for it has the double quality of a narcotic that both intoxicates and spreads a *fog.*

To be sure, apart from all the hasty hopes and faulty applications to the present with which I spoiled my first book, there still remains the great Dionysian question mark I raised—regarding music as well: what would a music have to be like that would no longer be of romantic origin, like German music—but *Dionysian?*

7

But, my dear sir, what in the world is romantic if *your* book isn't? Can deep hatred against "the Now," against "reality" and "modern ideas" be pushed further than you pushed it in your artists' metaphysics? believing sooner in the Nothing, sooner in the devil than in "the Now"? Is it not a deep bass of wrath and the lust for destruction that we hear humming underneath all of your contrapuntal vocal art and seduction of the ear, a furious resolve against everything that is "now," a will that is not too far removed from practical nihilism and seems to say: "sooner let nothing be true than that *you* should be right, than that *your* truth should be proved right!"

Listen yourself, my dear pessimist and art-deifier, but with open ears, to a single passage chosen from your book—to the not ineloquent dragon-slayer passage which may have an insidious pied-

---

[11] The allusion is to the time of Goethe when Germany, at her cultural zenith, was at her political nadir. The whole passage illustrates Nietzsche's conception of the "will to dominate" and the "will to power."

piper sound for young ears and hearts. How now? Isn't this the typical creed of the romantic of 1830, masked by the pessimism of 1850? Even the usual romantic finale is sounded—break, break-down, return and collapse before an old faith, before *the* old God. How now? Is your pessimists' book not itself a piece of anti-Hellen-ism and romanticism? Is it not itself something "equally intoxicat-ing and befogging," in any case a narcotic, even a piece of music, *German* music? But listen:

"Let us imagine a coming generation with such intrepidity of vision, with such a heroic penchant for the tremendous; let us imag-ine the bold stride of these dragon-slayers, the proud audacity with which they turn their back on all the weakling's doctrines of optim-ism in order to 'live resolutely' in wholeness and fullness: *would it not be necessary* for the tragic man of such a culture, in view of his self-education for seriousness and terror, to desire a new art, the *art of metaphysical comfort,* to desire tragedy as his own proper Helen, and to exclaim with Faust:

> *Should not my longing overleap the distance*
> *And draw the fairest form into existence?"* [12]

"Would it not be *necessary?*"—No, thrice no! O you young romantics: it would *not* be necessary! But it is highly probable that it will *end* that way, that *you* end that way—namely, "com-forted," as it is written, in spite of all self-education for serious-ness and terror, "comforted metaphysically"—in sum, as romantics end, as *Christians.*

No! You ought to learn the art of *this-worldly* comfort first; you ought to learn to laugh, my young friends, if you are hell-bent on remaining pessimists. Then perhaps, as laughers, you may some day dispatch all metaphysical comforts to the devil—metaphysics in front. Or, to say it in the language of that Dionysian monster who bears the name of Zarathustra:

"Raise up your hearts, my brothers, high, higher! And don't forget your legs! Raise up your legs, too, good dancers; and still better: stand on your heads!

"This crown of the laugher, the rose-wreath crown: I crown

---

12 Section 18 below.

myself with this crown; I myself pronounced holy my laughter. I did not find anyone else today strong enough for that.

"Zarathustra, the dancer; Zarathustra, the light one who beckons with his wings, preparing for a flight, beckoning to all birds, ready and heady, blissfully lightheaded;

"Zarathustra, the soothsayer; Zarathustra, the sooth-laugher; not impatient; not unconditional; one who loves leaps and side-leaps: I crown myself with this crown.

"This crown of the laugher, the rose-wreath crown: to you, my brothers, I throw this crown. Laughter I have pronounced holy: you higher men, *learn*—to laugh!"

Thus Spoke Zarathustra, Part IV.[13]

Sils-Maria, Oberengadin,
August 1886—

---

[13] "On the Higher Man," sections 17–20, quoted by Nietzsche with omissions.

THE
BIRTH OF TRAGEDY

Out of the Spirit of Music

Preface to Richard Wagner

To keep at a distance all the possible scruples, excitements, and misunderstandings that the thoughts united in this essay will occasion, in view of the peculiar character of our aesthetic public, and to be able to write these introductory remarks, too, with the same contemplative delight whose reflection—the distillation of good and elevating hours—is evident on every page, I picture the moment when you, my highly respected friend, will receive this essay. Perhaps after an evening walk in the winter snow, you will behold Prometheus unbound on the title page, read my name, and be convinced at once that, whatever this essay should contain, the author certainly has something serious and urgent to say; also that, as he hatched these ideas, he was communicating with you as if you were present, and hence could write down only what was in keeping with that presence. You will recall that it was during the same period when your splendid *Festschrift* on Beethoven came into being, amid the terrors and sublimities of the war that had just broken out, that I collected myself for these reflections. Yet anyone would be mistaken if he associated my reflections with the contrast between patriotic excitement and aesthetic enthusiasm, of courageous seriousness and a cheerful game: if he really read this essay, it would dawn on him, to his surprise, what a seriously German problem is faced here and placed right in the center of German hopes, as a vortex and turning point.[1] But perhaps such readers will find it offensive that an aesthetic problem should be taken so seriously—assuming they are unable to consider art more than a pleasant sideline, a readily dispensable tinkling of bells that accompanies the "seriousness of life," just as if nobody knew what was involved in such a contrast with the "seriousness of life." Let such "serious" readers learn something from the fact that I am convinced that art represents the highest task and the truly metaphysical activity of

---

[1] This image occurs also in section 15 below.

this life, in the sense of that man to whom, as my sublime predecessor on this path, I wish to dedicate this essay.

Basel, end of the year 1871

1

We shall have gained much for the science of aesthetics, once we perceive not merely by logical inference, but with the immediate certainty of vision, that the continuous development of art is bound up with the *Apollinian* and *Dionysian* duality—just as procreation depends on the duality of the sexes, involving perpetual strife with only periodically intervening reconciliations. The terms Dionysian and Apollinian we borrow from the Greeks, who disclose to the discerning mind the profound mysteries of their view of art, not, to be sure, in concepts, but in the intensely clear figures of their gods. Through Apollo and Dionysus, the two art deities of the Greeks, we come to recognize that in the Greek world there existed a tremendous opposition, in origin and aims,[1] between the Apollinian art of sculpture, and the nonimagistic, Dionysian art of music. These two different tendencies run parallel to each other, for the most part openly at variance; and they continually incite each other to new and more powerful births, which perpetuate an antagonism, only superficially reconciled by the common term "art"; till eventually,[2] by a metaphysical miracle of the Hellenic "will," they appear coupled with each other, and through this coupling ultimately generate an equally Dionysian and Apollinian form of art—Attic tragedy.

In order to grasp these two tendencies, let us first conceive of them as the separate art worlds of *dreams* and *intoxication*. These physiological phenomena present a contrast analogous to that existing between the Apollinian and the Dionysian. It was in dreams, says Lucretius, that the glorious divine figures first appeared to the souls of men; in dreams the great shaper beheld the splendid bodies of superhuman beings; and the Hellenic poet, if questioned about the mysteries of poetic inspiration, would likewise have suggested

---

[1] In the first edition: ". . . an opposition of style: two different tendencies run parallel in it, for the most part in conflict; and they . . ." Most of the changes in the revision of 1874 are as slight as this (compare the next footnote) and therefore not indicated in the following pages. This translation, like the standard German editions, follows Nietzsche's revision.

[2] First edition: "till eventually, at the moment of the flowering of the Hellenic 'will,' they appear fused to generate together the art form of Attic tragedy."

dreams and he might have given an explanation like that of Hans Sachs in the *Meistersinger:*

> *The poet's task is this, my friend,*
> *to read his dreams and comprehend.*
> *The truest human fancy seems*
> *to be revealed to us in dreams:*
> *all poems and versification*
> *are but true dreams' interpretation.*[3]

The beautiful illusion[4] of the dream worlds, in the creation of which every man is truly an artist, is the prerequisite of all plastic art, and, as we shall see, of an important part of poetry also. In our dreams we delight in the immediate understanding of figures; all forms speak to us; there is nothing unimportant or superfluous. But even when this dream reality is most intense, we still have, glimmering through it, the sensation that it is *mere appearance:* at least this is my experience, and for its frequency—indeed, normality—I could adduce many proofs, including the sayings of the poets.

Philosophical men even have a presentiment that the reality in which we live and have our being is also mere appearance, and that another, quite different reality lies beneath it. Schopenhauer actually indicates as the criterion of philosophical ability the occasional ability to view men and things as mere phantoms or dream images. Thus the aesthetically sensitive man stands in the same relation to the reality of dreams as the philosopher does to the reality of existence; he is a close and willing observer, for these images afford him an interpretation of life, and by reflecting on these processes he trains himself for life.

It is not only the agreeable and friendly images that he experiences as something universally intelligible: the serious, the trou-

---

[3] Wagner's original text reads:
> *Mein Freund, das grad' ist Dichters Werk,*
> *dass er sein Träumen deut' und merk'.*
> *Glaubt mir, des Menschen wahrster Wahn*
> *wird ihm im Traume aufgethan:*
> *all' Dichtkunst und Poëterei*
> *ist nichts als Wahrtraum-Deuterei.*

[4] *Schein* has been rendered in these pages sometimes as "illusion" and sometimes as "mere appearance."

bled, the sad, the gloomy, the sudden restraints, the tricks of accident, anxious expectations, in short, the whole divine comedy of
life, including the inferno, also pass before him, not like mere shadows on a wall—for he lives and suffers with these scenes—and yet
not without that fleeting sensation of illusion. And perhaps many
will, like myself, recall how amid the dangers and terrors of dreams
they have occasionally said to themselves in self-encouragement,
and not without success: "It is a dream! I will dream on!" I have
likewise heard of people who were able to continue one and the
same dream for three and even more successive nights—facts
which indicate clearly how our innermost being, our common
ground, experiences dreams with profound delight and a joyous necessity.

This joyous necessity of the dream experience has been embodied by the Greeks in their Apollo: Apollo, the god of all plastic
energies, is at the same time the soothsaying god. He, who (as the
etymology of the name indicates) is the "shining one," [5] the deity
of light, is also ruler over the beautiful illusion of the inner world of
fantasy. The higher truth, the perfection of these states in contrast
to the incompletely intelligible everyday world, this deep consciousness of nature, healing and helping in sleep and dreams, is at
the same time the symbolical analogue of the soothsaying faculty
and of the arts generally, which make life possible and worth living.
But we must also include in our image of Apollo that delicate
boundary which the dream image must not overstep lest it have a
pathological effect (in which case mere appearance would deceive
us as if it were crude reality). We must keep in mind that measured
restraint, that freedom from the wilder emotions, that calm of the
sculptor god. His eye must be "sunlike," as befits his origin; even
when it is angry and distempered it is still hallowed by beautiful
illusion. And so, in one sense, we might apply to Apollo the words
of Schopenhauer when he speaks of the man wrapped in the veil of
māyā [6] (*Welt als Wille und Vorstellung*, I, p. 416[7]): "Just as in a

---

[5] *Der "Scheinende."* The German words for illusion and appearance are
Schein and *Erscheinung.*

[6] A Sanskrit word usually translated as illusion. For detailed discussions see,
e.g., *A Source Book of Indian Philosophy,* ed. S. Radhakrishnan and Charles
Moore (Princeton, N.J., Princeton University Press, 1957); Heinrich Zimmer, *Philosophies of India,* ed. Joseph Campbell (New York, Meridian

stormy sea that, unbounded in all directions, raises and drops mountainous waves, howling, a sailor sits in a boat and trusts in his frail bark: so in the midst of a world of torments the individual human being sits quietly, supported by and trusting in the *principium individuationis.*" [8] In fact, we might say of Apollo that in him the unshaken faith in this *principium* and the calm repose of the man wrapped up in it receive their most sublime expression; and we might call Apollo himself the glorious divine image of the *principium individuationis,* through whose gestures and eyes all the joy and wisdom of "illusion," together with its beauty, speak to us.

In the same work Schopenhauer has depicted for us the tremendous *terror* which seizes man when he is suddenly dumfounded by the cognitive form of phenomena because the principle of sufficient reason, in some one of its manifestations, seems to suffer an exception. If we add to this terror the blissful ecstasy that wells from the innermost depths of man, indeed of nature, at this collapse of the *principium individuationis,* we steal a glimpse into the nature of the *Dionysian,* which is brought home to us most intimately by the analogy of intoxication.

Either under the influence of the narcotic draught, of which the songs of all primitive men and peoples speak, or with the potent coming of spring that penetrates all nature with joy, these Dionysian emotions awake, and as they grow in intensity everything subjective vanishes into complete self-forgetfulness. In the German Middle Ages, too, singing and dancing crowds, ever increasing in number, whirled themselves from place to place under this same Dionysian impulse. In these dancers of St. John and St. Vitus, we rediscover the Bacchic choruses of the Greeks, with their prehistory in Asia Minor, as far back as Babylon and the orgiastic Sacaea.[9] There are some who, from obtuseness or lack of experience,

---

Books, 1956); and Helmuth von Glasenapp, *Die Philosophie der Inder* (Stuttgart, Kröner, 1949), consulting the indices.

[7] This reference, like subsequent references to the same work, is Nietzsche's own and refers to the edition of 1873 edited by Julius Frauenstädt—still one of the standard editions of Schopenhauer's works.

[8] Principle of individuation.

[9] A Babylonian festival that lasted five days and was marked by general license. During this time slaves are said to have ruled their masters, and a

turn away from such phenomena as from "folk-diseases," with contempt or pity born of the consciousness of their own "healthy-mindedness." But of course such poor wretches have no idea how corpselike and ghostly their so-called "healthy-mindedness" looks when the glowing life of the Dionysian revelers roars past them.

Under the charm of the Dionysian not only is the union between man and man reaffirmed, but nature which has become alienated, hostile, or subjugated, celebrates once more her reconciliation with her lost son,[10] man. Freely, earth proffers her gifts, and peacefully the beasts of prey of the rocks and desert approach. The chariot of Dionysus is covered with flowers and garlands; panthers and tigers walk under its yoke. Transform Beethoven's "Hymn to Joy" into a painting; let your imagination conceive the multitudes bowing to the dust, awestruck—then you will approach the Dionysian. Now the slave is a free man; now all the rigid, hostile barriers that necessity, caprice, or "impudent convention" [11] have fixed between man and man are broken. Now, with the gospel of universal harmony, each one feels himself not only united, reconciled, and fused with his neighbor, but as one with him, as if the veil of *māyā* had been torn aside and were now merely fluttering in tatters before the mysterious primordial unity.

In song and in dance man expresses himself as a member of a higher community; he has forgotten how to walk and speak and is on the way toward flying into the air, dancing. His very gestures express enchantment. Just as the animals now talk, and the earth yields milk and honey, supernatural sounds emanate from him, too: he feels himself a god, he himself now walks about enchanted, in ecstasy, like the gods he saw walking in his dreams. He is no longer an artist, he has become a work of art: in these paroxysms of intoxication the artistic power of all nature reveals itself to the highest gratification of the primordial unity. The noblest clay, the most costly marble, man, is here kneaded and cut, and to the sound of the chisel strokes of the Dionysian world-artist rings out the cry

---

criminal was given all royal rights before he was put to death at the end of the festival. For references, see, e.g., *The Oxford Classical Dictionary.*

[10] In German, "the prodigal son" is *der verlorene Sohn* (the lost son).

[11] An allusion to Friedrich Schiller's hymn *An die Freude* (to joy), used by Beethoven in the final movement of his Ninth Symphony.

of the Eleusinian mysteries: "Do you prostrate yourselves, millions? Do you sense your Maker, world?" [12]

2

Thus far we have considered the Apollinian and its opposite, the Dionysian, as artistic energies which burst forth from nature herself, *without the mediation of the human artist*—energies in which nature's art impulses are satisfied in the most immediate and direct way—first in the image world of dreams, whose completeness is not dependent upon the intellectual attitude or the artistic culture of any single being; and then as intoxicated reality, which likewise does not heed the single unit, but even seeks to destroy the individual and redeem him by a mystic feeling of oneness. With reference to these immediate art-states of nature, every artist is an "imitator," that is to say, either an Apollinian artist in dreams, or a Dionysian artist in ecstasies, or finally—as for example in Greek tragedy—at once artist in both dreams and ecstasies; so we may perhaps picture him sinking down in his Dionysian intoxication and mystical self-abnegation, alone and apart from the singing revelers, and we may imagine how, through Apollinian dream-inspiration, his own state, i.e., his oneness with the inmost ground of the world, is revealed to him in a *symbolical dream image*.

So much for these general premises and contrasts. Let us now approach the *Greeks* in order to learn how highly these *art impulses of nature* were developed in them. Thus we shall be in a position to understand and appreciate more deeply that relation of the Greek artist to his archetypes which is, according to the Aristotelian expression, "the imitation of nature." In spite of all the dream literature and the numerous dream anecdotes of the Greeks, we can speak of their *dreams* only conjecturally, though with reasonable assurance. If we consider the incredibly precise and unerring plastic power of their eyes, together with their vivid, frank delight in colors, we can hardly refrain from assuming even for their dreams (to the shame of all those born later) a certain logic of line and contour, colors and groups, a certain pictorial sequence reminding us of their finest bas-reliefs whose perfection would cer-

---

[12] Quotation from Schiller's hymn.

tainly justify us, if a comparison were possible, in designating the
dreaming Greeks as Homers and Homer as a dreaming Greek—in
a deeper sense than that in which modern man, speaking of his
dreams, ventures to compare himself with Shakespeare.

On the other hand, we need not conjecture regarding the immense gap which separates the *Dionysian Greek* from the Dionysian barbarian. From all quarters of the ancient world—to say
nothing here of the modern—from Rome to Babylon, we can point
to the existence of Dionysian festivals, types which bear, at best,
the same relation to the Greek festivals which the bearded satyr,
who borrowed his name and attributes from the goat, bears to Dionysus himself. In nearly every case these festivals centered in extravagant sexual licentiousness, whose waves overwhelmed all family life and its venerable traditions; the most savage natural instincts
were unleashed, including even that horrible mixture of sensuality
and cruelty which has always seemed to me to be the real "witches'
brew." For some time, however, the Greeks were apparently perfectly insulated and guarded against the feverish excitements of
these festivals, though knowledge of them must have come to
Greece on all the routes of land and sea; for the figure of Apollo,
rising full of pride, held out the Gorgon's head to this grotesquely
uncouth Dionysian power—and really could not have countered
any more dangerous force. It is in Doric art that this majestically
rejecting attitude of Apollo is immortalized.

The opposition between Apollo and Dionysus became more
hazardous and even impossible, when similar impulses finally burst
forth from the deepest roots of the Hellenic nature and made a path
for themselves: the Delphic god, by a seasonably effected reconciliation, now contented himself with taking the destructive weapons
from the hands of his powerful antagonist. This reconciliation is
the most important moment in the history of the Greek cult: wherever we turn we note the revolutions resulting from this event. The
two antagonists were reconciled; the boundary lines to be observed
henceforth by each were sharply defined, and there was to be a
periodical exchange of gifts of esteem. At bottom, however, the
chasm was not bridged over. But if we observe how, under the
pressure of this treaty of peace, the Dionysian power revealed itself, we shall now recognize in the Dionysian orgies of the Greeks,
as compared with the Babylonian Sacaea with their reversion of

man to the tiger and the ape, the significance of festivals of world redemption and days of transfiguration. It is with them that nature for the first time attains her artistic jubilee; it is with them that the destruction of the *principium individuationis* for the first time becomes an artistic phenomenon.

The horrible "witches' brew" of sensuality and cruelty becomes ineffective; only the curious blending and duality in the emotions of the Dionysian revelers remind us—as medicines remind us of deadly poisons—of the phenomenon that pain begets joy, that ecstasy may wring sounds of agony from us. At the very climax of joy there sounds a cry of horror or a yearning lamentation for an irretrievable loss. In these Greek festivals, nature seems to reveal a sentimental [1] trait; it is as if she were heaving a sigh at her dismemberment into individuals. The song and pantomime of such dually-minded revelers was something new and unheard-of in the Homeric-Greek world; and the Dionysian *music* in particular excited awe and terror. If music, as it would seem, had been known previously as an Apollinian art, it was so, strictly speaking, only as the wave beat of rhythm, whose formative power was developed for the representation of Apollinian states. The music of Apollo was Doric architectonics in tones, but in tones that were merely suggestive, such as those of the cithara. The very element which forms the essence of Dionysian music (and hence of music in general) is carefully excluded as un-Apollinian—namely, the emotional power of the tone, the uniform flow of the melody, and the utterly incomparable world of harmony. In the Dionysian dithyramb man is incited to the greatest exaltation of all his symbolic faculties; something never before experienced struggles for utterance—the annihilation of the veil of *māyā,* oneness as the soul of the race and of nature itself. The essence of nature is now to be expressed symbolically; we need a new world of symbols; and the entire symbolism of the body is called into play, not the mere symbolism of the lips, face, and speech but the whole pantomime of dancing, forcing every member into rhythmic movement. Then the other symbolic powers suddenly press forward, particularly those of music, in rhythmics, dynamics, and harmony. To grasp this collective release

---

[1] *Sentimentalisch* (not *sentimental*): an allusion to Schiller's influential contrast of *naïve* (Goethean) poetry with his own *sentimentalische Dichtung.*

of all the symbolic powers, man must have already attained that height of self-abnegation which seeks to express itself symbolically through all these powers—and so the dithyrambic votary of Dionysus is understood only by his peers. With what astonishment must the Apollinian Greek have beheld him! With an astonishment that was all the greater the more it was mingled with the shuddering suspicion that all this was actually not so very alien to him after all, in fact, that it was only his Apollinian consciousness which, like a veil, hid this Dionysian world from his vision.

3

To understand this, it becomes necessary to level the artistic structure of the *Apollinian culture,* as it were, stone by stone, till the foundations on which it rests become visible. First of all we see the glorious *Olympian* figures of the gods, standing on the gables of this structure. Their deeds, pictured in brilliant reliefs, adorn its friezes. We must not be misled by the fact that Apollo stands side by side with the others as an individual deity, without any claim to priority of rank. For the same impulse that embodied itself in Apollo gave birth to this entire Olympian world, and in this sense Apollo is its father. What terrific need was it that could produce such an illustrious company of Olympian beings?

Whoever approaches these Olympians with another religion in his heart, searching among them for moral elevation, even for sanctity, for disincarnate spirituality, for charity and benevolence, will soon be forced to turn his back on them, discouraged and disappointed. For there is nothing here that suggests asceticism, spirituality, or duty. We hear nothing but the accents of an exuberant, triumphant life in which all things, whether good or evil, are deified.[1] And so the spectator may stand quite bewildered before this fantastic excess of life, asking himself by virtue of what magic potion these high-spirited men could have found life so enjoyable that, wherever they turned, their eyes beheld the smile of Helen, the ideal picture of their own existence, "floating in sweet sensuality." But to this spectator, who has already turned his back,

---

[1] This presage of the later coinage "beyond good and evil" is lost when *böse* is mistranslated as "bad" instead of "evil."

we must say: "Do not go away, but stay and hear what Greek folk wisdom has to say of this very life, which with such inexplicable gaiety unfolds itself before your eyes.

"There is an ancient story that King Midas hunted in the forest a long time for the wise Silenus, the companion of Dionysus, without capturing him. When Silenus at last fell into his hands, the king asked what was the best and most desirable of all things for man. Fixed and immovable, the demigod said not a word, till at last, urged by the king, he gave a shrill laugh and broke out into these words: 'Oh, wretched ephemeral race, children of chance and misery, why do you compel me to tell you what it would be most expedient for you not to hear? What is best of all is utterly beyond your reach: not to be born, not to *be*, to be *nothing*. But the second best for you is—to die soon.' " [2]

How is the world of the Olympian gods related to this folk wisdom? Even as the rapturous vision of the tortured martyr to his suffering.

Now it is as if the Olympian magic mountain [3] had opened before us and revealed its roots to us. The Greek knew and felt the terror and horror of existence. That he might endure this terror at all, he had to interpose between himself and life the radiant dream-birth of the Olympians. That overwhelming dismay in the face of the titanic powers of nature, the Moira [4] enthroned inexorably over all knowledge, the vulture of the great lover of mankind, Prometheus, the terrible fate of the wise Oedipus, the family curse of the Atridae which drove Orestes to matricide: in short, that entire philosophy of the sylvan god, with its mythical exemplars, which caused the downfall of the melancholy Etruscans—all this was again and again overcome by the Greeks with the aid of the Olympian *middle world* of art; or at any rate it was veiled and withdrawn from sight. It was in order to be able to live that the Greeks had to create these gods from a most profound need. Perhaps we may picture the process to ourselves somewhat as follows: out of the original Titanic divine order of terror, the Olympian divine order of joy gradually evolved through the Apollinian impulse toward

---

[2] Cf. Sophocles, *Oedipus at Colonus,* lines 1224ff.

[3] *Zauberberg,* as in the title of Thomas Mann's novel.

[4] Fate.

beauty, just as roses burst from thorny bushes. How else could this people, so sensitive, so vehement in its desires, so singularly capable of *suffering,* have endured existence, if it had not been revealed to them in their gods, surrounded with a higher glory?

The same impulse which calls art into being, as the complement and consummation of existence, seducing one to a continuation of life, was also the cause of the Olympian world which the Hellenic "will" made use of as a transfiguring mirror. Thus do the gods justify the life of man: they themselves live it—the only satisfactory theodicy! Existence under the bright sunshine of such gods is regarded as desirable in itself, and the real pain of Homeric men is caused by parting from it, especially by early parting: so that now, reversing the wisdom of Silenus, we might say of the Greeks that "to die soon is worst of all for them, the next worst—to die at all." Once heard, it will ring out again; do not forget the lament of the short-lived Achilles, mourning the leaflike change and vicissitudes of the race of men and the decline of the heroic age. It is not unworthy of the greatest hero to long for a continuation of life, even though he live as a day laborer.[5] At the Apollinian stage of development, the "will" longs so vehemently for this existence, the Homeric man feels himself so completely at one with it, that lamentation itself becomes a song of praise.

Here we should note that this harmony which is contemplated with such longing by modern man, in fact, this oneness of man with nature (for which Schiller introduced the technical term "naïve"), is by no means a simple condition that comes into being naturally and as if inevitably. It is not a condition that, like a terrestrial paradise, *must* necessarily be found at the gate of every culture. Only a romantic age could believe this, an age which conceived of the artist in terms of Rousseau's *Emile* and imagined that in Homer it had found such an artist Emile, reared at the bosom of nature. Where we encounter the "naïve" in art, we should recognize the highest effect of Apollinian culture—which always must first overthrow an empire of Titans and slay monsters, and which must have triumphed over an abysmal and terrifying view of the world and the keenest susceptibility to suffering through recourse to the most forceful and pleasurable illusions. But how rarely is the naïve at-

[5] An allusion to Homer's *Odyssey,* XI, lines 489ff.

tained—that consummate immersion in the beauty of mere appearance! How unutterably sublime is *Homer* therefore, who, as an individual being, bears the same relation to this Apollinian folk culture as the individual dream artist does to the dream faculty of the people and of nature in general.

The Homeric "naïveté" can be understood only as the complete victory of Apollinian illusion: this is one of those illusions which nature so frequently employs to achieve her own ends. The true goal is veiled by a phantasm: and while we stretch out our hands for the latter, nature attains the former by means of our illusion. In the Greeks the "will" wished to contemplate itself in the transfiguration of genius and the world of art; in order to glorify themselves, its creatures had to feel themselves worthy of glory; they had to behold themselves again in a higher sphere, without this perfect world of contemplation acting as a command or a reproach. This is the sphere of beauty, in which they saw their mirror images, the Olympians. With this mirroring of beauty the Hellenic will combated its artistically correlative talent for suffering and for the wisdom of suffering—and, as a monument of its victory, we have Homer, the naïve artist.

4

Now the dream analogy may throw some light on the naïve artist. Let us imagine the dreamer: in the midst of the illusion of the dream world and without disturbing it, he calls out to himself: "It is a dream, I will dream on." What must we infer? That he experiences a deep inner joy in dream contemplation; on the other hand, to be at all able to dream with this inner joy in contemplation, he must have completely lost sight of the waking reality and its ominous obtrusiveness. Guided by the dream-reading Apollo, we may interpret all these phenomena in roughly this way.

Though it is certain that of the two halves of our existence, the waking and the dreaming states, the former appeals to us as infinitely preferable, more important, excellent, and worthy of being lived, indeed, as that which alone is lived—yet in relation to that mysterious ground of our being of which we are the phenomena, I should, paradoxical as it may seem, maintain the very opposite estimate of the value of dreams. For the more clearly I perceive in

nature those omnipotent art impulses, and in them an ardent longing for illusion, for redemption through illusion, the more I feel
myself impelled to the metaphysical assumption that the truly existent primal unity, eternally suffering and contradictory, also needs
the rapturous vision, the pleasurable illusion, for its continuous
redemption. And we, completely wrapped up in this illusion and
composed of it, are compelled to consider this illusion as the truly
nonexistent—i.e., as a perpetual becoming in time, space, and
causality—in other words, as empirical reality. If, for the moment,
we do not consider the question of our own "reality," if we conceive of our empirical existence, and of that of the world in general,
as a continuously manifested representation of the primal unity, we
shall then have to look upon the dream as a *mere appearance of
mere appearance,* hence as a still higher appeasement of the primordial desire for mere appearance. And that is why the innermost
heart of nature feels that ineffable joy in the naïve artist and the
naïve work of art, which is likewise only "mere appearance of
mere appearance."

In a symbolic painting, *Raphael,* himself one of these immortal "naïve" ones, has represented for us this demotion of appearance to the level of mere appearance, the primitive process of the
naïve artist and of Apollinian culture. In his *Transfiguration,* the
lower half of the picture, with the possessed boy, the despairing
bearers, the bewildered, terrified disciples, shows us the reflection
of suffering, primal and eternal, the sole ground of the world: the
"mere appearance" here is the reflection of eternal contradiction,
the father of things. From this mere appearance arises, like ambro-
sial vapor, a new visionary world of mere appearances, invisible to
those wrapped in the first appearance—a radiant floating in purest
bliss, a serene contemplation beaming from wide-open eyes. Here
we have presented, in the most sublime artistic symbolism, that
Apollinian world of beauty and its substratum, the terrible wisdom
of Silenus; and intuitively we comprehend their necessary interde-
pendence. Apollo, however, again appears to us as the apotheosis
of the *principium individuationis,* in which alone is consummated
the perpetually attained goal of the primal unity, its redemption
through mere appearance. With his sublime gestures, he shows us
how necessary is the entire world of suffering, that by means of it
the individual may be impelled to realize the redeeming vision, and

then, sunk in contemplation of it, sit quietly in his tossing bark, amid the waves.

If we conceive of it at all as imperative and mandatory, this apotheosis of individuation knows but one law—the individual, i.e., the delimiting of the boundaries of the individual, *measure* in the Hellenic sense. Apollo, as ethical deity, exacts measure of his disciples, and, to be able to maintain it, he requires self-knowledge. And so, side by side with the aesthetic necessity for beauty, there occur the demands "know thyself" and "nothing in excess"; consequently overweening pride and excess are regarded as the truly hostile demons of the non-Apollinian sphere, hence as characteristics of the pre-Apollinian age—that of the Titans; and of the extra-Apollinian world—that of the barbarians. Because of his titanic love for man, Prometheus must be torn to pieces by vultures; because of his excessive wisdom, which could solve the riddle of the Sphinx, Oedipus must be plunged into a bewildering vortex of crime. Thus did the Delphic god interpret the Greek past.

The effects wrought by the *Dionysian* also seemed "titanic" and "barbaric" to the Apollinian Greek; while at the same time he could not conceal from himself that he, too, was inwardly related to these overthrown Titans and heroes. Indeed, he had to recognize even more than this: despite all its beauty and moderation, his entire existence rested on a hidden substratum of suffering and of knowledge, revealed to him by the Dionysian. And behold: Apollo could not live without Dionysus! The "titanic" and the "barbaric" were in the last analysis as necessary as the Apollinian.

And now let us imagine how into this world, built on mere appearance and moderation and artificially dammed up, there penetrated, in tones ever more bewitching and alluring, the ecstatic sound of the Dionysian festival; how in these strains all of nature's *excess* in pleasure, grief, and knowledge became audible, even in piercing shrieks; and let us ask ourselves what the psalmodizing artist of Apollo, with his phantom harp-sound, could mean in the face of this demonic folk-song! The muses of the arts of "illusion" paled before an art that, in its intoxication, spoke the truth. The wisdom of Silenus cried "Woe! woe!" to the serene Olympians. The individual, with all his restraint and proportion, succumbed to the self-oblivion of the Dionysian states, forgetting the precepts of Apollo. *Excess* revealed itself as truth. Contradiction, the bliss born of pain, spoke out from the very heart of nature. And so, wherever the Dionysian prevailed, the Apollinian was checked and destroyed. But, on the other hand, it is equally certain that, wherever the first Dionysian onslaught was successfully withstood, the authority and majesty of the Delphic god exhibited itself as more rigid and menacing than ever. For to me the *Doric* state[1] and Doric art are explicable only as a permanent military encampment of the Apollinian. Only incessant resistance to the titanic-barbaric nature of the Dionysian could account for the long survival of an art so defiantly prim and so encompassed with bulwarks, a training so warlike and rigorous, and a political structure so cruel and relentless.

Up to this point we have simply enlarged upon the observation made at the beginning of this essay: that the Dionysian and the Apollinian, in new births ever following and mutually augmenting one another, controlled the Hellenic genius; that out of the age of "bronze," with its wars of the Titans and its rigorous folk philosophy, the Homeric world developed under the sway of the Apollinian impulse to beauty; that this "naïve" splendor was again overwhelmed by the influx of the Dionysian; and that against this new power the Apollinian rose to the austere majesty of Doric art and the Doric view of the world. If amid the strife of these two hostile principles, the older Hellenic history thus falls into four great periods of art, we are now impelled to inquire after the final goal of these developments and processes, lest perchance we should regard the last-attained period, the period of Doric art, as the climax and aim of these artistic impulses. And here the sublime and celebrated art of *Attic tragedy* and the dramatic dithyramb presents itself as the common goal of both these tendencies whose mysterious union, after many and long precursory struggles, found glorius consummation in this child—at once Antigone and Cassandra.[2]

---

[1] Sparta.

[2] In footnote 32 of his first polemic (1872) Wilamowitz said: "Whoever explains these last words, to which Mephistopheles' remark about the witch's arithmetic [Goethe's *Faust,* lines 2565–66] applies, receives a suitable reward from me." It would seem that Sophocles' Antigone is here seen as representative of the Apollinian, while Aeschylus' Cassandra (in *Agamemnon*) is associated with the Dionysian.

5

We now approach the real goal of our investigation, which is directed toward knowledge of the Dionysian-Apollinian genius and its art product, or at least toward some feeling for and understanding of this mystery of union. Here we shall begin by seeking the first evidence in Greece of that new germ which subsequently developed into tragedy and the dramatic dithyramb. The ancients themselves give us a symbolic answer, when they place the faces of *Homer* and *Archilochus*,[1] as the forefathers and torchbearers of Greek poetry, side by side on gems, sculptures, etc., with a sure feeling that consideration should be given only to these two, equally completely original, from whom a stream of fire flows over the whole of later Greek history. Homer, the aged self-absorbed dreamer, the type of the Apollinian naïve artist, now beholds with astonishment the passionate head of the warlike votary of the muses, Archilochus, who was hunted savagely through life. Modern aesthetics, by way of interpretation, could only add that here the first "objective" artist confronts the first "subjective" artist. But this interpretation helps us little, because we know the subjective artist only as the poor artist, and throughout the entire range of art we demand first of all the conquest of the subjective, redemption from the "ego," and the silencing of the individual will and desire; indeed, we find it impossible to believe in any truly artistic production, however insignificant, if it is without objectivity, without pure contemplation devoid of interest.[2] Hence our aesthetics must first solve the problem of how the "lyrist" is possible as an artist—he who, according to the experience of all ages, is continually saying "I" and running through the entire chromatic scale of his passions and desires. Compared with Homer, Archilochus appalls us by his cries of hatred and scorn, by his drunken outbursts of desire. Therefore is not he, who has been called the first subjective artist, essentially the non-artist? But in this case, how explain the rever-

---

[1] An early Greek poet whose dates are disputed. He mentions an eclipse that some believe to be the one of 711 B.C., others that of 648 B.C. *The Oxford Classical Dictionary* considers the earlier date more probable. His mother was a slave, and he was killed in battle.

[2] This conception of contemplation devoid of interest, as well as much else that is indebted to Schopenhauer, was later expressly criticized by Nietzsche.

ence which was shown to him—the poet—in very remarkable utterances by the Delphic oracle itself, the center of "objective" art?

Schiller has thrown some light on the poetic process by a psychological observation, inexplicable but unproblematic to his own
mind. He confessed that before the act of creation he did not have
before him or within him any series of images in a causal arrangement, but rather a *musical mood.* ("With me the perception has at
first no clear and definite object; this is formed later. A certain
musical mood comes first, and the poetical idea only follows
later.") Let us add to this the most important phenomenon of all
ancient lyric poetry: they took for granted *the union,* indeed the
identity, of the *lyrist with the musician.* Compared with this, our
modern lyric poetry seems like the statue of a god without a head.
With this in mind we may now, on the basis of our aesthetical
metaphysics set forth above, explain the lyrist to ourselves in this
manner.

In the first place, as a Dionysian artist he has identified himself with the primal unity, its pain and contradiction. Assuming that
music has been correctly termed a repetition and a recast of the
world, we may say that he produces the copy of this primal unity as
music. Now, however, under the Apollinian dream inspiration, this
music reveals itself to him again as a *symbolic dream image.* The
inchoate, intangible reflection of the primordial pain in music, with
its redemption in mere appearance, now produces a second mirroring as a specific symbol or example. The artist has already surren-
dered his subjectivity in the Dionysian process. The image that now
shows him his identity with the heart of the world is a dream scene
that embodies the primordial contradiction and primordial pain,
together with the primordial pleasure, of mere appearance. The "I"
of the lyrist therefore sounds from the depth of his being: its "subjectivity," in the sense of modern aestheticians is a fiction. When
Archilochus, the first Greek lyrist, proclaims to the daughters of
Lycambes both his mad love and his contempt, it is not his passion
alone that dances before us in orgiastic frenzy; but we see Dionysus
and the Maenads, we see the drunken reveler Archilochus sunk
down in slumber—as Euripides depicts it in the *Bacchae,*[3] the
sleep on the high mountain pasture, in the noonday sun. And now

---

[3] Lines 677ff.

Apollo approaches and touches him with the laurel. Then the Dionysian-musical enchantment of the sleeper seems to emit image sparks, lyrical poems, which in their highest development are called tragedies and dramatic dithyrambs.

The plastic artist, like the epic poet who is related to him, is absorbed in the pure contemplation of images. The Dionysian musician is, without any images, himself pure primordial pain and its primordial re-echoing. The lyric genius is conscious of a world of images and symbols—growing out of his state of mystical self-abnegation and oneness. This world has a coloring, a causality, and a velocity quite different from those of the world of the plastic artist and the epic poet. For the latter lives in these images, and only in them, with joyous satisfaction. He never grows tired of contemplating lovingly even their minutest traits. Even the image of the angry Achilles is only an image to him whose angry expression he enjoys with the dreamer's pleasure in illusion. Thus, by this mirror of illusion, he is protected against becoming one and fused with his figures. In direct contrast to this, the images of the *lyrist* are nothing but *his very* self and, as it were, only different projections of himself, so he, as the moving center of this world, may say "I": of course, this self is not the same as that of the waking, empirically real man, but the only truly existent and eternal self resting at the basis of things, through whose images the lyric genius sees this very basis.

Now let us suppose that among these images he also beholds *himself* as nongenius, i.e., his subject, the whole throng of subjective passions and agitations of the will directed to a definite object which appears real to him. It might seem as if the lyric genius and the allied non-genius were one, as if the former had of its own accord spoken that little word "I." But this mere appearance will no longer be able to lead us astray, as it certainly led astray those who designated the lyrist as the subjective poet. For, as a matter of fact, Archilochus, the passionately inflamed, loving, and hating man, is but a vision of the genius, who by this time is no longer merely Archilochus, but a world-genius expressing his primordial pain symbolically in the symbol of the man Archilochus—while the subjectively willing and desiring man, Archilochus, can never at any time be a poet. It is by no means necessary, however, that the lyrist should see nothing but the phenomenon of the man Archilochus before him as a reflection of eternal being; and tragedy shows how far the visionary world of the lyrist may be removed from this phenomenon which, to be sure, is closest at hand.[4]

Schopenhauer, who did not conceal from himself the difficulty the lyrist presents in the philosophical contemplation of art, thought he had found a way out on which, however, I cannot follow him. Actually, it was in his profound metaphysics of music that he alone held in his hands the means for a solution. I believe I have removed the difficulty here in his spirit and to his honor. Yet he describes the peculiar nature of song as follows (*Welt als Wille und Vorstellung,* I, p. 295):

"It is the subject of the will, *i.e.,* his own volition, which fills the consciousness of the singer, often as a released and satisfied desire (joy), but still oftener as an inhibited desire (grief), always as an affect, a passion, a moved state of mind. Besides this, however, and along with it, by the sight of surrounding nature, the singer becomes conscious of himself as the subject of pure will-less knowing, whose unbroken blissful peace now appears, in contrast to the stress of desire, which is always restricted and always needy. The feeling of this contrast, this alternation, is really what the song as a whole expresses and what principally constitutes the lyrical state. In it pure knowing comes to us as it were to deliver us from willing and its strain; we follow, but only for moments; willing, the remembrance of our own personal ends, tears us anew from peaceful contemplation; yet ever again the next beautiful environment in which pure will-less knowledge presents itself to us lures us away from willing. Therefore, in the song and the lyrical mood, willing (the personal interest of the ends) and pure perception of the environment are wonderfully mingled; connections between them are sought and imagined; the subjective mood, the affection of the will, imparts its own hue to the perceived environment, and vice versa. Genuine song is the expression of the whole of this mingled and divided state of mind."

Who could fail to recognize in this description that lyric poetry is here characterized as an incompletely attained art that arrives at its goal infrequently and only, as it were, by leaps? Indeed, it is de-

---

[4] The poet's ego is closest at hand, but the tragic poet can use Cassandra or Hamlet as a mask no less than his own empirical self.

scribed as a semi-art whose *essence* is said to consist in this, that willing and pure contemplation, i.e., the unaesthetic and the aesthetic condition, are wonderfully mingled with each other. We contend, on the contrary, that the whole opposition between the subjective and objective, which Schopenhauer still uses as a measure of value in classifying the arts, is altogether irrelevant in aesthetics, since the subject, the willing individual that furthers his own egoistic ends, can be conceived of only as the antagonist, not as the origin of art. Insofar as the subject is the artist, however, he has already been released from his individual will, and has become, as it were, the medium through which the one truly existent subject celebrates his release in appearance. For to our humiliation *and* exaltation, one thing above all must be clear to us. The entire comedy of art is neither performed for our betterment or education nor are we the true authors of this art world. On the contrary, we may assume that we are merely images and artistic projections for the true author, and that we have our highest dignity in our significance as works of art—for it is only as an *aesthetic phenomenon* that existence and the world are eternally *justified*[5]—while of course our consciousness of our own significance hardly differs from that which the soldiers painted on canvas have of the battle represented on it. Thus all our knowledge of art is basically quite illusory, because as knowing beings we are not one and identical with that being which, as the sole author and spectator of this comedy of art, prepares a perpetual entertainment for itself. Only insofar as the genius in the act of artistic creation coalesces with this primordial artist of the world, does he know anything of the eternal essence of art; for in this state he is, in a marvelous manner, like the weird image of the fairy tale which can turn its eyes at will and behold itself; he is at once subject and object, at once poet, actor, and spectator.

6

In connection with Archilochus, scholarly research has discovered that he introduced the *folk song* into literature and on account

---

[5] This parenthetical remark, repeated in section 24, is one of the most famous dicta in *The Birth of Tragedy*. Cf. also p. 22 above.

of this deserved, according to the general estimate of the Greeks, his unique position beside Homer. But what is the folk song in contrast to the wholly Apollinian epos? What else but the *perpetuum vestigium* of a union of the Apollinian and the Dionysian? Its enormous diffusion among all peoples, further re-enforced by ever-new births, is testimony to the power of this artistic dual impulse of nature, which leaves its vestiges in the folk song just as the orgiastic movements of a people immortalize themselves in its music. Indeed, it might also be historically demonstrable that every period rich in folk songs has been most violently stirred by Dionysian currents, which we must always consider the substratum and prerequisite of the folk song.

First of all, however, we must conceive the folk song as the musical mirror of the world, as the original melody, now seeking for itself a parallel dream phenomenon and expressing it in poetry. *Melody is therefore primary and universal,* and so may admit of several objectifications in several texts. Likewise, in the naïve estimation of the people, it is regarded as by far the more important and essential element. Melody generates the poem out of itself, ever again: that is what *the strophic form of the folk song* signifies; a phenomenon which I had always beheld with astonishment, until at last I found this explanation. Anyone who in accordance with this theory examines a collection of folk songs, such as *Des Knaben Wunderhorn,*[1] will find innumerable instances of the way the continuously generating melody scatters image sparks all around, which in their variegation, their abrupt change, their mad precipitation, manifest a power quite unknown to the epic and its steady flow. From the standpoint of the epos, this unequal and irregular image world of lyrical poetry is simply to be condemned: and it certainly has been thus condemned by the solemn epic rhapsodists of the Apollinian festivals in the age of Terpander.[2]

Accordingly, we observe that in the poetry of the folk song, language is strained to its utmost that it may *imitate music;* and with Archilochus begins a new world of poetry, basically op-

---

[1] An anthology of medieval German folk songs (1806–08), edited by Achim von Arnim (1781–1831) and his brother-in-law, Clemens Brentano (1778–1842). The title means "The Boy's Magic Horn."

[2] Middle of the seventh century B.C. Terpander, a poet, was born in Lesbos and lived in Sparta.

posed to the Homeric. And in saying this we have indicated the only possible relation between poetry and music, between word and tone: the word, the image, the concept here seeks an expression analogous to music and now feels in itself the power of music. In this sense we may discriminate between two main currents in the history of the language of the Greek people, according to whether their language imitated the world of image and phenomenon or the world of music. One need only reflect more deeply on the linguistic difference with regard to color, syntactical structure, and vocabulary in Homer and Pindar, in order to understand the significance of this contrast; indeed, it becomes palpably clear that in the period between Homer and Pindar the *orgiastic flute tones of Olympus* must have been sounded, which, even in Aristotle's time, when music was infinitely more developed, transported people to drunken ecstasy, and which, in their primitive state of development, undoubtedly incited to imitation all the poetic means of expression of contemporaneous man.

I here call attention to a familiar phenomenon of our own times, against which our aesthetic raises many objections. Again and again we have occasion to observe that a Beethoven symphony compels its individual auditors to use figurative speech in describing it, no matter how fantastically variegated and even contradictory may be the composition and make-up of the different worlds of images produced by a piece of music. To exercise its poor wit on such compositions, and to overlook a phenomenon which is certainly worth explaining, are quite in keeping with this aesthetic. Indeed, even when the tone-poet expresses his composition in images, when for instance he designates a certain symphony as the "pastoral" symphony, or a passage in it as the "scene by the brook," or another as the "merry gathering of rustics," these two are only symbolical representations born of music—and not the imitated objects of music—representations which can teach us nothing whatsoever concerning the *Dionysian* content of music, and which indeed have no distinctive value of their own beside other images. We have now to transfer this process of a discharge of music in images to some fresh, youthful, linguistically creative people, in order to get some notion of the way in which the strophic folk song originates, and the whole linguistic capacity is excited by this new principle of the imitation of music.

If, therefore, we may regard lyric poetry as the imitative fulguration of music in images and concepts, we should now ask: "As what does music *appear* in the mirror of images and concepts?" It *appears as* will, taking the term in Schopenhauer's sense, i.e., as the opposite of the aesthetic, purely contemplative, and passive frame of mind. Here, however, we must make as sharp a distinction as possible between the concepts of essence and phenomenon; for music, according to its essence, cannot possibly be will. To be will it would have to be wholly banished from the realm of art—for the will is the unaesthetic-in-itself; but it *appears* as will. For in order to express its appearance in images, the lyrist needs all the agitations of passion, from the whisper of mere inclination to the roar of madness. Impelled to speak of music in Apollinian symbols, he conceives of all nature, and himself in it, as willing, as desiring, as eternal longing. But insofar as he interprets music by means of images, he himself rests in the calm sea of Apollinian contemplation, though everything around him that he beholds through the medium of music is in urgent and active motion. Indeed, when he beholds himself through this same medium, his own image appears to him as an unsatisfied feeling: his own willing, longing, moaning, rejoicing, are to him symbols by which he interprets music. This is the phenomenon of the lyrist: as Apollinian genius he interprets music through the image of the will, while he himself, completely released from the greed of the will, is the pure, undimmed eye of the sun.

Our whole discussion insists that lyric poetry is dependent on the spirit of music just as music itself in its absolute sovereignty does not *need* the image and the concept, but merely *endures* them as accompaniments. The poems of the lyrist can express nothing that did not already lie hidden in that vast universality and absoluteness in the music that compelled him to figurative speech. Language can never adequately render the cosmic symbolism of music, because music stands in symbolic relation to the primordial contradiction and primordial pain in the heart of the primal unity, and therefore symbolizes a sphere which is beyond and prior to all phenomena. Rather, all phenomena, compared with it, are merely symbols: hence *language,* as the organ and symbol of phenomena, can never by any means disclose the innermost heart of music; language, in its attempt to imitate it, can only be in superficial contact with music; while all the eloquence of lyric poetry cannot bring the deepest significance of the latter one step nearer to us.

7

We must now avail ourselves of all the principles of art considered so far, in order to find our way through the labyrinth, as we must call it, of *the origin of Greek tragedy*. I do not think I am unreasonable in saying that the problem of this origin has as yet not even been seriously posed, to say nothing of solved, however often the ragged tatters of ancient tradition have been sewn together in various combinations and torn apart again. This tradition tells us quite unequivocally *that tragedy arose from the tragic chorus,* and was originally only chorus and nothing but chorus. Hence we consider it our duty to look into the heart of this tragic chorus as the real proto-drama, without resting satisfied with such arty clichés as that the chorus is the "ideal spectator" or that it represents the people in contrast to the aristocratic region of the scene. This latter explanation has a sublime sound to many a politician—as if the immutable moral law had been embodied by the democratic Athenians in the popular chorus, which always won out over the passionate excesses and extravagances of kings. This theory may be ever so forcibly suggested by one of Aristotle's observations; still, it has no influence on the original formation of tragedy, inasmuch as the whole opposition of prince and people—indeed the whole politico-social sphere—was excluded from the purely religious origins of tragedy. But even regarding the classical form of the chorus in Aeschylus and Sophocles, which is known to us, we should deem it blasphemy to speak here of intimations of "constitutional popular representation." From this blasphemy, however, others have not shrunk. Ancient constitutions knew of no constitutional representation of the people in *praxi,* and it is to be hoped that they did not even "have intimations" of it in tragedy.

Much more famous than this political interpretation of the chorus is the idea of A. W. Schlegel,[1] who advises us to regard the

---

[1] One of the leading spirits of the early German romantic movement, especially renowned for his translations of about half of Shakespeare's plays; born 1767, died 1845.

chorus somehow as the essence and extract of the crowd of spectators—as the "ideal spectator." This view, when compared with the historical tradition that originally tragedy was only chorus, reveals itself for what it is—a crude, unscientific, yet brilliant claim that owes its brilliancy only to its concentrated form of expression, to the typically Germanic bias in favor of anything called "ideal," and to our momentary astonishment. For we are certainly astonished the moment we compare our familiar theatrical public with this chorus, and ask ourselves whether it could ever be possible to idealize from such a public something analogous to the Greek tragic chorus. We tacitly deny this, and now wonder as much at the boldness of Schlegel's claim as at the totally different nature of the Greek public. For we had always believed that the right spectator, whoever he might be, must always remain conscious that he was viewing a work of art and not an empirical reality. But the tragic chorus of the Greeks is forced to recognize real beings in the figures on the stage. The chorus of the Oceanides really believes that it sees before it the Titan Prometheus, and it considers itself as real as the god of the scene. But could the highest and purest type of spectator regard Prometheus as bodily present and real, as the Oceanides do? Is it characteristic of the ideal spectator to run onto the stage and free the god from his torments? We had always believed in an aesthetic public and considered the individual spectator the better qualified the more he was capable of viewing a work of art as art, that is, aesthetically. But now Schlegel tells us that the perfect, ideal spectator does not at all allow the world of the drama to act on him aesthetically, but corporally and empirically. Oh, these Greeks! we sigh; they upset all our aesthetics! But once accustomed to this, we repeated Schlegel's saying whenever the chorus came up for discussion.

Now the tradition, which is quite explicit, speaks against Schlegel. The chorus as such, without the stage—the primitive form of tragedy—and the chorus of ideal spectators do not go together. What kind of artistic genre could possibly be extracted from the concept of the spectator, and find its true form in the "spectator as such"? The spectator without the spectacle is an absurd notion. We fear that the birth of tragedy is to be explained neither by any high esteem for the moral intelligence of the masses nor by the concept of the spectator without a spectacle; and we consider the problem too deep to be even touched by such superficial considerations.

An infinitely more valuable insight into the significance of the chorus was displayed by Schiller in the celebrated Preface to his *Bride of Messina,* where he regards the chorus as a living wall that tragedy constructs around itself in order to close itself off from the world of reality and to preserve its ideal domain and its poetical freedom.

With this, his chief weapon, Schiller combats the ordinary conception of the natural, the illusion usually demanded in dramatic poetry. Although the stage day is merely artificial, the architecture only symbolical, and the metrical language ideal in character, nevertheless an erroneous view still prevails in the main, as he points out: it is not sufficient that one merely tolerates as poetic license what is actually the essence of all poetry. The introduction of the chorus, says Schiller, is the decisive step by which war is declared openly and honorably against all naturalism in art.

It would seem that to denigrate this view of the matter our would-be superior age has coined the disdainful catchword "pseudo-idealism." I fear, however, that we, on the other hand, with our present adoration of the natural and the real, have reached the opposite pole of all idealism, namely, the region of wax-work cabinets. There is an art in these, too, as there is in certain novels much in vogue at present; but we really should not be plagued with the claim that such art has overcome the "pseudo-idealism" of Goethe and Schiller.

It is indeed an "ideal" domain, as Schiller correctly perceived, in which the Greek satyr chorus, the chorus of primitive tragedy, was wont to dwell. It is a domain raised high above the actual paths of mortals. For this chorus the Greek built up the scaffolding of a fictitious *natural state* and on it placed fictitious *natural beings.* On this foundation tragedy developed and so, of course, it could dispense from the beginning with a painstaking portrayal of reality. Yet it is no arbitrary world placed by whim between heaven and earth; rather it is a world with the same reality and credibility that Olympus with its inhabitants possessed for the believing Hellene. The satyr, as the Dionysian chorist, lives in a religiously acknowledged reality under the sanction of myth and cult. That tragedy should begin with him, that he should be the voice of the Dionysian wisdom of tragedy, is just as strange a phenomenon for us as the general derivation of tragedy from the chorus.

Perhaps we shall have a point of departure for our inquiry if I put forward the proposition that the satyr, the fictitious natural being, bears the same relation to the man of culture that Dionysian music bears to civilization. Concerning the latter, Richard Wagner says that it is nullified [2] by music just as lamplight is nullified by the light of day. Similarly, I believe, the Greek man of culture felt himself nullified in the presence of the satyric chorus; and this is the most immediate effect of the Dionysian tragedy, that the state and society and, quite generally, the gulfs between man and man give way to an overwhelming feeling of unity leading back to the very heart of nature. The metaphysical comfort—with which, I am suggesting even now, every true tragedy leaves us—that life is at the bottom of things, despite all the changes of appearances, indestructibly powerful and pleasurable—this comfort appears in incarnate clarity in the chorus of satyrs, a chorus of natural beings who live ineradicably, as it were, behind all civilization and remain eternally the same, despite the changes of generations and of the history of nations.

With this chorus the profound Hellene, uniquely susceptible to the tenderest and deepest suffering, comforts himself, having looked boldly right into the terrible destructiveness of so-called world history as well as the cruelty of nature, and being in danger of longing for a Buddhistic negation of the will. [3] Art saves him, and through art—life.

For the rapture of the Dionysian state with its annihilation of the ordinary bounds and limits of existence contains, while it lasts, a *lethargic* element in which all personal experiences of the past become immersed. This chasm of oblivion separates the worlds of everyday reality and of Dionysian reality. But as soon as this everyday reality re-enters consciousness, it is experienced as such,

---

[2] *Aufgehoben:* one of Hegel's favorite words, which can also mean lifted up or preserved.

[3] Here Nietzsche's emancipation from Schopenhauer becomes evident, and their difference from each other concerns the central subject of the whole book: the significance of tragedy. Nietzsche writes about tragedy as the great life-affirming alternative to Schopenhauer's negation of the will. One can be as honest and free of optimistic illusions as Schopenhauer was, and still celebrate life as fundamentally powerful and pleasurable as the Greeks did.

with nausea: an ascetic, will-negating mood is the fruit of these states.

In this sense the Dionysian man resembles Hamlet: both have once looked truly into the essence of things, they have *gained knowledge,* and nausea inhibits action; for their action could not change anything in the eternal nature of things; they feel it to be ridiculous or humiliating that they should be asked to set right a world that is out of joint. Knowledge kills action; action requires the veils of illusion: that is the doctrine of Hamlet, not that cheap wisdom of Jack the Dreamer who reflects too much and, as it were, from an excess of possibilities does not get around to action. Not reflection, no—true knowledge, an insight into the horrible truth, outweighs any motive for action, both in Hamlet and in the Dionysian man.

Now no comfort avails any more; longing transcends a world after death, even the gods; existence is negated along with its glittering reflection in the gods or in an immortal beyond. Conscious of the truth he has once seen, man now sees everywhere only the horror or absurdity of existence; now he understands what is symbolic in Ophelia's fate; now he understands the wisdom of the sylvan god, Silenus: he is nauseated.

Here, when the danger to his will is greatest, *art* approaches as a saving sorceress, expert at healing. She alone knows how to turn these nauseous thoughts about the horror or absurdity of existence into notions with which one can live: these are the *sublime* as the artistic taming of the horrible, and the *comic* as the artistic discharge of the nausea of absurdity. The satyr chorus of the dithyramb is the saving deed of Greek art; faced with the intermediary world of these Dionysian companions, the feelings described here exhausted themselves.[4]

---

[4] Having finally broken loose from Schopenhauer, Nietzsche for the first time shows the brilliancy of his own genius. It is doubtful whether anyone before him had illuminated *Hamlet* so extensively in so few words: the passage invites comparison with Freud's great footnote on *Hamlet* in the first edition of *Die Traumdeutung* (interpretation of dreams), 1900. Even more obviously, the last three paragraphs invite comparison with existentialist literature, notably, but by no means only, Sartre's *La Nausée* (1938).

8

The satyr, like the idyllic shepherd of more recent times, is the offspring of a longing for the primitive and the natural; but how firmly and fearlessly the Greek embraced the man of the woods, and how timorously and mawkishly modern man dallied with the flattering image of a sentimental, flute-playing, tender shepherd! Nature, as yet unchanged by knowledge, with the bolts of culture still unbroken—that is what the Greek saw in his satyr who nevertheless was not a mere ape. On the contrary, the satyr was the archetype of man, the embodiment of his highest and most intense emotions, the ecstatic reveler enraptured by the proximity of his god, the sympathetic companion in whom the suffering of the god is repeated, one who proclaims wisdom from the very heart of nature, a symbol of the sexual omnipotence of nature which the Greeks used to contemplate with reverent wonder.

The satyr was something sublime and divine: thus he had to appear to the painfully broken vision of Dionysian man. The contrived shepherd in his dress-ups would have offended him: on the unconcealed and vigorously magnificent characters of nature, his eye rested with sublime satisfaction; here the true human being was disclosed, the bearded satyr jubilating to his god. Confronted with him, the man of culture shriveled into a mendacious caricature.

Schiller is right about these origins of tragic art, too: the chorus is a living wall against the assaults of reality because it—the satyr chorus—represents existence more truthfully, really, and completely than the man of culture does who ordinarily considers himself as the only reality. The sphere of poetry does not lie outside the world as a fantastic impossibility spawned by a poet's brain: it desires to be just the opposite, the unvarnished expression of the truth, and must precisely for that reason discard the mendacious finery of that alleged reality of the man of culture.

The contrast between this real truth of nature and the lie of culture that poses as if it were the only reality is similar to that between the eternal core of things, the thing-in-itself, and the whole world of appearances:[1] just as tragedy, with its metaphysical com-

---

[1] The word translated as "appearances" in this passage is *Erscheinungen*.

fort, points to the eternal life of this core of existence which abides through the perpetual destruction of appearances, the symbolism of the satyr chorus proclaims this primordial relationship between the thing-in-itself and appearance.[2] The idyllic shepherd of modern man is merely a counterfeit of the sum of cultural illusions that are allegedly nature; the Dionysian Greek wants truth and nature in their most forceful form—and sees himself changed, as by magic, into a satyr.

The reveling throng, the votaries of Dionysus jubilate under the spell of such moods and insights whose power transforms them before their own eyes till they imagine that they are beholding themselves as restored geniuses of nature, as satyrs. The later constitution of the chorus in tragedy is the artistic imitation of this natural phenomenon, though, to be sure, at this point the separation of Dionysian spectators and magically enchanted Dionysians became necessary. Only we must always keep in mind that the public at an Attic tragedy found itself in the chorus of the *orchestra,*[3] and there was at bottom no opposition between public and chorus: everything is merely a great sublime chorus of dancing and singing satyrs or of those who permit themselves to be represented by such satyrs.

Now we are ready to understand Schlegel's formulation in a deeper sense. The chorus is the "ideal spectator" [4] insofar as it is the only beholder, the beholder of the visionary world of the scene.[5] A public of spectators as we know it was unknown to the

---

[2] Here Nietzsche returns to Schopenhauer's perspective.

[3] "The Greek theatre appears to have been originally designed for the performance of dithyrambic choruses in honour of Dionysus. The centre of it was the *orchēstrā* ('dancing-place'), a circular space, in the middle of which stood the *thumelē* or altar of the god. Round more than half of the *orchestra,* forming a kind of horse-shoe, was the *theātron* ('seeing-place') proper, circular tiers of seats, generally cut out of the side of a hill . . . Behind the orchestra and facing the audience was the *skēnē* [called "scene" in the above translation], originally a wooden structure, a façade with three doors, through which, when the drama had developed from the dithyrambic chorus, the actors made their entrances" (*The Oxford Companion to Classical Literature,* ed. Sir Paul Harvey, revised edition, 1946, pp. 422f.).

[4] *Der "idealische Zuschauer."*

[5] *Der einzige* Schauer *ist, der Schauer der Visionswelt der Scene.* The word *Schauer* could also mean shudder, the shudder of holy awe; and while this is certainly not the primary meaning intended here, it somehow enters into the coloring of the sentence.

Greeks: in their theaters the terraced structure of concentric arcs made it possible for everybody to actually *overlook*[6] the whole world of culture around him and to imagine, in absorbed contemplation, that he himself was a chorist.

In the light of this insight we may call the chorus in its primitive form, in proto-tragedy, the mirror image in which the Dionysian man contemplates himself. This phenomenon is best made clear by imagining an actor who, being truly talented, sees the role he is supposed to play quite palpably before his eyes. The satyr chorus is, first of all, a vision of the Dionysian mass of spectators, just as the world of the stage, in turn, is a vision of this satyr chorus: the force of this vision is strong enough to make the eye insensitive and blind to the impression of "reality," to the men of culture who occupy the rows of seats all around. The form of the Greek theater recalls a lonely valley in the mountains: the architecture of the scene appears like a luminous cloud formation that the Bacchants swarming over the mountains behold from a height— like the splendid frame in which the image of Dionysus is revealed to them.

In the face of our learned views about elementary artistic processes, this artistic proto-phenomenon which we bring up here to help explain the tragic chorus is almost offensive, although nothing could be more certain than the fact that a poet is a poet only insofar as he sees himself surrounded by figures who live and act before him and into whose inmost nature he can see. Owing to a peculiar modern weakness, we are inclined to imagine the aesthetic protophenomenon in a manner much too complicated and abstract.

For a genuine poet, metaphor is not a rhetorical figure but a vicarious image that he actually beholds in place of a concept. A character is for him not a whole he has composed out of particular traits, picked up here and there, but an obtrusively alive person before his very eyes, distinguished from the otherwise identical vision of a painter only by the fact that it continually goes on living and acting. How is it that Homer's descriptions are so much more vivid

---

[6] *Übersehen,* like overlook, can mean both survey and ignore. Francis Golffing, in his translation, opts for "quite literally survey," which makes nonsense of the passage. The context unequivocally requires oblivion of the whole world of culture: nothing is between the beholder and the chorus. Golffing's translation is altogether more vigorous than it is reliable.

than those of any other poet? Because he visualizes so much more vividly. We talk so abstractly about poetry because all of us are usually bad poets. At bottom, the aesthetic phenomenon is simple: let anyone have the ability to behold continually a vivid play and to live constantly surrounded by hosts of spirits, and he will be a poet; let anyone feel the urge to transform himself and to speak out of other bodies and souls, and he will be a dramatist.

The Dionysian excitement is capable of communicating this artistic gift to a multitude, so they can see themselves surrounded by such a host of spirits while knowing themselves to be essentially one with them. This process of the tragic chorus is the *dramatic* proto-phenomenon: to see oneself transformed before one's own eyes and to begin to act as if one had actually entered into another body, another character. This process stands at the beginning of the origin of drama. Here we have something different from the rhapsodist who does not become fused with his images but, like a painter, sees them outside himself as objects of contemplation. Here we have a surrender of individuality and a way of entering into another character. And this phenomenon is encountered epidemically: a whole throng experiences the magic of this transformation.

The dithyramb is thus essentially different from all other choral odes. The virgins who proceed solemnly to the temple of Apollo, laurel branches in their hands, singing a processional hymn, remain what they are and retain their civic names: the dithyrambic chorus is a chorus of transformed characters whose civic past and social status have been totally forgotten: they have become timeless servants of their god who live outside the spheres of society. All the other choral lyric poetry of the Hellenes is merely a tremendous intensification of the Apollinian solo singer, while in the dithyramb we confront a community of unconscious actors who consider themselves and one another transformed.

Such magic transformation is the presupposition of all dramatic art. In this magic transformation the Dionysian reveler sees himself as a satyr, *and as a satyr, in turn, he sees the god,* which means that in his metamorphosis he beholds another vision outside himself, as the Apollinian complement of his own state. With this new vision the drama is complete.

In the light of this insight we must understand Greek tragedy as the Dionysian chorus which ever anew discharges itself in an Apollinian world of images. Thus the choral parts with which tragedy is interlaced are, as it were, the womb that gave birth to the whole of the so-called dialogue, that is, the entire world of the stage, the real drama. In several successive discharges this primal ground of tragedy radiates this vision of the drama which is by all means a dream apparition and to that extent epic in nature; but on the other hand, being the objectification of a Dionysian state, it represents not Apollinian redemption through mere appearance but, on the contrary, the shattering of the individual and his fusion with primal being. Thus the drama is the Dionysian embodiment of Dionysian insights and effects and thereby separated, as by a tremendous chasm, from the epic.

The *chorus* of the Greek tragedy, the symbol of the whole excited Dionysian throng, is thus fully explained by our conception. Accustomed as we are to the function of our modern stage chorus, especially in operas, we could not comprehend why the tragic chorus of the Greeks should be older, more original and important than the "action" proper, as the voice of tradition claimed unmistakably. And with this traditional primacy and originality we could not reconcile the fact that the chorus consisted only of humble beings who served—indeed, initially only of goatlike satyrs. Finally, there remained the riddle of the orchestra in front of the scene. But now we realize that the scene, complete with the action, was basically and originally thought of merely as a *vision;* the chorus is the only "reality" and generates the vision, speaking of it with the entire symbolism of dance, tone, and words. In its vision this chorus beholds its lord and master Dionysus and is therefore eternally the *serving* chorus: it sees how the god suffers and glorifies himself and therefore does not itself *act*. But while its attitude toward the god is wholly one of service, it is nevertheless the highest, namely the Dionysian, expression of *nature* and therefore pronounces in its rapture, as nature does, oracles and wise sayings: *sharing his suffering* it also shares something of his *wisdom* and proclaims the truth from the heart of the world. That is the origin of the fantastic and seemingly so offensive figure of the wise and rapturous satyr who is at the same time "the simple man" as opposed to the god—the image of nature and its strongest urges, even their symbol, and at the same time the proclaimer of her wisdom and art—musician, poet, dancer, and seer of spirits in one person.

Dionysus, the real stage hero and center of the vision, was, according both to this insight and to the tradition, not actually present at first, in the very oldest period of tragedy; he was merely imagined as present, which means that originally tragedy was only "chorus" and not yet "drama." Later the attempt was made to show the god as real and to represent the visionary figure together with its transfiguring frame as something visible for every eye—and thus "drama" in the narrower sense began. Now the dithyrambic chorus was assigned the task of exciting the mood of the listeners to such a Dionysian degree that, when the tragic hero appeared on the stage, they did not see the awkwardly masked human being but rather a visionary figure, born as it were from their own rapture.

Consider Admetus as he is brooding over the memory of his recently departed wife Alcestis, consuming himself in her spiritual contemplation, when suddenly a similarly formed, similarly walking woman's figure is led toward him, heavily veiled; let us imagine his sudden trembling unrest, his tempestuous comparisons, his instinctive conviction—and we have an analogy with what the spectator felt in his Dionysian excitement when he saw the approach on the stage of the god with whose sufferings he had already identified himself. Involuntarily, he transferred the whole magic image of the god that was trembling before his soul to that masked figure and, as it were, dissolved its reality into the unreality of spirits.

This is the Apollinian state of dreams in which the world of the day becomes veiled, and a new world, clearer, more understandable, more moving than the everyday world and yet more shadowy, presents itself to our eyes in continual rebirths. Accordingly, we recognize in tragedy a sweeping opposition of styles: the language, color, mobility, and dynamics of speech fall apart into the Dionysian lyrics of the chorus and, on the other hand, the Apollinian dream world, and become two utterly different spheres of expression. The Apollinian appearances in which Dionysus objectifies himself are no longer "an eternal sea, changeful strife, a glowing life," [7] like the music of the chorus, no longer those forces, merely felt and not condensed into images, in which the enraptured servant of Dionysus senses the nearness of the god: now the clarity

---

[7] Quoted from Goethe's *Faust,* lines 505–507.

and firmness of epic form addresses him from the scene; now Dionysus no longer speaks through forces but as an epic hero, almost in the language of Homer.

9

Everything that comes to the surface in the Apollinian part of Greek tragedy, in the dialogue, looks simple, transparent, and beautiful. In this sense, the dialogue is an image of the Hellene whose nature is revealed in the dance because in the dance the greatest strength remains only potential but betrays itself in the suppleness and wealth of movement. Thus the language of Sophocles' heroes amazes us by its Apollinian precision and lucidity, so we immediately have the feeling that we are looking into the innermost ground of their being, with some astonishment that the way to this ground should be so short. But suppose we disregard the character of the hero as it comes to the surface, visibly—after all, it is in the last analysis nothing but a bright image projected on a dark wall, which means appearance[1] through and through; suppose we penetrate into the myth that projects itself in these lucid reflections: then we suddenly experience a phenomenon that is just the opposite of a familiar optical phenomenon. When after a forceful attempt to gaze on the sun we turn away blinded, we see dark-colored spots before our eyes, as a cure, as it were. Conversely, the bright image projections of the Sophoclean hero—in short, the Apollinian aspect of the mask—are necessary effects of a glance into the inside and terrors of nature; as it were, luminous spots to cure eyes damaged by gruesome night. Only in this sense may we believe that we properly comprehend the serious and important concept of "Greek cheerfulness." The misunderstanding of this concept as cheerfulness in a state of unendangered comfort is, of course, encountered everywhere today.

Sophocles understood the most sorrowful figure of the Greek stage, the unfortunate Oedipus, as the noble human being who, in spite of his wisdom, is destined to error and misery but who eventually, through his tremendous suffering, spreads a magical power of blessing that remains effective even beyond his decease. The

---

[1] *Erscheinung*.

noble human being does not sin, the profound poet wants to tell us: though every law, every natural order, even the moral world may perish through his actions, his actions also produce a higher magical circle of effects which found a new world on the ruins of the old one that has been overthrown. That is what the poet wants to say to us insofar as he is at the same time a religious thinker. As a poet he first shows us a marvelously tied knot of a trial, slowly unraveled by the judge, bit by bit, for his own undoing. The genuinely Hellenic delight at this dialectical solution is so great that it introduces a trait of superior cheerfulness into the whole work, everywhere softening the sharp points of the gruesome presuppositions of this process.

In *Oedipus at Colonus* we encounter the same cheerfulness, but elevated into an infinite transfiguration. The old man, struck by an excess of misery, abandoned solely to *suffer* whatever befalls him, is confronted by the supraterrestrial cheerfulness that descends from the divine sphere and suggests to us that the hero attains his highest activity, extending far beyond his life, through his purely passive posture, while his conscious deeds and desires, earlier in his life, merely led him into passivity. Thus the intricate legal knot of the Oedipus fable that no mortal eye could unravel is gradually disentangled—and the most profound human joy overcomes us at this divine counterpart of the dialectic.

If this explanation does justice to the poet one may yet ask whether it exhausts the contents of the myth—and then it becomes evident that the poet's whole conception is nothing but precisely that bright image which healing nature projects before us after a glance into the abyss. Oedipus, the murderer of his father, the husband of his mother, the solver of the riddle of the Sphinx! What does the mysterious triad of these fateful deeds tell us?

There is a tremendously old popular belief, especially in Persia, that a wise magus can be born only from incest. With the riddle-solving and mother-marrying Oedipus in mind, we must immediately interpret this to mean that where prophetic and magical powers have broken the spell of present and future, the rigid law of individuation, and the real magic of nature, some enormously unnatural event—such as incest—must have occurred earlier, as a cause. How else could one compel nature to surrender her secrets if not by triumphantly resisting her, that is, by means of something unnatural? It is this insight that I find expressed in that horrible triad of Oedipus' destinies: the same man who solves the riddle of nature—that Sphinx of two species[2]—also must break the most sacred natural orders by murdering his father and marrying his mother. Indeed, the myth seems to wish to whisper to us that wisdom, and particularly Dionysian wisdom, is an unnatural abomination; that he who by means of his knowledge plunges nature into the abyss of destruction must also suffer the dissolution of nature in his own person. "The edge of wisdom turns against the wise: wisdom is a crime against nature": such horrible sentences are proclaimed to us by the myth; but the Hellenic poet touches the sublime and terrible Memnon's Column of myth like a sunbeam, so that it suddenly begins to sound—in Sophoclean melodies.[3]

Let me now contrast the glory of activity, which illuminates Aeschylus' *Prometheus,* with the glory of passivity. What the thinker Aeschylus had to say to us here, but what as a poet he only allows us to sense in his symbolic image, the youthful Goethe was able to reveal to us in the audacious words of his Prometheus:

> *Here I sit, forming men*
> *in my own image,*
> *a race to be like me,*
> *to suffer, to weep,*
> *to delight and to rejoice,*
> *and to defy you,*
> *as I do.*[4]

Man, rising to Titanic stature, gains culture by his own efforts and forces the gods to enter into an alliance with him because in his

---

[2] Lion and human. Actually, the Sphinx also has wings in ancient Greek representations.

Nietzsche's comments on incest are influenced by Wagner and should be compared with *The Case of Wagner,* section 4, third paragraph on p. 619.

[3] Memnon's Column was an ancient name given to one of the two colossal statues of the pharaoh Amenophis III, near the Egyptian Thebes between the Nile and the valley of the kings, across the river from Karnak. When the first rays of the sun struck the weathered statue in the morning, it is said to have produced a musical sound—a phenomenon that stopped when an earthquake damaged the statue still further. The "statue of Memnon" also appears in Ibsen's *Peer Gynt* (1867), in Act IV.

[4] Goethe's poem—original text and verse translation on facing pages—is included in *Twenty German Poets,* trans. W. Kaufmann.

very own wisdom he holds their existence and their limitations in his hands. But what is most wonderful in this Prometheus poem, which in its basic idea is the veritable hymn of impiety, is the profoundly Aeschylean demand for *justice*. The immeasurable suffering of the bold "individual" on the one hand and the divine predicament and intimation of a twilight of the gods on the other, the way the power of these two worlds of suffering compels a reconciliation, a metaphysical union—all this recalls in the strongest possible manner the center and main axiom of the Aeschylean view of the world which envisages Moira enthroned above gods and men as eternal justice.

In view of the astonishing audacity with which Aeschylus places the Olympian world on the scales of his justice, we must call to mind that the profound Greek possessed an immovably firm foundation for metaphysical thought in his mysteries, and all his skeptical moods could be vented against the Olympians. The Greek artist in particular had an obscure feeling of mutual dependence when it came to the gods; and precisely in the *Prometheus* of Aeschylus this feeling is symbolized. In himself the Titanic artist found the defiant faith that he had the ability to create men and at least destroy Olympian gods, by means of his superior wisdom which, to be sure, he had to atone for with eternal suffering. The splendid "ability" of the great genius for which even eternal suffering is a slight price, the stern pride of the *artist*—that is the content and soul of Aeschylus' poem, while Sophocles in his *Oedipus* sounds as a prelude the *holy man's* song of triumph.

But Aeschylus' interpretation of the myth does not exhaust the astounding depth of its terror. Rather the artist's delight in what becomes, the cheerfulness of artistic creation that defies all misfortune, is merely a bright image of clouds and sky mirrored in a black lake of sadness. The Prometheus story is an original possession of the entire Aryan community of peoples and evidences their gift for the profoundly tragic. Indeed, it does not seem improbable that this myth has the same characteristic significance for the Aryan character which the myth of the fall has for the Semitic character, and that these two myths are related to each other like brother and sister.[5] The presupposition of the Prometheus myth is

---

[5] After his emancipation from Wagner, Nietzsche came to consider the

to be found in the extravagant value which a naïve humanity attached to *fire* as the true palladium of every ascending culture. But that man should freely dispose of fire without receiving it as a present from heaven, either as a lightning bolt or as the warming rays of the sun, struck these reflective primitive men as sacrilege, as a robbery of divine nature. Thus the very first philosophical problem immediately produces a painful and irresolvable contradiction between man and god and moves it before the gate of every culture, like a huge boulder. The best and highest possession mankind can acquire is obtained by sacrilege and must be paid for with consequences that involve the whole flood of sufferings and sorrows with which the offended divinities have to afflict the nobly aspiring race of men. This is a harsh idea which, by the *dignity* it confers on sacrilege, contrasts strangely with the Semitic myth of the fall in which curiosity, mendacious deception, susceptibility to seduction, lust—in short, a series of pre-eminently feminine affects was considered the origin of evil. What distinguishes the Aryan notion is the sublime view of *active sin* as the characteristically Promethean virtue. With that, the ethical basis for pessimistic tragedy has been found: the justification of human evil, meaning both human guilt and the human suffering it entails.

The misfortune in the nature of things, which the contemplative Aryan is not inclined to interpret away—the contradiction at the heart of the world reveals itself to him as a clash of different worlds, e.g., of a divine and human one, in which each, taken as an individual, has right on its side, but nevertheless has to suffer for its individuation, being merely a single one beside another. In the heroic effort of the individual to attain universality, in the attempt to transcend the curse of individuation and to become the *one* world-being, he suffers in his own person the primordial contradiction that is concealed in things, which means that he commits sacrilege and suffers.

Thus the Aryans understand sacrilege as something masculine,[6] while the Semites understand sin as feminine,[7] just as the

---

terms "Aryan" and "Semitic" more problematic. See, e.g., his note: "Contra Aryan and Semitic. Where races are mixed, there is the source of great cultures" (*Werke, Musarion* edition, vol. XVI, pp. 373f.).

[6] *Der Frevel.*

[7] *Die Sünde.*

original sacrilege is committed by a man, the original sin by a woman. Also, the witches' chorus says:

> *If that is so, we do not mind it:*
> *With a thousand steps the women find it;*
> *But though they rush, we do not care:*
> *With one big jump the men get there.*[8]

Whoever understands this innermost kernel of the Prometheus story—namely, the necessity of sacrilege imposed upon the titanically striving individual—must also immediately feel how un-Apollinian this pessimistic notion is. For Apollo wants to grant repose to individual beings precisely by drawing boundaries between them and by again and again calling these to mind as the most sacred laws of the world, with his demands for self-knowledge and measure.

Lest this Apollinian tendency congeal the form to Egyptian rigidity and coldness, lest the effort to prescribe to the individual wave its path and realm might annul the motion of the whole lake, the high tide of the Dionysian destroyed from time to time all those little circles in which the one-sidedly Apollinian "will" had sought to confine the Hellenic spirit. The suddenly swelling Dionysian tide then takes the separate little wave-mountains of individuals on its back, even as Prometheus' brother, the Titan Atlas, does with the earth. This Titanic impulse to become, as it were, the Atlas for all individuals, carrying them on a broad back, higher and higher, farther and farther, is what the Promethean and the Dionysian have in common.

In this respect, the Prometheus of Aeschylus is a Dionysian mask, while in the aforementioned profound demand for justice Aeschylus reveals to the thoughtful his paternal descent from Apollo, the god of individuation and of just boundaries. So the dual nature of Aeschylus' Prometheus, his nature which is at the same time Dionysian and Apollinian, might be expressed thus in a conceptual formula: "All that exists is just and unjust and equally justified in both."

That is your world! A world indeed!—[9]

---

[8] Goethe's *Faust,* lines 3982–85.

[9] Goethe's *Faust,* line 409.

10

The tradition is undisputed that Greek tragedy in its earliest form had for its sole theme the sufferings of Dionysus and that for a long time the only stage hero was Dionysus himself. But it may be claimed with equal confidence that until Euripides, Dionysus never ceased to be the tragic hero; that all the celebrated figures of the Greek stage—Prometheus, Oedipus, etc.—are mere masks of this original hero, Dionysus. That behind all these masks there is a deity, that is one essential reason for the typical "ideality" of these famous figures which has caused so much astonishment. Somebody, I do not know who, has claimed that all individuals, taken as individuals, are comic and hence untragic—from which it would follow that the Greeks simply *could* not suffer individuals on the tragic stage. In fact, this is what they seem to have felt; and the Platonic distinction and evaluation of the "idea" and the "idol," the mere image, is very deeply rooted in the Hellenic character.

Using Plato's terms we should have to speak of the tragic figures of the Hellenic stage somewhat as follows: the one truly real Dionysus appears in a variety of forms, in the mask of a fighting hero, and entangled, as it were, in the net of the individual will. The god who appears talks and acts so as to resemble an erring, striving, suffering individual. That he *appears* at all with such epic precision and clarity is the work of the dream-interpreter, Apollo, who through this symbolic appearance interprets to the chorus its Dionysian state. In truth, however, the hero is the suffering Dionysus of the Mysteries, the god experiencing in himself the agonies of individuation, of whom wonderful myths tell that as a boy he was torn to pieces by the Titans and now is worshiped in this state as Zagreus. Thus it is intimated that this dismemberment, the properly Dionysian *suffering,* is like a transformation into air, water, earth, and fire, that we are therefore to regard the state of individuation as the origin and primal cause of all suffering, as something objectionable in itself. From the smile of this Dionysus sprang the Olympian gods, from his tears sprang man. In this existence as a dismembered god, Dionysus possesses the dual nature of a cruel, barbarized demon and a mild, gentle ruler. But the hope of the

epopts[1] looked toward a rebirth of Dionysus, which we must now
dimly conceive as the end of individuation. It was for this coming
third Dionysus that the epopts' roaring hymns of joy resounded.
And it is this hope alone that casts a gleam of joy upon the features
of a world torn asunder and shattered into individuals; this is symbolized in the myth of Demeter, sunk in eternal sorrow, who *rejoices* again for the first time when told that she may *once more*
give birth to Dionysus. This view of things already provides us with
all the elements of a profound and pessimistic view of the world,
together with the *mystery doctrine of tragedy:* the fundamental
knowledge of the oneness of everything existent, the conception of
individuation as the primal cause of evil, and of art as the joyous
hope that the spell of individuation may be broken in augury of a
restored oneness.

We have already suggested that the Homeric epos is the poem
of Olympian culture, in which this culture has sung its own song of
victory over the terrors of the war of the Titans. Under the predom-
inating influence of tragic poetry, these Homeric myths are now
born anew; and this metempsychosis reveals that in the meantime
the Olympian culture also has been conquered by a still more profound view of the world. The defiant Titan Prometheus has announced to his Olympian tormentor that some day the greatest
danger will menace his rule, unless Zeus should enter into an alliance with him in time. In Aeschylus we recognize how the terrified Zeus, fearful of his end, allies himself with the Titan. Thus the
former age of the Titans is once more recovered from Tartarus and
brought to the light.

The philosophy of wild and naked nature beholds with the
frank, undissembling gaze of truth the myths of the Homeric world
as they dance past: they turn pale, they tremble under the piercing
glance of this goddess[2]—till the powerful fist of the Dionysian artist forces them into the service of the new deity. Dionysian truth
takes over the entire domain of myth as the symbolism of *its*
knowledge which it makes known partly in the public cult of tragedy and partly in the secret celebrations of dramatic mysteries, but
always in the old mythical garb.

---

[1] Those initiated into the mysteries.
[2] Truth.

What power was it that freed Prometheus from his vultures and transformed the myth into a vehicle of Dionysian wisdom? It is the Heracleian power of music: having reached its highest manifestation in tragedy, it can invest myths with a new and most profound significance. This we have already characterized as the most powerful function of music. For it is the fate of every myth to creep by degrees into the narrow limits of some alleged historical reality, and to be treated by some later generation as a unique fact with historical claims: and the Greeks were already fairly on the way toward restamping the whole of their mythical juvenile dream sagaciously and arbitrarily into a historico-pragmatical *juvenile history*. For this is the way in which religions are wont to die out: under the stern, intelligent eyes of an orthodox dogmatism, the mythical premises of a religion are systematized as a sum total of historical events; one begins apprehensively to defend the credibility of the myths, while at the same time one opposes any continuation of their natural vitality and growth; the feeling for myth perishes, and its place is taken by the claim of religion to historical foundations. This dying myth was now seized by the new-born genius of Dionysian music; and in these hands it flourished once more with colors such as it had never yet displayed, with a fragrance that awakened a longing anticipation of a metaphysical world. After this final effulgence it collapses, its leaves wither, and soon the mocking Lucians of antiquity catch at the discolored and faded flowers carried away by the four winds. Through tragedy the myth attains its most profound content, its most expressive form; it rises once more like a wounded hero, and its whole excess of strength, together with the philosophic calm of the dying, burns in its eyes with a last powerful gleam.

What did you want, sacrilegious Euripides, when you sought to compel this dying myth to serve you once more? It died under your violent hands—and then you needed a copied, masked myth that, like the ape of Heracles, merely knew how to deck itself out in the ancient pomp. And just as the myth died on you, the genius of music died on you, too. Though with greedy hands you plundered all the gardens of music, you still managed only copied, masked music. And because you had abandoned Dionysus, Apollo abandoned you: rouse all the passions from their resting places and conjure them into your circle, sharpen and whet a sophistical dia-

lectic for the speeches of your heroes—your heroes, too, have only
copied, masked passions and speak only copied, masked speeches.

11

Greek tragedy met an end different from that of her older sister-
arts: she died by suicide, in consequence of an irreconcilable conflict; she died tragically, while all the others passed away calmly
and beautifully at a ripe old age. If it be consonant with a happy
natural state to take leave of life easily, leaving behind a fair posterity, the closing period of these older arts exhibits such a happy
natural state: slowly they sink from sight, and before their dying
eyes stand their fairer progeny, who lift up their heads impatiently,
with a bold gesture. But when Greek tragedy died, there rose everywhere the deep sense of an immense void. Just as Greek sailors in
the time of Tiberius once heard on a lonesome island the soul-
shaking cry, "Great Pan is dead," so the Hellenic world was now
pierced by the grievous lament: "Tragedy is dead! Poetry itself has
perished with her! Away with you, pale, meager epigones! Away to
Hades, that you may for once eat your fill of the crumbs of our
former masters!"

When a new artistic genre blossomed forth after all, and revered tragedy as its predecessor and mistress, it was noted with horror that she did indeed bear the features of her mother—but those
she had exhibited in her long death-struggle. It was *Euripides* who
fought this death struggle of tragedy; the later artistic genre is
known as *New Attic Comedy*.[1] In it the degenerate form of tragedy
lived on as a monument of its exceedingly painful and violent
death.

This connection helps to explain the passionate attachment

---

[1] The chief representative of the so-called Old Comedy was Aristophanes
(about 448–380 B.C.). "The New Comedy began to prevail about 336; its
characteristic features are the representation of contemporary life by means
of imaginary persons drawn from it, the development of plot and character,
the substitution of humour for wit, and the introduction of romantic love as
a theme. It resembles the tragedy of Euripides (the 'Ion' for example) more
than the comedy of Aristophanes. Of the chorus no more remains than a
band of musicians and dancers whose performances punctuate intervals in
the play. The New Comedy is in fact an obvious progenitor of the modern
drama. But the moral standard is surprisingly low. . . ." (*The Oxford Companion to Classical Literature, ed. cit.,* p. 116).

that the poets of the New Comedy felt for Euripides; so that we are no longer surprised at the wish of Philemon, who would have let himself be hanged at once, merely that he might visit Euripides in the lower world—if only he could be certain that the deceased still had possession of his reason. But if we desire, as briefly as possible, and without claiming to say anything exhaustive, to characterize what Euripides has in common with Menander and Philemon, and what appealed to them so strongly as worthy of imitation, it is sufficient to say that Euripides brought the *spectator* onto the stage. He who has perceived the material out of which the Promethean tragic writers prior to Euripides formed their heroes, and how remote from their purpose it was to bring the faithful mask of reality onto the stage, will also be aware of the utterly opposite tendency of Euripides. Through him the everyday man forced his way from the spectators' seats onto the stage; the mirror in which formerly only grand and bold traits were represented now showed the painful fidelity that conscientiously reproduces even the botched outlines of nature.

Odysseus, the typical Hellene of the older art, now sank, in the hands of the new poets, to the figure of the Graeculus, who, as the good-naturedly cunning house-slave, henceforth occupies the center of dramatic interest. What Euripides claims credit for in Aristophanes' *Frogs*,[2] namely, that his nostrums have liberated tragic art from its pompous corpulency, is apparent above all in his tragic heroes. The spectator now actually saw and heard his double on the Euripidean stage, and rejoiced that he could talk so well. But this joy was not all: one could even learn from Euripides how to speak oneself. He prides himself upon this in his contest with Aeschylus: from him the people have learned how to observe, debate, and draw conclusions according to the rules of art and with the cleverest sophistries. Through this revolution in ordinary language, he made the New Comedy possible. For henceforth it was no longer a secret how—and with what maxims—everyday life could be represented on the stage. Civic mediocrity, on which Euripides built all his political hopes, was now given a voice, while heretofore the demigod in tragedy and the drunken satyr, or demiman, in comedy, had deter-

---

[2] Lines 937ff. Aristophanes also lampoons Euripides in *The Acharnians* and in *Thesmophoriazousae*.

mined the character of the language. And so the Aristophanean Euripides prides himself on having portrayed the common, familiar, everyday life and activities of the people, about which all are qualified to pass judgment. If the entire populace now philosophized, managed land and goods, and conducted lawsuits with unheard-of circumspection, he deserved the credit, for this was the result of the wisdom he had inculcated in the people.

It was to a populace thus prepared and enlightened that the New Comedy could address itself: it was Euripides who had taught, as it were, the chorus; only now the chorus of spectators had to be trained. As soon as this chorus was trained to sing in the Euripidean key, there arose that drama which resembles a game of chess—the New Comedy, with its perpetual triumphs of cunning and craftiness. But Euripides—the chorus master—was praised continually: indeed, people would have killed themselves in order to learn still more from him, if they had not known that the tragic poets were quite as dead as tragedy. But with that, the Hellene had given up his belief in immortality; not only his belief in an ideal past, but also his belief in an ideal future. The words of the well-known epitaph, "frivolous and eccentric when an old man," [3] also suit aging Hellenism. The passing moment, wit, levity, and caprice are its highest deities; the fifth estate, that of the slaves, now comes to power, at least in sentiment; and if we may still speak at all of "Greek cheerfulness," it is the cheerfulness of the slave who has nothing of consequence to be responsible for, nothing great to strive for, and who does not value anything in the past or future higher than the present.

It was this semblance of "Greek cheerfulness" which so aroused the profound and formidable natures of the first four centuries of Christianity: this womanish flight from seriousness and terror, this craven satisfaction with easy enjoyment, seemed to them not only contemptible, but a specifically anti-Christian sentiment. And it is due to their influence that the conception of Greek antiquity which endured through the centuries clung with almost unconquerable persistency to that pink hue of cheerfulness—as if there had never been a sixth century with its birth of tragedy, its mysteries, its Py-

---

[3] Quotation from a six-line poem of the young Goethe, entitled "Grabschrift" (epitaph).

thagoras and Heraclitus, as if the works of art of the great period simply did not exist, though these phenomena can hardly be explained as having originated in any such senile and slavish pleasure in existence and cheerfulness, and point to a wholly different conception of the world as the ground of their existence.

The assertion made above, that Euripides brought the spectator onto the stage and thus qualified him to pass judgment on the drama, makes it appear as if the older tragic art had always suffered from bad relations with the spectator; and one might be tempted to extol as an advance over Sophocles the radical tendency of Euripides to produce a proper relation between art and the public. But "public," after all, is a mere word. In no sense is it a homogeneous and constant quantity. Why should the artist be bound to accommodate himself to a power whose strength lies solely in numbers? And if, by virtue of his endowments and aspirations, he should feel himself superior to every one of these spectators, how could he feel greater respect for the collective expression of all these subordinate capacities than for the relatively highest-endowed individual spectator? In truth, if ever a Greek artist throughout a long life treated his public with audacity and self-sufficiency, it was Euripides. When the masses threw themselves at his feet, he openly and with sublime defiance reversed his own tendency, the very tendency with which he had won over the masses. If this genius had had the slightest reverence for the pandemonium of the public, he would have broken down long before the middle of his career, beneath the heavy blows of his failures.

These considerations make it clear that our formula—that Euripides brought the spectator onto the stage in order to make him truly competent to pass judgment—was merely provisional; we must penetrate more deeply to understand his tendency. Conversely, it is well known that Aeschylus and Sophocles during the whole of their lives, and indeed long after, were in complete possession of the people's favor, so there can be no question of a false relation between art and the public in the case of these predecessors of Euripides. What was it then that forcibly drove this artist, so richly endowed, so constantly impelled to production, from the path warmed by the sun of the greatest names in poetry and covered by the cloudless heaven of popular favor? What strange consideration for the spectator led him to oppose the spectator? How

could he, out of too great a respect for his public—despise his public?

Euripides—and this is the solution of the riddle just propounded—undoubtedly felt himself, as a poet, superior to the
masses in general; but to two of his spectators he did not feel superior. He brought the masses onto the stage; but these two spectators he revered as the only competent judges and masters of his art.
Complying with their directions and admonitions, he transferred
the entire world of sentiments, passions, and experiences, hitherto
present at every festival performance as the invisible chorus on the
spectators' benches, into the souls of his stage-heroes. He yielded
to their demands, too, when for these new characters he sought out
a new language and a new tone. Only in their voices could he hear
any conclusive verdict on his work, and also the encouragement
that promised eventual success when, as usual, he found himself
condemned by the public judgment.

Of these two spectators, one is—Euripides himself, Euripides
as thinker, not as poet. It might be said of him, as of Lessing, that
his extraordinary fund of *critical* talent, if it did not create, at least
constantly stimulated his productive *artistic* impulse. With this gift,
with all the brightness and dexterity of his critical thinking, Euripides had sat in the theater and striven to recognize in the masterpieces of his great predecessors, as in paintings that have become
dark, feature after feature, line after line. And here he had experienced something which should not surprise anyone initiated into
the deeper secrets of Aeschylean tragedy. He observed something
incommensurable in every feature and in every line, a certain deceptive distinctness and at the same time an enigmatic depth, indeed an infinitude, in the background. Even the clearest figure
always had a comet's tail attached to it which seemed to suggest the
uncertain, that which could never be illuminated. A similar twilight
shrouded the structure of the drama, especially the significance of
the chorus. And how dubious the solution of the ethical problems
remained to him! How questionable the treatment of the myths!
How unequal the distribution of good and bad fortune! Even in the
language of the Old Tragedy there was much he found offensive, or
at least enigmatic; especially he found too much pomp for simple
affairs, too many tropes and monstrous expressions to suit the
plainness of the characters. So he sat in the theater, pondering un-

easily, and as a spectator he confessed to himself that he did not understand his great predecessors. But if the understanding was for him the real root of all enjoyment and creation, he had to inquire and look around to see whether no one else had the same opinion and also felt this incommensurability. But most people, and among them the finest individuals, had only a suspicious smile for him, and none could explain to him why the great masters were still in the right despite his scruples and objections. And in this state of torment, he found *that other spectator* who did not comprehend tragedy and therefore did not esteem it. Allied with him, he could now venture from his solitude to begin the tremendous struggle against the art of Aeschylus and Sophocles—not with polemical essays, but as a dramatic poet who opposed *his* conception of tragedy to the traditional one.—

12

Before we name this other spectator, let us pause here a moment to recall to our minds our previously described impression of the discordant and incommensurable elements in the nature of Aeschylean tragedy. Let us recall our surprise at the *chorus* and the *tragic hero* of that tragedy, neither of which we could reconcile with our own customs any more than with tradition—till we rediscovered this duality itself as the origin and essence of Greek tragedy, as the expression of two interwoven artistic impulses, *the Apollinian and the Dionysian.*

To separate this original and all-powerful Dionysian element from tragedy, and to reconstruct tragedy purely on the basis of an un-Dionysian art, morality, and world view—this is the tendency of Euripides as it now reveals itself to us in clear illumination.

In the evening of his life, Euripides himself propounded to his contemporaries the question of the value and significance of this tendency, using a myth. Is the Dionysian entitled to exist at all? Should it not be forcibly uprooted from Hellenic soil? Certainly, the poet tells us, if it were only possible: but the god Dionysus is too powerful; his most intelligent adversary—like Pentheus in the *Bacchae*—is unwittingly enchanted by him, and in this enchantment runs to meet his fate. The judgment of the two old men, Cadmus and Tiresias, seems also to be the judgment of the old poet: the reflection of the wisest individuals does not overthrow these old popular traditions, nor the perpetually self-propagating worship of Dionysus; rather it is proper to display a diplomatically cautious interest in the presence of such marvelous forces—although the possibility remains that the god may take offense at such lukewarm participation, and eventually transform the diplomat—like Cadmus—into a dragon. This is what we are told by a poet who opposed Dionysus with heroic valor throughout a long life—and who finally ended his career with a glorification of his adversary and with suicide, like a giddy man who, to escape the horrible vertigo he can no longer endure, casts himself from a tower.

This tragedy was a protest against the practicability of his own tendency; but alas, it had already been put into practice! The marvel had happened: when the poet recanted, his tendency had already triumphed. Dionysus had already been scared from the tragic stage, by a demonic power speaking through Euripides. Even Euripides was, in a sense, only a mask: the deity that spoke through him was neither Dionysus nor Apollo, but an altogether newborn demon, called *Socrates*.

This is the new opposition: the Dionysian and the Socratic—and the art of Greek tragedy was wrecked on this. Though Euripides may seek to comfort us by his recantation, he does not succeed: the most magnificent temple lies in ruins. What does the lamentation of the destroyer profit us, or his confession that it was the most beautiful of all temples? And even if Euripides has been punished by being changed into a dragon by the art critics of all ages—who could be content with so miserable a compensation?

Let us now approach this *Socratic* tendency with which Euripides combated and vanquished Aeschylean tragedy.

We must now ask ourselves, what could be the aim of the Euripidean design, which, in its most ideal form, would wish to base drama exclusively on the un-Dionysian? What form of drama still remained, if it was not to be born of the womb of music, in the mysterious twilight of the Dionysian? Only *the dramatized epos*—but in this Apollinian domain of art the *tragic* effect is certainly unattainable. The subject matter of the events represented is not decisive; indeed, I suggest that it would have been impossible for Goethe in his projected *Nausikaa* to have rendered tragically effec-

tive the suicide of this idyllic being, which was to have completed
the fifth act. So extraordinary is the power of the epic-Apollinian
that before our eyes it transforms the most terrible things by
the joy in mere appearance and in redemption through mere appearance. The poet of the dramatized epos cannot blend completely with his images any more than the epic rhapsodist can. He
is still that calm, unmoved contemplation which sees the images
before its wide-open eyes. The actor in this dramatized epos still
remains fundamentally a rhapsodist: the consecration of the inner
dream lies on all his actions, so that he is never wholly an actor.

How, then, is the Euripidean play related to this ideal of the
Apollinian drama? Just as the younger rhapsodist is related to the
solemn rhapsodist of old times. In the Platonic *Ion,* the younger
rhapsodist describes his own nature as follows: "When I am saying
anything sad, my eyes fill with tears; and when I am saying something awful and terrible, then my hair stands on end with fright and
my heart beats quickly." Here we no longer remark anything of
the epic absorption in mere appearance, or of the dispassionate
coolness of the true actor, who precisely in his highest activity is
wholly mere appearance and joy in mere appearance. Euripides is
the actor whose heart beats, whose hair stands on end; as Socratic
thinker he designs the plan, as passionate actor he executes it. Neither in the designing nor in the execution is he a pure artist. Thus
the Euripidean drama is a thing both cool and fiery, equally capable of freezing and burning. It is impossible for it to attain the
Apollinian effect of the epos, while, on the other hand, it has alienated itself as much as possible from Dionysian elements. Now, in
order to be effective at all, it requires new stimulants, which can no
longer lie within the sphere of the only two art-impulses, the Apollinian and the Dionysian. These stimulants are cool, paradoxical
thoughts, replacing Apollinian contemplation—and fiery *affects,* replacing Dionysian ecstasies; and, it may be added, thoughts and
affects copied very realistically and in no sense dipped into the
ether of art.

So we see that Euripides did not succeed in basing the drama
exclusively on the Apollinian, and his un-Dionysian tendency actually went astray and became naturalistic and inartistic. Now we
should be able to come closer to the character of *aesthetic Socratism,* whose supreme law reads roughly as follows, "To be beauti-

ful everything must be intelligible," as the counterpart to the Socratic dictum, "Knowledge is virtue." With this canon in his hands,
Euripides measured all the separate elements of the drama—language, characters, dramaturgic structure, and choric music—and
corrected them according to this principle.

The poetic deficiency and degeneration, which are so often
imputed to Euripides in comparison with Sophocles, are for the
most part products of this penetrating critical process, this audacious reasonableness.

The Euripidean *prologue* may serve as an example of the pro-
ductivity of this rationalistic method. Nothing could be more uncongenial to the technique of our own stage than the prologue in
the drama of Euripides. For a single person to appear at the outset
of the play, telling us who he is, what precedes the action, what has
happened so far, even what will happen in the course of the play,
would be condemned by a modern playwright as a willful, inexcus-
able abandonment of the effect of suspense. We know everything
that is going to happen; who would want to wait till it actually does
happen? After all, we do not even have the exciting relation of a
prophetic dream to a reality that comes to be later on. But Euripides did not think like that at all. The effect of tragedy never depended on epic suspense, on a fascinating uncertainty as to what is
to happen now and afterward, but rather on the great rhetorical-
lyrical scenes in which the passion and dialectic of the protagonist
swelled to a broad and powerful current. Everything laid the
ground for pathos, not for action: and whatever was not directed
toward pathos was considered objectionable. But what interferes
most with the hearer's pleasurable absorption in such scenes is any
missing link, any gap in the texture of the background story. So
long as the spectator has to figure out the meaning of this or that
person, or the presuppositions of this or that conflict of inclinations
and purposes, he cannot become completely absorbed in the activities and sufferings of the chief characters or feel breathless pity and
fear.

Aeschylean-Sophoclean tragedy employed the most ingenious
devices in the initial scenes to place in the spectator's hands, as if
by chance, all the threads necessary for a complete understanding
—a trait proving that noble artistry which, as it were, masks the
necessary formal element and makes it appear accidental. Yet Eu-

ripides thought he observed that during these first scenes the spectator was so anxious to solve the problem of the background history that the poetic beauties and the pathos of the exposition were lost on him. So he put the prologue even before the exposition, and placed it in the mouth of a person who could be trusted: often some deity had to guarantee the plot of the tragedy to the public, to remove every doubt as to the reality of the myth—somewhat as Descartes could prove the reality of the empirical world only by appealing to the truthfulness of God and his inability to utter falsehood. Euripides makes use of this same divine truthfulness once more at the close of his drama, in order to reassure the public as to the future of his heroes; this is the task of the notorious *deus ex machina*. Between this epic preview and epic prospect lies the dramatic-lyric present, the "drama" proper.

Thus Euripides as a poet is essentially an echo of his own conscious knowledge; and it is precisely on this account that he occupies such a remarkable position in the history of Greek art. With reference to his critical-productive activity, he must often have felt as if he had to bring to life for drama the beginning of the essay of Anaxagoras: "In the beginning all things were mixed together; then came the understanding and created order." Anaxagoras with his *"nous"* [1] is said to have appeared among philosophers as the first sober person[2] amid a crowd of drunken ones. Euripides may have conceived his relation to the other tragic poets in terms of a similar image. As long as the sole ruler and disposer of the universe, the *nous,* remained excluded from artistic activity, things were all mixed together in a primeval chaos: this was what Euripides must have thought; and so, as the first "sober" one among them, he had to condemn the "drunken" poets. Sophocles said of Aeschylus that he did what was right, though he did it unconsciously. This was surely not how Euripides saw it. He might have said that Aeschylus, *because* he created unconsciously, did what was *wrong*. The divine Plato, too, almost always speaks only ironically of the creative faculty of the poet, insofar as it is not con-

---

[1] The Greek word is translated as understanding (*Verstand*) in the preceding sentence. The quotation is not to be found in precisely this form in the extant fragments.

[2] Aristotle, *Metaphysics* 984b (A, end of Chapter 3).

scious insight, and places it on a par with the gift of the soothsayer and dream-interpreter: the poet is incapable of composing until he has become unconscious and bereft of understanding. Like Plato, Euripides undertook to show to the world the reverse of the "unintelligent" poet; his aesthetic principle that "to be beautiful everything must be conscious" is, as I have said, the parallel to the Socratic, "to be good everything must be conscious." So we may consider Euripides as the poet of aesthetic Socratism.

Socrates, however, was that *second spectator* who did not comprehend and therefore did not esteem the Old Tragedy; in alliance with him Euripides dared to be the herald of a new art. If it was this of which the older tragedy perished, then aesthetic Socratism was the murderous principle; but insofar as the struggle was directed against the Dionysian element in the older tragedy, we may recognize in Socrates the opponent of Dionysus. He is the new Orpheus who rose against Dionysus, and although he is destined to be torn to pieces by the Maenads of the Athenian court, he still put to flight the powerful god himself—who, as on his flight from Lycurgus the King of Edoni, sought refuge in the depths of the sea, namely the mystical flood of a secret cult which gradually covered the earth.

13

That Socrates was closely related to the tendency of Euripides did not escape the notice of contemporaneous antiquity. The most eloquent expression of this felicitous insight was the story current in Athens that Socrates used to help Euripides write his plays. Whenever an occasion arose to enumerate the demagogues of the day, the adherents of the "good old times" would mention both names in the same breath. To the influence of Socrates and Euripides they attributed the fact that the old Marathonian stalwart fitness of body and soul was being sacrificed more and more to a dubious enlightenment that involved the progressive degeneration of the powers of body and soul. It is in this tone, half indignant, half contemptuous, that Aristophanic comedy used to speak of both of them—to the consternation of modern men, who are quite willing to give up Euripides, but who cannot give sufficient expression to their astonishment that in Aristophanes Socrates should appear as the first and supreme *Sophist,* as the mirror and epitome of all sophistical tendencies. Their only consolation is to pillory Aristophanes himself as a dissolute, mendacious Alcibiades of poetry. Without here defending the profound instinct of Aristophanes against such attacks, I shall continue to show, by means of the sentiments of the time, the close connection between Socrates and Euripides. With this in view, we must remember particularly how Socrates, as an opponent of tragic art, refrained from attending tragedies and appeared among the spectators only when a new play of Euripides was to be performed. Most famous of all, however, is the juxtaposition of the two names by the Delphic oracle, which designated Socrates as the wisest of men and at the same time decided that the second prize in the contest of wisdom belonged to Euripides.

Sophocles was named third in order of rank—he who could boast that, as compared with Aeschylus, he did what was right because he *knew* what was right. Evidently it is precisely the degree of the brightness of this *knowledge* which distinguishes these three men in common as the three "knowing ones" of their time.

The most acute word, however, about this new and unprecedented value set on knowledge and insight was spoken by Socrates when he found that he was the only one who acknowledged to himself that he knew *nothing,* whereas in his critical peregrinations through Athens he had called on the greatest statesmen, orators, poets, and artists, and had everywhere discovered the conceit of knowledge. To his astonishment he perceived that all these celebrities were without a proper and sure insight, even with regard to their own professions, and that they practiced them only by instinct. "Only by instinct": with this phrase we touch upon the heart and core of the Socratic tendency. With it Socratism condemns existing art as well as existing ethics. Wherever Socratism turns its searching eyes it sees lack of insight and the power of illusion; and from this lack it infers the essential perversity and reprehensibility of what exists. Basing himself on this point, Socrates conceives it to be his duty to correct existence: all alone, with an expression of irreverence and superiority, as the precursor of an altogether different culture, art, and morality, he enters a world, to touch whose very hem would give us the greatest happiness.

This is what strikes us as so tremendously problematic whenever we consider Socrates, and again and again we are tempted to fathom the meaning and purpose of this most questionable phenomenon of antiquity. Who is it that may dare single-handed to negate the Greek genius that, as Homer, Pindar, and Aeschylus, as Phidias, as Pericles, as Pythia and Dionysus, as the deepest abyss and the highest height, is sure of our astonished veneration? What demonic power is this that dares to spill this magic potion into dust? What demigod is this to whom the chorus of the noblest spirits of mankind must call out:

> *Alas!*
> *You have shattered*
> *The beautiful world*
> *With brazen fist;*
> *It falls, it is scattered.*[1]

We are offered a key to the character of Socrates by the wonderful phenomenon known as "the *daimonion* of Socrates." In exceptional circumstances, when his tremendous intellect wavered, he found secure support in the utterances of a divine voice that spoke up at such moments. This voice, whenever it comes, always *dissuades*. In this utterly abnormal nature, instinctive wisdom appears only in order to *hinder* conscious knowledge occasionally. While in all productive men it is instinct that is the creative-affirmative force, and consciousness acts critically and dissuasively, in Socrates it is instinct that becomes the critic, and consciousness that becomes the creator—truly a monstrosity *per defectum!* Specifically, we observe here a monstrous *defectus* of any mystical disposition, so Socrates might be called the typical *non-mystic,* in whom, through a hypertrophy, the logical nature is developed as excessively as instinctive wisdom is in the mystic. But the logical urge that became manifest in Socrates was absolutely prevented from turning against itself; in its unbridled flood it displays a natural power such as we encounter to our awed amazement only in the very greatest instinctive forces. Anyone who, through the Platonic writings, has experienced even a breath of the divine naïveté and sureness of the Socratic way of life, will also feel how the enormous

---

[1] Goethe's *Faust,* lines 1607–11.

driving-wheel of logical Socratism is in motion, as it were, *behind* Socrates, and that it must be viewed through Socrates as through a shadow.

His own sense of this relationship found expression in the dignified seriousness with which he everywhere, even before his judges, insisted on his divine calling. At bottom, it was as impossible to refute him here as to approve of his instinct-disintegrating influence. In view of this indissoluble conflict, when he had at last been brought before the forum of the Greek state, only one kind of punishment was indicated: exile. Being thoroughly enigmatical, unclassifiable, and inexplicable, he might have been asked to leave the city, and posterity would never have been justified in charging the Athenians with an ignominious deed. But that he was sentenced to death, not exile, Socrates himself seems to have brought about with perfect awareness and without any natural awe of death. He went to his death with the calm with which, according to Plato's description, he leaves the Symposium at dawn, the last of the revelers, to begin a new day, while on the benches and on the earth his drowsy table companions remain behind to dream of Socrates, the true eroticist. *The dying Socrates* became the new ideal, never seen before, of noble Greek youths: above all, the typical Hellenic youth, Plato, prostrated himself before this image with all the ardent devotion of his enthusiastic soul.

14

Let us now imagine the one great Cyclops eye of Socrates fixed on tragedy, an eye in which the fair frenzy of artistic enthusiasm had never glowed. To this eye was denied the pleasure of gazing into the Dionysian abysses. What, then, did it have to see in the "sublime and greatly lauded" tragic art, as Plato called it? Something rather unreasonable, full of causes apparently without effects, and effects apparently without causes; the whole, moreover, so motley and manifold that it could not but be repugnant to a sober mind, and a dangerous tinder for sensitive and susceptible souls. We know the only kind of poetry he comprehended: the *Aesopian fable;* and this he favored no doubt with the smiling accommodation with which the good honest Gellert sings the praise of poetry in the fable of the bee and the hen:

Poems are useful: they can tell
The truth by means of parable
To those who are not very bright.

But to Socrates it seemed that tragic art did not even "tell the truth"; moreover, it addressed itself to "those who are not very bright," not to the philosopher: a twofold reason for shunning it. Like Plato, he reckoned it among the flattering arts which portray only the agreeable, not the useful; and therefore he required of his disciples abstinence and strict separation from such unphilosophical attractions—with such success that the youthful tragic poet Plato first burned his poems that he might become a student of Socrates. But where unconquerable propensities struggled against the Socratic maxims, their power, together with the impact of his tremendous character, was still great enough to force poetry itself into new and hitherto unknown channels.

An instance of this is Plato, who in condemning tragedy and art in general certainly did not lag behind the naïve cynicism of his master; he was nevertheless constrained by sheer artistic necessity to create an art form that was related to those forms of art which he repudiated. Plato's main objection to the older art—that it is the imitation of a phantom and hence belongs to a sphere even lower than the empirical world—could certainly not be directed against the new art; and so we find Plato endeavoring to transcend reality and to represent the idea which underlies this pseudo-reality. Thus Plato, the thinker, arrived by a detour where he had always been at home as a poet—at the point from which Sophocles and the older art protested solemnly against that objection. If tragedy had absorbed into itself all the earlier types of art, the same might also be said in an eccentric sense of the Platonic dialogue which, a mixture of all extant styles and forms, hovers midway between narrative, lyric, and drama, between prose and poetry, and so has also broken the strict old law of the unity of linguistic form. This tendency was carried still further by the *Cynic* writers, who in the greatest stylistic medley, oscillating between prose and metrical forms, realized also the literary image of the "raving Socrates" whom they represented in real life.

The Platonic dialogue was, as it were, the barge on which the shipwrecked ancient poetry saved herself with all her children:

crowded into a narrow space and timidly submitting to the single pilot, Socrates, they now sailed into a new world, which never tired of looking at the fantastic spectacle of this procession. Indeed, Plato has given to all posterity the model of a new art form, the model of the *novel*—which may be described as an infinitely enhanced Aesopian fable, in which poetry holds the same rank in relation to dialectical philosophy as this same philosophy held for many centuries in relation to theology: namely, the rank of *ancilla*.[1] This was the new position into which Plato, under the pressure of the demonic Socrates, forced poetry.

Here *philosophic thought* overgrows art and compels it to cling close to the trunk of dialectic. The *Apollinian* tendency has withdrawn into the cocoon of logical schematism; just as in the case of Euripides we noticed something analogous, as well as a transformation of the *Dionysian* into naturalistic affects. Socrates, the dialectical hero of the Platonic drama, reminds us of the kindred nature of the Euripidean hero who must defend his actions with arguments and counterarguments and in the process often risks the loss of our tragic pity; for who could mistake the *optimistic* element in the nature of dialectic, which celebrates a triumph with every conclusion and can breathe only in cool clarity and consciousness—the optimistic element which, having once penetrated tragedy must gradually overgrow its Dionysian regions and impel it necessarily to self-destruction—to the death-leap into the bourgeois drama. Consider the consequences of the Socratic maxims: "Virtue is knowledge; man sins only from ignorance; he who is virtuous is happy." In these three basic forms of optimism lies the death of tragedy. For now the virtuous hero must be a dialectician; now there must be a necessary, visible connection between virtue and knowledge, faith and morality; now the transcendental justice of Aeschylus is degraded to the superficial and insolent principle of "poetic justice" with its customary *deus ex machina*.[2]

---

[1] Handmaid.

[2] Aristotle had called Euripides "the most tragic of the poets" (*Poetics* 1453a). Although Nietzsche has more feeling for poetry—and tragedy—than Aristotle did, this estimate seems fairer than Nietzsche's conception of Euripides as the most optimistic. Surely, Euripides did not believe that "he who is virtuous is happy"—on the contrary—and the superabundance of dialectical fireworks in his tragedies, though it does dissipate the tragic emotion, usually illustrates the futility of reason, its inability to prevent tragedy.

As it confronts this new Socratic-optimistic stage world, how does the *chorus* appear now, and indeed the whole musical-Dionysian substratum of tragedy? As something accidental, a dispensable vestige of the origin of tragedy; while we have seen that the chorus can be understood only as the *cause* of tragedy, and of the tragic in general. This perplexity in regard to the chorus already manifests itself in Sophocles—an important indication that even with him the Dionysian basis of tragedy is beginning to break down. He no longer dares to entrust to the chorus the main share of the effect, but limits its sphere to such an extent that it now appears almost co-ordinate with the actors, just as if it were elevated from the orchestra into the scene; and thus its character is, of course, completely destroyed, even if Aristotle favors precisely this theory of the chorus. This alteration in the position of the chorus, which Sophocles at any rate recommended by his practice and, according to tradition, even by a treatise, is the first step toward the *destruction* of the chorus, whose phases follow one another with alarming rapidity in Euripides, Agathon, and the New Comedy. Optimistic dialectic drives *music* out of tragedy with the scourge of its syllogisms; that is, it destroys the essence of tragedy, which can be interpreted only as a manifestation and projection into images of Dionysian states, as the visible symbolizing of music, as the dream-world of a Dionysian intoxication.

If we must thus assume an anti-Dionysian tendency operating even prior to Socrates, which merely received in him an unprecedentedly magnificent expression, we must not draw back before the question of what such a phenomenon as that of Socrates indicates; for in view of the Platonic dialogues we are certainly not entitled to regard it as a merely disintegrating, negative force. And though there can be no doubt that the most immediate effect of the Socratic impulse tended to the dissolution of Dionysian tragedy, yet a profound experience in Socrates' own life impels us to ask whether there is *necessarily* only an antipodal relation between Socratism and art, and whether the birth of an "artistic Socrates" is altogether a contradiction in terms.

For with respect to art that despotic logician occasionally had the feeling of a gap, a void, half a reproach, a possibly neglected duty. As he tells his friends in prison, there often came to him one and the same dream apparition, which always said the same thing to him: "Socrates, practice music." Up to his very last days he comforts himself with the view that his philosophizing is the highest of the muses, and he finds it hard to believe that a deity should remind him of the "common, popular music." Finally, in prison, in order that he may thoroughly unburden his conscience, he does consent to practice this music for which he has but little respect. And in this mood he writes a prelude to Apollo and turns a few Aesopian fables into verse. It was something akin to the demonic warning voice that urged him to these practices; it was his Apollinian insight that, like a barbaric king, he did not understand the noble image of a god and was in danger of sinning against a deity—through his lack of understanding. The voice of the Socratic dream vision is the only sign of any misgivings about the limits of logic: Perhaps—thus he must have asked himself—what is not intelligible to me is not necessarily unintelligent? Perhaps there is a realm of wisdom from which the logician is exiled? Perhaps art is even a necessary correlative of, and supplement for science?

15

In the spirit of these last suggestive questions it must now be said how the influence of Socrates, down to the present moment and even into all future time, has spread over posterity like a shadow that keeps growing in the evening sun, and how it again and again prompts a regeneration of *art*—of art in the metaphysical, broadest and profoundest sense—and how its own infinity also guarantees the infinity of art.

Before this could be recognized, before the innermost dependence of every art on the Greeks, from Homer to Socrates, was demonstrated conclusively, we had to feel about these Greeks as the Athenians felt about Socrates. Nearly every age and stage of culture has at some time or other sought with profound irritation to free itself from the Greeks, because in their presence everything one has achieved oneself, though apparently quite original and sincerely admired, suddenly seemed to lose life and color and shriveled into a poor copy, even a caricature. And so time after time cordial anger erupts against this presumptuous little people that made bold for all time to designate everything not native as "barbaric." Who are they, one asks, who, though they display only an ephemeral historical splendor, ridiculously restricted institutions, a dubious excellence in their mores, and are marked by ugly vices, yet lay claim to that dignity and pre-eminence among peoples which characterize genius among the masses? Unfortunately, one was not lucky enough to find the cup of hemlock with which one could simply dispose of such a character; for all the poison that envy, calumny, and rancor created did not suffice to destroy that self-sufficient splendor. And so one feels ashamed and afraid in the presence of the Greeks, unless one prizes truth above all things and dares acknowledge even this truth: that the Greeks, as charioteers, hold in their hands the reins of our own and every other culture, but that almost always chariot and horses are of inferior quality and not up to the glory of their leaders, who consider it sport to run such a team into an abyss which they themselves clear with the leap of Achilles.

In order to vindicate the dignity of such a leader's position for Socrates, too, it is enough to recognize in him a type of existence unheard of before him: the type of the *theoretical man* whose significance and aim it is our next task to try to understand. Like the artist, the theoretical man finds an infinite delight in whatever exists, and this satisfaction protects him against the practical ethics of pessimism with its Lynceus eyes[1] that shine only in the dark. Whenever the truth is uncovered, the artist will always cling with rapt gaze to what still remains covering[2] even after such uncovering; but the theoretical man enjoys and finds satisfaction in the discarded covering and finds the highest object of his pleasure in the process of an ever happy uncovering that succeeds through his own efforts.

---

[1] Lynceus, one of the Argonauts, was so sharp-sighted he could see through the earth and distinguish objects almost ten miles away. Although the German word for "lynx" is *Luchs* and Nietzsche writes *Lynkeusaugen*, previous translations say "Lynx eyes."

[2] Previous translations have missed Nietzsche's point. The best commentary on his contrast is found in section 4 of the Preface to *The Gay Science*, reprinted at the end of *Nietzsche contra Wagner* (*Portable Nietzsche*, pp. 681–683). In this beautiful passage Nietzsche takes issue with those who "want by all means to unveil, uncover . . . We no longer believe that truth remains truth when the veils are withdrawn." We have learned "to stop courageously at the surface, the fold, the skin, to adore appearance, to believe in forms, tones, words, in the whole Olympus of appearance. Those Greeks were superficial—*out of profundity*. . . . Are we not, precisely in this respect, Greeks? Adorers of forms, of tones, of words? And therefore—*artists?*"

There would be no science if it were concerned only with that *one* nude goddess and with nothing else. For in that case her devotees would have to feel like men who wanted to dig a hole straight through the earth, assuming that each of them realized that even if he tried his utmost, his whole life long, he would only be able to dig a very small portion of this enormous depth, and even that would be filled in again before his own eyes by the labors of the next in line, so a third person would seem to do well if he picked a new spot for his drilling efforts. Now suppose someone proved convincingly that the goal of the antipodes cannot be reached in this direct manner: who would still wish to go on working in these old depths, unless he had learned meanwhile to be satisfied with finding precious stones or discovering laws of nature?

Therefore Lessing, the most honest theoretical man, dared to announce that he cared more for the search after truth than for truth itself [3]—and thus revealed the fundamental secret of science, to the astonishment, and indeed the anger, of the scientific community. Beside this isolated insight, born of an excess of honesty if not of exuberance, there is, to be sure, a profound *illusion* that first saw the light of the world in the person of Socrates: the unshakable faith that thought, using the thread of causality, can penetrate the deepest abysses of being, and that thought is capable not only of knowing being but even of *correcting* it. This sublime metaphysical illusion accompanies science as an instinct and leads science again

---

[3] "Not the truth in whose possession any man is, or thinks he is, but the honest effort he has made to find out the truth, is what constitutes the worth of a man. For it is not through the possession but through the inquiry after truth that his powers expand, and in this alone consists his ever growing perfection. Possession makes calm, lazy, proud—

"If God had locked up all truth in his right hand, and in his left the unique, ever-live striving for truth, albeit with the addition that I should always and eternally err, and he said to me, 'Choose!'—I should humbly clasp his left hand, saying: 'Father, give! Pure truth is after all for thee alone!'"

This celebrated passage is found at the end of the first section of *Eine Duplik* (a reply of the accused to the rejoinder of his accuser), 1778. Kierkegaard also admired this passage without feeling that he could follow Lessing's example: see *Concluding Unscientific Postscript,* the final section of Book Two, Part One, and, for some critical discussion, Kaufmann, *From Shakespeare to Existentialism,* rev. ed. (New York, Anchor Books, 1960), pp. 196f.). Nietzsche's treatment of Lessing in his second book, the "Meditation" on *David Friedrich Strauss, the Confessor and Writer* (1873), is discussed at length in Kaufmann, *Nietzsche,* Chapter 4, section 2.

and again to its limits at which it must turn into *art—which is really the aim of this mechanism.*

With the torch of this thought in our hands, let us now look at Socrates: he appears to us as the first who could not only live, guided by this instinct of science, but also—and this is far more—die that way. Hence the image of the *dying Socrates,* as the human being whom knowledge and reasons have liberated from the fear of death, is the emblem that, above the entrance gate of science, reminds all of its mission—namely, to make existence appear comprehensible and thus justified; and if reasons do not suffice, *myth* has to come to their aid in the end—myth which I have just called the necessary consequence, indeed the purpose, of science.

Once we see clearly how after Socrates, the mystagogue of science, one philosophical school succeeds another, wave upon wave; how the hunger for knowledge reached a never-suspected universality in the widest domain of the educated world, became the real task for every person of higher gifts, and led science onto the high seas from which it has never again been driven altogether; how this universality first spread a common net of thought over the whole globe, actually holding out the prospect of the lawfulness of an entire solar system; once we see all this clearly, along with the amazingly high pyramid of knowledge in our own time—we cannot fail to see in Socrates the one turning point and vortex of so-called world history. For if we imagine that the whole incalculable sum of energy used up for this world tendency had been used *not* in the service of knowledge but for the practical, i.e., egoistic aims of individuals and peoples, then we realize that in that case universal wars of annihilation and continual migrations of peoples would probably have weakened the instinctive lust for life to such an extent that suicide would have become a general custom and individuals might have experienced the final remnant of a sense of duty when, like the inhabitants of the Fiji Islands, they had strangled their parents and friends—a practical pessimism that might even have generated a gruesome ethic of genocide[4] motivated by pity, and which incidentally is, and was, present in the world wherever art did not appear in some form—especially as

---

[4] *Völkermord.*

religion and science—as a remedy and a preventive for this breath of pestilence.

By contrast with this practical pessimism, Socrates is the prototype of the theoretical optimist who, with his faith that the nature of things can be fathomed, ascribes to knowledge and insight the power of a panacea, while understanding error as the evil *par excellence*. To fathom the depths and to separate true knowledge from appearance and error, seemed to Socratic man the noblest, even the only truly human vocation. And since Socrates, this mechanism of concepts, judgments, and inferences has been esteemed as the highest occupation and the most admirable gift of nature, above all other capacities. Even the most sublime ethical deeds, the stirrings of pity, self-sacrifice, heroism, and that calm sea of the soul, so difficult to attain, which the Apollinian Greek called *sophrosune*,[5] were derived from the dialectic of knowledge by Socrates and his like-minded successors, down to the present, and accordingly designated as teachable.

Anyone who has ever experienced the pleasure of Socratic insight and felt how, spreading in ever-widening circles, it seeks to embrace the whole world of appearances, will never again find any stimulus toward existence more violent than the craving to complete this conquest and to weave the net impenetrably tight. To one who feels that way, the Platonic Socrates will appear as the teacher of an altogether new form of "Greek cheerfulness" and blissful affirmation of existence that seeks to discharge itself in actions—most often in maieutic and educational influences on noble youths, with a view to eventually producing a genius.

But science, spurred by its powerful illusion, speeds irresistibly toward its limits where its optimism, concealed in the essence of logic, suffers shipwreck. For the periphery of the circle of science has an infinite number of points; and while there is no telling how this circle could ever be surveyed completely, noble and gifted men nevertheless reach, e'er half their time[6] and inevitably, such

---

[5] Often rendered, not quite adequately, as temperance.

[6] "Before the middle of his existence" presumably alludes to the beginning of Dante's *Inferno*, not, like my translation, to Milton's sonnet on his blindness.

boundary points[7] on the periphery from which one gazes into what defies illumination. When they see to their horror how logic coils up at these boundaries and finally bites its own tail—suddenly the new form of insight breaks through, *tragic insight* which, merely to be endured, needs art as a protection and remedy.

Our eyes strengthened and refreshed by our contemplation of the Greeks, let us look at the highest spheres of the world around us; then we shall see how the hunger for insatiable and optimistic knowledge[8] that in Socrates appears exemplary has turned into tragic resignation and destitute need for art—while, to be sure, the same hunger on its lower levels can express itself in hostility to art and must particularly detest Dionysian-tragic art, as was illustrated earlier with the fight of Socratism against Aeschylean tragedy.

Here we knock, deeply moved, at the gates of present and future: will this "turning" [9] lead to ever-new configurations of genius and especially of the *Socrates who practices music?* [10] Will the net of art, even if it is called religion or science, that is spread over existence be woven even more tightly and delicately, or is it destined to be torn to shreds in the restless, barbarous, chaotic whirl that now calls itself "the present"?

Concerned but not disconsolate, we stand aside a little while, contemplative men to whom it has been granted to be witnesses of these tremendous struggles and transitions. Alas, it is the magic of these struggles that those who behold them must also take part and fight.[11]

---

[7] *Grenzpunkte.* Jaspers' celebrated *Grenzsituationen* are elaborations of the points here described. And Nietzsche's image of shipwreck (*Scheitern*) also became one of Jaspers' key terms. This passage is as close to Jaspers' existentialism" as section 7 is to Sartre's.

[8] In Nietzsche's text, knowledge is insatiable, not merely the hunger for it.

[9] *Umschlagen.* Cf. "has turned into tragic resignation" in the preceding paragraph.

[10] Even more obviously than the "artistic Socrates" near the end of the preceding section, this is surely an idealized self-portrait: Nietzsche played the piano and composed songs.

[11] The book might well end at this point—as the original version did: Friedrich Nietzsche: *Socrates und die griechische Tragödie: Ursprüngliche Fassung der Geburt der Tragödie aus dem Geiste der Musik* (Socrates and Greek tragedy: original version of *The Birth of Tragedy out of the Spirit of Music*), ed. Hans Joachim Mette (Munich, Beck, 1933). The discussion of the birth

16

By this elaborate historical example we have sought to make clear how just as tragedy perishes with the evanescence of the spirit of music, it is only from this spirit that it can be reborn. Lest this assertion seem too strange, it may be well to disclose the origin of this insight by considering the analogous phenomena of our own time; we must enter into the midst of those struggles, which, as I have just said, are being waged in the highest spheres of our contemporary world between insatiable optimistic knowledge and the tragic need of art. In my examination I shall leave out of account all those other antagonistic tendencies which at all times oppose art, especially tragedy, and which now are again extending their triumphant sway to such an extent that of the theatrical arts only the farce and the ballet, for example, put forth their blossoms, which perhaps not everyone cares to smell, in rather rich luxuriance. I will speak only of the noblest *opposition* to the tragic world-conception—and by this I mean science, which is at bottom optimistic, with its ancestor Socrates at its head. A little later on I shall also name those forces which seem to me to guarantee a *rebirth of tragedy*—and perhaps other blessed hopes for the German genius!

Before we plunge into the midst of these struggles, let us array ourselves in the armor of the insights we have acquired. In contrast to all those who are intent on deriving the arts from one exclusive principle, as the necessary vital source of every work of art, I shall keep my eyes fixed on the two artistic deities of the Greeks, Apollo and Dionysus, and recognize in them the living and conspicuous representatives of *two* worlds of art differing in their intrinsic essence and in their highest aims. I see Apollo as the transfiguring genius of the *principium individuationis* through which alone the redemption in illusion is truly to be obtained; while by the mystical triumphant cry of Dionysus the spell of individuation is broken, and the way lies open to the Mothers of Being,[1] to the innermost

---

and death of tragedy is finished in the main, and the following celebration of the rebirth of tragedy weakens the book and was shortly regretted by Nietzsche himself.

[1] An allusion to Goethe's *Faust,* lines 6216ff.

heart of things. This extraordinary contrast, which stretches like a yawning gulf between plastic art as the Apollinian, and music as the Dionysian art,[2] has revealed itself to only one of the great thinkers, to such an extent that, even without this clue to the symbolism of the Hellenic divinities, he conceded to music a character and an origin different from all the other arts, because, unlike them, it is not a copy of the phenomenon, but an immediate copy of the will itself, and therefore complements *everything physical in the world* and every phenomenon by representing *what is metaphysical,* the thing in itself. (Schopenhauer, *Welt als Wille und Vorstellung,* I, p. 310.)

To this most important insight of aesthetics (with which, in the most serious sense, aesthetics properly begins), Richard Wagner, by way of confirmation of its eternal truth, affixed his seal, when he asserted in his *Beethoven* that music must be evaluated according to aesthetic principles quite different from those which apply to all plastic arts, and not, in general, according to the category of beauty; although an erroneous aesthetics, inspired by a mistaken and degenerate art,[3] has, by virtue of the concept of beauty obtaining in the plastic domain, accustomed itself to demand of music an effect similar to that produced by works of plastic art, namely, the arousing of *delight in beautiful forms.* Having recognized this extraordinary contrast, I felt a strong need to approach the essence of Greek tragedy and, with it, the profoundest

---

[2] Nietzsche clearly did not mean to imply that all music is "Dionysian." Yet it did not occur to him at this time to consider Mozart's music as an alternative to Wagner's. Mozart is not mentioned in *The Birth of Tragedy.* He is mentioned elsewhere by the young Nietzsche, and all references express love and admiration. But it was only in 1880, in *The Wanderer and His Shadow* (section 165), after his break with Wagner, that Nietzsche offered a contrast of Wagner and Mozart in one of his books—without mentioning Wagner by name. Eventually, he included this passage and some comparable ones from *Beyond Good and Evil* (1886) in *Nietzsche contra Wagner.* When it occurred to Nietzsche that Mozart's music was not Dionysian, he also realized that Wagner's music was not really "Dionysian" either, but rather "romantic" and "decadent." See *Nietzsche contra Wagner* (in *The Portable Nietzsche,* especially pp. 667ff.) and section 370 of *The Gay Science* (in Kaufmann, *Nietzsche,* Chapter 12, section V).

[3] *Entartete Kunst:* the term was made infamous by the Nazis when they subsumed under it a great deal of modern art which was officially proscribed. But the Nazis wanted "beautiful forms" and raged against art which did not aim at "beauty," while Nietzsche criticizes the assumption that all art must aim at "beautiful forms."

revelation of the Hellenic genius; for I at last thought that I possessed a charm to enable me—far beyond the phraseology of our usual aesthetics—to represent vividly to my mind the fundamental problem of tragedy; whereby I was granted such a surprising and unusual insight into the Hellenic character that it necessarily seemed to me as if our classical-Hellenic science that bears itself so proudly had thus far contrived to subsist mainly on shadow plays and externals.

Perhaps we may touch on this fundamental problem by asking: what aesthetic effect results when the essentially separate art-forces, the Apollinian and the Dionysian, enter into simultaneous activity? Or more briefly: how is music related to image and concept? Schopenhauer, whom Richard Wagner, with special reference to this point, praises for an unsurpassable clearness and clarity of exposition, expresses himself most thoroughly on the subject in the following passage which I shall cite here at full length (*Welt als Wille und Vorstellung,* I, p. 309 [4]): "According to all this, we may regard the phenomenal world, or nature, and music as two different expressions of the same thing,[5] which is therefore itself the only medium of their analogy, so that a knowledge of it is demanded in order to understand that analogy. Music, therefore, if regarded as an expression of the world, is in the highest degree a universal language, which is related indeed to the universality of concepts, much as they are related to the particular things. Its universality, however, is by no means that empty universality of abstraction, but of quite a different kind, and is united with thorough and distinct definiteness. In this respect it resembles geometrical figures and numbers, which are the universal forms of all possible objects of experience and applicable to them all *a priori,* and yet are not abstract but perceptible and thoroughly determinate. All possible efforts, excitements, and manifestations of will, all that goes on in the heart of man and that reason includes in the wide, negative concept of feeling, may be expressed by the infinite number of possible melodies, but always in the universal, in the mere form, with-

---

[4] The reference is Nietzsche's own: see footnote 7, section 1. I have used the R. B. Haldane and J. Kemp translation of this long passage (*World as Will and Idea,* London, Kegan Paul, 1907, I, p. 239) but revised a number of inaccuracies.

[5] The will.

out the material, always according to the thing-in-itself, not the phenomenon, the inmost soul, as it were, of the phenomenon without the body. This deep relation which music has to the true nature of all things also explains the fact that suitable music played to any scene, action, event, or surrounding seems to disclose to us its most secret meaning, and appears as the most accurate and distinct commentary upon it. This is so truly the case that whoever gives himself up entirely to the impression of a symphony, seems to see all the possible events of life and the world take place in himself; yet if he reflects, he can find no likeness between the music and the things that passed before his mind. For, as we have said, music is distinguished from all the other arts by the fact that it is not a copy of the phenomenon, or, more accurately, of the adequate objectivity of the will, but an immediate copy of the will itself, and therefore complements everything physical in the world and every phenomenon by representing what is metaphysical, the thing in itself. We might, therefore, just as well call the world embodied music as embodied will; and this is the reason why music makes every painting, and indeed every scene of real life and of the world, at once appear with higher significance, certainly all the more, in proportion as its melody is analogous to the inner spirit of the given phenomenon. Therefore we are able to set a poem to music as a song, or a visible representation as a pantomime, or both as an opera. Such particular pictures of human life, set to the universal language of music, are never bound to it or correspond to it with stringent necessity; but they stand to it only in the relation of an example chosen at will to a general concept. In the determinateness of the real, they represent that which music expresses in the universality of mere form. For melodies are to a certain extent, like general concepts, an abstraction from the actual. This actual world, then, the world of particular things, affords the object of perception, the special and individual, the particular case, both to the universality of the concepts and to the universality of the melodies. But these two universalities are in a certain respect opposed to each other; for the concepts contain particulars only as the first forms abstracted from perception, as it were, the separated shell of things; thus they are, strictly speaking, *abstracta:* music, on the other hand, gives the inmost kernel which precedes all forms, or the heart of things. This relation may be very well expressed in the language of the schoolmen, by saying, the concepts are the *universalia post rem,* but music gives the *universalia ante rem,* and the real world the *universalia in re.* But that in general a relation is possible between a composition and a visible representation rests, as we have said, upon the fact that both are simply different expressions of the same inner being of the world. When now, in the particular case, such a relation is actually given, that is to say, when the composer has been able to express in the universal language of music the stirrings of will which constitute the heart of an event, then the melody of the song, the music of the opera, is expressive. But the analogy discovered by the composer between the two must have proceeded from the direct knowledge of the nature of the world unknown to his reason, and must not be an imitation produced with conscious intention by means of concepts, otherwise the music does not express the inner nature, the will itself, but merely gives an inadequate imitation of its phenomenon. All truly imitative music does this."

According to the doctrine of Schopenhauer, therefore, we understand music as the immediate language of the will, and we feel our fancy stimulated to give form to this invisible and yet so actively stirred spirit-world which speaks to us, and we feel prompted to embody it in an analogous example. On the other hand, image and concept, under the influence of a truly corresponding music, acquire a higher significance. Dionysian art therefore is wont to exercise two kinds of influences on the Apollinian art faculty: music incites to the *symbolic intuition* of Dionysian universality, and music allows the symbolic image to emerge *in its highest significance.* From these facts, intelligible in themselves and not inaccessible to a more penetrating examination, I infer the capacity of music to give birth to *myth* (the most significant example), and particularly the *tragic* myth: the myth which expresses Dionysian knowledge in symbols. In the phenomenon of the lyrist, I have shown how music strives to express its nature in Apollinian images. If now we reflect that music at its highest stage must seek to attain also to its highest objectification in images, we must deem it possible that it also knows how to find the symbolic expression for its unique Dionysian wisdom; and where shall we seek for this expression if not in tragedy and, in general, in the conception of the tragic?

From the nature of art as it is usually conceived according to the single category of appearance and beauty, the tragic cannot honestly be deduced at all; it is only through the spirit of music that we can understand the joy involved in the annihilation of the individual. For it is only in particular examples of such annihilation that we see clearly the eternal phenomenon of Dionysian art, which gives expression to the will in its omnipotence, as it were, behind the *principium individuationis,* the eternal life beyond all phenomena, and despite all annihilation. The metaphysical joy in the tragic is a translation of the instinctive unconscious Dionysian wisdom into the language of images: the hero, the highest manifestation of the will, is negated for our pleasure, because he is only phenomenon, and because the eternal life of the will is not affected by his annihilation. "We believe in eternal life," exclaims tragedy; while music is the immediate idea of this life. Plastic art has an altogether different aim: here Apollo overcomes the suffering of the individual by the radiant glorification of the *eternity of the phenomenon:* here beauty triumphs over the suffering inherent in life; pain is obliterated by lies from the features of nature. In Dionysian art and its tragic symbolism the same nature cries to us with its true, undissembled voice: "Be as I am! Amid the ceaseless flux of phenomena I am the eternally creative primordial mother, eternally impelling to existence, eternally finding satisfaction in this change of phenomena!"

17

Dionysian art, too, wishes to convince us of the eternal joy of existence: only we are to seek this joy not in phenomena, but behind them. We are to recognize that all that comes into being must be ready for a sorrowful end; we are forced to look into the terrors of the individual existence—yet we are not to become rigid with fear: a metaphysical comfort tears us momentarily from the bustle of the changing figures. We are really for a brief moment primordial being itself, feeling its raging desire for existence and joy in existence; the struggle, the pain, the destruction of phenomena, now appear necessary to us, in view of the excess of countless forms of existence which force and push one another into life, in view of the exuberant fertility of the universal will. We are pierced by the maddening sting of these pains just when we have become, as it were, one with the infinite primordial joy in existence, and when we anticipate, in Dionysian ecstasy, the indestructibility and eternity of this joy. In spite of fear and pity, we are the happy living beings, not as individuals, but as the *one* living being, with whose creative joy we are united.

The history of the rise of Greek tragedy now tells us with luminous precision how the tragic art of the Greeks was really born of the spirit of music. With this conception we believe we have done justice for the first time to the primitive and astonishing significance of the chorus. At the same time, however, we must admit that the meaning of tragic myth set forth above never became clear in transparent concepts to the Greek poets, not to speak of the Greek philosophers: their heroes speak, as it were, more superficially than they act; the myth does not at all obtain adequate objectification in the spoken word. The structure of the scenes and the visual images reveal a deeper wisdom than the poet himself can put into words and concepts: the same is also observable in Shakespeare, whose Hamlet, for instance, similarly, talks more superficially than he acts, so that the previously mentioned lesson of Hamlet is to be deduced, not from his words, but from a profound contemplation and survey of the whole.

With respect to Greek tragedy, which of course presents itself to us only as word-drama, I have even intimated that the lack of congruity between myth and expression might easily lead us to regard it as shallower and less significant than it really is, and accordingly to attribute to it a more superficial effect than it must have had according to the testimony of the ancients: for how easily one forgets that what the word-poet did not succeed in doing, namely, attain the highest spiritualization and ideality of the myth, he might very well succeed in doing every moment as creative musician! To be sure, we are almost forced to construct for ourselves by scholarly research the superior power of the musical effect in order to experience something of the incomparable comfort which must have been characteristic of true tragedy. Even this musical superiority, however, would only have been felt by us had we been Greeks; for in the entire development of Greek music—as compared with the infinitely richer music known and familiar to us—we imagine we hear only the youthful song of the musical genius modestly intoned. The Greeks, as the Egyptian priests say, are eternal children, and in tragic art too they are only children who do not know what a sublime plaything originated in their hands and—was quickly demolished.

That striving of the spirit of music toward visual and mythical objectification, which increases from the beginnings of lyric poetry up to Attic tragedy, suddenly breaks off after attaining a luxuriant development, and disappears, as it were, from the surface of Hellenic art; while the Dionysian world view born of this striving lives on in the mysteries and, in its strangest metamorphoses and debasements, does not cease to attract serious natures. Will it not some day rise once again out of its mystic depths as art?

Here we are detained by the question, whether the power, by virtue of whose opposing influence tragedy perished, has for all time sufficient strength to prevent the artistic reawakening of tragedy and the tragic world view. If ancient tragedy was diverted from its course by the dialectical desire for knowledge and the optimism of science, this fact might lead us to believe that there is an eternal conflict between *the theoretic* and *the tragic world view;* and only after the spirit of science has been pursued to its limits, and its claim to universal validity destroyed by the evidence of these limits may we hope for a rebirth of tragedy—a form of culture for which we should have to use the symbol *of the music-practicing Socrates* in the sense spoken of above.[1] In this contrast, I understand by the spirit of science the faith that first came to light in the person of Socrates—the faith in the explicability of nature and in knowledge as a panacea.

He who recalls the immediate consequences of this restlessly progressing spirit of science will realize at once that *myth* was annihilated by it, and that, because of this annihilation, poetry was driven like a homeless being from her natural ideal soil. If we have been right in assigning to music the power of again giving birth to myth, we may similarly expect to find the spirit of science on the path where it inimically opposes this mythopoeic power of music. This takes place in the development of the *New Attic Dithyramb,* the music of which no longer expressed the inner essence, the will itself, but only rendered the phenomenon inadequately, in an imitation by means of concepts. From this intrinsically degenerate music

[1] Section 15, text for note 10.

the genuinely musical natures turned away with the same repugnance that they felt for the art-destroying tendency of Socrates. The unerring instinct of Aristophanes was surely right when it included Socrates himself, the tragedy of Euripides, and the music of the New Dithyrambic poets in the same feeling of hatred, recognizing in all three phenomena the signs of a degenerate culture.

In this New Dithyramb, music is outrageously manipulated so as to be the imitative counterfeit of a phenomenon, for instance, of a battle or a storm at sea; and thus, of course, it has been utterly robbed of its mythopoeic power. For if it seeks to arouse pleasure only by impelling us to seek external analogies between a vital or natural process and certain rhythmical figures and characteristic sounds of music; if our understanding is to content itself with the perception of these analogies; we are reduced to a frame of mind which makes impossible any reception of the mythical; for the myth wants to be experienced vividly as a unique example of a universality and truth that gaze into the infinite. The truly Dionysian music presents itself as such a general mirror of the universal will: the vivid event refracted in this mirror expands at once for our consciousness to the copy of an external truth. Conversely, such a vivid event is at once divested of every mythical character by the tone-painting of the New Dithyramb; music now becomes a wretched copy of the phenomenon, and therefore infinitely poorer than the phenomenon itself. And through this poverty it still further reduces the phenomenon for our consciousness, so that now, for example, a musically imitated battle of this sort exhausts itself in marches, signal sounds, etc., and our imagination is arrested precisely by these superficialities. Tone-painting is thus in every respect the opposite of true music with its mythopoeic power: through it the phenomenon, poor in itself, is made still poorer, while through Dionysian music the individual phenomenon is enriched and expanded into an image of the world. It was a great triumph for the un-Dionysian spirit when, by the development of the New Dithyramb, it had estranged music from itself and reduced it to be the slave of phenomena. Euripides, who, though in a higher sense, must be considered a thoroughly unmusical nature, is for this very reason a passionate adherent of the New Dithyrambic Music, and with the liberality of a robber makes use of all its effective tricks and mannerisms.

In another direction also we see at work the power of this un-Dionysian myth-opposing spirit, when we turn our attention to the prevalence of *character representation* and psychological refinement in tragedy from Sophocles onward. The character must no longer be expanded into an eternal type, but, on the contrary, must develop individually through artistic subordinate traits and shadings, through the nicest precision of all lines, in such a manner that the spectator is in general no longer conscious of the myth, but of the vigorous truth to nature and the artist's imitative power. Here also we observe the victory of the phenomenon over the universal, and the delight in a unique, almost anatomical preparation; we are already in the atmosphere of a theoretical world, where scientific knowledge is valued more highly than the artistic reflection of a universal law.

The movement in the direction of character delineation proceeds rapidly: while Sophocles still portrays complete characters and employs myth for their refined development, Euripides already draws only prominent individual traits of character, which can express themselves in violent bursts of passion. In the New Attic Comedy, however, there are only masks with *one* expression: frivolous old men, duped panders, and cunning slaves, recurring incessantly. Where now is the mythopoeic spirit of music? What still remains of music is either excitatory or reminiscent music, that is, either a stimulant for dull and faded nerves, or tone-painting. As regards the former, it hardly matters about the text set to it: as soon as his heroes and choruses begin to sing, everything becomes pretty slovenly in Euripides; to what pass must things have come with his impertinent successors?

The new un-Dionysian spirit, however, reveals itself most plainly in the *dénouements* of the new dramas. In the Old Tragedy one could sense at the end that metaphysical comfort without which the delight in tragedy cannot be explained at all. The reconciling tones from another world sound purest, perhaps, in the *Oedipus at Colonus*. Now that the genius of music has fled from tragedy, tragedy, strictly speaking, is dead: for from what source shall we now draw this metaphysical comfort? The new spirit, therefore, sought for an earthly resolution of the tragic dissonance. The hero, after being sufficiently tortured by fate, earned a well-deserved reward through a splendid marriage or tokens of divine favor. The hero had turned gladiator on whom, after he had been nicely beaten and covered with wounds, freedom was occasionally bestowed. The *deus ex machina* took the place of metaphysical comfort.

I will not say that the tragic world view was everywhere completely destroyed by this intruding un-Dionysian spirit: we only know that it had to flee from art into the underworld as it were, in the degenerate form of a secret cult. Over the widest extent of the Hellenic character, however, there raged the consuming blast of this spirit, which manifests itself in the form of "Greek cheerfulness," which we have already spoken of as a senile, unproductive love of existence. This cheerfulness stands opposed to the splendid "naïveté" of the earlier Greeks, which, according to the characterization given above, must be conceived as the blossom of the Apollinian culture springing from a dark abyss, as the victory which the Hellenic will, through its mirroring of beauty, obtains over suffering and the wisdom of suffering.

The noblest manifestation of that other form of "Greek cheerfulness," the Alexandrian, is the cheerfulness of the *theoretical man*. It exhibits the same characteristic symptoms that I have just deduced from the spirit of the un-Dionysian: it combats Dionysian wisdom and art, it seeks to dissolve myth, it substitutes for a metaphysical comfort an earthly consonance, in fact, a *deus ex machina* of its own, the god of machines and crucibles, that is, the powers of the spirits of nature recognized and employed in the service of a higher egoism; it believes that it can correct the world by knowledge, guide life by science, and actually confine the individual within a limited sphere of solvable problems, from which he can cheerfully say to life: "I desire you; you are worth knowing."

18

It is an eternal phenomenon: the insatiable will always finds a way to detain its creatures in life and compel them to live on, by means of an illusion spread over things. One is chained by the Socratic love of knowledge and the delusion of being able thereby to heal the eternal wound of existence; another is ensnared by art's seductive veil of beauty fluttering before his eyes; still another by the metaphysical comfort that beneath the whirl of phenomena eternal life flows on indestructibly—to say nothing of the more vulgar and almost more powerful illusions which the will always has at hand. These three stages of illusion are actually designed only for the more nobly formed natures, who actually feel profoundly the weight and burden of existence, and must be deluded by exquisite stimulants into forgetfulness of their displeasure. All that we call culture is made up of these stimulants; and, according to the proportion of the ingredients, we have either a dominantly *Socratic* or *artistic* or *tragic* culture; or, if historical exemplifications are permitted, there is either an Alexandrian or a Hellenic or a Buddhistic culture.[1]

Our whole modern world is entangled in the net of Alexandrian[2] culture. It proposes as its ideal the theoretical man equipped with the greatest forces of knowledge, and laboring in the service of science, whose archetype and progenitor is Socrates. All our educational methods originally have this ideal in view: every other form of existence must struggle on laboriously beside it, as something tolerated, but not intended. In an almost alarming manner the cultured man was for a long time found only in the form of the scholar: even our poetical arts have been forced to evolve from scholarly imitations, and in the main effect, that of rhyme, we still recognize the origin of our poetic form from artificial experiments with a nonindigenous, really scholarly language. How unintelligible

---

[1] All editions published by Nietzsche himself contain these words, and Wilamowitz cited this passage both in 1872 (p. 6) and in 1873 (p. 6). The standard editions of Nietzsche's collected works substitute "an Indian (Brahmanic) culture" for "Buddhistic culture." According to volume I (p. 599) of the so-called Grossoktav edition of Nietzsche's *Werke* (1905), this change is based on "a penciled correction in Nietzsche's own hand in his copy of the *second* version." It would seem that both "Buddhistic" and "Brahmanic" depend on some misconception; neither seems to make much sense.

[2] It is not uncommon to distinguish the Alexandrian period of Greek literature from the immediately preceding Attic period. The great tragic poets, as well as Thucydides, Plato, and Aristotle are associated with Athens and belong to the immensely creative fifth and fourth centuries, along with Phidias and Praxiteles. The glories of Alexandria, the intellectual capital of the Hellenic world from about 300 to 30 B.C., include no remotely comparable creative achievements but are its immense library, which far surpassed any previous collection, and its often exceedingly erudite scholars. To be sure, one still wrote poetry and vast amounts of prose, but on the whole the achievements of the scientists and scholars were more remarkable. Nietzsche is plainly suggesting that nineteenth-century Germany is in important respects strikingly similar to Alexandrian civilization.

must *Faust,* the modern cultured man, who is in himself intelligible, have appeared to a true Greek—Faust, storming unsatisfied through all the faculties, devoted to magic and the devil from a desire for knowledge; Faust, whom we have but to place beside Socrates for the purpose of comparison, in order to see that modern man is beginning to divine the limits of this Socratic love of knowledge and yearns for a coast in the wide waste of the ocean of knowledge. When Goethe on one occasion said to Eckermann with reference to Napoleon: "Yes, my good friend, there is also a productiveness of deeds," he reminded us in a charmingly naïve manner that the nontheorist is something incredible and astounding to modern man; so that we again have need of the wisdom of Goethe to discover that such a surprising form of existence is not only comprehensible, but even pardonable.

Now we must not hide from ourselves what is concealed in the womb of this Socratic culture: optimism, with its delusion of limitless power. We must not be alarmed if the fruits of this optimism ripen—if society, leavened to the very lowest strata by this kind of culture, gradually begins to tremble with wanton agitations and desires, if the belief in the earthly happiness of all, if the belief in the possibility of such a general intellectual culture changes into the threatening demand for such an Alexandrian earthly happiness, into the conjuring up of a Euripidean *deus ex machina.*

Let us mark this well: the Alexandrian culture, to be able to exist permanently, requires a slave class, but with its optimistic view of life it denies the necessity of such a class, and consequently, when its beautifully seductive and tranquillizing utterances about the "dignity of man" and the "dignity of labor" are no longer effective, it gradually drifts toward a dreadful destruction. There is nothing more terrible than a class of barbaric slaves who have learned to regard their existence as an injustice, and now prepare to avenge, not only themselves, but all generations. In the face of such threatening storms, who dares to appeal with any confidence to our pale and exhausted religions, the very foundations of which have degenerated into scholarly religions? Myth, the necessary prerequisite of every religion, is already paralyzed everywhere, and even in this domain the optimistic spirit, which we have just designated as the germ of destruction in our society, has attained the mastery.

While the disaster slumbering in the womb of theoretical culture gradually begins to frighten modern man, and he anxiously ransacks the stores of his experience for means to avert the danger, though he has no great faith in these means; while he, therefore, begins to divine the consequences of his situation—great men, universally gifted, have contrived, with an incredible amount of thought, to make use of the paraphernalia of science itself, to point out the limits and the relativity of knowledge generally, and thus to deny decisively the claim of science to universal validity and universal aims. And their demonstration diagnosed for the first time the illusory notion which pretends to be able to fathom the innermost essence of things with the aid of causality. The extraordinary courage and wisdom of *Kant* and *Schopenhauer* have succeeded in gaining the most difficult victory, the victory over the optimism concealed in the essence of logic—an optimism that is the basis of our culture. While this optimism, resting on apparently unobjectionable *aeternae veritates*,[3] had believed that all the riddles of the universe could be known and fathomed, and had treated space, time, and causality as entirely unconditional laws of the most universal validity, Kant showed that these really served only to elevate the mere phenomenon, the work of *māyā,* to the position of the sole and highest reality, as if it were the innermost and true essence of things, thus making impossible any knowledge of this essence or, in Schopenhauer's words, lulling the dreamer still more soundly asleep.

With this insight a culture is inaugurated that I venture to call a tragic culture. Its most important characteristic is that wisdom takes the place of science as the highest end—wisdom that, uninfluenced by the seductive distractions of the sciences, turns with unmoved eyes to a comprehensive view of the world, and seeks to grasp, with sympathetic feelings of love, the eternal suffering as its own.

Let us imagine a coming generation with such intrepidity of vision, with such a heroic penchant for the tremendous; let us imagine the bold stride of these dragon-slayers, the proud audacity with which they turn their back on all the weaklings' doctrines of optim-

---

[3] Eternal verities.

ism in order to "live resolutely" in wholeness and fullness:[4] would it not be necessary for the tragic man of such a culture, in view of his self-education for seriousness and terror, to desire a new art, the art of metaphysical comfort, to desire tragedy as his own proper Helen, and to exclaim with Faust:

> *Should not my longing overleap the distance*
> *And draw the fairest form into existence?* [5]

But now that the Socratic culture can only hold the scepter of its infallibility with trembling hands; now that it has been shaken from two directions—once by the fear of its own consequences which it at length begins to surmise, and again because it no longer has its former naïve confidence in the eternal validity of its foundation—it is a sad spectacle to see how the dance of its thought rushes longingly toward ever-new forms, to embrace them, and then, shuddering, lets them go suddenly as Mephistopheles does the seductive Lamiae.[6] It is certainly the sign of the "breach" of which everyone speaks as the fundamental malady of modern culture, that the theoretical man, alarmed and dissatisfied at his own consequences, no longer dares entrust himself to the terrible icy current of existence: he runs timidly up and down the bank. So thoroughly has he been pampered by his optimistic views that he no longer wants to have anything whole, with all of nature's cruelty attaching to it. Besides, he feels that a culture based on the principles of science must be destroyed when it begins to grow *illogical,* that is, to retreat before its own consequences. Our art reveals this universal distress: in vain does one depend imitatively on all the great productive periods and natures; in vain does one accumulate the entire "world-literature" around modern man for his comfort; in vain does one place oneself in the midst of the art styles and artists of all ages, so that one may give names to them as Adam did to the

---

[4] The quotation is from Goethe's poem *"Generalbeichte"* (general confession), written in 1802—an exuberant anti-Philistine manifesto.

[5] This whole paragraph is ridiculed by Nietzsche himself in the final section of his "Attempt at a Self-Criticism," printed as a preface to the "new edition" of 1886 and included above in the present English version. The quotation is from Goethe's *Faust,* Part II, lines 7438ff.

[6] In Goethe's *Faust,* Part II, lines 7769ff. (in the classical Walpurgis Night).

beasts: one still remains eternally hungry, the "critic" without joy
and energy, the Alexandrian man, who is at bottom a librarian and
corrector of proofs, and wretchedly goes blind from the dust of
books and from printers' errors.

19

We cannot indicate the innermost modern content of this Socratic culture more distinctly than by calling it *the culture of the
opera:* for it is in this department that this culture has expressed its
aims and perceptions with special naïveté, which is surprising
when we compare the genesis of the opera and the facts of operatic
development with the eternal truths of the Apollinian and Dionysian. I recall first of all the origin of the *stilo rappresentativo*[1] and
the recitative. Is it credible that this thoroughly externalized operatic music, incapable of devotion, could be received and cherished
with enthusiastic favor, as a rebirth, as it were, of all true music, by
the very age in which had appeared the ineffably sublime and sacred music of Palestrina? And who, on the other hand, would think
of making only the diversion-craving luxuriousness of those Florentine circles and the vanity of their dramatic singers responsible
for the love of the opera which spread with such rapidity? That in
the same age, even among the same people, this passion for a half-
musical mode of speech should awaken alongside of the vaulted
structure of Palestrina harmonies which all medieval Christendom
had been building up, I can explain to myself only by a cooperating,
extra-artistic tendency in the essence of the recitative.

The listener who insists on distinctly hearing the words under
the music has his desire fulfilled by the singer in that the latter
speaks rather than sings, intensifying the pathetic expression of the
words by means of this half-song. By this intensification of the
pathos he facilitates the understanding of the words and overcomes
the remaining half of the music. The specific danger now threatening him is that in some unguarded moment he may stress the music
unduly, which would immediately entail the destruction of the
pathos of the speech and the distinctness of the words; while, on
the other hand, he feels himself continually impelled to musical

---

[1] Representational style.

discharge and a virtuoso exhibition of his vocal talent. Here the "poet" comes to his aid, who knows how to provide him with abundant opportunities for lyrical interjections, repetitions of words and sentences, etc.—at which places the singer, now in the purely musical element, can rest himself without paying any attention to the words. This alternation of emotionally impressive speech which, however, is only half sung, with interjections which are wholly sung, an alternation characteristic of the *stilo rappresentativo,* this rapidly changing endeavor to affect now the concepts and imagination of the hearer, now his musical sense, is something so utterly unnatural and likewise so intrinsically contradictory both to the Apollinian and Dionysian artistic impulses, that one has to infer an origin of the recitative lying outside all artistic instincts. According to this description, the recitative must be defined as a mixture of epic and lyric delivery, not by any means as an intrinsically stable mixture, a state not to be attained in the case of such totally disparate elements, but as an entirely superficial mosaic conglutination, such as is totally unprecedented in the domain of nature and experience. *But this was not the opinion of the inventors of the recitative:* they themselves, together with their age, believed rather that the mystery of antique music has been solved by this *stilo rappresentativo,* in which, so they thought, was to be found the only explanation of the enormous influence of an Orpheus, an Amphion, and even of Greek tragedy. The new style was looked upon as the reawakening of the most effective music, ancient Greek music: indeed, in accordance with the universal and popular conception of the Homeric *as the primitive world,* they could abandon themselves to the dream of having descended once more into the paradisiacal beginnings of mankind, where music also must have had that unsurpassed purity, power, and innocence of which the poets, in their pastoral plays, could give such touching accounts. Here we can see into the innermost development of this thoroughly modern variety of art, the opera: art here responds to a powerful need, but it is a nonaesthetic need: the yearning for the idyllic, the faith in the primordial existence of the artistic and good man. The recitative was regarded as the rediscovered language of this primitive man; opera as the rediscovered country of this idyllically or heroically good creature, who simultaneously with every action follows a natural artistic impulse, who accomplishes his speech with a little singing, in order that he may immediately break forth into full song at the slightest emotional excitement.

It is now a matter of indifference to us that the humanists of the time combated the old ecclesiastical conception of man as inherently corrupt and lost, with this newly created picture of the paradisiacal artist: so that opera is to be understood as the opposition dogma of the good man, but may also, at the same time, provide a consolation for that pessimism which, owing to the frightful uncertainty of all conditions of life, attracted precisely the serious-minded men of the time. For us, it is enough to have perceived that the essential charm, and therefore the genesis, of this new art form lies in the gratification of an altogether nonaesthetic need, in the optimistic glorification of man as such, in the conception of the primitive man as the man naturally good and artistic—a principle of the opera that has gradually changed into a threatening and terrible *demand* which, in face of contemporary socialistic movements, we can no longer ignore. The "good primitive man" wants his rights: what paradisiacal prospects!

Besides this I place another equally obvious confirmation of my view that opera is based on the same principles as our Alexandrian culture. Opera is the birth of the theoretical man, the critical layman, not of the artist: one of the most surprising facts in the history of all the arts. It was the demand of thoroughly unmusical hearers that before everything else the words must be understood, so that according to them a rebirth of music is to be expected only when some mode of singing has been discovered in which text-word lords it over counterpoint like master over servant. For the words, it is argued, are as much nobler than the accompanying harmonic system as the soul is nobler than the body.

It was in accordance with the laically unmusical crudeness of these views that the combination of music, image, and words was effected in the beginnings of the opera. In the spirit of this aesthetic the first experiments were made in the leading amateur circles of Florence by the poets and singers patronized there. The man incapable of art creates for himself a kind of art precisely because he is the inartistic man as such. Because he does not sense the Dionysian depth of music, he changes his musical taste into an appreciation of the understandable word-and-tone-rhetoric of the passions in the *stilo rappresentativo,* and into the voluptuousness of the arts of song. Because he is unable to behold a vision, he forces the machinist and the decorative artist into his service. Because he cannot comprehend the true nature of the artist, he conjures up the "artistic primitive man" to suit his taste, that is, the man who sings and recites verses under the influence of passion. He dreams himself back into a time when passion sufficed to generate songs and poems; as if emotion had ever been able to create anything artistic.

The premise of the opera is a false belief concerning the artistic process: the idyllic belief that every sentient man is an artist. This belief would make opera the expression of the taste of the laity in art, dictating their laws with the cheerful optimism of the theoretical man.

Should we desire to combine the two conceptions that have just been shown to have influenced the origin of opera, it would merely remain for us to speak of an *idyllic tendency of the opera*. In this connection we need only avail ourselves of the expressions and explanation of Schiller. Nature and the ideal, he says, are either objects of grief, when the former is represented as lost, the latter unattained; or both are objects of joy, in that they are represented as real. The first case furnishes the elegy in its narrower signification, the second the idyll in its widest sense.

Here we must at once call attention to the common characteristic of these two conceptions in the genesis of opera, namely, that in them the ideal is not felt as unattained or nature as lost. This sentiment supposes that there was a primitive age of man when he lay close to the heart of nature, and, owing to this naturalness, had at once attained the ideal of mankind in a paradisiacal goodness and artistry. From this perfect primitive man all of us were supposed to be descended. We were even supposed to be faithful copies of him; only we had to cast off a few things in order to recognize ourselves once more as this primitive man, on the strength of a voluntary renunciation of superfluous learnedness, of superabundant culture. It was to such a concord of nature and the ideal, to an idyllic reality, that the cultured Renaissance man let himself be led back by his operatic imitation of Greek tragedy. He made use of this tragedy as Dante made use of Vergil, in order to be conducted to the gates of paradise; while from this point he continued unassisted and passed over from an imitation of the highest Greek art-form to a "restoration of all things," to an imitation of man's original art-

world. What a cheerful confidence there is about these daring endeavors, in the very heart of theoretical culture!—solely to be explained by the comforting belief, that "man-in-himself" is the
eternally virtuous hero of the opera, the eternally piping or singing
shepherd, who must always in the end rediscover himself as such,
should he ever at any time have really lost himself; to be considered solely as the fruit of that optimism, which here rises like a
sweetishly seductive column of vapor from the depth of the Socratic world view.

Therefore, the features of the opera do not by any means exhibit the elegiac sorrow of an eternal loss, but rather the cheerfulness of eternal rediscovery, the comfortable delight in an idyllic
reality which one can at least always imagine as real. But in this
process one may some day grasp the fact that this supposed reality
is nothing but a fantastically silly dawdling, at which everyone who
could judge it by the terrible seriousness of true nature, and compare it with actual primitive scenes of the beginnings of mankind,
would be impelled to call out, nauseated: Away with the phantom!

Nevertheless, it would be a mistake to imagine that it is possible merely by a vigorous shout to frighten away such a playful
thing as the opera, as if it were a specter. He who would destroy the
opera must take up the struggle against Alexandrian cheerfulness,
which expresses itself so naïvely in opera concerning its favorite
idea. Indeed, opera is its specific form of art. But what may art
itself expect from the operation of an art form whose beginnings lie
entirely outside of the aesthetic province and which has stolen over
from a half-moral sphere into the artistic domain, deceiving us only
occasionally about its hybrid origin? By what sap is this parasitic
opera nourished, if not by that of true art? Must we not suppose
that the highest and, indeed, the truly serious task of art—to save
the eye from gazing into the horrors of night and to deliver the
subject by the healing balm of illusion from the spasms of the agitations of the will—must degenerate under the influence of its idyllic
seductions and Alexandrian flatteries to become an empty and
merely distracting diversion? What will become of the eternal
truths of the Dionysian and Apollinian when the styles are mixed in
this fashion, as I have shown to be the essence of the *stilo rappresentativo?* A style in which music is regarded as the servant, the
text as the master, where music is compared with the body, the text

with the soul? where at best the highest aim will be directed toward a paraphrastic tone-painting, just as formerly in the New Attic Dithyramb? where music is completely alienated from its true dignity as the Dionysian mirror of the world, so that the only thing left to it, as the slave of phenomena, is to imitate the formal character of phenomena, and to arouse a superficial pleasure in the play of lines and proportions. Closely observed, this fatal influence of the opera on music is seen to coincide exactly with the universal development of modern music; the optimism lurking in the genesis of the opera and in the character of the culture thereby represented, has, with alarming rapidity, succeeded in divesting music of its Dionysian-cosmic mission and impressing on it a playfully formal and pleasurable character: a change comparable to the metamorphosis of the Aeschylean man into the cheerful Alexandrian.

If, however, in the exemplification here indicated, we have rightly associated the disappearance of the Dionysian spirit with a most striking, but hitherto unexplained, transformation and degeneration of the Hellenic man—what hopes must revive in us when the most certain auspices guarantee *the reverse process, the gradual awakening of the Dionysian spirit* in our modern world! It is impossible that the divine strength of Herakles should languish for ever in ample bondage to Omphale.[2] Out of the Dionysian root of the German spirit a power has arisen which, having nothing in common with the primitive conditions of Socratic culture, can neither be explained nor excused by it, but which is rather felt by this culture as something terribly inexplicable and overwhelmingly hostile—*German music* as we must understand it, particularly in its vast solar orbit from Bach to Beethoven, from Beethoven to Wagner.

Even under the most favorable circumstances what can the knowledge-craving Socratism of our days do with this demon rising from unfathomable depths? Neither by means of the flourishes and arabesques of operatic melody, nor with the aid of the arithmetical counting board of fugue and contrapuntal dialectic is the formula to be found by whose thrice-powerful light one might subdue this

---

[2] A queen of Lydia by whom Herakles claimed to have been detained for a year of bondage, according to Sophocles, *Trachiniae,* lines 248ff. In Ovid's *Heroïdes,* 9.53ff., the story is elaborated.

demon and compel it to speak. What a spectacle, when our latter-day aestheticians, with a net of "beauty" peculiar to themselves, pursue and clutch at the genius of music whirling before display activities which are not to be judged by the standard of eternal beauty any more than by the standard of the sublime. Let us but observe these patrons of music at close range, as they really are, indefatigably crying: "Beauty! beauty!" Do they really bear the stamp of nature's darling children who are fostered and nourished at the breast of the beautiful, or are they not rather seeking a mendacious cloak for their own coarseness, an aesthetical pretext for their own insensitive sobriety; here I am thinking of Otto Jahn, for example.[3] But let the liar and the hypocrite beware of German music: for amid all our culture it is really the only genuine, pure, and purifying fire-spirit from which and toward which, as in the teaching of the great Heraclitus of Ephesus, all things move in a double orbit: all that we now call culture, education, civilization, must some day appear before the unerring judge, Dionysus.

Let us recollect further that Kant and Schopenhauer made it possible for the spirit of *German philosophy,* streaming from similar sources, to destroy scientific Socratism's complacent delight in existence by establishing its boundaries; how through this delimitation was introduced an infinitely profounder and more serious view

---

[3] Otto Jahn was born in 1813, like Nietzsche's father, Richard Wagner, and Kierkegaard, and died in 1869. He was a professor of classical philology at Bonn, first a friend and later a foe of Nietzsche's teacher Ritschl. His many publications included articles on Greek tragedies and on ancient sculptures and vase paintings, a life of Mozart, and essays on music. To explain the above remark, it may be relevant to recall a passage in one of Nietzsche's letters to Rohde, October 8, 1868: "Recently I have also read . . . Jahn's essays on music, including those on Wagner. It requires some enthusiasm to do justice to such a man, while Jahn has an instinctive aversion and listens only with ears that are half plugged. Nevertheless I agree with him on many points; especially insofar as he considers Wagner the representative of a modern dilettantism that absorbs and digests all artistic interests. But precisely from this point of view one can hardly be astonished enough at how imposing every single artistic talent is in this man, and what inexhaustible energy is here coupled with such many-sided artistic talents, while 'education,' the more motley and comprehensive it is, usually appears with weak eyes, feeble legs, and unnerved loins. Moreover, Wagner has a dimension of feelings that remains altogether hidden from O. Jahn: Jahn simply remains a . . . healthy man for whom the myth of Tannhäuser and the atmosphere of Lohengrin remain a closed world. What I like about Wagner is what I like about Schopenhauer: the ethical air, the Faustian fragrance, cross, death, and tomb, etc."

of ethical problems and of art, which we may designate as Dionysian wisdom comprised in concepts. To what then does the mystery
of this oneness of German music and philosophy point if not to a
new form of existence, concerning whose character we can only
inform ourselves by surmise from Hellenic analogies? For to us
who stand on the boundary line between two different forms of
existence, the Hellenic prototype retains this immeasurable value,
that all these transitions and struggles are imprinted upon it in a
classically instructive form; except that we, as it were, pass through
the chief epochs of the Hellenic genius, analogically in *reverse*
order, and seem now, for instance, to be passing backward from
the Alexandrian age to the period of tragedy. At the same time we
have the feeling that the birth of a tragic age simply means a return
to itself of the German spirit, a blessed self-rediscovery after powerful intrusive influences had for a long time compelled it, living
as it did in a helpless and unchaste barbarism, to servitude under
their form. Now at last, upon returning to the primitive source of
its being, it may venture to stride along boldly and freely before the
eyes of all nations without being attached to the lead strings of a
Romanic civilization; if only it can learn constantly from one people—the Greeks, from whom to be able to learn at all is itself a
high honor and a rare distinction. And when were we in greater
need of these highest of all teachers than at present, when we are
experiencing a *rebirth of tragedy* and are in danger alike of not
knowing whence it comes and of being unable to make clear to
ourselves whither it tends?

20

Some day, before an impartial judge, it may be decided in
what time and in what men the German spirit has so far striven
most resolutely to learn from the Greeks; and if we confidently assume that this unique praise must be accorded to the noblest intellectual efforts of Goethe, Schiller, and Winckelmann, we should
certainly have to add that since their time and the more immediate
consequences of their efforts, the endeavor to attain to culture and
to the Greeks on the same path has grown incomprehensibly feebler and feebler. That we may not despair utterly of the German
spirit, must we not conclude that, in some essential matter, even

these champions did not penetrate into the core of the Hellenic nature, to establish a permanent alliance between German and Greek culture? So an unconscious recognition of this shortcoming may have prompted the disheartening doubt, even in very serious people, whether after such predecessors they could possibly advance further on this path of culture or could reach the goal at all. Accordingly, we see that opinions concerning the value of the Greeks for education have been degenerating in the most alarming manner since that time. Expressions of compassionate condescension may be heard in the most varied camps of the spirit—and of lack of spirit. Elsewhere, ineffectual rhetoric plays with the phrases "Greek harmony," "Greek beauty," "Greek cheerfulness." And those very circles whose dignified task it might be to draw indefatigably from the Greek reservoir for the good of German culture, the teachers of the higher educational institutions, have learned best to come to terms with the Greeks easily and in good time, often by skeptically abandoning the Hellenic ideal and completely perverting the true purpose of antiquarian studies. Whoever in these circles has not completely exhausted himself in his endeavor to be a dependable corrector of old texts or a linguistic microscopist who apes natural history is probably trying to assimilate Greek antiquity "historically," along with other antiquities, at any rate according to the method and with the supercilious airs of our present cultured historiography.

The cultural power of our higher educational institutions has perhaps never been lower or feebler than at present. The "journalist," the paper slave of the day, triumphs over the professor in all matters pertaining to culture; and nothing remains to the latter but the metamorphosis, often experienced by now, of fluttering also like a cheerful cultured butterfly, with the "light elegance" peculiar to this sphere, employing the journalist's style. In what painful confusion must the cultured class of such a period gaze at the phenomenon which perhaps is to be comprehended analogically only by means of the profoundest principle of the hitherto unintelligible Hellenic genius—the phenomenon of the reawakening of the Dionysian spirit and the rebirth of tragedy?

There has never been another period in the history of art in which so-called culture and true art have been so estranged and opposed as we may observe them to be at present. We can understand why so feeble a culture hates true art; it fears destruction from its hands. But has not an entire cultural form, namely, the Socratic-Alexandrian, exhausted itself after culminating in such a daintily tapering point as our present culture? If heroes like Goethe and Schiller could not succeed in breaking open the enchanted gate which leads into the Hellenic magic mountain; if with their most dauntless striving they could not go beyond the longing gaze which Goethe's Iphigenia casts from barbaric Tauris to her home across the ocean, what could the epigones of such heroes hope for—unless, amid the mystic tones of reawakened tragic music, the gate should open for them suddenly of its own accord, from an entirely different side, quite overlooked in all previous cultural endeavors.

Let no one try to blight our faith in a yet-impending rebirth of Hellenic antiquity; for this alone gives us hope for a renovation and purification of the German spirit through the fire magic of music.[1] What else could we name that might awaken any comforting expectations for the future in the midst of the desolation and exhaustion of contemporary culture? In vain we look for a single vigorously developed root, for a spot of fertile and healthy soil: everywhere there is dust and sand; everything has become rigid and languishes. One who is disconsolate and lonely could not choose a better symbol than the knight with death and devil, as Dürer has drawn him for us, the armored knight with the iron, hard look, who knows how to pursue his terrible path, undeterred by his gruesome companions, and yet without hope, alone with his horse and dog. Our Schopenhauer was such a Dürer knight; he lacked all hope, but he desired truth. He has no peers.

But how suddenly the desert of our exhausted culture, just described in such gloomy terms, is changed when it is touched by the Dionysian magic! A tempest seizes everything that has outlived itself, everything that is decayed, broken, and withered, and, whirling, shrouds it in a cloud of red dust to carry it into the air like a vulture. Confused, our eyes look after what has disappeared; for what they see has been raised as from a depression into golden light, so full and green, so amply alive, immeasurable and full of yearning. Tragedy is seated amid this excess of life, suffering, and

---

[1] This request that no one should trouble our faith because it alone gives us hope, contrasts very sharply with Nietzsche's later attitude toward faith.

pleasure, in sublime ecstasy, listening to a distant melancholy song that tells of the mothers of being whose names are: Delusion, Will, Woe.[2]

Yes, my friends, believe with me in Dionysian life and the rebirth of tragedy. The age of the Socratic man is over; put on wreaths of ivy, put the thyrsus into your hand, and do not be surprised when tigers and panthers lie down, fawning, at your feet. Only dare to be tragic men; for you are to be redeemed. You shall accompany the Dionysian pageant from India to Greece. Prepare yourselves for hard strife, but believe in the miracles of your god.

21

Returning from these hortatory tones to the mood befitting contemplation, I repeat that we can learn only from the Greeks what such an almost miraculously sudden awakening of tragedy means for the innermost life ground of a people. It is the people of the tragic mysteries that fights the battles against the Persians; and the people that fought these wars in turn needs tragedy as a necessary potion to recover. Who would have supposed that precisely this people, after it had been deeply agitated through several generations by the strongest spasms of the Dionysian demon, should still have been capable of such a uniformly vigorous effusion of the simplest political feeling, the most natural patriotic instincts, and original manly desire to fight? After all, one feels in every case in which Dionysian excitement gains any significant extent how the Dionysian liberation from the fetters of the individual finds expression first of all in a diminution of, in indifference to, indeed, in hostility to, the political instincts. Just as certainly, Apollo who forms states is also the genius of the *principium individuationis,* and state and patriotism cannot live without an affirmation of the individual personality. But from orgies a people can take one path only, the path to Indian Buddhism, and in order that this may be endurable at all with its yearning for the nothing, it requires these rare ecstatic states with their elevation above space, time, and the individual. These states in turn demand a philosophy

---

[2] *Wahn, Wille, Wehe.* This passage reads like a parody of Wagner, but certainly was not meant to be satirical.

that teaches men how to overcome by the force of an idea the indescribable displeasure of the states that lie between. Where the political drives are taken to be absolutely valid, it is just as necessary that a people should go the path toward the most extreme secularization whose most magnificent but also most terrifying expression may be found in the Roman *imperium*.

Placed between India and Rome, and pushed toward a seductive choice, the Greeks succeeded in inventing a third form, in classical purity—to be sure, one they did not long use themselves, but one that precisely for that reason gained immortality. For that the favorites of the gods die early, is true in all things; but it is just as certain that they then live eternally with the gods. After all, one should not demand of what is noblest of all that it should have the durable toughness of leather. That staunch perseverance which characterized, for example, the national instincts of the Romans, probably does not belong among the necessary predicates of perfection. But let us ask by means of what remedy it was possible for the Greeks during their great period, in spite of the extraordinary strength of their Dionysian and political instincts, not to exhaust themselves either in ecstatic brooding or in a consuming chase after worldly power and worldly honor, but rather to attain that splendid mixture which resembles a noble wine in making one feel fiery and contemplative at the same time. Here we must clearly think of the tremendous power that stimulated, purified, and discharged the whole life of the people: *tragedy*. We cannot begin to sense its highest value until it confronts us, as it did the Greeks, as the quintessence of all prophylactic powers of healing, as the mediator that worked among the strongest and in themselves most fatal qualities of the people.

Tragedy absorbs the highest ecstasies of music, so that it truly brings music, both among the Greeks and among us, to its perfection; but then it places the tragic myth and the tragic hero next to it, and he, like a powerful Titan, takes the whole Dionysian world upon his back and thus relieves us of this burden. On the other hand, by means of the same tragic myth, in the person of the tragic hero, it knows how to redeem us from the greedy thirst for this existence, and with an admonishing gesture it reminds us of another existence and a higher pleasure for which the struggling hero prepares himself by means of his destruction, not by means of his triumphs. Between the universal validity of its music and the listener, receptive in his Dionysian state, tragedy places a sublime parable, the myth, and deceives the listener into feeling that the music is merely the highest means to bring life into the vivid world of myth. Relying on this noble deception, it may now move its limbs in dithyrambic dances and yield unhesitatingly to an ecstatic feeling of freedom in which it could not dare to wallow as pure music without this deception. The myth protects us against the music, while on the other hand it alone gives music the highest freedom. In return, music imparts to the tragic myth an intense and convincing metaphysical significance that word and image without this singular help could never have attained. And above all, it is through music that the tragic spectator is overcome by an assured premonition of a highest pleasure[1] attained through destruction and negation, so he feels as if the innermost abyss of things spoke to him perceptibly.

If these last sentences have perhaps managed to give only a preliminary expression to these difficult ideas and are immediately intelligible only to few, I nevertheless may not desist at this point from trying to stimulate my friends to further efforts and must ask them to use a single example of our common experience in order to prepare themselves for a general insight. In giving this example, I must not appeal to those who use the images of what happens on the stage, the words and emotions of the acting persons, in order to approach with their help the musical feeling; for these people do not speak music as their mother tongue and, in spite of this help, never get beyond the entrance halls of musical perception, without ever being able to as much as touch the inner sanctum. Some of them, like Gervinus,[2] do not even reach the entrance halls. I must appeal only to those who, immediately related to music, have in it, as it were, their motherly womb, and are related to things almost exclusively through unconscious musical relations. To these genuine musicians I direct the question whether they can imagine a human being who would be able to perceive the third act of *Tristan and Isolde,* without any aid of word and image, purely as a tremen-

---

[1] An allusion to Faust's last words in lines 11,585f. of Goethe's play.

[2] G. G. Gervinus, author of *Shakespeare,* 2 vols., Leipzig, 1850, 3rd ed., 1862; English tr., *Shakespeare Commentaries,* 1863.

dous symphonic movement, without expiring in a spasmodic un-harnessing of all the wings of the soul?

Suppose a human being has thus put his ear, as it were, to the heart chamber of the world will and felt the roaring desire for exist-ence pouring from there into all the veins of the world, as a thun-dering current or as the gentlest brook, dissolving into a mist—how could he fail to break suddenly? How could he endure to perceive the echo of innumerable shouts of pleasure and woe in the "wide space of the world night," enclosed in the wretched glass capsule of the human individual, without inexorably fleeing toward his pri-mordial home, as he hears this shepherd's dance of metaphysics? But if such a work could nevertheless be perceived as a whole, without denial of individual existence; if such a creation could be created without smashing its creator—whence do we take the solu-tion of such a contradiction?

Here the tragic myth and the tragic hero intervene between our highest musical emotion and this music—at botton only as symbols of the most universal facts, of which only music can speak so directly. But if our feelings were those of entirely Dionysian beings, myth as a symbol would remain totally ineffective and un-noticed, and would never for a moment keep us from listening to the re-echo of the *universalia ante rem*.[3] Yet here the *Apollinian* power erupts to restore the almost shattered individual with the healing balm of blissful illusion: suddenly we imagine we see only Tristan, motionless, asking himself dully: "The old tune, why does it wake me?" And what once seemed to us like a hollow sigh from the core of being now merely wants to tell us how "desolate and empty the sea." [4] And where, breathless, we once thought we were being extinguished in a convulsive distention of all our feelings, and little remained to tie us to our present existence, we now hear and see only the hero wounded to death, yet not dying, with his despair-ing cry: "Longing! Longing! In death still longing! for very longing not dying!" And where, formerly after such an excess and super-abundance of consuming agonies, the jubilation of the horn cut through our hearts almost like the ultimate agony, the rejoicing

---

[3] The universals before (antedating) the thing.

[4] *Wie "öd und leer das Meer,"* also quoted from *Tristan und Isolde* by T. S. Eliot in *The Waste Land* (1922), line 42.

Kurwenal now stands between us and this "jubilation in itself," his face turned toward the ship which carries Isolde. However powerfully pity affects us, it nevertheless saves us in a way from the primordial suffering of the world, just as the symbolic image of the myth saves us from the immediate perception of the highest world-idea, just as thought and word save us from the uninhibited effusion of the unconscious will. The glorious Apollinian illusion makes it appear as if even the tone world confronted us as a sculpted world, as if the fate of Tristan and Isolde had been formed and molded in it, too, as in an exceedingly tender and expressive material.

Thus the Apollinian tears us out of the Dionysian universality and lets us find delight in individuals; it attaches our pity to them, and by means of them it satisfies our sense of beauty which longs for great and sublime forms; it presents images of life to us, and incites us to comprehend in thought the core of life they contain. With the immense impact of the image, the concept, the ethical teaching, and the sympathetic emotion, the Apollinian tears man from his orgiastic self-annihilation and blinds him to the universality of the Dionysian process, deluding him into the belief that he is seeing a single image of the world (*Tristan and Isolde,* for instance), and that, *through music,* he is merely supposed to *see* it still better and more profoundly. What can the healing magic of Apollo not accomplish when it can even create the illusion that the Dionysian is really in the service of the Apollinian and capable of enhancing its effects—as if music were essentially the art of presenting an Apollinian content?

By means of the pre-established harmony between perfect drama and its music, the drama attains a superlative vividness unattainable in mere spoken drama. In the independently moving lines of the melody all the living figures of the scene simplify themselves before us to the distinctness of curved lines, and the harmonies of these lines sympathize in a most delicate manner with the events on the stage. These harmonies make the relations of things immediately perceptible to us in a sensuous, by no means abstract manner, and thus we perceive that it is only in these relations that the essence of a character and of a melodic line is revealed clearly. And while music thus compels us to see more and more profoundly than usual, and we see the action on the stage as a delicate web, the world of the stage is expanded infinitely and illuminated for our spiritualized eye. How could a word-poet furnish anything analogous, when he strives to attain this internal expansion and illumination of the visible stage-world by means of a much more imperfect mechanism, indirectly, proceeding from word and concept? Although musical tragedy also avails itself of the word, it can at the same time place beside it the basis and origin of the word, making the development of the word clear to us, from the inside.

Concerning the process just described, however, we may still say with equal assurance that it is merely a glorious appearance, namely, the aforementioned Apollinian *illusion* whose influence aims to deliver us from the Dionysian flood and excess. For, at bottom, the relation of music to drama is precisely the reverse: music is the real idea of the world, drama is but the reflection of this idea, a single silhouette of it. The identity between the melody and the living figure, between the harmony and the character relations of that figure, is true in a sense opposite to what one would suppose on the contemplation of musical tragedy. Even if we agitate and enliven the figure in the most visible manner, and illuminate it from within, it still remains merely a phenomenon from which no bridge leads us to true reality, into the heart of the world. But music speaks out of this heart; and though countless phenomena of the kind were to accompany this music, they could never exhaust its essence, but would always be nothing more than its externalized copies.

As for the intricate relationship of music and drama, nothing can be explained, while everything may be confused, by the popular and thoroughly false contrast of soul and body; but the unphilosophical crudeness of this contrast seems to have become—who knows for what reasons—a readily accepted article of faith among our aestheticians, while they have learned nothing of the contrast of the phenomenon and the thing-in-itself—or, for equally unknown reasons, have not cared to learn anything about it.

Should our analysis have established that the Apollinian element in tragedy has by means of its illusion gained a complete victory over the primoridal Dionysian element of music, making music subservient to its aims, namely, to make the drama as vivid as possible—it would certainly be necessary to add a very important qualification: at the most essential point this Apollinian illusion is broken and annihilated. The drama that, with the aid of music, unfolds itself before us with such inwardly illumined distinctness in all its movements and figures, as if we saw the texture coming into being on the loom as the shuttle flies to and fro—attains as a whole an effect that transcends *all Apollinian artistic effects*. In the total effect of tragedy, the Dionysian predominates once again. Tragedy closes with a sound which could never come from the realm of Apollinian art. And thus the Apollinian illusion reveals itself as what it really is—the veiling during the performance of the tragedy of the real Dionysian effect; but the latter is so powerful that it ends by forcing the Apollinian drama itself into a sphere where it begins to speak with Dionysian wisdom and even denies itself and its Apollinian visibility. Thus the intricate relation of the Apollinian and the Dionysian in tragedy may really be symbolized by a fraternal union of the two deities: Dionysus speaks the language of Apollo; and Apollo, finally the language of Dionysus; and so the highest goal of tragedy and of all art is attained.

22

Let the attentive friend imagine the effect of a true musical tragedy purely and simply, as he knows it from experience. I think I have so portrayed the phenomenon of this effect in both its phases that he can now interpret his own experiences. For he will recollect how with regard to the myth which passed in front of him, he felt himself exalted to a kind of omniscience, as if his visual faculty were no longer merely a surface faculty but capable of penetrating into the interior, and as if he now saw before him, with the aid of music, the waves of the will, the conflict of motives, and the swelling flood of the passions, sensuously visible, as it were, like a multitude of vividly moving lines and figures; and he felt he could dip into the most delicate secrets of unconscious emotions. While he thus becomes conscious of the highest exaltation of his instincts for clarity and transfiguration, he nevertheless feels just as definitely that this long series of Apollinian artistic effects still does *not* generate that blessed continuance in will-less contemplation which the plastic artist and the epic poet, that is to say, the strictly Apollinian artists, evoke in him with their artistic productions: to wit, the justification of the world of the *individuatio* attained by this contemplation—which is the climax and essence of Apollinian art. He beholds the transfigured world of the stage and nevertheless denies it. He sees the tragic hero before him in epic clearness and beauty, and nevertheless rejoices in his annihilation. He comprehends the action deep down, and yet likes to flee into the incomprehensible. He feels the actions of the hero to be justified, and is nevertheless still more elated when these actions annihilate their agent. He shudders at the sufferings which will befall the hero, and yet anticipates in them a higher, much more overpowering joy. He sees more extensively and profoundly than ever, and yet wishes he were blind.

How must we derive this curious internal bifurcation, this blunting of the Apollinian point, if not from the *Dionysian* magic that, though apparently exciting the Apollinian emotions to their highest pitch, still retains the power to force into its service his excess of Apollinian force?

The *tragic myth* is to be understood only as a symbolization of Dionysian wisdom through Apollinian artifices. The myth leads the world of phenomena to its limits where it denies itself and seeks to flee back again into the womb of the true and only reality, where it then seems to commence its metaphysical swansong, like Isolde:

> In the rapture ocean's
> billowing roll,
> in the fragrance waves'
> ringing sound,
> in the world breath's
> wafting whole—
> to drown, to sink—
> unconscious—highest joy! [1]

---

[1]   In des Wonnemeeres
      wogendem Schwall,
      in der Duft-Wellen
      tönendem Schall,
      in des Weltathems
      wehendem All—
      ertrinken—versinken—
         unbewusst—höchste Lust!

Thus we use the experiences of the truly aesthetic listener to bring to mind the tragic artist himself as he creates his figures like a fecund divinity of individuation (so his work can hardly be understood as an "imitation of nature") and as his vast Dionysian impulse then devours his entire world of phenomena, in order to let us sense beyond it, and through its destruction, the highest artistic primal joy, in the bosom of the primordially One. Of course, our aestheticians have nothing to say about this return to the primordial home, or the fraternal union of the two art-deities, nor of the excitement of the hearer which is Apollinian as well as Dionysian; but they never tire of characterizing the struggle of the hero with fate, the triumph of the moral world order, or the purgation of the emotions through tragedy, as the essence of the tragic. And their indefatigability makes me think that perhaps they are not aesthetically sensitive at all, but react merely as moral beings when listening to a tragedy.

Never since Aristotle has an explanation of the tragic effect been offered from which aesthetic states or an aesthetic activity of the listener could be inferred. Now the serious events are supposed to prompt pity and fear to discharge themselves in a way that relieves us; now we are supposed to feel elevated and inspired by the triumph of good and noble principles, at the sacrifice of the hero in the interest of a moral vision of the universe. I am sure that for countless men precisely this, and only this, is the effect of tragedy, but it plainly follows that all these men, together with their interpreting aestheticians, have had no experience of tragedy as a supreme *art*.

The pathological discharge, the catharsis of Aristotle, of which philologists are not sure whether it should be included among medical or moral phenomena, recalls a remarkable notion of Goethe's. "Without a lively pathological interest," he says, "I, too, have never yet succeeded in elaborating a tragic situation of any kind, and hence I have rather avoided than sought it. Can it perhaps have been yet another merit of the ancients that the deepest pathos was with them merely aesthetic play, while with us the truth of nature must co-operate in order to produce such a work?"

We can now answer this profound final question in the affirmative after our glorious experiences, having found to our astonishment that the deepest pathos can indeed be merely aesthetic play in the case of musical tragedy. Therefore we are justified in believing that now for the first time the primal phenomenon of the tragic can be described with some degree of success. Anyone who still persists in talking only of those vicarious effects proceeding from extra-aesthetic spheres, and who does not feel that he is above the pathological-moral process, should despair of his aesthetic nature: should we recommend to him as an innocent equivalent the interpretation of Shakespeare after the manner of Gervinus and the diligent search for poetic justice? [2]

Thus the aesthetic *listener* is also reborn with the rebirth of tragedy. In his place in the theater, a curious *quid pro quo*[3] used to sit with half moral and half scholarly pretensions—the "critic." Everything in his sphere so far has been artificial and merely whitewashed with an appearance of life. The performing artist was really at a loss how to deal with a listener who comported himself so critically; so he, as well as the dramatist or operatic composer who inspired him, searched anxiously for the last remains of life in a being so pretentiously barren and incapable of enjoyment. So far, however, such "critics" have constituted the audience: the student, the schoolboy, even the most innocuous female had been unwittingly prepared by education and newspapers for this kind of perception of works of art. Confronted with such a public, the nobler natures among the artists counted upon exciting their moral-religious emotions, and the appeal to the moral world-order intervened vicariously where some powerful artistic magic ought to enrapture the genuine listener. Or some more imposing, or at all events exciting, trend of the contemporary political and social world was so vividly presented by the dramatist that the listener could forget his critical exhaustion and abandon himself to emotions similar to those felt in patriotic or warlike moments, or before the tribune of parliament, or at the condemnation of crime and vice—an alienation from the true aims of art that sometimes had to result in an outright cult of tendentiousness. But what happened next is what has always happened to all artificial arts: a rapid degeneration of such tendentiousness. The attempt, for example, to use the theater as an institution for the moral education of the peo-

---

[2] See section 21, note 2.
[3] One thing in place of another.

ple, still taken seriously in Schiller's time, is already reckoned among the incredible antiques of a dated type of education. While the critic got the upper hand in the theater and concert hall, the journalist in the schools, and the press in society, art degenerated into a particularly lowly topic of conversation, and aesthetic criticism was used as a means of uniting a vain, distracted, selfish, and moreover piteously unoriginal sociability whose character is suggested by Schopenhauer's parable of the porcupines.[4] As a result, art has never been so much talked about and so little esteemed. But is it still possible to have intercourse with a person capable of conversing about Beethoven or Shakespeare?[5] Let each answer this question according to his own feelings: he will at any rate show by his answer his conception of "culture," provided he at least tries to answer the question, and has not already become dumfounded with astonishment.

On the other hand, many a being more nobly and delicately endowed by nature, though he may have gradually become a critical barbarian in the manner described, might have something to say about the unexpected as well as totally unintelligible effect that a successful performance of *Lohengrin,* for example, had on him—except that perhaps there was no helpful interpreting hand to guide him; so the incomprehensibly different and altogether incomparable sensation that thrilled him remained isolated and, like a mys-

---

[4] The parable is found at the end of Schopenhauer's *Parerga und Paralipomena,* vol. II (1851), section 396: "On a cold winter day, a group of porcupines huddled together closely to save themselves by their mutual warmth from freezing. But soon they felt the mutual quills and drew apart. Whenever the need for warmth brought them closer together again, this second evil was repeated, so that they were tossed back and forth between these two kinds of suffering until they discovered a moderate distance that proved most tolerable.— Thus the need for company, born of the emptiness and monotony inside them, drives men together; but their many revolting qualities and intolerable faults repel them again. The medium distance that they finally discover and that makes association possible is politeness and good manners. Whoever does not keep this distance is told, among the British: keep your distance!— To be sure, this only permits imperfect satisfaction of the need for mutual warmth, but it also keeps one from feeling the prick of the quills.— But whoever possesses much inner warmth of his own will prefer to avoid company lest he cause or suffer annoyance." I have quoted this parable in its entirety; *keep your distance* is English in the original.

[5] Cf. T. S. Eliot's "Love Song of J. Alfred Prufrock": "In the room the women come and go/Talking of Michelangelo."

terious star, became extinct after a short period of brilliance. But it was then that he had an inkling of what an aesthetic listener is.

23

Whoever wishes to test rigorously to what extent he himself is related to the true aesthetic listener or belongs to the community of the Socratic-critical persons needs only to examine sincerely the feeling with which he accepts miracles represented on the stage: whether he feels his historical sense, which insists on strict psychological causality, insulted by them, whether he makes a benevolent concession and admits the miracle as a phenomenon intelligible to childhood but alien to him, or whether he experiences anything else. For in this way he will be able to determine to what extent he is capable of understanding *myth* as a concentrated image of the world that, as a condensation of phenomena, cannot dispense with miracles. It is probable, however, that almost everyone, upon close examination, finds that the critical-historical spirit of our culture has so affected him that he can only make the former existence of myth credible to himself by means of scholarship, through intermediary abstractions. But without myth every culture loses the healthy natural power of its creativity: only a horizon defined by myths completes and unifies a whole cultural movement. Myth alone saves all the powers of the imagination and of the Apollinian dream from their aimless wanderings. The images of the myth have to be the unnoticed omnipresent demonic guardians, under whose care the young soul grows to maturity and whose signs help the man to interpret his life and struggles. Even the state knows no more powerful unwritten laws than the mythical foundation that guarantees its connection with religion and its growth from mythical notions.

By way of comparison let us now picture the abstract man, untutored by myth; abstract education; abstract morality; abstract law; the abstract state; let us imagine the lawless roving of the artistic imagination, unchecked by any native myth; let us think of a culture that has no fixed and sacred primordial site but is doomed to exhaust all possibilities and to nourish itself wretchedly on all other cultures—there we have the present age, the result of that

Socratism which is bent on the destruction of myth. And now the mythless man stands eternally hungry, surrounded by all past ages, and digs and grubs for roots, even if he has to dig for them among the remotest antiquities. The tremendous historical need of our unsatisfied modern culture, the assembling around one of countless other cultures, the consuming desire for knowledge—what does all this point to, if not to the loss of myth, the loss of the mythical home, the mythical maternal womb? Let us ask ourselves whether the feverish and uncanny excitement of this culture is anything but the greedy seizing and snatching at food of a hungry man—and who would care to contribute anything to a culture that cannot be satisfied no matter how much it devours, and at whose contact the most vigorous and wholesome nourishment is changed into "history and criticism"?

We should also have to regard our German character with sorrowful despair, if it had already become inextricably entangled in, or even identical with, its culture, as we may observe to our horror in the case of civilized France. What for a long time was the great advantage of France and the cause of her vast superiority, namely, this very identity of people and culture, might compel us in view of this sight to congratulate ourselves that this so questionable culture of ours has as yet nothing in common with the noble core of our people's character.[1] On the contrary, all our hopes stretch out longingly toward the perception that beneath this restlessly palpitating cultural life and convulsion there is concealed a glorious, intrinsically healthy, primordial power that, to be sure, stirs vigorously only at intervals in stupendous moments, and then continues to dream of a future awakening. It is from this abyss that the German Reformation came forth; and in its chorales the future tune of German music resounded for the first time. So deep, courageous, and spiritual, so exuberantly good and tender did this chorale of

---

[1] This pro-German and anti-French passage echoes Wagner and is utterly at odds with Nietzsche's later works. Indeed, even his second book, the essay on *David Strauss* (1873), published the year after the first edition of *The Birth*, begins with "the bad and dangerous consequences of the war" of 1870–71; and the first paragraph ends with the prospect of *"the defeat—yes, the extirpation of the German spirit in favor of the 'German Reich.'"* After his break with Wagner, Nietzsche expressed his admiration for the French again and again; and no major German writer has ever equaled Nietzsche's stringent criticisms of his own people.

Luther sound—as the first Dionysian luring call breaking forth from dense thickets at the approach of spring. And in competing echoes the solemnly exuberant procession of Dionysian revelers responded, to whom we are indebted for German music—and to whom we shall be indebted for *the rebirth of German myth.*

I know that I must now lead the sympathizing and attentive friend to an elevated position of lonely contemplation, where he will have but few companions, and I call out encouragingly to him that we must hold fast to our luminous guides, the Greeks. To purify our aesthetic insight, we have previously borrowed from them the two divine figures who rule over separate realms of art, and concerning whose mutual contact and enhancement we have acquired some notion through Greek tragedy. It had to appear to us that the demise of Greek tragedy was brought about through a remarkable and forcible dissociation of these two primordial artistic drives. To this process there corresponded a degeneration and transformation of the character of the Greek people, which calls for serious reflection on how necessary and close the fundamental connections are between art and the people, myth and custom, tragedy and the state. This demise of tragedy was at the same time the demise of myth. Until then the Greeks had felt involuntarily impelled to relate all their experiences immediately to their myths, indeed to understand them only in this relation. Thus even the immediate present had to appear to them right away *sub specie aeterni*[2] and in a certain sense as timeless.

But the state no less than art dipped into this current of the timeless to find rest in it from the burden and the greed of the moment. And any people—just as, incidentally, also any individual—is worth only as much as it is able to press upon its experiences the stamp of the eternal; for thus it is, as it were, desecularized and shows its unconscious inward convictions of the relativity of time and of the true, that is metaphysical, significance of life. The opposite of this happens when a people begins to comprehend itself historically and to smash the mythical works that surround it. At that point we generally find a decisive secularization, a break with the unconscious metaphysics of its previous existence, together with all its ethical consequences. Greek

---

[2] Under the aspect of the eternal.

art and pre-eminently Greek tragedy delayed above all the destruction of myth. One had to destroy tragedy, too, in order to be able to live away from the soil of home, uninhibited, in the wilderness of thought, custom, and deed. Even now this metaphysical drive still tries to create for itself a certainly attenuated form of transfiguration, in the Socratism of science that strives for life; but on the lower steps, this same drive led only to a feverish search that gradually lost itself in a pandemonium of myths and superstitions that were collected from all over and piled up in confusion: nevertheless the Greek sat among them with an unstilled heart until he learned to mask this fever with Greek cheerfulness and Greek frivolity, becoming a *Graeculus*,[3] or he numbed his mind completely in some dark Oriental superstition.

Since the reawakening of Alexandrian-Roman antiquity in the fifteenth century we have approximated this state in the most evident manner, after a long interlude that is difficult to describe. On the heights we encounter the same overabundant lust for knowledge, the same unsatisfied delight in discovery, the same tremendous secularization, and beside it a homeless roving, a greedy crowding around foreign tables, a frivolous deification of the present, or a dully dazed retreat—everything *sub specie saeculi*,[4] of the "present age." And these same symptoms allow us to infer the same lack at the heart of this culture, the destruction of myth. It scarcely seems possible to be continually successful at transplanting a foreign myth without irreparably damaging the tree by this transplantation. In one case it may perhaps be strong and healthy enough to eliminate this foreign element in a terrible fight; usually, however, it must consume itself, sick and withered or in diseased superfoetation.

We think so highly of the pure and vigorous core of the German character that we dare to expect of it above all others this elimination of the forcibly implanted foreign elements, and consider it possible that the German spirit will return to itself. Some may suppose that this spirit must begin its fight with the elimination of everything Romanic. If so they may recognize an external preparation and encouragement in the victorious fortitude and bloody

---

[3] A contemptuous term for a Greek. See section 11.
[4] Under the aspect of the times, or the spirit of the age.

glory of the last war; but one must still seek the inner necessity in the ambition to be always worthy of the sublime champions on this way, Luther as well as our great artists and poets. But let him never believe that he could fight similar fights without the gods of his house, or his mythical home, without "bringing back" all German things! And if the German should hesitantly look around for a leader who might bring him back again into his long lost home whose ways and paths he scarcely knows anymore, let him merely listen to the ecstatically luring call of the Dionysian bird that hovers above him and wants to point the way for him.

24

Among the peculiar art effects of musical tragedy we had to emphasize an Apollinian *illusion* by means of which we were supposed to be saved from the immediate unity with Dionysian music, while our musical excitement could discharge itself in an Apollinian field and in relation to a visible intermediary world that had been interposed. At the same time we thought that we had observed how precisely through this discharge the intermediary world of the action on the stage, and the drama in general, had been made visible and intelligible from the inside to a degree that in all other Apollinian art remains unattained. Where the Apollinian receives wings from the spirit of music and soars, we thus found the highest intensification of its powers, and in this fraternal union of Apollo and Dionysus we had to recognize the apex of the Apollinian as well as the Dionysian aims of art.

To be sure, the Apollinian projection that is thus illuminated from inside by music does not achieve the peculiar effect of the weaker degrees of Apollinian art. What the epic or the animated stone can do, compelling the contemplative eye to find calm delight in the world of individuation, that could not be attained here, in spite of a higher animation and clarity. We looked at the drama and with penetrating eye reached its inner world of motives—and yet we felt as if only a parable passed us by, whose most profound meaning we almost thought we could guess and that we wished to draw away like a curtain in order to behold the primordial image behind it. The brightest clarity of the image did not suffice us, for this seemed to wish just as much to reveal something as to conceal something. Its revelation, being like a parable, seemed to summon us to tear the veil and to uncover the mysterious background; but at the same time this all-illuminated total visibility cast a spell over the eyes and prevented them from penetrating deeper.

Those who have never had the experience of having to see at the same time that they also longed to transcend all seeing will scarcely be able to imagine how definitely and clearly these two processes coexist and are felt at the same time, as one contemplates the tragic myth. But all truly aesthetic spectators will confirm that among the peculiar effects of tragedy this coexistence is the most remarkable. Now transfer this phenomenon of the aesthetic spectator into an analogous process in the tragic artist, and you will have understood the genesis of the *tragic myth*. With the Apollinian art sphere he shares the complete pleasure in mere appearance and in seeing, yet at the same time he negates this pleasure and finds a still higher satisfaction in the destruction of the visible world of mere appearance.

The content of the tragic myth is, first of all, an epic event and the glorification of the fighting hero. But what is the origin of this enigmatic trait that the suffering and the fate of the hero, the most painful triumphs, the most agonizing oppositions of motives, in short, the exemplification of this wisdom of Silenus, or, to put it aesthetically, that which is ugly and disharmonic, is represented ever anew in such countless forms and with such a distinct preference—and precisely in the most fruitful and youthful period of a people? Surely a higher pleasure must be perceived in all this.

That life is really so tragic would least of all explain the origin of an art form—assuming that art is not merely imitation of the reality of nature but rather a metaphysical supplement of the reality of nature, placed beside it for its overcoming. The tragic myth, too, insofar as it belongs to art at all, participates fully in this metaphysical intention of art to transfigure. But what does it transfigure when it presents the world of appearance in the image of the suffering hero? Least of all the "reality" of this world of appearance, for it says to us: "Look there! Look closely! This is your life, this is the hand on the clock of your existence."

And the myth should show us this life in order to thus transfigure it for us? But if not, in what then lies the aesthetic pleasure with which we let these images, too, pass before us? I ask about the

aesthetic pleasure, though I know full well that many of these images also produce at times a moral delight, for example, under the
form of pity or moral triumph. But those who would derive the
effect of the tragic solely from these moral sources—which, to be
sure, has been the custom in aesthetics all too long—should least of
all believe that they have thus accomplished something for art,
which above all must demand purity in its sphere. If you would
explain the tragic myth, the first requirement is to seek the pleasure
that is peculiar to it in the purely aesthetic sphere, without trans-
gressing into the region of pity, fear, or the morally sublime. How
can the ugly and the disharmonic, the content of the tragic myth,
stimulate aesthetic pleasure?

Here it becomes necessary to take a bold running start and
leap into a metaphysics of art, by repeating the sentence written
above,[1] that existence and the world seem justified only as an aesthetic phenomenon. In this sense, it is precisely the tragic myth that
has to convince us that even the ugly and disharmonic are part of
an artistic game that the will in the eternal amplitude of its pleasure
plays with itself. But this primordial phenomenon of Dionysian art
is difficult to grasp, and there is only one direct way to make it intelligible and grasp it immediately: through the wonderful significance
of *musical dissonance*. Quite generally, only music, placed beside
the world, can give us an idea of what is meant by the justification
of the world as an aesthetic phenomenon. The joy aroused by the
tragic myth has the same origin as the joyous sensation of dissonance in music. The Dionysian, with its primordial joy experienced
even in pain, is the common source of music and tragic myth.

Is it not possible that by calling to our aid the musical relation
of dissonance we may meanwhile have made the difficult problem
of the tragic effect much easier? For we now understand what it
means to wish to see tragedy and at the same time to long to get
beyond all seeing: referring to the artistically employed disso-
nances, we should have to characterize the corresponding state by
saying that we desire to hear and at the same time long to get beyond all hearing. That striving for the infinite, the wing-beat of
longing that accompanies the highest delight in clearly perceived
reality, reminds us that in both states we must recognize a Diony-

[1] Section 5.

sian phenomenon: again and again it reveals to us the playful construction and destruction of the individual world as the overflow of a primordial delight. Thus the dark Heraclitus compares the world-building force to a playing child that places stones here and there and builds sand hills only to overthrow them again.

In order, then, to form a true estimate of the Dionysian capacity of a people, we must think not only of their music, but also just as necessarily of their tragic myth, as the second witness of this capacity. Considering this extremely close relationship between music and myth, one must suppose that a degeneration and depravation of the one will involve a deterioration of the other, if the weakening of the myth really expresses a weakening of the Dionysian capacity. Concerning both, however, a glance at the development of the German character should not leave us in any doubt. In the opera, just as in the abstract character of our mythless existence, in an art degenerated to mere entertainment as well as in a life guided by concepts, the inartistic as well as life-consuming nature of Socratic optimism had revealed itself to us. Yet we were comforted by indications that nevertheless in some inaccessible abyss the German spirit still rests and dreams, undestroyed, in glorious health, profundity, and Dionysian strength, like a knight sunk in slumber; and from this abyss the Dionysian song rises to our ears to let us know that this German knight is still dreaming his primordial Dionysian myth in blissfully serious visions. Let no one believe that the German spirit has forever lost its mythical home when it can still understand so plainly the voices of the birds that tell of that home. Some day it will find itself awake in all the morning freshness following a tremendous sleep: then it will slay dragons, destroy vicious dwarfs,[2] wake Brünnhilde—and even Wotan's spear will not be able to stop its course!

My friends, you who believe in Dionysian music, you also know what tragedy means to us. There we have tragic myth reborn from music—and in this myth we can hope for everything and forget what is most painful. What is most painful for all of us, how-

---

[2] In his otherwise immensely perceptive and interesting interpretation, in the chapter on *The Birth of Tragedy* in *Ecce Homo,* Nietzsche claims at the end of section 1 that the "vicious dwarfs" (see also the next paragraph) represent "Christian priests." The imagery, of course, is taken from the Siegfried myth. See p. 727 below.

ever, is—the prolonged degradation in which the German genius has lived, estranged from house and home, in the service of vicious dwarfs. You understand my words—as you will also, in conclusion, understand my hopes.

25

Music and tragic myth are equally expressions of the Dionysian capacity of a people, and they are inseparable.[1] Both derive from a sphere of art that lies beyond the Apollinian; both transfigure a region in whose joyous chords dissonance as well as the terrible image of the world fade away charmingly; both play with the sting of displeasure, trusting in their exceedingly powerful magic arts; and by means of this play both justify the existence of even the "worst world." Thus the Dionysian is seen to be, compared to the Apollinian, the eternal and original artistic power that first calls the whole world of phenomena into existence—and it is only in the midst of this world that a new transfiguring illusion[2] becomes necessary in order to keep the animated world of individuation alive.

If we could imagine dissonance become man—and what else is man?—this dissonance, to be able to live, would need a splendid illusion[3] that would cover dissonance with a veil of beauty. This is the true artistic aim of Apollo in whose name we comprehend all those countless illusions of the beauty of mere appearance[4] that at every moment make life worth living at all and prompt the desire to live on in order to experience the next moment.

Of this foundation of all existence—the Dionysian basic ground of the world—not one whit more may enter the consciousness of the human individual than can be overcome again by this Apollinian power of transfiguration. Thus these two art drives must unfold their powers in a strict proportion, according to the law of eternal justice. Where the Dionysian powers rise up as impetuously as we experience them now, Apollo, too, must already have de-

---

[1] The rhapsody on Wagner continues, heedless of Mozart and Beethoven, Handel and Haydn, and scores of others.

[2] *Verklärungsschein* could also mean a transfiguring halo.

[3] *Illusion.*

[4] *Illusionen des schönen Scheins.*

scended among us, wrapped in a cloud; and the next generation will probably behold his most ample beautiful effects.

That this effect should be necessary, everybody should be able to feel most assuredly by means of intuition, provided he has ever felt, if only in a dream, that he was carried back into an ancient Greek existence. Walking under lofty Ionic colonnades, looking up toward a horizon that was cut off by pure and noble lines, finding reflections of his transfigured shape in the shining marble at his side, and all around him solemnly striding or delicately moving human beings, speaking with harmonious voices and in a rhythmic language of gestures—in view of this continual influx of beauty, would he not have to exclaim, raising his hand to Apollo: "Blessed people of Hellas! How great must Dionysus be among you if the god of Delos considers such magic necessary to heal your dithyrambic madness!"

To a man in such a mood, however, an old Athenian, looking up at him with the sublime eyes of Aeschylus, might reply: "But say this, too, curious stranger: how much did this people have to suffer to be able to become so beautiful! But now follow me to witness a tragedy, and sacrifice with me in the temple of both deities!"

SEVENTY-FIVE
APHORISMS
from Five Volumes

CONTENTS

Seventy-Five Aphorisms from Five Volumes   147

INDEX TO *Seventy-Five Aphorisms from Five Volumes*   809

Human, All-Too-Human (1878)

Dual prehistory of good and evil.— The concept of good and evil has a dual prehistory; *first,* in the soul of the ruling tribes and castes. Whoever has the power to repay good with good, evil with evil, and also actually repays, thus being grateful and vengeful, is called good; whoever is powerless and unable to repay is considered bad. As one who is good, one belongs to the "good," a community that possesses communal feeling because all individuals are knit together by the sense of repayment. As one who is bad, one belongs to the "bad," a group of subjected, impotent human beings who have no communal feeling. The good are a caste, the bad a mass like dust. Good and bad are for a time the same as noble and low, master and slave. But the *enemy* is not considered evil, he can repay. Trojan and Greek are both good in Homer. Not he that does us harm but he that is contemptible is considered bad. In the community of the good, good is inherited; it is impossible that a bad person should grow out of such good soil. If one of the good nevertheless does something unworthy of the good, then one has recourse to excuses; one blames a god, for example, saying that he struck the good man with delusion and madness.

Then, in the soul of the oppressed, the powerless. Here all *other* human beings are considered hostile, ruthless, exploiting, cruel, cunning, whether they be noble or low. Evil is the characteristic word for man, indeed for every living being believed in, for example for a god; human or divine means as much as devilish or evil. The signs of graciousness, helpfulness, pity are taken anxiously as wiles, as preludes to a disastrous conclusion, soporifics and craft, in short, as refined malice. As long as individuals have such an attitude, a community can hardly come into being; at best, only its rudiments: hence, wherever this conception of good and evil rules, the ruination of individuals, their tribes and races, is near.

Our current morality has grown on the soil of the *ruling* tribes and castes.[1]

92

Origin of justice.—Justice (fairness)[2] originates among those who are approximately *equally powerful,* as Thucydides (in the terrible conversation between the Athenian and Melian ambassadors) comprehended correctly: where there is no clearly recognizable predominance and a fight would mean inconclusive mutual damage, there the idea originates that one might come to an understanding and negotiate one's claims: the initial character of justice is the character of a trade. Each satisfies the other inasmuch as each receives what he esteems more than the other does. One gives another what he wants, so that it becomes his, and in return one receives what one wants. Thus justice is repayment and exchange on the assumption of an approximately equal power position; revenge originally belongs in the domain of justice, being an exchange. Gratitude, too.

Justice naturally derives from prudent concern with self-preservation; that means, from the egoism of the consideration: "Why should I harm myself uselessly and perhaps not attain my goal anyway?"

So much on the *origin* of justice. In accordance with their intellectual habits, men have *forgotten* the original purpose of so-called just, fair actions, and for millennia children have been taught to admire and emulate such actions. Hence it has gradually come

---

[1] The theme of this section is taken up again in *Beyond Good and Evil* (1886), section 260, where we gain the distinct impression—though Nietzsche is not as emphatic as in the last sentence above—that our current morality is a mixed type. It would seem that this became his considered view, notwithstanding the widespread misapprehension that he considered modern morality an example of "slave morality." Most important: as the above aphorism makes abundantly clear, Nietzsche is not concerned to divide the men among whom he lives into masters and slaves; he is concerned with the history, the genesis, the genealogy of morals. And in the Preface to the *Genealogy of Morals* (1887), Nietzsche refers to several early aphorisms, including this one.

[2] *Die Gerechtigkeit (Billigkeit)* . . .

to appear as if a just action were unegoistic; but the high esteem for it depends on this appearance, and this esteem, moreover, continues to grow all the time, like all esteem; for whatever is highly esteemed becomes the object of striving, emulation, and multiplication, coupled with many sacrifices, and grows further because the value of the effort and zeal is added by every individual to the value of the thing he esteems.

How little the world would look moral without forgetfulness! A poet might say that God made forgetfulness the guard he placed at the threshold of human dignity.

96

Mores and moral.[3]— Being moral or ethical means obeying ancient established law or custom. Whether one submits to it with difficulty or gladly, that is immaterial; it is enough that one does it. *"Good"* is what one calls those who do what is moral as if they did it by nature, after long heredity—in other words, easily and gladly —whatever may be moral in this sense (practicing revenge, for example, when practicing revenge belongs, as it did among the more ancient Greeks, to good mores). He is called good because he is good "for something"; but because benevolence, pity, and that sort of thing have always been felt to be, through many changes in mores, "good for something" and useful, it has come to pass that now the benevolent and helpful are pre-eminently considered "good."

Being evil is being "not *moral*" (immoral), practicing immorality, resisting tradition, however reasonable or stupid tradition may be. Harming the neighbor, however, has been felt to be preeminently harmful in all the moral laws of different ages, until now the word "evil" is associated primarily with the deliberate harming of the neighbor.

---

[3] *Sitte und sittlich:* wherever Nietzsche pairs these words, they are translated as above, and *unsittlich* is rendered as immoral. Elsewhere, Nietzsche often uses such words as *Moral, moralisch, Immoralist*—e.g., in *Beyond Good and Evil* and in the *Genealogy of Morals* (not only in the title of the latter book) —and morality, morals, moral, and immoralist have been used to render them.

Not "egoistic" and "unegoistic" is the fundamental pair of contraries that has led men to distinguish moral and immoral, good and evil, but rather: being tied to a tradition and law, and detachment from them. How the tradition *originated* is indifferent; in any case it was without any regard for good and evil or any immanent categorical imperative, but above all in order to preserve a *community*, a people: every superstitious custom that originated on the basis of some misinterpreted accident involves a tradition that it is moral to follow; for detaching oneself from it is dangerous, even more dangerous for the community than for the individual (because the deity punishes the community—and the individual only indirectly—for the sacrilege and the violation of divine privileges). Now every tradition becomes ever more venerable the more remote its origins are and the more they have been forgotten; the veneration shown it is accumulated, generation upon generation; finally, the tradition becomes holy and inspires reverence; and thus the *morality of pious regard for the old* [4] is certainly a much more ancient morality than that which demands unegoistic actions.

136

On Christian asceticism and holiness.—Strongly as individual thinkers have endeavored to present the rare phenomena of morality that are usually called asceticism and holiness as if they were marvels that it would almost be sacrilege and desecration to illuminate by raising the torch of rational explanation up to their face— the temptation to commit this sacrilege is just as strong. A powerful impulse of nature has led men in all ages to protest against these phenomena as such; science, insofar as it is, as mentioned, an imitation of nature, at least takes the liberty to object to their alleged inexplicability and even unapproachability. To be sure, so far it has not succeeded: these phenomena are still unexplained, much to the delight of the said admirers of moral marvels. For, to speak generally: the unexplained should by all means be unexplainable, the unexplainable by all means unnatural, supernatural, miraculous—

---

[4] *Moral der Pietät* (emphasis in the original).

thus goes the demand in the souls of all the religious and metaphysicians (of artists, too, if they are at the same time thinkers); while the scientific person sees in this demand the "evil principle."

The general first probability one encounters as one contemplates holiness and asceticism is this: their nature is *complicated;* for almost everywhere, in the physical world as well as in the moral world, one has succeeded in reducing the allegedly miraculous to the complicated which depends on many conditions. Let us dare then to begin by isolating single impulses in the souls of holy men and ascetics, and to conclude by thinking of them as grown together.

137

There is a *defiance of oneself* among whose most sublimated expressions some forms of asceticism belong. For certain human beings have such a great need to exercise their force and lust to rule that, lacking other objects, or because they have always failed elsewhere, they finally have recourse to tyrannizing certain parts of their own nature, as it were sections or stages of themselves.

Thus some thinkers profess views that evidently do not serve to increase or improve their reputations; some practically conjure up the disrespect of others for them, although it would be easy for them to remain highly respected, simply by keeping still. Others recant former opinions and are not afraid of henceforth being called inconsistent: on the contrary, they exert themselves to that end and behave like exuberant riders who like their horse best when it has gone wild, is covered with sweat, and shying.

Thus man ascends the highest mountains on dangerous paths, to laugh scornfully at his anxiety and his trembling knees; thus the philosopher professes views of asceticism, humility, and sanctity in whose splendor his own image is made exceedingly ugly. This breaking of oneself, this mockery of one's own nature, this *spernere se sperni*[5] of which religions have made so much, is really a very high degree of vanity. The whole morality of the Sermon on the Mount belongs here: man experiences a veritable voluptuousness

---

[5] Scorn of one's being scorned.

in violating himself by means of exaggerated demands and in then deifying this tyrannically demanding force in his soul.

In every ascetic morality man adores part of himself as God and to that end needs to diabolicize the rest.

142

To sum up what has been said here: that state of the soul which the holy man or the man who is becoming holy enjoys is composed of elements which all of us know quite well; they merely take on a different coloring when they are influenced by nonreligious ideas, and then they are usually reproached by men just as much as they can count—or at least could count in former times— on admiration, even worship, when associated with religion and the ultimate meaning of existence.

Sometimes the holy man practices that defiance against himself which is closely related to the lust to rule at any price and which gives even the loneliest the feeling of power; sometimes his swollen feeling changes from the craving to let his passions run their course into the craving to make them collapse like wild horses under the powerful pressure of a proud soul; sometimes he wants the complete cessation of all feelings that disturb, torment, provoke —a wakeful sleep, an enduring rest in the lap of a dumb, animal- or plant-like indolence; sometimes he seeks a fight and inflames it within himself because boredom fixes him with a yawning countenance: he scourges his self-deification with self-contempt and cruelty, he delights in the wild rebellion of his desires, in the sharp pain of sin, even in the idea that he is lost; he knows how to lay a snare for his affects, that of the most extreme lust to rule, for example, so that it changes into the most extreme humiliation and this contrast completely unbalances his hounded soul; and finally: if he should crave visions or conversation with the dead or with divine beings, this is at bottom a rare kind of voluptuousness that he desires, but perhaps that voluptuousness in which all the others are tied up into one knot. Novalis,[6] one of the authorities on questions

---

[6] Pseudonym of Friedrich von Hardenberg (1772–1801), widely considered the greatest of the early German romantic poets. Cf. *Twenty German Poets: A Bilingual Collection* (New York, Modern Library, 1963), pp. 63–69.

of holiness, both by experience and by instinct, once expressed the whole secret with a naïve joy: "It is marvelous enough that the association of voluptuousness, religion, and cruelty has not long attracted the attention of men to their close kinship and common tendency."

143

Not what the holy man *is* but what he *signifies* in the eyes of those who are not holy gives him his world-historical value. It was because one was *wrong* about him, because one *misinterpreted* the states of his soul and drew as sharp a line as possible between oneself and him, as if he were something utterly incomparable and strangely superhuman—that he gained that extraordinary power with which he could dominate the imagination of whole peoples and ages. He did not know himself; he understood the writing of his moods, inclinations, and actions according to an art of interpretation which was just as extravagant and artificial as the pneumatic interpretation of the Bible. What was eccentric and sick in his nature, with its fusion of spiritual poverty, faulty knowledge, spoilt health, and overexcited nerves remained concealed from his own eyes and from the eyes of those who looked at him. He was not an especially good person, even less an especially wise person; but he *signified* something that exceeded all human measure of goodness and wisdom. The faith in him supported the faith in the divine and miraculous, in a religious meaning of all existence, in an impending final day of judgment. In the evening splendor of the world-end's sunset that illuminated the Christian peoples, the shadowy figure of the holy man grew into something enormous—indeed, to such a height that even in our time, which no longer believes in God, there are still thinkers who believe in the holy man.[7]

144

It scarcely needs saying that this sketch of the holy man, being drawn after the average of the whole species, can be countered with

---

[7] For example—but not only—Schopenhauer.

many sketches that tend to produce a more agreeable feeling. Single exceptions stand out from the species, whether by virtue of great mildness and humanitarianism or by the magic of unusual energy; others are attractive in the highest degree because certain delusions inundate their whole nature with light—as is the case, for example, with the celebrated founder of Christianity who considered himself the inborn son of God and therefore felt he was without sin; thus, by virtue of an illusion—which should not be judged too harshly, for the whole of antiquity was full of sons of gods —he attained the same goal, the feeling of complete freedom from sin, complete lack of responsibility, which is now available to everybody by means of science!

I have also ignored the holy men of India who occupy an intermediate stage between the Christian holy man and the Greek philosopher, and thus do not represent a pure type: knowledge, science—insofar as science existed—raising oneself above other men through the logical discipline and training of thought, were just as much demanded among the Buddhists, as a sign of holiness, as the same qualities were repudiated and pronounced heretical in the Christian world where they were held to be signs of unholiness.

Mixed Opinions
and Maxims (1879)

89

Mores and their victim.— The origin of mores may be found in two thoughts: "society is worth more than the individual," and "enduring advantage is to be preferred to ephemeral advantage"— from which it follows that the enduring advantage of society must be given precedence, unconditionally, over the advantage of the individual, especially over his momentary well-being but also over his enduring advantage and even his continued existence. Whether the individual suffers from an institution that is good for the whole, whether it causes him to atrophy or perish—mores must be preserved, sacrifices must be made. But such an attitude *originates* only in those who are *not* its victims—for they claim in their behalf that the individual may be worth more than many, also that present enjoyment, the moment in paradise, may have to be valued higher than a pallid continuation of painless or complacent states. The philosophy of the sacrificial animal, however, is always sounded too late; and so we retain mores and *morality*[1]—which is no more than the feeling for the whole quintessence of mores under which one lives and has been brought up—brought up not as an individual but as a member of a whole, as a digit of a majority.— Thus it happens constantly that an individual brings to bear upon himself, by means of his morality, the tyranny of the majority.[2]

130

Readers' bad manners.— A reader is doubly guilty of bad manners against the author when he praises his second book at the expense of the first (or vice versa) and then asks the author to be grateful for that.

137

The worst readers.— The worst readers are those who proceed like plundering soldiers: they pick up a few things they can use, soil and confuse the rest, and blaspheme the whole.

145

Value of honest books.— Honest books make the reader honest, at least by luring into the open his hatred and aversion which his sly prudence otherwise knows how to conceal best. But against a book one lets oneself go, even if one is very reserved toward people.

---

[1] *So bleibt es bei der Sitte und der* Sittlichkeit.
[2] *Sich selbst* . . . majorisiert.

157

Sharpest criticism.—— One criticizes a person, a book, most sharply when one pictures their ideal.

168

Praise of aphorisms.—— A good aphorism is too hard for the tooth of time and is not consumed by all millennia, although it serves every time for nourishment: thus it is the great paradox of literature, the intransitory amid the changing, the food that always remains esteemed, like salt, and never loses its savor, as even that does.

200

Original.—— Not that one is the first to see something new, but that one sees *as new* what is old, long familiar, seen and overlooked by everybody, is what distinguishes truly original minds. The first discoverer is ordinarily that wholly common creature, devoid of spirit and addicted to fantasy—accident.

201

Philosophers' error.—— The philosopher supposes that the value of his philosophy lies in the whole, in the structure; but posterity finds its value in the stone which he used for building, and which is used many more times after that for building—better. Thus it finds the value in the fact that the structure can be destroyed and *nevertheless* retains value as building material.

206

Why scholars are nobler[3] than artists.—— Science requires *nobler* natures than poetry does: they have to be simpler, less ambitious,

---

[3] *Edler.*

more abstinent, quieter, not so concerned about posthumous fame, and forget themselves over matters that rarely seem worthy in the eyes of many of such a sacrifice of one's personality. To this must be added another loss of which they are conscious: the type of their work, the continual demand for the greatest sobriety, weakens their *will;* the fire is not kept as strong as on the hearth of poetic natures—and therefore they often lose their highest strength and bloom at an earlier age than those men do—and, as mentioned, they *realize* this danger. In any case they *appear* less gifted because they shine less, and they will be considered inferior to what they are.

251

In parting.— Not how one soul comes close to another but how it moves away shows me their kinship and how much they belong together.

298

Virtue has not been invented by the Germans.— Goethe's nobility[4] and lack of envy, Beethoven's noble[5] hermit's resignation, Mozart's charm and grace of the heart, Handel's unbendable manliness and freedom under the law, Bach's confident and transfigured inner life that does not even find it necessary to renounce splendor and success—are these in any way *German* qualities?— But if not, it at least shows for what Germans should strive and what they can attain.

309

Siding against oneself.— Our adherents never forgive us if we take sides against ourselves: for in their eyes this means not only rejecting their love but also exposing their intelligence.

---

[4] *Vornehmheit.*
[5] *Edle.*

325

Opinions.— Most people are nothing and are considered nothing until they have dressed themselves up in general convictions and public opinions—in accordance with the tailor philosophy: clothes make people. Of the exceptional person, however, it must be said: *only he that wears it makes the costume;*[6] here opinions cease to be public and become something other than masks, finery, and disguises.

341

Loving the master.— Not as apprentices do, loves a master a master.[7]

346

Being misunderstood.— When one is misunderstood as a whole, it is impossible to remove completely a single misunderstanding. One has to realize this lest one waste superfluous energy on one's defense.

404

How duty acquires splendor.— The means for changing your iron duty to gold in everyone's eyes is this: always keep a little more than you promise.

405

Prayer to men.— "Forgive us our virtues"—thus one should pray to men.

---

[6] *Erst der Träger macht die Tracht.*
[7] Based on Nietzsche's relationship to Wagner.

408

The journey to Hades.— I, too, have been in the underworld, like Odysseus, and shall be there often yet; and not only rams have I sacrificed to be able to speak with a few of the dead, but I have not spared my own blood. Four pairs it was that did not deny themselves to my sacrifice: Epicurus and Montaigne, Goethe and Spinoza, Plato and Rousseau, Pascal and Schopenhauer. With these I must come to terms when I have long wandered alone; they may call me right and wrong; to them will I listen when in the process they call each other right and wrong. Whatsoever I say, resolve, or think up for myself and others—on these eight I fix my eyes and see their eyes fixed on me.

May the living forgive me that occasionally *they* appear to me as shades, so pale and somber, so restless and, alas, so lusting for life—while those men then seem so alive to me as if now, *after* death, they could never again grow weary of life. But *eternal aliveness* is what counts: what matters "eternal life" or any life! [8]

The Wanderer
and His Shadow (1880)

33

Elements of revenge.— The word "revenge" is said so quickly, it almost seems as if it could not contain more than one root concept and feeling. And so people are still trying to find this root—just as our economists still have not got tired of smelling such a unity in the

---

[8] This is the final aphorism with which the book, published in 1879, ended. In a later note (*Musarion* edition, 1920–29, vol. XIV, p. 109) Nietzsche jotted down: "My ancestors: *Heraclitus, Empedocles, Spinoza, Goethe.*" And his eyes were much more consistently fixed on Socrates than on Epicurus and Montaigne. His references to Pascal and Rousseau, especially Rousseau, are generally very critical.

word "value" and of looking for the original root concept of value. As if all words were not pockets into which now this and now that has been put, and now many things at once! [1] Thus "revenge," too, is now this and now that, and now something very composite.

Let us distinguish, *first,* that return blow of resistance which is almost an involuntary reflex, executed even against lifeless objects that have harmed us (such as moving machines): the sense of this countermove is to stop the harm by bringing the machine to a halt. Occasionally, the strength of the counterblow must be so strong to succeed in this that it smashes the machine; but where that is too strong to be destructible immediately by an individual, he will nevertheless strike as hard as he can—making, as it were, an all-out-attempt. One behaves the same way against persons who harm one, as long as one feels the harm immediately: if you want to call this action an act of revenge, all right; but consider that it is only *self-preservation* that has here put its rational machinery into motion, and that in the last analysis one does not think at all of the harming person in such a case but only of oneself: we act that way *without* any wish to do harm in return, merely in order to *get away* with life and limb.

Time is needed—when instead of concentrating on oneself one begins to think about one's opponent, asking oneself how one can hurt him the most. This happens in the *second* type of revenge: reflection on the other person's vulnerability and capacity for suffering is its presupposition; one wants to hurt. Protecting oneself against further harm, on the other hand, is so little a consideration for the seeker of such vengeance that he almost regularly brings about further harm to himself and quite often anticipates this in cold blood. In the first type of revenge it was fear of a second blow that made the counterblow as strong as possible; here we find almost total indifference to what the opponent *will* do yet; the strength of the counterblow is determined solely by what he *has*

---

[1] A remarkably clear and vivid statement of a point that is widely held to be one of Ludwig Wittgenstein's major contributions to philosophy; cf. Wittgenstein's *Philosophical Investigations* (1953), sections 65ff. The great antipode of Nietzsche and Wittgenstein is Plato's theory of ideas, which holds that all the instances called by the same name participate in the same idea or form which alone embodies to perfection the quality named.

done to us. But what has he done? And what use is it to us if he now suffers after we have suffered on his account? What matters is a *restoration,* while the act of revenge of the first type serves only *self-preservation.* Perhaps we have lost through our opponent possessions, rank, friends, children: such losses are not brought back by revenge; the restoration concerns solely a *loss incidental* to all these losses. The revenge of restoration does not protect against further harm; it does not make good the harm suffered—except in one case. If our *honor* has suffered from our opponent, then revenge can *restore* it. But this has suffered damage in every instance in which suffering has been inflicted on us deliberately; for our opponent thus demonstrated that he did not *fear* us. By revenge we demonstrate that we do not fear him either: this constitutes the equalization, the restoration. (The intent of showing one's utter lack of *fear* goes so far in some persons that the danger their revenge involves for them—loss of health or life or other damage—is for them an indispensable condition of all revenge. Therefore they choose the means of a duel although the courts offer them help in obtaining satisfaction for the insult: but they do not accept an undangerous restoration of their honor as sufficient, because it cannot demonstrate their lack of fear.)

In the first type of revenge it is fear that strikes the counterblow; here, on the other hand, it is the absence of fear that, as I have tried to show, *wants to prove* itself by means of the counterblow.

Nothing therefore seems more different than the inner motivation of the two ways of action that are called by one name, "revenge." Nevertheless it happens quite frequently that the person seeking revenge is unclear about what really induced him to act: perhaps he delivered the counterblow from fear and in order to preserve himself, but later, when he has time to think about the point of his injured honor, he convinces himself that he avenged himself for his honor's sake—after all, this motive is *nobler* than the other one. Moreover, it is also important whether he believes his honor to have been injured in the eyes of others (the world) or only in the eyes of the opponent who insulted him: in the latter case he will prefer secret revenge, in the former public revenge.

Depending on whether he projects himself strongly or weakly into the soul of his opponent and the spectators, his revenge will be more embittered or tamer; if he lacks this type of imagination entirely, he will not think of revenge at all, for in that case the feeling for "honor" is not present in him and hence cannot be injured. Just so, he will not think of revenge if he *despises* the doer and the spectators of the deed—because they, being despised, cannot accord him any honor and hence also cannot take it away. Finally, he will forgo revenge in the not unusual case in which he loves the doer: to be sure, he thus loses honor in his opponent's eyes and perhaps thus becomes less worthy of being loved in return. But even forgoing all such counterlove is a sacrifice that love is prepared to make if only it does not *have to hurt* the beloved being: that would mean hurting oneself more than this sacrifice hurts.

Thus: everybody will revenge himself unless he is without honor or full of contempt or full of love for the person who has harmed and insulted him. Even when he has recourse to the courts he wants revenge as a private person—but *besides,* being a member of society who thinks further and considers the future, he also wants society's revenge on one who does not *honor* it. Thus judicial punishment *restores* both private honor and the honor of society— which means, punishment is revenge.

Indubitably, it also contains that other element of revenge which we described first, insofar as society uses punishment for its *self-preservation* and deals a counterblow in *self-defense.* Punishment desires to prevent *further* damage; it desires to *deter.* Thus both of these so different elements of revenge are actually *tied together* in punishment, and perhaps this is the main support of that above-mentioned conceptual confusion by virtue of which the individual who revenges himself usually does not *know what* he really *wants.*

194

Dreams.— On the rare occasions when our dreams succeed and achieve perfection—most dreams are bungled—they are symbolic chains of scenes and images in place of a narrative poetic language; they circumscribe our experiences or expectations or situations with such poetic boldness and decisiveness that in the morning we are always amazed at ourselves when we remember our dreams. We use up too much artistry in our dreams—and therefore often are impoverished during the day.

202

Tourists.— They climb mountains like animals, stupid and sweating; one has forgotten to tell them that there are beautiful views on the way up.

203

Too much and too little.— All men now live through too much and think through too little: they suffer at the same time from extreme hunger and from colic, and therefore become thinner and thinner, no matter how much they eat.— Whoever says now, "I have not lived through anything"—is an ass.

204

End and goal.— Not every end is the goal. The end of a melody is not its goal; and yet: as long as the melody has not reached its end, it also hasn't reached its goal. A parable.

208

How to have all men against you.— If anyone dared to say now, "Whoever is not for me, is against me," [2] he would immediately have all men against him.— This does our time honor.

249

Positive and negative.— This thinker needs nobody to refute him: for that he suffices himself.

[2] Mat. 12:30; Luke 11:23.

263

Way to equality.— A few hours of mountain climbing turn a villain and a saint into two rather equal creatures. Exhaustion is the shortest way to *equality* and *fraternity*—and *liberty* is added eventually by sleep.

297

Not to wish to see too soon.— As long as one lives through an experience, one must surrender to the experience and shut one's eyes instead of becoming an observer *immediately*. For that would disturb the good digestion of the experience: instead of wisdom one would acquire indigestion.

298

From the practice of wise men.— To become wise, one must *wish* to have certain experiences and run, as it were, into their gaping jaws. This, of course, is very dangerous; many a wise guy has been swallowed.

301

A testimony of love.— Somebody said: "About two persons I have never reflected very thoroughly: that is the testimony of my love for them." [3]

302

How one tries to improve bad arguments.— Some people throw a bit of their personality after their bad arguments, as if that might straighten their paths and turn them into right and good arguments—just as a man in a bowling alley, after he has let go of the ball, still tries to direct it with gestures.

---

[3] Nietzsche may have thought particularly of his mother and sister.

307

When taking leave is needed.— From what you would know and measure, you must take leave, at least for a time. Only after having left town, you see how high its towers rise above the houses.

317

Opinions and fish.— Possessing opinions is like possessing fish, assuming one has a fish pond. One has to go fishing and needs some luck—then one has one's own fish, one's own opinions. I am speaking of live opinions, of live fish. Others are satisfied if they own a cabinet of fossils—and in their heads, "convictions." [4]

322

Death.— The certain prospect of death could sweeten every life with a precious and fragrant drop of levity—and now you strange apothecary souls have turned it into an ill-tasting drop of poison that makes the whole of life repulsive.

323

Remorse.— Never give way to remorse, but immediately say to yourself: that would merely mean adding a second stupidity to the first.— If you have done harm, see how you can do good.— If you are punished for your actions, bear the punishment with the feeling that you *are* doing good—by deterring others from falling prey to the same folly. Every evildoer who is punished may feel that he is a benefactor of humanity.

326

Don't touch!— There are terrible people who, instead of solving a problem, bungle it and make it more difficult for all who come

---

[4] See section 333 below. About convictions, cf. *The Antichrist*, sections 50ff. (*Portable Nietzsche*, pp. 631ff.).

after. Whoever can't hit the nail on the head should, please, not hit it at all.

333

Dying for the "truth."— We should not let ourselves be burnt for our opinions: we are not that sure of them. But perhaps for this: that we may have and change our opinions.

The Dawn (1881)

1

Rationality ex post facto.— Whatever lives long is gradually so saturated with reason that its irrational origins become improbable. Does not almost every accurate history of the origin of something sound paradoxical and sacrilegious to our feelings? Doesn't the good historian *contradict* all the time?

18

The morality of voluntary suffering.— What is the supreme enjoyment for men who live in the state of war of those small, continually endangered communities which are characterized by the strictest mores? In other words, for vigorous, vindictive, vicious, suspicious souls who are prepared for what is most terrible and hardened by deprivations and mores? The enjoyment of *cruelty;* and in these circumstances it is even accounted among the *virtues* of such a soul if it is inventive and insatiable in cruelty. The community feels refreshed by cruel deeds, and casts off for once the gloom of continual anxiety and caution. Cruelty belongs to the most ancient festive joys of mankind. Hence one supposes that the *gods,* too, feel refreshed and festive when one offers them the sight of cruelty; and so the idea creeps into the world that *voluntary suffering,* torture one has chosen oneself, has value and makes good sense.

Gradually, the mores shape a communal practice in accordance with this idea: all extravagant well-being henceforth arouses some mistrust, and all hard and painful states more and more confidence. One supposes that the gods might look upon us ungraciously because of our happiness, and graciously because of our suffering—not by any means with pity. For pity is considered contemptible and unworthy of a strong and terrible soul. Rather, graciously, because it delights them and puts them into good spirits; for those who are cruel enjoy the supreme titillation of the feeling of power.[1]

Thus the concept of the "most moral man" of the community comes to contain the virtue of frequent suffering, deprivation, a hard way of life, and of cruel self-mortification—*not,* to say this again and again, as a means of self-discipline, self-control, and the desire for individual happiness, but as a virtue that makes the community look good to the evil gods, steaming up to them like a continual sacrifice of atonement upon some altar. All those spiritual leaders of peoples who succeeded in stirring something in the inert but fertile mud of their mores, had need not only of madness but also of voluntary torture to engender faith—and most and first of all, as always, their faith in themselves. The more their own spirit moved along novel paths and was therefore tormented by pangs of conscience and anxieties, the more cruelly they raged against their own flesh, their own desires, and their own health—as if they wanted to offer the deity some substitute gratification in case it should perhaps be embittered on account of customs one had neglected and fought against and new goals one had championed.

Let us not believe too quickly that now we have rid ourselves completely of such a logic of feeling. Let the most heroic souls question themselves about this. Every smallest step on the field of free thought and the individually formed life has always been fought for with spiritual and physical torments: not only moving forward, no, above all moving, motion, change have required innumerable martyrs, all through the long path-seeking and basic mil-

---

[1] This was written before Nietzsche developed his conception of the will to power. The function of *The Dawn* in the development of this idea is discussed in detail in Chapter 6 of Kaufmann's *Nietzsche*.

lennia of which, to be sure, people don't think when they talk, as usual, about "world history," that ridiculously small segment of human existence. And even in this so-called world history, which is at bottom much ado about the latest news, there is no really more important theme than the primordial tragedy of the martyrs *who wanted to move the swamps.*

Nothing has been bought more dearly than that little bit of human reason and of a feeling of freedom that now constitutes our pride. But it is this very pride that now makes it almost impossible for us to feel with those vast spans of time characterized by the "morality of mores" [2] which antedate "world history" as the *real and decisive main history that determined the character of humanity*—when suffering was a virtue, cruelty a virtue, dissimulation a virtue, revenge a virtue, the slander of reason a virtue, while well-being was a danger, the craving for knowledge a danger, peace a danger, pity a danger, being pitied ignominy, work ignominy, madness divine, change immoral [3] and pregnant with disaster.

You think that all this has changed, and that humanity must thus have changed its character? You who think you know men, learn to know yourselves better!

112

On the natural history of duty and right.— Our duties—are the rights others have against us. How did the others acquire these rights? By taking us to be capable of contracts and of repayment, as equal and similar to them; by entrusting us with something on this basis and educating, correcting, and supporting us. We do our duty—that means: we justify this idea of our power on the basis of which we have been treated this way; we give back in the same measure in which one has given to us. Thus it is our pride that bids us do our duty—we want to regain our sovereignty when we balance what others have done for us with something we do for them —for in this way they have intruded into the sphere of our power

---

[2] *Sittlichkeit der Sitte.*

[3] *Unsittlich:* practically by definition.

and would keep their hand in it constantly if we did not repay them with our "duty," which means that we intrude into their power. The rights of others can relate only to what is within our power; it would be unreasonable if they wanted something from us that does not belong to us. To be more precise one should say: only to what they suppose is within our power, assuming that it is the same thing we suppose to be within our power. The same error could easily be made on both sides: the sense of a duty depends on our sharing with the others the same *faith* about the extent of our power: namely, that we promise certain things and are *capable* of incurring these duties ("freedom of the will").

My *rights:* they define that part of my power which the others have not only conceded to me but in which they wish to preserve me. What leads the others to do this? First, their prudence and fear and caution—whether they expect something similar in return from us (protection of their rights), or consider a fight with us dangerous or pointless, or see in every diminution of our strength a disadvantage for themselves because it would render us unfit for an alliance with them against a third and hostile power. Then, deeding or ceding. In this case the others have power enough, more than enough, to be able to give some of it away and to guarantee the piece they give away to the person who receives it—in which case a slight feeling of power is assumed in the person who accepts the present. Thus rights originate: recognized and guaranteed degrees of power. If the proportions of power are changed drastically, rights pass away, and new rights come to be—which is apparent in international law with its constant passing away and coming to be. If our power is decreased drastically, the feelings of those who have so far guaranteed our rights change: they consider whether they can restore us to our old full possession—and if they feel incapable of that, then they deny our "rights" henceforth. Just so, when our power is increased drastically, the feelings of those change who have so far recognized it and whose recognition we now no longer need: they may try to reduce our power to its former measure, they may wish to interfere, invoking their "duty"—but this is just a waste of words. Where right *rules,* a state and degree of power is preserved, and a diminution and increase are resisted. The right of

others is the concession of our feeling of power to the feeling of
power among these others. When our power is proved to have been
profoundly shaken and broken, our rights cease; on the other hand,
when we have become a great deal more powerful, the rights of
others cease for us, at least in the form in which we have so far
conceded them.

The "fair person" constantly needs the fine tact of a scale
for the degrees of power and right which, in view of the transitory
nature of human affairs, will always be balanced only for a short
time, while for the most part they either sink or rise: to be fair is
therefore difficult and requires much practice, good will, and a
great deal of good *spirit*.—

231

Of German virtue.— How degenerate in taste, how slavish
before offices, classes, robes, pomp, and splendor must a people
have been when it evaluated the simple [*schlicht*] as the bad
[*schlecht*], the simple man as the bad man! One should counter
the moral arrogance of the Germans with this one little word,
schlecht, and nothing more.[4]

232

From a disputation.— A: My friend, you have talked yourself
hoarse. B: Then I stand refuted. Let us not discuss the matter any
further.

236

Punishment.— A strange thing, our punishment! It does not
cleanse the criminal, it is no atonement; on the contrary, it pollutes
worse than the crime does.

---

[4] The etymology is sound—and the aphorism invites comparison with *Genealogy of Morals,* I, section 4. See p. 464 below.

The Gay Science (1882)

51

Sense of truth.— I think well of all skepticism to which I may reply: "Let us try it." But I no longer want to hear anything of all those things and questions which do not permit experiments. This is the limit of my "sense of truth": for there courage has lost its rights.

108

New struggles.— After Buddha was dead, his shadow was still shown for centuries in a cave—a tremendous, gruesome shadow. God is dead: but given the way men are, there may still be caves for thousands of years in which his shadow will be shown.— And we—we still have to vanquish his shadow, too.[1]

121

Life no argument.— We have fixed up a world for ourselves in which we can live—assuming bodies, lines, planes, causes and effects, motion and rest, form and content: without these articles of faith, nobody now would endure life. But that does not mean that they have been proved. Life is no argument; the conditions of life could include error.[2]

129

The conditions of God.— "God himself cannot exist without wise men"—Luther said, and was right. But "God can exist even less without unwise men"—that good old Luther did not say.

---

[1] Cf. section 125 (*Portable Nietzsche*, pp. 95f.).
[2] Cf. *Beyond Good and Evil*, section 4, p. 201f., below.

130

A dangerous resolve.— The Christian resolve to find the world ugly and bad has made the world ugly and bad.

142

Incense.— Buddha said: "Do not flatter your benefactor." This saying should be repeated in a Christian church—right away it clears the air of everything Christian.

163

After a great victory.— What is best about a great victory is that it rids the victor of fear of defeat. "Why not also lose for once?" he says to himself; "now I am rich enough for that."

173

Being deep and appearing deep.— Whoever knows he is deep, strives for clarity; whoever would like to appear deep to the crowd, strives for obscurity. For the crowd considers anything deep if only it cannot see to the bottom: the crowd is so timid and afraid of going into the water.

200

Laughter.— Laughter means: being *schadenfroh*,[3] but with a good conscience.

205

Need.— A need is considered the cause of the origin: in truth, it is often merely an effect of what did originate.

---

[3] The word is famous for being untranslatable: it signifies taking a mischievous delight in the discomfort of another person.

228

Against mediators.— Those who wish to be mediators between two resolute thinkers are marked as mediocre: they lack eyes to see the unparalleled; seeing things as similar and making them the same is the mark of weak eyes.

231

"Thorough."— Those slow in knowledge suppose that slowness belongs to knowledge.[4]

232

Dreams.— We have no dreams at all or interesting ones. We should learn to be awake the same way—not at all or in an interesting manner.

258

Those who deny chance.— No victor believes in chance.

273

Whom do you call bad?— Those who always want to put to shame.

274

What do you consider most humane?— To spare someone shame.

275

What is the seal of attained freedom?— No longer being ashamed in front of oneself.

---

[4] Cf. section 381, below, and *Beyond Good and Evil*, section 27.

292

To the preachers of morals.— I have no wish to establish morals, but I have this advice for those who do: if you want to do the best things and states out of all honor and worth, then continue to talk about them as you have been doing. Place them at the head of your morality and talk from morning till night of the happiness of virtue, of peace of soul, of justice and immanent retribution: the way you are carrying on, all these good things finally acquire a popularity and are shouted about in the streets; but at the same time all of their gold will be worn off, and even worse—all the gold that was *in* them will have been changed to lead. Truly, you are masters of inverse alchemy, of the devaluation of the most valuable things. Why don't you reach, experimentally, for another recipe, lest you keep attaining the opposite of what you seek: *deny* these good things, deprive them of the mob's acclaim and their constant currency; restore them to the concealed bashfulness of solitary souls; say that *morality is something forbidden.* Perhaps you will in that way gain the support for these things of the only type of men that matter—those who are *heroic.* But then they must have a quality that inspires fear, and not, as hitherto, nausea. Should we not say of morality today what Master Eckhart[5] said: "I ask God that he rid me of God."

312

My dog.— I have given a name to my pain and call it "dog": it is just as faithful, just as obtrusive and shameless, just as entertaining, just as clever as any other dog—and I can scold it and vent my bad moods on it, as others do with their dogs, servants, and wives.

---

[5] Meister Eckhart (1260–1327) was the greatest German mystic of the Middle Ages.

316

Prophetic men.— You have no feeling for the fact that prophetic men are men who suffer a great deal: you merely suppose that they have been granted a beautiful "gift," and you would even like to have it yourself. But I shall express myself in a parable. How much may animals suffer from the electricity in the air and clouds! We see how some species have a prophetic faculty regarding the weather; monkeys, for example (as may be observed even in Europe, and not only in zoos—namely, on Gibraltar). But we do not heed that it is their *pains* that make them prophets. When a strong positive electrical charge, under the influence of an approaching cloud that is as yet far from visible, suddenly changes into negative electricity, these animals behave as if an enemy were drawing near and prepare for defense or escape; most often they try to hide: they do not understand bad weather as a kind of weather but as an enemy whose hand they already *feel.*

322

Parable.— Those thinkers in whom all stars move in cyclic orbits are not the most profound: whoever looks into himself as into vast space and carries galaxies in himself also knows how irregular all galaxies are; they lead into the chaos and labyrinth of existence.

325

What belongs to greatness.— Who will attain anything great if he does not possess the strength and the will to *inflict* great suffering? Being able to suffer is the least thing: weak women and even slaves often attain mastery in that. But not to perish of inner distress and uncertainty when one inflicts great suffering and hears the cry of this suffering—that is great, that belongs to greatness.[6]

---

[6] This aphorism is surely quite as much prompted by personal experience as the three that precede it: Nietzsche is thinking of the suffering that his ideas

327

Taking seriously.— In the great majority, the intellect is a clumsy, gloomy, creaking machine that is difficult to start. They call it "taking the matter seriously," when they work with this machine and want to think well: how onerous they must find thinking well! The lovely beast, man, seems to lose its good spirits every time it thinks well: it becomes "serious." And "where laughter and gaiety are found, the quality of thought is poor"—that is the prejudice of this serious beast against all "gay science."— Well, then, let us prove that it is a prejudice.[7]

332

The bad hour.— Every philosopher has probably had a bad hour when he thought: what do I matter if one does not accept my bad arguments, too?— And then some mischievous[8] little bird flew past him and twittered: "What do you matter? What do you matter?"

381 [9]

On the question of being understandable.— One does not only wish to be understood when one writes; one wishes just as surely *not* to be understood. It is not by any means necessarily an objection to a book when anybody finds it impossible to understand: perhaps that was part of the author's intention—he did not want to be understood by just "anybody." Every more noble spirit

---

and books inflict on his mother, the Wagner circle, and those whose pieties he offends.

[7] This aphorism, and the whole conception of the "gay science," should be recalled in connection with Nietzsche's inquiry concerning "ascetic ideals" in the *Genealogy*. Science and scholarship, he argues there, involve variations of asceticism. But his solution does not consist in renouncing reason: he wants to develop a "gay science."

[8] *Schadenfrohes.*

[9] From the Fifth Book, added in 1887.

and taste selects its audience when it wishes to communicate itself; and choosing them, it at the same time erects barriers against "the others." All the more subtle laws of any style have their origin at this point: they at the same time keep away, create a distance, forbid "entrance," understanding, as said above—while they open the ears of those whose ears are related to ours.

And let me say this among ourselves and about my own case: I don't want either my ignorance or the liveliness of my temperament to keep me from being understandable for *you,* my friends— not the liveliness, however much it compels me to tackle a matter swiftly to tackle it at all. For I approach deep problems like cold baths: quickly into them and quickly out again. That one does not get to the depths that way, not deep enough down, is the superstition of those afraid of the water, the enemies of cold water; they speak without experience. The freezing cold makes one swift.

And to ask this incidentally: does a matter necessarily remain ununderstood and unfathomed merely because it has been touched only in flight, glanced at, in a flash? Is it absolutely imperative that one settles down on it? that one has brooded over it as over an egg? *Diu noctuque incubando,* as Newton said of himself? At least there are truths that are singularly shy and ticklish and cannot be caught except suddenly—that must be *surprised* or left alone.

Finally, my brevity has yet another value: given such questions as concern me, I must say many things briefly in order that they may be heard still more briefly. For, being an immoralist, one has to take steps against corrupting innocents—I mean, asses and old maids of both sexes whom life offers nothing but their innocence. Even more, my writings should inspire, elevate, and encourage them to be virtuous. I cannot imagine anything on earth that would be a merrier sight than inspired old asses and maids who feel excited by the sweet sentiments of virtue; and "this I have seen"— thus spoke Zarathustra.

So much regarding brevity. Matters stand worse with my ignorance which I do not try to conceal from myself. There are hours when I feel ashamed of it—to be sure, also hours when I feel ashamed of feeling ashamed. Perhaps all of us philosophers are in a bad position nowadays regarding knowledge: science keeps growing, and the most scholarly among us are close to discovering that they know too little. But it would be still worse if it were different —and we knew *too much;* our task is and remains above all not to mistake ourselves for others. We *are* something different from scholars, although it is unavoidable for us to be also, among other things, scholarly. We have different needs, grow differently, and also have a different digestion: we need more, we also need less. How much a spirit needs for its nourishment, for this there is no formula; but if its taste is for independence, for quick coming and going, for roaming, perhaps for adventures for which only the swiftest are a match, it is better for such a spirit to live in freedom with little to eat than unfree and stuffed. It is not fat but the greatest possible suppleness and strength that a good dancer desires from his nourishment—and I would not know what the spirit of a philosopher might wish more to be than a good dancer. For the dance is his ideal, also his art, and finally also his only piety, his "service of God."

BEYOND
GOOD and EVIL

*Prelude
to a
Philosophy of the Future*

———◆———

FOR
David

CONTENTS

TRANSLATOR'S PREFACE *181*

NIETZSCHE'S PREFACE *192*

On the Prejudices of Philosophers 197

The Free Spirit 223

What Is Religious 247

Epigrams and Interludes 267

Natural History of Morals 285

We Scholars 309

Our Virtues 333

Peoples and Fatherlands 361

What Is Noble 389

From High Mountains: *Aftersong 428*

INDEX *813*

Translator's Preface

Nietzsche was controversial to the marrow. He sought controversy and is still controversial. But the area of agreement about him is growing. What the Germans and the French have known for some time is gradually being recognized in the English-speaking world as well: Nietzsche was one of the greatest German writers and philosophers of all time and one of the most interesting and influential Europeans of the nineteenth century. *Beyond Good and Evil* is one of his most important books, and its nine parts with their descriptive subtitles are designed to give the reader a comprehensive idea of Nietzsche's thought and style.

For all that, the book, like all of Nietzsche's best volumes, is easily misunderstood. For readers who come to it with no previous knowledge of Nietzsche or with erroneous preconceptions about him, I have ventured to offer something of a commentary in the form of copious footnotes. *All of the footnotes are mine; none are Nietzsche's.*

I have chosen to use notes for elucidation of major and minor points in the text rather than a long introduction or interlarded commentaries because such notes can provide immediate clarification or interpretation for the reader who requires such assistance. On the other hand, the reader can skip the notes if he wishes, and read Nietzsche straight through without the intrusion of the editor's commentaries.

Another possibility would have been to offer the commentary on facing pages, as I myself have done in the case of Hegel's long Preface to the *Phenomenology*. But Nietzsche's book is not *that* difficult: one can read it like an ordinary book, and many pages require no elucidation. Everything considered, then, it seemed best to offer the commentary in the form of notes—none on some pages, several on others.

To keep down the length of the commentary and to avoid excessive repetition of material available elsewhere, I have referred to detailed discussion of many points in my own *Nietzsche* volume.

2

A word about the text: it was originally published in 1886, following *Thus Spoke Zarathustra,* which is generally and rightly regarded as Nietzsche's first attempt to present his whole philosophy. All of his previous works had been stages in his development: with *Zarathustra* the final phase begins; a comprehensive vision has been attained but is far from easy to communicate. *Zarathustra,* though much of the work consists of apparently direct preaching, is a form of "indirect communication," to use Kierkegaard's term: the form is literary and there is an abundance of symbolism. For those who know the author well, the book is a stunning epitome of his thought; for those who do not, some other approach is needed. It was with this in mind that Nietzsche wrote *Beyond Good and Evil.* And on September 22, 1886, he wrote Jacob Burckhardt: "Please read this book (although it says the same things as my *Zarathustra,* but differently, very differently—)."

The first edition was the only one that Nietzsche himself supervised. In a letter to his friend Franz Overbeck, he wrote: "I am making the experiment of having something published at *my* expense: assuming 300 copies will be sold, my expenses will be covered and I might be able to repeat the experiment some time. The firm of C. G. Naumann permits the use of its highly respectable name. This between us. The neglect by Schm.[1] was monstrous: for ten years now no copies distributed to bookstores; neither any review copies . . . no promotion—in short, my writings beginning with *Human, All-Too-Human* are 'anecdota.' Of *Zarathustra* 60–70 copies each[2] have been sold, etc., etc."[3]

---

[1] Ernst Schmeitzner had been Nietzsche's publisher.

[2] The reference is to the first three parts, published separately in 1883 and 1884. Of Part Four, only forty copies had been printed privately, and only seven were distributed among friends.

[3] Written from Sils Maria, summer 1886; Number 255 in *Friedrich Nietzsches Briefwechsel mit Franz Overbeck* (Friedrich Nietzsche's correspondence with Franz Overbeck), Leipzig, 1916, p. 341.

The book of which Nietzsche had hoped to sell 300 copies was *Beyond Good and Evil,* but a year later, June 8, 1887, he writes Peter Gast: "This time, for *Bey. G. & E.,* everything necessary (and even a little more than that) has been done as far as the book trade is concerned: so Herr Schmeitzner cannot be blamed any more, as I had done so far. *In spite of all this*—the result is the same as with Schmeitzner: rather, it is still worse! Altogether only 114 copies have been sold (while 66 copies have been given away to newspapers and journals).

"Instructive! Namely, one simply does not want my literature; and I—may no longer afford the luxury of print." [4]

By 1903, 17,000 copies were in print; by 1906, 36,000. Since then new editions and translations into other languages have mushroomed.

The first edition has become a great rarity and has never been reprinted exactly as published in 1886. All subsequent editions contain a few very minor deviations. Karl Schlechta's edition of Nietzsche's works in three volumes [5] is widely considered vastly superior to all previous editions, at least philologically, although it contains much less of Nietzsche's *Nachlass* [6] than some earlier editions; and Schlechta claims unequivocally that he has followed the original edition, published by C. G. Naumann (Leipzig, 1886), [7] but he has not. Where the standard editions differ from the original edition, he follows the later editions. [8] No matter of philosophical substance is involved; the deviations are very small; but the fact remains astonishing. Notwithstanding all sorts of sensational claims, none of the scholarly corrections of the older editions of Nietzsche's writings, published since World War II, are important philosophi-

---

[4] *Friedrich Nietzsches Briefe an Peter Gast* (Friedrich Nietzsche's letters to Peter Gast), Leipzig, 1908.

[5] *Werke in drei Bänden,* Munich, 1954–56; *Nietzsche–Index,* Munich, 1965.

[6] The notes, fragments, lectures, and drafts he had not published himself. Moreover, the three volumes include only 278 of Nietzsche's thousands of published letters and none of his early scholarly articles.

[7] "Philological Postscript," in Vol. III, p. 1,387.

[8] Sections 65a, 73a, 186, 237, 247, 269, and 270.

cally, and it is ironical that the editions of Schlechta and Podach[9] are by no means models of belated philological soundness.[10] This translation follows the first edition. In my footnote commentary, deviations of the later editions are pointed out.

I have taken two liberties. Nietzsche occasionally uses dots, usually four, as a punctuation mark; for example, but by no means there alone, at the end of sections 62 and 227. In serious works in the English-speaking world dots are so generally taken to indicate omissions that it did not seem advisable to follow Nietzsche's usage. Dashes have therefore been used instead. Moreover, Nietzsche often employs dots or dashes in the middle of lengthy paragraphs. In such cases I have often begun a new paragraph to mark the break; and beyond that, I have generally broken up long paragraphs. The reader may always assume that in the original a numbered section constitutes a single paragraph; even if it is as long as the whole Preface or sections 25, 26, and 28.

3

Beyond Good and Evil has been translated into English twice before. The first translator, Helen Zimmern, was an English writer who had met Nietzsche in Sils Maria in the summer of 1886—the period when the book was completed, printed, and published. Indeed, Nietzsche mentions her in the margin of the letter to Franz Overbeck previously cited: "Till the middle of September I shall stay here. There is no dearth of old acquaintances . . . Miss Helen Zimmern . . ."

In the index of names at the end of Nietzsche's *Briefe an Peter Gast,* Helen Zimmern is identified as an "English writer"; in the index to *Briefe an Mutter und Schwester* (letters to mother and sister, Leipzig, 1909), as "engl. Litteratin," which is less respectful. Neither volume mentions that she translated *Beyond Good and Evil.* What Nietzsche wrote (September 19, 1886) about her to his

---

[9] *Friedrich Nietzsche Werke des Zusammenbruchs* (the work of Nietzsche's collapse), Heidelberg, 1961.

[10] See W. Kaufmann, "Nietzsche in the Light of His Suppressed Manuscripts," *Journal of the History of Philosophy,* October 1964.

mother or sister was: "I had the privilege of introducing this 'champion of women's rights' (Frl. von Salis) to another 'champion' who is my neighbor at meals, Miss Helen Zimmern, who is extremely clever, incidentally not an Englishwoman—but Jewish. May heaven have mercy on the European intellect if one wanted to subtract the Jewish intellect from it."[11] In 1885, the year before, Nietzsche's sister had married Bernhard Förster, one of the leaders of the German anti-Semitic movement.[12]

Helen Zimmern (1846–1934), two years Nietzsche's junior, had published *Arthur Schopenhauer: His Life and His Philosophy* (1876) and *Gotthold Ephraim Lessing: His Life and His Works* (1878); she also published many other books and translations, including several from the Italian. About her version of *Beyond Good and Evil,* Dr. Oscar Levy reported in 1913 in a short essay on "The Nietzsche Movement in England" (in the last volume, the eighteenth, of his edition of *The Complete Works*): "But in 1907 the party had somewhat recovered its spirit, and as a last experiment brought out a translation of *Beyond Good and Evil*—this time at private risk, for no publisher could be induced to take up an author twice repudiated. This translation was one which had been made nearly ten years ago, but until then had never seen, and was never expected to see, the light of publicity. It turned out to be a success —a half-hearted success perhaps, but one that at last told the few inmates of the Nietzschean ark that the waters of democracy had diminished, and that at least some higher peaks of humanity were free from the appalling deluge. The success encouraged them once more to take up their old project of the publication of the complete works. . . ."

---

[11] Cf. the similar remarks about her in letters to Gast, July 20, 1886, and January 6, 1888: "Of course Jewish:—it is terrific to what extent this race now holds the 'spirit [Geistigkeit]' in Europe in its hands," and, "the clever Englishwoman (resp., Jewess) who introduced Schopenhauer to the English. . . . (Summer before last she was in Sils Maria, sitting next to me at meals)."

[12] Cf. Kaufmann, *Nietzsche: Philosopher, Psychologist, Antichrist,* Chapter 1, section III, where Nietzsche's letters about the marriage and his opposition to anti-Semitism are quoted. For full-length portraits of the Försters see E. F. Podach, *Gestalten um Nietzsche* (persons around Nietzsche, Weimar, 1932), Chapter 4.

The "inmates" in England were a very different lot from those who were by then writing about Nietzsche in Germany and France: English professional *philosophers,* for example, had developed curious versions of Hegelianism after Hegel had gone into eclipse on the continent, and at the beginning of the twentieth century the young G. E. Moore and Bertrand Russell were trying to emancipate philosophy from the influence of the leading Idealists, F. H. Bradley and J. M. E. McTaggart. The tone of the English Nietzscheans, in turn, helped to create a public image of Nietzsche that did not attract philosophers to him.

It was over fifty years after *Beyond Good and Evil* had originally appeared in 1886 that professional philosophers began to publish studies of Nietzsche's philosophy in English.

Meanwhile, the Zimmern translation of *Beyond Good and Evil* found its way into the Modern Library, and it was until 1955 the only version through which myriads of readers knew the book. In preparing the present edition, I hoped at first that I might merely revise her version, modernizing her somewhat Victorian prose and correcting mistakes; but I soon gave up. The mistakes were too numerous, and in Nietzsche's case nuances are so important that it would be difficult to say at what point an infelicitous rendering becomes downright wrong.

The second translator, Marianne Cowan, is not a philosopher either. Her version is modern and very readable. But the merits are somewhat offset by errors of understanding, and therefore I have pointed out a few such instances in my notes.

Often it seems helpful to call the reader's attention to crucial passages in some of Nietzsche's other works. These are cited in each instance according to sections, to enable the reader to find them in any edition; but in the case of material included in a volume of Nietzsche translations that I published in 1954 [13] I have also given the page numbers in parentheses.

---

[13] *The Portable Nietzsche,* which contains complete versions of *Zarathustra, Twilight of the Idols, Antichrist,* and *Nietzsche contra Wagner,* as well as selections from Nietzsche's other books, his notes, and his letters.

4

About the title of the book: like many of Nietzsche's titles, phrases, and coinages, it is brilliant, unforgettable, and usually misconstrued. The following sections of the book are relevant to an understanding of what Nietzsche meant by "beyond good and evil": the author's Preface and sections 2, 4, 32, 33, 56, 153, 164, 202, 212, the end of 241, 260, and 284. This is not to say that the other sections are not relevant nor that the reader would be best advised to look up these passages first. Rather, it would be well to read the book with an open mind and a readiness to distinguish the many connotations of its striking title. And it might be helpful to read the editor's note for section 250 at the start.

To an extent at least it may help many readers to relate several themes of the book to other great writers, and some such comparisons will be found in the notes. One theme, however, should be stated here at the outset. Ibsen's Dr. Thomas Stockmann says at the end of *An Enemy of the People:* "*He* is the strongest man in the world that stands alone." This leitmotif of the play illustrates Kierkegaard's influence on Ibsen, to which Georg Brandes referred in a letter to Nietzsche, March 7, 1888: "Intellectually, he has been very dependent on Kierkegaard." We may recall Kierkegaard's remarks on "That Individual"[14] with its refrain "The crowd is untruth." The fourth act of Ibsen's play could almost be subtitled "Variations on a Theme by Kierkegaard." Witness Dr. Stockmann's words:

> The most dangerous enemy of truth and freedom among us—is the compact majority. Yes, the damned, compact, liberal majority . . .
>
> The majority has *might*—unfortunately—but *right* it is not. Right—are I and a few others. The minority is always right. . . .
>
> I have a mind to make a revolution against the lie that the majority is in the possession of truth. What kind of truths

---

[14] Included in *Existentialism from Dostoevsky to Sartre,* ed. Walter Kaufmann (New York, Meridian Books, 1956), pp. 92–99.

are those around which the majority usually gathers? They are truths that have become so old that they are on the way toward becoming shaky. But once a truth has become that old, it is also on the way toward becoming a lie . . . A normally constituted truth lives, let us say, as a rule seventeen or eighteen years; at most twenty, rarely more. But such aged truths are always exceedingly thin. Nevertheless it is only at that stage that the majority makes their acquaintance . . . All these majority truths . . . are rather like rancid, spoiled . . . hams. And that is the source of the moral scurvy that rages all around us. . . ."

A generation later, Freud said on the second page of his autobiographical *Selbstdarstellung* (Leipzig, 1925) that, as a Jew at an anti-Semitic university, "I learned early to know the lot of standing in opposition and being placed under a ban by the 'compact majority.' Thus the ground was laid for a certain independence of judgment."

One reasonable perspective for *Beyond Good and Evil* is to see it somewhere between Kierkegaard and Ibsen on the one hand and Freud and Sartre on the other. And considering how much Nietzsche has to say about "nobility" in this book, it is good to recall that the old Freud said in a letter about Nietzsche: "In my youth he signified a nobility which I could not attain." [15]

Such sections as 212 and 296, to name only two among a great many, invite comparison with some of the phrases cited here. But it would be pointless to attempt a long list, for what is at stake is not just a verbal similarity here or there but rather one way of seeing the whole book. There are many others.

It would be foolish for a translator, and even for a commentator, to attempt to foist his own estimate of a book with which he has been living for some time on those who will henceforth share his experience to some extent. But in the spirit of Zarathustra's

---

[15] Included by Ernest Jones in his *Life and Work of Sigmund Freud* (New York, Basic Books, 1957), III, 460. For details of the image of Nietzsche communicated to Freud in the early eighteen-eighties by his friend Dr. Paneth who met Nietzsche in Nice, see Kaufmann, *From Shakespeare to Existentialism* (Garden City, N. Y., Anchor Books, 1960), pp. 323f.

"This is *my* way; where is yours?" [16] I shall venture a suggestion.

This is one of the great books of the nineteenth century, indeed of any century, despite much with which the modern reader might disagree. There is much in it with which I too do not agree; but that is also true of Plato's and Aristotle's writings, of all great philosophical works and, making due allowances for the different genre, of Dante's and Dostoevsky's ideas and of the Bible. There are some passages that strike me as blemishes without which the book would be better; for example, the tedious remarks about women, the mercifully briefer comments on the English, and the poem at the end.

It is possible to say briefly what makes the book great: the prophetic independence of its spirit; the hundreds of doors it opens for the mind, revealing new vistas, problems, and relationships; and what it contributes to our understanding of much of recent thought and literature and history. Readers might ask, for example, about the relation of various passages to psychoanalysis, to analytical philosophy, or to existentialism. But even a far longer list would not do justice to the book. There remains another dimension. This is one of those rare books in which one encounters not only a great thinker but also a fascinating human being of exceptional complexity and integrity.

One final caution. *Beyond Good and Evil* is not a collection of aphorisms for browsing. Each of the nine major parts, with the possible exception of part four, is meant to be read straight through. Each pursues one complex of problems, and what is said in one section is frequently qualified decisively in the next, or a few pages later. The often surprising developments of an idea constitute one of the major charms of this work. And it is in part on their account that this book, like all great books—for this is part of their definition or, as Nietzsche might say, a criterion for the order of rank—needs to be read more than once. It is a book to reread and live with.

September 1965   W. K.

---

[16] End of the chapter "On the Spirit of Gravity" in Part III (*Portable Nietzsche*, p. 307).

Jenseits

von Gut und Böse.

Vorspiel

einer

Philosophie der Zukunft.

Von

Friedrich Nietzsche.

Leipzig

Druck und Verlag von C. G. Naumann.

1886.

Preface

Supposing truth is a woman—what then? Are there not grounds for the suspicion that all philosophers, insofar as they were dogmatists, have been very inexpert about women? That the gruesome seriousness, the clumsy obtrusiveness with which they have usually approached truth so far[1] have been awkward and very improper methods for winning a woman's heart? What is certain is that she has not allowed herself to be won—and today every kind of dogmatism is left standing dispirited and discouraged. *If* it is left standing at all! For there are scoffers who claim that it has fallen, that all dogmatism lies on the ground—even more, that all dogmatism is dying.

Speaking seriously, there are good reasons why all philosophical dogmatizing, however solemn and definitive its airs used to be, may nevertheless have been no more than a noble childishness and tyronism. And perhaps the time is at hand when it will be comprehended again and again *how little* used to be sufficient to furnish the cornerstone for such sublime and unconditional philosophers' edifices as the dogmatists have built so far: any old popular superstition from time immemorial (like the soul superstition which, in the form of the subject and ego superstition, has not even yet ceased to do mischief); some play on words perhaps, a seduction by grammar, or an audacious generalization of very narrow, very personal, very human, all too human facts.

The dogmatists' philosophy was, let us hope, only a promise across millennia—as astrology was in still earlier times when perhaps more work, money, acuteness, and patience were lavished in its service than for any real science so far: to astrology and its "supra-terrestrial" claims we owe the grand style of architecture in Asia and Egypt. It seems that all great things first have to bestride

---

[1] *Bisher* (so far) is a word that recurs constantly throughout *Beyond Good and Evil*. It helps to color the word "beyond" in the title.

the earth in monstrous and frightening masks in order to inscribe themselves in the hearts of humanity with eternal demands: dogmatic philosophy was such a mask; for example, the Vedanta doctrine in Asia and Platonism in Europe.

Let us not be ungrateful to it, although it must certainly be conceded that the worst, most durable, and most dangerous of all errors so far was a dogmatist's error—namely, Plato's invention of the pure spirit and the good as such. But now that it is overcome, now that Europe is breathing freely again after this nightmare and at least can enjoy a healthier—sleep, we, *whose task is wakefulness itself,* are the heirs of all that strength which has been fostered [2] by the fight against this error. To be sure, it meant standing truth on her head and denying *perspective,* the basic condition of all life, when one spoke of spirit and the good as Plato did. Indeed, as a physician one might ask: "How could the most beautiful growth of antiquity, Plato, contract such a disease? Did the wicked Socrates corrupt him after all? Could Socrates have been the corrupter of youth after all? And did he deserve his hemlock?"

But the fight against Plato or, to speak more clearly and for "the people," the fight against the Christian-ecclesiastical pressure of millennia—for Christianity is Platonism for "the people"—has created in Europe a magnificent tension of the spirit the like of which had never yet existed on earth: with so tense a bow we can now shoot for the most distant goals. To be sure, European man experiences this tension as need and distress; twice already attempts have been made in the grand style to unbend the bow—once by means of Jesuitism, the second time by means of the democratic enlightenment which, with the aid of freedom of the press and newspaper-reading, might indeed bring it about that the spirit would no longer experience itself so easily as a "need." (The Germans have invented gunpowder—all due respect for that!—but then they made up for that: they invented the press.)[3] But we who

---

[2] *Grossgezüchtet: züchten* means to breed, grow, or cultivate animals, plants, or qualities. Nietzsche uses the word frequently, and in these pages it is most often rendered by "cultivate." In his usage the connotation is generally spiritual.

[3] Cf. the Preface to *The Antichrist:* "One must be skilled in living on moun-

are neither Jesuits nor democrats, nor even German enough, we *good Europeans*[4] and free, *very* free spirits—we still feel it, the whole need of the spirit and the whole tension of its bow. And perhaps also the arrow, the task, and—who knows?—the *goal*——

Sils Maria, Upper Engadine,
June 1885.[5]

---

tains—seeing the wretched ephemeral babble of politics and national self-seeking *beneath* oneself" (*Portable Nietzsche,* p. 568). In the daily newspaper the concern with ephemeral matters is institutionalized and cultivated at the expense of genuine "spirituality."

[4] Nietzsche's coinage, initially introduced by him in *Human, All-Too-Human* (1878), section 475 (*Portable Nietzsche,* pp. 61-63).

[5] The book was written "summer 1885 in the Upper Engadine and the following winter in Nizza" (letter to Georg Brandes, April 10, 1888). This is borne out by other letters, except that additions and revisions were made until June 1886. The book was printed in June and July and published the beginning of August 1886.

CONTENTS[1]

On the Prejudices of Philosophers   197

The Free Spirit   223

What Is Religious   247

Epigrams and Interludes   267

Natural History of Morals   285

We Scholars   309

Our Virtues   333

Peoples and Fatherlands   361

What Is Noble   389

From High Mountains: Aftersong   428

---

[1] The Table of Contents appears here in the original edition but not in the later standard editions or in Schlechta.

PART ONE

ON THE PREJUDICES
OF PHILOSOPHERS

Part[1] *One*

1

The will to truth which will still tempt us to many a venture, that famous truthfulness of which all philosophers so far have spoken with respect—what questions has this will to truth not laid before us! What strange, wicked, questionable questions! That is a long story even now—and yet it seems as if it had scarcely begun. Is it any wonder that we should finally become suspicious, lose patience, and turn away impatiently? that we should finally learn from this Sphinx to ask questions, too? *Who* is it really that puts questions to us here? *What* in us really wants "truth"?

Indeed we came to a long halt at the question about the cause of this will—until we finally came to a complete stop before a still more basic question. We asked about the *value* of this will. Suppose we want truth: *why not rather* untruth? and uncertainty? even ignorance?

The problem of the value of truth came before us—or was it we who came before the problem? Who of us is Oedipus here? Who the Sphinx? It is a rendezvous, it seems, of questions and question marks.

And though it scarcely seems credible, it finally almost seems to us as if the problem had never even been put so far—as if we were the first to see it, fix it with our eyes, and *risk* it. For it does involve a risk, and perhaps there is none that is greater.

2

"How *could* anything originate out of its opposite? for example, truth out of error? or the will to truth out of the will to

---

[1] Marianne Cowan has suggested in the preface to her translation that Nietzsche divided this book "into 'articles' like articles of faith," and she sees "irony in this." But there is no warrant for rendering *Hauptstück* as "article": it means "major part." Kant's *Critique of Pure Reason* and *Critique of Practical Reason* are both divided into *Hauptstücke*. So is Nietzsche's own *Human, All-Too-Human*. The term is obviously particularly appropriate for books subdivided into many short sections.

deception? or selfless deeds out of selfishness? or the pure and sunlike gaze of the sage out of lust? Such origins are impossible; whoever dreams of them is a fool, indeed worse; the things of the highest value must have another, *peculiar* origin—they cannot be derived from this transitory, seductive, deceptive, paltry world, from this turmoil of delusion and lust. Rather from the lap of Being, the intransitory, the hidden god, the 'thing-in-itself'—there must be their basis, and nowhere else."

This way of judging constitutes the typical prejudgment and prejudice which give away the metaphysicians of all ages; this kind of valuation looms in the background of all their logical procedures; it is on account of this "faith" that they trouble themselves about "knowledge," about something that is finally baptized solemnly as "the truth." The fundamental faith of the metaphysicians is *the faith in opposite values*.[2] It has not even occurred to the most cautious among them that one might have a doubt right here at the threshold where it was surely most necessary—even if they vowed to themselves, *"de omnibus dubitandum."* [3]

For one may doubt, first, whether there are any opposites at all, and secondly whether these popular valuations and opposite values on which the metaphysicians put their seal, are not perhaps merely foreground estimates, only provisional perspectives, perhaps even from some nook, perhaps from below, frog perspectives, as it were, to borrow an expression painters use. For all the value that the true, the truthful, the selfless may deserve, it would still be possible that a higher and more fundamental value for life might have to be ascribed to deception, selfishness, and lust. It might even be possible that what constitutes the value of these good and revered things is precisely that they are insidiously related, tied to, and involved with these wicked, seemingly opposite things—maybe even one with them in essence. Maybe!

But who has the will to concern himself with such dangerous maybes? For that, one really has to wait for the advent of a new

---

[2] Nietzsche's attack on this faith is prefigured in the title of the book. This aphorism invites comparison with the first aphorism of *Human, All-Too-Human.*

[3] "All is to be doubted." Descartes.

species of philosophers, such as have somehow another and converse taste and propensity from those we have known so far—philosophers of the dangerous "maybe" in every sense.

And in all seriousness: I see such new philosophers coming up.

3

After having looked long enough between the philosopher's lines and fingers, I say to myself: by far the greater part of conscious thinking must still be included among instinctive activities, and that goes even for philosophical thinking. We have to relearn here, as one has had to relearn about heredity and what is "innate." As the act of birth deserves no consideration in the whole process and procedure of heredity, so "being conscious" is not in any decisive sense the *opposite* of what is instinctive: most of the conscious thinking of a philosopher is secretly guided and forced into certain channels by his instincts.

Behind all logic and its seeming sovereignty of movement, too, there stand valuations or, more clearly, physiological demands for the preservation of a certain type of life. For example, that the definite should be worth more than the indefinite, and mere appearance worth less than "truth"—such estimates might be, in spite of their regulative importance for *us,* nevertheless mere foreground estimates, a certain kind of *niaiserie*[4] which may be necessary for the preservation of just such beings as we are. Supposing, that is, that not just man is the "measure of things" [5]—

4

The falseness of a judgment is for us not necessarily an objection to a judgment; in this respect our new language may sound strangest. The question is to what extent it is life-promoting, life-preserving, species-preserving, perhaps even species-cultivating.

---

[4] Folly, stupidity, silliness: one of Nietzsche's favorite French words.
[5] "Man is the measure of all things." Protagoras, born about 480 B.C.

And we are fundamentally inclined to claim that the falsest judgments (which include the synthetic judgments *a priori*)[6] are the
most indispensable for us; that without accepting the fictions of
logic, without measuring reality against the purely invented world
of the unconditional and self-identical, without a constant falsification of the world by means of numbers, man could not live—that
renouncing false judgments would mean renouncing life and a
denial of life. To recognize untruth as a condition of life—that certainly means resisting accustomed value feelings in a dangerous
way; and a philosophy that risks this would by that token alone
place itself beyond good and evil.

5

What provokes one to look at all philosophers half suspiciously, half mockingly, is not that one discovers again and again
how innocent they are—how often and how easily they make mistakes and go astray; in short, their childishness and childlikeness—
but that they are not honest enough in their work, although they all
make a lot of virtuous noise when the problem of truthfulness is
touched even remotely. They all pose as if they had discovered and
reached their real opinions through the self-development of a
cold, pure, divinely unconcerned dialectic (as opposed to the mystics of every rank, who are more honest and doltish—and talk of
"inspiration"); while at bottom it is an assumption, a hunch, indeed a kind of "inspiration"—most often a desire of the heart that
has been filtered and made abstract—that they defend with reasons they have sought after the fact. They are all advocates who resent that name, and for the most part even wily spokesmen for

---

[6] One of Kant's central questions was, "How are synthetic judgments *a
priori* possible?" He meant judgments that are known for certain to be true,
independently of experience, but not by definition. His examples include the
judgment that every event has a cause. Hans Vaihinger, a leading Kant
scholar who published a book on *Nietzsche als Philosoph* (1902; 4th ed.
1916), later published his own theory of necessary fictions under the title,
Die Philosophie des Als-Ob (1911; English tr. by C. K. Ogden, 1924: *The
Philosophy of "As If"*), devoting the final chapter to a detailed discussion
of Nietzsche's similar ideas. Cf. section 11 below.

their prejudices which they baptize "truths"—and *very* far from having the courage of the conscience that admits this, precisely this, to itself; very far from having the good taste of the courage which also lets this be known, whether to warn an enemy or friend, or, from exuberance, to mock itself.

The equally stiff and decorous Tartuffery of the old Kant as he lures us on the dialectical bypaths that lead to his "categorical imperative"—really lead astray and seduce—this spectacle makes us smile, as we are fastidious and find it quite amusing to watch closely the subtle tricks of old moralists and preachers of morals. Or consider the hocus-pocus of mathematical form with which Spinoza clad his philosophy—really "the love of *his* wisdom," to render that word fairly and squarely—in mail and mask, to strike terror at the very outset into the heart of any assailant who should dare to glance at that invincible maiden and Pallas Athena: how much personal timidity and vulnerability this masquerade of a sick hermit betrays!

6

Gradually it has become clear to me what every great philosophy so far has been: namely, the personal confession of its author and a kind of involuntary and unconscious memoir; also that the moral (or immoral) intentions in every philosophy constituted the real germ of life from which the whole plant had grown.

Indeed, if one would explain how the abstrusest metaphysical claims of a philosopher really came about, it is always well (and wise) to ask first: at what morality does all this (does *he*) aim? Accordingly, I do not believe that a "drive to knowledge" is the father of philosophy; but rather that another drive has, here as elsewhere, employed understanding (and misunderstanding) as a mere instrument. But anyone who considers the basic drives of man to see to what extent they may have been at play just here as *inspiring* spirits (or demons and kobolds) will find that all of them have done philosophy at some time—and that every single one of them would like only too well to represent just *itself* as the ultimate purpose of existence and the legitimate *master* of all the other drives. For every drive wants to be master—and it attempts to philosophize in *that spirit*.

To be sure: among scholars who are really scientific men, things may be different—"better," if you like—there you may really find something like a drive for knowledge, some small, independent clockwork that, once well wound, works on vigorously *without* any essential participation from all the other drives of the scholar. The real "interests" of the scholar therefore lie usually somewhere else—say, in his family, or in making money, or in politics. Indeed, it is almost a matter of total indifference whether his little machine is placed at this or that spot in science, and whether the "promising" young worker turns himself into a good philologist or an expert on fungi or a chemist: it does not *characterize* him that he becomes this or that. In the philosopher, conversely, there is nothing whatever that is impersonal;[7] and above all, his morality bears decided and decisive witness to *who he is*— that is, in what order of rank the innermost drives of his nature stand in relation to each other.

7

How malicious philosophers can be! I know of nothing more venomous than the joke Epicurus permitted himself against Plato and the Platonists; he called them *Dionysiokolakes*. That means literally—and this is the foreground meaning—"flatterers of Dionysius," in other words, tyrant's baggage and lickspittles; but in addition to this he also wants to say, "they are all *actors*, there is nothing genuine about them" (for *Dionysokolax* was a popular name for an actor).[8] And the latter is really the malice that Epicurus aimed at Plato: he was peeved by the grandiose manner, the *mise en scène*[9] at which Plato and his disciples were so expert—at

---

[7] Nietzsche is thinking of the "great" philosophers. Now that there are literally thousands of "philosophers," these tend to be more akin to their colleagues in other departments than to the men discussed here.

[8] The reference is to Epicurus' fragment 238, and the ambiguity is due to the fact that Dionysius was the name of the Sicilian tyrant whom Plato had tried for several years to convert to his own philosophy.

[9] Staging.

which Epicurus was not an expert—he, that old schoolmaster from Samos, who sat, hidden away, in his little garden at Athens and wrote three hundred books—who knows? perhaps from rage and ambition against Plato?

It took a hundred years until Greece found out who this garden god, Epicurus, had been.— Did they find out?—

8

There is a point in every philosophy when the philosopher's "conviction" appears on the stage—or to use the language of an ancient Mystery:

Adventavit asinus,
Pulcher et fortissimus.[10]

9

"According to nature" you want to *live?* O you noble Stoics, what deceptive words these are! Imagine a being like nature, wasteful beyond measure, indifferent beyond measure, without purposes and consideration, without mercy and justice, fertile and desolate and uncertain at the same time; imagine indifference itself as a power—how *could* you live according to this indifference? Living—is that not precisely wanting to be other than this nature? Is not living—estimating, preferring, being unjust, being limited, wanting to be different? And supposing your imperative "live according to nature" meant at bottom as much as "live according to life"—how could you *not* do that? Why make a principle of what you yourselves are and must be?

In truth, the matter is altogether different: while you pretend rapturously to read the canon of your law in nature, you want something opposite, you strange actors and self-deceivers! Your pride wants to impose your morality, your ideal, on nature—even on nature—and incorporate them in her; you demand that she should be nature "according to the Stoa," and you would like all

---

[10] "The ass arrived, beautiful and most brave."

existence to exist only after your own image—as an immense eternal glorification and generalization of Stoicism. For all your love of truth, you have forced yourselves so long, so persistently, so rigidly-hypnotically to see nature the wrong way, namely Stoically, that you are no longer able to see her differently. And some abysmal arrogance finally still inspires you with the insane hope that *because* you know how to tyrannize yourselves—Stoicism is self-tyranny—nature, too, lets herself be tyrannized: is not the Stoic—a *piece* of nature?

But this is an ancient, eternal story: what formerly happened with the Stoics still happens today, too, as soon as any philosophy begins to believe in itself. It always creates the world in its own image; it cannot do otherwise. Philosophy is this tyrannical drive itself, the most spiritual will to power, to the "creation of the world," to the *causa prima*.[11]

10

The eagerness and subtlety—I might even say, shrewdness—with which the problem of "the real and the apparent world" is today attacked all over Europe makes one think and wonder; and anyone who hears nothing in the background except a "will to truth," certainly does not have the best of ears. In rare and isolated instances it may really be the case that such a will to truth, some extravagant and adventurous courage, a metaphysician's ambition to hold a hopeless position, may participate and ultimately prefer even a handful of "certainty" to a whole carload of beautiful possibilities; there may actually be puritanical fanatics of conscience who prefer even a certain nothing to an uncertain something to lie down on—and die. But this is nihilism and the sign of a despairing, mortally weary soul—however courageous the gestures of such a virtue may look.

It seems, however, to be otherwise with stronger and livelier thinkers who are still eager for life. When they side *against* appearance, and speak of "perspective," with a new arrogance; when they

---

11 First cause.

rank the credibility of their own bodies about as low as the credibility of the visual evidence that "the earth stands still," and thus, apparently in good humor, let their securest possession go (for in what does one at present believe more firmly than in one's body?) —who knows if they are not trying at bottom to win back something that was formerly an even *securer* possession, something of the ancient domain of the faith of former times, perhaps the "immortal soul," perhaps "the old God," in short, ideas by which one could live better, that is to say, more vigorously and cheerfully, than by "modern ideas"? There is *mistrust* of these modern ideas in this attitude, a disbelief in all that has been constructed yesterday and today; there is perhaps some slight admixture of satiety and scorn, unable to endure any longer the *bric-a-brac* of concepts of the most diverse origin, which is the form in which so-called positivism offers itself on the market today; a disgust of the more fastidious taste at the village-fair motleyness and patchiness of all these reality-philosophasters in whom there is nothing new or genuine, except this motleyness. In this, it seems to me, we should agree with these skeptical anti-realists and knowledge-microscopists of today: their instinct, which repels them from *modern* reality, is unrefuted—what do their retrograde bypaths concern us! The main thing about them is *not* that they wish to go "back," but that they wish to get—*away*. A little *more* strength, flight, courage, and artistic power, and they would want to *rise*—not return!

11

It seems to me that today attempts are made everywhere to divert attention from the actual influence Kant exerted on German philosophy, and especially to ignore prudently the value he set upon himself. Kant was first and foremost proud of his table of categories; with that in his hand he said: "This is the most difficult thing that could ever be undertaken on behalf of metaphysics."

Let us only understand this "could be"! He was proud of having *discovered* a new faculty in man, the faculty for synthetic judgments, *a priori*. Suppose he deceived himself in this matter; the development and rapid flourishing of German philosophy depended nevertheless on his pride, and on the eager rivalry of the younger generation to discover, if possible, something still prouder—at all events "new faculties"!

But let us reflect; it is high time to do so. "How are synthetic judgments *a priori possible?*" Kant asked himself—and what really is his answer? *"By virtue of a faculty"* [12]—but unfortunately not in five words, but so circumstantially, venerably, and with such a display of German profundity and curlicues that people simply failed to note the comical *niaiserie allemande*[13] involved in such an answer. People were actually beside themselves with delight over this new faculty, and the jubilation reached its climax when Kant further discovered a moral faculty in man—for at that time the Germans were still moral and not yet addicted to *Realpolitik*.

The honeymoon of German philosophy arrived. All the young theologians of the Tübingen seminary went into the bushes —all looking for "faculties." And what did they not find—in that innocent, rich, and still youthful period of the German spirit, to which romanticism, the malignant fairy, piped and sang, when one could not yet distinguish between "finding" and "inventing"! [14] Above all, a faculty for the "surprasensible": Schelling christened it intellectual intuition, and thus gratified the most heartfelt cravings of the Germans, whose cravings were at bottom pious. One can do no greater wrong to the whole of this exuberant and enthusiastic movement, which was really youthfulness, however boldly it disguised itself in hoary and senile concepts, than to take it seriously, or worse, to treat it with moral indignation. Enough, one grew older and the dream vanished. A time came when people scratched their heads, and they still scratch them today. One had been dreaming, and first and foremost—old Kant. "By virtue of a faculty"—he had said, or at least meant. But is that—an answer? An explanation? Or is it not rather merely a repetition of the ques-

---

12 *Vermöge eines Vermögens:* by virtue of some virtue, or by means of a means.
13 German foolishness.
14 *"Finden"* und *"erfinden."*

tion? How does opium induce sleep? "By virtue of a faculty," namely the *virtus dormitiva,* replies the doctor in Molière,

> *Quia est in eo virtus dormitiva,*
> *Cujus est natura sensus assoupire.*[15]

But such replies belong in comedy, and it is high time to replace the Kantian question, "How are synthetic judgments *a priori* possible?" by another question, "Why is belief in such judgments *necessary?*"—and to comprehend that such judgments must be *believed* to be true, for the sake of the preservation of creatures like ourselves; though they might, of course, be *false* judgments for all that! Or to speak more clearly and coarsely: synthetic judgments *a priori* should not "be possible" at all; we have no right to them; in our mouths they are nothing but false judgments. Only, of course, the belief in their truth is necessary, as a foreground belief and visual evidence belonging to the perspective optics of life.

Finally, to call to mind the enormous influence that "German philosophy"—I hope you understand its right to quotation marks—has exercised throughout the whole of Europe, there is no doubt that a certain *virtus dormitiva* had a share in it: it was a delight to the noble idlers, the virtuous, the mystics, artists, three-quarter Christians, and political obscurantists of all nations, to find, thanks to German philosophy, an antidote to the still predominant sensualism which overflowed from the last century into this, in short—"*sensus assoupire.*"

12

As for materialistic atomism, it is one of the best refuted theories there are, and in Europe perhaps no one in the learned world is now so unscholarly as to attach serious significance to it, except for convenient household use (as an abbreviation of the means of expression)—thanks chiefly to the Dalmatian Boscovich: he and the Pole Copernicus have been the greatest and most successful opponents of visual evidence so far. For while Copernicus

---

[15] "Because it contains a sleepy faculty whose nature it is to put the senses to sleep."

has persuaded us to believe, contrary to all the senses, that the earth does *not* stand fast, Boscovich has taught us to abjure the belief in the last part of the earth that "stood fast"—the belief in "substance," in "matter," in the earth-residuum and particle-atom:[16] it is the greatest triumph over the senses that has been gained on earth so far.

One must, however, go still further, and also declare war, relentless war unto death, against the "atomistic need" which still leads a dangerous afterlife in places where no one suspects it, just like the more celebrated "metaphysical need": one must also, first of all, give the finishing stroke to that other and more calamitous atomism which Christianity has taught best and longest, the *soul atomism*. Let it be permitted to designate by this expression the belief which regards the soul as something indestructible, eternal, indivisible, as a monad, as an *atomon:* this belief ought to be expelled from science! Between ourselves, it is not at all necessary to get rid of "the soul" at the same time, and thus to renounce one of the most ancient and venerable hypotheses—as happens frequently to clumsy naturalists who can hardly touch on "the soul" without immediately losing it. But the way is open for new versions and refinements of the soul-hypothesis; and such conceptions as "mortal soul," and "soul as subjective multiplicity," and "soul as social structure of the drives and affects," [17] want henceforth to

---

[16] "Boscovich, an eighteenth-century Jesuit philosopher somewhat out of the main stream of science . . . had defined atoms only as centers of force, and not as particles of matter in which powers somehow inhere" (Charles Coulston Gillispie, *The Edge of Objectivity: An Essay in the History of Scientific Ideas,* Princeton, N.J., Princeton University Press, 1960, p. 455).
[17] *Affekt:* I have rendered this term consistently as "affect": good dictionaries include the relevant meanings. "Feeling" comes close to Nietzsche's meaning but fails to suggest the fact that the term is somewhat technical and carries overtones of Spinoza's *affectus* and a long philosophical tradition. Moreover, "feeling" is needed to render *Gefühl,* which occurs several times in this section.

In his discussion of Spinoza's *affectus,* Stuart Hampshire uses "affection" and places the word in quotation marks (*Spinoza,* Baltimore, Penguin Books, 1951, pp. 135f.). In James Mark Baldwin's *Dictionary of Philosophy and Psychology,* vol. I (1901), "affect" is defined as "A stimulus or motive to action which is AFFECTIVE (q.v.) or felt, not presented as an end," a usage "suggested by Baldwin," while "affection" is suggested as

have citizens' rights in science. When the *new* psychologist puts an end to the superstitions which have so far flourished with almost tropical luxuriance around the idea of the soul, he practically exiles himself into a new desert and a new suspicion—it is possible that the older psychologists had a merrier and more comfortable time of it; eventually, however, he finds that precisely thereby he also condemns himself to *invention*—and—who knows?—perhaps to discovery.

13

Physiologists should think before putting down the instinct of self-preservation as the cardinal instinct of an organic being. A living thing seeks above all to *discharge* its strength—life itself is *will to power;* self-preservation is only one of the indirect and most frequent *results.*

In short, here as everywhere else, let us beware of *superfluous* teleological principles—one of which is the instinct of self-preservation (we owe it to Spinoza's inconsistency).[18] Thus method, which must be essentially economy of principles, demands it.

14

It is perhaps just dawning on five or six minds that physics, too, is only an interpretation and exegesis of the world (to suit us, if I may say so!) and *not* a world-explanation; but insofar as it is

---

an equivalent of the German *Affekt,* which is defined as "passing emotional states . . . The best writers distinguish it from passion, as having less vehemence, and as less distinctly, if at all, connected with a sensuous basis. . . . St. Augustine, as quoted and adopted by Aquinas, says: 'Those mental states (*motus animi*) which the Greeks call *pathē,* and Cicero *perturbationes,* are by some called *affectus,* or *affectiones* by others, keeping to the literal rendering of the Greek *passiones.*'"

My reason for preferring "affect" to "affection" is that the former is readily recognized as a technical term, while the latter is very apt to be misunderstood as suggesting a mild form of love.

[18] Nietzsche admired Spinoza for, among other things, his critique of teleology.

based on belief in the senses, it is regarded as more, and for a long time to come must be regarded as more—namely, as an explanation. Eyes and fingers speak in its favor, visual evidence and palpableness do, too: this strikes an age with fundamentally plebeian tastes as fascinating, persuasive, and *convincing*—after all, it follows instinctively the canon of truth of eternally popular sensualism. What is clear, what is "explained"? Only what can be seen and felt—every problem has to be pursued to that point. Conversely, the charm of the Platonic way of thinking, which was a *noble* way of thinking, consisted precisely in *resistance* to obvious sense-evidence—perhaps among men who enjoyed even stronger and more demanding senses than our contemporaries, but who knew how to find a higher triumph in remaining masters of their senses—and this by means of pale, cold, gray concept nets which they threw over the motley whirl of the senses—the mob of the senses, as Plato said. In this overcoming of the world, and interpreting of the world in the manner of Plato, there was an *enjoyment* different from that which the physicists of today offer us—and also the Darwinists and anti-teleologists among the workers in physiology, with their principle of the "smallest possible force" and the greatest possible stupidity. "Where man cannot find anything to see or to grasp, he has no further business"—that is certainly an imperative different from the Platonic one, but it may be the right imperative for a tough, industrious race of machinists and bridge-builders of the future, who have nothing but *rough* work to do.

15

To study physiology with a clear conscience, one must insist that the sense organs are *not* phenomena in the sense of idealistic philosophy; as such they could not be causes! Sensualism, therefore, at least as a regulative hypothesis, if not as a heuristic principle.

What? And others even say that the external world is the work of our organs? But then our body, as a part of this external world, would be the work of our organs! But then our organs themselves would be—the work of our organs! It seems to me that this is a complete *reductio ad absurdum,*[19] assuming that the concept of a *causa sui*[20] is something fundamentally absurd. Consequently, the external world is *not* the work of our organs—?

16

There are still harmless self-observers who believe that there are "immediate certainties"; for example, "I think," or as the superstition of Schopenhauer put it, "I will"; as though knowledge here got hold of its object purely and nakedly as "the thing in itself," without any falsification on the part of either the subject or the object. But that "immediate certainty," as well as "absolute knowledge" and the "thing in itself," involve a *contradictio in adjecto,*[21] I shall repeat a hundred times; we really ought to free ourselves from the seduction of words!

Let the people suppose that knowledge means knowing things entirely; the philosopher must say to himself: When I analyze the process that is expressed in the sentence, "I think," I find a whole series of daring assertions that would be difficult, perhaps impossible, to prove; for example, that it is *I* who think, that there must necessarily be something that thinks, that thinking is an activity and operation on the part of a being who is thought of as a cause, that there is an "ego," and, finally, that it is already determined what is to be designated by thinking—that I *know* what thinking is. For if I had not already decided within myself what it is, by what standard could I determine whether that which is just happening is not perhaps "willing" or "feeling"? In short, the assertion "I think" assumes that I *compare* my state at the present moment with other states of myself which I know, in order to determine what it is; on account of this retrospective connection with further "knowledge," it has, at any rate, no immediate certainty for me.

In place of the "immediate certainty" in which the people may believe in the case at hand, the philosopher thus finds a series of

---

[19] Reduction to the absurd.
[20] Something that is its own cause—a term traditionally applied to God.
[21] Contradiction between the noun and the adjective.

metaphysical questions presented to him, truly searching questions of the intellect; to wit: "From where do I get the concept of thinking? Why do I believe in cause and effect? What gives me the right to speak of an ego, and even of an ego as cause, and finally of an ego as the cause of thought?" Whoever ventures to answer these metaphysical questions at once by an appeal to a sort of *intuitive* perception, like the person who says, "I think, and know that this, at least, is true, actual, and certain"—will encounter a smile and two question marks from a philosopher nowadays. "Sir," the philosopher will perhaps give him to understand, "it is improbable that you are not mistaken; but why insist on the truth?"—

17

With regard to the superstitions of logicians, I shall never tire of emphasizing a small terse fact, which these superstitious minds hate to concede—namely, that a thought comes when "it" wishes, and not when "I" wish, so that it is a falsification of the facts of the case to say that the subject "I" is the condition of the predicate "think." *It* thinks; but that this "it" is precisely the famous old "ego" is, to put it mildly, only a supposition, an assertion, and assuredly not an "immediate certainty." After all, one has even gone too far with this "it thinks"—even the "it" contains an *interpretation* of the process, and does not belong to the process itself. One infers here according to the grammatical habit: "Thinking is an activity; every activity requires an agent; consequently—"

It was pretty much according to the same schema that the older atomism sought, besides the operating "power," that lump of matter in which it resides and out of which it operates—the atom. More rigorous minds, however, learned at last to get along without this "earth-residuum," and perhaps some day we shall accustom ourselves, including the logicians, to get along without the little "it" (which is all that is left of the honest little old ego).

18

It is certainly not the least charm of a theory that it is refutable; it is precisely thereby that it attracts subtler minds. It seems that the hundred-times-refuted theory of a "free will" owes its persistence to this charm alone; again and again someone comes along who feels he is strong enough to refute it.

19

Philosophers are accustomed to speak of the will as if it were the best-known thing in the world; indeed, Schopenhauer has given us to understand that the will alone is really known to us, absolutely and completely known, without subtraction or addition. But again and again it seems to me that in this case, too, Schopenhauer only did what philosophers are in the habit of doing—he adopted a *popular prejudice* and exaggerated it. Willing seems to me to be above all something *complicated,* something that is a unit only as a word—and it is precisely in this one word that the popular prejudice lurks, which has defeated the always inadequate caution of philosophers. So let us for once be more cautious, let us be "unphilosophical": let us say that in all willing there is, first, a plurality of sensations, namely, the sensation of the state *"away from which,"* the sensation of the state *"towards which,"* the sensations of this *"from"* and *"towards"* themselves, and then also an accompanying muscular sensation, which, even without our putting into motion "arms and legs," begins its action by force of habit as soon as we "will" anything.

Therefore, just as sensations (and indeed many kinds of sensations) are to be recognized as ingredients of the will, so, secondly, should thinking also: in every act of the will there is a ruling thought—let us not imagine it possible to sever this thought from the "willing," as if any will would then remain over!

Third, the will is not only a complex of sensation and thinking, but it is above all an *affect,* and specifically the affect of the command. That which is termed "freedom of the will" is essentially the affect of superiority in relation to him who must obey: "I am free, 'he' must obey"—this consciousness is inherent in every will; and equally so the straining of the attention, the straight look that fixes itself exclusively on one aim, the unconditional evaluation that "this and nothing else is necessary now," the inward certainty that obedience will be rendered—and whatever else belongs to the position of the commander. A man who *wills* commands something within himself that renders obedience, or that he believes renders obedience.

But now let us notice what is strangest about the will—this manifold thing for which the people have only one word: inasmuch as in the given circumstances we are at the same time the commanding *and* the obeying parties, and as the obeying party we know the sensations of constraint, impulsion, pressure, resistance, and motion, which usually begin immediately after the act of will; inasmuch as, on the other hand, we are accustomed to disregard this duality, and to deceive ourselves about it by means of the synthetic concept "I," a whole series of erroneous conclusions, and consequently of false evaluations of the will itself, has become attached to the act of willing—to such a degree that he who wills believes sincerely that willing *suffices* for action. Since in the great majority of cases there has been exercise of will only when the effect of the command—that is, obedience; that is, the action—was to be *expected,* the *appearance* has translated itself into the feeling, as if there were *a necessity of effect.* In short, he who wills believes with a fair amount of certainty that will and action are somehow one; he ascribes the success, the carrying out of the willing, to the will itself, and thereby enjoys an increase of the sensation of power which accompanies all success.

"Freedom of the will"—that is the expression for the complex state of delight of the person exercising volition, who commands and at the same time identifies himself with the executor of the order—who, as such, enjoys also the triumph over obstacles, but thinks within himself that it was really his will itself that overcame them. In this way the person exercising volition adds the feelings of delight of his successful executive instruments, the useful "under-wills" or under-souls—indeed, our body is but a social structure composed of many souls—to his feelings of delight as commander. *L'effet c'est moi:*[22] what happens here is what happens in every well-constructed and happy commonwealth; namely, the governing

---

22 "*I* am the effect."

class identifies itself with the successes of the commonwealth. In all willing it is absolutely a question of commanding and obeying, on the basis, as already said, of a social structure composed of many "souls." Hence a philosopher should claim the right to include willing as such within the sphere of morals—morals being understood as the doctrine of the relations of supremacy under which the phenomenon of "life" comes to be.

20

That individual philosophical concepts are not anything capricious or autonomously evolving, but grow up in connection and relationship with each other; that, however suddenly and arbitrarily they seem to appear in the history of thought, they nevertheless belong just as much to a system as all the members of the fauna of a continent—is betrayed in the end also by the fact that the most diverse philosophers keep filling in a definite fundamental scheme of possible philosophies. Under an invisible spell, they always revolve once more in the same orbit; however independent of each other they may feel themselves with their critical or systematic wills, something within them leads them, something impels them in a definite order, one after the other—to wit, the innate systematic structure and relationship of their concepts. Their thinking is, in fact, far less a discovery than a recognition, a remembering, a return and a homecoming to a remote, primordial, and inclusive household of the soul, out of which those concepts grew originally: philosophizing is to this extent a kind of atavism of the highest order.

The strange family resemblance of all Indian, Greek, and German philosophizing is explained easily enough. Where there is affinity of languages, it cannot fail, owing to the common philosophy of grammar—I mean, owing to the unconscious domination and guidance by similar grammatical functions—that everything is prepared at the outset for a similar development and sequence of philosophical systems; just as the way seems barred against certain other possibilities of world-interpretation. It is highly probable that philosophers within the domain of the Ural-Altaic languages (where the concept of the subject is least developed) look otherwise "into the world," and will be found on paths of thought different from those of the Indo-Germanic peoples and the Muslims: the spell of certain grammatical functions is ultimately also the spell of *physiological* valuations and racial conditions.

So much by way of rejecting Locke's superficiality regarding the origin of ideas.

21

The *causa sui* is the best self-contradiction that has been conceived so far, it is a sort of rape and perversion of logic; but the extravagant pride of man has managed to entangle itself profoundly and frightfully with just this nonsense. The desire for "freedom of the will" in the superlative metaphysical sense, which still holds sway, unfortunately, in the minds of the half-educated; the desire to bear the entire and ultimate responsibility for one's actions oneself, and to absolve God, the world, ancestors, chance, and society involves nothing less than to be precisely this *causa sui* and, with more than Münchhausen's audacity, to pull oneself up into existence by the hair, out of the swamps of nothingness.[23] Sup-

---

[23] Cf. Sartre's famous dictum: "If man as the existentialist sees him is not definable, it is because to begin with he is nothing. He will not be anything until later, and then he will be what he makes of himself. . . . Man simply is. Not that he is simply what he conceives himself to be, but he is what he wills . . . Man is nothing else but that which he makes of himself. That is the first principle of existentialism. . . . Before that projection of the self nothing exists . . . Man is responsible for what he is. Thus, the first effect of existentialism is that it puts every man in possession of himself as he is, and places the entire responsibility for his existence squarely upon his own shoulders" ("Existentialism Is a Humanism," included in *Existentialism from Dostoevsky to Sartre,* ed. Walter Kaufmann, pp. 290f.).

Reading this without knowing that *Beyond Good and Evil* was published in 1886 and Sartre's lecture in 1946, one would scarcely guess at Nietzsche's immense influence on existentialism in general and Sartre in particular; one might even suppose that Nietzsche was here polemicizing against Sartre. Cf. also section 8 of "The Four Great Errors" in *Twilight of the Idols* (*Portable Nietzsche,* p. 500), where some implications of the above passage in *Beyond Good and Evil* are developed briefly.

pose someone were thus to see through the boorish simplicity of this celebrated concept of "free will" and put it out of his head altogether, I beg of him to carry his "enlightenment" a step further, and also put out of his head the contrary of this monstrous conception of "free will": I mean "unfree will," which amounts to a misuse of cause and effect. One should not wrongly reify "cause" and "effect," as the natural scientists do (and whoever, like them, now "naturalizes" in his thinking), according to the prevailing mechanical doltishness which makes the cause press and push until it "effects" its end; one should use "cause" and "effect" only as pure concepts, that is to say, as conventional fictions for the purpose of designation and communication—*not* for explanation. In the "in-itself" there is nothing of "causal connections," of "necessity," or of "psychological non-freedom"; there the effect does *not* follow the cause, there is no rule of "law." It is *we* alone who have devised cause, sequence, for-each-other, relativity, constraint, number, law, freedom, motive, and purpose; and when we project and mix this symbol world into things as if it existed "in itself," we act once more as we have always acted—*mythologically*. The "unfree will" is mythology; in real life it is only a matter of *strong* and *weak* wills.

It is almost always a symptom of what is lacking in himself when a thinker senses in every "causal connection" and "psychological necessity" something of constraint, need, compulsion to obey, pressure, and unfreedom; it is suspicious to have such feelings—the person betrays himself. And in general, if I have observed correctly, the "unfreedom of the will" is regarded as a problem from two entirely opposite standpoints, but always in a profoundly *personal* manner: some will not give up their "responsibility," their belief in *themselves,* the personal right to *their* merits at any price (the vain races belong to this class). Others, on the contrary, do not wish to be answerable for anything, or blamed for anything, and owing to an inward self-contempt, seek to *lay the blame for themselves somewhere else.* The latter, when they write books, are in the habit today of taking the side of criminals; a sort of socialist pity is their most attractive disguise. And as a matter of fact, the fatalism of the weak-willed embellishes itself surprisingly when it can pose as *"la religion de la souffrance humaine"*;[24] that is *its* "good taste."

22

Forgive me as an old philologist who cannot desist from the malice of putting his finger on bad modes of interpretation: but "nature's conformity to law," of which you physicists talk so proudly, as though—why, it exists only owing to your interpretation and bad "philology." It is no matter of fact, no "text," but rather only a naïvely humanitarian emendation and perversion of meaning, with which you make abundant concessions to the democratic instincts of the modern soul! "Everywhere equality before the law; nature is no different in that respect, no better off than we are"—a fine instance of ulterior motivation, in which the plebeian antagonism to everything privileged and autocratic as well as a second and more refined atheism are disguised once more. *"Ni Dieu, ni maître"* [25]—that is what you, too, want; and therefore "cheers for the law of nature!"—is it not so? But as said above, that is interpretation, not text; and somebody might come along who, with opposite intentions and modes of interpretation, could read out of the same "nature," and with regard to the same phenomena, rather the tyrannically inconsiderate and relentless enforcement of claims of power—an interpreter who would picture the unexceptional and unconditional aspects of all "will to power" so vividly that almost every word, even the word "tyranny" itself, would eventually seem unsuitable, or a weakening and attenuating metaphor—being too human—but he might, nevertheless, end by asserting the same about this world as you do, namely, that it has a "necessary" and "calculable" course, *not* because laws obtain in it, but because they are absolutely *lacking,* and every power draws its ultimate consequences at every moment. Supposing that this also is only in-

---

24 "The religion of human suffering."
25 "Neither God nor master."

terpretation—and you will be eager enough to make this objection?—well, so much the better.

23

All psychology so far has got stuck in moral prejudices and fears; it has not dared to descend into the depths. To understand it as morphology and *the doctrine of the development of the will to power,* as I do—nobody has yet come close to doing this even in thought—insofar as it is permissible to recognize in what has been written so far a symptom of what has so far been kept silent. The power of moral prejudices has penetrated deeply into the most spiritual world, which would seem to be the coldest and most devoid of presuppositions, and has obviously operated in an injurious, inhibiting, blinding, and distorting manner. A proper physio-psychology has to contend with unconscious resistance in the heart of the investigator, it has "the heart" against it: even a doctrine of the reciprocal dependence of the "good" and the "wicked" drives, causes (as refined immorality) distress and aversion in a still hale and hearty conscience—still more so, a doctrine of the derivation of all good impulses from wicked ones. If, however, a person should regard even the affects of hatred, envy, covetousness, and the lust to rule as conditions of life, as factors which, fundamentally and essentially, must be present in the general economy of life (and must, therefore, be further enhanced if life is to be further enhanced)— he will suffer from such a view of things as from seasickness. And yet even this hypothesis is far from being the strangest and most painful in this immense and almost new domain of dangerous insights; and there are in fact a hundred good reasons why everyone should keep away from it who—*can.*

On the other hand, if one has once drifted there with one's bark, well! all right! let us clench our teeth! let us open our eyes and keep our hand firm on the helm! We sail right *over* morality, we crush, we destroy perhaps the remains of our own morality by daring to make our voyage there—but what matter are *we!* Never yet did a *profounder* world of insight reveal itself to daring travelers and adventurers, and the psychologist who thus "makes a sacrifice"—it is *not* the *sacrifizio dell' intelletto*,[26] on the contrary! —will at least be entitled to demand in return that psychology shall be recognized again[27] as the queen of the sciences, for whose service and preparation the other sciences exist. For psychology is now again the path to the fundamental problems.

---

[26] Sacrifice of the intellect.
[27] "Again" is surely open to objections.

PART TWO

THE FREE SPIRIT

Part Two

24

O *sancta simplicitas!* [1] In what strange simplification and falsification man lives! One can never cease wondering once one has acquired eyes for this marvel! How we have made everything around us clear and free and easy and simple! how we have been able to give our senses a passport to everything superficial, our thoughts a divine desire for wanton leaps and wrong inferences! how from the beginning we have contrived to retain our ignorance in order to enjoy an almost inconceivable freedom, lack of scruple and caution, heartiness, and gaiety of life—in order to enjoy life! And only on this now solid, granite foundation of ignorance could knowledge rise so far—the will to knowledge on the foundation of a far more powerful will: the will to ignorance, to the uncertain, to the untrue! Not as its opposite, but—as its refinement!

Even if *language,* here as elsewhere, will not get over its awkwardness, and will continue to talk of opposites where there are only degrees and many subtleties of gradation; even if the inveterate Tartuffery of morals, which now belongs to our unconquerable "flesh and blood," infects the words even of those of us who know better—here and there we understand it and laugh at the way in which precisely science at its best seeks most to keep us in this *simplified,* thoroughly artificial, suitably constructed and suitably falsified world—at the way in which, willy-nilly, it loves error, because, being alive, it loves life.

25

After such a cheerful commencement, a serious word would like to be heard; it appeals to the most serious. Take care, philosophers and friends, of knowledge, and beware of martyrdom! Of

---

[1] Holy simplicity!

suffering "for the truth's sake"! Even of defending yourselves! It spoils all the innocence and fine neutrality of your conscience; it makes you headstrong against objections and red rags; it stupefies, animalizes, and brutalizes when in the struggle with danger, slander, suspicion, expulsion, and even worse consequences of hostility, you have to pose as protectors of truth upon earth—as though "the truth" were such an innocuous and incompetent creature as to require protectors! and you of all people, you knights of the most sorrowful countenance,[2] dear loafers and cobweb-spinners of the spirit! After all, you know well enough that it cannot be of any consequence if *you* of all people are proved right; you know that no philosopher so far has been proved right, and that there might be a more laudable truthfulness in every little question mark that you place after your special words and favorite doctrines (and occasionally after yourselves) than in all the solemn gestures and trumps before accusers and law courts.[3] Rather, go away. Flee into concealment. And have your masks and subtlety,[4] that you may be mistaken for what you are not, or feared a little. And don't forget the garden, the garden with golden trelliswork. And have people around you who are as a garden—or as music on the waters in the evening, when the day is turning into memories. Choose the *good* solitude, the free, playful, light solitude that gives you, too, the right to remain good in some sense. How poisonous, how crafty, how bad, does every long war make one, that cannot be waged openly by means of force! How *personal* does a long fear make one, a long watching of enemies, of possible enemies! These outcasts of society, these long-pursued, wickedly persecuted ones—also the compulsory recluses, the Spinozas or Giordano Brunos—always become in the end, even under the most spiritual masquerade, and

---

[2] For the role of Don Quixote, alluded to above, in Nietzsche's thought, see Kaufmann, *Nietzsche*, Chapter 1, note 40.

[3] Compare Nietzsche's splendid formulation in a note of the 1880's: "A very popular error: having the courage of one's convictions; rather it is a matter of having the courage for an *attack* on one's convictions!!!" (*Werke*, Musarion edition, Munich, 1920-29, XVI, p. 318.

[4] *Feinheit* (subtlety) can also mean fineness or, depending on the context, delicacy, sensitivity, nicety, elegance, purity. In this translation it has been generally rendered as "subtlety" and sometimes as "refinement."

perhaps without being themselves aware of it, sophisticated vengeance-seekers and poison-brewers (let someone lay bare the foundation of Spinoza's ethics and theology!), not to speak of the stupidity of moral indignation, which is the unfailing sign in a philosopher that his philosophical sense of humor has left him. The martyrdom of the philosopher, his "sacrifice for the sake of truth," forces into the light whatever of the agitator and actor lurks in him; and if one has so far contemplated him only with artistic curiosity, with regard to many a philosopher it is easy to understand the dangerous desire to see him also in his degeneration (degenerated into a "martyr," into a stage- and platform-bawler). Only, that it is necessary with such a desire to be clear *what* spectacle one will see in any case—merely a satyr play, merely an epilogue farce, merely the continued proof that the long, real tragedy *is at an end,* assuming that every philosophy was in its genesis a long tragedy.

26

Every choice human being strives instinctively for a citadel and a secrecy where he is saved from the crowd, the many, the great majority—where he may forget "men who are the rule," being their exception—excepting only the one case in which he is pushed straight to such men by a still stronger instinct, as a seeker after knowledge in the great and exceptional sense. Anyone who, in intercourse with men, does not occasionally glisten in all the colors of distress, green and gray with disgust, satiety, sympathy, gloominess, and loneliness, is certainly not a man of elevated tastes; supposing, however, that he does not take all this burden and disgust upon himself voluntarily, that he persistently avoids it, and remains, as I said, quietly and proudly hidden in his citadel, one thing is certain: he was not made, he was not predestined, for knowledge. If he were, he would one day have to say to himself: "The devil take my good taste! but the rule is more interesting than the exception—than myself, the exception!" And he would go *down,*[5] and above all, he would go "inside."

---

[5] An echo of the Prologue to *Zarathustra*.

The long and serious study of the *average* man, and consequently much disguise, self-overcoming, familiarity, and bad contact (all contact is bad contact except with one's equals)—this constitutes a necessary part of the life-history of every philosopher, perhaps the most disagreeable, odious, and disappointing part. If he is fortunate, however, as a favorite child of knowledge should be, he will encounter suitable shortcuts and helps for his task; I mean so-called cynics, those who simply recognize the animal, the commonplace, and "the rule" in themselves, and at the same time still have that degree of spirituality and that itch which makes them talk of themselves and their likes *before witnesses*—sometimes they even wallow in books, as on their own dung.

Cynicism is the only form in which base souls approach honesty; and the higher man must listen closely to every coarse or subtle cynicism, and congratulate himself when a clown without shame or a scientific satyr speaks out precisely in front of him.

There are even cases where enchantment mixes with the disgust—namely, where by a freak of nature genius is tied to some such indiscreet billygoat and ape, as in the case of the Abbé Galiani,[6] the profoundest, most clear-sighted, and perhaps also filthiest man of his century—he was far profounder than Voltaire and consequently also a good deal more taciturn. It happens more frequently, as has been hinted, that a scientific head is placed on an ape's body, a subtle exceptional understanding in a base soul, an occurrence by no means rare, especially among doctors and physiologists of morality. And whenever anyone speaks without bitterness, quite innocently, of man as a belly with two requirements, and a head with one; whenever anyone sees, seeks, and *wants* to see only hunger, sexual lust, and vanity as the real and only mo-

---

[6] Abbé Ferdinand Galiani (1728-87) is characterized in *The Oxford Companion to French Literature* (Oxford, Clarendon Press, 1959) as "a Neapolitan, of diminutive size, secretary at the embassy in Paris from 1759 . . . of considerable learning and originality of views, somewhat of a buffoon, much appreciated in the literary and philosophical society of the day . . . His *Dialogues sur les blés*, a work remarkable for lively wit as well as force of argument, combating the doctrines of the more extreme physiocrats, appeared in 1770, after his departure from Paris in 1769." His letters to Mme d'Épinay, Mme Geoffrin, and Mme Necker have also been published.

tives of human actions; in short, when anyone speaks "badly"—
and not even *"wickedly"*—of man, the lover of knowledge should
listen subtly and diligently; he should altogether have an open ear
wherever people talk without indignation. For the indignant and
whoever perpetually tears and lacerates with his own teeth himself (or as a substitute, the world, or God, or society) may indeed,
morally speaking, stand higher than the laughing and self-satisfied
satyr, but in every other sense they are a more ordinary, more indifferent, and less instructive case. And no one *lies* as much as the
indignant do.

27

It is hard to be understood, especially when one thinks and
lives *gāngāsrotagati*[7] among men who think and live differently—
namely, *kūrmagati,*[8] or at best "the way frogs walk," *mandūkagati*[9] (I obviously do everything to be "hard to understand" myself!)—and one should be cordially grateful for the good will to
some subtlety of interpretation. As regards "the good friends,"
however, who are always too lazy and think that as friends they

---

[7] In the original edition: gangasrotagati. Although the second "o" is clearly
a misprint, it has not been corrected in later editions or in the English translations. *Gati* means gait; *srota,* the current of a river, and *ganga* is the river
Ganges. So the word means: as the current of the Ganges moves. (For the
information about the Sanskrit words, also in the two following notes, I
am indebted to Professor Samuel D. Atkins.)

[8] As the tortoise moves. In the original edition and in subsequent editions
and translations the diacritical mark is missing.

[9] In the original edition: mandeikagati, without diacritical marks. The "ei"
is a misprint, perhaps due to the misreading of a handwritten "u"—but has
been perpetuated in subsequent editions and translations.
Far from being *merely* playful or concerned with style to the exclusion
of philosophy, this section touches on a crucial problem: Nietzsche's *tempo*
is a major reason for the long delay in his reception as a philosopher; and
three quarters of a century after the appearance of *Beyond Good and Evil*
the *tempo* of articles in British and American philosophical journals had
slowed down to the point where many philosophers were bound to feel that
anything written *gāngāsrotagati* simply could not be philosophy. Even Wittgenstein, though he had never followed the fashion of moving like the tortoise, had at least proceeded *mandūkagati.* For this whole question of philosophical style and *tempo* see Kaufmann, *Critique of Religion and Philosophy* (Garden City, N.Y., Anchor Books), sections 3-10.

have a right to relax, one does well to grant them from the outset
some leeway and romping place for misunderstanding: then one
can even laugh—or get rid of them altogether, these good friends
—and also laugh.

28

What is most difficult to render from one language into another is the *tempo* of its style, which has its basis in the character
of the race, or to speak more physiologically, in the average *tempo*
of its metabolism. There are honestly meant translations that, as
involuntary vulgarizations, are almost falsifications of the original,
merely because its bold and merry *tempo* (which leaps over and
obviates all dangers in things and words) could not be translated.
A German is almost incapable of *presto*[10] in his language; thus also,
as may be reasonably inferred, of many of the most delightful and
daring *nuances* of free, free-spirited thought. And just as the buffoon and satyr are foreign to him in body and conscience, so Aristophanes and Petronius are untranslatable for him. Everything
ponderous, viscous, and solemnly clumsy, all long-winded and boring types of style are developed in profuse variety among Germans
—forgive me the fact that even Goethe's prose, in its mixture of
stiffness and elegance, is no exception, being a reflection of the
"good old time" to which it belongs, and a reflection of German
taste at a time when there still was a "German taste"—a rococo
taste *in moribus et artibus*.[11]

Lessing is an exception, owing to his histrionic nature which
understood much and understood how to do many things. He was
not the translator of Bayle for nothing and liked to flee to the
neighborhood of Diderot and Voltaire, and better yet that of the
Roman comedy writers. In *tempo,* too, Lessing loved free thinking and escape from Germany. But how could the German language, even in the prose of a Lessing, imitate the *tempo* of Machia-

---

[10] Rapid tempo.
[11] In morals and arts.

velli,[12] who in his *Principe* [*The Prince*] lets us breathe the dry,
refined air of Florence and cannot help presenting the most serious matters in a boisterous *allegrissimo,*[13] perhaps not without a
malicious artistic sense of the contrast he risks—long, difficult,
hard, dangerous thoughts and the *tempo* of the gallop and the very
best, most capricious humor?

Who, finally, could venture on a German translation of Petronius, who, more than any great musician so far, was a master of
presto in invention, ideas, and words? What do the swamps of the
sick, wicked world, even the "ancient world," matter in the end,
when one has the feet of a wind as he did, the rush, the breath, the
liberating scorn of a wind that makes everything healthy by making everything *run!* And as for Aristophanes—that transfiguring,
complementary spirit for whose sake one *forgives* everything
Hellenic for having existed, provided one has understood in its full
profundity *all* that needs to be forgiven and transfigured here—
there is nothing that has caused me to meditate more on *Plato's*
secrecy and sphinx nature than the happily preserved *petit fait*[14]
that under the pillow of his deathbed there was found no "Bible,"
nor anything Egyptian, Pythagorean, or Platonic—but a volume of
Aristophanes. How could even Plato have endured life—a Greek
life he repudiated—without an Aristophanes?

29

Independence is for the very few; it is a privilege of the
strong. And whoever attempts it even with the best right but without inner constraint proves that he is probably not only strong, but
also daring to the point of recklessness. He enters into a labyrinth,
he multiplies a thousandfold the dangers which life brings with it
in any case, not the least of which is that no one can see how and
where he loses his way, becomes lonely, and is torn piecemeal by

---

[12] In the original edition and in the standard editions; Macchiavelli.
[13] Extremely brisk and lively manner.
[14] Small fact.

some minotaur of conscience. Supposing one like that comes to grief, this happens so far from the comprehension of men that they neither feel it nor sympathize. And he cannot go back any longer. Nor can he go back to the pity of men.—

30

Our highest insights must—and should—sound like follies and sometimes like crimes when they are heard without permission by those who are not predisposed and predestined for them.[15] The difference between the exoteric and the esoteric, formerly known to philosophers—among the Indians as among the Greeks, Persians, and Muslims, in short, wherever one believed in an order of rank and *not* in equality and equal rights—does not so much consist in this, that the exoteric approach comes from outside and sees, estimates, measures, and judges from the outside, not the inside: what is much more essential is that the exoteric approach sees things from below, the esoteric looks *down from above*. There are heights of the soul from which even tragedy ceases to look tragic; and rolling together all the woe of the world—who could dare to decide whether its sight would *necessarily* seduce us and compel us to feel pity and thus double this woe?

What serves the higher type of men as nourishment or delectation must almost be poison for a very different and inferior type. The virtues of the common man might perhaps signify vices and weaknesses in a philosopher. It could be possible that a man of a high type, when degenerating and perishing, might only at that point acquire qualities that would require those in the lower sphere into which he had sunk to begin to venerate him like a saint. There are books that have opposite values for soul and health, depending on whether the lower soul, the lower vitality, or the higher and more vigorous ones turn to them: in the former case, these books are dangerous and lead to crumbling and disintegration; in the latter, heralds' cries that call the bravest to *their*

---

[15] This theme is taken up again in several later sections, where the concept of the mask is discussed; e.g., section 40.

courage. Books for all the world are always foul-smelling books: the smell of small people clings to them. Where the people eat and drink, even where they venerate, it usually stinks. One should not go to church if one wants to breathe *pure* air.

31

When one is young, one venerates and despises without that art of nuances which constitutes the best gain of life, and it is only fair that one has to pay dearly for having assaulted men and things in this manner with Yes and No. Everything is arranged so that the worst of tastes, the taste for the unconditional, should be cruelly fooled and abused until a man learns to put a little art into his feelings and rather to risk trying even what is artificial—as the real artists of life do.

The wrathful and reverent attitudes characteristic of youth do not seem to permit themselves any rest until they have forged men and things in such a way that these attitudes may be vented on them—after all, youth in itself has something of forgery and deception. Later, when the young soul, tortured by all kinds of disappointments, finally turns suspiciously against itself, still hot and wild, even in its suspicion and pangs of conscience—how wroth it is with itself now! how it tears itself to pieces, impatiently! how it takes revenge for its long self-delusion, just as if it had been a deliberate blindness! In this transition one punishes oneself with mistrust against one's own feelings; one tortures one's own enthusiasm with doubts; indeed, one experiences even a good conscience as a danger, as if it were a way of wrapping oneself in veils and the exhaustion of subtler honesty—and above all one takes sides, takes sides on principle, *against* "youth."— Ten years later one comprehends that all this, too—was still youth.

32

During the longest part of human history—so-called prehistorical times—the value or disvalue of an action was derived from its consequences. The action itself was considered as little as its origin. It was rather the way a distinction or disgrace still reaches back today from a child to its parents, in China: it was the retroactive force of success or failure that led men to think well or ill of an action. Let us call this period the *pre-moral* period of mankind: the imperative "know thyself!" was as yet unknown.

In the last ten thousand years, however, one has reached the point, step by step, in a few large regions on the earth, where it is no longer the consequences but the origin of an action that one allows to decide its value. On the whole this is a great event which involves a considerable refinement of vision and standards; it is the unconscious aftereffect of the rule of aristocratic values and the faith in "descent"—the sign of a period that one may call *moral* in the narrower sense. It involves the first attempt at self-knowledge. Instead of the consequences, the origin: indeed a reversal of perspective! Surely, a reversal achieved only after long struggles and vacillations. To be sure, a calamitous new superstition, an odd narrowness of interpretation, thus become dominant: the origin of an action was interpreted in the most definite sense as origin in an *intention;* one came to agree that the value of an action lay in the value of the intention. The intention as the whole origin and prehistory of an action—almost to the present day this prejudice dominated moral praise, blame, judgment, and philosophy on earth.

But today—shouldn't we have reached the necessity of once more resolving on a reversal and fundamental shift in values, owing to another self-examination of man, another growth in profundity? Don't we stand at the threshold of a period which should be designated negatively, to begin with, as *extra-moral?* After all, today at least we immoralists have the suspicion that the decisive value of an action lies precisely in what is *unintentional* in it, while everything about it that is intentional, everything about it that can be seen, known, "conscious," still belongs to its surface and skin—which, like every skin, betrays something but *conceals* even more. In short, we believe that the intention is merely a sign and symptom that still requires interpretation—moreover, a sign that means too much and therefore, taken by itself alone, almost nothing. We believe that morality in the traditional sense, the morality of intentions, was a prejudice, precipitate and perhaps provisional

—something on the order of astrology and alchemy—but in any case something that must be overcome. The overcoming of morality, in a certain sense even the self-overcoming of morality—let this be the name for that long secret work which has been saved up for the finest and most honest, also the most malicious, consciences of today, as living touchstones of the soul.

33

There is no other way: the feelings of devotion, self-sacrifice for one's neighbor, the whole morality of self-denial must be questioned mercilessly and taken to court—no less than the aesthetics of "contemplation devoid of all interest" which is used today as a seductive guise for the emasculation of art, to give it a good conscience. There is too much charm and sugar in these feelings of "for others," "*not* for myself," for us not to need to become doubly suspicious at this point and to ask: "are these not perhaps—*seductions?*"

That they *please*—those who have them and those who enjoy their fruits, and also the mere spectator—this does not yet constitute an argument in their *favor* but rather invites caution. So let us be cautious.

34

Whatever philosophical standpoint one may adopt today, from every point of view the *erroneousness* of the world in which we think we live is the surest and firmest fact that we can lay eyes on: we find reasons upon reasons for it which would like to lure us to hypotheses concerning a deceptive principle in "the essence of things." But whoever holds our thinking itself, "the spirit," in other words, responsible for the falseness of the world—an honorable way out which is chosen by every conscious or unconscious *advocatus dei*[16]—whoever takes this world, along with space, time,

---

[16] Advocate of God: Nietzsche's coinage, modeled after *advocatus diaboli*, devil's advocate.

form, movement, to be falsely *inferred*—anyone like that would at least have ample reason to learn to be suspicious at long last of all thinking. Wouldn't thinking have put over on us the biggest hoax yet? And what warrant would there be that it would not continue to do what it has always done?

In all seriousness: the innocence of our thinkers is somehow touching and evokes reverence, when today they still step before consciousness with the request that it should please give them *honest* answers; for example, whether it is "real," and why it so resolutely keeps the external world at a distance, and other questions of that kind. The faith in "immediate certainties" is a *moral* naïveté that reflects honor on us philosophers; but—after all we should not be *"merely* moral" men. Apart from morality, this faith is a stupidity that reflects little honor on us. In bourgeois life everpresent suspicion may be considered a sign of "bad character" and hence belong among things imprudent; here, among us, beyond the bourgeois world and its Yes and No—what should prevent us from being imprudent and saying: a philosopher has nothing less than a *right* to "bad character," as the being who has so far always been fooled best on earth; he has a *duty* to suspicion today, to squint maliciously out of every abyss of suspicion.

Forgive me the joke of this gloomy grimace and trope; for I myself have learned long ago to think differently, to estimate differently with regard to deceiving and being deceived, and I keep in reserve at least a couple of jostles for the blind rage with which the philosophers resist being deceived. Why *not?* It is no more than a moral prejudice that truth is worth more than mere appearance; it is even the worst proved assumption there is in the world. Let at least this much be admitted: there would be no life at all if not on the basis of perspective estimates and appearances; and if, with the virtuous enthusiasm and clumsiness of some philosophers, one wanted to abolish the "apparent world" altogether—well, supposing *you* could do that, at least nothing would be left of your "truth" either. Indeed, what forces us at all to suppose that there is an essential opposition of "true" and "false"? Is it not sufficient to assume degrees of apparentness and, as it were, lighter and darker shadows and shades of appearance—different "values," to use the language of painters? Why couldn't the world *that concerns us*—be a fiction? And if somebody asked, "but to a fiction there surely belongs an author?"—couldn't one answer simply: *why?* Doesn't this "belongs" perhaps belong to the fiction, too? Is it not permitted to be a bit ironical about the subject no less than the predicate and object? Shouldn't philosophers be permitted to rise above faith in grammar? All due respect for governesses—but hasn't the time come for philosophy to renounce the faith of governesses? [17]

35

O Voltaire! O humaneness! O nonsense! There is something about "truth," about the *search* for truth; and when a human being is too human about it—*"il ne cherche le vrai que pour faire le bien"* [18]—I bet he finds nothing.

36

Suppose nothing else were "given" as real except our world of desires and passions, and we could not get down, or up, to any other "reality" besides the reality of our drives—for thinking is merely a relation of these drives to each other: is it not permitted to make the experiment and to ask the question whether this "given" would not be *sufficient* for also understanding on the basis of this kind of thing the so-called mechanistic (or "material") world? I mean, not as a deception, as "mere appearance," an "idea" (in the sense of Berkeley and Schopenhauer) but as holding the same rank of reality as our affect—as a more primitive form of the world of affects in which everything still lies contained in a powerful unity

---

[17] Cf.: "It might be amusing, perhaps even instructive, to compare Ryle on ordinary language with W. D. Ross on *prima facie* duties. There is a close resemblance between Oxford deontology and Oxford linguisticism, not least in the assumption that duties, like verbal habits, are 'learnt in the nursery' [Ryle's phrase], and that what nurse has told us goes for the rest of the world, too" (John Passmore. "Professor Ryle's Use of 'Use' and 'Usage,'" *The Philosophical Review,* LXIII [January 1954], 62).

[18] "He seeks the true only to do the good."

before it undergoes ramifications and developments in the organic process (and, as is only fair, also becomes tenderer and weaker) —as a kind of instinctive life in which all organic functions are still synthetically intertwined along with self-regulation, assimilation, nourishment, excretion, and metabolism—as a *pre-form* of life.

In the end not only is it permitted to make this experiment; the conscience of *method* demands it. Not to assume several kinds of causality until the experiment of making do with a single one has been pushed to its utmost limit (to the point of nonsense, if I may say so)—that is a moral of method which one may not shirk today —it follows "from its definition," as a mathematician would say. The question is in the end whether we really recognize the will as *efficient,* whether we believe in the causality of the will: if we do —and at bottom our faith in this is nothing less than our faith in causality itself—then we have to make the experiment of positing the causality of the will hypothetically as the only one. "Will," of course, can affect only "will"—and not "matter" (not "nerves," for example). In short, one has to risk the hypothesis whether will does not affect will wherever "effects" are recognized—and whether all mechanical occurrences are not, insofar as a force is active in them, will force, effects of will.

Suppose, finally, we succeeded in explaining our entire instinctive life as the development and ramification of *one* basic form of the will—namely, of the will to power, as *my* proposition has it; suppose all organic functions could be traced back to this will to power and one could also find in it the solution of the problem of procreation and nourishment—it is *one* problem—then one would have gained the right to determine *all* efficient force univocally as —*will to power*. The world viewed from inside, the world defined and determined according to its "intelligible character"—it would be "will to power" and nothing else.—

37

"What? Doesn't this mean, to speak with the vulgar: God is refuted, but the devil is not?" On the contrary! On the contrary, my friends. And, the devil—who forces you to speak with the vulgar?

38

What happened most recently in the broad daylight of modern times in the case of the French Revolution—that gruesome farce which, considered closely, was quite superfluous, though noble and enthusiastic spectators from all over Europe contemplated it from a distance and interpreted it according to their own indignations and enthusiasms for so long, and so passionately, that *the text finally disappeared under the interpretation*—could happen once more as a noble posterity might misunderstand the whole past and in that way alone make it tolerable to look at.

Or rather: isn't this what has happened even now? haven't we ourselves been this "noble posterity"? And isn't now precisely the moment when, insofar as we comprehend this, it is all over?

39

Nobody is very likely to consider a doctrine true merely because it makes people happy or virtuous—except perhaps the lovely "idealists" who become effusive about the good, the true, and the beautiful and allow all kinds of motley, clumsy, and benevolent desiderata to swim around in utter confusion in their pond. Happiness and virtue are no arguments. But people like to forget—even sober spirits—that making unhappy and evil are no counterarguments. Something might be true while being harmful and dangerous in the highest degree. Indeed, it might be a basic characteristic of existence that those who would know it completely would perish, in which case the strength of a spirit should be measured according to how much of the "truth" one could still barely endure—or to put it more clearly, to what degree one would *require* it to be thinned down, shrouded, sweetened, blunted, falsified.[19]

But there is no doubt at all that the evil and unhappy are more favored when it comes to the discovery of certain *parts* of truth,

---

[19] This is relevant to Nietzsche's conception of an order of rank and the themes of Part IX below.

and that the probability of their success here is greater—not to speak of the evil who are happy, a species the moralists bury in silence. Perhaps hardness and cunning furnish more favorable conditions for the origin of the strong, independent spirit and philosopher than that gentle, fine, conciliatory good-naturedness and art of taking things lightly which people prize, and prize rightly, in a scholar. Assuming first of all that the concept "philosopher" is not restricted to the philosopher who writes books—or makes books of *his* philosophy.

A final trait for the image of the free-spirited philosopher is contributed by Stendhal whom, considering German taste, I do not want to fail to stress—for he goes against the German taste. *"Pour être bon philosophe,"* says this last great psychologist, *"il faut être sec, clair, sans illusion. Un banquier, qui a fait fortune, a une partie du caractère requis pour faire des découvertes en philosophie, c'est-à-dire pour voir clair dans ce qui est."* [20]

40

Whatever is profound loves masks; what is most profound even hates image and parable. Might not nothing less than the *opposite* be the proper disguise for the shame of a god? [21] A questionable question: it would be odd if some mystic had not risked something to that effect in his mind. There are occurrences of such a delicate nature that one does well to cover them up with some rudeness to conceal them; there are actions of love and extravagant generosity after which nothing is more advisable than to take a stick and give any eyewitness a sound thrashing: that would muddle his memory. Some know how to muddle and abuse their own memory in order to have their revenge at least against this only witness: shame is inventive.

It is not the worst things that cause the worst shame: there is

---

[20] "To be a good philosopher, one must be dry, clear, without illusion. A banker who has made a fortune has one character trait that is needed for making discoveries in philosophy, that is to say, for seeing clearly into what is."

[21] Cf. section 30 above.

not only guile behind a mask—there is so much graciousness in cunning. I could imagine that a human being who had to guard something precious and vulnerable might roll through life, rude and round as an old green wine cask with heavy hoops: the refinement of his shame would want it that way.

A man whose sense of shame has some profundity encounters his destinies and delicate decisions, too, on paths which few ever reach and of whose mere existence his closest intimates must not know: his mortal danger is concealed from their eyes, and so is his regained sureness of life. Such a concealed man who instinctively needs speech for silence and for burial in silence and who is inexhaustible in his evasion of communication, *wants* and sees to it that a mask of him roams in his place through the hearts and heads of his friends. And supposing he did not want it, he would still realize some day that in spite of that a mask of him is there—and that this is well. Every profound spirit needs a mask: even more, around every profound spirit a mask is growing continually, owing to the constantly false, namely *shallow,* interpretation of every word, every step, every sign of life he gives.[22]—

41

One has to test oneself to see that one is destined for independence and command—and do it at the right time. One should not dodge one's tests, though they may be the most dangerous

---

[22] This section is obviously of great importance for the student of Nietzsche: it suggests plainly that the surface meaning noted by superficial browsers often masks Nietzsche's real meaning, which in extreme cases may approximate the opposite of what the words might suggest to hasty readers. In this sense "beyond good and evil" and "will to power," "master morality" and "hardness" and "cruelty" may be masks that elicit reactions quite inappropriate to what lies behind them. Specific examples will be found on later pages.

Karl Jaspers has called attention to the similarity between Nietzsche and Kierkegaard at this point, in his lecture on Kierkegaard and Nietzsche (*Existentialism from Dostoevsky to Sartre,* ed. Kaufmann, New York, Meridian Books, 1956, p. 165). See also Jaspers' *Nietzsche* (1936, pp. 358ff.; pp. 405ff. of the English version, Tucson, University of Arizona Press, 1965, which unfortunately omits the references for the quotations).

game one could play and are tests that are taken in the end before no witness or judge but ourselves.

Not to remain stuck to a person—not even the most loved— every person is a prison, also a nook.[23] Not to remain stuck to a fatherland—not even if it suffers most and needs help most—it is less difficult to sever one's heart from a victorious fatherland. Not to remain stuck to some pity—not even for higher men into whose rare torture and helplessness some accident allowed us to look.[24] Not to remain stuck to a science—even if it should lure us with the most precious finds that seem to have been saved up precisely for us.[25] Not to remain stuck to one's own detachment, to that voluptuous remoteness and strangeness of the bird who flees ever higher to see ever more below him—the danger of the flier. Not to remain stuck to our own virtues and become as a whole the victim of some detail in us, such as our hospitality, which is the danger of dangers for superior and rich souls who spend themselves lavishly, almost indifferently, and exaggerate the virtue of generosity into a vice. One must know how *to conserve oneself:* the hardest test of independence.

42

A new species of philosophers is coming up: I venture to baptize them with a name that is not free of danger. As I unriddle them, insofar as they allow themselves to be unriddled—for it belongs to their nature to *want* to remain riddles at some point— these philosophers of the future may have a right—it might also be a wrong—to be called *attempters.*[26] This name itself is in the end a mere attempt and, if you will, a temptation.

---

23 *Winkel* has been translated here and elsewhere as "nook"; but it can also mean angle, which would make sense here though not in many of the other passages.
24 This might be an allusion to Richard Wagner; but this is a point Nietzsche considered important generally, and it is developed at length in Part IV of *Zarathustra.*
25 In German usage, classical philology, which Nietzsche had given up in order to devote himself entirely to his own writing, is a science.
26 *Versucher* could also mean tempters (which does not seem intended here,

43

Are these coming philosophers new friends of "truth"? That is probable enough, for all philosophers so far have loved their truths. But they will certainly not be dogmatists. It must offend their pride, also their taste, if their truth is supposed to be a truth for everyman —which has so far been the secret wish and hidden meaning of all dogmatic aspirations. "My judgment is *my* judgment": no one else is easily entitled to it—that is what such a philosopher of the future may perhaps say of himself.

One must shed the bad taste of wanting to agree with many. "Good" is no longer good when one's neighbor mouths it. And how should there be a "common good"! The term contradicts itself: whatever can be common always has little value. In the end it must be as it is and always has been: great things remain for the great, abysses for the profound, nuances and shudders for the refined, and, in brief, all that is rare for the rare.[27]—

44

Need I still say expressly after all this that they, too, will be free, *very* free spirits, these philosophers of the future—though just as certainly they will not be merely free spirits but something more, higher, greater, and thoroughly different that does not want to be misunderstood and mistaken for something else. But saying this I

---

at least as the primary meaning) or experimenters (which is meant but would spoil the triple play on words): *Versuch* (attempt or experiment) and *Versuchung* (temptation). For some discussion of Nietzsche's "experimentalism" see Kaufmann's *Nietzsche,* Chapter 2, section III. See also section 210 below.

[27] It is interesting to compare this critique of dogmatism with Hegel's. Hegel had insisted that dogmatism is wrong in supposing that an isolated proposition can be the form of the truth; nothing is accomplished by repeating such formulations: their significance depends on the meaning assigned to the terms and on the context; hence only the system can be the form of the truth. For a comparison of Hegel's and Nietzsche's views of systems see Kaufmann's *Nietzsche,* Chapter 2, section II; the remainder of the chapter deals with Nietzsche's "experimentalism" and its "existential" quality.

feel an *obligation*—almost as much to them as to ourselves who are their heralds and precursors, we free spirits—to sweep away a stupid old prejudice and misunderstanding about the lot of us: all too long it has clouded the concept "free spirit" like a fog.

In all the countries of Europe, and in America, too, there now is something that abuses this name: a very narrow, imprisoned, chained type of spirits who want just about the opposite of what accords with our intentions and instincts—not to speak of the fact that regarding the *new* philosophers who are coming up they must assuredly be closed windows and bolted doors. They belong, briefly and sadly, among the *levelers*—these falsely so-called "free spirits"—being eloquent and prolifically scribbling slaves of the democratic taste and its "modern ideas"; they are all human beings without solitude, without their own solitude, clumsy good fellows whom one should not deny either courage or respectable decency —only they are unfree and ridiculously superficial, above all in their basic inclination to find in the forms of the old society as it has existed so far just about the cause of *all* human misery and failure —which is a way of standing truth happily upon her head! What they would like to strive for with all their powers is the universal green-pasture happiness of the herd, with security, lack of danger, comfort, and an easier life for everyone; the two songs and doctrines which they repeat most often are "equality of rights" and "sympathy for all that suffers"—and suffering itself they take for something that must be *abolished*.

We opposite men, having opened our eyes and conscience to the question where and how the plant "man" has so far grown most vigorously to a height—we think that this has happened every time under the opposite conditions, that to this end the dangerousness of his situation must first grow to the point of enormity, his power of invention and simulation (his "spirit") had to develop under prolonged pressure and constraint into refinement and audacity, his life-will had to be enhanced into an unconditional power-will. We think that hardness, forcefulness, slavery, danger in the alley and the heart, life in hiding, stoicism, the art of experiment and devilry of every kind, that everything evil, terrible, tyrannical in man, everything in him that is kin to beasts of prey and serpents, serves the enhancement of the species "man" as much as its opposite does. Indeed, we do not even say enough when we say only that much; and at any rate we are at this point, in what we say and keep silent about, at the *other* end from all modern ideology and herd desiderata—as their antipodes perhaps?

Is it any wonder that we "free spirits" are not exactly the most communicative spirits? that we do not want to betray in every particular *from what* a spirit can liberate himself and *to what* he may then be driven? And as for the meaning of the dangerous formula "beyond good and evil," with which we at least guard against being mistaken for others: we *are* something different from *"libres-penseurs," "liberi pensatori," "Freidenker,"* [28] and whatever else all these goodly advocates of "modern ideas" like to call themselves.

At home, or at least having been guests, in many countries of the spirit; having escaped again and again from the musty agreeable nooks into which preference and prejudice, youth, origin, the accidents of people and books or even exhaustion from wandering seemed to have banished us; full of malice against the lures of dependence that lie hidden in honors, or money, or offices, or enthusiasms of the senses; grateful even to need and vacillating sickness because they always rid us from some rule and its "prejudice," grateful to god, devil, sheep, and worm in us; curious to a vice, investigators to the point of cruelty, with uninhibited fingers for the unfathomable, with teeth and stomachs for the most indigestible, ready for every feat that requires a sense of acuteness and acute senses, ready for every venture, thanks to an excess of "free will," with fore- and back-souls into whose ultimate intentions nobody can look so easily, with fore- and backgrounds which no foot is likely to explore to the end; concealed under cloaks of light, conquerors even if we look like heirs and prodigals, arrangers and collectors from morning till late, misers of our riches and our crammed drawers, economical in learning and forgetting, inventive in schemas, occasionally proud of tables of categories, occasionally pedants, occasionally night owls of work even in broad daylight;

---

[28] Free-thinkers.

yes, when it is necessary even scarecrows—and today it is necessary; namely, insofar as we are born, sworn, jealous friends of *solitude,* of our own most profound, most midnightly, most middaily solitude: that is the type of man we are, we free spirits! And perhaps *you* have something of this, too, you that are coming? you *new* philosophers?—

PART THREE

WHAT IS RELIGIOUS[1]

---

[1] The German title is *Das religiöse Wesen*. The word *Wesen* is not easy to translate. In philosophical prose it is most often rendered by "essence," but in many contexts "being" is called for; e.g., a natural being, a human being. Above, either "the religious nature" or "the religious being" might do. But in section 47 Nietzsche speaks of "the religious neurosis—or what I call *'das religiöse Wesen'*"; and this puts one in mind of contexts in which *Wesen* means character, conduct, manners, airs, and even ado: *viel Wesen* means much ado. *Finanzwesen* means financial affairs, or the financial establishment, or finances. *Bankwesen,* banks or banking in general; *Minenwesen,* mining; and *Kriegswesen,* military art—these last examples come from a dictionary.

Part Three

45

The human soul and its limits, the range of inner human experiences reached so far, the heights, depths, and distances of these experiences, the whole history of the soul *so far* and its as yet unexhausted possibilities—that is the predestined hunting ground for a born psychologist and lover of the "great hunt." But how often he has to say to himself in despair: "One hunter! alas, only a single one! and look at this huge forest, this primeval forest!" And then he wishes he had a few hundred helpers and good, well-trained hounds that he could drive into the history of the human soul to round up *his* game. In vain: it is proved to him again and again, thoroughly and bitterly, how helpers and hounds for all the things that excite his curiosity cannot be found. What is wrong with sending scholars into new and dangerous hunting grounds, where courage, sense, and subtlety in every way are required, is that they cease to be of any use precisely where the *"great hunt,"* but also the great danger, begins: precisely there they lose their keen eye and nose.

To figure out and determine, for example, what kind of a history the problem of *science and conscience*[2] has so far had in the soul of *homines religiosi*,[3] one might perhaps have to be as profound, as wounded, as monstrous as Pascal's intellectual conscience was—and then one would still need that vaulting heaven of bright, malicious spirituality that would be capable of surveying from above, arranging, and forcing into formulas this swarm of dangerous and painful experiences.

But who would do me this service? But who would have time to wait for such servants? They obviously grow too rarely; they are so improbable in any age. In the end one has to do everything *one-*

---

[2] *Wissen und Gewissen:* literally, knowledge and conscience.
[3] Religious men.

self in order to know a few things oneself: that is, one has *a lot* to do.

But a curiosity of my type remains after all the most agreeable of all vices—sorry, I meant to say: the love of truth has its reward in heaven and even on earth.—

46

The faith demanded, and not infrequently attained, by original Christianity, in the midst of a skeptical and southern free-spirited world that looked back on, and still contained, a centuries-long fight between philosophical schools, besides the education for tolerance given by the *imperium Romanum*[4]—this faith is *not* that ingenuous and bearlike subalterns' faith with which, say, a Luther or a Cromwell, or some other northern barbarian of the spirit, clung to his god and to Christianity. It is much closer to the faith of Pascal, which resembles in a gruesome manner a continual suicide of reason—a tough, long-lived, wormlike reason that cannot be killed all at once and with a single stroke.

From the start, the Christian faith is a sacrifice: a sacrifice of all freedom, all pride, all self-confidence of the spirit; at the same time, enslavement and self-mockery, self-mutilation. There is cruelty and religious Phoenicianism in this faith which is expected of an over-ripe, multiple, and much-spoiled conscience: it presupposes that the subjection of the spirit *hurts* indescribably; that the whole past and the habits of such a spirit resist the *absurdissimum*[5] which "faith" represents to it.

Modern men, obtuse to all Christian nomenclature, no longer feel the gruesome superlative that struck a classical taste in the paradoxical formula "god on the cross." Never yet and nowhere has there been an equal boldness in inversion, anything as horrible, questioning, and questionable as this formula: it promised a revaluation of all the values of antiquity.

It is the Orient, *deep* Orient, it is the Oriental slave who re-

---

[4] Roman Empire.
[5] Height of absurdity.

venged himself in this way on Rome and its noble and frivolous tolerance, on the Roman "catholicity" of faith. It has always been not faith but the freedom from faith, that half-stoical and smiling unconcern with the seriousness of faith, that enraged slaves in their masters—against their masters. "Enlightenment" enrages: for the slave wants the unconditional; he understands only what is tyrannical, in morals, too; he loves as he hates, without nuance, to the depths, to the point of pain, of sickness—his abundant *concealed* suffering is enraged against the noble taste that seems to *deny* suffering. Nor was skepticism concerning suffering, at bottom merely a pose of aristocratic morality, the least cause of the origin of the last great slave rebellion which began with the French Revolution.

47

Wherever on earth the religious neurosis has appeared we find it tied to three dangerous dietary demands: solitude, fasting, and sexual abstinence. But one cannot decide with certainty what is cause and what effect, and *whether* any relation of cause and effect is involved here. The final doubt seems justified because among its most regular symptoms, among both savage and tame peoples, we also find the most sudden, most extravagant voluptuousness which then, just as suddenly, changes into a penitential spasm and denial of the world and will—both perhaps to be interpreted as masked epilepsy? But nowhere should one resist interpretation more: no other type has yet been surrounded by such a lavish growth of nonsense and superstition, no other type seems to have interested men, even philosophers, more. The time has come for becoming a bit cold right here, to learn caution—better yet: to look away, *to go away*.

Even in the background of the most recent philosophy, that of Schopenhauer, we find, almost as the problem-in-itself, this gruesome question mark of the religious crisis and awakening. How is the denial of the will *possible*? how is the saint possible? This really seems to have been the question over which Schopenhauer became a philosopher and began. And so it was a genuinely Schopenhauerian conclusion when his most convinced adherent (perhaps also the last one, as far as Germany is concerned), namely, Richard Wagner, finished his life's work at precisely this point and in the end brought this horrible and eternal type on the stage as Kundry, *type vécu,*[6] in the flesh—at the very time when the psychiatrists of almost all the countries of Europe had occasion to study it at close quarters, wherever the religious neurosis—or what I call *"das religiöse Wesen"* [7]—had its latest epidemic outbreak and pageant in the "Salvation Army."

Let us ask what precisely about this whole phenomenon of the saint has seemed so enormously interesting to men of all types and ages, even to philosophers. Beyond any doubt, it was the air of the miraculous that goes with it—namely, the immediate *succession of opposites,* of states of the soul that are judged morally in opposite ways. It seemed palpable that a "bad man" was suddenly transformed into a "saint," a good man. The psychology we have had so far suffered shipwreck at this point: wasn't this chiefly because it had placed itself under the dominion of morals, because it, too, *believed* in opposite moral values and saw, read, *interpreted* these opposites into the text and the facts?

What? The "miracle" merely a mistake of interpretation? A lack of philology?

48

It seems that Catholicism is much more intimately related to the Latin races than all of Christianity in general is to us northerners—and unbelief therefore means something altogether different in Catholic and Protestant countries: among *them,* a kind of rebellion against the spirit of the race, while among us it is rather a return to the spirit (or anti-spirit) of the race. We northerners are undoubtedly descended from barbarian races, which also shows in

---

[6] A type that has lived.
[7] The title of this part of the book. See note 1 above.

our talent for religion: we have *little* talent for it. We may except the Celts, who therefore also furnished the best soil for the spread of the Christian infection to the north: in France the Christian ideal came to flourish as much as the pale sun of the north permitted it. How strangely pious for our taste are even the most recent French skeptics insofar as they have any Celtic blood! How Catholic, how un-German Auguste Comte's sociology smells to us with its Roman logic of the instincts! How Jesuitical that gracious and clever cicerone of Port-Royal, Sainte-Beuve, in spite of all his hostility against the Jesuits! And especially Ernest Renan: how inaccessible the language of such a Renan sounds to us northerners: at one instant after another some nothing of religious tension unbalances his soul, which is, in the more refined sense, voluptuous and inclined to stretch out comfortably. Let us speak after him these beautiful sentences—and how much malice and high spirits stir immediately in our probably less beautiful and harder, namely more German, soul as a response!

"Disons donc hardiment que la religion est un produit de l'homme normal, aue l'homme est le plus dans le vrai quand il est le plus religieux et le plus assuré d'une destinée infinie. . . . C'est quand il est bon qu'il veut que la vertu corresponde à un ordre éternel, c'est quand il contemple les choses d'une manière désintéressée qu'il trouve la morte révoltante et absurde. Comment ne pas supposer que c'est dans ces moments-là, que l'homme voit le mieux?" [8]

These sentences are so utterly *antipodal* to my ears and habits that on finding them my first wrath wrote on the margin *"la niaiserie religieuse par excellence!"* But my subsequent wrath actually took a fancy to them—these sentences standing truth on her head! It is so neat, so distinguished to have one's own antipodes!

---

[8] "So let us make bold to say that religion is a product of the normal man, that man is closest to the truth when he is most religious and most certain of an infinite destiny. . . . It is when he is good that he wants virtue to correspond to an eternal order; it is when he contemplates things in a disinterested manner that he finds death revolting and absurd. How can we but suppose that it is in moments like this that man sees best?"

49

What is amazing about the religiosity of the ancient Greeks is the enormous abundance of gratitude it exudes: it is a very noble type of man that confronts nature and life in *this* way.[9]

Later, when the rabble gained the upper hand in Greece, *fear* became rampant in religion, too—and the ground was prepared for Christianity.—

50

The passion for God: there are peasant types, sincere and obtrusive, like Luther—the whole of Protestantism lacks southern *delicatezza*.[10] There is sometimes an Oriental ecstasy worthy of a slave who, without deserving it, has been pardoned and elevated— for example, in Augustine, who lacks in a truly offensive manner all nobility of gestures and desires. There is a womanly tenderness and lust that presses bashfully and ignorantly toward a *unio mystica et physica*[11]—as in Madame de Guyon.[12] In many cases it appears oddly enough as a disguise for the puberty of a girl or youth; here and there even as the hysteria of an old maid, also as her final ambition—and in several such instances the church has proclaimed the female a saint.

---

[9] In other words, that affirms life as a great boon, in spite of all its terrors: this shows great strength and a remarkable and noble freedom from resentment.

[10] Delicacy.

[11] Mystical and physical union.

[12] Madame Guyon (Jeanne-Marie Bouvier de la Motte-Guyon, 1648-1717), was a French mystic who is considered one of the chief advocates of Quietism, introduced before 1675 by Miguel Molinos (1640-96), a Spanish priest who was arrested by the Roman Inquisition in 1685 and sentenced to perpetual imprisonment in 1687. Madame Guyon was imprisoned from 1695 to 1703. The Quietist doctrine was condemned by Innocent XII in 1699. (These dates are taken from *The Oxford Companion to French Literature*, Oxford, Clarendon Press, 1959.)

51

So far the most powerful human beings have still bowed worshipfully before the saint as the riddle of self-conquest and deliberate final renunciation. Why did they bow? In him—and as it were behind the question mark of his fragile and miserable appearance —they sensed the superior force that sought to test itself in such a conquest, the strength of the will in which they recognized and honored their own strength and delight in dominion: they honored something in themselves when they honored the saint. Moreover, the sight of the saint awakened a suspicion in them: such an enormity of denial, of anti-nature will not have been desired for nothing, they said to and asked themselves. There may be a reason for it, some very great danger about which the ascetic, thanks to his secret comforters and visitors, might have inside information. In short, the powerful of the world learned a new fear before him; they sensed a new power, a strange, as yet unconquered enemy— it was the "will to power" that made them stop before the saint. They had to ask him——

52

In the Jewish "Old Testament," the book of divine justice, there are human beings, things, and speeches in so grand a style that Greek and Indian literature have nothing to compare with it. With terror and reverence one stands before these tremendous remnants of what man once was, and will have sad thoughts about ancient Asia and its protruding little peninsula Europe, which wants by all means to signify as against Asia the "progress of man." To be sure, whoever is himself merely a meager, tame domestic animal and knows only the needs of domestic animals (like our educated people of today, including the Christians of "educated" Christianity) has no cause for amazement or sorrow among these ruins— the taste for the Old Testament is a touchstone for "great" and "small" [13]—perhaps he will find the *New* Testament, the book of grace, still rather more after his heart (it contains a lot of the real, tender, musty true-believer and small-soul smell). To have glued this New Testament, a kind of rococo of taste in every respect, to the Old Testament to make *one* book, as the "Bible," as "the book par excellence"—that is perhaps the greatest audacity and "sin against the spirit" that literary Europe has on its conscience.[14]

53

Why atheism today?—"The father" in God has been thoroughly refuted; ditto, "the judge," "the rewarder." Also his "free will": he does not hear—and if he heard he still would not know how to help. Worst of all: he seems incapable of clear communication: is he unclear?

This is what I found to be causes for the decline of European theism, on the basis of a great many conversations, asking and listening. It seems to me that the religious instinct is indeed in the process of growing powerfully—but the theistic satisfaction it refuses with deep suspicion.

54

What is the whole of modern philosophy doing at bottom? Since Descartes—actually more despite him than because of his precedent—all the philosophers seek to assassinate the old soul concept, under the guise of a critique of the subject-and-predicate concept—which means an attempt on the life of the basic presupposition of the Christian doctrine. Modern philosophy, being an epistemological skepticism, is, covertly or overtly, *anti-Christian*—although, to say this for the benefit of more refined ears, by no means anti-religious.

---

[13] Another suggestion for an "order of rank." Cf. section 39, note 19 above.
[14] Cf. *The Genealogy of Morals,* Third Essay, section 22, p. 580 below.

For, formerly, one believed in "the soul" as one believed in grammar and the grammatical subject: one said, "I" is the condition, "think" is the predicate and conditioned—thinking is an activity to which thought *must* supply a subject as cause. Then one tried with admirable perseverance and cunning to get out of this net—and asked whether the opposite might not be the case: "think" the condition, "I" the conditioned; "I" in that case only a synthesis which is *made* by thinking. At bottom, *Kant* wanted to prove that, starting from the subject, the subject could not be proved—nor could the object: the possibility of a *merely apparent existence* of the subject, "the soul" in other words, may not always have remained strange to him—that thought which as Vedanta philosophy existed once before on this earth and exercised tremendous power.

55

There is a great ladder of religious cruelty, with many rungs; but three of these are the most important.

Once one sacrificed human beings to one's god, perhaps precisely those whom one loved most: the sacrifices of the first-born in all prehistoric religions belong here, as well as the sacrifice of the Emperor Tiberius in the Mithras grotto of the isle of Capri, that most gruesome of all Roman anachronisms.

Then, during the moral epoch of mankind, one sacrificed to one's god one's own strongest instincts, one's "nature": *this* festive joy lights up the cruel eyes of the ascetic, the "anti-natural" enthusiast.

Finally—what remained to be sacrificed? At long last, did one not have to sacrifice for once whatever is comforting, holy, healing; all hope, all faith in hidden harmony, in future blisses and justices? didn't one have to sacrifice God himself and, from cruelty against oneself, worship the stone, stupidity, gravity, fate, the nothing? To sacrifice God for the nothing—this paradoxical mystery of the final cruelty was reserved for the generation that is now coming up: all of us already know something of this.—

56

Whoever has endeavored with some enigmatic longing, as I have, to think pessimism through to its depths and to liberate it from the half-Christian, half-German narrowness and simplicity in which it has finally presented itself to our century, namely, in the form of Schopenhauer's philosophy; whoever has really, with an Asiatic and supra-Asiatic eye, looked into, down into the most world-denying of all possible ways of thinking—beyond good and evil and no longer, like the Buddha and Schopenhauer, under the spell and delusion of morality—may just thereby, without really meaning to do so, have opened his eyes to the opposite ideal: the ideal of the most high-spirited, alive, and world-affirming human being who has not only come to terms and learned to get along with whatever was and is, but who wants to have *what was and is* repeated into all eternity,[15] shouting insatiably *da capo*[16]—not only to himself but to the whole play and spectacle, and not only to a spectacle but at bottom to him who needs precisely this spectacle— and who makes it necessary because again and again he needs him- self—and makes himself necessary—— What? And this wouldn't be—*circulus vitiosus deus?* [17]

57

With the strength of his spiritual eye and insight grows dis- tance and, as it were, the space around man: his world becomes more profound; ever new stars, ever new riddles and images be- come visible for him. Perhaps everything on which the spirit's eye has exercised its acuteness and thoughtfulness was nothing but an

---

[15] An allusion to Nietzsche's doctrine of the eternal recurrence of all events. Cf. the penultimate chapter of *Thus Spoke Zarathustra*, especially sections 10 and 11 (*Portable Nietzsche*, pp. 435f.), and, for critical expositions, Kaufmann's *Nietzsche*, Chapter 11, section II, and A. Danto's *Nietzsche as Philosopher* (New York, Macmillan, 1965), Chapter 7.

[16] From the beginning: a musical direction.

[17] A vicious circle made god? or: God is a vicious circle? or, least likely: the circle is a vicious god?

occasion for this exercise, a playful matter, something for children and those who are childish. Perhaps the day will come when the most solemn concepts which have caused the most fights and suffering, the concepts "God" and "sin," will seem no more important to us than a child's toy and a child's pain seem to an old man—and perhaps "the old man" will then be in need of another toy and another pain—still child enough, an eternal child!

58

Has it ever been really noted to what extent a genuinely religious life (both its microscopic favorite occupation of self-examination and that tender composure which calls itself "prayer" and is a continual readiness for the "coming of God") requires a leisure class, or half-leisure—I mean leisure with a good conscience, from way back, by blood, to which the aristocratic feeling that work *disgraces* is not altogether alien—the feeling that it makes soul and body common. And that consequently our modern, noisy, time-consuming industriousness, proud of itself, stupidly proud, educates and prepares people, more than anything else does, precisely for "unbelief."

Among those, for example, who now live in Germany at a distance from religion I find people whose "free-thinking" is of diverse types and origins, but above all a majority of those in whom industriousness has, from generation unto generation, dissolved the religious instincts, so they no longer even know what religions are good for and merely register their presence in the world with a kind of dumb amazement. They feel abundantly committed, these good people, whether to their business or to their pleasures, not to speak of the "fatherland" and the newspapers and "family obligations": it seems that they simply have no time left for religion, the more so because it remains unclear to them whether it involves another business or another pleasure—for it is not possible, they say to themselves, that one goes to church merely to dampen one's good spirits. They are not enemies of religious customs; when participation in such customs is required in certain cases, by the state, for example, they do what is required, as one does so many things—with a patient and modest seriousness and without much curiosity and discomfort: they simply live too much apart and outside to feel any need for any pro and con in such matters.

Those indifferent in this way include today the great majority of German middle-class Protestants, especially in the great industrious centers of trade and traffic; also the great majority of industrious scholars and the other accessories of the universities (excepting the theologians, whose presence and possibility there pose ever increasing and ever subtler riddles for a psychologist). Pious or even merely churchly people rarely have the slightest idea *how much* good will—one might say caprice—is required of a German scholar today if he is to take the problem of religion seriously. On the basis of his whole trade (and, as noted, on the basis of the tradelike industriousness to which he is committed by his modern conscience) he is inclined toward a superior, almost good-natured amusement in the face of religion, occasionally mixed with a dash of disdain for the "uncleanliness" of the spirit which he assumes wherever a church is still acknowledged. The scholar succeeds only with the help of history (*not* on the basis of his own personal experience) to muster a reverent seriousness and a certain shy consideration in the face of religion. But even if he raises his feeling into real gratitude toward it,[18] he still has not personally approached, not even by a single step, what still exists now as church or piety; perhaps even the opposite. The practical indifference toward religious matters into which he has been born and brought up is generally sublimated in him into caution and cleanliness that shun contact with religious men and matters; and it may be precisely the depth of his tolerance and humanity that bids him dodge the subtle distress involved in tolerance.

Every age has its own divine type of naïveté for whose invention other ages may envy it—and how much naïveté, venerable, childlike, and boundlessly clumsy naïveté lies in the scholar's faith in his superiority, in the good conscience of his tolerance, in the un-

---

18 In other words, even if he rises above all resentment and sees only the good done by religion.

suspecting simple certainty with which his instinct treats the religious man as an inferior and lower type that he has outgrown, leaving it behind, *beneath* him—him, that presumptuous little dwarf and rabble man, the assiduous and speedy head- and handiworker of "ideas," of "modern ideas"!

59

Anyone who has looked deeply into the world may guess how much wisdom lies in the superficiality of men. The instinct that preserves them teaches them to be flighty, light, and false. Here and there one encounters an impassioned and exaggerated worship of "pure forms," among both philosophers and artists: let nobody doubt that whoever stands that much in *need* of the cult of surfaces must at some time have reached *beneath* them with disastrous results.

Perhaps there even exists an order of rank among these burnt children, these born artists who can find the enjoyment of life only in the intention of *falsifying* its image (as it were, in a longwinded revenge on life): the degree to which life has been spoiled for them might be inferred from the degree to which they wish to see its image falsified, thinned down, transcendentalized, deified—the *homines religiosi* might be included among artists, as their highest rank.

It is the profound, suspicious fear of an incurable pessimism that forces whole millennia to bury their teeth in and cling to a religious interpretation of existence: the fear of that instinct which senses that one might get a hold of the truth *too soon*, before man has become strong enough, hard enough, artist enough.

Piety, the "life in God," seen in this way, would appear as the subtlest and final offspring of the *fear* of truth, as an artist's worship and intoxication before the most consistent of all falsifications, as the will to the inversion of truth, to untruth at any price. It may be that until now there has been no more potent means for beautifying man himself than piety: it can turn man into so much art, surface, play of colors, graciousness that his sight no longer makes one suffer.—

60

To love man *for God's sake*—that has so far been the noblest and most remote feeling attained among men. That the love of man is just one more stupidity and brutishness if there is no ulterior intent to sanctify it; that the inclination to such love of man must receive its measure, its subtlety, its grain of salt and dash of ambergris from some higher inclination—whoever the human being may have been who first felt and "experienced" this, however much his tongue may have stumbled [19] as it tried to express such *délicatesse,* let him remain holy and venerable for us for all time as the human being who has flown highest yet and gone astray most beautifully!

61

The philosopher as *we* understand him, we free spirits—as the man of the most comprehensive responsibility who has the conscience for the over-all development of man—this philosopher will make use of religions for his project of cultivation[20] and education, just as he will make use of whatever political and economic states are at hand. The selective and cultivating[21] influence, always destructive as well as creative and form-giving, which can be exerted with the help of religions, is always multiple and different according to the sort of human beings who are placed under its spell and protection. For the strong and independent who are prepared and predestined to command and in whom the reason and art of a governing race become incarnate, religion is one more means for overcoming resistances, for the ability to rule—as a bond that unites rulers and subjects and betrays and delivers the consciences of the latter, that which is most concealed and intimate and would like to elude obedience, to the former. And if a few individuals of such

---

[19] Probably an allusion to Exodus 4:10: the context requires us to think of Moses, in any case.

[20] *Seinem Züchtungs- und Erziehungswerke.*

[21] *Züchtende.*

noble descent are inclined through lofty spirituality to prefer a more withdrawn and contemplative life and reserve for themselves only the most subtle type of rule (over selected disciples or brothers in some order), then religion can even be used as a means for obtaining peace from the noise and exertion of *cruder* forms of government, and purity from the *necessary* dirt of all politics. That is how the Brahmins, for example, understood things: by means of a religious organization they gave themselves the power of nominating the kings of the people while they themselves kept and felt apart and outside, as men of higher and supra-royal tasks.

Meanwhile religion also gives to some of the ruled the instruction and opportunity to prepare themselves for future ruling and obeying: those slowly ascending classes—in which, thanks to fortunate marital customs, the strength and joy of the will, the will to self-control is ever growing—receive enough nudges and temptations from religion to walk the paths to higher spirituality, to test the feelings of great self-overcoming, of silence and solitude. Asceticism and puritanism are almost indispensable means for educating and ennobling a race that wishes to become master over its origins among the rabble and that works its way up toward future rule.

To ordinary human beings, finally—the vast majority who exist for service and the general advantage, and who *may* exist only for that—religion gives an inestimable contentment with their situation and type, manifold peace of the heart, an ennobling of obedience, one further happiness and sorrow with their peers and something transfiguring and beautifying, something of a justification for the whole everyday character, the whole lowliness, the whole half-brutish poverty of their souls. Religion and religious significance spread the splendor of the sun over such ever-toiling human beings and make their own sight tolerable to them. Religion has the same effect which an Epicurean philosophy has on sufferers of a higher rank: it is refreshing, refining, makes, as it were, the most of suffering, and in the end even sanctifies and justifies. Perhaps nothing in Christianity or Buddhism is as venerable as their art of teaching even the lowliest how to place themselves through piety in an illusory higher order of things and thus to maintain their contentment with the real order, in which their life is hard enough—and precisely this hardness is necessary.

62

In the end, to be sure—to present the other side of the account of these religions, too, and to expose their uncanny dangerousness—one always pays dearly and terribly when religions do *not* want to be a means of education and cultivation in the philosopher's hand but insist on having their own *sovereign* way, when they themselves want to be ultimate ends and not means among other means. There is among men as in every other animal species an excess of failures, of the sick, degenerating, infirm, who suffer necessarily; the successful cases are, among men too, always the exception—and in view of the fact that man is the *as yet undetermined animal,* the rare exception. But still worse: the higher type of man that a man represents, the greater the improbability that he will turn out *well.* The accidental, the law of absurdity in the whole economy of mankind, manifests itself most horribly in its destructive effect on the higher men whose complicated conditions of life can only be calculated with great subtlety and difficulty.

What, then, is the attitude of the above-mentioned two greatest religions toward this *excess* of cases that did not turn out right? They seek to preserve, to preserve alive whatever can possibly be preserved; indeed, as a matter of principle, they side with these cases as religions for *sufferers;* they agree with all those who suffer life like a sickness and would like to make sure that every other feeling about life should be considered false and should become impossible. Even if the very highest credit is given to this considerate and preserving care, which, besides being directed toward all the others, was and is also directed toward the highest type of man, the type that so far has almost always suffered most; nevertheless, in a total accounting, the *sovereign* religions we have had so far are among the chief causes that have kept the type "man" on a lower rung—they have preserved too much of *what ought to perish*. What we have to thank them for is inestimable; and who could be rich enough in gratitude not to be impoverished in view of all that the "spiritual men" of Christianity, for example, have so far done for Europe! And yet, when they gave comfort to sufferers, courage to the oppressed and despairing, a staff and support to the dependent, and lured away from society into monasteries and penitentiaries for the soul those who had been destroyed inwardly and who had become savage: how much more did they have to do besides, in order to work with a good conscience and on principle, to preserve all that was sick and that suffered—which means, in fact and in truth, to *worsen the European race?* Stand all valuations *on their head—that* is what they had to do. And break the strong, sickly o'er[22] great hopes, cast suspicion on the joy in beauty, bend everything haughty, manly, conquering, domineering, all the instincts characteristic of the highest and best-turned-out type of "man," into unsureness, agony of conscience, self-destruction—indeed, invert all love of the earthly and of dominion over the earth into hatred of the earth and the earthly—*that* is the task the church posed for itself and had to pose, until in its estimation "becoming unworldly," "unsensual," and "higher men" were fused into a single feeling.

Suppose we could contemplate the oddly painful and equally crude and subtle comedy of European Christianity with the mocking and aloof eyes of an Epicurean god, I think our amazement and laughter would never end: doesn't it seem that a single will dominated Europe for eighteen centuries—to turn man into a *sublime miscarriage?* Anyone, however, who approached this almost deliberate degeneration and atrophy of man represented by the Christian European (Pascal, for example), feeling the opposite kind of desire, not in an Epicurean spirit but rather with some divine hammer in his hand, would surely have to cry out in wrath, in pity, in horror: "O you dolts, you presumptuous, pitying dolts, what have you done! Was that work for your hands? How have you bungled and botched my beautiful stone! What presumption!"

I meant to say: Christianity has been the most calamitous

---

[22] An allusion to Hamlet's "sicklied o'er by the pale cast of thought."

kind of arrogance yet. Men, not high and hard enough to have any right to try to form *man* as artists; men, not strong and far-sighted enough to *let* the foreground law of thousandfold failure and ruin prevail, though it cost them sublime self-conquest; men, not noble enough to see the abysmally different order of rank, chasm of rank, between man and man—*such* men have so far held sway over the fate of Europe, with their "equal before God," until finally a smaller, almost ridiculous type, a herd animal, something eager to please, sickly, and mediocre has been bred, the European of today—

PART FOUR

---◄◉►---

EPIGRAMS AND INTERLUDES

Part Four

63

Whoever is a teacher through and through takes all things seriously only in relation to his students—even himself.

64

"Knowledge for its own sake"—that is the last snare of morality: with that one becomes completely entangled in it once more.

65

The attraction of knowledge would be small if one did not have to overcome so much shame on the way.

65a[1]

One is most dishonest to one's god: he is not *allowed* to sin.

66

The inclination to depreciate himself, to let himself be robbed, lied to, and taken advantage of, could be the modesty[2] of a god among men.

67

Love of *one* is a barbarism; for it is exercised at the expense of all others. The love of God, too.

---

[1] In the original edition of 1886 and in the second edition of 1891 this section bears the same number (65) as that preceding it. In the third and fourth editions of 1893 and 1894, the editor introduced minor changes and renumbered all the sections from this point on. In the standard editions (the so-called Grossoktav and the Musarion editions) this section is distinguished from the one preceding it by the addition of an "a." Schlechta, whose edition of the works in three volumes is widely considered impeccable philologically, follows the standard editions although he purports to follow the edition of 1886. Similar instances will be noted in subsequent notes.

[2] *Scham:* in most other places (see sections 40 and 65 above) this word has been translated as "shame."

68

"I have done that," says my memory. "I cannot have done that," says my pride, and remains inexorable. Eventually—memory yields.[3]

69

One has watched life badly if one has not also seen the hand that considerately—kills.

70

If one has character one also has one's typical experience, which recurs repeatedly.

71

The sage as astronomer.— As long as you still experience the stars as something "above you" you lack the eye of knowledge.

72

Not the intensity but the duration of high feelings makes high men.

73

Whoever reaches his ideal transcends it *eo ipso*.

73a[4]

Many a peacock hides his peacock tail from all eyes—and calls that his pride.

74

A man with spirit is unbearable if he does not also have at least two other things: gratitude[5] and cleanliness.

---

[3] Freud's theory of repression *in nuce*—or *in ovo*. Other sections that put one in mind of Freud include 3 above and 75 below; but this list could easily be lengthened.

[4] See section 65a, note 1, above.

[5] Again, as in sections 49 and 58, gratitude is virtually an antonym of resentment.

75

The degree and kind of a man's sexuality reach up into the ultimate pinnacle of his spirit.

76

Under peaceful conditions a warlike man sets upon himself.

77

With one's principles one wants to bully one's habits, or justify, honor, scold, or conceal them: two men with the same principles probably aim with them at something basically different.

78

Whoever despises himself still respects himself as one who despises.

79

A soul that knows it is loved but does not itself love betrays its sediment: what is at the bottom comes up.

80

A matter that becomes clear ceases to concern us.— What was on the mind of that god who counseled: "Know thyself!" Did he mean: "Cease to concern yourself! Become objective!"— And Socrates?— And "scientific men"?—

81

It is terrible to die of thirst in the ocean. Do you have to salt your truth so heavily that it does not even—quench thirst any more?

82

"Pity for all"—would be hardness and tyranny toward *you*, my dear neighbor!—

83

Instinct.— When the house burns one forgets even lunch.— Yes, but one eats it later in the ashes.

84

Woman learns to hate to the extent to which her charms—decrease.

85

The same affects in man and woman are yet different in *tempo:* therefore man and woman do not cease to misunderstand each other.

86

Women themselves always still have in the background of all personal vanity an impersonal contempt—for "woman."—

87

Tethered heart, free spirit.— If one tethers one's heart severely and imprisons it, one can give one's spirit many liberties: I have said that once before. But one does not believe me, unless one already knows it—

88

One begins to mistrust very clever people when they become embarrassed.

89

Terrible experiences pose the riddle whether the person who has them is not terrible.

90

Heavy, heavy-spirited people become lighter precisely through what makes others heavier, through hatred and love, and for a time they surface.

91

So cold, so icy that one burns one's fingers on him! Every hand is startled when touching him.— And for that very reason some think he glows.

92

Who has not, for the sake of his good reputation—sacrificed himself once?—

93

Affability contains no hatred of men, but for that very reason too much contempt for men.

94

A man's maturity—consists in having found again the seriousness one had as a child, at play.

95

To be ashamed of one's immorality—that is a step on the staircase at whose end one is also ashamed of one's morality.

96

One should part from life as Odysseus parted from Nausicaa—blessing it rather than in love with it.

97

What? A great man? I always see only the actor of his own ideal.

98

If we train our conscience, it kisses us while it hurts us.

99

The voice of disappointment:[6] "I listened for an echo and heard nothing but praise—"

100

In front of ourselves we all pose as simpler than we are: thus we take a rest from our fellow men.

---

[6] Emphasized in most editions, but not in that of 1886 nor in Schlechta's.

101

Today the man of knowledge might well feel like God become animal.

102

Discovering that one is loved in return really ought to disenchant the lover with the beloved. "What? this person is modest enough to love even you? Or stupid enough? Or—or—"

103

Danger in happiness.[7]— "Now everything redounds to my best, now I love every destiny—who feels like being my destiny?"

104

Not their love of men but the impotence of their love of men keeps the Christians of today from—burning us.[8]

105

The *pia fraus*[9] offends the taste (the "piety") of the free spirit, who has "the piety of the search for knowledge," even more than the *impia fraus*. Hence his profound lack of understanding for the church, a characteristic of the type "free spirit"—*his* unfreedom.

106

In music the passions enjoy themselves.

107

Once the decision has been made, close your ear even to the best counterargument: sign of a strong character. Thus an occasional will to stupidity.

---

[7] See note 6 above.

[8] If Christians were really passionately concerned for the salvation of their fellow men in the hereafter, they would still burn those whose heresies lead legions into eternal damnation.

[9] "Pious fraud" or holy lie; here juxtaposed with "impious fraud" or unholy lie. The former means deceiving men for the sake of their own salvation, as in Plato's *Republic*, 414C.

108

There are no moral phenomena at all, but only a moral interpretation of phenomena—

109

A criminal is frequently not equal to his deed: he makes it smaller and slanders it.[10]

110

The lawyers defending a criminal are rarely artists enough to turn the beautiful terribleness of his deed to his advantage.

111

Our vanity is hardest to wound when our pride has just been wounded.

112

Those who feel predestined to see and not to believe will find all believers too noisy and obtrusive: they fend them off.

113

"You want to prepossess him in your favor? Then pretend to be embarrassed in his presence—"

114

The enormous expectation in sexual love and the sense of shame in this expectation spoils all perspective for women from the start.

115

Where neither love nor hatred is in the game, a woman's game is mediocre.

---

[10] One of Sartre's leitmotifs; cf. Electra in *Les Mouches* (*The Flies*) and the problem of *Les Mains sales* (*Dirty Hands*).

116

The great epochs of our life come when we gain the courage to rechristen our evil as what is best in us.

117

The will to overcome an affect is ultimately only the will of another, or of several other, affects.

118

There is an innocence in admiration; it is found in those to whom it has never yet occurred that they, too, might be admired some day.

119

The disgust with dirt can be so great that it keeps us from cleaning ourselves—from "justifying" ourselves.

120

Sensuality often hastens the growth of love so much that the roots remain weak and are easily torn up.

121

It was subtle of God to learn Greek when he wished to become an author—and not to learn it better.

122

Enjoying praise is in some people merely a courtesy of the heart—and just the opposite of vanity of the spirit.

123

Even concubinage has been corrupted—by marriage.

124

Whoever rejoices on the very stake triumphs not over pain but at the absence of pain that he had expected. A parable.

125

When we have to change our mind about a person, we hold the inconvenience he causes us very much against him.

126

A people[11] is a detour of nature to get to six or seven great men.— Yes, and then to get around them.

127

Science offends the modesty of all real women. It makes them feel as if one wanted to peep under their skin—yet worse, under their dress and finery.

128

The more abstract the truth is that you would teach, the more you have to seduce the senses to it.

129

The devil has the broadest perspectives for God; therefore he keeps so far away from God—the devil being the most ancient friend of wisdom.

130

What a man *is* begins to betray itself when his talent decreases —when he stops showing what he *can do*. Talent, too, is finery; finery, too, is a hiding place.

131

The sexes deceive themselves about each other—because at bottom they honor and love only themselves (or their own ideal, to put it more pleasantly). Thus man likes woman peaceful—but woman is *essentially* unpeaceful, like a cat, however well she may have trained herself to seem peaceable.

---

[11] *Ein Volk:* the polemical and sarcastic thrust of this epigram depends on the heavy reliance of German nationalism—both in Nietzsche's time and in the twentieth century—on the mystique of the *Volk.*

132

One is best punished for one's virtues.

133

Whoever does not know how to find the way to *his* ideal lives more frivolously and impudently than the man without an ideal.

134

All credibility, all good conscience, all evidence of truth come only from the senses.

135

Pharisaism is not a degeneration in a good man: a good deal of it is rather the condition of all being good.

136

One seeks a midwife for his thoughts, another someone whom he can help: origin of a good conversation.

137

When associating with scholars and artists we easily miscalculate in opposite directions: behind a remarkable scholar one finds, not infrequently, a mediocre man, and behind a mediocre artist quite often—a very remarkable man.

138

When we are awake we also do what we do in our dreams: we invent and make up the person with whom we associate—and immediately forget it.

139

In revenge and in love woman is more barbarous than man.

140

Rule as a riddle.— "If the bond shan't burst—bite upon it first."

141

The abdomen is the reason why man does not easily take himself for a god.

142

The chastest words I have heard: *"Dans le véritable amour c'est l'âme, qui enveloppe le corps."* [12]

143

Our vanity desires that what we do best should be considered what is hardest for us. Concerning the origin of many a morality.

144

When a woman has scholarly inclinations there is usually something wrong with her sexually. Sterility itself disposes one toward a certain masculinity of taste; for man is, if I may say so, "the sterile animal."

145

Comparing man and woman on the whole, one may say: woman would not have the genius for finery if she did not have an instinct for a *secondary* role.

146

Whoever fights monsters should see to it that in the process he does not become a monster. And when you look long into an abyss, the abyss also looks into you.

147

From old Florentine novels; also—from life: *"Buona femmina e mala femmina vuol bastone."* [13] Sacchetti, Nov. 86.

148

Seducing one's neighbor to a good opinion and afterwards be-

---

[12] "In true love it is the soul that envelops the body."
[13] "Good and bad women want a stick."

lieving piously in this opinion—who could equal women in this art?—

149

What a time experiences as evil is usually an untimely echo of what was formerly experienced as good—the atavism of a more ancient ideal.

150

Around the hero everything turns into a tragedy; around the demi-god, into a satyr play; and around God—what? perhaps into "world"?—

151

Having a talent is not enough: one also requires your permission for it—right, my friends?

152

"Where the tree of knowledge stands, there is always Paradise": thus speak the oldest and the youngest serpents.

153

Whatever is done from love always occurs beyond good and evil.

154

Objections, digressions, gay mistrust, the delight in mockery are signs of health: everything unconditional belongs in pathology.

155

The sense of the tragic gains and wanes with sensuality.

156

Madness is rare in individuals—but in groups, parties, nations, and ages it is the rule.

157

The thought of suicide is a powerful comfort: it helps one through many a dreadful night.

158

To our strongest drive, the tyrant in us, not only our reason bows but also our conscience.

159

One *has* to repay good and ill—but why precisely to the person who has done us good or ill?

160

One no longer loves one's insight enough once one communicates it.

161

Poets treat their experiences shamelessly: they exploit them.

162

"Our neighbor[14]—is not our neighbor but *his* neighbor"—thus thinks every nation.

163

Love brings the high and concealed characteristics of the lover into the light—what is rare and exceptional in him: to that extent it easily deceives regarding his normality.

164

Jesus said to his Jews: "The law was for servants—love God as I love him, as his son! What are morals to us sons of God!"

165

Regarding all parties.— A shepherd always needs a bell-wether—or he himself must occasionally be a wether.

---

[14] In the religious sense.

166

Even when the mouth lies, the way it looks still tells the truth.

167

In men who are hard, intimacy involves shame—and is precious.

168

Christianity gave Eros poison to drink: he did not die of it but degenerated—into a vice.

169

Talking much about oneself can also be a means to conceal oneself.

170

Praise is more obtrusive than a reproach.

171

In a man devoted to knowledge, pity seems almost ridiculous, like delicate hands on a cyclops.

172

From love of man one occasionally embraces someone at random (because one cannot embrace all): but one must not tell him this—

173

One does not hate as long as one still despises, but only those whom one esteems equal or higher.

174

You utilitarians, you, too, love everything *useful* only as a *vehicle* for your inclinations; you, too, really find the noise of its wheels insufferable?

175

In the end one loves one's desire and not what is desired.

176

The vanity of others offends our taste only when it offends our vanity.

177

Perhaps nobody yet has been truthful enough about what "truthfulness" is.

178

One does not credit clever people with their follies: what a loss of human rights!

179

The consequences of our actions take hold of us, quite indifferent to our claim that meanwhile we have "improved."

180

There is an innocence in lying which is the sign of good faith in a cause.

181

It is inhuman to bless where one is cursed.

182

The familiarity of those who are superior embitters because it may not be returned.—

183

"Not that you lied to me, but that I no longer believe you, has shaken me"—

184

The high spirits of kindness may look like malice.

185

"I don't like him."— Why?— "I am not equal to him."—
Has any human being ever answered that way?

PART FIVE

NATURAL HISTORY
OF MORALS

Part Five

186

The moral sentiment in Europe today is as refined, old, diverse, irritable, and subtle, as the "science of morals" that accompanies it is still young, raw, clumsy, and butterfingered—an attractive contrast that occasionally even becomes visible and incarnate in the person of a moralist. Even the term "science of morals" is much too arrogant considering what it designates, and offends *good* taste—which always prefers more modest terms.

One should own up in all strictness to what is still necessary here for a long time to come, to what alone is justified so far: to collect material, to conceptualize and arrange a vast realm of subtle feelings of value and differences of value which are alive, grow, beget, and perish—and perhaps attempts to present vividly some of the more frequent and recurring forms of such living crystallizations—all to prepare a *typology* of morals.

To be sure, so far one has not been so modest. With a stiff seriousness that inspires laughter, all our philosophers demanded something far more exalted, presumptuous, and solemn from themselves as soon as they approached the study of morality: they wanted to supply a *rational foundation* for morality—and every philosopher so far has believed that he has provided such a foundation. Morality itself, however, was accepted as "given." How remote from their clumsy pride was that task which they considered insignificant and left in dust and must—the task of description—although the subtlest fingers and senses can scarcely be subtle enough for it.

Just because our moral philosophers knew the facts of morality only very approximately in arbitrary extracts or in accidental epitomes—for example, as the morality of their environment, their class, their church, the spirit of their time, their climate and part of the world—just because they were poorly informed and not even very curious about different peoples, times, and past ages—they never laid eyes on the real problems of morality; for these emerge only when we compare *many* moralities. In all "science of morals" so far one thing was *lacking,* strange as it may sound: the problem of morality itself; what was lacking was any suspicion that there was something problematic here. What the philosophers called "a rational foundation for morality" and tried to supply was, seen in the right light, merely a scholarly variation of the common *faith* in the prevalent morality; a new means of *expression* for this faith; and thus just another fact within a particular morality; indeed, in the last analysis a kind of denial that this morality might ever be considered problematic—certainly the very opposite of an examination, analysis, questioning, and vivisection of this very faith.

Listen, for example, with what almost venerable innocence Schopenhauer still described his task, and then draw your conclusions about the scientific standing of a "science" whose ultimate masters still talk like children and little old women: "The principle," he says (p. 136 of *Grundprobleme der Moral*),[1] "the fundamental

---

[1] First edition of 1886 and second edition of 1891: "das Princip, sagt er (S. 136 der Grundprobleme der Moral), der Grundsatz . . ."

Musarion edition of the *Werke:* "das Princip, sagt er (S. 137 der Grundprobleme der Ethik), der Grundsatz . . ."

Schlechta's edition, which purports to follow the original edition, actually departs even a little further from it than the Musarionausgabe: "das Princip" sagt er (S. 137 der Grundprobleme der Ethik), "der Grundsatz . . ."

The correct title of Schopenhauer's book is *Die beiden Grundprobleme der Ethik* (the two fundamental problems of ethics), and in the original edition of 1841 the quoted passage is found on p. 138. Nietzsche neither placed the title in quotes nor italicized it, and his slight variation of the title is less odd than the fact that on Schopenhauer's own title page of 1841 the title of the second essay, which Nietzsche cites, is given as *"Ueber das Fundament der Moral, nicht* gekrönt von der K. Dänischen Societät der Wissenschaften, zu Kopenhagen, den 30. Januar 1840" ("On the Foundation of Morals, not awarded a prize by the Danish Royal Society . . ."). Turning the page, one finds the table of contents, in which the title of the second essay is given as follows: *"Preisschrift über die Grundlage der Moral"* (Prize essay on the basis of morals). (The heading on p. 101 agrees with the table of contents, not with Schopenhauer's title page.) If Schopenhauer could say in one instance *Fundament* and in the other *Grundlage,* Nietzsche might as well say *Moral* instead of *Ethik;* moreover, the word in the title that concerned Nietzsche was *Moral,* not *Ethik.*

The editors who changed the title and page reference given by Nietzsche failed to insert three dots in the quotation itself, to indicate a minor omis-

proposition on whose contents all moral philosophers are *really*[2] agreed—*neminem laede, immo omnes, quantum potes, juva*[3]— that is *really* the proposition for which all moralists endeavor to find the rational foundation . . . the *real* basis of ethics for which one has been looking for thousands of years as for the philosopher's stone."

The difficulty of providing a rational foundation for the principle cited may indeed be great—as is well known, Schopenhauer did not succeed either—and whoever has once felt deeply how insipidly false and sentimental this principle is in a world whose essence is will to power, may allow himself to be reminded that Schopenhauer, though a pessimist, *really*—played the flute. Every day, after dinner: one should read his biography on that. And incidentally: a pessimist, one who denies God and the world but *comes to a stop* before morality—who affirms morality and plays the flute—the *laede neminem* morality—what? is that really—a pessimist?

187

Even apart from the value of such claims as "there is a categorical imperative in us," one can still always ask: what does such a claim tell us about the man who makes it? There are moralities which are meant to justify their creator before others. Other moralities are meant to calm him and lead him to be satisfied with himself. With yet others he wants to crucify himself and humiliate himself. With others he wants to wreak revenge, with others conceal himself, with others transfigure himself and place himself way up, at a distance. This morality is used by its creator to forget, that one to have others forget him or something about him. Some moralists want to vent their power and creative whims on humanity; some others,

---

sion of two and a half lines between "agreed" and the Latin quotation. This omission does not change the sense and is in no way unfair to Schopenhauer.

[2] "Really" and "real": *eigentlich*. The emphasis is Nietzsche's, not Schopenhauer's.

[3] "Hurt no one; rather, help all as much as you can."

perhaps including Kant, suggest with their morality: "What deserves respect in me is that I can obey—and you *ought* not to be different from me."— In short, moralities are also merely a *sign language of the affects*.

188

Every morality is, as opposed to *laisser aller*,[4] a bit of tyranny against "nature"; also against "reason"; but this in itself is no objection, as long as we do not have some other morality which permits us to decree that every kind of tyranny and unreason is impermissible. What is essential and inestimable in every morality is that it constitutes a long compulsion: to understand Stoicism or Port-Royal or Puritanism, one should recall the compulsion under which every language so far has achieved strength and freedom— the metrical compulsion of rhyme and rhythm.

How much trouble the poets and orators of all peoples have taken—not excepting a few prose writers today in whose ear there dwells an inexorable conscience—"for the sake of some foolishness," as utilitarian dolts say, feeling smart—"submitting abjectly to capricious laws," as anarchists say, feeling "free," even "free-spirited." But the curious fact is that all there is or has been on earth of freedom, subtlety, boldness, dance, and masterly sureness, whether in thought itself or in government, or in rhetoric and persuasion, in the arts just as in ethics, has developed only owing to the "tyranny of such capricious laws"; and in all seriousness, the probability is by no means small that precisely this is "nature" and "natural"—and *not* that *laisser aller*.

Every artist knows how far from any feeling of letting himself go his "most natural" state is—the free ordering, placing, disposing, giving form in the moment of "inspiration"—and how strictly and subtly he obeys thousandfold laws precisely then, laws that precisely on account of their hardness and determination defy all formulation through concepts (even the firmest concept is, com-

---

[4] Letting go.

pared with them, not free of fluctuation, multiplicity, and ambiguity).

What is essential "in heaven and on earth" seems to be, to say it once more, that there should be *obedience* over a long period of time and in a *single* direction: given that, something always develops, and has developed, for whose sake it is worth while to live on earth; for example, virtue, art, music, dance, reason, spirituality—something transfiguring, subtle, mad, and divine. The long unfreedom of the spirit, the mistrustful constraint in the communicability of thoughts, the discipline thinkers imposed on themselves to think within the directions laid down by a church or court, or under Aristotelian presuppositions, the long spiritual will to interpret all events under a Christian schema and to rediscover and justify the Christian god in every accident—all this, however forced, capricious, hard, gruesome, and anti-rational, has shown itself to be the means through which the European spirit has been trained to strength, ruthless curiosity, and subtle mobility, though admittedly in the process an irreplaceable amount of strength and spirit had to be crushed, stifled, and ruined (for here, as everywhere, "nature" manifests herself as she is, in all her prodigal and indifferent magnificence which is outrageous but noble).

That for thousands of years European thinkers thought merely in order to prove something—today, conversely, we suspect every thinker who "wants to prove something"—that the conclusions that *ought* to be the result of their most rigorous reflection were always settled from the start, just as it used to be with Asiatic astrology, and still is today with the innocuous Christian-moral interpretation of our most intimate personal experiences "for the glory of God" and "for the salvation of the soul"—this tyranny, this caprice, this rigorous and grandiose stupidity has *educated* the spirit. Slavery is, as it seems, both in the cruder and in the more subtle sense, the indispensable means of spiritual discipline and cultivation,[5] too. Consider any morality with this in mind: what there is in it of "nature" teaches hatred of the *laisser aller,* of any all-too-great

---

[5] *Zucht und Züchtung.*

freedom, and implants the need for limited horizons and the nearest tasks—teaching the *narrowing of our perspective,* and thus in a certain sense stupidity, as a condition of life and growth.

"You shall obey—someone and for a long time: *else* you will perish and lose the last respect for yourself"—this appears to me to be the moral imperative of nature which, to be sure, is neither "categorical" as the old Kant would have it (hence the "else") nor addressed to the individual (what do individuals matter to her?), but to peoples, races, ages, classes—but above all to the whole human animal, to *man.*

189

Industrious races find it very troublesome to endure leisure: it was a masterpiece of *English* instinct to make the Sabbath so holy and so boring that the English begin unconsciously to lust again for their work- and week-day. It is a kind of cleverly invented, cleverly inserted *fast,* the like of which is also encountered frequently in the ancient world (although, in fairness to southern peoples, not exactly in regard to work). There have to be fasts of many kinds; and wherever powerful drives and habits prevail, legislators have to see to it that intercalary days are inserted on which such a drive is chained and learns again to hunger. Viewed from a higher vantage point, whole generations and ages that make their appearance, infected with some moral fanaticism, seem to be such times of constraint and fasting during which a drive learns to stoop and submit, but also to *purify* and *sharpen* itself. A few philosophical sects, too, permit such an interpretation (for example, the Stoa in the midst of Hellenistic culture with its lascivious atmosphere, overcharged with aphrodisiac odors).

This is also a hint for an explanation of the paradox: why it was precisely during the most Christian period of Europe and altogether only under the pressure of Christian value judgments that the sex drive sublimated [6] itself into love (*amour-passion*).

---

[6] Nietzsche was the first to use *sublimiren* in its specifically modern sense, which is widely associated with Freud. On the history of this interesting term see Kaufmann's *Nietzsche,* Chapter 7, section II.

190

There is something in the morality of Plato that does not really belong to Plato but is merely encountered in his philosophy—one might say, in spite of Plato: namely, the Socratism for which he was really too noble. "Nobody wants to do harm to himself, therefore all that is bad is done involuntarily. For the bad do harm to themselves: this they would not do if they knew that the bad is bad. Hence the bad are bad only because of an error; if one removes the error, one necessarily makes them—good."

This type of inference smells of the *rabble* that sees nothing in bad actions but the unpleasant consequences and really judges, "it is *stupid* to do what is bad," while "good" is taken without further ado to be identical with "useful and agreeable." In the case of every moral utilitarianism one may immediately infer the same origin and follow one's nose: one will rarely go astray.

Plato did everything he could in order to read something refined and noble into the proposition of his teacher—above all, himself. He was the most audacious of all interpreters and took the whole Socrates only the way one picks a popular tune and folk song from the streets in order to vary it into the infinite and impossible—namely, into all of his own masks and multiplicities. In a jest, Homeric at that: what is the Platonic Socrates after all if not *prosthe Platōn opithen te Platōn messē te Chimaira.*[7]

191

The ancient theological problem of "faith" and "knowledge" —or, more clearly, of instinct and reason—in other words, the question whether regarding the valuation of things instinct deserves more authority than rationality, which wants us to evaluate

---

[7] "Plato in front and Plato behind, in the middle Chimaera." Cf. *Iliad,* VI:181, where Chimaera is described: "Lion in front and serpent behind, in the middle a goat." For Nietzsche's complex and seemingly contradictory view of Socrates, see Kaufmann's *Nietzsche,* Chapter 13.

and act in accordance with reasons, with a "why?"—in other words, in accordance with expedience and utility—this is still the ancient moral problem that first emerged in the person of Socrates and divided thinking people long before Christianity. Socrates himself, to be sure, with the taste of his talent—that of a superior dialectician—had initially sided with reason; and in fact, what did he do his life long but laugh at the awkward incapacity of noble Athenians who, like all noble men, were men of instinct and never could give sufficient information about the reasons for their actions? In the end, however, privately and secretly, he laughed at himself, too: in himself he found, before his subtle conscience and self-examination, the same difficulty and incapacity. But is that any reason, he encouraged himself, for giving up the instincts? One has to see to it that they as well as reason receive their due—one must follow the instincts but persuade reason to assist them with good reasons. This was the real *falseness* of that great ironic, so rich in secrets; he got his conscience to be satisfied with a kind of self-trickery: at bottom, he had seen through the irrational element in moral judgments.

Plato, more innocent in such matters and lacking the craftiness of the plebeian, wanted to employ all his strength—the greatest strength any philosopher so far has had at his disposal—to prove to himself that reason and instinct of themselves tend toward one goal, the good, "God." And since Plato, all theologians and philosophers are on the same track—that is, in moral matters it has so far been instinct, or what the Christians call "faith," or "the herd," as I put it, that has triumphed. Perhaps Descartes should be excepted, as the father of rationalism (and hence the grandfather of the Revolution) who conceded authority to reason alone: but reason is merely an instrument, and Descartes was superficial.

192

Whoever has traced the history of an individual science finds a clue in its development for understanding the most ancient and common processes of all "knowledge and cognition." There as here it is the rash hypotheses, the fictions, the good dumb will to "believe," the lack of mistrust and patience that are developed first; our senses learn only late, and never learn entirely, to be subtle, faithful, and cautious organs of cognition. Our eye finds it more comfortable to respond to a given stimulus by reproducing once more an image that it has produced many times before, instead of registering what is different and new in an impression. The latter would require more strength, more "morality." Hearing something new is embarrassing and difficult for the ear; foreign music we do not hear well. When we hear another language we try involuntarily to form the sounds we hear into words that sound more familiar and more like home to us: thus the German, for example, transformed *arcubalista,* when he heard that, into *Armbrust.*[8] What is new finds our senses, too, hostile and reluctant; and even in the "simplest" processes of sensation the affects dominate, such as fear, love, hatred, including the passive affects of laziness.

Just as little as a reader today reads all of the individual words (let alone syllables) on a page—rather he picks about five words at random out of twenty and "guesses" at the meaning that probably belongs to these five words—just as little do we see a tree exactly and completely with reference to leaves, twigs, color, and form; it is so very much easier for us simply to improvise some approximation of a tree. Even in the midst of the strangest experiences we still do the same: we make up the major part of the experience and can scarcely be forced *not* to contemplate some event as its "inventors." All this means: basically and from time immemorial we are—*accustomed to lying.* Or to put it more virtuously and hypocritically, in short, more pleasantly: one is much more of an artist than one knows.

In an animated conversation I often see the face of the person with whom I am talking so clearly and so subtly determined in accordance with the thought he expresses, or that I believe has been produced in him, that this degree of clarity far surpasses my powers of vision: so the subtle shades of the play of the muscles and the expression of the eyes *must* have been made up by me. Probably the person made an altogether different face, or none at all.

---

[8] Literally, arm-breast; both words mean crossbow.

193

Quidquid luce fuit, tenebris agit:[9] but the other way around, too. What we experience in dreams—assuming that we experience it often—belongs in the end just as much to the over-all economy of our soul as anything experienced "actually": we are richer or poorer on account of it, have one need more or less, and finally are led a little by the habits of our dreams even in broad daylight and in the most cheerful moments of our wide-awake spirit.

Suppose someone has flown often in his dreams and finally, as soon as he dreams, he is conscious of his power and art of flight as if it were his privilege, also his characteristic and enviable happiness. He believes himself capable of realizing every kind of arc and angle simply with the lightest impulse; he knows the feeling of a certain divine frivolity, an "upward" without tension and constraint, a "downward" without condescension and humiliation—without *gravity!* How could a human being who had had such dream experiences and dream habits fail to find that the word "happiness" had a different color and definition in his waking life, too? How could he fail to—desire happiness differently? "Rising" as described by poets must seem to him, compared with this "flying," too earthbound, muscle-bound, forced, too "grave."

194

The difference among men becomes manifest not only in the difference between their tablets of goods—in the fact that they consider different goods worth striving for and also disagree about what is more and less valuable, about the order of rank of the goods they recognize in common—it becomes manifest even more in what they take for really *having* and *possessing* something good.

Regarding a woman, for example, those men who are more modest consider the mere use of the body and sexual gratification a sufficient and satisfying sign of "having," of possession. Another

---

9 "What occurred in the light, goes on in the dark."

type, with a more suspicious and demanding thirst for possession, sees the "question mark," the illusory quality of such "having" and wants subtler tests, above all in order to know whether the woman does not only give herself to him but also gives up for his sake what she has or would like to have: only then does she seem to him "possessed." A third type, however, does not reach the end of his mistrust and desire for having even so: he asks himself whether the woman, when she gives up everything for him, does not possibly do this for a phantom of him. He wants to be known deep down, abysmally deep down, before he is capable of being loved at all; he dares to let himself be fathomed. He feels that his beloved is fully in his possession only when she no longer deceives herself about him, when she loves him just as much for his devilry and hidden insatiability as for his graciousness, patience, and spirituality.

One type wants to possess a people—and all the higher arts of a Cagliostro and Catiline suit him to that purpose. Someone else, with a more subtle thirst for possession, says to himself: "One may not deceive where one wants to possess." The idea that a mask of him might command the heart of the people[10] irritates him and makes him impatient: "So I must *let* myself be known, and first must know myself."

Among helpful and charitable people one almost regularly encounters that clumsy ruse which first doctors the person to be helped—as if, for example, he "deserved" help, required just *their* help, and would prove to be profoundly grateful for all help, faithful and submissive. With these fancies they dispose of the needy as of possessions, being charitable and helpful people from a desire for possessions. One finds them jealous if one crosses or anticipates them when they want to help.

Involuntarily, parents turn children into something similar to themselves—they call that "education." Deep in her heart, no mother doubts that the child she has borne is her property; no father contests his own right to subject it to *his* concepts and valuations. Indeed, formerly it seemed fair for fathers (among the ancient Germans, for example) to decide on the life or death of the new-

---

[10] This, of course, was what happened to Nietzsche himself after his death.

born as they saw fit. And like the father, teachers, classes, priests, and princes still see, even today, in every new human being an unproblematic opportunity for another possession. So it follows——

195

The Jews—a people "born for slavery," as Tacitus and the whole ancient world say; "the chosen people among the peoples," as they themselves say and believe—the Jews have brought off that miraculous feat of an inversion of values, thanks to which life on earth has acquired a novel and dangerous attraction for a couple of millennia: their prophets have fused "rich," "godless," "evil," "violent," and "sensual" into one and were the first to use the word "world" as an opprobrium. This inversion of values (which includes using the word "poor" as synonymous with "holy" and "friend") constitutes the significance of the Jewish people: they mark the beginning of the slave rebellion in morals.[11]

196

Countless dark bodies are to be *inferred* near the sun—and we shall never see them. Among ourselves, this is a parable; and a psychologist of morals reads the whole writing of the stars only as a parable- and sign-language which can be used to bury much in silence.

197

We misunderstand the beast of prey and the man of prey (for example, Cesare Borgia)[12] thoroughly, we misunderstand "na-

---

[11] But compare section 52 above; also *Human, All-Too-Human*, section 475, and *The Dawn*, section 205 (*Portable Nietzsche*, pp. 61ff.; 86f.); and, above all, sections 248 and 250 below. For a discussion of Nietzsche's image of the Jews and the many pertinent passages in his writings, see Kaufmann, *Nietzsche*, Chapter 10.

[12] It has often been alleged that Cesare Borgia was Nietzsche's ideal, but an examination of all of Nietzsche's references to him shows that this is plainly false (Kaufmann, *Nietzsche*, Chapter 7, section III). One can consider a type healthy without admiring it or urging others to emulate it.

ture," as long as we still look for something "pathological" at the bottom of these healthiest of all tropical monsters and growths, or even for some "hell" that is supposed to be innate in them; yet this is what almost all moralists so far have done. Could it be that moralists harbor a hatred of the primeval forest and the tropics? And that the "tropical man" must be discredited at any price, whether as sickness and degeneration of man or as his own hell and self-torture? Why? In favor of the "temperate zones"? In favor of temperate men? Of those who are "moral"? Who are mediocre?— This for the chapter "Morality as Timidity."

198

All these moralities that address themselves to the individual, for the sake of his "happiness," as one says—what are they but counsels for behavior in relation to the degree of *dangerousness* in which the individual lives with himself; recipes against his passions, his good and bad inclinations insofar as they have the will to power and want to play the master; little and great prudences and artifices that exude the nook odor of old nostrums and of the wisdom of old women; all of them baroque and unreasonable in form —because they address themselves to "all," because they generalize where one must not generalize. All of them speak unconditionally, take themselves for unconditional, all of them flavored with more than one grain of salt and tolerable only—at times even seductive—when they begin to smell over-spiced and dangerous, especially "of the other world." All of it is, measured intellectually, worth very little and not by a long shot "science," much less "wisdom," but rather, to say it once more, three times more, prudence, prudence, prudence, mixed with stupidity, stupidity, stupidity—whether it be that indifference and statue coldness against the hot-headed folly of the affects which the Stoics advised and administered; or that laughing-no-more and weeping-no-more of Spinoza, his so naïvely advocated destruction of the affects through their analysis and vivisection; or that tuning down of the affects to a harmless mean according to which they may be satisfied, the Aristotelianism of morals; even morality as enjoyment of the affects in a deliberate thinness and spiritualization by means of the symbolism of art, say, as music, or as love of God and of man for God's sake—for in religion the passions enjoy the rights of citizens again, assuming that——; finally even that accommodating and playful surrender to the affects, as Hafiz and Goethe taught it, that bold dropping of the reins, that spiritual-physical *licentia morum*[13] in the exceptional case of wise old owls and sots[14] for whom it "no longer holds much danger." This, too, for the chapter "Morality as Timidity."

199

Inasmuch as at all times, as long as there have been human beings, there have also been herds of men (clans, communities, tribes, peoples, states, churches) and always a great many people who obeyed, compared with the small number of those commanding—considering, then, that nothing has been exercised and cultivated better and longer among men so far than obedience—it may fairly be assumed that the need for it is now innate in the average man, as a kind of *formal conscience* that commands: "thou shalt unconditionally do something, unconditionally not do something else," in short, "thou shalt." This need seeks to satisfy itself and to fill its form with some content. According to its strength, impatience, and tension, it seizes upon things as a rude appetite, rather indiscriminately, and accepts whatever is shouted into its ears by someone who issues commands—parents, teachers, laws, class prejudices, public opinions.

The strange limits of human development, the way it hesitates, takes so long, often turns back, and moves in circles, is due to the fact that the herd instinct of obedience is inherited best, and at the expense of the art of commanding. If we imagine this instinct progressing for once to its ultimate excesses, then those who command

---

13 Moral license.

14 The association of Goethe and Hafiz is suggested by Goethe's great collection of poems, *West-Östlicher Divan* (West-Eastern Divan, 1819), in which he identifies himself with the Persian poet. But the old Goethe, unlike Hafiz, was certainly no sot.

and are independent would eventually be lacking altogether; or they would secretly suffer from a bad conscience and would find it necessary to deceive themselves before they could command—as if they, too, merely obeyed. This state is actually encountered in Europe today: I call it the moral hypocrisy of those commanding. They know no other way to protect themselves against their bad conscience than to pose as the executors of more ancient or higher commands (of ancestors, the constitution, of right, the laws, or even of God). Or they even borrow herd maxims from the herd's way of thinking, such as "first servants of their people" or "instruments of the common weal."

On the other side, the herd man in Europe today gives himself the appearance of being the only permissible kind of man, and glorifies his attributes, which make him tame, easy to get along with, and useful to the herd, as if they were the truly human virtues: namely, public spirit, benevolence, consideration, industriousness, moderation, modesty, indulgence, and pity. In those cases, however, where one considers leaders and bellwethers indispensable, people today make one attempt after another to add together clever herd men by way of replacing commanders: all parliamentary constitutions, for example, have this origin. Nevertheless, the appearance of one who commands unconditionally strikes these herd-animal Europeans as an immense comfort and salvation from a gradually intolerable pressure, as was last attested in a major way by the effect of Napoleon's appearance. The history of Napoleon's reception is almost the history of the higher happiness attained by this whole century in its most valuable human beings and moments.

200

In an age of disintegration that mixes races indiscriminately, human beings have in their bodies the heritage of multiple origins, that is, opposite, and often not merely opposite, drives and value standards that fight each other and rarely permit each other any rest. Such human beings of late cultures and refracted lights will on the average be weaker human beings: their most profound desire is that the war they *are* should come to an end. Happiness appears to them, in agreement with a tranquilizing (for example, Epicurean or Christian) medicine and way of thought, pre-eminently as the happiness of resting, of not being disturbed, of satiety, of finally attained unity, as a "sabbath of sabbaths," to speak with the holy rhetorician Augustine who was himself such a human being.

But when the opposition and war in such a nature have the effect of one more charm and incentive of life—and if, moreover, in addition to his powerful and irreconcilable drives, a real mastery and subtlety in waging war against oneself, in other words, self-control, self-outwitting, has been inherited or cultivated, too—then those magical, incomprehensible, and unfathomable ones arise, those enigmatic men predestined for victory and seduction, whose most beautiful expression is found in Alcibiades and Caesar (to whose company I should like to add that *first* European after my taste, the Hohenstaufen Frederick II),[15] and among artists perhaps Leonardo da Vinci. They appear in precisely the same ages when that weaker type with its desire for rest comes to the fore: both types belong together and owe their origin to the same causes.

201

As long as the utility reigning in moral value judgments is solely the utility of the herd, as long as one considers only the preservation of the community, and immorality is sought exactly and exclusively in what seems dangerous to the survival of the community—there can be no morality of "neighbor love." Supposing that even then there was a constant little exercise of consideration, pity, fairness, mildness, reciprocity of assistance; supposing that even in that state of society all those drives are active that later receive the honorary designation of "virtues" and eventually almost

---

[15] Medieval German emperor, 1215-50. The members of the Stefan George Circle cultivated "monumentalistic" historiography, in the sense of Nietzsche's second "Untimely Meditation," and penned portraits of great men partly aimed to show the qualities that constitute human greatness. Two of their most celebrated studies are Friedrich Gundolf's *Caesar* (1924) and Ernst Kantorowicz's *Kaiser Friedrich II* (1927). Another such study is Ernst Bertram's *Nietzsche* (1918), whose faults are summed up in the subtitle: "Attempt at a Mythology."

coincide with the concept of "morality"—in that period they do not yet at all belong in the realm of moral valuations; they are still *extra-moral*. An act of pity, for example, was not considered either good or bad, moral or immoral, in the best period of the Romans; and even when it was praised, such praise was perfectly compatible with a kind of disgruntled disdain as soon as it was juxtaposed with an action that served the welfare of the whole, of the *res publica*.[16]

In the last analysis, "love of the neighbor" is always something secondary, partly conventional and arbitrary-illusory in relation to *fear of the neighbor*. After the structure of society is fixed on the whole and seems secure against external dangers, it is this fear of the neighbor that again creates new perspectives of moral valuation. Certain strong and dangerous drives, like an enterprising spirit, foolhardiness, vengefulness, craftiness, rapacity, and the lust to rule, which had so far not merely been honored insofar as they were socially useful—under different names, to be sure, from those chosen here—but had to be trained and cultivated to make them great (because one constantly needed them in view of the dangers to the whole community, against the enemies of the community), are now experienced as doubly dangerous, since the channels to divert them are lacking, and, step upon step, they are branded as immoral and abandoned to slander.

Now the opposite drives and inclinations receive moral honors; step upon step, the herd instinct draws its conclusions. How much or how little is dangerous to the community, dangerous to equality, in an opinion, in a state or affect, in a will, in a talent—that now constitutes the moral perspective: here, too, fear is again the mother of morals.

The highest and strongest drives, when they break out passionately and drive the individual far above the average and the flats of the herd conscience, wreck the self-confidence of the community, its faith in itself, and it is as if its spine snapped. Hence just these drives are branded and slandered most. High and independent spirituality, the will to stand alone, even a powerful reason are

---

[16] Commonwealth.

experienced as dangers; everything that elevates an individual above the herd and intimidates the neighbor is henceforth called *evil;* and the fair, modest, submissive, conforming mentality, the *mediocrity* of desires attains moral designations and honors. Eventually, under very peaceful conditions, the opportunity and necessity for educating one's feelings to severity and hardness is lacking more and more; and every severity, even in justice, begins to disturb the conscience; any high and hard nobility and self-reliance is almost felt to be an insult and arouses mistrust; the "lamb," even more the "sheep," gains in respect.

There is a point in the history of society when it becomes so pathologically soft and tender that among other things it sides even with those who harm it, criminals, and does this quite seriously and honestly. Punishing somehow seems unfair to it, and it is certain that imagining "punishment" and "being supposed to punish" hurts it, arouses fear in it. "Is it not enough to render him *undangerous?* Why still punish? Punishing itself is terrible." With this question, herd morality, the morality of timidity, draws its ultimate consequence. Supposing that one could altogether abolish danger, the reason for fear, this morality would be abolished, too, *eo ipso:* it would no longer be needed, it would no longer *consider itself* necessary.

Whoever examines the conscience of the European today will have to pull the same imperative out of a thousand moral folds and hideouts—the imperative of herd timidity: "we want that some day there should be *nothing any more to be afraid of!*" Some day—throughout Europe, the will and way to this day is now called "progress." [17]

---

[17] Cf. F. D. Roosevelt's celebrated demand for "freedom from fear." The idea that much of man's conduct and culture can be explained in terms of fear was first explored extensively by Nietzsche in *The Dawn* (1881). For some discussion and pertinent quotations, see Kaufmann's *Nietzsche,* Chapter 6, section II; for Nietzsche's own opposition to punishment and resentment, *ibid.,* Chapter 12, section V. Nietzsche's critique of one type of opposition to punishment, above, should be compared with *Twilight of the Idols,* section 37 (*Portable Nietzsche,* pp. 538ff.), and Rilke's *Sonnets to Orpheus,* II.9 (original and translation in *Twenty German Poets,* ed. and trans. W. Kaufmann, New York, Modern Library, 1963, pp. 234f.).

202

Let us immediately say once more what we have already said a hundred times, for today's ears resist such truths—*our* truths. We know well enough how insulting it sounds when anybody counts man, unadorned and without metaphor, among the animals; but it will be charged against us as almost a *guilt* that precisely for the men of "modern ideas" we constantly employ such expressions as "herd," "herd instincts," and so forth. What can be done about it? We cannot do anything else; for here exactly lies our novel insight. We have found that in all major moral judgments Europe is now of one mind, including even the countries dominated by the influence of Europe: plainly, one now *knows* in Europe what Socrates thought he did not know and what that famous old serpent once promised to teach—today one "knows" what is good and evil.[18]

Now it must sound harsh and cannot be heard easily when we keep insisting: that which here believes it knows, that which here glorifies itself with its praises and reproaches, calling itself good, that is the instinct of the herd animal, man, which has scored a breakthrough and attained prevalence and predominance over other instincts—and this development is continuing in accordance with the growing physiological approximation and assimilation of which it is the symptom. *Morality in Europe today is herd animal morality*—in other words, as we understand it, merely *one* type of human morality beside which, before which, and after which many other types, above all *higher* moralities, are, or ought to be, possible. But this morality resists such a "possibility," such an "ought"

---

[18] Cf. *Zarathustra*, "On Old and New Tablets," section 2 (*Portable Nietzsche*, p. 308): "When I came to men I found them sitting on an old conceit: the conceit that they have long known what is good and evil for man . . . whoever wanted to sleep well still talked of good and evil before going to sleep."

And in Shaw's *Major Barbara* (Act III) Undershaft says: "What! no capacity for business, no knowledge of law, no sympathy with art, no pretension to philosophy; only a simple knowledge of the secret that has puzzled all the philosophers, baffled all the lawyers . . . : the secret of right and wrong. Why, man, you are a genius, a master of masters, a god! At twenty-four, too!"

with all its power: it says stubbornly and inexorably, "I am morality itself, and nothing besides is morality." Indeed, with the help of a religion which indulged and flattered the most sublime herd-animal desires, we have reached the point where we find even in political and social institutions an ever more visible expression of this morality: the *democratic* movement is the heir of the Christian movement.

But there are indications that its tempo is still much too slow and sleepy for the more impatient, for the sick, the sufferers of the instinct mentioned: witness the ever madder howling of the anarchist dogs who are baring their fangs more and more obviously and roam through the alleys of European culture. They seem opposites of the peacefully industrious democrats and ideologists of revolution, and even more so of the doltish philosophasters and brotherhood enthusiasts who call themselves socialists and want a "free society"; but in fact they are at one with the lot in their thorough and instinctive hostility to every other form of society except that of the *autonomous* herd (even to the point of repudiating the very concepts of "master" and "servant"—*ni dieu ni maître*[19] runs a socialist formula). They are at one in their tough resistance to every special claim, every special right and privilege (which means in the last analysis, *every* right: for once all are equal nobody needs "rights" any more). They are at one in their mistrust of punitive justice (as if it were a violation of those who are weaker, a wrong against the *necessary* consequence of all previous society). But they are also at one in the religion of pity, in feeling with all who feel, live, and suffer (down to the animal, up to "God"—the excess of a "pity with God" belongs in a democratic age). They are at one, the lot of them, in the cry and the impatience of pity, in their deadly hatred of suffering generally, in their almost feminine inability to remain spectators, to *let* someone suffer. They are at one in their involuntary plunge into gloom and unmanly tenderness under whose spell Europe seems threatened by a new Buddhism. They are at one in their faith in the morality of *shared* pity, as if that were

---

[19] "Neither god nor master"; cf. section 22 above.

morality in itself, being the height, the *attained* height of man, the sole hope of the future, the consolation of present man, the great absolution from all former guilt. They are at one, the lot of them, in their faith in the community as the *savior,* in short, in the herd, in "themselves"—

203

We have a different faith; to us the democratic movement is not only a form of the decay of political organization but a form of the decay, namely the diminution, of man, making him mediocre and lowering his value. Where, then, must *we* reach with our hopes?

Toward *new philosophers;* there is no choice; toward spirits strong and original enough to provide the stimuli for opposite valuations and to revalue and invert "eternal values"; toward forerunners, toward men of the future who in the present tie the knot and constraint that forces the will of millennia upon *new* tracks. To teach man the future of man as his *will,* as dependent on a human will, and to prepare great ventures and over-all attempts of discipline and cultivation by way of putting an end to that gruesome dominion of nonsense and accident that has so far been called "history"—the nonsense of the "greatest number" is merely its ultimate form: at some time new types of philosophers and commanders will be necessary for that, and whatever has existed on earth of concealed, terrible, and benevolent spirits, will look pale and dwarfed by comparison. It is the image of such leaders that *we* envisage: may I say this out loud, you free spirits? The conditions that one would have partly to create and partly to exploit for their genesis; the probable ways and tests that would enable a soul to grow to such a height and force that it would feel the *compulsion* for such tasks; a revaluation of values under whose new pressure and hammer a conscience would be steeled, a heart turned to bronze, in order to endure the weight of such responsibility; on the other hand, the necessity of such leaders, the frightening danger that they might fail to appear or that they might turn out badly or degenerate—these are *our* real worries and gloom—do you know that, you free spirits?—these are the heavy distant thoughts and storms that pass over the sky of *our* life.

There are few pains as sore as once having seen, guessed, felt how an extraordinary human being strayed from his path and degenerated.[20] But anyone who has the rare eye for the over-all danger that "man" himself *degenerates;* anyone who, like us, has recognized the monstrous fortuity that has so far had its way and play regarding the future of man—a game in which no hand, and not even a finger, of God took part as a player; anyone who fathoms the calamity that lies concealed in the absurd guilelessness and blind confidence of "modern ideas" and even more in the whole Christian-European morality—suffers from an anxiety that is past all comparisons. With a single glance he sees what, given a favorable accumulation and increase of forces and tasks, might yet *be made of man;* he knows with all the knowledge of his conscience how man is still unexhausted for the greatest possibilities and how often the type "man" has already confronted enigmatic decisions and new paths—he knows still better from his most painful memories what wretched things have so far usually broken a being of the highest rank that was in the process of becoming, so that it broke, sank, and became contemptible.

The *over-all degeneration of man* down to what today appears to the socialist dolts and flatheads as their "man of the future"— as their ideal—this degeneration and diminution of man into the perfect herd animal (or, as they say, to the man of the "free society"), this animalization of man into the dwarf animal of equal rights and claims, is *possible,* there is no doubt of it. Anyone who has once thought through this possibility to the end knows one kind of nausea that other men don't know—but perhaps also a new *task!*—

[20] Perhaps an allusion to Richard Wagner.

PART SIX

WE SCHOLARS[1]

---

[1] *Wir Gelehrten.* This can only mean "Scholars," not "Intellectuals" (Cowan translation).

Part Six

204

At the risk that moralizing will here, too, turn out to be what it has always been—namely, according to Balzac, an intrepid *montrer ses plaies*[2]—I venture to speak out against an unseemly and harmful shift in the respective ranks of science[3] and philosophy, which is now threatening to become established, quite unnoticed and as if it were accompanied by a perfectly good conscience. I am of the opinion that only *experience*—experience always seems to mean bad experience?—can entitle us to participate in the discussion of such higher questions of rank, lest we talk like blind men about colors—*against* science the way women and artists do ("Oh, this dreadful science!" sigh their instinct and embarrassment; "it always gets to the *bottom* of things!").

The scholar's[4] declaration of independence, his emancipation from philosophy, is one of the more refined effects of the democratic order—and disorder: the self-glorification and self-exaltation of scholars[5] now stand in full bloom, in their finest spring, everywhere—which is not meant to imply that in this case self-praise smells pleasant.[6] "Freedom from all masters!" that is what the instinct of the rabble wants in this case, too; and after science has most happily rid itself of theology whose "handmaid" it was too long, it now aims with an excess of high spirits and a lack of understanding to lay down laws for philosophy and to play the "master" herself—what am I saying? the *philosopher*.

My memory—the memory of a scientific man, if you'll for-

---

[2] "Showing one's wounds."

[3] *Wissenschaft* might just as well be rendered as "scholarship" in this section —and in much German literature: the term does not have primary reference to the natural sciences as it does in twentieth-century English.

[4] *Des wissenschaftlichen Menschen.*

[5] *Des Gelehrten.*

[6] An allusion the German proverb: "Self-praise stinks."

give me—is bulging with naïvetés of overbearing that I have heard about philosophy and philosophers from the lips of young natural scientists and old physicians (not to speak of the most learned [7] and conceited [8] of all scholars, the philologists and schoolmen, who are both by profession). Sometimes it was the specialist and nook dweller who instinctively resisted any kind of synthetic enterprise and talent; sometimes the industrious worker who had got a whiff of *otium*[9] and the noble riches in the psychic economy of the philosopher which had made him feel defensive and small. Sometimes it was that color blindness of the utility man who sees nothing in philosophy but a series of *refuted* systems and a prodigal effort that "does nobody any good." Sometimes the fear of masked mysticism and a correction of the limits of knowledge leaped forward; sometimes lack of respect for individual philosophers that had involuntarily generalized itself into lack of respect for philosophy.

Most frequently, finally, I found among young scholars that what lay behind the arrogant contempt for philosophy was the bad aftereffect of—a philosopher to whom they now denied allegiance on the whole without, however, having broken the spell of his cutting evaluation of other philosophers—with the result of an over-all irritation with all philosophy. (Schopenhauer's aftereffect on our most modern Germany, for example, seems to me to be of this kind: with his unintelligent wrath against Hegel [10] he has succeeded in wrenching the whole last generation of Germans out of the context of German culture—a culture that was, considering everything, an elevation and divinatory subtlety of the *historical sense*. But precisely at this point Schopenhauer was poor, unreceptive, and un-German to the point of genius.)

Altogether, taking a large view, it may have been above all what was human, all too human, in short, the wretchedness of the most recent philosophy itself that most thoroughly damaged re-

---

[7] *Gebildet.*
[8] *Eingebildet.*
[9] Leisure.
[10] Cf. section 252 below.

spect for philosophy and opened the gates to the instinct of the rabble. Let us confess how utterly our modern world lacks the whole type[11] of a Heraclitus, Plato, Empedocles, and whatever other names these royal and magnificent hermits of the spirit had; and how it is with considerable justification that, confronted with such representatives of philosophy as are today, thanks to fashion, as much on top as they are really at the bottom—in Germany, for example, the two lions of Berlin, the anarchist Eugen Dühring and the amalgamist Eduard von Hartmann[12]—a solid man of science *may* feel that he is of a better type and descent. It is especially the sight of those hodgepodge philosophers who call themselves "philosophers of reality" or "positivists" that is capable of injecting a dangerous mistrust into the soul of an ambitious young scholar: these are at best scholars and specialists themselves—that is palpable—they are all losers who have been *brought back* under the hegemony of science, after having desired *more* of themselves at some time without having had the right to this "more" and its responsibilities—and who now represent, in word and deed, honorably, resentfully, and vengefully, the *unbelief* in the masterly task and masterfulness of philosophy.

Finally: how could it really be otherwise? Science is flourishing today and her good conscience is written all over her face, while the level to which all modern philosophy has gradually sunk, this rest of philosophy today, invites mistrust and displeasure, if not mockery and pity. Philosophy reduced to "theory of knowledge," in fact no more than a timid epochism and doctrine of abstinence— a philosophy that never gets beyond the threshold and takes pains to *deny* itself the right to enter—that is philosophy in its last throes, an end, an agony, something inspiring pity. How could such a philosophy—*dominate!*

---

[11] The German word *Art* in this context *could* mean manner, but the same word near the end of the sentence plainly means type.
[12] Eugen Dühring (1833-1921) and Eduard von Hartmann (1842-1906) were highly regarded at the time. Dühring was a virulent anti-Semite; Hartmann attempted to amalgamate Schopenhauer's philosophy with Hegel's.

205

The dangers for a philosopher's development are indeed so manifold today that one may doubt whether this fruit can still ripen at all. The scope and the tower-building of the sciences has grown to be enormous, and with this also the probability that the philosopher grows weary while still learning or allows himself to be detained somewhere to become a "specialist"—so he never attains his proper level, the height for a comprehensive look, for looking around, for looking *down*. Or he attains it too late, when his best time and strength are spent—or impaired, coarsened, degenerated, so his view, his over-all value judgment does not mean much any more. It may be precisely the sensitivity of his intellectual conscience that leads him to delay somewhere along the way and to be late: he is afraid of the seduction to become a dilettante, a millipede, an insect with a thousand antennae; he knows too well that whoever has lost his self-respect cannot command or *lead* in the realm of knowledge—unless he would like to become a great actor, a philosophical Cagliostro and pied piper, in short, a seducer. This is in the end a question of taste, even if it were not a question of conscience.

Add to this, by way of once more doubling the difficulties for a philosopher, that he demands of himself a judgment, a Yes or No, not about the sciences but about life and the value of life— that he is reluctant to come to believe that he has a right, or even a duty, to such a judgment, and must seek his way to this right and faith only from the most comprehensive—perhaps most disturbing and destructive[13]—experiences, and frequently hesitates, doubts, and lapses into silence.

Indeed, the crowd has for a long time misjudged and mistaken the philosopher, whether for a scientific man and ideal scholar or for a religiously elevated, desensualized,[14] "desecular-

---

13 *Störendsten, zerstörendsten.*
14 *Entsinnlichten.* Cowan mistakenly translates this word as "demoralized."

ized" enthusiast and sot of God.[15] And if a man is praised today for living "wisely" or "as a philosopher," it hardly means more than "prudently and apart." Wisdom—seems to the rabble a kind of escape, a means and trick for getting well out of a wicked game. But the genuine philosopher—as it seems to *us*, my friends?—lives "unphilosophically" and "unwisely," above all *imprudently,* and feels the burden and the duty of a hundred attempts and temptations of life—he risks *himself* constantly, he plays the wicked game—

206

Compared to a genius—that is, to one who either *begets* or *gives birth,* taking both terms in their most elevated sense—the scholar, the scientific average man, always rather resembles an old maid: like her he is not conversant with the two most valuable functions of man. Indeed, one even concedes to both, to the scholars and to old maids, as it were by way of a compensation, that they are respectable—one stresses their respectability—and yet feels annoyed all over at having to make this concession.

Let us look more closely: what is the scientific man? To begin with, a type of man that is not noble, with the virtues of a type of man that is not noble, which is to say, a type that does not dominate and is neither authoritative nor self-sufficient: he has industriousness, patient acceptance of his place in rank and file, evenness and moderation in his abilities and needs, an instinct for his equals and for what they need; for example, that bit of independence and green pasture without which there is no quiet work, that claim to honor and recognition (which first of all presupposes literal recognition and recognizability), that sunshine of a good name, that constant attestation of his value and utility which is needed to overcome again and again the internal *mistrust* which is the sediment in the hearts of all dependent men and herd animals.

---

[15] An allusion to the conception of Spinoza as "God-intoxicated." Cowan: "divine alcoholic."

The scholar also has, as is only fair, the diseases and bad manners of a type that is not noble: he is rich in petty envy and has lynx eyes for what is base in natures to whose heights he cannot attain. He is familiar, but only like those who let themselves go, not *flow;* and just before those who flow like great currents he freezes and becomes doubly reserved: his eye becomes like a smooth and reluctant lake with not a ripple of delight or sympathy. The worst and most dangerous thing of which scholars are capable comes from their sense of the mediocrity of their own type—from that Jesuitism of mediocrity which instinctively works at the annihilation of the uncommon man and tries to break every bent bow or, preferably, to unbend it. Unbending—considerately, of course, with a solicitous hand—*unbending* with familiar pity, that is the characteristic art of Jesuitism which has always known how to introduce itself as a religion of pity.—

207

However gratefully we may welcome an *objective* spirit—and is there anyone who has never been mortally sick of everything subjective and of his accursed ipsissimosity? [16]—in the end we also have to learn caution against our gratitude and put a halt to the exaggerated manner in which the "unselfing" and depersonalization of the spirit is being celebrated nowadays as if it were the goal itself and redemption and transfiguration. This is particularly characteristic of the pessimist's school, which also has good reasons for according the highest honors to "disinterested knowledge."

The objective person who no longer curses and scolds like the pessimist, the *ideal* scholar in whom the scientific instinct, after thousands of total and semi-failures, for once blossoms and blooms to the end, is certainly one of the most precious instruments there are; but he belongs in the hand of one more powerful. He is only an instrument; let us say, he is a *mirror*—he is no "end in himself." The objective man is indeed a mirror: he is accustomed to sub-

---

[16] Coinage, formed from *ipsissima* (very own).

mit before whatever wants to be known, without any other pleasure than that found in knowing and "mirroring"; he waits until something comes, and then spreads himself out tenderly lest light footsteps and the quick passage of spiritlike beings should be lost on his plane and skin.

Whatever still remains in him of a "person" strikes him as accidental, often arbitrary, still more often disturbing: to such an extent has he become a passageway and reflection of strange forms and events even to himself. He recollects "himself" only with an effort and often mistakenly; he easily confuses himself with others, he errs about his own needs and is in this respect alone unsubtle and slovenly. Perhaps his health torments him, or the pettiness and cramped atmosphere of wife and friend, or the lack of companions and company—yes, he forces himself to reflect on his torments—in vain. Already his thoughts roam—to a *more general* case, and tomorrow he knows no more than he did yesterday how he might be helped. He has lost any seriousness for himself, also time: he is cheerful, *not* for lack of distress, but for lack of fingers and handles for *his* need. His habit of meeting every thing and experience halfway, the sunny and impartial hospitality with which he accepts everything that comes his way, his type of unscrupulous benevolence, of dangerous unconcern about Yes and No—alas, there are cases enough in which he has to pay for these virtues! And as a human being he becomes all too easily the *caput mortuum*[17] of these virtues.

If love and hatred are wanted from him—I mean love and hatred as God, woman, and animal understand them—he will do what he can and give what he can. But one should not be surprised if it is not much—if just here he proves inauthentic, fragile, questionable, and worm-eaten. His love is forced, his hatred artificial and rather *un tour de force,* a little vanity and exaggeration. After all, he is genuine only insofar as he may be objective: only in his cheerful "totalism" he is still "nature" and "natural." His mirror soul, eternally smoothing itself out, no longer knows how to af-

---

[17] Dross.

firm or negate; he does not command, neither does he destroy. *"Je ne méprise presque rien,"* [18] he says with Leibniz: one should not overlook and underestimate that *presque.*[19]

Neither is he a model man; he does not go before anyone, nor behind; altogether he places himself too far apart to have any reason to take sides for good or evil. When confusing him for so long with the *philosopher,* with the Caesarian cultivator and cultural dynamo,[20] one accorded him far too high honors and overlooked his most essential characteristics: he is an instrument, something of a slave though certainly the most sublime type of slave, but in himself nothing—*presque rien!* The objective man is an instrument, a precious, easily injured and clouded instrument for measuring and, as an arrangement of mirrors, an artistic triumph that deserves care and honor; but he is no goal, no conclusion and sunrise,[21] no complementary man in whom the *rest* of existence is justified, no termination—and still less a beginning, a begetting and first cause, nothing tough, powerful, self-reliant that wants to be master —rather only a delicate, carefully dusted, fine, mobile pot for forms that still has to wait for some content and substance in order to "shape" itself accordingly—for the most part, a man without substance and content, a "selfless" man. Consequently, also nothing for women, *in parenthesi.*—

208

When a philosopher suggests these days that he is not a skeptic—I hope this is clear from the description just given of the objective spirit—everybody is annoyed. One begins to look at him apprehensively, one would like to ask, to ask so much—— Indeed, among timid listeners, of whom there are legions now, he is henceforth considered dangerous. It is as if at his rejection of skepticism they heard some evil, menacing rumbling in the distance, as if a new explosive were being tried somewhere, a dynamite of the

---

18 "I despise almost nothing."

19 Almost.

20 *Dem cäsarischen Züchter und Gewaltmenschen der Cultur.*

21 *Ausgang und Aufgang;* literally, going out and going up.

spirit, perhaps a newly discovered Russian *nihiline*,[22] a pessimism *bonae voluntatis*[23] that does not merely say No, want No, but— horrible thought!—*does* No.

Against this type of "good will"—a will to the actual, active denial of life—there is today, according to common consent, no better soporific and sedative than skepticism, the gentle, fair, lulling poppy of skepticism; and even *Hamlet* is now prescribed by the doctors of the day against the "spirit" [24] and its underground rumblings. "Aren't our ears filled with wicked noises as it is?" asks the skeptic as a friend of quiet, and almost as a kind of security police; "this subterranean No is terrible! Be still at last, you pessimistic moles!"

For the skeptic, being a delicate creature, is frightened all too easily; his conscience is trained to quiver at every No, indeed even at a Yes that is decisive and hard, and to feel as if it had been bitten.[25] Yes and No—that goes against his morality; conversely, he likes to treat his virtue to a feast of noble abstinence, say, by repeating Montaigne's "What do I know?" or Socrates' "I know that I know nothing." Or: "Here I don't trust myself, here no door is open to me." Or: "Even if one were open, why enter right away?" Or: "What use are all rash hypotheses? Entertaining no hypotheses at all might well be part of good taste. Must you insist on immediately straightening what is crooked? on filling up every hole with oakum? Isn't there time? Doesn't time have time? O you devilish brood, are you incapable of *waiting*? The uncertain has its charms,

---

[22] Coinage, modeled on "nicotine"; cf. *Antichrist,* section 2 (*Portable Nietzsche,* p. 570).

[23] Of good will.

[24] The Cowan translation has, instead of "against the 'spirit' " [*gegen den "Geist"*], "to cure mind," which misses the point of the remark about *Hamlet.*

Nietzsche had argued in one of the most brilliant passages of his first book, *The Birth of Tragedy,* that Hamlet is no skeptic: "Action requires the veils of illusion: that is the doctrine of Hamlet, not that cheap wisdom of Jack the Dreamer who reflects too much . . . Not reflection, no—true knowledge, an insight into the horrible truth, outweighs any motive for action" (section 7).

[25] In German, conscience bites. Cf. the medieval "agenbite of inwit" of which James Joyce makes much in *Ulysses.*

too; the sphinx, too, is a Circe; Circe, too, was a philosopher."

Thus a skeptic consoles himself; and it is true that he stands in need of some consolation. For skepticism is the most spiritual expression of a certain complex physiological condition that in ordinary language is called nervous exhaustion and sickliness; it always develops when races or classes that have long been separated are crossed suddenly and decisively. In the new generation that, as it were, has inherited in its blood diverse standards and values, everything is unrest, disturbance, doubt, attempt; the best forces have an inhibiting effect, the very virtues do not allow each other to grow and become strong; balance, a center of gravity, and perpendicular poise are lacking in body and soul. But what becomes sickest and degenerates most in such hybrids is the *will:* they no longer know independence of decisions and the intrepid sense of pleasure in willing—they doubt the "freedom of the will" even in their dreams.

Our Europe of today, being the arena of an absurdly sudden attempt at a radical mixture of classes, and *hence* races, is therefore skeptical in all its heights and depths—sometimes with that mobile skepticism which leaps impatiently and lasciviously from branch to branch, sometimes dismal like a cloud overcharged with question marks—and often mortally sick of its will. Paralysis of the will: where today does one not find this cripple sitting? And often in such finery! How seductive the finery looks! This disease enjoys the most beautiful pomp- and lie-costumes; and most of what today displays itself in the showcases, for example, as "objectivity," "being scientific," *"l'art pour l'art,"* "pure knowledge, free of will," is merely dressed-up skepticism and paralysis of the will: for this diagnosis of the European sickness I vouch.

The sickness of the will is spread unevenly over Europe: it appears strongest and most manifold where culture has been at home longest; it disappears to the extent to which the "barbarian" still—or again—claims his rights under the loose garments of Western culture. In France today the will is accordingly most seriously sick, which is as easy to infer as it is palpable. And France, having always possessed a masterly skill at converting even the most calamitous turns of its spirit into something attractive and seductive, now really shows its cultural superiority over Europe by being the school and display of all the charms of skepticism.

The strength to will, and to will something for a long time, is a little greater in Germany, and more so in the German north than in the center of Germany; but much stronger yet in England, Spain, and Corsica, here in association with indolence, there with hard heads—not to speak of Italy, which is too young to know what it wants and still has to prove whether it is able to will—but it is strongest and most amazing by far in that enormous empire in between, where Europe, as it were, flows back into Asia, in Russia. There the strength to will has long been accumulated and stored up, there the will—uncertain whether as a will to negate or a will to affirm—is waiting menacingly to be discharged, to borrow a pet phrase of our physicists today. It may well take more than Indian wars and complications in Asia to rid Europe of its greatest danger: internal upheavals would be needed, too, the shattering of the empire into small units, and above all the introduction of the parliamentary nonsense, including the obligation for everybody to read his newspaper with his breakfast.

I do not say this because I want it to happen: the opposite would be rather more after my heart—I mean such an increase in the menace of Russia that Europe would have to resolve to become menacing, too, namely, *to acquire one will* by means of a new caste that would rule Europe, a long, terrible will of its own that would be able to cast its goals millennia hence—so the long-drawn-out comedy of its many splinter states as well as its dynastic and democratic splinter wills would come to an end. The time for petty politics is over: the very next century will bring the fight for the dominion of the earth—the *compulsion* to large-scale politics.

209

To what extent the new warlike age into which we Europeans have evidently entered may also favor the development of another and stronger type of skepticism, on that I want to comment for the present only in the form of a parable which those who like German history should understand readily. That unscrupulous enthusiast for handsome and very tall grenadiers who, as King of Prussia,[26] brought into being a military and skeptical genius—and thus, when you come right down to it, that new type of German which has just now come to the top triumphantly—the questionable, mad father of Frederick the Great himself had the knack and lucky claw of genius, though only at one point: he knew what was missing in Germany at that time, and what lack was a hundred times more critical and urgent than, say, the lack of education and social graces—his antipathy against the young Frederick came from the fear of a deep instinct. *Men were missing;* and he suspected with the most bitter dismay that his own son was not man enough. In this he was deceived: but who, in his place, wouldn't have deceived himself about that? He saw his son surrender to atheism, to *esprit,* to the hedonistic frivolity of clever Frenchmen: in the background he saw that great vampire, the spider of skepticism; he suspected the incurable misery of a heart that is no longer hard enough for evil or good, of a broken will that no longer commands, no longer is capable of commanding. Meanwhile there grew up in his son that more dangerous and harder new type of skepticism— who knows *how much* it owed precisely to the hatred of the father and the icy melancholy of a will condemned to solitude?—the skepticism of audacious manliness which is most closely related to the genius for war and conquest and first entered Germany in the shape of the great Frederick.

This skepticism despises and nevertheless seizes; it undermines and takes possession; it does not believe but does not lose itself in the process; it gives the spirit dangerous freedom, but it is severe on the heart; it is the *German* form of skepticism which, in the form of a continued Frederickianism that had been sublimated spiritually, brought Europe for a long time under the hegemony of the German spirit and its critical and historical mistrust. Thanks to the unconquerably strong and tough virility of the great German philologists and critical historians (viewed properly, all of them were also artists of destruction and dissolution), a *new* concept of the German spirit crystallized gradually in spite of all romanticism

---

[26] Frederick William I, reigned 1713-40.

in music and philosophy, and the inclination to virile skepticism became a decisive trait, now, for example, as an intrepid eye, now as the courage and hardness of analysis, as the tough will to undertake dangerous journeys of exploration and spiritualized North Pole expeditions under desolate and dangerous skies.[27]

There may be good reasons why warmblooded and superficial humanitarians cross themselves just when they behold this spirit—*cet esprit fataliste, ironique, méphistophélique,*[28] Michelet calls it, not without a shudder. But if we want to really feel what a distinction such fear of the "man" in the German spirit confers—a spirit through which Europe was after all awakened from her "dogmatic slumber" [29]—we have to remember the former conception which was replaced by this one: it was not so long ago that a masculinized woman could dare with unbridled presumption to commend the Germans to the sympathy of Europe as being gentle, goodhearted, weak-willed, and poetic dolts.[30] At long last we ought to understand deeply enough Napoleon's surprise when he came to see Goethe: it shows what people had associated with the "German spirit" for centuries. *"Voilà un homme!"*—that meant: "But this is a *man!* And I had merely expected a German." [31]—

---

[27] It is essential for understanding Nietzsche to realize that he is not "for" or "against" skepticism, but that he analyzes one type of skepticism with disdain (section 208) before describing another with which he clearly identifies himself. It is equally characteristic that when he joins his countrymen in admiration of Frederick the Great, he pays tribute to him not for his exploits and conquests but rather for his skepticism, and that his praise of "tough virility" is aimed at the sublimated, spiritual version found, for example, in philologists and historians. For Nietzsche's anti-romanticism cf., e.g., *The Gay Science* (1887), section 370, cited at length and discussed in Kaufmann's *Nietzsche,* Chapter 12, section V.

[28] "That fatalistic, ironical, Mephistophelic spirit." "Mephistophelic" obviously refers to Goethe's Mephistopheles, not to Marlowe's. For Goethe's conception see *Goethe's Faust: The Original German and a New Translation and Introduction* by Walter Kaufmann (Garden City, Anchor Books, 1962), pp. 22-25.

[29] Allusion to Kant's famous dictum, in the Preface to his *Prolegomena* (1783), that it was Hume who had first interrupted his "dogmatic slumber."

[30] Allusion to Madame de Staël's *De l'Allemagne* (Paris, 1810).

[31] For Nietzsche's conception of Goethe see, e.g., *Twilight of the Idols,* sections 49-51 (*Portable Nietzsche,* pp. 553-55.). Cf. also the title of one of Nietzsche's last works, *Ecce Homo* (written in 1888).

210

Suppose then that some trait in the image of the philosophers of the future poses the riddle whether they would not perhaps have to be skeptics in the sense suggested last, this would still designate only one feature and *not* them as a whole. With just as much right one could call them critics: and certainly they will be men of experiments.[32] With the name in which I dared to baptize them I have already stressed expressly their attempts and delight in attempts: was this done because as critics in body and soul they like to employ experiments in a new, perhaps wider, perhaps more dangerous sense? Does their passion for knowledge force them to go further with audacious and painful experiments than the softhearted and effeminate taste of a democratic century could approve?

No doubt, these coming philosophers will be least able to dispense with those serious and by no means unproblematic qualities which distinguish the critic from the skeptic; I mean the certainty of value standards, the deliberate employment of a unity of method, a shrewd courage, the ability to stand alone and give an account of themselves. Indeed, they admit to a pleasure in saying No and in taking things apart, and to a certain levelheaded cruelty that knows how to handle a knife surely and subtly, even when the heart bleeds. They will be *harder* (and perhaps not always only against themselves) than humane people might wish; they will not dally with "Truth" to be "pleased" or "elevated" or "inspired" by her. On the contrary, they will have little faith that *truth* of all things should be accompanied by such amusements for our feelings.

They will smile, these severe spirits, if somebody should say in front of them: "This thought elevates me; how could it fail to be true?" Or: "This work delights me; how could it fail to be beautiful?" Or: "This artist makes me greater; how could he fail to be great?" Perhaps they do not merely have a smile but feel a gen-

---

[32] *Experimente*. In the following, as earlier, *Versuch* is rendered as "attempt." Cf. section 42 above.

uine nausea over everything that is enthusiastic, idealistic, feminine, hermaphroditic in this vein. And whoever knew how to follow them into the most secret chambers of their hearts would scarcely find any intention there to reconcile "Christian feelings" with "classical taste" and possibly even with "modern parliamentarism" (though such conciliatory attempts are said to occur even among philosophers in our very unsure and consequently very conciliatory century).

Critical discipline and every habit that is conducive to cleanliness and severity in matters of the spirit will be demanded by these philosophers not only of themselves: they could display them as their kind of jewels—nevertheless they still do not want to be called critics on that account. They consider it no small disgrace for philosophy when people decree, as is popular nowadays: "Philosophy itself is criticism and critical science—and nothing whatever besides." This evaluation of philosophy may elicit applause from all the positivists of France and Germany (and it might even have pleased the heart and taste of *Kant*—one should remember the titles of his major works); our new philosophers will say nevertheless: critics are instruments of the philosopher and for that very reason, being instruments, a long ways from being philosophers themselves. Even the great Chinese of Königsberg[33] was merely a great critic.—

211

I insist that people should finally stop confounding philosophical laborers, and scientific men generally, with philosophers; precisely at this point we should be strict about giving "each his due," and not far too much to those and far too little to these.

It may be necessary for the education of a genuine philosopher that he himself has also once stood on all these steps on which his servants, the scientific laborers of philosophy, remain standing —*have to* remain standing. Perhaps he himself must have been

---

[33] Kant. Cf. *Antichrist,* section 11 (*Portable Nietzsche,* p. 577).

critic and skeptic and dogmatist and historian and also poet and collector and traveler and solver of riddles and moralist and seer and "free spirit" and almost everything in order to pass through the whole range of human values and value feelings and to be *able* to see with many different eyes and consciences, from a height and into every distance, from the depths into every height, from a nook into every expanse. But all these are merely preconditions of his task: this task itself demands something different—it demands that he *create values.*

Those philosophical laborers after the noble model of Kant and Hegel have to determine and press into formulas, whether in the realm of *logic* or *political* (moral) thought or *art,* some great data of valuations—that is, former *positings* of values, creations of value which have become dominant and are for a time called "truths." It is for these investigators to make everything that has happened and been esteemed so far easy to look over, easy to think over, intelligible and manageable, to abbreviate everything long, even "time," and to *overcome* the entire past—an enormous and wonderful task in whose service every subtle pride, every tough will can certainly find satisfaction. *Genuine philosophers, however, are commanders and legislators:* they say, "*thus* it *shall* be!" They first determine the Whither and For What of man, and in so doing have at their disposal the preliminary labor of all philosophical laborers, all who have overcome the past. With a creative hand they reach for the future, and all that is and has been becomes a means for them, an instrument, a hammer. Their "knowing" is *creating,* their creating is a legislation, their will to truth is—*will to power.*

Are there such philosophers today? Have there been such philosophers yet? *Must* there not be such philosophers? [34]—

---

[34] The dichotomy proposed in this section is highly questionable: we find both analyses and normative suggestions in the works of the major moral philosophers from Plato and Aristotle to Spinoza and Kant; and normative thinkers or legislators who are not also analysts are not philosophers. Yet Nietzsche's point that something vital is lacking in the work of those who are merely "laborers" is certainly worth pondering, and the immediately following section offers a far superior suggestion about the ethos of the "true" philosopher.

212

More and more it seems to me that the philosopher, being *of necessity* a man of tomorrow and the day after tomorrow, has always found himself, and *had* to find himself, in contradiction to his today: his enemy was ever the ideal of today. So far all these extraordinary furtherers of man whom one calls philosophers, though they themselves have rarely felt like friends of wisdom but rather like disagreeable fools and dangerous question marks, have found their task, their hard, unwanted, inescapable task, but eventually also the greatness of their task, in being the bad conscience of their time.

By applying the knife vivisectionally to the chest of the very *virtues of their time,* they betrayed what was their own secret: to know of a *new* greatness of man, of a new untrodden way to his enhancement. Every time they exposed how much hypocrisy, comfortableness, letting oneself go and letting oneself drop, how many lies lay hidden under the best honored type of their contemporary morality, how much virtue was *outlived.* Every time they said: "We must get there, that way, where *you* today are least at home."

Facing a world of "modern ideas" that would banish everybody into a corner and "specialty," a philosopher—if today there could be philosophers—would be compelled to find the greatness of man, the concept of "greatness," precisely in his range and multiplicity, in his wholeness in manifoldness. He would even determine value and rank in accordance with how much and how many things one could bear and take upon himself, how *far* one could extend his responsibility.

Today the taste of the time and the virtue of the time weakens and thins down the will; nothing is as timely as weakness of the will. In the philosopher's ideal, therefore, precisely strength of the will, hardness, and the capacity for long-range decisions must belong to the concept of "greatness"—with as much justification as the opposite doctrine and the ideal of a dumb, renunciatory, humble, selfless humanity was suitable for an opposite age, one that suffered, like the sixteenth century, from its accumulated energy of will and from the most savage floods and tidal waves of selfishness.

In the age of Socrates, among men of fatigued instincts, among the conservatives of ancient Athens who let themselves go—"toward happiness," as they said; toward pleasure, as they acted—and who all the while still mouthed the ancient pompous words to which their lives no longer gave them any right, *irony* may have been required for greatness of soul,[35] that Socratic sarcastic assurance of the old physician and plebeian who cut ruthlessly into his own flesh, as he did into the flesh and heart of the "noble," with a look that said clearly enough: "Don't dissemble in front of me! Here—we are equal."

Today, conversely, when only the herd animal receives and dispenses honors in Europe, when "equality of rights" could all too

---

[35] Aristotle's discussion of greatness of soul (*megalopsychia*) is worth quoting here, at least in part, because it evidently influenced Nietzsche. The valuations that find expression in Aristotle's account are exceedingly remote from those of the New Testament and help us understand Nietzsche's contrast of master morality and slave morality, introduced below (section 260). Moreover, in his long discussion of "what is noble," Nietzsche emulates Aristotle's descriptive mode.

"A person is thought to be great-souled if he claims much and deserves much [as Socrates did in the *Apology* when he said he deserved the greatest honor Athens could bestow]. . . . He that claims less than he deserves is small-souled. . . . The great-souled man is justified in despising other people—his estimates are correct; but most proud men have no good ground for their pride. . . . He is fond of conferring benefits, but ashamed to receive them, because the former is a mark of superiority and the latter of inferiority. . . . It is also characteristic of the great-souled men never to ask help from others, or only with reluctance, but to render aid willingly; and to be haughty towards men of position and fortune, but courteous towards those of moderate station. . . . He must be open both in love and in hate, since concealment shows timidity; and care more for the truth than for what people will think; . . . he is outspoken and frank, except when speaking with ironical self-depreciation, as he does to common people. . . . He does not bear a grudge, for it is not a mark of greatness of soul to recall things against people, especially the wrongs they have done you, but rather to overlook them. He is . . . not given to speaking evil himself, even of his enemies, except when he deliberately intends to give offence. . . . Such then being the great-souled man, the corresponding character on the side of deficiency is the small-souled man, and on that of excess the vain man" (*Nicomachean Ethics* IV.3, Rackham translation Cambridge, Mass., Harvard University Press, 1947).
The whole passage is relevant and extremely interesting.

easily be changed into equality in violating rights—I mean, into a common war on all that is rare, strange, privileged, the higher man, the higher soul, the higher duty, the higher responsibility, and the abundance of creative power and masterfulness—today the concept of greatness entails being noble, wanting to be by oneself, being able to be different, standing alone and having to live independently. And the philosopher will betray something of his own ideal when he posits: "He shall be greatest who can be loneliest, the most concealed, the most deviant, the human being beyond good and evil, the master of his virtues, he that is overrich in will. Precisely this shall be called *greatness:* being capable of being as manifold as whole, as ample as full." And to ask it once more: today—is greatness *possible?*

213

What a philosopher is, that is hard to learn because it cannot be taught: one must "know" it, from experience—or one should have the pride *not* to know it. But nowadays all the world talks of things of which it *cannot* have any experience, and this is most true, and in the worst way, concerning philosophers and philosophical states: exceedingly few know them, may know them, and all popular opinions about them are false.

That genuinely philosophical combination, for example, of a bold and exuberant spirituality that runs *presto* and a dialectical severity and necessity that takes no false step is unknown to most thinkers and scholars from their own experience, and therefore would seem incredible to them if somebody should speak of it in their presence. They picture every necessity as a kind of need, as a painstaking having-to-follow and being-compelled. And thinking itself they consider something slow and hesitant, almost as toil, and often enough as "worthy of the *sweat* of the noble"—but not in the least as something light, divine, closely related to dancing and high spirits. "Thinking" and taking a matter "seriously," considering it "grave"—for them all this belongs together: that is the only way they have "experienced" it.

Artists seem to have more sensitive noses in these matters,

knowing only too well that precisely when they no longer do any-thing "voluntarily" but do everything of necessity, their feeling of freedom, subtlety, full power, of creative placing, disposing, and forming reaches its peak—in short, that necessity and "freedom of the will" then become one in them.

Ultimately, there is an order of rank among states of the soul, and the order of rank of problems accords with this. The highest problems repulse everyone mercilessly who dares approach them without being predestined for their solution by the height and power of his spirituality. What does it avail when nimble smarties or clumsy solid mechanics and empiricists push near them, as is common today, trying with their plebeian ambition to enter the "court of courts." Upon such carpets coarse feet may never step: the primeval law of things takes care of that; the doors remain closed to such obtrusiveness, even if they crash and crush their heads against them.

For every high world one must be born; or to speak more clearly, one must be *cultivated* for it: a right to philosophy—taking that word in its great sense—one has only by virtue of one's ori-gins; one's ancestors, one's "blood" [36] decide here, too. Many gen-erations must have labored to prepare the origin of the philosopher; every one of his virtues must have been acquired, nurtured, inher-ited, and digested singly, and not only the bold, light, delicate gait and course of his thoughts but above all the readiness for great re-sponsibilities, the loftiness of glances that dominate and look down, feeling separated from the crowd and its duties and virtues, the af-fable protection and defense of whatever is misunderstood and slandered, whether it be god or devil, the pleasure and exercise of the great justice, the art of command, the width of the will, the slow eye that rarely admires, rarely looks up, rarely loves[37]—

---

[36] *"Geblüt."* Nietzsche's conception of "blood" is discussed, and other rele-vant passages are quoted, in Kaufmann's *Nietzsche,* at the end of Chapter 10.

[37] The element of snobbery and the infatuation with "dominating" and "looking down" are perhaps more obvious than Nietzsche's perpetual sub-limation and spiritualization of these and other similar qualities. It may be interesting to compare Nietzsche's view with Dr. Thomas Stockmann's in Act IV of Ibsen's *An Enemy of the People:*
"What a difference there is between a cultivated and an uncultivated ani-

mal family! Just look at a common barnyard hen. . . . But now take a cultivated Spanish or Japanese hen, or take a noble pheasant or a turkey; indeed, you'll see the difference. And then I refer you to dogs, which are so amazingly closely related to us men. Consider first a common plebeian dog—I mean, a disgusting, shaggy, moblike cur that merely runs down the streets and fouls the houses. And then compare the cur with a poodle that for several generations is descended from a noble house where it received good food and has had occasion to hear harmonious voices and music. Don't you suppose that the poodle's brain has developed in a way quite different from the cur's? You can count on it. It is such cultivated young poodles that jugglers can train to do the most astonishing tricks. A common peasant cur could never learn anything of the kind, even if stood on its head."

Not only do Nietzsche and Ibsen's Dr. Stockmann share Lamarck's belief in the heredity of acquired characteristics; both are concerned with spiritual nobility and realize that—to put it plainly—of two brothers one may have it and the other not. Thus Stockmann says a little later: "But that's how it always goes when plebeian descent is still in one's limbs and one has not worked one's way up to spiritual nobility. . . . That kind of rabble of which I am speaking isn't to be found only in the lower strata. . . . My brother Peter—he is also a plebeian straight out of the book."

PART SEVEN

OUR VIRTUES

Part Seven

214

Our virtues?—It is probable that we, too, still have our virtues, although in all fairness they will not be the simpleminded and four-square virtues for which we hold our grandfathers in honor—and at arm's length. We Europeans of the day after tomorrow, we first-born of the twentieth century—with all our dangerous curiosity, our multiplicity and art of disguises, our mellow and, as it were, sweetened cruelty in spirit and senses—*if* we should have virtues we shall presumably have only virtues which have learned to get along best with our most secret and cordial inclinations, with our most ardent needs. Well then, let us look for them in our labyrinths —where, as is well known, all sorts of things lose themselves, all sorts of things are lost for good. And is there anything more beautiful than *looking for* one's own virtues? Doesn't this almost mean: *believing* in one's own virtue? But this "believing in one's virtue"—isn't this at bottom the same thing that was formerly called one's "good conscience," that venerable long pigtail of a concept which our grandfathers fastened to the backs of their heads, and often enough also to the backside of their understanding? So it seems that however little we may seem old-fashioned and grandfatherly-honorable to ourselves in other matters, in one respect we are nevertheless the worthy grandsons of these grandfathers, we last Europeans with a good conscience: we, too, still wear their pigtail.— Alas, if you knew how soon, very soon—all will be different!—

215

As in the realm of stars the orbit of a planet is in some cases determined by two suns; as in certain cases suns of different colors shine near a single planet, sometimes with red light, sometimes with green light, and then occasionally illuminating the planet at the same time and flooding it with colors—so we modern men are determined, thanks to the complicated mechanics of our "starry sky," by *different* moralities; our actions shine alternately in different colors, they are rarely univocal—and there are cases enough in which we perform actions *of many colors*.

216

Love one's enemies? I think this has been learned well: it is done thousands of times today, in small ways and big ways. Indeed, at times something higher and more sublime is done: we learn to *despise* when we love, and precisely when we love best—but all of this unconsciously, without noise, without pomp, with that modesty and concealed goodness which forbids the mouth solemn words and virtue formulas. Morality as a pose—offends our taste today. That, too, is progress—just as it was progress when religion as a pose finally offended our fathers' taste, including hostility and Voltairian bitterness against religion (and everything that formerly belonged to the gestures of free-thinkers). It is the music in our conscience, the dance in our spirit, with which the sound of all puritan litanies, all moral homilies and old-fashioned respectability won't go.

217

Beware of those who attach great value to being credited with moral tact and subtlety in making moral distinctions. They never forgive us once they have made a mistake *in front of* us (or, worse, *against* us): inevitably they become our instinctive slanderers and detractors, even if they should still remain our "friends."

Blessed are the forgetful: for they get over their stupidities, too.

218

The psychologists of France—and where else are any psychologists left today?—still have not exhausted their bitter and manifold delight in the *bêtise bourgeoise*,[1] just as if——enough, this betrays something. Flaubert, for example, that solid citizen of Rouen, in the end no longer saw, heard, or tasted anything else any more: this was his kind of self-torture and subtler cruelty. Now, for a change—since this is becoming boring—I propose another source of amusement: the unconscious craftiness with which all good, fat, solid, mediocre spirits react to higher spirits and their tasks—that subtle, involved, Jesuitical craftiness which is a thousand times more subtle than not only the understanding and taste of this middle class is at its best moments, but even the understanding of its victims—which proves once again that "instinct" is of all the kinds of intelligence that have been discovered so far —the most intelligent. In short, my dear psychologists, study the philosophy of the "norm" in its fight against the "exception": there you have a spectacle that is good enough for gods and godlike malice! Or, still more clearly: vivisect the "good man," the *"homo bonae voluntatis"* [2]—*yourselves!*

219

Moral judgments and condemnations constitute the favorite revenge of the spiritually limited against those less limited—also a sort of compensation for having been ill-favored by nature—finally an opportunity for acquiring spirit and *becoming* refined—malice spiritualized. It pleases them deep down in their hearts that there are standards before which those overflowing with the wealth and privileges of the spirit are their equals: they fight for the "equality of all men before God" and almost *need* faith in God just for that. They include the most vigorous foes of atheism. Anyone who said to them, "high spirituality is incomparable with any kind of solidity and respectability of a merely moral man" would enrage them— and I shall beware of doing this. Rather I want to flatter them with my proposition, that high spirituality itself exists only as the ulti-

---

[1] Bourgeois stupidity.
[2] "Man of good will."

mate product of moral qualities; that it is a synthesis of all those states which are attributed to "merely moral" men, after they have been acquired singly through long discipline and exercise, perhaps through whole chains of generations; that high spirituality is the spiritualization of justice and of that gracious severity which knows that it is its mission to maintain the *order of rank* in the world, among things themselves—and not only among men.

220

In view of the modern popularity of praise of the "disinterested," we should bring to consciousness, perhaps not without some danger, what it is that elicits the people's interest, and what are the things about which the common man is deeply and profoundly concerned—including the educated, even the scholars, and unless all appearances deceive, perhaps even the philosophers. Then the fact emerges that the vast majority of the things that interest and attract choosier and more refined tastes and every higher nature seem to the average man totally "uninteresting"; and when he nevertheless notices a devotion to such matters he calls it *"désintéressé"* and wonders how it is possible to act "without interest." There have been philosophers who have known how to lend to this popular wonder a seductive and mystical-transcendental expression[3] (—perhaps because they did not know the higher nature from experience?)—instead of positing the naked truth, which is surely not hard to come by, that the "disinterested" action is an *exceedingly* interesting and interested action, assuming——

"And love?"— What? Even an action done from love is supposed to be "unegoistic"? But you dolts! "And the praise of sacrifices?"— But anyone who has really made sacrifices knows that he wanted and got something in return—perhaps something of himself in return for something of himself—that he gave up here in order to have more there, perhaps in order to *be* more or at least to feel that he was "more." But this a realm of questions and answers in which a choosier spirit does not like to dwell: even now truth finds

---

[3] Notably Kant.

it necessary to stifle her yawns when she is expected to give answers. In the end she is a woman: she should not be violated.

221

It does happen, said a moralistic pedant and dealer in trifles, that I honor and exalt a man free of self-interest—not because he is free of self-interest but because he seems to me to be entitled to profit another human being at his own expense. Enough; the question is always who *he* is, and who the *other* person is. In a person, for example, who is called and made to command, self-denial and modest self-effacement would not be a virtue but the waste of a virtue: thus it seems to me. Every unegoistic morality that takes itself for unconditional and addresses itself to all does not only sin against taste: it is a provocation to sins of omission, one *more* seduction under the mask of philanthropy—and precisely a seduction and injury for the higher, rarer, privileged. Moralities must be forced to bow first of all before the *order of rank;* their presumption must be brought home to their conscience—until they finally reach agreement that it is *immoral* to say: "what is right for one is fair for the other."

Thus my moralistic pedant and *bonhomme:*[4] does he deserve to be laughed at for thus admonishing moralities to become moral? But one should not be too right if one wants to have those who laugh on one's own side; a grain of wrong actually belongs to good taste.

222

Where pity is preached today—and, if you listen closely, this is the only religion preached now—psychologists should keep their

---

[4] What the "moralistic pedant" says, especially after the "Enough" (several lines above), seems very close, to put it mildly, to Nietzsche's own position. Yet Nietzsche here dissociates himself from these remarks and ascribes them to a "pedant"—not because they are wrong but because he considers it pedantic and self-righteous to be so unhumorously and completely right. See sections 30 and 40 above. With the final sentence of section 221 compare *Ecce Homo,* Chapter 1, end of section 5, p. 685 below.

ears open: through all the vanity, through all the noise that characterizes these preachers (like all preachers) they will hear a hoarse, groaning, genuine sound of *self-contempt*. This belongs to that darkening and uglification of Europe which has been growing for a century now (and whose first symptoms were registered in a thoughtful letter Galiani wrote to Madame d'Épinay)[5]—*unless it is the cause of this process*. The man of "modern ideas," this proud ape, is immeasurably dissatisfied with himself: that is certain. He suffers—and his vanity wants him to suffer only with others, to feel pity.—

223

The hybrid European—all in all, a tolerably ugly plebeian—simply needs a costume: he requires history as a storage room for costumes. To be sure, he soon notices that not one fits him very well; so he keeps changing. Let anyone look at the nineteenth century with an eye for these quick preferences and changes of the style masquerade; also for the moments of despair over the fact that "nothing is becoming." It is no use to parade as romantic or classical, Christian or Florentine, baroque or "national," *in moribus et artibus:* it "does not look good." But the "spirit," especially the "historical spirit," finds its advantage even in this despair: again and again a new piece of prehistory or a foreign country is tried on, put on, taken off, packed away, and above all *studied:* we are the first age that has truly studied "costumes"—I mean those of moralities, articles of faith, tastes in the arts, and religions—prepared like no previous age for a carnival in the grand style, for the laughter and high spirits of the most spiritual revelry, for the transcendental heights of the highest nonsense and Aristophanean derision of the world. Perhaps this is where we shall still discover the realm of our *invention,* that realm in which we, too, can still be original, say, as parodists of world history and God's buffoons—perhaps, even if nothing else today has any future, our *laughter* may yet have a future.

---

[5] See note for section 26 above.

224

The *historical sense* (or the capacity for quickly guessing the order of rank of the valuations according to which a people, a society, a human being has lived; the "divinatory instinct" for the relations of these valuations, for the relation of the authority of values to the authority of active forces)—this historical sense to which we Europeans lay claim as our specialty has come to us in the wake of that enchanting and mad *semi-barbarism* into which Europe had been plunged by the democratic mingling of classes and races: only the nineteenth century knows this sense, as its sixth sense. The past of every form and way of life, of cultures that formerly lay right next to each other or one on top of the other, now flows into us "modern souls," thanks to this mixture; our instincts now run back everywhere; we ourselves are a kind of chaos. Finally, as already mentioned, "the spirit" sees its advantage in this.

Through our semi-barbarism in body and desires we have secret access in all directions, as no noble age ever did; above all, access to the labyrinths of unfinished cultures and to every semi-barbarism that ever existed on earth. And insofar as the most considerable part of human culture so far was semi-barbarism, "historical sense" almost means the sense and instinct for everything, the taste and tongue for everything—which immediately proves it to be an *ignoble* sense. We enjoy Homer again, for example: perhaps it is our most fortunate advantage that we know how to relish Homer whom the men of a noble culture (say, the French of the seventeenth century, like Saint-Évremond, who reproached him for his *esprit vaste,*[6] and even their afterglow, Voltaire) cannot and could not assimilate so easily—whom to enjoy they scarcely permitted themselves. The very definite Yes and No of their palate, their easy nausea, their hesitant reserve toward everything foreign, their horror of the poor taste even of a lively curiosity, and altogether the reluctance of every noble and self-sufficient culture to own a new desire, a dissatisfaction with what is one's own, and ad-

---

[6] Vast or comprehensive spirit.

miration for what is foreign—all this inclines and disposes them unfavorably even against the best things in the world which are not theirs or *could* not become their prey. No sense is more incomprehensible for such people than the historical sense and its submissive plebeian curiosity.

It is no different with Shakespeare, that amazing Spanish-Moorish-Saxon synthesis of tastes that would have all but killed an ancient Athenian of Aeschylus' circle with laughter or irritation. But we—accept precisely this wild abundance of colors, this medley of what is most delicate, coarsest, and most artificial, with a secret familiarity and cordiality; we enjoy him as a superb subtlety of art saved up especially for us; and the disgusting odors and the proximity of the English rabble in which Shakespeare's art and taste live we do not allow to disturb us any more than on the Chiaja of Naples, where we go our way with all our senses awake, enchanted and willing, though the sewer smells of the plebeian quarters fill the air.

As men of the "historical sense" we also have our virtues; that cannot be denied: we are unpretentious, selfless, modest, courageous, full of self-overcoming, full of devotion, very grateful, very patient, very accommodating; but for all that we are perhaps not paragons of good taste. Let us finally own it to ourselves: what we men of the "historical sense" find most difficult to grasp, to feel, to taste once more, to love once more, what at bottom finds us prejudiced and almost hostile, is precisely the perfection and ultimate maturity of every culture and art,[7] that which is really noble in a work or human being, the moment when their sea is smooth and they have found halcyon self-sufficiency, the golden and cold aspect of all things that have consummated themselves.

Perhaps our great virtue of the historical sense is necessarily opposed to *good* taste, at least to the very best taste; and precisely the highest little strokes of luck and transfigurations of human life that briefly light up here and there we can recapture only poorly,

---

[7] When Nietzsche wrote this, the taste for archaic and primitive art was not yet widespread and classical art was still considered the norm: Praxiteles and Raphael were supposed to be the ultimate in beauty. Nietzsche thus foresees developments of the twentieth century.

hesitantly, by forcing ourselves—those moments and marvels when great power voluntarily stopped this side of the immeasurable and boundless, when an excess of subtle delight in sudden restraint and petrification, in standing firm and taking one's measure, was enjoyed on still trembling ground. *Measure* is alien to us; let us own it; our thrill is the thrill of the infinite, the unmeasured. Like a rider on a steed that flies forward, we drop the reins before the infinite, we modern men, like semi-barbarians—and reach *our* bliss only where we are most—*in danger*.

225

Whether it is hedonism or pessimism, utilitarianism or eudaemonism—all these ways of thinking that measure the value of things in accordance with *pleasure* and *pain,* which are mere epiphenomena and wholly secondary, are ways of thinking that stay in the foreground and naïvetés on which everyone conscious of *creative* powers and an artistic conscience will look down not without derision, nor without pity. Pity with *you*—that, of course, is not pity in your sense: it is not pity with social "distress," with "society" and its sick and unfortunate members, with those addicted to vice and maimed from the start, though the ground around us is littered with them; it is even less pity with grumbling, sorely pressed, rebellious slave strata who long for dominion, calling it "freedom." *Our* pity is a higher and more farsighted pity: we see how *man* makes himself smaller, how *you* make him smaller—and there are moments when we behold *your* very pity with indescribable anxiety, when we resist this pity—when we find *your* seriousness more dangerous than any frivolity. You want, if possible—and there is no more insane "if possible"—*to abolish suffering*. And we? It really seems that *we* would rather have it higher and worse than ever. Well-being as you understand it—that is no goal, that seems to us an *end,* a state that soon makes man ridiculous and contemptible—that makes his destruction[8] *desirable*.

---

[8] *Untergang.* Compare with this whole passage the Prologue of *Zarathustra,* especially sections 3-6, where Nietzsche plays with the words *Untergang, Übermensch* (overman), and *überwinden* (overcome) and contrasts the

The discipline of suffering, of *great* suffering—do you not know that only *this* discipline has created all enhancements of man so far? That tension of the soul in unhappiness which cultivates its strength, its shudders face to face with great ruin, its inventiveness and courage in enduring, persevering, interpreting, and exploiting suffering, and whatever has been granted to it of profundity, secret, mask, spirit, cunning, greatness—was it not granted to it through suffering, through the discipline of great suffering? In man *creature* and *creator* are united: in man there is material, fragment, excess, clay, dirt, nonsense, chaos; but in man there is also creator, form-giver, hammer hardness, spectator divinity, and seventh day: do you understand this contrast? And that *your* pity is for the "creature in man," for what must be formed, broken, forged, torn, burnt, made incandescent, and purified—that which *necessarily* must and *should* suffer? And *our* pity—do you not comprehend for whom our *converse* pity is when it resists your pity as the worst of all pamperings and weaknesses?

Thus it is pity *versus* pity.

But to say it once more: there are higher problems than all problems of pleasure, pain, and pity; and every philosophy that stops with them is a naïveté.—

226

We immoralists!— This world that concerns *us,* in which *we* fear and love, this almost invisible and inaudible world of subtle commanding and subtle obeying, in every way a world of the "almost," involved, captious, peaked, and tender—indeed, it is defended well against clumsy spectators and familiar curiosity. We have been spun into a severe yarn and shirt of duties and *cannot* get out of that—and in this we are "men of duty," we, too. Occasionally, that is true, we dance in our "chains" and between our "swords"; more often, that is no less true, we gnash our teeth and feel impatient with all the secret hardness of our destiny. But we

overman with "the last man" who has "invented happiness" and is contemptible.

can do what we like—the dolts and appearances speaks against us, saying: "These are men *without* duty." We always have the dolts and appearances against us.

227

Honesty,[9] supposing that this is our virtue from which we cannot get away, we free spirits—well, let us work on it with all our malice and love and not weary of "perfecting" ourselves in *our* virtue, the only one left us. May its splendor remain spread out one day like a gilded blue mocking evening light over this aging culture and its musty and gloomy seriousness! And if our honesty should nevertheless grow weary one day and sigh and stretch its limbs and find us too hard, and would like to have things better, easier, tenderer, like an agreeable vice—let us remain *hard,* we last Stoics! And let us dispatch to her assistance whatever we have in us of devilry: our disgust with what is clumsy and approximate, our *"nitimur in vetitum,"* [10] our adventurous courage, our seasoned and choosy curiosity, our subtlest, most disguised, most spiritual will to power and overcoming of the world that flies and flutters covetously around all the realms of the future—let us come to the assistance of our "god" with all our "devils"!

It is probable that we shall be misunderstood and mistaken for others on this account: what matter?[11] And even if they were right!

---

[9] *Redlichkeit.*

[10] "We strive for the forbidden." The quotation is from Ovid's *Amores,* III, 4, 17.

[11] Cf. *Schopenhauer as Educator* (1874), section 4: ". . . He will be mistaken for another and long be considered an ally of powers which he abominates. . . ." There, too, this is pictured as a consequence of honesty and courage. But when Nietzsche wrote *Ecce Homo,* in 1888, he no longer felt: "what matter?" Thus the first section of the Preface ends: "Under these circumstances I have a duty against which my habits, even more the pride of my instincts, revolt at bottom—namely, to say: *Hear me! For I am such and such a person. Above all, do not mistake me for someone else!"* There is also a note of the period 1885-88, published posthumously: "One generally mistakes me for someone else: I confess it; also that I should be done a great service if someone else were to defend and define me against these mistakes [*Verwechselungen*]" (*Werke,* Musarion editon, vol. XIV, 318f.).

Have not all gods so far been such devils who have become holy and been rebaptized? And what ultimately do we know of ourselves? And how the spirit that leads us would like to be *called?* (It is a matter of names.) And how many spirits we harbor?

Our honesty, we free spirits—let us see to it that it does not become our vanity, our finery and pomp, our limit, our stupidity. Every virtue inclines toward stupidity; every stupidity, toward virtue. "Stupid to the point of holiness," they say in Russia; let us see to it that out of honesty we do not finally become saints and bores. Is not life a hundred times too short—for boredom? One really would have to believe in eternal life to——

228

May I be forgiven the discovery that all moral philosophy so far has been boring and was a soporific and that "virtue" has been impaired more for me by its *boring* advocates than by anything else, though I am not denying their general utility. It is important that as few people as possible should think about morality; hence it is *very* important that morality should not one day become interesting. But there is no reason for worry. Things still stand today as they have always stood: I see nobody in Europe who has (let alone, *promotes*) any awareness that thinking about morality could become dangerous, captious, seductive—that there might be any *calamity* involved.

Consider, for example, the indefatigable, inevitable British utilitarians, how they walk clumsily and honorably in Bentham's footsteps, walking along (a Homeric simile says it more plainly), even as he himself had already walked in the footsteps of the honorable Helvétius[12] (no, he was no dangerous person, this Helvétius, *ce sénateur Pococurante,*[13] to speak with Galiani). Not a new idea, no trace of a subtler version or twist of an old idea, not even a real

---

[12] Claude Adrien Helvétius (1715-71) was a French philosopher whose ancestors had borne the name of Schweitzer. He was a materialist and utilitarian.

[13] *Poco:* little; *curante:* careful, caring; *pococurante:* easygoing.

history of what had been thought before: altogether an *impossible* literature, unless one knows how to flavor it with some malice.

For into these moralists, too (one simply has to read them with ulterior thoughts, if one *has* to read them), that old English vice has crept which is called *cant* and consists in *moral Tartuffery;* only this time it hides in a new, scientific, form. A secret fight against a bad conscience is not lacking either, as it is only fair that a race of former Puritans will have a bad conscience whenever it tries to deal with morality scientifically. (Isn't a moral philosopher the opposite of a Puritan? Namely, insofar as he is a thinker who considers morality questionable, as calling for question marks, in short as a problem? Should moralizing not be—immoral?)

Ultimately they all want *English* morality to be proved right— because this serves humanity best, or "the general utility," or "the happiness of the greatest number"—no, the happiness of *England.* With all their powers they want to prove to themselves that the striving for *English* happiness—I mean for comfort and fashion[14] (and at best a seat in Parliament)—is at the same time also the right way to virtue; indeed that whatever virtue has existed in the world so far must have consisted in such striving.

None of these ponderous herd animals with their unquiet consciences (who undertake to advocate the cause of egoism as the cause of the general welfare) wants to know or even sense that "the general welfare" is no ideal, no goal, no remotely intelligible concept, but only an emetic—that what is fair for one *cannot* by any means for that reason alone also be fair for others; that the demand of one morality for all is detrimental for the higher men; in short, that there is an order of rank between man and man, hence also between morality and morality. They are a modest and thoroughly mediocre type of man, these utilitarian Englishmen, and, as said above, insofar as they are boring one cannot think highly enough of their utility. They should even be *encouraged:* the following rhymes represent an effort in this direction.

> Hail, dear drudge and patient fretter!
> "More drawn out is always better,"

---

[14] Nietzsche uses the English words "comfort" and "fashion."

Stiffness grows in head and knee,
No enthusiast and no joker,
Indestructibly mediocre,
Sans génie et sans esprit! [15]

229

In late ages that may be proud of their humanity, so much fear remains, so much *superstitious* fear of the "savage cruel beast" whose conquest is the very pride of these more humane ages, that even palpable truths remain unspoken for centuries, as if by some agreement, because they look as if they might reanimate that savage beast one has finally "mortified." Perhaps I dare something when I let one of these truths slip out: let others catch it again and give it "milk of the pious ways of thinking" [16] to drink until it lies still and forgotten in its old corner.

We should reconsider cruelty and open our eyes. We should at long last learn impatience lest such immodest fat errors keep on strutting about virtuously and saucily, as have been fostered about tragedy, for example, by philosophers both ancient and modern. Almost everything we call "higher culture" is based on the spiritualization of *cruelty,* on its becoming more profound: this is my proposition. That "savage animal" has not really been "mortified"; it lives and flourishes, it has merely become—divine.

What constitutes the painful voluptuousness of tragedy is cruelty; what seems agreeable in so-called tragic pity, and at bottom in everything sublime, up to the highest and most delicate shudders of metaphysics, receives its sweetness solely from the admixture of

---

[15] *Heil euch, brave Karrenschieber,*
  Stets "je länger desto lieber,"
  Steifer stets an Kopf und Knie,
  Unbegeistert, ungespässig,
  Unverwüstlich-mittelmässig,
  Sans génie et sans esprit!
The phrase in quotes is a German cliché.

[16] Quoted from Tell's famous monologue in Schiller's *Wilhelm Tell,* Act IV, Scene 3. Schiller had earlier translated *Macbeth* into German and was, no doubt, influenced by "the milk of human kindness."

cruelty. What the Roman in the arena, the Christian in the ecstasies of the cross, the Spaniard at an auto-da-fe or bullfight, the Japanese of today when he flocks to tragedies, the laborer in a Parisian suburb who feels a nostalgia for bloody revolutions, the Wagnerienne who "submits to" *Tristan and Isolde,* her will suspended—what all of them enjoy and seek to drink in with mysterious ardor are the spicy potions of the great Circe, "cruelty."

To see this we must, of course, chase away the clumsy psychology of bygone times which had nothing to teach about cruelty except that it came into being at the sight of the sufferings of *others*. There is also an abundant, over-abundant enjoyment at one's own suffering, at making oneself suffer—and wherever man allows himself to be persuaded to self-denial in the *religious* sense, or to self-mutilation, as among Phoenicians and ascetics, or altogether to desensualization, decarnalization, contrition, Puritanical spasms of penitence, vivisection of the conscience, and *sacrifizio dell'intelletto*[17] à la Pascal, he is secretly lured and pushed forward by his cruelty, by those dangerous thrills of cruelty turned *against oneself*.

Finally consider that even the seeker after knowledge forces his spirit to recognize things against the inclination of the spirit, and often enough also against the wishes of his heart—by way of saying No where he would like to say Yes, love, and adore—and thus acts as an artist and transfigurer of cruelty. Indeed, any insistence on profundity and thoroughness is a violation, a desire to hurt the basic will of the spirit which unceasingly strives for the apparent and superficial—in all desire to know there is a drop of cruelty.

230

What I have just said of a "basic will of the spirit" may not be readily understood: permit me an explanation.

That commanding something which the people call "the spirit" wants to be master in and around its own house and wants to feel that it is master; it has the will from multiplicity to simplicity, a will that ties up, tames, and is domineering and truly masterful. Its

---

[17] Sacrifice of the intellect.

needs and capacities are so far the same as those which physiologists posit for everything that lives, grows, and multiplies. The
spirit's power to appropriate the foreign stands revealed in its inclination to assimilate the new to the old, to simplify the manifold,
and to overlook or repulse whatever is totally contradictory—just
as it involuntarily emphasizes certain features and lines in what is
foreign, in every piece of the "external world," retouching and falsifying the whole to suit itself. Its intent in all this is to incorporate
new "experiences," to file new things in old files—growth, in a
word—or, more precisely, the *feeling* of growth, the feeling of increased power.

An apparently opposite drive serves this same will: a suddenly erupting decision in favor of ignorance, of deliberate exclusion, a shutting of one's windows, an internal No to this or that
thing, a refusal to let things approach, a kind of state of defense
against much that is knowable, a satisfaction with the dark, with the
limiting horizon, a Yea and Amen to ignorance—all of which is
necessary in proportion to a spirit's power to appropriate, its "digestive capacity," to speak metaphorically—and actually "the
spirit" is relatively most similar to a stomach.

Here belongs also the occasional will of the spirit to let itself
be deceived, perhaps with a capricious intimation of the fact that
such and such is *not* the case, that one merely accepts such and such
a delight in all uncertainty and ambiguity, a jubilant self-enjoyment
in the arbitrary narrowness and secrecy of some nook, in the all
too near, in the foreground, in what is enlarged, diminished. dis-
placed, beautified, a self-enjoyment in the caprice of all these expressions of power.

Here belongs also, finally, that by no means unproblematic
readiness of the spirit to deceive other spirits and to dissimulate in
front of them, that continual urge and surge of a creative, form-
giving, changeable force: in this the spirit enjoys the multiplicity
and craftiness of its masks, it also enjoys the feeling of its security
behind them: after all, it is surely its Protean arts that defend and
conceal it best.

This will to mere appearance, to simplification, to masks, to
cloaks, in short, to the surface—for every surface is a cloak—is

countered by that sublime inclination of the seeker after knowledge who insists on profundity, multiplicity, and thoroughness, with a *will* which is a kind of cruelty of the intellectual conscience and taste. Every courageous thinker will recognize this in himself, assuming only that, as fit, he has hardened and sharpened his eye for himself long enough and that he is used to severe discipline, as well as severe words. He will say: "there is something cruel in the inclination of my spirit"; let the virtuous and kindly try to talk him out of that!

Indeed, it would sound nicer if we were said, whispered, reputed[18] to be distinguished not by cruelty but by "extravagant honesty," we free, *very* free spirits—and perhaps *that* will actually be our—posthumous reputation.[19] Meanwhile—for there is plenty of time until then—we ourselves are probably least inclined to put on the garish finery of such moral word tinsels: our whole work so far makes us sick of this taste and its cheerful luxury. These are beautiful, glittering, jingling, festive words: honesty, love of truth, love of wisdom, sacrifice for knowledge, heroism of the truthful— they have something that swells one's pride. But we hermits and marmots have long persuaded ourselves in the full secrecy of a hermit's conscience that this worthy verbal pomp, too, belongs to the old mendacious pomp, junk, and gold dust of unconscious human vanity, and that under such flattering colors and make-up as well, the basic text of *homo natura* must again be recognized.

To translate man back into nature; to become master over the many vain and overly enthusiastic interpretations and connotations that have so far been scrawled and painted over that eternal basic text of *homo natura;* to see to it that man henceforth stands before man as even today, hardened in the discipline of science, he stands before the *rest* of nature, with intrepid Oedipus eyes and sealed Odysseus ears, deaf to the siren songs of old metaphysical bird catchers who have been piping at him all too long, "you are more, you are higher, you are of a different origin!"—that may be a

---

[18] *Nachsagte, nachraunte, nachrühmte:* literally, "said after, whispered after, praised after us an extravagant honesty."

[19] *Nachruhm:* literally, after-fame.

strange and insane task, but it is a *task*—who would deny that? Why did we choose this insane task? Or, putting it differently: "why have knowledge at all?"

Everybody will ask us that. And we, pressed this way, we who have put the same question to ourselves a hundred times, we have found and find no better answer—

231

Learning changes us; it does what all nourishment does which also does not merely "preserve"—as physiologists know. But at the bottom of us, really "deep down," there is, of course, something unteachable, some granite of spiritual *fatum*,[20] of predetermined decision and answer to predetermined selected questions. Whenever a cardinal problem is at stake, there speaks an unchangeable "this is I"; about man and woman, for example, a thinker cannot relearn but only finish learning—only discover ultimately how this is "settled in him." At times we find certain solutions of problems that inspire strong faith in *us;* some call them henceforth *their* "convictions." Later—we see them only as steps to self-knowledge, signposts to the problem we *are*—rather, to the great stupidity we are, to our spiritual *fatum,* to what is *unteachable* very "deep down." [21]

After this abundant civility that I have just evidenced in relation to myself I shall perhaps be permitted more readily to state a few truths about "woman as such"—assuming that it is now known from the outset how very much these are after all only—*my* truths.

232

Woman wants to become self-reliant—and for that reason she is beginning to enlighten men about "woman as such": *this* is one of the worst developments of the general *uglification* of Europe. For what must these clumsy attempts of women at scientific self-

---

20 Fate.
21 Cf. Freud.

exposure bring to light! Woman has much reason for shame; so much pedantry, superficiality, schoolmarmishness, petty presumption, petty licentiousness and immodesty lies concealed in woman —one only needs to study her behavior with children!—and so far all this was at bottom best repressed and kept under control by *fear* of man. Woe when "the eternally boring in woman" [22]—she is rich in that!—is permitted to venture forth! When she begins to unlearn thoroughly and on principle her prudence and art—of grace, of play, of chasing away worries, of lightening burdens and taking things lightly—and her subtle aptitude for agreeable desires!

Even now female voices are heard which—holy Aristophanes! —are frightening: they threaten with medical explicitness what woman *wants* from man, first and last. Is it not in the worst taste when woman sets about becoming scientific that way? So far enlightenment of this sort was fortunately man's affair, man's lot—we remained "among ourselves" in this; and whatever women write about "woman," we may in the end reserve a healthy suspicion whether woman really *wants* enlightenment about herself— whether she *can* will it—

Unless a woman seeks a new adornment for herself that way —I do think adorning herself is part of the Eternal-Feminine? —she surely wants to inspire fear of herself—perhaps she seeks mastery. But she does not *want* truth: what is truth to woman? From the beginning, nothing has been more alien, repugnant, and hostile to woman than truth—her great art is the lie, her highest concern is mere appearance and beauty. Let us men confess it: we honor and love precisely *this* art and *this* instinct in woman—we who have a hard time and for our relief like to associate with beings under whose hands, eyes, and tender follies our seriousness, our gravity and profundity [23] almost appear to us like folly.

Finally I pose the question: has ever a woman conceded pro-

---

[22] Allusion to "the Eternal-Feminine" in the penultimate line of Goethe's *Faust*.

[23] The embarrassing contrast with Nietzsche's own remarks in section 230, toward the end of the paragraph to which notes 18 and 19 refer, speaks for itself. If anything redeems section 232, and much of the remainder of Part VII, it is surely the disclaimer in 231.

fundity to a woman's head, or justice to a woman's heart? And is it not true that on the whole "woman" has so far been despised most by woman herself—and by no means by us?

We men wish that woman should not go on compromising herself through enlightenment—just as it was man's thoughtfulness and consideration for woman that found expression in the church decree: *mulier taceat in ecclesia!* [24] It was for woman's good when Napoleon gave the all too eloquent Madame de Staël to understand: *mulier taceat in politicis!* [25] And I think it is a real friend of women that counsels them today: *mulier taceat de muliere!* [26]

233

It betrays a corruption of the instincts—quite apart from the fact that it betrays bad taste—when a woman adduces Madame Roland or Madame de Staël or Monsieur George Sand, of all people, as if they proved anything in *favor* of "woman as such." Among men these three are the three *comical* women as such— nothing more!—and precisely the best involuntary *counterarguments* against emancipation and feminine vainglory.

234

Stupidity in the kitchen; woman as cook: the gruesome thoughtlessness to which the feeding of the family and of the master of the house is abandoned! Woman does not understand what food *means*—and wants to be cook. If woman were a thinking creature, she, as cook for millennia, would surely have had to discover the greatest physiological facts, and she would have had to gain possession of the art of healing. Bad cooks—and the utter lack of reason in the kitchen—have delayed human development longest and impaired it most: nor have things improved much even today. A lecture for finishing-school girls.

---

[24] Woman should be silent in church.
[25] Woman should be silent when it comes to politics.
[26] Woman should be silent about woman.

235

There are expressions and bull's-eyes of the spirit, there are epigrams, a little handful of words, in which a whole culture, a whole society is suddenly crystallized. Among these belongs the occasional remark of Madame de Lambert to her son: *"mon ami, ne vous permettez jamais que de folies, qui vous feront grand plaisir"* [27]—incidentally the most motherly and prudent word ever directed to a son.

236

What Dante and Goethe believed about woman—the former when he sang, *"ella guardava suso, ed io in lei,"* [28] and the latter when he translated this, "the Eternal-Feminine attracts us *higher"* —I do not doubt that every nobler woman will resist this faith, for she believes the same thing about the Eternal-Masculine—

237

SEVEN EPIGRAMS ON WOMAN

❊

How the longest boredom flees,   when a man comes on his knees!

❊

Science and old age at length   give weak virtue, too, some strength.

❊

Black dress and a silent part   make every woman appear—smart.

---

[27] "My friend, permit yourself nothing but follies—that will give you great pleasure."
[28] "She looked up, and I at her."

❈

Whom I thank for my success?   God!—and my dear tailoress.

❈

Young: flower-covered den.   Old: a dragon denizen.

❈

Noble name, the legs are fine,   man as well: that he were mine!

❈

Ample meaning, speech concise[29]*—she-ass, watch for slippery ice!*

❈

237a[30]

Men have so far treated women like birds who had strayed to them from some height: as something more refined and vulnerable, wilder, stranger, sweeter, and more soulful—but as something one has to lock up lest it fly away.

238

To go wrong on the fundamental problem of "man and woman," to deny the most abysmal antagonism between them and the necessity of an eternally hostile tension, to dream perhaps of equal rights, equal education, equal claims and obligations—that is a *typical* sign of shallowness, and a thinker who has proved shallow in this dangerous place—shallow in his instinct—may be consid-

---

[29] *Kurze Rede, langer Sinn* inverts *der langen Rede kurzer Sinn* (the brief meaning of the long speech), a familiar German quotation from Schiller's *Die Piccolomini,* Act I, Scene 2. Cf. *Twilight of the Idols,* section 51, and the succeeding section 1 of the last chapter of *Twilight* (*Portable Nietzsche,* pp. 555-57).

[30] In the first two editions a new section begins at this point, but it is numbered 237, repeating the preceding number. In the standard editions, including Schlechta's (which falsely claims to follow the original edition), the second 237 is omitted, and the verse and prose are offered as a single section.

ered altogether suspicious, even more—betrayed, exposed: probably he will be too "short" for all fundamental problems of life, of
the life yet to come, too, and incapable of attaining *any* depth.[31] A
man, on the other hand, who has depth, in his spirit as well as in
his desires, including that depth of benevolence which is capable of
severity and hardness and easily mistaken for them, must always
think about woman as *Orientals* do: he must conceive of woman as
a possession, as property that can be locked, as something predestined for service and achieving her perfection in that. Here he must
base himself on the tremendous reason of Asia, on Asia's superiority in the instincts, as the Greeks did formerly, who were Asia's
best heirs and students: as is well known, from Homer's time to the
age of Pericles, as their culture *increased* along with the range of
their powers, they also gradually became *more severe,* in brief,
more Oriental, against woman. *How* necessary, *how* logical, *how*
humanely desirable even, this was—is worth pondering.

239

In no age has the weaker sex been treated with as much respect by men as in ours: that belongs to the democratic inclination
and basic taste, just like disrespectfulness for old age. No wonder
that this respect is immediately abused. One wants more, one learns
to demand, finally one almost finds this tribute of respect insulting,
one would prefer competition for rights, indeed even a genuine
fight: enough, woman loses her modesty. Let us immediately add
that she also loses taste. She unlearns her *fear* of man: but the
woman who "unlearns fear" surrenders her most womanly instincts.

---

[31] Fortunately for Nietzsche, this is surely wrong. But it is worth asking
which, if any, of his other ideas are of a piece with his secondhand wisdom
about "woman": probably his embarrassingly frequent invocation of "severity" and "hardness" and other such terms—the almost ritual repetition of
the words, not necessarily, if at all, the spiritualized conceptions he develops
with their aid—and perhaps also the tenor of his remarks about democracy
and parliaments. Goethe said: "The greatest human beings are always connected with their century by means of some weakness" (*Elective Affinities*).
At these points Nietzsche's deliberate "untimeliness" now seems time-bound,
dated, and as shallow as what he attacked.

That woman ventures forth when the aspect of man that inspires fear—let us say more precisely, when the *man* in man is no longer desired and cultivated—that is fair enough, also comprehensible enough. What is harder to comprehend is that, by the same token—woman degenerates. This is what is happening today: let us not deceive ourselves about that.

Wherever the industrial spirit has triumphed over the military and aristocratic spirit, woman now aspires to the economic and legal self-reliance of a clerk: [32] "woman as clerk" is inscribed on the gate to the modern society that is taking shape now. As she thus takes possession of new rights, aspires to become "master" [33] and writes the "progress" of woman upon her standards and banners, the opposite development is taking place with terrible clarity: *woman is retrogressing*.

Since the French Revolution, woman's influence in Europe has *decreased* proportionately as her rights and claims have increased; and the "emancipation of woman," insofar as that is demanded and promoted by women themselves (and not merely by shallow males) is thus seen to be an odd symptom of the increasing weakening and dulling of the most feminine instincts. There is *stupidity* in this movement, an almost masculine stupidity of which a woman who had turned out well—and such women are always prudent—would have to be thoroughly ashamed.

To lose the sense for the ground on which one is most certain of victory; to neglect practice with one's proper weapons; to let oneself go before men, perhaps even "to the point of writing a book," when formerly one disciplined oneself to subtle and cunning humility; to work with virtuous audacity against men's faith in a basically different ideal that he takes to be *concealed* in woman, something Eternally-and-Necessarily-Feminine—to talk men emphatically and loquaciously out of their notion that woman must be maintained, taken care of, protected, and indulged like a more delicate, strangely wild, and often pleasant domestic animal; the awkward and indignant search for everything slavelike and serflike

---

[32] *Commis.*
[33] *"Herr."*

that has characterized woman's position in the order of society so far, and still does (as if slavery were a counterargument and not instead a condition of every higher culture, every enhancement of culture)—what is the meaning of all this if not a crumbling of feminine instincts, a defeminization?

To be sure, there are enough imbecilic friends and corrupters of woman among the scholarly asses of the male sex who advise woman to defeminize herself in this way and to imitate all the stupidities with which "man" in Europe, European "manliness," is sick: they would like to reduce woman to the level of "general education," probably even of reading the newspapers and talking about politics. Here and there they even want to turn women into freethinkers and scribblers—as if a woman without piety would not seem utterly obnoxious and ridiculous to a profound and godless man.

Almost everywhere one ruins her nerves with the most pathological and dangerous kind of music (our most recent German music) and makes her more hysterical by the day and more incapable of her first and last profession—to give birth to strong children. Altogether one wants to make her more "cultivated" and, as is said, make the weaker sex *strong* through culture—as if history did not teach us as impressively as possible that making men "cultivated" and making them weak—weakening, splintering, and sicklying over the *force of the will*—have always kept pace, and that the most powerful and influential women of the world (most recently Napoleon's mother) owed their power and ascendancy over men to the force of their will—and not to schoolmasters!

What inspires respect for woman, and often enough even fear, is her *nature,* which is more "natural" than man's, the genuine, cunning suppleness of a beast of prey, the tiger's claw under the glove, the naïveté of her egoism, her uneducability and inner wildness, the incomprehensibility, scope, and movement of her desires and virtues—

What, in spite of all fear, elicits pity for this dangerous and beautiful cat "woman" is that she appears to suffer more, to be more vulnerable, more in need of love, and more condemned to disappointment than any other animal. Fear and pity: with these feelings man has so far confronted woman, always with one foot in tragedy[34] which tears to pieces as it enchants.[35]

What? And this should be the end? And the breaking of woman's magic spell is at work? The "borification" of woman is slowly dawning? O Europe! Europe! We know the horned animal you always found most attractive; it still threatens you! Your old fable could yet become "history"—once more an immense stupidity might become master over you and carry you off. And this time no god would hide in it; no, only an "idea," a "modern idea"!——

---

[34] Ever since Aristotle's *Poetics* (1449b), pity and fear have been associated with tragedy. Cf. also 1452a, 1453b.

[35] Allusion to Schiller's famous line about fate in classical tragedy (in "Shakespeare's Shadow"): "which elevates man when it crushes man."

PART EIGHT

PEOPLES AND FATHERLANDS

Part Eight

240

I heard once again for the first time—Richard Wagner's overture to the *Meistersinger:* [1] it is magnificent, overcharged, heavy, late art that has the pride of presupposing two centuries of music as still living, if it is to be understood: it is to the credit of the Germans that such pride did not miscalculate. What flavors and forces, what seasons and climes are not mixed here! It strikes us now as archaic, now as strange, tart, and too young, it is just as capricious as it is pompous-traditional, it is not infrequently saucy, still more often coarse and rude—it has fire and courage and at the same time the loose dun skin of fruit that ripens too late. It flows broad and full—and suddenly a moment of inexplicable hesitation, like a gap opening up between cause and effect, a pressure triggering dreams, almost nightmares—but already the old width and breadth are regained by the current of well-being, the most manifold well-being, of old and new happiness, very much including the artist's happiness with himself which he has no wish to hide, his amazed, happy sharing of the knowledge that the means he has employed here are masterly—new artistic devices, newly acquired, not yet tested, as he seems to let us know.

Altogether, no beauty, no south, nothing of southern and subtle brightness of the sky, nothing of gracefulness, no dance, scarcely any will to logic; even a certain clumsiness that is actually stressed, as if the artist wished to say to us, "that is part of my intention"; cumbersome drapery, something capricious, barbarian, and solemn, a flurry of erudite preciousness and lace; something German in the best and worst senses of the word, something manifold, formless, and inexhaustible in a German way; a certain German powerfulness and overfulness of the soul which is not afraid of hiding behind the refinements of decay—which perhaps really feels most at

---

[1] Nietzsche discusses Wagner at greater length in *The Birth of Tragedy, The Case of Wagner,* and *Nietzsche contra Wagner.*

home there; a truly genuine token of the German soul which is at the same time young and superannuated, overly mellow and still overrich in future. This kind of music expresses best what I think of the Germans: they belong to the day before yesterday and the day after tomorrow—*as yet they have no today*.

241

We "good Europeans"—we, too, know hours when we permit ourselves some hearty fatherlandishness, a plop and relapse into old loves and narrownesses—I have just given a sample of that— hours of national agitations, patriotic palpitations, and various other sorts of archaizing sentimental inundations. More ponderous spirits than we are may require more time to get over what with us takes only hours and in a few hours has run its course: some require half a year, others half a life, depending on the speed and power of their digestion and metabolism. Indeed, I could imagine dull[2] and sluggish races who would require half a century even in our rapidly moving Europe to overcome such atavistic attacks of fatherlandishness and soil addiction and to return to reason, meaning "good Europeanism."

As I am digressing to this possibility, it so happens that I become an ear-witness of a conversation between two old "patriots": apparently both were hard of hearing and therefore spoke that much louder.

"*He* thinks and knows as much of philosophy as a peasant or a fraternity student," said one; "he is still innocent. But what does it matter today? This is the age of the masses: they grovel on their bellies before anything massive. In *politicis,* too. A statesman who piles up for them another tower of Babel, a monster of empire and power, they call 'great'; what does it matter that we, more cautious

---

[2] *Dumpf* has no perfect equivalent in English. It can mean hollow or muted when applied to a sound, heavy and musty applied to air, dull applied to wits, and is a cousin of the English words, dumb and damp. Goethe still used it with a positive connotation when he wrote poetry about inarticulate feelings; Nietzsche uses the word often—with a strongly negative, anti-romantic connotation.

and reserved, do not yet abandon the old faith that only a great thought can give a deed or cause greatness. Suppose a statesman put his people in a position requiring them to go in for 'great politics' from now on, though they were ill-disposed for that by nature and ill prepared as well, so that they would find it necessary to sacrifice their old and secure virtues for the sake of a novel and dubious mediocrity—suppose a statesman actually condemned his people to 'politicking' although so far they had had better things to do and think about, and deep down in their souls they had not got rid of a cautious disgust with the restlessness, emptiness, and noisy quarrelsomeness of peoples that really go in for politicking—suppose such a statesman goaded the slumbering passions and lusts of his people, turning their diffidence and delight in standing aside into a blot, their cosmopolitanism and secret infinity into a serious wrong, devaluating their most cordial inclinations, inverting their conscience, making their spirit narrow, their taste 'national'— what! a statesman who did all this, for whom his people would have to atone for all future time, if they have any future, such a statesman should be *great?*"

"Without a doubt!" the other patriot replied vehemently; "otherwise he would not have been *able* to do it. Perhaps it was insane to want such a thing? But perhaps everything great was merely insane when it started."

"An abuse of words!" his partner shouted back; "strong! strong! strong and insane! *Not* great!"

The old men had obviously become heated as they thus flung their truths into each other's faces; but I, in my happiness and beyond, considered how soon one stronger will become master over the strong; also that for the spiritual flattening[3] of a people there is a compensation, namely the deepening of another people.

---

[3] *Verflachung* (becoming shallower) contrasted with *Vertiefung* (becoming more profound). The first people is, without a doubt, Germany; the statesman, Bismarck; and the second people probably France. Of course, the points made are also meant to apply more generally, but this evaluation of Bismarck at the zenith of his success and power certainly shows an amazing independence of spirit, and without grasping the full weight of the final sentence one cannot begin to understand Nietzsche's conceptions of the will to power or of "beyond good and evil."

242

Call that in which the distinction of the European is sought "civilization" or "humanization" or "progress," or call it simply—without praise or blame—using a political formula, Europe's *democratic* movement: behind all the moral and political foregrounds to which such formulas point, a tremendous *physiological* process is taking place and gaining momentum. The Europeans are becoming more similar to each other; they become more and more detached from the conditions under which races originate that are tied to some climate or class; they become increasingly independent of any *determinate* milieu that would like to inscribe itself for centuries in body and soul with the same demands. Thus an essentially supra-national and nomadic type of man is gradually coming up, a type that possesses, physiologically speaking, a maximum of the art and power of adaptation as its typical distinction.

The tempo of this process of the *"evolving European"* may be retarded by great relapses, but perhaps it will gain in vehemence and profundity and grow just on their account: the still raging storm and stress of "national feeling" belongs here, also that anarchism which is just now coming up. But this process will probably lead to results which would seem to be least expected by those who naïvely promote and praise it, the apostles of "modern ideas." The very same new conditions that will on the average lead to the leveling and mediocritization of man—to a useful, industrious, handy, multi-purpose herd animal—are likely in the highest degree to give birth to exceptional human beings of the most dangerous and attractive quality.

To be sure, that power of adaptation which keeps trying out changing conditions and begins some new work with every generation, almost with every decade, does not make possible the *powerfulness* of the type, and the over-all impression of such future Europeans will probably be that of manifold garrulous workers who will be poor in will, extremely employable, and as much in need of a master and commander as of their daily bread. But while the democratization of Europe leads to the production of a type that is prepared for *slavery* in the subtlest sense, in single, exceptional cases the *strong* human being will have to turn out stronger and richer than perhaps ever before—thanks to the absence of prejudice from his training, thanks to the tremendous manifoldness of practice, art, and mask. I meant to say: the democratization of Europe is at the same time an involuntary arrangement for the cultivation of *tyrants*—taking that word in every sense, including the most spiritual.

243

I hear with pleasure that our sun is swiftly moving toward the constellation of *Hercules*—and I hope that man on this earth will in this respect follow the sun's example? And we first of all, we good Europeans!—

244

There was a time when it was customary to attribute "profundity" to the Germans, as a distinction. Now that the most successful type of the new Germanism lusts after utterly different honors and perhaps misses "pluck" in everything profound, some doubt may almost be timely and patriotic as to whether that former praise was not based on self-deception—in short, whether German profundity is not at bottom something different and worse, and something that, thank God, one is about to shake off successfully. Let us make the attempt to relearn about German profundity: nothing more is needed for this than a little vivisection of the German soul.

The German soul is above all manifold, of diverse origins, more put together and superimposed than actually built: that is due to where it comes from. A German who would make bold to say, "two souls, alas, are dwelling in my breast," [4] would violate the truth rather grossly or, more precisely, would fall short of the truth by a good many souls. As a people of the most monstrous mixture

---

[4] Goethe's *Faust,* line 1112.

and medley of races, perhaps even with a preponderance of the pre-Aryan element, as "people of the middle" in every sense, the Germans are more incomprehensible, comprehensive, contradictory, unknown, incalculable, surprising, even frightening than other people are to themselves: they elude *definition* and would be on that account alone the despair of the French.

It is characteristic of the Germans that the question, "what is German?" never dies out among them. Kotzebue surely knew his Germans well enough: "we have been recognized!" they jubilated —but *Sand,* too, thought he knew them.[5] Jean Paul[6] knew what he was doing when he declared himself wrathfully against Fichte's mendacious but patriotic flatteries and exaggerations—but it is probable that Goethe did not think about the Germans as Jean Paul did, although he considered him right about Fichte. What did Goethe really think about the Germans?

But there were many things around him about which he never spoke clearly, and his life long he was a master of subtle silence— he probably had good reasons for that. What is certain is that it was not "the Wars of Liberation"[7] that made him look up more cheerfully, any more than the French Revolution; the event on whose account he *rethought* his *Faust,* indeed the whole problem of man, was the appearance of Napoleon. There are words of Goethe in which he deprecates with impatient hardness, as if he belonged to a foreign country, what the Germans take pride in: the celebrated German *Gemüt*[8] he once defined as "indulgence toward the weaknesses of others as well as one's own." Was he wrong in that? It is characteristic of the Germans that one is rarely completely wrong about them.

---

[5] August Friedrich Ferdinand von Kotzebue (1761-1819), a popular German writer in his time who had his differences with Goethe and also published attacks on Napoleon, was assassinated by Karl Ludwig Sand (1795-1820), a theology student who took the poet for a Russian spy. Sand was executed.

[6] Pen name of Johann Paul Friedrich Richter (1763-1825), one of the most renowned German writers of the romantic period.

[7] Against Napoleon.

[8] A word without any exact equivalent in English. It is variously rendered as feeling, soul, heart, while *gemütlich* might be translated as comfortable or cozy.

The German soul has its passageways and inter-passageways; there are caves, hideouts, and dungeons in it; its disorder has a good deal of the attraction of the mysterious; the German is an expert on secret paths to chaos. And just as everything loves its simile, the German loves clouds and everything that is unclear, becoming, twilit, damp, and overcast: whatever is in any way uncertain, unformed, blurred, growing, he feels to be "profound." The German himself *is* not, he *becomes,* he "develops." "Development" is therefore the truly German find and hit in the great realm of philosophical formulas—a governing concept that, united with German beer and German music, is at work trying to Germanize the whole of Europe.

Foreigners stand amazed and fascinated before the riddles posed for them by the contradictory nature at the bottom of the German soul (brought into a system by Hegel and finally set to music by Richard Wagner). "Good-natured and vicious"—such a conjunction, preposterous in relation to any other people, is unfortunately justified all too often in Germany: let anyone live for a while among Swabians! The ponderousness of the German scholar, his social bad taste, gets along alarmingly well with an inner rope-dancing and easy boldness which has taught all the gods what fear is. Whoever wants a demonstration of the "German soul" *ad oculos*[9] should merely look into German taste, into German arts and customs: What boorish indifference to "taste"! How the noblest stands right next to the meanest! How disorderly and rich this whole psychic household is! The German *drags* his soul along: whatever he experiences he drags. He digests his events badly, he never gets "done" with them; German profundity is often merely a hard and sluggish "digestion." And just as all chronic invalids, all dyspeptics, love comfort, Germans love "openness" and *"Bieder-keit":* how *comfortable* it is to be open and *"bieder"!* [10]

Perhaps the German of today knows no more dangerous and successful disguise than this confiding, accommodating, cards-on-

[9] For the eyes.

[10] The word has no exact English equivalent but might be rendered "four-square."

the-table manner of German *honesty:* this is his true Mephistopheles-art; with that he can "still go far." The German lets himself go while making faithful blue, empty, German eyes—and immediately foreigners confound him with his dressing gown.

I meant to say: whatever "German profundity" may be—when we are entirely among ourselves, perhaps we permit ourselves to laugh at it?—we shall do well to hold its semblance and good name in honor in the future, too, and not to trade our old reputation as a people of profundity too cheaply for Prussian "pluck" and Berlin wit and sand.[11] It is clever for a people to make and let itself be considered profound, awkward, good-natured, honest, and not clever: it might even be—profound. Finally, one should live up to one's name: it is not for nothing that one is called the *"tiusche" Volk,* the *Täusche-Volk,* deceiver people.[12]—

245

The "good old time" is gone, in Mozart we hear its swan song. How fortunate *we* are that his rococo still speaks to us, that his "good company," his tender enthusiasms, his childlike delight in curlicues and Chinese touches, his courtesy of the heart, his longing for the graceful, those in love, those dancing, those easily moved to tears, his faith in the south, may still appeal to some *residue* in us. Alas, some day all this will be gone—but who may doubt that the understanding and taste for Beethoven will go long before that! Beethoven was after all merely the final chord of transition in style, a style break, and not, like Mozart, the last chord of a centuries-old great European taste.

Beethoven is the interlude of a mellow old soul that constantly breaks and an over-young future soul that constantly *comes;* on his music lies that twilight of eternal losing and eternal extravagant hoping—the same light in which Europe was bathed when it

---

[11] The area around Berlin was at one time called "the sandbox of the Holy Roman Empire."

[12] This is by no means the accepted German etymology of *deutsch.*

dreamed with Rousseau, danced around the freedom tree of the Revolution, and finally almost worshiped before Napoleon. But how quickly *this* feeling pales now; how difficult is mere *knowledge* of this feeling even today—how strange to our ears sounds the language of Rousseau, Schiller, Shelley, Byron, in whom, taken *together,* the same fate of Europe found its way into words that in Beethoven knew how to sing!

Whatever German music came after that belongs to romanticism, a movement that was, viewed historically, still briefer, still more fleeting, still more superficial than that great *entr'acte,* that transition of Europe from Rousseau to Napoleon and to the rise of democracy. Weber: but what are *Freischütz* and *Oberon* to us today! Or Marschner's *Hans Heiling* and *Vampyr!* Or even Wagner's *Tannhäuser.* That is music that has died away though it is not yet forgotten. All this music of romanticism, moreover, was not noble enough to remain valid anywhere except in the theater and before crowds; it was from the start second-rate music that was not considered seriously by genuine musicians.

It is different with Felix Mendelssohn, that halcyon master who, on account of his lighter, purer, more enchanted soul, was honored quickly and just as quickly forgotten: as the beautiful *intermezzo* of German music. But as for Robert Schumann, who was very serious and also was taken seriously from the start—he was the last to found a school—is it not considered a good fortune among us today, a relief, a liberation, that this Schumann romanticism has been overcome?

Schumann, fleeing into the "Saxon Switzerland" [13] of his soul, half like Werther, half like Jean Paul, certainly not like Beethoven, certainly not like Byron—his Manfred music is a mistake and misunderstanding to the point of an injustice—Schumann with his taste which was basically a *small* taste (namely, a dangerous propensity, doubly dangerous among Germans, for quiet lyricism and sottishness of feeling), constantly walking off to withdraw shyly

---

[13] A very rugged and picturesque mountain range about fifteen miles southeast of Dresden, not comparable in height, extent, or magnificence to the Swiss Alps.

and retire, a noble tender-heart who wallowed in all sorts of anonymous bliss and woe, a kind of girl and *noli me tangere*[14] from the start: this Schumann was already a merely *German* event in music, no longer a European one, as Beethoven was and, to a still greater extent, Mozart. With him German music was threatened by its greatest danger: losing *the voice for the soul of Europe* and descending to mere fatherlandishness.

246

What torture books written in German are for anyone who has a *third* ear! How vexed one stands before the slowly revolving swamp of sounds that do not sound like anything and rhythms that do not dance, called a "book" among Germans! Yet worse is the German who *reads* books! How lazily, how reluctantly, how badly he reads! How many Germans know, and demand of themselves that they should know, that there is *art* in every good sentence—art that must be figured out if the sentence is to be understood! A misunderstanding about its tempo, for example—and the sentence itself is misunderstood.

That one must not be in doubt about the rhythmically decisive syllables, that one experiences the break with any excessively severe symmetry as deliberate and attractive, that one lends a subtle and patient ear to every *staccato*[15] and every *rubato,*[16] that one figures out the meaning in the sequence of vowels and diphthongs and how delicately and richly they can be colored and change colors as they follow each other—who among book-reading Germans has enough good will to acknowledge such duties and demands and to listen to that much art and purpose in language? In the end one simply does not have "the ear for that"; and thus the strongest contrasts of style go unheard, and the subtlest artistry is *wasted* as on the deaf.

---

14 "Touch me not!" John 20:17.

15 A musical term, meaning detached, disconnected, with breaks between successive notes.

16 *Tempo rubato,* literally robbed time, is a tempo in which some notes are shortened in order that others may be lengthened.

These were my thoughts when I noticed how clumsily and un-discerningly two masters in the art of prose were confounded—one whose words drop hesitantly and coldly, as from the ceiling of a damp cave—he counts on their dull sound and resonance—and another who handles his language like a flexible rapier, feeling from his arm down to his toes the dangerous delight of the quivering, over-sharp blade that desires to bite, hiss, cut.[17]—

247[18]

How little German style has to do with sound and the ears is shown by the fact that precisely our good musicians write badly. The German does not read aloud, not for the ear but only with the eye: meanwhile his ears are put away in a drawer. In antiquity men read—when they did read, which happened rarely enough—to themselves, aloud, with a resounding voice; one was surprised when anyone read quietly, and secretly asked oneself for the reasons. With a resounding voice: that means, with all the crescendos, inflections, and reversals of tone and changes in tempo in which the ancient *public* world took delight.

The laws of written style were then the same as those for spoken style; and these laws depended partly on the amazing development and the refined requirements of ear and larynx, partly on the strength, perseverance, and power of ancient lungs. A period in the classical sense is above all a physiological unit, insofar as it is held together by a single breath. Such periods as are found in Demosthenes and Cicero, swelling twice and coming down twice, all within a single breath, are delights for the men of *antiquity* who, from their own training, knew how to esteem their virtue and how rare and difficult was the delivery of such a period. *We* really have no right to the *great* period, we who are modern and in every sense short of breath.[19]

---

[17] The second master is surely Nietzsche, and the whole passage may give some idea of the difficulty of translating him.

[18] In the first two editions this appears as 247a, although there is no section 247.

[19] But *Beyond Good and Evil* is full of examples, most of which have been

All of these ancients were after all themselves dilettantes in rhetoric, hence connoisseurs, hence critics and thus drove their rhetoricians to extremes; just as in the last century, when all Italians and Italiennes knew how to sing, virtuosity in singing (and with that also the art of melody) reached its climax among them. In Germany, however, there really was (until quite recently, when a kind of platform eloquence began shyly and clumsily enough to flap its young wings) only a single species of public and *roughly* artful rhetoric: that from the pulpit.

In Germany the preacher alone knew what a syllable weighs, or a word, and how a sentence strikes, leaps, plunges, runs, runs out; he alone had a conscience in his ears, often enough a bad conscience; for there is no lack of reasons why Germans rarely attain proficiency in rhetoric, and almost always too late. The masterpiece of German prose is therefore, fairly enough, the masterpiece of its greatest preacher: the *Bible* has so far been the best German book. Compared with Luther's Bible, almost everything else is mere "literature"—something that did not grow in Germany and therefore also did not grow and does not grow into German hearts—as the Bible did.

248

There are two types of genius: one which above all begets and wants to beget, and another which prefers being fertilized and giving birth. Just so, there are among peoples of genius those to whom the woman's problem of pregnancy and the secret task of forming, maturing, and perfecting has been allotted—the Greeks, for example, were a people of this type; also the French—and others who must fertilize and become the causes of new orders of life—like the Jews,[20] the Romans, and, asking this in all modesty, the Germans?

---

preserved in translation, though a few have been broken up into shorter sentences. Plainly it is part of the aim of these sections to tell the reader how the present book wants to be read.

[20] Nietzsche inverts the anti-Semitic cliché that the Jews are uncreative parasites who excel, if at all, only as performers and interpreters. (Cf. also, e.g., section 52 above and his praise of Mendelssohn in section 245.) The image of the Jews "lusting after foreign races" *was* a cliché of German anti-Semi-

Peoples, tormented and enchanted by unknown fevers and irresistibly pressed beyond themselves, in love and lusting after foreign races (after those who like "being fertilized"), and at the same time domineering like all that knows itself to be full of creative powers and hence "by the grace of God." These two types of genius seek each other, like man and woman; but they also misunderstand each other—like man and woman.

249

Every people has its own Tartuffery and calls it its virtues.—What is best in us we do not know—we cannot know.

250

What Europe owes to the Jews? Many things, good and bad, and above all one thing that is both of the best and of the worst: the grand style in morality, the terribleness and majesty of infinite demands, infinite meanings, the whole romanticism and sublimity of moral questionabilities—and hence precisely the most attractive, captious, and choicest part of those plays of color and seductions to life in whose afterglow the sky of our European culture, its evening sky, is burning now—perhaps burning itself out. We artists among the spectators and philosophers are—grateful for this to the Jews.[21]

---

tism, but it is entirely characteristic of Nietzsche's style of thinking and writing that the phrase is "spiritualized" (to use his own term) and moreover used in a context which makes plain—for those who read and do not merely browse—that Nietzsche's meaning is utterly opposed to that previously associated with the words. His famous "revaluation" begins with *words* that receive new values.

Nietzsche's conception of the Greeks and Romans also inverts the usual view. In his frequent insistence on the debt of the Greeks to earlier civilizations he was at least half a century ahead of his time.

[21] Cf. section 195 above. In the light of these two sections it seems probable that the reference to the Germans ("in all modesty") in section 248 alludes to Nietzsche's own ambitions. He is hoping to initiate a "revaluation" comparable to that ascribed to the Jews in section 195: they are his model. Of course, he does not agree with the values he ascribes to them; but the whole book represents an effort to rise "beyond" simpleminded agreement and

251

It must be taken into the bargain if all sorts of clouds and disturbances—in brief, little attacks of hebetation—pass over the spirit of a people that is suffering, and *wants* to suffer, of nationalistic nerve fever and political ambition. Examples among the Germans today include now the anti-French stupidity, now the anti-Jewish, now the anti-Polish, now the Christian-romantic, now the Wagnerian, now the Teutonic, now the Prussian (just look at the wretched historians, these Sybels and Treitschkes[22] and their

---

disagreement, beyond the vulgar faith in antithetic values, "beyond good and evil." The point of that title is *not* that the author considers himself beyond good and evil in the crudest sense, but it is in part that he is beyond saying such silly things as "the Jews are good" or "the Jews are evil"; or "free spirits" or "scholars" or "virtues" or "honesty" or "humaneness" are "good" or "evil." Everywhere he introduces distinctions, etching first one type and then another—both generally confounded under a single label. He asks us to shift perspectives, or to perceive hues and gradations instead of simple black and white. This has led superficial readers to suppose that he contradicts himself or that he never embraces any meaningful conclusions (Karl Jaspers); but this book abounds in conclusions. Only one can never be sure what they are as long as one tears sentences and half-sentences out of context (the method of Bertram and Jaspers)—or even whole aphorisms: section 240 is meant to be read before section 241, not in isolation.

[22] Heinrich von Sybel (1817-95) and Heinrich von Treitschke (1834-96) were among the leading German historians of their time. Sybel was for many years a member of the Prussian parliament. At one time a critic of Bismarck, he strongly supported many of Bismarck's policies, beginning in 1866. In 1875 Bismarck appointed him director of the Prussian archives. His major works include *Die deutsche Nation und das Kaiserreich* (the German nation and the Empire; 1862) and *Die Begründung des deutschen Reiches durch Wilhelm I* (1889-94; English version, *The Founding of the German Empire by William I*, trans. Marshall Livingston, 1890-98).

Treitschke, born at Dresden, was a Liberal as a young man. By 1866, when Prussia went to war against Austria, "his sympathies with Prussia were so strong that he went to Berlin [from Freiburg, where he had been a professor], became a Prussian subject, and was appointed editor of the *Preussische Jahrbücher*" (*Encyclopaedia Britannica,* 11th ed.). In 1871 he became a member of the new imperial parliament, and in 1874 a professor of history at Berlin. He became "the chief panegyrist of the house of Hohenzollern. He did more than anyone to mould the minds of the rising generation, and he carried them with him even in his violent attacks on all opinions and all parties which appeared in any way to be injurious to the rising power of Germany. He supported the government in its attempts to subdue by legisla-

thickly bandaged heads!) and whatever other names these little mistifications[23] of the German spirit and conscience may have. Forgive me, for during a brief daring sojourn in very infected territory I, too, did not altogether escape this disease and began like everyone else to develop notions about matters that are none of my business: the first sign of the political infection. For example about the Jews: only listen!

I have not met a German yet who was well disposed toward the Jews; and however unconditionally all the cautious and politically-minded repudiated real anti-Semitism,[24] even this caution and policy are not directed against the species of this feeling itself but only against its dangerous immoderation, especially against the insipid and shameful expression of this immoderate feeling—about this, one should not deceive oneself. That Germany has amply *enough* Jews, that the German stomach, the German blood has trouble (and will still have trouble for a long time) digesting even this quantum of "Jew"—as the Italians, French, and English have done, having a stronger digestive system—that is the clear testimony and language of a general instinct to which one must listen, in accordance with which one must act. "Admit no more new Jews! And especially close the doors to the east (also to Austria)!" thus commands the instinct of a people whose type is still weak and indefinite, so it could easily be blurred or extinguished by a stronger race. The Jews, however, are beyond any doubt the strongest, toughest, and purest race now living in Europe; they know how to prevail even under the worst conditions (even better than under favorable conditions), by means of virtues that today one would like to mark as vices—thanks above all to a resolute faith that

---

tion the Socialists, Poles, and Catholics; and he was one of the few men of eminence who gave the sanction of his name to the attacks on the Jews which began in 1878. As a strong advocate of colonial expansion, he was also a bitter enemy of Great Britain, and he was to a large extent responsible for the anti-British feeling of German Chauvinism during the last years of the 19th century" (*ibid.*).

Although all of Nietzsche's references to Treitschke are vitriolic (there are three in *Ecce Homo*), uninformed writers have occasionally linked Nietzsche and Treitschke as if both had been German nationalists.

[23] *Benebelungen.* Could also be translated "befoggings."

[24] *Antisemiterei* is more derogatory than *Antisemitismus.*

need not be ashamed before "modern ideas"; they change, *when* they change, always only as the Russian Empire makes its conquests—being an empire that has time and is not of yesterday—namely, according to the principle, "as slowly as possible."

A thinker who has the development of Europe on his conscience will, in all his projects for this future, take into account the Jews as well as the Russians as the provisionally surest and most probable factors in the great play and fight of forces. What is called a "nation" in Europe today, and is really rather a *res facta* than a *res nata* (and occasionally can hardly be told from a *res ficta et picta*)[25] is in any case something evolving, young, and easily changed, not yet a race, let alone such an *aere perennius*[26] as the Jewish type: these "nations" really should carefully avoid every hotheaded rivalry and hostility! That the Jews, if they wanted it—or if they were forced into it, which seems to be what the anti-Semites want—*could* even now have preponderance, indeed quite literally mastery over Europe, that is certain; that they are *not* working and planning for that is equally certain.

Meanwhile they want and wish rather, even with some importunity, to be absorbed and assimilated by Europe; they long to be fixed, permitted, respected somewhere at long last, putting an end to the nomads' life, to the "Wandering Jew"; and this bent and impulse (which may even express an attenuation of the Jewish instincts) should be noted well and *accommodated:* to that end it might be useful and fair to expel the anti-Semitic screamers from the country.[27] Accommodated with all caution, with selection; ap-

---

[25] Something made; something born; something fictitious and unreal.

[26] More enduring than bronze: quotation from Horace's *Odes*, III, 30.1.

[27] None of this prevented Richard Oehler from quoting a passage from this section, out of context, in one of the first Nazi books on Nietzsche, after saying: "To wish to give proof regarding Nietzsche's thoughts in order to establish that they agree with the race views and strivings of the National Socialist movement would be carrying coals to Newcastle" (*Friedrich Nietzsche und die deutsche Zukunft,* Leipzig [Friedrich Nietzsche and the German future], 1935, p. 86). Oehler knew better: he had been one of the editors of the collected works and had even then compiled elaborate indices for two editions—one of these indices comprised two and a half large volumes—and later he compiled a third one for yet another edition. But the Nazis' occa-

proximately as the English nobility does. It is obvious that the stronger and already more clearly defined types of the new Germanism can enter into relations with them with the least hesitation; for example, officers of the nobility from the March Brandenburg:[28] it would be interesting in many ways to see whether the hereditary art of commanding and obeying—in both of these, the land just named is classical today—could not be enriched with[29] the genius of money and patience (and above all a little spirituality, which is utterly lacking among these officers). But here it is proper to break off my cheerful Germanomania and holiday oratory; for I am beginning to touch on what is *serious* for me, the "European problem" as I understand it, the cultivation of a new caste that will rule Europe.

252

They are no philosophical race, these Englishmen: Bacon signifies an *attack* on the philosophical spirit; Hobbes, Hume, and Locke a debasement and lowering of the value of the concept of "philosophy" for more than a century. It was *against* Hume that Kant arose, and rose; it was Locke of whom Schelling said, *understandably, "je méprise Locke"*;[30] in their fight against the English-mechanistic doltification of the world, Hegel and Schopenhauer were of one mind (with Goethe)—these two hostile brother geniuses in philosophy who strove apart toward opposite poles of the German spirit and in the process wronged each other as only brothers wrong each other.[31]

---

sional use and perversion of Nietzsche was completely devoid of the most elementary scruples. For other examples see Kaufmann's *Nietzsche,* Chapter 10.

[28] The region around Berlin. In 1701 the Elector of Brandenburg was crowned the first King of Prussia, and in 1871 the kings of Prussia, his descendants, became German Emperors.

[29] *Hinzutun, hinzuzüchten.*

[30] "I despise Locke."

[31] In fact, Hegel, who was then very famous and influential, never wronged Schopenhauer, who was young, unknown, and deliberately provocative; but

What was lacking in England, and always has been lacking there, was known well enough to that semi-actor and rhetorician, the insipid muddlehead Carlyle, who tried to conceal behind passionate grimaces what he knew of himself—namely, what was *lacking* in Carlyle: real *power* of spirituality, real *profundity* of spiritual perception; in brief, philosophy.

It is characteristic of such an unphilosophical race that it clings firmly to Christianity: they *need* its discipline to become "moralized" and somewhat humanized. The English, being gloomier, more sensual, stronger in will, and more brutal than the Germans, are precisely for that reason more vulgar, also more pious than the Germans: they stand more in *need* of Christianity. For more sensitive nostrils even this English Christianity still has a typically English odor of *spleen* and alcoholic dissipation against which it is needed for good reasons as a remedy—the subtler poison against the coarser: a subtler poisoning is indeed for clumsy peoples some progress, a step toward spiritualization. English clumsiness and peasant seriousness is still disguised most tolerably —or rather elucidated and reinterpreted—by the language of Christian gestures and by prayers and singing of psalms. And for those brutes of sots and rakes who formerly learned how to grunt morally under the sway of Methodism and more recently again as a "Salvation Army," a penitential spasm may really be the relatively highest achievement of "humanity" to which they can be raised: that much may be conceded in all fairness. But what is offensive even in the most humane Englishman is his lack of music, speaking metaphorically (but not only metaphorically): in the movements of his soul and body he has no rhythm and dance, indeed not even the desire for rhythm and dance, for "music." Listen to him speak; watch the most beautiful Englishwomen *walk*—there are no more beautiful doves and swans in any country in the world—finally listen to them sing! But I am asking too much—

Schopenhauer attacked Hegel after his death in the strongest terms, in print. See Walter Kaufmann, *Hegel* (Garden City, N.Y., Doubleday, 1965), section 54. It is remarkable how completely Nietzsche emancipated himself from Schopenhauer's view of Hegel, considering Nietzsche's early enthusiasm for Schopenhauer.

253

There are truths that are recognized best by mediocre minds because they are most congenial to them; there are truths that have charm and seductive powers only for mediocre spirits: we come up against this perhaps disagreeable proposition just now, since the spirit of respectable but mediocre Englishmen—I name Darwin, John Stuart Mill, and Herbert Spencer—is beginning to predominate in the middle regions of European taste. Indeed, who would doubt that it is useful that *such* spirits should rule at times? It would be a mistake to suppose that the spirits of a high type that soar on their own paths would be particularly skillful at determining and collecting many small and common facts and then drawing conclusions from them: on the contrary, being exceptions, they are from the start at a disadvantage when it comes to the "rule." Finally, they have more to do than merely to gain knowledge— namely, to *be* something new, to *signify* something new, to *represent* new values. Perhaps the chasm between *know* and *can* is greater, also uncannier, than people suppose: those who can do things in the grand style, the creative, may possibly have to be lacking in knowledge—while, on the other hand, for scientific discoveries of the type of Darwin's a certain narrowness, aridity, and industrious diligence, something English in short, may not be a bad disposition.

Finally, we should not forget that the English with their profound normality have once before caused an over-all depression of the European spirit: what people call "modern ideas" or "the ideas of the eighteenth century" or also "French ideas"—that, in other words, against which the *German* spirit has risen with a profound disgust—was of English origin; there is no doubt of that. The French have merely been apes and mimes of these ideas; also their best soldiers; unfortunately, their first and most thoroughgoing *victims* as well: for over this damnable Anglomania of "modern ideas" the *âme française*[32] has in the end become so thin and emaciated

---

[32] French soul.

that today one recalls her sixteenth and seventeenth centuries, her profound and passionate strength, and her inventive nobility almost with disbelief. Yet we must hang on to this proposition of historical fairness with our very teeth, defending it against momentary appearances: European *noblesse*—of feeling, of taste, of manners, taking the word, in short, in every higher sense—is the work and invention of *France;* European vulgarity, the plebeianism of modern ideas, that of *England.*—[33]

254

Even now France is still the seat of the most spiritual and sophisticated culture in Europe and the foremost school of taste—but one has to know how to find this "France of taste." [34] Those who belong to it stay well hidden: it may be a small number in whom it lives—at that, perhaps human beings whose legs might be sturdier, some of them fatalists, somber and sick, some of them overly delicate and artificial, such as have the *ambition* to hide. One point they all have in common: they plug their ears against the raging stupidity and the noisy twaddle of the democratic bourgeois. Indeed, the foreground today is taken up by a part of France that has become stupid and coarse: recently, at Victor Hugo's funeral,[35] it celebrated a veritable orgy of bad taste and at the same time self-admiration. They have in common one other point as well: the good will to resist any spiritual Germanization—and a still better incapacity to succeed.

Perhaps Schopenhauer is even now more at home and in-

---

[33] Nietzsche's influence on French letters since the turn of the century has been second only to his influence on German literature and thought; his reputation in England has been negligible. The British writers of the first rank who were influenced greatly by him were Irish: Shaw, Yeats, and Joyce.

[34] Parts of this section were later included by Nietzsche, slightly revised, in *Nietzsche contra Wagner,* in the chapter "Where Wagner Belongs" (*Portable Nietzsche,* pp. 671f.). He also used section 256 in the same chapter of *Nietzsche contra Wagner* and in the following one, and sections 269 and 270 for the chapter "The Psychologist Speaks Up" (pp. 677ff.).

[35] Victor Hugo died May 22, 1885.

digenous in this France of the spirit, which is also a France of pessimism, than he ever was in Germany—not to speak of Heinrich Heine, who has long become part of the very flesh and blood of the subtler and more demanding lyric poets of Paris, or of Hegel, who today exerts an almost tyrannical influence through Taine, who is the *foremost* historian now living. But as for Richard Wagner: the more French music learns to form itself in accordance with the actual needs of the *âme moderne*,[36] the more it will "Wagnerize"—that one can predict—and it is doing enough of that even now.

Nevertheless, there are three things to which the French can still point with pride today, as their heritage and possession and an enduring mark of their ancient cultural superiority over Europe, in spite of all voluntary and involuntary Germanization and vulgarization of their taste. First, the capacity for artistic passions, for that devotion to "form" for which the phrase *l'art pour l'art* has been invented along with a thousand others: that sort of thing has not been lacking in France for the last three centuries and has made possible again and again, thanks to their reverence for the "small number," a kind of chamber music in literature for which one looks in vain in the rest of Europe.

The second thing on which the French can base a superiority over Europe is their old, manifold, *moralistic*[37] culture, as a result of which we find, on the average, even in the little *romanciers* of the newspapers and in chance *boulevardiers de Paris* a psychological oversensitivity and curiosity of which in Germany, for example, one simply has no idea (let alone the thing itself). For this the Germans lack a few centuries of moralistic work which, as mentioned, France did not spare herself; anyone who calls the Germans "naïve" on that account praises them for a defect. (By way of contrast to the German inexperience and innocence *in voluptate psychologica*,[38] which is none too distantly related to the tediousness of

---

[36] Modern soul.

[37] The negative overtones of "moralistic" in current English usage are out of place in this context; Nietzsche is plainly thinking of the French term *moraliste*.

[38] In the delight of psychology.

German company, and as the most consummate expression of a typically French curiosity and inventiveness for this realm of delicate thrills, one may consider Henri Beyle,[39] that remarkable anticipatory and precursory human being who ran with a Napoleonic tempo through *his* Europe, through several centuries of the European soul, as an explorer and discoverer of this soul: it required two generations to *catch up* with him in any way, to figure out again a few of the riddles that tormented and enchanted him, this odd epicurean and question mark of a man who was France's last great psychologist.)

There is yet a third claim to superiority. The French character contains a halfway successful synthesis of the north and the south which allows them to comprehend many things and to do things which an Englishman could never understand. Their temperament, periodically turned toward and away from the south, in which from time to time Provençal and Ligurian blood foams over, protects them against the gruesome northern gray on gray and the sunless concept-spooking and anemia—the disease of *German* taste against whose excesses one has now prescribed for oneself, with considerable resolution, blood and iron,[40] which means "great politics" (in accordance with a dangerous healing art which teaches me to wait and wait but so far has not taught me any hope.) Even now one still encounters in France an advance understanding and

---

[39] The great French novelist (1783-1842) who is better known by his pen name, Stendhal. Nietzsche's writings abound in tributes to him; e.g., section 39 above.

[40] Bismarck's famous phrase. On May 12, 1859, writing to the cabinet minister Schleinitz from St. Petersburg, Bismarck spoke of "an infirmity of Prussia that sooner or later we shall have to cure *ferro et igni.*" In an evening session of the budget commission of the Prussian parliament, September 30, 1862, he said: "It is not by speeches and majority resolutions that the great questions of the time are decided—that was the mistake of 1848 and 1849—but by iron and blood." And on January 28, 1886, Bismarck said to the Parliament: "It is not my fault that at that time I was misunderstood. It was a matter of military questions, and I said: Place as great a military force as possible, in other words as much blood and iron as possible, in the hand of the king of Prussia, then he will be able to make the politics you desire; with speeches and riflemen's festivals and songs it cannot be made; it can be made only with blood and iron."

accommodation of those rarer and rarely contented human beings who are too comprehensive to find satisfaction in any fatherland-ishness and know how to love the south in the north and the north in the south—the born Midlanders, the "good Europeans."

It was for them that *Bizet* made music, this last genius to see a new beauty and seduction—who discovered a piece of *the south of music.*

255

Against German music all kinds of precautions seem to me to be indicated. Suppose somebody loves the south as I love it, as a great school of convalescence, in the most spiritual as well as the most sensuous sense, as an uncontainable abundance of sun and transfiguration by the sun that suffuses an existence that believes and glories in itself: well, such a person will learn to be somewhat on his guard against German music, because in corrupting his taste again it also corrupts his health again.

If such a southerner, not by descent but by *faith,* should dream of the future of music, he must also dream of the redemption of music from the north, and in his ears he must have the prelude of a more profound, more powerful, perhaps more evil and mysterious music, a supra-German music that does not fade away at the sight of the voluptuous blue sea and the brightness of the Mediterranean sky, nor does it turn yellow and then pale as all German music does—a supra-European music that prevails even before the brown sunsets of the desert, a music whose soul is related to palm trees and feels at home and knows how to roam among great, beautiful, lonely beasts of prey—

I could imagine a music whose rarest magic would consist in its no longer knowing anything of good and evil, only now and then some sailor nostalgia, some golden shadows and delicate weak-nesses would pass over it—an art that from a great distance would behold, fleeing toward it, the colors of a setting *moral* world that had almost become unintelligible—and that would be hospitable and profound enough to receive such late fugitives.—

256

Owing to the pathological estrangement which the insanity of nationality has induced, and still induces, among the peoples of Europe; owing also to the shortsighted and quick-handed politicians who are at the top today with the help of this insanity, without any inkling that their separatist policies can of necessity only be *entr'acte* policies; owing to all this and much else that today simply cannot be said, the most unequivocal portents are now being overlooked, or arbitrarily and mendaciously reinterpreted—that *Europe wants to become one.*

In all the more profound and comprehensive men of this century, the over-all direction of the mysterious workings of their soul was to prepare the way for this new *synthesis* and to anticipate experimentally the European of the future: only in their foregrounds or in weaker hours, say in old age, did they belong to the "fatherlandish"—they were merely taking a rest from themselves when they became "patriots." I am thinking of such human beings as Napoleon, Goethe, Beethoven, Stendhal, Heinrich Heine, Schopenhauer: do not hold it against me when I include Richard Wagner, too, with them, for one should not allow oneself to be led astray about him by his own misunderstandings—geniuses of his type rarely have the right to understand themselves. Even less, to be sure, by the indecent noise with which people in France now close themselves off against him and resist him: the fact remains nevertheless that the *late French romanticism* of the forties and Richard Wagner belong together most closely and intimately. In all the heights and depths of their needs they are related, fundamentally related: it is Europe, the one Europe, whose soul surges and longs to get further and higher through their manifold and impetuous art —where? into a new light? toward a new sun? But who could express precisely what all these masters of new means of language could not express precisely? What is certain is that the same storm and stress tormented them and that they *sought* in the same way, these last great seekers!

Literature dominated all of them up to their eyes and ears—

they were the first artists steeped in world literature—and most of them were themselves writers, poets, mediators and mixers of the arts and senses (as a musician, Wagner belongs among painters; as a poet, among musicians; as an artist in general, among actors); all of them were fanatics of *expression* "at any price"—I should stress Delacroix, who was most closely related to Wagner—all of them great discoverers in the realm of the sublime, also of the ugly and gruesome, and still greater discoverers concerning effects, display, and the art of display windows—all of them talents far beyond their genius—virtuosos through and through, with uncanny access to everything that seduces, allures, compels, overthrows; born enemies of logic and straight lines, lusting after the foreign, the exotic, the tremendous, the crooked, the self-contradictory; as human beings, Tantaluses of the will, successful plebeians who knew themselves to be incapable, both in their lives and works, of a noble tempo, a *lento*[41]—take Balzac, for example—unbridled workers, almost self-destroyers through work; antinomians and rebels against custom, ambitious and insatiable without balance and enjoyment; all of them broke and collapsed in the end before the Christian cross (with right and reason: for who among them would have been profound and original[42] enough for a philosophy of the *Antichrist?*)—on the whole, an audaciously daring, magnificently violent type of higher human beings who soared, and tore others along, to the heights—it fell to them to first teach their century—and it is the century of the *crowd!*—the concept "higher man"—

Let the German friends of Richard Wagner ponder whether there is in Wagner's art anything outright German, or whether it is not just its distinction that it derives from *supra-German* sources and impulses. Nor should it be underestimated to what extent Paris was indispensable for the development of his type, and at the decisive moment the depth of his instincts led him to Paris. His entire manner and self-apostolate could perfect itself only when he saw the model of the French socialists. Perhaps it will be found after a subtler comparison that, to the honor of Richard Wagner's Ger-

---

[41] Slow tempo.
[42] *Ursprünglich.*

man nature, his doings were in every respect stronger, more audacious, harder, and higher than anything a Frenchman of the nineteenth century could manage—thanks to the fact that we Germans
are still closer to barbarism than the French. Perhaps Wagner's
strangest creation is inaccessible, inimitable, and beyond the feelings of the whole, so mature, Latin race, not only today but forever: the figure of Siegfried, that *very free* man who may indeed be
much too free, too hard, too cheerful, too healthy, too *anti-
Catholic* for the taste of ancient and mellow cultured peoples. He
may even have been a sin against romanticism, this anti-romantic
Siegfried: well, Wagner more than atoned for this sin in his old and
glum days when—anticipating a taste that has since then become
political—he began, if not to walk, at least to preach, with his
characteristic religious vehemence, *the way to Rome.*

Lest these final words be misunderstood, I will enlist the assistance of a few vigorous rhymes which will betray to less subtle ears,
too, what I want—what I have against the "final Wagner" and his
Parsifal music:

—Is this still German?—
Out of a German heart, this sultry screeching?
a German body, this self-laceration?
German, this priestly affectation,
this incense-perfumed sensual preaching?
German, this halting, plunging, reeling,
this so uncertain bim-bam pealing?
this nunnish ogling, *Ave* leavening,
this whole falsely ecstatic heaven overheavening?
—Is this still German?—
You still stand at the gate, perplexed?
Think! What you hear is *Rome—Rome's faith without the text.*

PART NINE

WHAT IS NOBLE [1]

---

[1] *Vornehm*. See section 212 above, especially the last paragraph.

Part Nine

257

Every enhancement of the type "man" has so far been the work of an aristocratic society—and it will be so again and again—a society that believes in the long ladder of an order of rank and differences in value between man and man, and that needs slavery in some sense or other. Without that *pathos of distance* which grows out of the ingrained difference between strata[2]—when the ruling caste constantly looks afar and looks down upon subjects and instruments and just as constantly practices obedience and command, keeping down and keeping at a distance—that other, more mysterious pathos could not have grown up either—the craving for an ever new widening of distances within the soul itself, the development of ever higher, rarer, more remote, further-stretching, more comprehensive states—in brief, simply the enhancement of the type "man," the continual "self-overcoming of man," to use a moral formula in a supra-moral sense.

To be sure, one should not yield to humanitarian illusions about the origins of an aristocratic society (and thus of the presupposition of this enhancement of the type "man"): truth is hard. Let us admit to ourselves, without trying to be considerate, how every higher culture on earth so far has *begun*. Human beings whose nature was still natural, barbarians in every terrible sense of the word, men of prey who were still in possession of unbroken strength of will and lust for power, hurled themselves upon weaker, more civilized, more peaceful races, perhaps traders or cattle raisers, or upon mellow old cultures whose last vitality was even then

---

[2] *Stände: Stand* can mean—apart from position, state, condition—class, rank, profession, and *Stände* can mean the estates of the realm. Asked to indicate her *Stand* on a questionnaire, a German woman might write, even after World War II: *Strassenbahnschaffnerswitwe*, that is, "widow of a streetcar conductor."

flaring up in splendid fireworks of spirit and corruption. In the beginning, the noble caste was always the barbarian caste: their predominance did not lie mainly in physical strength but in strength of the soul—they were more *whole* human beings (which also means, at every level, "more whole beasts").

258

Corruption as the expression of a threatening anarchy among the instincts and of the fact that the foundation of the affects, which is called "life," has been shaken: corruption is something totally different depending on the organism in which it appears. When, for example, an aristocracy, like that of France at the beginning of the Revolution, throws away its privileges with a sublime disgust and sacrifices itself to an extravagance of its own moral feelings, that is corruption; it was really only the last act of that centuries-old corruption which had led them to surrender, step by step, their governmental prerogatives, demoting themselves to a mere *function* of the monarchy (finally even to a mere ornament and showpiece). The essential characteristic of a good and healthy aristocracy, however, is that it experiences itself *not* as a function (whether of the monarchy or the commonwealth) but as their *meaning* and highest justification—that it therefore accepts with a good conscience the sacrifice of untold human beings who, *for its sake,* must be reduced and lowered to incomplete human beings, to slaves, to instruments. Their fundamental faith simply has to be that society must *not* exist for society's sake but only as the foundation and scaffolding on which a choice type of being is able to raise itself to its higher task and to a higher state of *being*[3]—comparable to those sun-seeking vines of Java—they are called *Sipo Matador* —that so long and so often enclasp an oak tree with their tendrils until eventually, high above it but supported by it, they can unfold their crowns in the open light and display their happiness.

---

[3] Cf. the outlook of the heroes of the *Iliad.*

259

Refraining mutually from injury, violence, and exploitation and placing one's will on a par with that of someone else—this may become, in a certain rough sense, good manners among individuals if the appropriate conditions are present (namely, if these men are actually similar in strength and value standards and belong together in *one* body). But as soon as this principle is extended, and possibly even accepted as the *fundamental principle of society,* it immediately proves to be what it really is—a will to the *denial* of life, a principle of disintegration and decay.

Here we must beware of superficiality and get to the bottom of the matter, resisting all sentimental weakness: life itself is *essentially* appropriation, injury, overpowering of what is alien and weaker; suppression, hardness, imposition of one's own forms, incorporation and at least, at its mildest, exploitation—but why should one always use those words in which a slanderous intent has been imprinted for ages?

Even the body within which individuals treat each other as equals, as suggested before—and this happens in every healthy aristocracy—if it is a living and not a dying body, has to do to other bodies what the individuals within it refrain from doing to each other: it will have to be an incarnate will to power, it will strive to grow, spread, seize, become predominant—not from any morality or immorality but because it is *living* and because life simply *is* will to power. But there is no point on which the ordinary consciousness of Europeans resists instruction as on this: everywhere people are now raving, even under scientific disguises, about coming conditions of society in which "the exploitative aspect" will be removed—which sounds to me as if they promised to invent a way of life that would dispense with all organic functions. "Exploitation" does not belong to a corrupt or imperfect and primitive society: it belongs to the *essence* of what lives, as a basic organic function; it is a consequence of the will to power, which is after all the will of life.

If this should be an innovation as a theory—as a reality it is the *primordial fact* of all history: people ought to be honest with themselves at least that far.

260

Wandering through the many subtler and coarser moralities which have so far been prevalent on earth, or still are prevalent, I found that certain features recurred regularly together and were closely associated—until I finally discovered two basic types and one basic difference.

There are *master morality* and *slave morality*[4]—I add immediately that in all the higher and more mixed cultures there also appear attempts at mediation between these two moralities, and yet more often the interpenetration and mutual misunderstanding of both, and at times they occur directly alongside each other— even in the same human being, within a *single* soul.[5] The moral discrimination of values has originated either among a ruling group whose consciousness of its difference from the ruled group was accompanied by delight—or among the ruled, the slaves and dependents of every degree.

In the first case, when the ruling group determines what is "good," the exalted, proud states of the soul are experienced as conferring distinction and determining the order of rank. The noble human being separates from himself those in whom the opposite of such exalted, proud states finds expression: he despises them. It should be noted immediately that in this first type of morality the opposition of "good" and *"bad"* means approximately the same as "noble" and "contemptible." (The opposition of "good" and *"evil"* has a different origin.) One feels contempt for the cowardly, the

---

[4] While the ideas developed here, and explicated at greater length a year later in the first part of the *Genealogy of Morals,* had been expressed by Nietzsche in 1878 in section 45 of *Human, All-Too-Human,* this is the passage in which his famous terms "master morality" and "slave morality" are introduced. See p. 147f., above.

[5] These crucial qualifications, though added immediately, have often been overlooked. "Modern" moralities are clearly mixtures; hence their manifold tensions, hypocrisies, and contradictions.

anxious, the petty, those intent on narrow utility; also for the suspicious with their unfree glances, those who humble themselves, the doglike people who allow themselves to be maltreated, the begging flatterers, above all the liars: it is part of the fundamental faith of all aristocrats that the common people lie. "We truthful ones"— thus the nobility of ancient Greece referred to itself.

It is obvious that moral designations were everywhere first applied to *human beings* and only later, derivatively, to actions. Therefore it is a gross mistake when historians of morality start from such questions as: why was the compassionate act praised? The noble type of man experiences *itself* as determining values; it does not need approval; it judges, "what is harmful to me is harmful in itself"; it knows itself to be that which first accords honor to things; it is *value-creating*. Everything it knows as part of itself it honors: such a morality is self-glorification. In the foreground there is the feeling of fullness, of power that seeks to overflow, the happiness of high tension, the consciousness of wealth that would give and bestow: the noble human being, too, helps the unfortunate, but not, or almost not, from pity, but prompted more by an urge begotten by excess of power. The noble human being honors himself as one who is powerful, also as one who has power over himself, who knows how to speak and be silent, who delights in being severe and hard with himself and respects all severity and hardness. "A hard heart Wotan put into my breast," says an old Scandinavian saga: a fitting poetic expression, seeing that it comes from the soul of a proud Viking. Such a type of man is actually proud of the fact that he is *not* made for pity, and the hero of the saga therefore adds as a warning: "If the heart is not hard in youth it will never harden." Noble and courageous human beings who think that way are furthest removed from that morality which finds the distinction of morality precisely in pity, or in acting for others, or in *désintéressement;* faith in oneself, pride in oneself, a fundamental hostility and irony against "selflessness" belong just as definitely to noble morality as does a slight disdain and caution regarding compassionate feelings and a "warm heart."

It is the powerful who *understand* how to honor; this is their art, their realm of invention. The profound reverence for age and tradition—all law rests on this double reverence—the faith and prejudice in favor of ancestors and disfavor of those yet to come are typical of the morality of the powerful; and when the men of "modern ideas," conversely, believe almost instinctively in "progress" and "the future" and more and more lack respect for age, this in itself would sufficiently betray the ignoble origin of these "ideas."

A morality of the ruling group, however, is most alien and embarrassing to the present taste in the severity of its principle that one has duties only to one's peers; that against beings of a lower rank, against everything alien, one may behave as one pleases or "as the heart desires," and in any case "beyond good and evil"— here pity and like feelings may find their place.[6] The capacity for, and the duty of, long gratitude and long revenge—both only among one's peers—refinement in repaying, the sophisticated concept of friendship, a certain necessity for having enemies (as it were, as drainage ditches for the affects of envy, quarrelsomeness, exuberance—at bottom, in order to be capable of being good *friends*): all these are typical characteristics of noble morality which, as suggested, is not the morality of "modern ideas" and therefore is hard to empathize with today, also hard to dig up and uncover.[7]

---

[6] The final clause that follows the dash, omitted in the Cowan translation, is crucial and qualifies the first part of the sentence: a noble person has no *duties* to animals but treats them in accordance with his feelings, which means, if he is noble, with pity.

The ruling masters, of course, are not always noble in this sense, and this is recognized by Nietzsche in *Twilight of the Idols,* in the chapter "The 'Improvers' of Mankind," in which he gives strong expression to his distaste for Manu's laws concerning outcastes (*Portable Nietzsche,* pp. 503-05); also in *The Will to Power* (ed. W. Kaufmann, New York, Random House, 1967), section 142. Indeed, in *The Antichrist,* section 57, Nietzsche contradicts outright his formulation above: "When the exceptional human being treats the mediocre more tenderly than himself and his peers, this is not mere courtesy of the heart—it is simply his *duty*."

More important: Nietzsche's obvious distaste for slave morality and the fact that he makes a point of liking master morality better does not imply that he endorses master morality. Cf. the text for note 5 above.

[7] Clearly, master morality cannot be discovered by introspection nor by the observation of individuals who are "masters" rather than "slaves." Both of these misunderstandings are widespread. What is called for is rather a rereading of, say, the *Iliad* and, to illustrate "slave morality," the New Testament.

It is different with the second type of morality, *slave morality*. Suppose the violated, oppressed, suffering, unfree, who are uncertain of themselves and weary, moralize: what will their moral valuations have in common? Probably, a pessimistic suspicion about the whole condition of man will find expression, perhaps a condemnation of man along with his condition. The slave's eye is not favorable to the virtues of the powerful: he is skeptical and suspicious, *subtly* suspicious, of all the "good" that is honored there—he would like to persuade himself that even their happiness is not genuine. Conversely, those qualities are brought out and flooded with light which serve to ease existence for those who suffer: here pity, the complaisant and obliging hand, the warm heart, patience, industry, humility, and friendliness are honored—for here these are the most useful qualities and almost the only means for enduring the pressure of existence. Slave morality is essentially a morality of utility.

Here is the place for the origin of that famous opposition of "good" and "evil": into evil one's feelings project power and dangerousness, a certain terribleness, subtlety, and strength that does not permit contempt to develop. According to slave morality, those who are "evil" thus inspire fear; according to master morality it is precisely those who are "good" that inspire, and wish to inspire, fear, while the "bad" are felt to be contemptible.

The opposition reaches its climax when, as a logical consequence of slave morality, a touch of disdain is associated also with the "good" of this morality—this may be slight and benevolent—because the good human being has to be *undangerous* in the slaves' way of thinking: he is good-natured, easy to deceive, a little stupid perhaps, *un bonhomme*.[8] Wherever slave morality becomes preponderant, language tends to bring the words "good" and "stupid" closer together.

One last fundamental difference: the longing for *freedom,* the instinct for happiness and the subtleties of the feeling of free-

---

[8] Literally "a good human being," the term is used for precisely the type described here.

dom belong just as necessarily to slave morality and morals as artful and enthusiastic reverence and devotion are the regular symptom of an aristocratic way of thinking and evaluating.

This makes plain why love *as passion*—which is our European specialty—simply must be of noble origin: as is well known, its invention must be credited to the Provençal knight-poets, those magnificent and inventive human beings of the *"gai saber"* [9] to whom Europe owes so many things and almost owes itself.—

261

Among the things that may be hardest to understand for a noble human being is vanity: he will be tempted to deny it, where another type of human being could not find it more palpable. The problem for him is to imagine people who seek to create a good opinion of themselves which they do not have of themselves—and thus also do not "deserve"—and who nevertheless end up *believing* this good opinion themselves. This strikes him half as such bad taste and lack of self-respect, and half as so baroquely irrational, that he would like to consider vanity as exceptional, and in most cases when it is spoken of he doubts it.

He will say, for example: "I may be mistaken about my value and nevertheless demand that my value, exactly as I define it, should be acknowledged by others as well—but this is no vanity (but conceit or, more frequently, what is called 'humility' or 'modesty')." Or: "For many reasons I may take pleasure in the good opinion of others: perhaps because I honor and love them and all their pleasures give me pleasure; perhaps also because their good opinion confirms and strengthens my faith in my own good opinion; perhaps because the good opinion of others, even in cases

---

[9] "Gay science": in the early fourteenth century the term was used to designate the art of the troubadours, codified in *Leys d'amors.* Nietzsche subtitled his own *Fröhliche Wissenschaft* (1882), *"la gaya scienza,"* placed a quatrain on the title page, began the book with a fifteen-page "Prelude in German Rhymes," and in the second edition (1887) added, besides a Preface and Book V, an "Appendix" of further verses.

where I do not share it, is still useful to me or promises to become so—but all that is not vanity."

The noble human being must force himself, with the aid of history, to recognize that, since time immemorial, in all somehow dependent social strata the common man *was* only what he was *considered:* not at all used to positing values himself, he also attached no other value to himself than his masters attached to him (it is the characteristic *right of masters* to create values).

It may be understood as the consequence of an immense atavism that even now the ordinary man still always *waits* for an opinion about himself and then instinctively submits to that—but by no means only a "good" opinion; also a bad and unfair one (consider, for example, the great majority of the self-estimates and self-underestimates that believing women accept from their father-confessors, and believing Christians quite generally from their church).

In accordance with the slowly arising democratic order of things (and its cause, the intermarriage of masters and slaves), the originally noble and rare urge to ascribe value to oneself on one's own and to "think well" of oneself will actually be encouraged and spread more and more now; but it is always opposed by an older, ampler, and more deeply ingrained propensity—and in the phenomenon of "vanity" this older propensity masters the younger one. The vain person is delighted by *every* good opinion he hears of himself (quite apart from all considerations of its utility, and also apart from truth or falsehood), just as every bad opinion of him pains him: for he submits to both, he *feels* subjected to them in accordance with that oldest instinct of submission that breaks out in him.

It is "the slave" in the blood of the vain person, a residue of the slave's craftiness—and how much "slave" is still residual in woman, for example!—that seeks to *seduce* him to good opinions about himself; it is also the slave who afterwards immediately prostrates himself before these opinions as if he had not called them forth.

And to say it once more: vanity is an atavism.

262

A *species*[10] comes to be, a type becomes fixed and strong, through the long fight with essentially constant *unfavorable* conditions. Conversely, we know from the experience of breeders[11] that species accorded superabundant nourishment and quite generally extra protection and care soon tend most strongly toward variations of the type and become rich in marvels and monstrosities (including monstrous vices).

Now look for once at an aristocratic commonwealth—say, an ancient Greek *polis*,[12] or Venice—as an arrangement, whether voluntary or involuntary, for *breeding:* [13] human beings are together there who are dependent on themselves and want their species to prevail, most often because they *have to* prevail or run the terrible risk of being exterminated. Here that boon, that excess, and that protection which favor variations are lacking; the species needs itself as a species, as something that can prevail and make itself durable by virtue of its very hardness, uniformity, and simplicity of form, in a constant fight with its neighbors or with the oppressed who are rebellious or threaten rebellion. Manifold experience teaches them to which qualities above all they owe the fact that, despite all gods and men, they are still there, that they have always triumphed: these qualities they call virtues, these virtues alone they cultivate.[14] They do this with hardness, indeed they want hardness; every aristocratic morality is intolerant—in the education of youth, in their arrangements for women, in their marriage customs, in the relations of old and young, in their penal laws (which take into account deviants only)—they consider intolerance itself a virtue, calling it "justice."

In this way a type with few but very strong traits, a species of

---

[10] Throughout this section *Art* is rendered as species, and *Typus* as type. Elsewhere, *Art* is often translated as type.

[11] *Züchter.*

[12] City-state.

[13] *Züchtung.*

[14] *Züchtet sie gross.*

severe, warlike, prudently taciturn men, close-mouthed and closely linked (and as such possessed of the subtlest feeling for the charms and *nuances* of association), is fixed beyond the changing generations; the continual fight against ever constant *unfavorable* conditions is, as mentioned previously, the cause that fixes and hardens a type.

Eventually, however, a day arrives when conditions become more fortunate and the tremendous tension decreases; perhaps there are no longer any enemies among one's neighbors, and the means of life, even for the enjoyment of life, are superabundant. At one stroke the bond and constraint of the old discipline[15] are torn: it no longer seems necessary, a condition of existence—if it persisted it would only be a form of *luxury,* an archaizing *taste.* Variation, whether as deviation (to something higher, subtler, rarer) or as degeneration and monstrosity, suddenly appears on the scene in the greatest abundance and magnificence; the individual dares to be individual and different.

At these turning points of history we behold beside one another, and often mutually involved and entangled, a splendid, manifold, junglelike growth and upward striving, a kind of *tropical* tempo in the competition to grow, and a tremendous ruin and self-ruination, as the savage egoisms that have turned, almost exploded, against one another wrestle "for sun and light" and can no longer derive any limit, restraint, or consideration from their previous[16] morality. It was this morality itself that dammed up such enormous strength and bent the bow in such a threatening manner; now it is "outlived." The dangerous and uncanny point has been reached where the greater, more manifold, more comprehensive life transcends and *lives beyond* the old morality; the "individual" appears, obliged to give himself laws and to develop his own arts and wiles for self-preservation, self-enhancement, self-redemption.

All sorts of new what-fors and wherewithals; no shared formulas any longer; misunderstanding allied with disrespect; decay, cor-

---

[15] *Zucht.*

[16] *Bisherigen:* elsewhere *bisher* has always been rendered as "so far"; see Preface, note 1.

ruption, and the highest desires gruesomely entangled; the genius of the race overflowing from all cornucopias of good and bad; a calamitous simultaneity of spring and fall, full of new charms and veils that characterize young, still unexhausted, still unwearied corruption. Again danger is there, the mother of morals, great danger, this time transposed into the individual, into the neighbor and friend, into the alley, into one's own child, into one's own heart, into the most personal and secret recesses of wish and will: what may the moral philosophers emerging in this age have to preach now?

These acute observers and loiterers discover that the end is approaching fast, that everything around them is corrupted and corrupts, that nothing will stand the day after tomorrow, except *one* type of man, the incurably *mediocre*. The mediocre alone have a chance of continuing their type and propagating—they are the men of the future, the only survivors: "Be like them! Become mediocre!" is now the only morality that still makes sense, that still gets a hearing.

But this morality of mediocrity is hard to preach: after all, it may never admit what it is and what it wants. It must speak of measure and dignity and duty and neighbor love—it will find it difficult *to conceal its irony*.—

263

There is an *instinct for rank* which, more than anything else, is a sign of a *high* rank; there is a delight in the nuances of reverence that allows us to infer noble origin and habits. The refinement, graciousness, and height of a soul is tested dangerously when something of the first rank passes by without being as yet protected by the shudders of authority against obtrusive efforts and ineptitudes—something that goes its way unmarked, undiscovered, tempting, perhaps capriciously concealed and disguised, like a living touchstone. Anyone to whose task and practice it belongs to search out souls will employ this very art in many forms in order to determine the ultimate value of a soul and the unalterable, innate order of rank to which it belongs: he will test it for its *instinct of reverence*.

Différence engendre haine:[17] the baseness of some people suddenly spurts up like dirty water when some holy vessel, some precious thing from a locked shrine, some book with the marks of a great destiny, is carried past; and on the other hand there is a reflex of silence, a hesitation of the eye, a cessation of all gestures that express how a soul *feels* the proximity of the most venerable. The way in which reverence for the *Bible* has on the whole been maintained so far in Europe is perhaps the best bit of discipline and refinement of manners that Europe owes to Christianity: such books of profundity and ultimate significance require some external tyranny of authority for their protection in order to gain those millennia of *persistence* which are necessary to exhaust them and figure them out.

Much is gained once the feeling has finally been cultivated in the masses (among the shallow and in the high-speed intestines of every kind) that they are not to touch everything; that there are holy experiences before which they have to take off their shoes and keep away their unclean hands—this is almost their greatest advance toward humanity. Conversely, perhaps there is nothing about so-called educated people and believers in "modern ideas" that is as nauseous as their lack of modesty and the comfortable insolence of their eyes and hands with which they touch, lick, and finger everything; and it is possible that even among the common people, among the less educated, especially among peasants, one finds today more *relative* nobility of taste and tactful reverence than among the newspaper-reading *demi-monde* of the spirit, the educated.

264

One cannot erase from the soul of a human being what his ancestors liked most to do and did most constantly: whether they

---

[17] Difference engenders hatred.

were, for example, assiduous savers and appurtenances of a desk and cash box, modest and bourgeois in their desires, modest also in their virtues; or whether they lived accustomed to commanding from dawn to dusk, fond of rough amusements and also perhaps of even rougher duties and responsibilities; or whether, finally, at some point they sacrificed ancient prerogatives of birth and possessions in order to live entirely for their faith—their "god"—as men of an inexorable and delicate conscience which blushes at every compromise. It is simply not possible that a human being should *not* have the qualities and preferences of his parents and ancestors in his body, whatever appearances may suggest to the contrary. This is the problem of race.[18]

If one knows something about the parents, an inference about the child is permissible: any disgusting incontinence, any nook envy, a clumsy insistence that one is always right—these three things together have always constituted the characteristic type of the plebeian—that sort of thing must as surely be transferred to the child as corrupted blood; and with the aid of the best education one will at best *deceive* with regard to such a heredity.

And what else is the aim of education and "culture" today? In our very popularity-minded—that is, plebeian—age, "education" and "culture" *have* to be essentially the art of deceiving—about one's origins, the inherited plebs in one's body and soul. An educator who today preached truthfulness above all and constantly challenged his students, "be true! be natural! do not pretend!"—even such a virtuous and guileless ass would learn after a while to reach for that *furca* of Horace to *naturam expellere:* with what success? "Plebs" *usque recurret.*[19]—

---

18 Here, as elsewhere, Nietzsche gives expression to his Lamarckian belief in the heredity of acquired characteristics, shared by Samuel Butler and Bernard Shaw but anathema to Nazi racists and almost universally rejected by geneticists. His Lamarckism is not just an odd fact about Nietzsche but symptomatic of his conception of body and spirit: he ridiculed belief in "pure" spirit but believed just as little in any "pure" body; he claimed that neither could be understood without the other. For a detailed discussion see Kaufmann, *Nietzsche,* Chapter 10.

19 Horace's *Epistles,* I.10, 24: "Try with a pitchfork to drive out nature, she always returns."

265

At the risk of displeasing innocent ears I propose: egoism belongs to the nature of a noble soul—I mean that unshakable faith that to a being such as "we are" other beings must be subordinate by nature and have to sacrifice themselves. The noble soul accepts this fact of its egoism without any question mark, also without any feeling that it might contain hardness, constraint, or caprice, rather as something that may be founded in the primordial law of things: if it sought a name for this fact it would say, "it is justice itself." Perhaps it admits under certain circumstances that at first make it hesitate that there are some who have rights equal to its own; as soon as this matter of rank is settled it moves among these equals with their equal privileges, showing the same sureness of modesty and delicate reverence that characterize its relations with itself—in accordance with an innate heavenly mechanism understood by all stars. It is merely another aspect of its egoism, this refinement and self-limitation in its relations with its equals—every star is such an egoist—it honors *itself* in them and in the rights it cedes to them; it does not doubt that the exchange of honors and rights is of the nature of all social relations and thus also belongs to the natural condition of things.

The noble soul gives as it takes, from that passionate and irritable instinct of repayment that lies in its depth. The concept "grace" [20] has no meaning or good odor *inter pares;* [21] there may be a sublime way of letting presents from above happen to one, as it were, and to drink them up thirstily like drops—but for this art and gesture the noble soul has no aptitude. Its egoism hinders it: quite generally it does not like to look "up"—but either *ahead,* horizontally and slowly, or down: *it knows itself to be at a height.*

266

"Truly high respect one can have only for those who do not *seek* themselves."—Goethe to Rat Schlosser.

---

[20] *"Gnade."*
[21] Among equals.

267

The Chinese have a proverb that mothers even teach children: *siao-sin*—"make your heart *small!*" This is the characteristic fundamental propensity in late civilizations: I do not doubt that an ancient Greek would recognize in us Europeans of today, too, such self-diminution; this alone would suffice for us to "offend his taste."—

268

What, in the end, is common? [22]
Words are acoustical signs for concepts; concepts, however, are more or less definite image signs for often recurring and associated sensations, for groups of sensations. To understand one another, it is not enough that one use the same words; one also has to use the same words for the same species of inner experiences; in the end one has to have one's experience in *common*.

Therefore the human beings of *one* people understand one another better than those belonging to different peoples even if they employ the same language; or rather when human beings have long lived together under similar conditions (of climate, soil, danger, needs, and work), what *results*[23] from this is people who "understand [24] one another"—a people. In all souls an equal number of often recurring experiences has come to be predominant over experiences that come more rarely: on the basis of the former one understands the other, quickly and ever more quickly—the history of language is the history of a process of abbreviation—and on the basis of such quick understanding one associates, ever more closely.

The greater the danger is, the greater is the need to reach agreement quickly and easily about what must be done; not mis-

---

[22] *Die Gemeinheit:* commonness; but it usually means vulgarity, meanness, baseness.
[23] *Entsteht.* ·
[24] *"Sich versteht."*

understanding one another in times of danger is what human beings simply cannot do without in their relations. In every friendship or love affair one still makes this test: nothing of that sort can endure once one discovers that one's partner associates different feelings, intentions, nuances, desires, and fears with the same words. (Fear of the "eternal misunderstanding"—that is the benevolent genius which so often keeps persons of different sex from rash attachments to which their senses and hearts prompt them—this and *not* some Schopenhauerian "genius of the species"!)

Which group of sensations is aroused, expresses itself, and issues commands in a soul most quickly, is decisive for the whole order of rank of its values and ultimately determines its table of goods. The values of a human being betray something of the *structure* of his soul and where it finds its conditions of life, its true need.

Assuming next that need has ever brought close to one another only such human beings as could suggest with similar signs similar requirements and experiences, it would follow on the whole that easy communicability of need—which in the last analysis means the experience of merely average and *common* experiences—must have been the most powerful of all powers at whose disposal man has been so far. The human beings who are more similar, more ordinary, have had, and always have, an advantage; those more select, subtle, strange, and difficult to understand, easily remain alone, succumb to accidents, being isolated, and rarely propagate. One must invoke tremendous counter-forces in order to cross this natural, all too natural *progressus in simile,* the continual development of man toward the similar, ordinary, average, herdlike— *common!*

269

The more a psychologist—a born and inevitable psychologist and unriddler of souls—applies himself to the more exquisite cases and human beings, the greater becomes the danger that he might suffocate from pity.[25] He *needs* hardness and cheerfulness more

---

[25] Cf. *Zarathustra,* Part IV.

than anyone else. For the corruption, the ruination of the higher men, of the souls of a stranger type, is the rule: it is terrible to have such a rule always before one's eyes. The manifold torture of the psychologist who has discovered this ruination, who discovers this whole inner hopelessness of the higher man, this eternal "too late" in every sense, first in one case and then *almost* always through the whole of history—may perhaps lead him one day to turn against his own lot, embittered, and to make an attempt at self-destruction—may lead to his own "corruption."

In almost every psychologist one will perceive a telltale preference for and delight in association with everyday, well-ordered people: this reveals that he always requires a cure, that he needs a kind of escape and forgetting, away from all that with which his insights, his incisions, his "craft" have burdened his conscience. He is characterized by fear of his memory. He is easily silenced by the judgments of others; he listens with an immobile face as they venerate, admire, love, and transfigure where he has *seen*—or he even conceals his silence by expressly agreeing with some foreground opinion. Perhaps the paradox of his situation is so gruesome that precisely where he has learned the greatest pity coupled with the greatest contempt, the crowd, the educated, the enthusiasts learn the greatest veneration—the veneration for "great men" and prodigies for whose sake one blesses and honors the fatherland, the earth, the dignity of humanity, and oneself, and to whom one refers the young, toward whom one educates them—

And who knows whether what happened in all great cases so far was not always the same: that the crowd adored a god—and that the "god" was merely a poor sacrificial animal. Success has always been the greatest liar—and the "work" itself is a success; the great statesman, the conqueror, the discoverer is disguised by his creations, often beyond recognition; the "work," whether of the artist or the philosopher, invents the man who has created it, who is supposed to have created it; "great men," as they are venerated, are subsequent pieces of wretched minor fiction; in the world of historical values, counterfeit *rules*.

Those great poets, for example—men like Byron, Musset, Poe, Leopardi, Kleist, Gogol (I do not dare mention greater names, but I mean them) [26]—are and perhaps must be men of fleeting moments, enthusiastic, sensual, childish, frivolous and sudden in mistrust and trust; with souls in which they usually try to conceal some fracture; often taking revenge with their works for some inner contamination, often seeking with their high flights to escape into forgetfulness from an all-too-faithful memory; often lost in the mud and almost in love with it, until they become like the will-o'-the-wisps around swamps and *pose* as stars—the people may then call them idealists—often fighting against a long nausea, with a recurring specter of unbelief that chills and forces them to languish for *gloria* and to gobble their "belief in themselves" from the hands of intoxicated flatterers—what *torture* are these great artists and all the so-called higher men for anyone who has once guessed their true nature! [27]

It is easy to understand that *these* men should so readily receive from woman—clairvoyant in the world of suffering and, unfortunately, also desirous far beyond her strength to help and save —those eruptions of boundless and most devoted *pity* which the multitude, above all the venerating multitude, does not understand and on which it lavishes inquisitive and self-satisfied interpretations. This pity deceives itself regularly about its powers; woman would like to believe that love can achieve *anything*—that is her characteristic *faith*. Alas, whoever knows the heart will guess how poor, stupid, helpless, arrogant, blundering, more apt to destroy than to save is even the best and profoundest love!

It is possible that underneath the holy fable and disguise of

---

[26] The parenthesis is not found in the first two editions of 1886 and 1891, but it appears in all standard editions, including Schlechta's, although he purports to follow the original edition. When Nietzsche included this passage in *Nietzsche contra Wagner* in slightly revised form, the remark was set off by dashes instead of parentheses and read, "I do not mention far greater names, but I mean them" (*Portable Nietzsche,* p. 678). The third edition of *Beyond Good and Evil* (1894) has "far greater names."

According to the table comparing the page numbers of the different editions of *Beyond Good and Evil* in Vol. VII (1903) of the Grossoktav edition of the *Werke,* the third edition of *Beyond* was dated 1893, the fourth 1894, and the page numbers of both are the same; but the Princeton University Library has a copy of the *Dritte Auflage* (third edition) dated 1894.

[27] Another leitmotif of *Zarathustra,* Part IV.

Jesus' life there lies concealed one of the most painful cases of the martyrdom of *knowledge about love:* the martyrdom of the most innocent and desirous heart, never sated by any human love; *demanding* love, to be loved and nothing else, with hardness, with insanity, with terrible eruptions against those who denied him love; the story of a poor fellow, unsated and insatiable in love, who had to invent hell in order to send to it those who did not *want* to love him—and who finally, having gained kowledge about human love, had to invent a god who is all love, all *ability* to love—who has mercy on human love because it is so utterly wretched and unknowing. Anyone who feels that way, who *knows* this about love—*seeks* death.

But why pursue such painful matters? Assuming one does not have to.—

270

The spiritual haughtiness and nausea of every man who has suffered profoundly—it almost determines the order of rank *how* profoundly human beings can suffer—his shuddering certainty, which permeates and colors him through and through, that by virtue of his suffering he *knows more* than the cleverest and wisest could possibly know, and that he knows his way and has once been "at home" in many distant, terrifying worlds of which *"you* know nothing"—this spiritual and silent haughtiness of the sufferer, this pride of the elect of knowledge, of the "initiated," of the almost sacrificed, finds all kinds of disguises necessary to protect itself against contact with obtrusive and pitying hands and altogether against everything that is not its equal in suffering. Profound suffering makes noble; it separates.

One of the most refined disguises is Epicureanism, and a certain ostentatious courage of taste which takes suffering casually and resists everything sad and profound. There are "cheerful people" who employ cheerfulness because they are misunderstood on its account—they *want* to be misunderstood. There are "scientific men" who employ science because it creates a cheerful appearance, and because being scientific suggests that a human being is superficial—they *want* to seduce others to this false inference. There are free, insolent spirits who would like to conceal and deny that they are broken, proud, incurable hearts (the cynicism of Hamlet—the case of Galiani); [28] and occasionally even foolishness is the mask for an unblessed all-too-certain knowledge.

From which it follows that it is characteristic of more refined humanity to respect "the mask" and not to indulge in psychology and curiosity in the wrong place.

271

What separates two people most profoundly is a different sense and degree of cleanliness. What avails all decency and mutual usefulness and good will toward each other—in the end the fact remains: "They can't stand each other's smell!"

The highest instinct of cleanliness places those possessed of it in the oddest and most dangerous lonesomeness, as saints: for precisely this is saintliness—the highest spiritualization of this instinct. Whether one is privy to someone's indescribable abundance of pleasure in the bath, or whether one feels some ardor and thirst that constantly drives the soul out of the night into the morning and out of the dim and "dark moods" into what is bright, brilliant, profound, and refined—just as such a propensity *distinguishes*—it is a noble propensity—it also *separates*.

The saint's pity is pity with the *dirt* of what is human, all too human. And there are degrees and heights where he experiences even pity itself as a pollution, as dirty—

272

Signs of nobility: never thinking of degrading our duties into duties for everybody; not wanting to delegate, to share, one's own responsibility; counting one's privileges and their exercise among one's *duties*.

---

[28] The parenthesis is not found in the first four editions (see note 26 above), but in most subsequent editions, including Schlechta's. In *Nietzsche contra Wagner* we read, instead of the parenthesis: "—the case of Hamlet."

273

A human being who strives for something great considers everyone he meets on his way either as a means or as a delay and obstacle—or as a temporary resting place. His characteristic high-grade *graciousness* toward his fellow men becomes possible only once he has attained his height and rules. Impatience and his consciousness that until then he is always condemned to comedy—for even war is a comedy and conceals, just as every means conceals the end—spoil all of his relations to others: this type of man knows solitude and what is most poisonous in it.

274

The problem of those who are waiting.—It requires strokes of luck and much that is incalculable if a higher man in whom the solution of a problem lies dormant is to get around to action in time —to "eruption," one might say. In the average case it does *not* happen, and in nooks all over the earth sit men who are waiting, scarcely knowing in what way they are waiting, much less that they are waiting in vain. Occasionally the call that awakens—that accident which gives the "permission" to act—comes too late, when the best youth and strength for action has already been used up by sitting still; and many have found to their horror when they "leaped up" that their limbs had gone to sleep and their spirit had become too heavy. "It is too late," they said to themselves, having lost their faith in themselves and henceforth forever useless.

Could it be that in the realm of the spirit "Raphael without hands," taking this phrase in the widest sense, is perhaps not the exception but the rule? [29]

---

[29] An allusion to an oft-quoted sentence from Lessing's *Emilia Galotti,* Act I, Scene 4: "Or do you think, my Prince, that Raphael would not have been the greatest artistic [literally: painterly] genius if he had been born by some misfortune without hands?"

This section reminds us forcefully that Nietzsche is not proposing any easy bifurcation of mankind: not only are appearances misleading, as he points out again and again, but he considers the belief in opposite values an

Genius is perhaps not so rare after all—but the five hundred *hands* it requires to tyrannize the *kairos,* "the right time," seizing chance by its forelock.

275

Anyone who does not *want* to see what is lofty in a man looks that much more keenly for what is low in him and mere foreground —and thus betrays himself.

276

In all kinds of injury and loss the lower and coarser soul is better off than the nobler one: the dangers for the latter must be greater; the probability that it will come to grief and perish is actually, in view of the multiplicity of the conditions of its life, tremendous.

In a lizard a lost finger is replaced again; not so in man.

277

—Bad enough! The same old story! When one has finished building ones' house, one suddenly realizes that in the process one has learned something that one really needed to know in the worst way—before one began. The eternal distasteful "too late!"

The melancholy of everything *finished!* [30]—

278

Wanderer, who are you? I see you walking on your way without scorn, without love, with unfathomable eyes; moist and sad like

---

inveterate prejudice (see, e.g., section 2) and insists on a scale of subtle shades, degrees, and nuances.

[30] This section may signal the approaching end of the book. And the immediately following sections, being less continuous than the preceding, may also have been placed here from a sense of "where else?"—the end being at hand. In a sense, to be sure, they belong in Part IX, "What Is Noble," for they deal with the feelings of the uncommon man who lives apart; but they seem more personal.

a sounding lead that has returned to the light, unsated, from every depth—what did it seek down there?—with a breast that does not sigh, with a lip that conceals its disgust, with a hand that now reaches only slowly: who are you? what have you done? Rest here: this spot is hospitable to all—recuperate! And whoever you may be: what do you like now? what do you need for recreation? Name it: whatever I have I offer to you!

"Recreation? Recreation? You *are* inquisitive! What are you saying! But give me, please——"

What? What? Say it!

"Another mask! A second mask!" [31]—

279

Men of profound sadness betray themselves when they are happy: they have a way of embracing happiness as if they wanted to crush and suffocate it, from jealousy: alas, they know only too well that it will flee.

280

"Too bad! What? Isn't he going—back?"

Yes, but you understand him badly when you complain. He is going back like anybody who wants to attempt a big jump.—

281

—"Will people believe me? But I demand that they should believe me: I have always thought little and badly of myself, only on very rare occasions, only when I had to, always without any desire for 'this subject,' more than ready to digress from 'myself'; always without faith in the result, owing to an unconquerable mistrust of the *possibility* of self-knowledge which went so far that even in the concept of 'immediate knowledge,' which theoreticians permit themselves, I sensed a *contradictio in adjecto:* this whole

---

[31] See sections 30, 40, 289, and 290.

fact is almost the most certain thing I do know about myself. There must be a kind of aversion in me to *believing* anything definite about myself.

"Does this perhaps point to a riddle? Probably; but fortunately none for my own teeth.

"Perhaps it betrays the species to which I belong?

"But not to me—and of that I am glad."

282

—"But whatever happened to you?"

"I don't know," he said hesitantly; "perhaps the Harpies flew over my table."

Nowadays it happens occasionally that a mild, moderate, reticent person suddenly goes into a rage, smashes dishes, upends the table, screams, raves, insults everybody—and eventually walks off, ashamed, furious with himself—where? what for? To starve by himself? To suffocate on his recollection?

If a person has the desires of a high and choosy soul and only rarely finds his table set and his food ready, his danger will be great at all times; but today it is extraordinary. Thrown into a noisy and plebeian age with which he does not care to eat out of the same dishes, he can easily perish of hunger and thirst or, if eventually he "falls to" after all—of sudden nausea.

Probably all of us have sat at tables where we did not belong; and precisely the most spiritual among us, being hardest to nourish, know that dangerous dyspepsia which comes of a sudden insight and disappointment about our food and our neighbors at the table—the *after-dinner nausea*.

283

It involves subtle and at the same time noble self-control, assuming that one wants to praise at all, if one always praises only where one does *not* agree: for in the other case one would after all praise oneself, which offends good taste. Still this kind of self-control furnishes a neat occasion and provocation for constant misunderstandings. To be in a position to afford this real luxury of taste and morality, one must not live among dolts of the spirit but rather among people whose misunderstandings and blunders are still amusing owing to their subtlety—or one will have to pay dearly for it!

"He praises me: *hence* he thinks I am right"—this asinine inference spoils half our life for us hermits, for it leads asses to seek our neighborhood and friendship.

284

To live with tremendous and proud composure; always beyond—. To have and not to have one's affects, one's pro and con, at will; to condescend to them, for a few hours; to *seat* oneself on them as on a horse, often as on an ass—for one must know how to make use of their stupidity as much as of their fire. To reserve one's three hundred foregrounds; also the dark glasses; for there are cases when nobody may look into our eyes, still less into our "grounds." And to choose for company that impish and cheerful vice, courtesy. And to remain master of one's four virtues: of courage, insight, sympathy, and solitude.[32] For solitude is a virtue for us, as a sublime bent and urge for cleanliness which guesses how all contact between man and man—"in society"—involves inevitable uncleanliness. All community makes men—somehow, somewhere, sometime "common."

---

[32] But see section 227: "Honesty, supposing that this is our virtue . . ." And *Dawn*, section 556 (quoted in full): "*The good four.*—*Honest* with ourselves and whoever *else* is our friend; *courageous* with the enemy; *magnanimous* with the vanquished; *courteous*—always: thus the four cardinal virtues want us." Plato's four cardinal virtues had been wisdom, courage, temperance, and justice (*Republic* 427ff.). In German, the four terms in the *Dawn* are: *redlich, tapfer, grossmütig, höflich;* the four above: *Mut, Einsicht, Mitgefühl, Einsamkeit. Mut* and *Tapferkeit* are synonyms and mean courage. Honesty and insight are clearly related but not synonymous, and this is also true of magnanimity and sympathy. (The literal meaning of sympathy and *Mitgefühl* is the same and neither is restricted to suffering; both mean feeling with others what they feel.) The inclusion of sympathy among the four virtues is noteworthy, particularly as it occurs in "What Is Noble" in *Beyond Good and Evil.*

285

The greatest events and thoughts—but the greatest thoughts are the greatest events—are comprehended last: the generations that are contemporaneous with them do not *experience* such events —they live right past them. What happens is a little like what happens in the realm of stars. The light of the remotest stars comes last to men; and until it has arrived man *denies* that there are—stars there. "How many centuries does a spirit require to be comprehended?"—that is a standard, too; with that, too, one creates an order of rank and etiquette that is still needed—for spirit and star.[33]

286

"Here the vision is free, the spirit exalted." [34]

But there is an opposite type of man that is also on a height and also has free vision—but looks *down*.

287

—What is noble? What does the word "noble" still mean to us today? What betrays, what allows one to recognize the noble human being, under this heavy, overcast sky of the beginning rule of the plebs that makes everything opaque and leaden?

---

[33] Cf. *Zarathustra*, Part II: "the greatest events—they are not our loudest but our stillest hours. Not around the inventors of new noise, but around the inventors of new values does the world revolve; it revolves *inaudibly*" ("On Great Events," p. 243); and "Thoughts that come on doves' feet guide the world" ("The Stillest Hour," p. 258). The implications for Nietzsche's alleged bifurcation of humanity should not be overlooked: We are in no position to tell who among our contemporaries is great.

[34] Goethe's *Faust*, lines 11989f. This aphorism makes little sense unless one recognizes the quotation and knows that Doctor Marianus thus leads up to his apostrophe to the queen of heaven.— One may wonder whether it could possibly be noble to insist so often that one is looking *down;* but at least Nietzsche does not purport to speak of himself.

It is not actions that prove him—actions are always open to many interpretations, always unfathomable—nor is it "works." Among artists and scholars today one finds enough of those who betray by their works how they are impelled by a profound desire for what is noble; but just this need *for* what is noble is fundamentally different from the needs of the noble soul itself and actually the eloquent and dangerous mark of its lack. It is not the works, it is the *faith* that is decisive here, that determines the order of rank —to take up again an ancient religious formula in a new and more profound sense: some fundamental certainty that a noble soul has about itself, something that cannot be sought, nor found, nor perhaps lost.

The noble soul has reverence for itself.[35]

288

There are human beings who have spirit in an inevitable way; they may turn and twist as they please and hold their hands over their giveaway eyes (as if a hand did not give away secrets!)—in the end it always will out that they have something they conceal, namely spirit. One of the subtlest means for keeping up the deception at least as long as possible and of successfully appearing more stupid than one is—which in ordinary life is often as desirable as an umbrella—is called *enthusiasm,* if we include what belongs with it; for example, virtue. For as Galiani, who should know, says: *vertu est enthousiasme.*

289

In the writings[36] of a hermit one always also hears something of the echo of the desolate regions, something of the whispered

---

[35] Cf. Aristotle's *Nicomachean Ethics* (1169a): "The good man ought to be a lover of self, since he will then act nobly, and so both benefit himself and his fellows; but the bad man ought not to be a lover of self, since he will follow his base passions, and so injure both himself and his neighbours" (Rackham translation). Cf. also the long note for section 212 above.

[36] "Footsteps" in the Cowan translation depends on misreading *Schritten* instead of *Schriften.*

tones and the furtive look of solitude; in his strongest words, even in his cry, there still vibrates a new and dangerous kind of silence —of burying something in silence. When a man has been sitting alone with his soul in confidential discord and discourse, year in and year out, day and night; when in his cave—it may be a labyrinth or a gold mine—he has become a cave bear or a treasure digger or a treasure guard and dragon; then even his concepts eventually acquire a peculiar twilight color, an odor just as much of depth as of must, something incommunicable and recalcitrant that blows at every passerby like a chill.

The hermit does not believe that any philosopher—assuming that every philosopher was first of all a hermit—ever expressed his real and ultimate opinions in books: does one not write books precisely to conceal what one harbors? [37] Indeed, he will doubt whether a philosopher could *possibly* have "ultimate and real" opinions, whether behind every one of his caves there is not, must not be, another deeper cave—a more comprehensive, stranger, richer world beyond the surface, an abysmally deep ground behind every ground, under every attempt to furnish "grounds." [38] Every philosophy is a foreground philosophy—that is a hermit's judgment: "There is something arbitrary in his stopping *here* to look back and look around, in his not digging deeper *here* but laying his spade aside; there is also something suspicious about it." Every philosophy also *conceals* a philosophy; every opinion is also a hideout, every word also a mask.

290

Every profound thinker is more afraid of being understood than of being misunderstood. The latter may hurt his vanity, but the former his heart, his sympathy, which always says: "Alas, why do *you* want to have as hard a time as I did?"

---

[37] *Um zu verbergen, was man bei sich birgt.* See sections 30 and 40 above.
[38] *Ein Abgrund hinter jedem Grunde, unter jeder "Begründung."*

291

Man, a manifold, mendacious, artificial, and opaque animal, uncanny to the other animals less because of his strength than because of his cunning and shrewdness, has invented the good conscience to enjoy his soul for once as *simple;* and the whole of morality is a long undismayed forgery which alone makes it at all possible to enjoy the sight of the soul. From this point of view much more may belong in the concept of "art" than is generally believed.

292

A philosopher—is a human being who constantly experiences, sees, hears, suspects, hopes, and dreams extraordinary things; who is struck by his own thoughts as from outside, as from above and below, as by *his* type of experiences and lightning bolts; who is perhaps himself a storm pregnant with new lightnings; a fatal human being around whom there are constant rumblings and growlings, crevices, and uncanny doings. A philosopher—alas, a being that often runs away from itself, often is afraid of itself—but too inquisitive not to "come to" again—always back to himself.

293

A man who says, "I like this, I take this for my own and want to protect it and defend it against anybody"; a man who is able to manage something, to carry out a resolution, to remain faithful to a thought, to hold a woman, to punish and prostrate one who presumed too much; a man who has his wrath and his sword and to whom the weak, the suffering, the hard pressed, and the animals, too, like to come[39] and belong by nature, in short a man who is by nature a *master*—when such a man has pity, well, *this* pity has value. But what good is the pity of those who suffer. Or those who, worse, *preach* pity.

---

[39] *Gern zufallen:* literally, they like to fall to him or to his lot.

Almost everywhere in Europe today we find a pathological sensitivity and receptivity to pain; also a repulsive incontinence in lamentation, an increase in tenderness that would use religion and philosophical bric-a-brac to deck itself out as something higher— there is a veritable cult of suffering. The *unmanliness* of what is baptized as "pity" in the circles of such enthusiasts is, I should think, what always meets the eye first.

This newest kind of bad taste should be exorcized vigorously and thoroughly; and I finally wish that one might place around one's heart and neck the good amulet *"gai saber"*—"gay science," to make it plain to the plain.[40]

294

The Olympian vice.— In despite of that philosopher who, being a real Englishman, tried to bring laughter into ill repute among all thinking men—"laughing is a bad infirmity of human nature, which every thinking mind will strive to overcome" (Hobbes)[41]—

---

[40] *Um es den Deutschen zu verdeutlichen.* Cf. section 260, note 9.

[41] Translated into English from Nietzsche's German. Though the words appear in quotation marks, there seem to be only five passages in which Hobbes discusses laughter—never in quite these words. (Two of these are found in the Latin works and add nothing to the quotations that follow.) Hobbes explained laughter by invoking the will to power, albeit without using that term.

The first and longest discussion is found in *Human Nature* (1640), Chapter IX.13: "There is a passion that hath no name; but the sign of it is that distortion of the countenance which we call *laughter,* which is always *joy.* . . . Whatsoever it be that moveth to laughter, it must be *new* and *unexpected.* Men laugh often, especially such as are greedy of applause from every thing they do well, at their *own* actions performed never so little beyond their own expectations; as also at their own *jests:* and in this case it is manifest, that the passion of laughter proceedeth from a *sudden conception* of some *ability* in himself that laugheth. Also men laugh at the *infirmities* of others, by comparison wherewith their own abilities are set off and illustrated. Also men laugh at *jests,* the *wit* whereof always consisteth in the elegant *discovering* and conveying to our minds some *absurdity* of *another:* and in this case also the passion of laughter proceedeth from the *sudden* imagination of our own odds and eminency. . . . For when a jest is broken upon ourselves, or friends of whose dishonour we participate, we never laugh thereat. I may therefore conclude, that the passion of laughter is nothing else but *sudden glory* arising from some sudden *conception* of some *eminency* in ourselves, by comparison with the *infirmity* of others, or

I should actually risk an order of rank among philosophers depending on the rank of their laughter—all the way up to those capable of *golden* laughter. And supposing that gods, too, philosophize, which has been suggested to me by many an inference—I

---

with our own formerly: for men laugh at the follies of themselves past . . . Besides, it is vain glory, and an argument of little worth, to think the infirmity of another, sufficient matter for his triumph."

The parallel passage in the *Leviathan* (1651), Part I, Chapter 6, p. 27, which is much shorter, ends: "And it is incident most to them, that are conscious of the fewest abilities in themselves; who are forced to keep themselves in their own favour, by observing the imperfections of other men. And therefore much Laughter at the defects of others is a signe of Pusillanimity. For of great minds, one of the proper workes is, to help and free others from scorn; and compare themselves onely with the most able."

Finally, in "The Answer of Mr. Hobbes to Sir William Davenant's Preface before Gondibert" (Paris, Jan. 10, 1650; reprinted in *The English Works of Thomas Hobbes,* vol. IV, 1840) Hobbes says (pp. 454f.): "Great persons, that have their minds employed on great designs, have not leisure enough to laugh, and are pleased with the contemplation of their own power and virtues, so as they need not the infirmities and vices of other men to recommend themselves to their own favour by comparison, as all men do when they laugh."

Hobbes is evidently thinking quite literally of laughter while for Nietzsche laughter represents an attitude toward the world, toward life, and toward oneself. In *The Gay Science* (1882) he had written: "Laughter means: to rejoice at another's expense [*schadenfroh sein*], but with a good conscience" (section 200). And still earlier, in *Human, All-Too-Human* (1878): "Descending below the animals.— When man neighs with laughter, he surpasses all animals by his vulgarity" (section 553). But in the second volume of the same work (1879) we find an aphorism (section 173): "*Laughing and smiling.*— The more joyous and certain his spirit becomes, the more man unlearns loud laughter; instead a more spiritual smile constantly wells up in him. . . ." And in a note of that period (*Musarion* edition, IX, 413): "Everything *sudden* pleases if it does no *harm;* hence wit. . . . For a tension is thus released. . . ." And another note (same page): "Caricature is the beginning of art. That something *signifies,* delights. That whatever signifies, should mock and be laughed at, delights still more. Laughing at something is the first sign of a higher psychic life (as in the fine arts)."

In spite of the title *The Gay Science,* Nietzsche's celebration of laughter is encountered first and foremost in *Zarathustra.* To cite all the relevant passages (*Portable Nietzsche* pp. 248, 272, 294, 310, 341, 342, 427) would be pointless, but the three most significant should be mentioned.

"Not by wrath does one kill but by laughter. Come, let us kill the spirit of gravity!" ("On Reading and Writing," p. 153).

"As yet he has not learned laughter or beauty. Gloomy this hunter returned from the woods of knowledge. . . . But I do not like these tense souls. . . . As yet his knowledge has not learned to smile. . . . Gracefulness

should not doubt that they also know how to laugh the while in a superhuman and new way—and at the expense of all serious things. Gods enjoy mockery: it seems they cannot suppress laughter even during holy rites.

295

The genius of the heart, as that great concealed one possesses it, the tempter god[42] and born pied piper of consciences whose voice knows how to descend into the netherworld of every soul; who does not say a word or cast a glance in which there is no consideration and ulterior enticement; whose mastery includes the knowledge of how to seem—not what he is but what is to those who follow him one *more* constraint to press ever closer to him in order to follow him ever more inwardly and thoroughly—the genius of the heart who silences all that is loud and self-satisfied, teaching it to listen; who smooths rough souls and lets them taste a new desire—to lie still as a mirror, that the deep sky may mirror itself in them—the genius of the heart who teaches the doltish and rash hand to hesitate and reach out more delicately; who guesses the concealed and forgotten treasure, the drop of graciousness and sweet spirituality under dim and thick ice, and is a divining rod for every grain of gold that has long lain buried in the dungeon of much mud and sand; the genius of the heart from whose touch everyone walks away richer, not having received grace and sur-

---

is part of the graciousness of the great-souled. . . . Verily, I have often laughed at the weaklings who thought themselves good because they had no claws" ("On Those Who Are Sublime," pp. 228-31, one of the most important chapters in Nietzsche's writings).

"What has so far been the greatest sin here on earth? Was it not the word of him who said, 'Woe unto those who laugh here'? . . . He did not love enough: else he would also have loved us who laugh. But he hated and mocked us: howling and gnashing of teeth he promised us. . . . Laughter I have pronounced holy; you higher men, *learn* to laugh!" ("On the Higher Man," sections 16 and 20, pp. 405-408).

For Nietzsche laughter becomes less a physical phenomenon than a symbol of joyous affirmation of life and of the refusal to bow before the spirit of gravity.

[42] Cf. section 42, note: *Versucher-Gott* could also mean "god of experimenters."

prised, not as blessed and oppressed by alien goods, but richer in himself, newer to himself than before, broken open, blown at and sounded out by a thawing wind, perhaps more unsure, tenderer, more fragile, more broken, but full of hopes that as yet have no name, full of new will and currents, full of new dissatisfaction and undertows——but what am I doing, my friends? [43]

Of whom am I speaking to you? Have I forgotten myself so far that I have not even told you his name? Unless you have guessed by yourselves who this questionable spirit and god is who wants to be *praised* in such fashion. For just as happens to everyone who from childhood has always been on his way and in foreign parts, many strange and not undangerous spirits have crossed my path, too, but above all he of whom I was speaking just now, and he again and again—namely, no less a one than the god *Dionysus,* that great ambiguous one and tempter god to whom I once offered, as you know, in all secrecy and reverence, my first-

---

[43] Some of the features of this portrait bring to mind Socrates. In this connection section 212 might be reread; also the beginning of section 340 of *The Gay Science:* "The dying Socrates.— I admire the courage and wisdom of Socrates in everything he did, said—and did not say. This mocking and enamored monster and pied piper of Athens, who made the most arrogant youths tremble and sob, was not only the wisest talker who ever lived: he was just as great in his silence. . . ."

The image of the pied piper recurs in the first sentence of the present section—and the Preface to *Twilight of the Idols* where Nietzsche calls himself "an old psychologist and pied piper" (*Portable Nietzsche,* p. 466). With the praise of Socrates' greatness "in his silence" compare Nietzsche's comment on *Beyond Good and Evil* in *Ecce Homo,* where he praises the book for "the subtlety of its form, of its intent, of its art of *silence,*" all of which he contrasts with *Zarathustra.*

Finally, the section on the genius of the heart should be compared with the words of the Platonic Socrates, on the last page of the *Theaetetus:* "Supposing you should ever henceforth try to conceive afresh, Theaetetus, if you succeed your embryo thoughts will be the better as a consequence of today's scrutiny; and if you remain barren, you will be gentler . . . having the good sense not to fancy you know what you do not know. For that, and no more, is all that my art can effect; nor have I any of that knowledge possessed by all the great and admirable men of our own day or of the past. But this midwife's art is a gift from heaven; my mother had it for women, and I for young men of a generous spirit and for all in whom beauty dwells" (F. M. Cornford translation).

born—as the last, it seems to me, who offered him a *sacrifice:* for I have found no one who understood what I was doing then.[44]

Meanwhile I have learned much, all too much, more about the philosophy of this god, and, as I said, from mouth to mouth— I, the last disciple and initiate of the god Dionysus—and I suppose I might begin at long last to offer you, my friends, a few tastes of this philosophy, insofar as this is permitted to me? In an undertone, as is fair, for it concerns much that is secret, new, strange, odd, uncanny.

Even that Dionysus is a philosopher, and that gods, too, thus do philosophy, seems to me to be a novelty that is far from innocuous and might arouse suspicion precisely among philosophers. Among you, my friends, it will not seem so offensive, unless it comes too late and not at the right moment; for today, as I have been told, you no longer like to believe in God and gods. Perhaps I shall also have to carry frankness further in my tale than will always be pleasing to the strict habits of your ears? Certainly the god in question went further, very much further, in dialogues of this sort and was always many steps ahead of me.

Indeed, if it were permitted to follow human custom in according to him many solemn pomp-and-virtue names, I should have to give abundant praise to his explorer and discoverer courage, his daring honesty, truthfulness, and love of wisdom. But such a god has no use whatever for all such venerable junk and pomp. "Keep that," he would say, "for yourself and your likes and

---

[44] Although "first-born" is plural in the original (*Erstlinge*), the primary reference is certainly to *The Birth of Tragedy.* From the Preface added to the new edition of 1886 (the same year that saw the publication of *Beyond Good and Evil*) it is plain that by now Nietzsche felt that he himself had not fully understood in 1872 what he was doing.

More important: the Dionysus of his later works is no longer the Dionysus of *The Birth of Tragedy.* In the early work, Dionysus stands for uncontrolled, frenzied, intoxicated passion and is contrasted with Apollo; in the later works, Dionysus stands for controlled and creatively employed passion—the mature Goethe is now called Dionysian (*Twilight,* section 49, *Portable Nietzsche,* pp. 553f.)—and is contrasted with "the Crucified" (end of *Ecce Homo*) and the extirpation of the passions and the denial of this world.

whoever else has need of it! I—have no reason for covering my nakedness."

One guesses: this type of deity and philosopher is perhaps lacking in shame?

Thus he once said: "Under certain circumstances I love what is human"—and with this he alluded to Ariadne who was present[45] —"man is to my mind an agreeable, courageous, inventive animal that has no equal on earth; it finds its way in any labyrinth. I am well disposed towards him: I often reflect how I might yet advance him and make him stronger, more evil, and more profound than he is."

"Stronger, more evil, and more profound?" I asked startled. "Yes," he said once more; "stronger, more evil, and more profound; also more beautiful"—and at that the tempter god smiled with his halcyon smile as though he had just paid an enchanting compliment. Here we also see: what this divinity lacks is not only a sense of shame—and there are also other good reasons for conjecturing that in several respects all of the gods could learn from us humans. We humans are—more humane.[46]—

296

Alas, what are you after all, my written and painted thoughts! It was not long ago that you were still so colorful, young, and malicious, full of thorns and secret spices—you made me sneeze and laugh—and now? You have already taken off your novelty, and some of you are ready, I fear, to become truths: they already look so immortal, so pathetically decent, so dull! And has it ever been different? What things do we copy, writing and painting, we mandarins with Chinese brushes, we immortalizers of things that *can* be written—what are the only things we are able to paint? Alas, always only what is on the verge of withering and losing its fragrance! Alas, always only storms that are passing, ex-

---

[45] There is a large literature, much of it inordinately pretentious and silly, about Nietzsche's conception of Ariadne. For a very brief explanation, see Kaufmann's *Nietzsche,* Chapter 1, section II.

[46] *"Wir Menschen sind—menschlicher. . . ."*

hausted, and feelings that are autumnal and yellow! Alas, always only birds that grew weary of flying and flew astray and now can be caught by hand—by *our* hand! We immortalize what cannot live and fly much longer—only weary and mellow things! And it is only your *afternoon,* you, my written and painted thoughts, for which alone I have colors, many colors perhaps, many motley caresses and fifty yellows and browns and greens and reds: but nobody will guess from that how you looked in your morning, you sudden sparks and wonders of my solitude, you my old beloved—*wicked* thoughts!

From High Mountains

AFTERSONG

TRANSLATOR'S NOTE

"Aus hohen Bergen. Nachgesang." In the original edition this title occupies a right-hand page by itself, facing section 296, and the poem begins on the next right-hand page. The asterisks at the beginning and end of the poem are found in the original edition.

My translation, though relatively faithful, is not entirely literal; and this is one reason for furnishing the original text, too—in fairness to both author and reader. There is another reason: fairness to the translator; for the poem is not one of Nietzsche's best. (The five dots occurring four times in the German text do not mark an omission but are among Nietzsche's characteristic punctuation devices: sometimes they are used to indicate that a thought breaks off or that something remains unsaid; here they plainly suggest a long pause.)

More of Nietzsche's verse, also with the original and translation on facing pages, is included in *Twenty German Poets: A Bilingual Collection*.[1] One of those poems, "To the Mistral: A Dancing Song," has a somewhat similar rhyme scheme but strikes me as a much better poem than "From High Mountains."

I confess that I do not admire the present poem—except for one magnificent line which defies translation:

Nur wer sich wandelt, bleibt mit mir verwandt.

My version does not capture the play on words but tries to communicate the meaning: "One has to change to stay akin to me." Or: "Only those who change remain related to me." This rendering is far from perfect but it at least rectifies the misreading of the line in L. A. Magnus' translation of the poem appended to Helen Zimmern's version of *Beyond Good and Evil:* "None but new kith are native of my land!"

---

[1] Edited, translated, and introduced by Walter Kaufmann (New York, Modern Library, 1963).

Nietzsche had sent an earlier version[2] of this poem to Heinrich von Stein, with the comment: "This is for you, my dear friend, to remember Sils Maria and in gratitude for your letter, *such* a letter." [3] In his reply the "dear friend" gave expression to his Wagner worship and asked Nietzsche to participate by letter in his weekly discussions with two friends about articles in the *Wagner-Lexicon*.[4] The poem seems sentimental to me, but Nietzsche did know loneliness as few men have ever known it.

W.K.

---

[2] In that version the order of the second and third stanzas was reversed, as was that of the seventh and eighth, and the tenth and eleventh. Moreover, the wording was slightly different in several places, and the last two stanzas were missing entirely.

[3] *Friedrich Nietzsches Gesammelte Briefe* (Friedrich Nietzsche's collected letters) vol. III (2nd ed., Leipzig, 1905), pp. 243-45, end of November 1884, from Nizza. Heinrich von Stein's letter is printed in *ibid.*, pp. 240-42.

[4] *Ibid.*, pp. 245ff.

Aus hohen Bergen.

NACHGESANG.

*   *   *

*   *   *   *

Oh Lebens Mittag! Feierliche Zeit!
      Oh Sommergarten!
Unruhig Glück im Stehn und Spähn und Warten:—
Der Freunde harr' ich, Tag und Nacht bereit,
Wo bleibt ihr Freunde? Kommt! 's ist Zeit! 's ist Zeit!

War's nicht für euch, dass sich des Gletschers Grau
      Heut schmückt mit Rosen?
Euch sucht der Bach, sehnsüchtig drängen, stossen
Sich Wind und Wolke höher heut in's Blau,
Nach euch zu spähn aus fernster Vogel-Schau.

Im Höchsten ward für euch mein Tisch gedeckt:—
      Wer wohnt den Sternen
So nahe, wer des Abgrunds grausten Fernen?
Mein Reich—welch Reich hat weiter sich gereckt?
Und meinen Honig—wer hat ihn geschmeckt? . . . . .

—Da *seid* ihr, Freunde!—Weh, doch *ich* bin's nicht,
      Zu dem ihr wolltet?
Ihr zögert, staunt—ach, dass ihr lieber grolltet!
Ich—bin's nicht mehr? Vertauscht Hand, Schritt, Gesicht?
Und was ich bin, euch Freunden—bin ich's nicht?

Ein Andrer ward ich? Und mir selber fremd?
      Mir selbst entsprungen?
Ein Ringer, der zu oft sich selbst bezwungen?
Zu oft sich gegen eigne Kraft gestemmt,
Durch eignen Sieg verwundet und gehemmt?

From High Mountains

———

AFTERSONG

* * *

* * * * * *

O noon of life! O time to celebrate!
        O summer garden!
Restlessly happy and expectant, standing,
Watching all day and night, for friends I wait:
Where are you, friends? Come! It is time! It's late!

The glacier's gray adorned itself for you
        Today with roses;
The brook seeks you, and full of longing rises
The wind, the cloud, into the vaulting blue
To look for you from dizzy bird's-eye view.

Higher than mine no table has been set:
        Who lives so near
The stars or dread abysses half as sheer?
My realm, like none, is almost infinite,
And my sweet honey—who has tasted it?——

—There you are, friends!—Alas, the man you sought
        You do not find here?
You hesitate, amazed? Anger were kinder!
I—changed so much? A different face and gait?
And what I am—for you, friends, I am not?

Am I another? Self-estranged? From me—
        Did I elude?
A wrestler who too oft himself subdued?
Straining against his strength too frequently,
Wounded and stopped by his own victory?

Ich suchte, wo der Wind am schärfsten weht?
　　　Ich lernte wohnen,
Wo Niemand wohnt, in öden Eisbär-Zonen,
Verlernte Mensch und Gott, Fluch und Gebet?
Ward zum Gespenst, das über Gletscher geht?

—Ihr alten Freunde! Seht! Nun blickt ihr bleich,
　　　Voll Lieb' und Grausen!
Nein, geht! Zürnt nicht! Hier—könntet *ihr* nicht hausen:
Hier zwischen fernstem Eis- und Felsenreich—
Hier muss man Jäger sein und gemsengleich.

Ein *schlimmer* Jäger ward ich!—Seht, wie steil
　　　Gespannt mein Bogen!
Der Stärkste war's, der solchen Zug gezogen— —:
Doch wehe nun! Gefährlich ist *der* Pfeil,
Wie *kein* Pfeil,—fort von hier! Zu eurem Heil! . . . . .

Ihr wendet euch?—Oh Herz, du trugst genung,
　　　Stark blieb dein Hoffen:
Halt *neuen* Freunden deine Thüren offen!
Die alten lass! Lass die Erinnerung!
Warst einst du jung, jetzt—bist du besser jung!

Was je uns knüpfte, Einer Hoffnung Band,—
　　　Wer liest die Zeichen,
Die Liebe einst hineinschrieb, noch, die bleichen?
Dem Pergament vergleich ich's, das die Hand
Zu fassen *scheut,*—ihm gleich verbräunt, verbrannt.

Nicht Freunde mehr, das sind—wie nenn' ich's doch?—
　　　Nur Freunds-Gespenster!
Das klopft mir wohl noch Nachts an Herz und Fenster,
Das sieht mich an und spricht: „wir *waren's* doch?"—
—Oh welkes Wort, das einst wie Rosen roch!

Oh Jugend-Sehnen, das sich missverstand!
　　　Die *ich* ersehnte,
Die ich mir selbst verwandt-verwandelt wähnte,
Dass *alt* sie wurden, hat sie weggebannt:
Nur wer sich wandelt, bleibt mit mir verwandt.

Oh Lebens Mittag! Zweite Jugendzeit!
　　　Oh Sommergarten!
Unruhig Glück im Stehn und Spähn und Warten!

I sought where cutting winds are at their worst?
> *I learned to dwell*
Where no one lives, in bleakest polar hell,
Unlearned mankind and god, prayer and curse?
Became a ghost that wanders over glaciers?

—My ancient friends! Alas! You show the shock
> *Of love and fear!*
No, leave! Do not be wroth! You—can't live here—
Here, among distant fields of ice and rock—
Here one must be a hunter, chamois-like.

A wicked archer I've become.—The ends
> *Of my bow kiss;*
Only the strongest bends his bow like this.
No arrow strikes like that which my bow sends:
Away from here—for your own good, my friends!——

You leave?—My heart: no heart has borne worse hunger;
> *Your hope stayed strong:*
Don't shut your gates; new friends may come along.
Let old ones go. Don't be a memory-monger!
Once you were young—now you are even younger.

What once tied us together, one hope's bond—
> *Who reads the signs*
Love once inscribed on it, the pallid lines?
To parchment I compare it that the hand
Is loath to touch—discolored, dark, and burnt.

No longer friends—there is no word for those—
> *It is a wraith*
That knocks at night and tries to rouse my faith,
And looks at me and says: "Once friendship was—"
—O wilted word, once fragrant as the rose.

Youth's longing misconceived inconstancy.
> *Those whom I deemed*
Changed to my kin, the friends of whom I dreamed,
Have aged and lost our old affinity:
One has to change to stay akin to me.

O noon of life! Our second youthful state!
> *O summer garden!*
Restlessly happy and expectant, standing,

Der Freunde harr' ich, Tag und Nacht bereit,
Der *neuen* Freunde! Kommt! 's ist Zeit! 's ist Zeit!

* * *

Dies Lied ist aus,—der Sehnsucht süsser Schrei
      Erstarb im Munde:
Ein Zaubrer that's, der Freund zur rechten Stunde,
Der Mittags-Freund—nein! fragt nicht, wer es sei—
Um Mittag war's, da wurde Eins zu Zwei . . . . .

Nun feiern wir, vereinten Siegs gewiss,
      Das Fest der Feste:
Freund *Zarathustra* kam, der Gast der Gäste!
Nun lacht die Welt, der grause Vorhang riss,
Die Hochzeit kam für Licht und Finsterniss . . . . .

*   *   *   *
  *   *
   * *

Looking all day and night, for friends I wait:
For new *friends! Come! It's time! It's late!*

＊　　　＊
＊

This song is over—*longing's dulcet cry*
      Died in my mouth:
A wizard did it, friend in time of drought,
The friend of noon—no, do not ask me who—
At noon it was that one turned into two——

Sure of our victory, we celebrate
      The feast of feasts:
Friend Zarathustra came, the guest of guests!
The world now laughs, rent are the drapes of fright,
The wedding is at hand of dark and light——

＊　　＊　　　　　　＊　　＊
＊　　　　　　　　＊

＊　　＊
＊

On the
GENEALOGY
of MORALS

CONTENTS

EDITOR'S INTRODUCTION *439*

NIETZSCHE'S PREFACE *451*

I. *"Good and Evil," "Good and Bad"* *460*

II. *"Guilt," "Bad Conscience," and the Like* *493*

III. *What is the Meaning of Ascetic Ideals?* *533*

INDEX *823*

Editor's Introduction

1

Of all of Nietzsche's books, the *Genealogy of Morals* comes closest, at least in form, to Anglo-American philosophy: it consists of three inquiries, each self-contained and yet related to the other two. Even those who suppose, erroneously, that *Beyond Good and Evil* is a book for browsing, a collection of aphorisms that may be read in any order whatever, generally recognize that the *Genealogy* comprises three essays. Moreover, all three essays deal with morality, a subject close to the heart of British and American philosophy; and Nietzsche's manner is much more sober and single-minded than usual.

Yet it should be noted that the title page is followed by these words: "A Sequel to My Last Book, *Beyond Good and Evil,* Which It Is Meant to Supplement and Clarify." [1] In other words, Nietzsche did not suppose that the *Genealogy* could be readily understood by itself, and in the final section of the preface he explained emphatically at some length that he presupposed not only a passing acquaintance with his earlier books but actually a rather close study of them.

Moreover, Nietzsche refers the reader, especially (but not only) in the preface, to a large number of specific passages in his earlier works. It is easy to resent all this as tedious and self-important—and to misunderstand the book and Nietzsche's philosophy generally. It is fashionable to read hastily, as if, for example, one knew all about Nietzsche's contrast of master and slave morality before one had even begun to read him. But if one reads snippets here and there, projecting ill-founded preconceptions into the gaps, one is apt to misconstrue Nietzsche's moral philosophy completely—as Loeb and Leopold did when, as youngsters, they supposed that a brutal and senseless murder would prove them masters. Similar misunderstandings mar many academic interpretations;

---

[1] *Dem letztveröffentlichten* "Jenseits von Gut und Böse" *zur Ergänzung und Verdeutlichung beigegeben.*

but professors naturally react differently: they feel outraged by Nietzsche and do violence, on a different level, to *him*.

To understand Nietzsche's conceptions of master and slave morality, one should read *Beyond Good and Evil,* section 260, and *Human, All-Too-Human,* section 45—and keep in mind the title of our book, which deals with the *origins* of morality. Nietzsche distinguishes moralities that originated in ruling classes from moralities that originated among the oppressed.

Unfortunately, some of the aphoristic material in his earlier works to which Nietzsche refers us is not easy to come by, and the larger part of it has never been translated adequately. Most of these aphorisms have therefore been included in the present volume, in new translations. And some commentary, in the form of footnotes, may not be supererogatory.

The extent of such a commentary poses insoluble problems: if there is too little of it, students may feel that they get no help where they need it; if there is too much, it becomes an affront to the reader's knowledge and intelligence and a monument of pedantry. No mean can possibly be right for all.

At the end of his Preface Nietzsche says that it won't do simply to read an aphorism, one must also decipher it; and he claims that his whole third inquiry is a paradigm case of a commentary on a single aphorism. Taking my cue from this suggestion, I have selected one exceptionally interesting section in the third essay and given it a much more detailed commentary than the rest of the book: section 24, which deals with the intellectual conscience and with truth. But this is not to suggest that this section is self-contained; on the contrary, the argument is continued in the following section—and so is the commentary.

2

The title of our book is ambiguous, but it is clear which meaning Nietzsche intended. *Zur Genealogie der Moral* could mean "Toward a (literally, "Toward the") Genealogy of Morals" (or Morality); it could also mean—and does mean—"On the Genealogy of Morals." How can one tell?

There is one, and only one, sure way. In many of Nietzsche's books, the aphorisms or sections have brief titles; and several of these (about two dozen) begin with the word *Zur*. So do a great many of his notes, including more than two dozen of those included in the posthumous collection, *The Will to Power*. In the case of the notes, to be sure, the titles were sometimes added by Peter Gast, Nietzsche's worshipful friend and editor; but even titles contributed by Gast have some evidential value, as he had presumably acquired some feeling for Nietzsche's usage.

The upshot: In no title does Nietzsche's *Zur* or *Zum* clearly mean "Toward," and he used *Zur* again and again in contexts in which "Toward" makes no sense at all, and "On" is the only possible meaning; for example, the heading of section 381, in the fifth book of *The Gay Science*—published in 1887 as was the *Genealogy of Morals*—reads: *Zur Frage der Verständlichkeit,* "On the Question of Being Understandable." To be sure, if that same phrase were found in Heidegger, one would not hesitate to translate it, "toward the question of understandability": Heidegger is always on the way toward the point from which it may be possible some day to ask a question. But not Nietzsche. It is not enough to know the language; one must also acquire some feeling for an author. Toward the latter end, an excellent prescription would be to read Nietzsche "On the Question of Being Understandable"; and this aphorism is included in the present volume.

3

Speaking of intelligibility: why does Nietzsche use the French word *ressentiment?* First of all, the German language lacks any close equivalent to the French term. That alone would be sufficient excuse for Nietzsche, though perhaps not for a translator, who could use "resentment."

Secondly, Nietzsche's emergence from the influence of Wagner, who extolled everything Germanic and excoriated the French, was marked by an attitude more Francophile than that of any other major German writer—at least since Leibniz (1646–1716), who preferred to write in French. Nietzsche saw himself as the heir of the French *moralistes* and as a "good European."

In 1805 Hegel wrote to Johann Heinrich Voss, who had translated Homer into German dactylic hexameters: "I should like to say of my aspirations that I shall try to teach philosophy to speak German." [2] Avoiding Greek, Latin, and French terms, Hegel created an involved German terminology, devising elaborate locutions that make his prose utterly forbidding. And a little over a century later, Heidegger tried to do much the same thing. Yet Hegel was assuredly wrong when he went on to say, in the next sentence of his letter: "Once that is accomplished, it will be infinitely more difficult to give shallowness the appearance of profound speech." On the contrary. Nothing serves as well as obscurity to make shallowness look profound.

Modern readers who do not know foreign languages may wonder whether Nietzsche's abundant use of French phrases, and occasionally also of Latin, Greek, and Italian (sometimes he uses English words, too) does not make for obscurity. If it does, this is obscurity of an altogether different kind and easily removed—by a brief footnote, for example. Nietzsche likes brevity as much as he likes being a good European; and he hates nationalism as much as he hates saying approximately, at great length, what can be said precisely, in one word.

One is tempted to add that the kind of obscurantism he abominated involves irremediable ambiguities which lead to endless discussion, while his terms, whether German or foreign, are unequivocal. That is true up to a point—but not quite. Nietzsche had an almost pathological weakness for one particular kind of ambiguity, which, to be sure, is not irremediable: he loved words and phrases that mean one thing out of context and almost the opposite in the context he gives them. He loved language as poets do and relished these "revaluations." All of them involve a double meaning, one exoteric and one esoteric, one—to put it crudely—wrong, and the other right. The former is bound to lead astray hasty readers, browsers, and that rapidly growing curse of our time—the non-readers who do not realize that galloping consumption is a disease. The body of knowledge keeps increasing at incredible speed,

---

[2] The letter is lost, but three drafts have survived. The quotation is from the final draft, May 1805. See Kaufmann's *Hegel* (Garden City, N.Y., Anchor Books, 1966), Chapter VII, p. 316.

but the literature of nonknowledge grows even faster. Books multiply like mushrooms, or rather like toadstools—mildew would be still more precise—and even those who read books come perforce to depend more and more on knowledge *about* books, writers, and, if at all possible—for this is the intellectual, or rather the nonintellectual, equivalent of a bargain—*movements*. As long as one knows about existentialism, one can talk about a large number of authors without having actually read their books.

Nietzsche diagnosed this disease in its early stages, long before it had reached its present proportions—yet wrote in a manner that insured his being misunderstood by the kind of reader and nonreader he despised. Why? He gave reasons more than once; for example, in *Beyond Good and Evil,* sections 30, 40, 230, 270, 278, 289, and 290, and in the aforementioned section 381 of *The Gay Science.* And I have attempted a different sort of explanation in an essay on "Philosophy versus Poetry." [3]

The *Genealogy* contains several examples of misleading slogans, but *ressentiment* is actually not one of them. That term is univocal, but—to ask this once more—why couldn't we substitute "resentment" for it in an English translation? Apart from the fact that something of the flavor of Nietzsche's style and thought would be lost, this is a point at which Nietzsche succeeded in teaching psychology to speak—Nietzschean. His conception of *ressentiment* constitutes one of his major contributions to psychology—and helps to illuminate the widespread misunderstanding of Nietzsche.

To begin with the first point: At the beginning of his own lengthy essay on "[The role of] *Ressentiment* in the Construction of Moralities," [4] Max Scheler says: "Among the exceedingly few discoveries made in recent times concerning the origin of moral value judgments, Friedrich Nietzsche's discovery of *ressentiment* as the source of such value judgments is the most profound, even if his more specific claim that Christian morality and in particular Chris-

---

[3] Chapter 14 of *From Shakespeare to Existentialism* (Boston, Mass., Beacon Press, 1959; rev. ed., Garden City, N.Y., Doubleday Anchor Books, 1960).

[4] "Das Ressentiment im Aufbau der Moralen" in *Vom Umsturz der Werte* (collapse of values), Leipzig, Der Neue Geist Verlag, 1915; 2nd ed., 1919, vol. I, pp. 43–236.

tian love are the finest 'flower of resssentiment' should turn out to be false." [5]

Scheler, one of the outstanding German philosophers of the first quarter of the twentieth century, converted to Roman Catholicism and persuaded some of his disciples to follow his example—but later abandoned Christianity as well as all theism. In the essay on *ressentiment* he argued: "We believe that Christian values are particularly prone to being reinterpreted into values of *ressentiment* and have also been understood that way particularly often, but that the *core of Christian ethics did not grow on the soil of ressentiment*. Yet we also believe that the *core of bourgeois morality,* which since the thirteenth century has begun more and more to supersede Christian morality until it attained its supreme achievement in the French Revolution, does have its roots in *ressentiment.*" Even where he disagreed with Nietzsche, Scheler emphasized that he considered Nietzsche's account singularly profound and worthy of the most serious consideration.[6]

Readers ready to jump to the conclusion that Nietzsche confounded true Christianity with its bourgeois misinterpretation while Scheler obviously understood Christianity far better should ponder Scheler's footnote: "The possible unity of style of warlike and Christian morality is demonstrated in detail in my book *Der Genius des Krieges und der deutsche Krieg* (The genius of war and the German war), 1915." [7] To be sure, most Christians in England, France, and the United States felt the same way in 1915, but the question remains whether Scheler's reading of Christianity was not designed to be heard gladly in the twentieth century, around 1915, when the essay on *ressentiment,* too, appeared. In any case, this essay does not compare in originality and importance with Nietzsche's *Genealogy,* but it deserves mention as an attempt to develop Nietzsche's ideas, and it shows how the term *ressentiment* has become established.

Nietzsche's conception of *ressentiment* also throws light on

---

[5] *Ibid.,* p. 49. Both here and on p. 106 Scheler claims erroneously that Nietzsche used the phrase in single quotes in *Genealogy,* essay I, section 8.

[6] *Ibid.,* pp. 106f.

[7] *Ibid.,* p. 143.

the reception of his ideas. By way of contrast, consider Max Weber, perhaps the greatest sociologist of the century, and certainly *one* of the greatest. Weber's sociology of religion owes a great deal to Nietzsche's *Genealogy*. But why is it generally recognized that Weber was by no means an anti-Semite, although he found the clue to the Jewish religion in the alleged fact that the Jews were a pariah people, while Nietzsche's comments on slave morality and the slave rebellion in morals have so often been considered highly offensive and tinged by anti-Semitism? (Nietzsche's many references to anti-Semitism are invariably scathing: see the indices in this volume.) Could it be that a scholar is given the benefit of every doubt so long as he does not have the presumption to write well?

To write about Nietzsche "scholars" with the lack of inhibition with which *they* have written about Nietzsche, mixing moralistic denunciations with attempts at psychiatric explanations, would be utterly unthinkable. Why? The answer is clearly not that Nietzsche really was an inferior scholar and did eventually become insane. Most Nietzsche "scholars" cannot hold a candle to his learning or originality, and the closer they are to meriting psychological explanations, the worse it would be to offer any.

Could the reason for the disparity in treatment be that Nietzsche is dead? We are in no danger of hurting his feelings or his career; and he cannot hit back. He is no longer a member of the family; he has left us and is fair game. But Max Weber is dead, too; yet he is still treated as a member of the guild. Clearly, there must be another reason. Nietzsche wrote too well and was too superior. That removed him from the immunity of our community, quite as much as the commission of a crime. But where the transgression has been spiritual or intellectual, and those offended are the intellectual community, the revenge, too, is intellectual. The pent-up resentment against fellow members of the community—sloppy scholars and writers as well as those who excite envy—all this rancor that cannot be vented against living colleagues, at least not in print, may be poured out against a few great scapegoats.

There are many reasons for Nietzsche's being one of the great scapegoats of all time. During World War I British intellectuals found it convenient to contribute to the war effort by denouncing a German intellectual of stature whom one could discuss in print without losing a lot of time reading him—and Nietzsche had said many nasty things about the British.[8] Henceforth Nietzsche was a marked man, and World War II contributed its share to this type of disgraceful literature. But there are even more such studies in German—which is scarcely surprising. After all, Nietzsche said far more wicked things—incomparably more and worse—about the Germans than he ever did about the British. And as the literature shows us beyond a doubt: Christian scholars also needed outlets for their rancor. For all that, it would be wrong to think in terms of any strict tit-for-tat, as if each group the dead man had offended then felt justified in hitting back once he was dead. Once it was established that this writer was a scapegoat, *anybody* was allowed to play and vent his own *ressentiment* on him, no matter what its source.

Apart from these considerations, Nietzsche's reception cannot be understood. To be sure, reactions of *that* sort do not exhaust this story. There is also Nietzsche's influence on Rilke and German poetry, on Thomas Mann and the German novel, on Karl Jaspers and German philosophy, on Gide and Malraux, Sartre and Camus, Freud and Buber, Shaw and Yeats. But to understand that, one only has to read them—and him.

4

One final word about the contents and spirit of the *Genealogy*. All three inquiries deal with the origins of moral phenomena, as the title of the book indicates. The first essay, which contrasts "Good and Evil" with "Good and Bad," juxtaposes master and slave morality; the second essay considers "guilt," the "bad conscience," and related matters; and the third, ascetic ideals. The most common misunderstanding of the book is surely to suppose that Nietzsche considers slave morality, the bad conscience, and ascetic ideals evil; that he suggests that mankind would be better off if only

---

[8] To give at least one example, consider Ernest Barker's Oxford pamphlet on *Nietzsche and Treitschke* (London, Oxford University Press, 1914).

these things had never appeared; and that in effect he glorifies un-
conscionable brutes.

Any such view is wrong in detail and can be refuted both by
considering in context the truncated quotations that have been adduced to buttress it and by citing a large number of other passages.
I have tried to do this in my book on *Nietzsche,*[9] and this is not the
place to repeat the demonstration. But this sort of misinterpretation involves not only hundreds of particular misreadings, it also
involves a misreading of the *Genealogy* and, even more generally,
of Nietzsche's attitude toward history and the world. In conclusion,
something needs to be said about that.

The *Genealogy* is intended as a supplement and clarification
of *Beyond Good and Evil*. And while that title suggests an attempt
to rise above the slave morality that contrasts good and evil, it also
signifies a very broad attack on *"the faith in opposite values."* [10]
Decidedly, it is not Nietzsche's concern in the *Genealogy* to tell us
that master morality is good, while slave morality is evil; or to
persuade us that the bad conscience and ascetic ideals are bad,
while a brutish state antedating both phenomena is good. Of
course, it is his plan to open new perspectives and to make us see
what he discusses in unwonted, different ways. If you are bent on
using terms like good and bad, you might say that he tries to show
us, among other things, how moral valuations, phenomena, and
ideals that are usually not questioned have their bad or dark side.
Ordinarily, we see the foreground only; Nietzsche seeks to show us
the background.

In a nutshell: when Nietzsche has shown us the dark side of
the bad conscience, he says, "The bad conscience is an illness,
there is no doubt about that, but an illness as pregnancy is an illness" (II, section 19). His love of fate, his *amor fati,* should not
be forgotten. The second chapter of *Ecce Homo* ends: "My formula for greatness in a human being is *amor fati:* that one wants

---

[9] Princeton University Press, 1950; rev. ed., Meridian Books, 1956; 3rd rev.
ed., Princeton University Press and Vintage Books, 1968.

[10] Section 2, on p. 199ff. For a list of other sections that illuminate the title
of the book, see section 4 of my Preface, p. 187 above.

nothing to be different, not forward, not backward, not in all eternity. Not merely to bear what is necessary, still less conceal it—all idealism is mendaciousness in the face of what is necessary—but *love* it."

In the imagery of the first chapter of *Zarathustra,* it is not Nietzsche's intention to malign or to glorify either the camel or the lion—either the ascetic "spirit that would bear much, and kneels down like a camel" or the blond beast. Indeed, Zarathustra is eloquent in his praise of the camel, and it is plain that much of his description fits Nietzsche himself, who was certainly no stranger to ascetic ideals. But the point is that both camel and lion represent mere stages in the development of the spirit; and insofar as Nietzsche feels dissatisfied with both, it is because he would not have us settle for either: he wants us to climb higher—which, however, cannot be done without passing through these stages. And what lies beyond? What is the goal? Here we return to the image of pregnancy: the third stage is represented by the child. "The child is innocence and forgetting, a new beginning, a game, a self-propelled wheel, a first movement, a sacred 'Yes.' For the game of creation, my brothers, a sacred 'Yes' is needed."

Without acquiring a bad conscience, without learning to be profoundly dissatisfied with ourselves, we cannot envisage higher norms, a new state of being, self-perfection. Without ascetic ideals, without self-control and cruel self-discipline, we cannot attain that self-mastery which Nietzsche ever praises and admires. But to settle down with a nagging bad conscience, to remain an ascetic and mortify oneself, is to fall short of Nietzsche's "Dionysian" vision. What he celebrates is neither the camel nor the lion but the creator.

"*Goethe* . . . fought the mutual extraneousness of reason, senses, feeling, and will . . . he disciplined himself into wholeness, he *created* himself. . . . Such a spirit who has *become free* stands amid the cosmos with a joyous and trusting fatalism, in the *faith* . . . that all is redeemed and affirmed in the whole—*he does not negate any more.* Such a faith, however, is the highest of all possible faiths: I have baptized it with the name of *Dionysus.*" [11]

---

11 *Twilight of the Idols,* section 49 (*The Portable Nietzsche,* translated, with an introduction, prefaces, and notes, by Walter Kaufmann, New York, The Viking Press, 1954; paperback edition, 1958, pp. 553f.).

ON THE
GENEALOGY OF MORALS

A Polemic[1]

---

[1] *Eine Streitschrift.*

Preface

1

We are unknown to ourselves, we men of knowledge—and with good reason. We have never sought ourselves—how could it happen that we should ever *find* ourselves? It has rightly been said: "Where your treasure is, there will your heart be also";[1] *our* treasure is where the beehives of our knowledge are. We are constantly making for them, being by nature winged creatures and honey-gatherers of the spirit; there is one thing alone we really care about from the heart—"bringing something home." Whatever else there is in life, so-called "experiences"—which of us has sufficient earnestness for them? Or sufficient time? Present experience has, I am afraid, always found us "absent-minded": we cannot give our hearts to it—not even our ears! Rather, as one divinely preoccupied and immersed in himself into whose ear the bell has just boomed with all its strength the twelve beats of noon suddenly starts up and asks himself: "what really was that which just struck?" so we sometimes rub our ears *afterward* and ask, utterly surprised and disconcerted, "what really was that which we have just experienced?" and moreover: "who *are* we really?" and, afterward as aforesaid, count the twelve trembling bell-strokes of our experience, our life, our *being*—and alas! miscount them.—So we are necessarily strangers to ourselves, we do not comprehend ourselves, we *have* to misunderstand ourselves, for us the law "Each is furthest from himself" applies to all eternity—we are not "men of knowledge" with respect to ourselves.

2

My ideas on the *origin* of our moral prejudices—for this is the subject of this polemic—received their first, brief, and provisional

---

[1] Matthew 6:21.

expression in the collection of aphorisms that bears the title *Human, All-Too-Human. A Book for Free Spirits*. This book was begun in Sorrento during a winter when it was given to me to pause as a wanderer pauses and look back across the broad and dangerous country my spirit had traversed up to that time. This was in the winter of 1876–77; the ideas themselves are older. They were already in essentials the same ideas that I take up again in the present treatises—let us hope the long interval has done them good, that they have become riper, clearer, stronger, more perfect! *That* I still cleave to them today, however, that they have become in the meantime more and more firmly attached to one another, indeed entwined and interlaced with one another, strengthens my joyful assurance that they might have arisen in me from the first not as isolated, capricious, or sporadic things but from a common root, from a *fundamental will* of knowledge, pointing imperiously into the depths, speaking more and more precisely, demanding greater and greater precision. For this alone is fitting for a philosopher. We have no right to *isolated* acts of any kind: we may not make isolated errors or hit upon isolated truths. Rather do our ideas, our values, our yeas and nays, our ifs and buts, grow out of us with the necessity with which a tree bears fruit—related and each with an affinity to each, and evidence of *one* will, *one* health, *one* soil, *one* sun.—Whether *you* like them, these fruits of ours?—But what is that to the trees! What is that to *us*, to us philosophers!

3

Because of a scruple peculiar to me that I am loth to admit to—for it is concerned with *morality,* with all that has hitherto been celebrated on earth as morality—a scruple that entered my life so early, so uninvited, so irresistibly, so much in conflict with my environment, age, precedents, and descent that I might almost have the right to call it my *"a priori"*—my curiosity as well as my suspicions were bound to halt quite soon at the question of where our good and evil really *originated*. In fact, the problem of the origin of evil pursued me even as a boy of thirteen: at an age in which you have "half childish trifles, half God in your heart," [2] I

---

[2] Goethe's *Faust,* lines 3781f.

devoted to it my first childish literary trifle, my first philosophical effort—and as for the "solution" of the problem I posed at that time, well, I gave the honor to God, as was only fair, and made him the *father* of evil. Was *that* what my *"a priori"* demanded of me? that new immoral, or at least unmoralistic *"a priori"* and the alas! so anti-Kantian, enigmatic "categorical imperative" which spoke through it and to which I have since listened more and more closely, and not merely listened?

Fortunately I learned early to separate theological prejudice from moral prejudice and ceased to look for the origin of evil *behind* the world. A certain amount of historical and philological schooling, together with an inborn fastidiousness of taste in respect to psychological questions in general, soon transformed my problem into another one: under what conditions did man devise these value judgments good and evil? *and what value do they themselves possess?* Have they hitherto hindered or furthered human prosperity? Are they a sign of distress, of impoverishment, of the degeneration of life? Or is there revealed in them, on the contrary, the plenitude, force, and will of life, its courage, certainty, future?

Thereupon I discovered and ventured divers answers; I distinguished between ages, peoples, degrees of rank among individuals; I departmentalized my problem; out of my answers there grew new questions, inquiries, conjectures, probabilities—until at length I had a country of my own, a soil of my own, an entire discrete, thriving, flourishing world, like a secret garden the existence of which no one suspected.—Oh how *fortunate* we are, we men of knowledge, provided only that we know how to keep silent long enough!

4

The first impulse to publish something of my hypotheses concerning the origin of morality was given me by a clear, tidy, and shrewd—also precocious—little book in which I encountered distinctly for the first time an upside-down and perverse species of genealogical hypothesis, the genuinely *English* type, that attracted me—with that power of attraction which everything contrary, everything antipodal possesses. The title of the little book was *The*

Origin of the Moral Sensations; its author Dr. Paul Rée; the year in which it appeared 1877. Perhaps I have never read anything to which I would have said to myself No, proposition by proposition, conclusion by conclusion, to the extent that I did to this book: yet quite without ill-humor or impatience. In the above-mentioned work, on which I was then engaged, I made opportune and inopportune reference to the propositions of that book, not in order to refute them—what have I to do with refutations!—but, as becomes a positive spirit, to replace the improbable with the more probable, possibly one error with another. It was then, as I have said, that I advanced for the first time those genealogical hypotheses to which this treatise is devoted—ineptly, as I should be the last to deny, still constrained, still lacking my own language for my own things and with much backsliding and vacillation. One should compare in particular what I say in *Human, All-Too-Human,* section 45, on the twofold prehistory of good and evil (namely, in the sphere of the noble and in that of the slaves); likewise, section 136, on the value and origin of the morality of asceticism; likewise, sections 96 and 99 and volume II, section 89, on the "morality of mores," that much older and more primitive species of morality which differs *toto caelo*[3] from the altruistic mode of evaluation (in which Dr. Rée, like all English moral genealogists, sees moral evaluation *as such*); likewise, section 92, *The Wanderer,* section 26, and *Dawn,* section 112, on the origin of justice as an agreement between two approximately equal powers (equality as the presupposition of all compacts, consequently of all law); likewise *The Wanderer,* sections 22 and 33, on the origin of punishment, of which the aim of intimidation is neither the essence nor the source (as Dr. Rée thinks—it is rather only introduced, under certain definite circumstances, and always as an incidental, as something added).[4]

---

[3] Diametrically: literally, by the whole heavens.

[4] Nietzsche always gives page references to the first editions. I have substituted section numbers, which are the same in all editions and translations; and on pp. 145–78 most of the sections cited are offered in my translations.

For Nietzsche's relation to Rée, see Rudolph Binion, *Frau Lou,* Princeton, N.J., Princeton University Press, 1968.

5

Even then my real concern was something much more important than hypothesis-mongering, whether my own or other people's, on the origin of morality (or more precisely: the latter concerned me solely for the sake of a goal to which it was only one means among many). What was at stake was the *value* of morality—and over this I had to come to terms almost exclusively with my great teacher Schopenhauer, to whom that book of mine, the passion and the concealed contradiction of that book, addressed itself as if to a contemporary (—for that book, too, was a "polemic"). What was especially at stake was the value of the "unegoistic," the instincts of pity, self-abnegation, self-sacrifice, which Schopenhauer had gilded, deified, and projected into a beyond for so long that at last they became for him "value-in-itself," on the basis of which he *said No* to life and to himself. But it was against precisely *these* instincts that there spoke from me an ever more fundamental mistrust, an ever more corrosive skepticism! It was precisely here that I saw the *great* danger to mankind, its sublimest enticement and seduction—but to what? to nothingness?—it was precisely here that I saw the beginning of the end, the dead stop, a retrospective weariness, the will turning *against* life, the tender and sorrowful signs of the ultimate illness: I understood the ever spreading morality of pity that had seized even on philosophers and made them ill, as the most sinister symptom of a European culture that had itself become sinister, perhaps as its by-pass to a new Buddhism? to a Buddhism for Europeans? to—*nihilism?*

For this overestimation of and predilection for pity on the part of modern philosophers is something new: hitherto philosophers have been at one as to the *worthlessness* of pity. I name only Plato, Spinoza, La Rochefoucauld and Kant—four spirits as different from one another as possible, but united in one thing: in their low estimation of pity.

6

This problem of the *value* of pity and of the morality of pity (—I am opposed to the pernicious modern effeminacy of feeling—) seems at first to be merely something detached, an isolated question mark; but whoever sticks with it and *learns* how to ask questions here will experience what I experienced—a tremendous new prospect opens up for him, a new possibility comes over him like a vertigo, every kind of mistrust, suspicion, fear leaps up, his belief in morality, in all morality, falters—finally a new demand becomes audible. Let us articulate this *new demand:* we need a *critique* of moral values, *the value of these values themselves must first be called in question*—and for that there is needed a knowledge of the conditions and circumstances in which they grew, under which they evolved and changed (morality as consequence, as symptom, as mask, as tartufferie, as illness, as misunderstanding; but also morality as cause, as remedy, as stimulant, as restraint, as poison), a knowledge of a kind that has never yet existed or even been desired. One has taken the *value* of these "values" as given, as factual, as beyond all question; one has hitherto never doubted or hesitated in the slightest degree in supposing "the good man" to be of greater value than "the evil man," of greater value in the sense of furthering the advancement and prosperity of man in general (the future of man included). But what if the reverse were true? What if a symptom of regression were inherent in the "good," likewise a danger, a seduction, a poison, a narcotic, through which the present was possibly living *at the expense of the future?* Perhaps more comfortably, less dangerously, but at the same time in a meaner style, more basely?— So that precisely morality would be to blame if the *highest power and splendor* actually possible to the type man was never in fact attained? So that precisely morality was the danger of dangers?

7

Let it suffice that, after this prospect had opened up before me, I had reasons to look about me for scholarly, bold, and industrious comrades (I am still looking). The project is to traverse with quite novel questions, and as though with new eyes, the enormous, distant, and so well hidden land of morality—of morality that has actually existed, actually been lived; and does this not mean virtually to *discover* this land for the first time?

If I considered in this connection the above-mentioned Dr. Rée, among others, it was because I had no doubt that the very nature of his inquiries would compel him to adopt a better method for reaching answers. Have I deceived myself in this? My desire, at any rate, was to point out to so sharp and disinterested an eye as his a better direction in which to look, in the direction of an actual *history of morality,* and to warn him in time against gazing around haphazardly in the blue after the English fashion. For it must be obvious which color is a hundred times more vital for a genealogist of morals than blue: namely *gray,* that is, what is documented, what can actually be confirmed and has actually existed, in short the entire long hieroglyphic record, so hard to decipher, of the moral past of mankind!

This was unknown to Dr. Rée; but he had read Darwin—so that in his hypotheses, and after a fashion that is at least entertaining, the Darwinian beast and the ultramodern unassuming moral milksop who "no longer bites" politely link hands, the latter wearing an expression of a certain good-natured and refined indolence, with which is mingled even a grain of pessimism and weariness, as if all these things—the problems of morality—were really not worth taking quite so seriously. But to me, on the contrary, there seems to be nothing *more* worth taking seriously, among the rewards for it being that some day one will perhaps be allowed to take them *cheerfully.* For cheerfulness—or in my own language *gay science*—is a reward: the reward of a long, brave, industrious, and subterranean seriousness, of which, to be sure, not everyone is capable. But on the day we can say with all our hearts, "Onwards!

our old morality too is part *of the comedy!*" we shall have discovered a new complication and possibility for the Dionysian drama of "The Destiny of the Soul"—and one can wager that the grand old eternal comic poet of our existence will be quick to make use of it!

8

If this book is incomprehensible to anyone and jars on his ears, the fault, it seems to me, is not necessarily mine. It is clear enough, assuming, as I do assume, that one has first read my earlier writings and has not spared some trouble in doing so: for they are, indeed, not easy to penetrate.[5] Regarding my *Zarathustra,* for example, I do not allow that anyone knows that book who has not at some time been profoundly wounded and at some time profoundly delighted by every word in it; for only then may he enjoy the privilege of reverentially sharing in the halcyon element out of which that book was born and in its sunlight clarity, remoteness, breadth, and certainty. In other cases, people find difficulty with the aphoris-

---

[5] See also the end of Nietzsche's Preface to the new edition of *The Dawn,* written in the fall of 1886: ". . . to read *well,* that means reading slowly, deeply, with consideration and caution . . ." The last four words do not adequately render *rück- und vorsichtig,* which can also mean, looking backward and forward—i.e., with a regard for the context, including also the writer's earlier and later works. Cf. *Beyond Good and Evil,* my note on section 250.

Yet Arthur Danto voices a very common assumption when he says on the first page of the first chapter of his *Nietzsche as Philosopher* (New York, Macmillan, 1965): "No one of them [i.e., Nietzsche's books] presupposes an acquaintance with any other . . . his writings may be read in pretty much any order, without this greatly impeding the comprehension of his ideas." This is as wrong as Danto's claim on the same page that "it would be difficult even for a close reader to tell the difference between those works he [Nietzsche] saw through the press [e.g., the *Genealogy*] and those [*sic*] pieced together by his editors [i.e., *The Will to Power*]." Indeed, Danto, like most readers, approaches Nietzsche as if "any given aphorism or essay might as easily have been placed in one volume as in another"; he bases his discussions on short snippets, torn from their context, and frequently omits phrases without indicating that he has done so; and he does not bother to consider all or most of the passages that are relevant to the topics he discusses.

This is one of the few books in English that deal with Nietzsche as a philosopher, and Danto's standing as a philosopher inspires confidence; but his account of Nietzsche's moral and epistemological ideas unfortunately depends on this untenable approach. See also the first footnote to the second essay, below.

tic form: this arises from the fact that today this form is *not taken seriously enough*. An aphorism, properly stamped and molded, has not been "deciphered" when it has simply been read; rather, one has then to begin its *exegesis,* for which is required an art of exegesis. I have offered in the third essay of the present book an example of what I regard as "exegesis" in such a case—an aphorism is prefixed to this essay, the essay itself is a commentary on it. To be sure, one thing is necessary above all if one is to practice reading as an *art* in this way, something that has been unlearned most thoroughly nowadays—and therefore it will be some time before my writings are "readable"—something for which one has almost to be a cow and in any case *not* a "modern man": *rumination*.

Sils-Maria, Upper Engadine,
July 1887

First Essay
"Good and Evil," "Good and Bad"

1

These English psychologists, whom one has also to thank for the only attempts hitherto to arrive at a history of the origin of morality—they themselves are no easy riddle; I confess that, as living riddles, they even possess one essential advantage over their books —*they are interesting!* These English psychologists—what do they really want? One always discovers them voluntarily or involuntarily at the same task, namely at dragging the *partie honteuse*[1] of our inner world into the foreground and seeking the truly effective and directing agent, that which has been decisive in its evolution, in just that place where the intellectual pride of man would least *desire* to find it (in the *vis inertiae*[2] of habit, for example, or in forgetfulness, or in a blind and chance mechanistic hooking-together of ideas, or in something purely passive, automatic, reflexive, molecular, and thoroughly stupid)—what is it really that always drives these psychologists in just *this* direction? Is it a secret, malicious, vulgar, perhaps self-deceiving instinct for belittling man? Or possibly a pessimistic suspicion, the mistrustfulness of disappointed idealists grown spiteful and gloomy? Or a petty subterranean hostility and rancor toward Christianity (and Plato) that has perhaps not even crossed the threshold of consciousness? Or even a lascivious taste for the grotesque, the painfully paradoxical, the questionable and absurd in existence? Or finally—something of each of them, a little vulgarity, a little gloominess, a little anti-Christianity, a little itching and need for spice?

But I am told they are simply old, cold, and tedious frogs, creeping around men and into men as if in their own proper ele-

---

1 Shame.
2 Inertia.

ment, that is, in a *swamp*. I rebel at that idea; more, I do not believe it; and if one may be allowed to hope where one does not know, then I hope from my heart they may be the reverse of this—that these investigators and microscopists of the soul may be fundamentally brave, proud, and magnanimous animals, who know how to keep their hearts as well as their sufferings in bounds and have trained themselves to sacrifice all desirability to truth, *every* truth, even plain, harsh, ugly, repellent, unchristian, immoral truth.—For such truths do exist.—

2

All respect then for the good spirits that may rule in these historians of morality! But it is, unhappily, certain that the *historical spirit* itself is lacking in them, that precisely all the good spirits of history itself have left them in the lurch! As is the hallowed custom with philosophers, the thinking of all of them is *by nature* unhistorical; there is no doubt about that. The way they have bungled their moral genealogy comes to light at the very beginning, where the task is to investigate the origin of the concept and judgment "good." "Originally"—so they decree—"one approved unegoistic actions and called them good from the point of view of those to whom they were done, that is to say, those to whom they were *useful;* later one *forgot* how this approval originated and, simply because unegoistic actions were always *habitually* praised as good, one also felt them to be good—as if they were something good in themselves." One sees straightaway that this primary derivation already contains all the typical traits of the idiosyncrasy of the English psychologists—we have "utility," "forgetting," "habit," and finally "error," all as the basis of an evaluation of which the higher man has hitherto been proud as though it were a kind of prerogative of man as such. This pride *has* to be humbled, this evaluation disvalued: has that end been achieved?

Now it is plain to me, first of all, that in this theory the source of the concept "good" has been sought and established in the wrong place: the judgment "good" did *not* originate with those to whom "goodness" was shown! Rather it was "the good" themselves, that is to say, the noble, powerful, high-stationed and high-minded, who felt and established themselves and their actions as good, that is, of the first rank, in contradistinction to all the low, low-minded, common and plebeian. It was out of this *pathos of distance*[1] that they first seized the right to create values and to coin names for values: what had they to do with utility! The viewpoint of utility is as remote and inappropriate as it possibly could be in face of such a burning eruption of the highest rank-ordering, rank-defining value judgments: for here feeling has attained the antithesis of that low degree of warmth which any calculating prudence, any calculus of utility, presupposes—and not for once only, not for an exceptional hour, but for good. The pathos of nobility and distance, as aforesaid, the protracted and domineering fundamental total feeling on the part of a higher ruling order in relation to a lower order, to a "below"—*that* is the origin of the antithesis "good" and "bad." (The lordly right of giving names extends so far that one should allow oneself to conceive the origin of language itself as an expression of power on the part of the rulers: they say "this *is* this and this," they seal every thing and event with a sound and, as it were, take possession of it.) It follows from this origin that the word "good" was definitely *not* linked from the first and by necessity to "unegoistic" actions, as the superstition of these genealogists of morality would have it. Rather it was only when aristocratic value judgments *declined* that the whole antithesis "egoistic" "unegoistic" obtruded itself more and more on the human conscience—it is, to speak in my own language, the *herd instinct* that through this antithesis at last gets its word (and its *words*) in. And even then it was a long time before that instinct attained such dominion that moral evaluation was actually stuck and halted at this antithesis (as, for example, is the case in contemporary Europe: the prejudice that takes "moral," "unegoistic," *"désintéressé"* as concepts of equivalent value already rules today with the force of a "fixed idea" and brain-sickness).

---

[1] Cf. *Beyond Good and Evil,* section 257, p. 391 above.

3

In the second place, however: quite apart from the historical untenability of this hypothesis regarding the origin of the value judgment "good," it suffers from an inherent psychological absurdity. The utility of the unegoistic action is supposed to be the source of the approval accorded it, and this source is supposed to have been *forgotten*—but how is this forgetting *possible?* Has the utility of such actions come to an end at some time or other? The opposite is the case: this utility has rather been an everyday experience at all times, therefore something that has been underlined again and again: consequently, instead of fading from consciousness, instead of becoming easily forgotten, it must have been impressed on the consciousness more and more clearly. How much more reasonable is that opposing theory (it is not for that reason more true—) which Herbert Spencer,[1] for example, espoused: that the concept "good" is essentially identical with the concept "useful," "practical," so that in the judgments "good" and "bad" mankind has summed up and sanctioned precisely its *unforgotten* and *unforgettable* experiences regarding what is useful-practical and what is harmful-impractical. According to this theory, that which has always proved itself useful is good: therefore it may claim to be "valuable in the highest degree," "valuable in itself." This road to an explanation is, as aforesaid, also a wrong one, but at least the explanation is in itself reasonable and psychologically tenable.

4

The signpost to the *right* road was for me the question: what was the real etymological significance of the designations for "good" coined in the various languages? I found they all led back to the *same conceptual transformation*—that everywhere "noble," "aristocratic" in the social sense, is the basic concept from which

---

[1] Herbert Spencer (1820–1903) was probably the most widely read English philosopher of his time. He applied the principle of evolution to many fields, including sociology and ethics.

"good" in the sense of "with aristocratic soul," "noble," "with a soul of a high order," "with a privileged soul" necessarily developed: a development which always runs parallel with that other in which "common," "plebeian," "low" are finally transformed into the concept "bad." The most convincing example of the latter is the German word *schlecht* [bad] itself: which is identical with *schlicht* [plain, simple]—compare *schlechtweg* [plainly], *schlechterdings* [simply]—and orginally designated the plain, the common man, as yet with no inculpatory implication and simply in contradistinction to the nobility. About the time of the Thirty Years' War, late enough therefore, this meaning changed into the one now customary.[1]

With regard to a moral genealogy this seems to me a *fundamental* insight; that it has been arrived at so late is the fault of the retarding influence exercised by the democratic prejudice in the modern world toward all questions of origin. And this is so even in the apparently quite objective domain of natural science and physiology, as I shall merely hint here. But what mischief this prejudice is capable of doing, especially to morality and history, once it has been unbridled to the point of hatred is shown by the notorious case of Buckle;[2] here the *plebeianism* of the modern spirit, which is of English origin, erupted once again on its native soil, as violently as a mud volcano and with that salty, noisy, vulgar eloquence with which all volcanos have spoken hitherto.—

5

With regard to *our* problem, which may on good grounds be called a *quiet* problem and one which fastidiously directs itself to few ears, it is of no small interest to ascertain that through those words and roots which designate "good" there frequently still shines the most important nuance by virtue of which the noble felt themselves to be men of a higher rank. Granted that, in the

---

[1] Cf. *Dawn*, section 231, included in the present volume.

[2] Henry Thomas Buckle (1821–1862), English historian, is known chiefly for his *History of Civilization* (1857ff.). The suggestion in the text is developed more fully in section 876 of *The Will to Power*.

majority of cases, they designate themselves simply by their superiority in power (as "the powerful," "the masters," "the commanders") or by the most clearly visible signs of this superiority, for example, as "the rich," "the possessors" (this is the meaning of *arya;* and of corresponding words in Iranian and Slavic). But they also do it by a *typical character trait:* and this is the case that concerns us here. They call themselves, for instance, "the truthful"; this is so above all of the Greek nobility, whose mouthpiece is the Megarian poet Theognis.[1] The root of the word coined for this, *esthlos,*[2] signifies one who *is,* who possesses reality, who is actual, who is true; then, with a subjective turn, the true as the truthful: in this phase of conceptual transformation it becomes a slogan and catchword of the nobility and passes over entirely into the sense of "noble," as distinct from the *lying* common man, which is what

---

[1] Nietzsche's first publication, in 1867 when he was still a student at the University of Leipzig, was an article in a leading classical journal, *Rheinisches Museum,* on the history of the collection of the maxims of Theognis ("Zur Geschichte der Theognideischen Spruchsammlung"). Theognis of Megara lived in the sixth century B.C.

[2] Greek: good, brave. Readers who are not classical philologists may wonder as they read this section how well taken Nietzsche's points about the Greeks are. In this connection one could obviously cite a vast literature, but in this brief commentary it will be sufficient to quote Professor Gerald F. Else's monumental study *Aristotle's Poetics: The Argument* (Cambridge, Mass., Harvard University Press, 1957), a work equally notable for its patient and thorough scholarship and its spirited defense of some controversial interpretations. On the points at issue here, Else's comments are not, I think, controversial; and that is the reason for citing them here.

"The dichotomy is mostly taken for granted in Homer: there are not many occasions when the heaven-wide gulf between heroes and commoners even has to be mentioned.[30] [30 Still, one finds 'good' (*esthloi*) and 'bad' (*kakoi*) explicitly contrasted a fair number of times: B366, Z489, I319, . . .] In the . . . seventh and sixth centuries, on the other hand, the antithesis grows common. In Theognis it amounts to an obsession . . . Greek thinking begins with and for a long time holds to the proposition that mankind is divided into 'good' and 'bad,' and these terms are quite as much social, political, and economic as they are moral. . . . The dichotomy is absolute and exclusive for a simple reason: it began as the aristocrats' view of society and reflects their idea of the gulf between themselves and the 'others.' In the minds of a comparatively small and close-knit group like the Greek aristocracy there are only two kinds of people, 'we' and 'they'; and of course 'we' are the good people, the proper, decent, good-looking, right-thinking ones, while 'they' are the rascals, the poltroons, the good-for-nothings . . . Aristotle knew and sympathized with this older aristocratic, 'practical' ideal, not as superior to the contemplative, but at least as next best to it" (p. 75).

Theognis takes him to be and how he describes him—until finally, after the decline of the nobility, the word is left to designate nobility of soul and becomes as it were ripe and sweet. In the word *kakos*,[3] as in *deilos*[4] (the plebeian in contradistinction to the *agathos*[5]), cowardice is emphasized: this perhaps gives an indication in which direction one should seek the etymological origin of *agathos*, which is susceptible of several interpretations. The Latin *malus*[6] (beside which I set *melas*[7]) may designate the common man as the dark-colored, above all as the black-haired man (*"hic niger est*[8]—"), as the pre-Aryan occupant of the soil of Italy who was distinguished most obviously from the blond, that is Aryan, conqueror race by his color; Gaelic, at any rate, offers us a precisely similar case—*fin* (for example in the name *Fin-Gal*), the distinguishing word for nobility, finally for the good, noble, pure, orginally meant the blond-headed, in contradistinction to the dark, black-haired aboriginal inhabitants.

The Celts, by the way, were definitely a blond race; it is wrong to associate traces of an essentially dark-haired people which appear on the more careful ethnographical maps of Germany with any sort of Celtic origin or blood-mixture, as Virchow[9] still does: it is rather the *pre-Aryan* people of Germany who emerge in these places. (The same is true of virtually all Europe: the suppressed race has gradually recovered the upper hand again, in coloring, shortness of skull, perhaps even in the intellectual and social in-

---

[3] Greek: bad, ugly, ill-born, mean, craven.

[4] Greek: cowardly, worthless, vile, wretched.

[5] Greek: good, well-born, gentle, brave, capable.

[6] Bad.

[7] Greek: black, dark.

[8] Quoted from Horace's *Satires,* I.4, line 85: "He that backbites an absent friend . . . and cannot keep secrets, is black, O Roman, beware!" *Niger,* originally "black," also came to mean unlucky and, as in this quotation, wicked. Conversely, *candidus* means white, bright, beautiful, pure, guileless, candid, honest, happy, fortunate. And in *Satires,* I.5, 41, Horace speaks of "the whitest souls earth ever bore" (*animae qualis neque candidiores terra tulit*).

[9] Rudolf Virchow (1821–1902) was one of the greatest German pathologists, as well as a liberal politician, a member of the German Reichstag (parliament), and an opponent of Bismarck.

stincts: who can say whether modern democracy, even more modern anarchism and especially that inclination for *"commune,"* for the most primitive form of society, which is now shared by all the socialists of Europe, does not signify in the main a tremendous *counterattack*—and that the conqueror and *master race,*[10] the Aryan, is not succumbing physiologically, too?

I believe I may venture to interpret the Latin *bonus*[11] as "the warrior," provided I am right in tracing *bonus* back to an earlier *duonus*[12] (compare *bellum = duellum = duen-lum,* which seems to me to contain *duonus*). Therefore *bonus* as the man of strife, of dissention (*duo*), as the man of war: one sees what constituted the "goodness" of a man in ancient Rome. Our German *gut* [good] even: does it not signify "the godlike," the man of "godlike race"? And is it not identical with the popular (originally noble) name of the Goths? The grounds for this conjecture cannot be dealt with here.—

6

To this rule that a concept denoting political superiority always resolves itself into a concept denoting superiority of soul it is not necessarily an exception (although it provides occasions for exceptions) when the highest caste is at the same time the *priestly* caste and therefore emphasizes in its total description of itself a predicate that calls to mind its priestly function. It is then, for example, that "pure" and "impure" confront one another for the first time as designations of station; and here too there evolves a "good" and a "bad" in a sense no longer referring to station. One should be warned, moreover, against taking these concepts "pure" and "impure" too ponderously or broadly, not to say symbolically: all the concepts of ancient man were rather at first

[10] For a detailed discussion both of this concept and of Nietzsche's attitude toward the Jews and anti-Semitism, see Kaufmann's *Nietzsche,* Chapter 10: "The Master-Race."

[11] Good.

[12] Listed in Harper's Latin Dictionary as the old form of *bonus,* with the comment: "for *duonus,* cf. *bellum.*" And *duellum* is identified as an early and poetic form of *bellum* (war).

incredibly uncouth, coarse, external, narrow, straightforward, and altogether *unsymbolical* in meaning to a degree that we can scarcely conceive. The "pure one" is from the beginning merely a man who washes himself, who forbids himself certain foods that produce skin ailments, who does not sleep with the dirty women of the lower strata, who has an aversion to blood—no more, hardly more! On the other hand, to be sure, it is clear from the whole nature of an essentially priestly aristocracy why antithetical valuations could in precisely this instance soon become dangerously deepened, sharpened, and internalized; and indeed they finally tore chasms between man and man that a very Achilles of a free spirit would not venture to leap without a shudder. There is from the first something *unhealthy* in such priestly aristocracies and in the habits ruling in them which turn them away from action and alternate between brooding and emotional explosions, habits which seem to have as their almost invariable consequence that intestinal morbidity and neurasthenia which has afflicted priests at all times; but as to that which they themselves devised as a remedy for this morbidity—must one not assert that it has ultimately proved itself a hundred times more dangerous in its effects than the sickness it was supposed to cure? Mankind itself is still ill with the effects of this priestly naïveté in medicine! Think, for example, of certain forms of diet (abstinence from meat), of fasting, of sexual continence, of flight "into the wilderness" (the Weir Mitchell isolation cure[1]—without, to be sure, the subsequent fattening and over-feeding which constitute the most effective remedy for the hysteria induced by the ascetic ideal): add to these the entire antisensualistic metaphysic of the priests that makes men indolent and overrefined, their autohypnosis in the manner of fakirs and Brahmins —Brahma used in the shape of a glass knob and a fixed idea—and finally the only-too-comprehensible satiety with all this, together with the radical cure for it, *nothingness* (or God—the desire for a *unio mystica* with God is the desire of the Buddhist for nothingness, Nirvana—and no more!). For with the priests *everything* becomes more dangerous, not only cures and remedies, but also arro-

---

[1] The cure developed by Dr. Silas Weir Mitchell (1829–1914, American) consisted primarily in isolation, confinement to bed, dieting, and massage.

gance, revenge, acuteness, profligacy, love, lust to rule, virtue, disease—but it is only fair to add that it was on the soil of this *essentially dangerous* form of human existence, the priestly form, that man first became *an interesting animal,* that only here did the human soul in a higher sense acquire *depth* and become *evil*—and these are the two basic respects in which man has hitherto been superior to other beasts!

7

One will have divined already how easily the priestly mode of valuation can branch off from the knightly-aristocratic and then develop into its opposite; this is particularly likely when the priestly caste and the warrior caste are in jealous opposition to one another and are unwilling to come to terms. The knightly-aristocratic value judgments presupposed a powerful physicality, a flourishing, abundant, even overflowing health, together with that which serves to preserve it: war, adventure, hunting, dancing, war games, and in general all that involves vigorous, free, joyful activity. The priestly-noble mode of valuation presupposes, as we have seen, other things: it is disadvantageous for it when it comes to war! As is well known, the priests are the *most evil enemies*—but why? Because they are the most impotent. It is because of their impotence that in them hatred grows to monstrous and uncanny proportions, to the most spiritual and poisonous kind of hatred. The truly great haters in world history have always been priests; likewise the most ingenious[1] haters: other kinds of spirit [2] hardly come into consideration when compared with the spirit of priestly vengefulness. Human history would be altogether too stupid a thing without the spirit that the impotent have introduced into it—let us take at once the most notable example. All that has been done on earth against "the noble," "the powerful," "the masters," "the rulers," fades into nothing compared with what the *Jews* have done against them; the Jews, that priestly people, who in opposing their enemies and conquerors were ultimately satisfied with nothing less than a radical

---

[1] *Geistreich.*
[2] *Geist.*

revaluation of their enemies' values, that is to say, an act of the *most spiritual revenge*. For this alone was appropriate to a priestly people, the people embodying the most deeply repressed [3] priestly vengefulness. It was the Jews who, with awe-inspiring consistency, dared to invert the aristocratic value-equation (good = noble = powerful = beautiful = happy = beloved of God) and to hang on to this inversion with their teeth, the teeth of the most abysmal hatred (the hatred of impotence), saying "the wretched alone are the good; the poor, impotent, lowly alone are the good; the suffering, deprived, sick, ugly alone are pious, alone are blessed by God, blessedness is for them alone—and you, the powerful and noble, are on the contrary the evil, the cruel, the lustful, the insatiable, the godless to all eternity; and you shall be in all eternity the unblessed, accursed, and damned!" . . . One knows *who* inherited this Jewish revaluation . . . In connection with the tremendous and immeasurably fateful initiative provided by the Jews through this most fundamental of all declarations of war, I recall the proposition I arrived at on a previous occasion (*Beyond Good and Evil*, section 195)[4]—that with the Jews there begins *the slave revolt in morality:* that revolt which has a history of two thousand years behind it and which we no longer see because it—has been victorious.

8

But you do not comprehend this? You are incapable of seeing something that required two thousand years to achieve victory?— There is nothing to wonder at in that: all *protracted* things are hard to see, to see whole. *That,* however, is what has happened: from the trunk of that tree of vengefulness and hatred, Jewish hatred— the profoundest and sublimest kind of hatred, capable of creating ideals and reversing values, the like of which has never existed on earth before—there grew something equally incomparable, a *new love,* the profoundest and sublimest kind of love—and from what other trunk could it have grown?

---

[3] *Zurückgetretensten.*
[4] See p. 298 above, including the commentary in note 11.

One should not imagine it grew up as the denial of that thirst for revenge, as the opposite of Jewish hatred! No, the reverse is true! That love grew out of it as its crown, as its triumphant crown spreading itself farther and farther into the purest brightness and sunlight, driven as it were into the domain of light and the heights in pursuit of the goals of that hatred—victory, spoil, and seduction—by the same impulse that drove the roots of that hatred deeper and deeper and more and more covetously into all that was profound and evil. This Jesus of Nazareth, the incarnate gospel of love, this "Redeemer" who brought blessedness and victory to the poor, the sick, and the sinners—was he not this seduction in its most uncanny and irresistible form, a seduction and bypath to precisely those *Jewish* values and new ideals? Did Israel not attain the ultimate goal of its sublime vengefulness precisely through the bypath of this "Redeemer," this ostensible opponent and disintegrator of Israel? Was it not part of the secret black art of truly *grand* politics of revenge, of a farseeing, subterranean, slowly advancing, and premeditated revenge, that Israel must itself deny the real instrument of its revenge before all the world as a mortal enemy and nail it to the cross, so that "all the world," namely all the opponents of Israel, could unhesitatingly swallow just this bait? And could spiritual subtlety imagine any *more dangerous* bait than this? Anything to equal the enticing, intoxicating, overwhelming, and undermining power of that symbol of the "holy cross," that ghastly paradox of a "God on the cross," that mystery of an unimaginable ultimate cruelty and self-crucifixion of God *for the salvation of man?*

What is certain, at least, is that *sub hoc signo*[1] Israel, with its vengefulness and revaluation of all values, has hitherto triumphed again and again over all other ideals, over all *nobler* ideals.——

9

"But why are you talking about *nobler* ideals! Let us stick to the facts: the people have won—or 'the slaves' or 'the mob' or 'the herd' or whatever you like to call them—if this has happened

---

[1] Under this sign.

through the Jews, very well! in that case no people ever had a more world-historic mission. 'The masters' have been disposed of; the morality of the common man has won. One may conceive of this victory as at the same time a blood-poisoning (it has mixed the races together)—I shan't contradict; but this in-toxication has undoubtedly been *successful*. The 'redemption' of the human race (from 'the masters,' that is) is going forward; everything is visibly becoming Judaized, Christianized, mob-ized (what do the words matter!). The progress of this poison through the entire body of mankind seems irresistible, its pace and tempo may from now on even grow slower, subtler, less audible, more cautious—there is plenty of time.— To this end, does the church today still have any *necessary* role to play? Does it still have the right to exist? Or could one do without it? *Quaeritur.*[2] It seems to hinder rather than hasten this progress. But perhaps that is its usefulness.— Certainly it has, over the years, become something crude and boorish, something repellent to a more delicate intellect, to a truly modern taste. Ought it not to become at least a little more refined?— Today it alienates rather than seduces.— Which of us would be a free spirit if the church did not exist? It is the church, and not its poison, that repels us.— Apart from the church, we, too, love the poison.—"

This is the epilogue of a "free spirit" to my speech; an honest animal, as he has abundantly revealed, and a democrat, moreover; he had been listening to me till then and could not endure to listen to my silence. For at this point I have much to be silent about.

10

The slave revolt in morality begins when *ressentiment*[1] itself becomes creative and gives birth to values: the *ressentiment* of natures that are denied the true reaction, that of deeds, and compensate themselves with an imaginary revenge. While every noble morality develops from a triumphant affirmation of itself, slave morality from the outset says No to what is "outside," what is "different," what is "not itself"; and *this* No is its creative deed. This inversion of the value-positing eye—this *need* to direct one's

---

2 One asks.

1 Resentment. The term is discussed above, in section 3 of the Introduction.

view outward instead of back to oneself—is of the essence of *ressentiment:* in order to exist, slave morality always first needs a hostile external world; it needs, physiologically speaking, external stimuli in order to act at all—its action is fundamentally reaction.

The reverse is the case with the noble mode of valuation: it acts and grows spontaneously, it seeks its opposite only so as to affirm itself more gratefully and triumphantly—its negative concept "low," "common," "bad" is only a subsequently-invented pale, contrasting image in relation to its positive basic concept—filled with life and passion through and through—"we noble ones, we good, beautiful, happy ones!" When the noble mode of valuation blunders and sins against reality, it does so in respect to the sphere with which it is *not* sufficiently familiar, against a real knowledge of which it has indeed inflexibly guarded itself: in some circumstances it misunderstands the sphere it despises, that of the common man, of the lower orders; on the other hand, one should remember that, even supposing that the affect of contempt, of looking down from a superior height, *falsifies* the image of that which it despises, it will at any rate still be a much less serious falsification than that perpetrated on its opponent—*in effigie* of course—by the submerged hatred, the vengefulness of the impotent. There is indeed too much carelessness, too much taking lightly, too much looking away and impatience involved in contempt, even too much joyfulness, for it to be able to transform its object into a real caricature and monster.

One should not overlook the almost benevolent nuances that the Greek nobility, for example, bestows on all the words it employs to distinguish the lower orders from itself; how they are continuously mingled and sweetened with a kind of pity, consideration, and forbearance, so that finally almost all the words referring to the common man have remained as expressions signifying "unhappy," "pitiable" (compare *deilos,*[2] *deilaios,*[3] *poneros,*[4] *mochtheros,*[5] the

---

[2] All of the footnoted words in this section are Greek. The first four mean *wretched,* but each has a separate note to suggest some of its other connotations. *Deilos:* cowardly, worthless, vile.

[3] Paltry.

[4] Oppressed by toils, good for nothing, worthless, knavish, base, cowardly.

[5] Suffering hardship, knavish.

last two of which properly designate the common man as work-slave and beast of burden)—and how on the other hand "bad," "low," "unhappy" have never ceased to sound to the Greek ear as one note with a tone-color in which "unhappy" preponderates: this as an inheritance from the ancient nobler aristocratic mode of evaluation, which does not belie itself even in its contempt (—philologists should recall the sense in which *oïzyros*,[6] *anolbos*,[7] *tlēmōn*,[8] *dystychein*,[9] *xymphora*[10] are employed). The "well-born" *felt* themselves to be the "happy"; they did not have to establish their happiness artificially by examining their enemies, or to persuade themselves, *deceive* themselves, that they were happy (as all men of *ressentiment* are in the habit of doing); and they likewise knew, as rounded men replete with energy and therefore *necessarily* active, that happiness should not be sundered from action—being active was with them necessarily a part of happiness (whence *eu prattein*[11] takes its origin)—all very much the opposite of "happiness" at the level of the impotent, the oppressed, and those in whom poisonous and inimical feelings are festering, with whom it appears as essentially narcotic, drug, rest, peace, "sabbath," slackening of tension and relaxing of limbs, in short *passively*.

While the noble man lives in trust and openness with himself (*gennaios*[12] "of noble descent" underlines the nuance "upright" and probably also "naïve"), the man of *ressentiment* is neither upright nor naïve nor honest and straightforward with himself. His soul *squints*; his spirit loves hiding places, secret paths and back doors, everything covert entices him as *his* world, *his* security, *his* refreshment; he understands how to keep silent, how not to forget, how to wait, how to be provisionally self-deprecating and humble. A race of such men of *ressentiment* is bound to become eventually *cleverer* than any noble race; it will also honor cleverness to a far greater degree: namely, as a condition of existence of the first im-

---

6 Woeful, miserable, toilsome; wretch.

7 Unblest, wretched, luckless, poor.

8 Wretched, miserable.

9 To be unlucky, unfortunate.

10 Misfortune.

11 To do well in the sense of faring well.

12 High-born, noble, high-minded.

portance; while with noble men cleverness can easily acquire a subtle flavor of luxury and subtlety—for here it is far less essential than the perfect functioning of the regulating *unconscious* instincts or even than a certain imprudence, perhaps a bold recklessness whether in the face of danger or of the enemy, or that enthusiastic impulsiveness in anger, love, reverence, gratitude, and revenge by which noble souls have at all times recognized one another. *Ressentiment* itself, if it should appear in the noble man, consummates and exhausts itself in an immediate reaction, and therefore does not *poison*: on the other hand, it fails to appear at all on countless occasions on which it inevitably appears in the weak and impotent.

To be incapable of taking one's enemies, one's accidents, even one's misdeeds seriously for very long—that is the sign of strong, full natures in whom there is an excess of the power to form, to mold, to recuperate and to forget (a good example of this in modern times is Mirabeau,[13] who had no memory for insults and vile actions done him and was unable to forgive simply because he—forgot). Such a man shakes off with a *single* shrug many vermin that eat deep into others; here alone genuine "love of one's enemies" is possible—supposing it to be possible at all on earth. How much reverence has a noble man for his enemies!—and such reverence is a bridge to love.— For he desires his enemy for himself, as his mark of distinction; he can endure no other enemy than one in whom there is nothing to despise and *very much* to honor! In contrast to this, picture "the enemy" as the man of *ressentiment* conceives him—and here precisely is his deed, his creation: he has conceived "the evil enemy," *"the Evil One,"* and this in fact is his basic concept, from which he then evolves, as an afterthought and pendant, a "good one"—himself!

11

This, then, is quite the contrary of what the noble man does, who conceives the basic concept "good" in advance and spontaneously out of himself and only then creates for himself an idea of

---

[13] Honoré Gabriel Riqueti, Comte de Mirabeau (1749–1791), was a celebrated French Revolutionary statesman and writer.

"bad"! This "bad" of noble origin and that "evil" out of the caul-
dron of unsatisfied hatred—the former an after-production, a side
issue, a contrasting shade, the latter on the contrary the original
thing, the beginning, the distinctive *deed* in the conception of a
slave morality—how different these words "bad" and "evil" are,
although they are both apparently the opposite of the same concept
"good." But it is *not* the same concept "good": one should ask
rather precisely *who* is "evil" in the sense of the morality of *ressentiment*. The answer, in all strictness, is: *precisely* the "good
man" of the other morality, precisely the noble, powerful man, the
ruler, but dyed in another color, interpreted in another fashion, seen
in another way by the venomous eye of *ressentiment*.

Here there is one thing we shall be the last to deny: he who
knows these "good men" only as enemies knows only *evil enemies*, and the same men who are held so sternly in check *inter
pares*[1] by custom, respect, usage, gratitude, and even more by mutual suspicion and jealousy, and who on the other hand in their
relations with one another show themselves so resourceful in consideration, self-control delicacy, loyalty, pride, and friendship—
once they go outside, where the strange, the *stranger* is found, they
are not much better than uncaged beasts of prey. There they savor
a freedom from all social constraints, they compensate themselves
in the wilderness for the tension engendered by protracted confinement and enclosure within the peace of society, they go *back* to the
innocent conscience of the beast of prey, as triumphant monsters
who perhaps emerge from a disgusting[2] procession of murder, arson, rape, and torture, exhilarated and undisturbed of soul, as if it
were no more than a students' prank, convinced they have provided
the poets with a lot more material for song and praise. One cannot
fail to see at the bottom of all these noble races the beast of prey,
the splendid *blond beast*[3] prowling about avidly in search of spoil

---

[1] Among equals.

[2] *Scheusslichen.*

[3] This is the first appearance in Nietzsche's writings of the notorious "blond
beast." It is encountered twice more in the present section; a variant appears
in section 17 of the second essay; and then the *blonde Bestie* appears once
more in *Twilight*, "The 'Improvers' of Mankind," section 2 (*Portable Nietzsche*, p. 502). That is all. For a detailed discussion of these passages see

and victory; this hidden core needs to erupt from time to time, the animal has to get out again and go back to the wilderness: the Roman, Arabian, Germanic, Japanese nobility, the Homeric heroes, the Scandinavian Vikings—they all shared this need.

It is the noble races that have left behind them the concept "barbarian" wherever they have gone; even their highest culture betrays a consciousness of it and even a pride in it (for example, when Pericles says to his Athenians in his famous funeral oration "our boldness has gained access to every land and sea, everywhere raising imperishable monuments to its goodness *and wickedness*"). This "boldness" of noble races, mad, absurd, and sudden in its expression, the incalculability, even incredibility of their undertakings —Pericles specially commends the *rhathymia*[4] of the Athenians—

Kaufmann's *Nietzsche,* Chapter 7, section III: ". . . The 'blond beast' is not a racial concept and does not refer to the 'Nordic race' of which the Nazis later made so much. Nietzsche specifically refers to Arabs and Japanese . . . —and the 'blondness' presumably refers to the beast, the lion."

Francis Golffing, in his free translation of the *Genealogy,* deletes the blond beast three times out of four; only where it appears the second time in the original text, he has "the blond Teutonic beast." This helps to corroborate the myth that the blondness refers to the Teutons. Without the image of the lion, however, we lose not only some of Nietzsche's poetry as well as any chance to understand one of his best known coinages; we also lose an echo of the crucial first chapter of *Zarathustra,* where the lion represents the second stage in "The Three Metamorphoses" of the spirit—above the obedient camel but below the creative child (*Portable Nietzsche,* pp. 138f.).

Arthur Danto has suggested that if lions were black and Nietzsche had written "Black Beast," the expression would "provide support for African instead of German nationalists" (*Nietzsche as Philosopher,* New York, Macmillan, 1965, p. 170). Panthers *are* black and magnificent animals, but anyone calling Negroes black beasts and associating them with "a disgusting procession of murder, arson, rape, and torture," adding that "the animal has to get out again and go back to the wilderness," and then going on to speak of "their hair-raising cheerfulness and profound joy in all destruction," would scarcely be taken to "provide support for . . . nationalists." On the contrary, he would be taken for a highly prejudiced critic of the Negro.

No other German writer of comparable stature has been a more extreme critic of German nationalism than Nietzsche. For all that, it is plain that in this section he sought to describe the behavior of the ancient Greeks and Romans, the Goths and the Vandals, not that of nineteenth-century Germans.

[4] Thucydides, 2.39. In *A Historical Commentary on Thucydides,* vol. II (Oxford, Clarendon Press, 1956; corrected imprint of 1966), p. 118, A. W. Gomme comments on this word: "in its original sense, 'ease of mind,' 'without anxiety' . . . But ease of mind can in certain circumstances become

their indifference to and contempt for security, body, life, comfort, their hair-raising[5] cheerfulness and profound joy in all destruction, in all the voluptuousness of victory and cruelty—all this came together, in the minds of those who suffered from it, in the image of the "barbarian," the "evil enemy," perhaps as the "Goths," the "Vandals." The deep and icy mistrust the German still arouses today whenever he gets into a position of power is an echo of that inextinguishable horror with which Europe observed for centuries that raging of the blond Germanic beast (although between the old Germanic tribes and us Germans there exists hardly a conceptual relationship, let alone one of blood).

I once drew attention to the dilemma in which Hesiod found himself when he concocted his succession of cultural epochs and sought to express them in terms of gold, silver, and bronze: he knew no way of handling the contradiction presented by the glorious but at the same time terrible and violent world of Homer except by dividing one epoch into two epochs, which he then placed one behind the other—first the epoch of the heroes and demigods of Troy and Thebes, the form in which that world had survived in the memory of the noble races who were those heroes' true descendants; then the bronze epoch, the form in which that same world appeared to the descendants of the downtrodden, pillaged, mistreated, abducted, enslaved: an epoch of bronze, as aforesaid, hard, cold, cruel, devoid of feeling or conscience, destructive and bloody.

Supposing that what is at any rate believed to be the "truth" really is true, and the *meaning of all culture* is the reduction of the beast of prey "man" to a tame and civilized animal, a *domestic animal,* then one would undoubtedly have to regard all those instincts of reaction and *ressentiment* through whose aid the noble races and their ideals were finally confounded and overthrown as the actual *instruments of culture*; which is not to say that the *bearers* of these instincts themselves represent culture. Rather is the reverse not merely probable—no! today it is *palpable!* These bear-

---

carelessness, remissness, frivolity: Demosthenes often accused the Athenians of *rhathymia* . . ."

[5] *Entsetzliche.*

ers of the oppressive instincts that thirst for reprisal, the descendants of every kind of European and non-European slavery, and especially of the entire pre-Aryan populace—they represent the *regression* of mankind! These "instruments of culture" are a disgrace to man and rather an accusation and counterargument against "culture" in general! One may be quite justified in continuing to fear the blond beast at the core of all noble races and in being on one's guard against it: but who would not a hundred times sooner fear where one can also admire than *not* fear but be permanently condemned to the repellent sight of the ill-constituted, dwarfed, atrophied, and poisoned? [6] And is that not *our* fate? What today constitutes *our* antipathy to "man"?—for we *suffer* from man, beyond doubt.

Not fear; rather that we no longer have anything left to fear in man; that the maggot[7] "man" is swarming in the foreground; that the "tame man," the hopelessly mediocre and insipid[8] man, has already learned to feel himself as the goal and zenith, as the meaning of history, as "higher man"—that he has indeed a certain right to feel thus, insofar as he feels himself elevated above the surfeit of ill-constituted, sickly, weary and exhausted people of which Europe is beginning to stink today, as something at least relatively well-constituted, at least still capable of living, at least affirming life.

12

At this point I cannot suppress a sigh and a last hope. What is it that I especially find utterly unendurable? That I cannot cope with, that makes me choke and faint? Bad air! Bad air! The ap-

---

[6] If the present section is not clear enough to any reader, he might turn to *Zarathustra*'s contrast of the *overman* and the *last man* (Prologue, sections 3–5) and, for good measure, read also the first chapter or two of Part One. Then he will surely see how Aldous Huxley's *Brave New World* and George Orwell's *1984*—but especially the former—are developments of Nietzsche's theme. Huxley, in his novel, uses Shakespeare as a foil; Nietzsche, in the passage above, Homer.

[7] *Gewürm* suggests wormlike animals; *wimmelt* can mean swarm or crawl but is particularly associated with maggots—in a cheese, for example.

[8] *Unerquicklich.*

proach of some ill-constituted thing; that I have to smell the entrails of some ill-constituted soul!

How much one is able to endure: distress, want, bad weather,
sickness, toil, solitude. Fundamentally one can cope with everything else, born as one is to a subterranean life of struggle; one
emerges again and again into the light, one experiences again and
again one's golden hour of victory—and then one stands forth as
one was born, unbreakable, tensed, ready for new, even harder,
remoter things, like a bow that distress only serves to draw tauter.

But grant me from time to time—if there are divine goddesses
in the realm beyond good and evil—grant me the sight, but *one*
glance of something perfect, wholly achieved, happy, mighty, triumphant, something still capable of arousing fear! Of a man who justifies *man,* of a complementary and redeeming lucky hit on the part
of man for the sake of which one may still *believe in man!*

For this is how things are: the diminution and leveling of European man constitutes *our* greatest danger, for the sight of him
makes us weary.— We can see nothing today that wants to grow
greater, we suspect that things will continue to go down, down, to
become thinner, more good-natured, more prudent, more comfortable, more mediocre, more indifferent, more Chinese, more Christian—there is no doubt that man is getting "better" all the time.

Here precisely is what has become a fatality for Europe—together with the fear of man we have also lost our love of him, our
reverence for him, our hopes for him, even the will to him. The
sight of man now makes us weary—what is nihilism today if it is
not *that*?— We are weary *of man.*

13

But let us return: the problem of the *other* origin of the
"good," of the good as conceived by the man of *ressentiment,* demands its solution.

That lambs dislike great birds of prey does not seem strange:
only it gives no ground for reproaching these birds of prey for bearing off little lambs. And if the lambs say among themselves: "these
birds of prey are evil; and whoever is least like a bird of prey, but

rather its opposite, a lamb—would he not be good?" there is no reason to find fault with this institution of an ideal, except perhaps that the birds of prey might view it a little ironically and say: "*we* don't dislike them at all, these good little lambs; we even love them: nothing is more tasty than a tender lamb."

To demand of strength that it should *not* express itself as strength, that it should *not* be a desire to overcome, a desire to throw down, a desire to become master, a thirst for enemies and resistances and triumphs, is just as absurd as to demand of weakness that it should express itself as strength. A quantum of force is equivalent to a quantum of drive, will, effect—more, it is nothing other than precisely this very driving, willing, effecting, and only owing to the seduction of language (and of the fundamental errors of reason that are petrified in it) which conceives and misconceives all effects as conditioned by something that causes effects, by a "subject," can it appear otherwise. For just as the popular mind separates the lightning from its flash and takes the latter for an *action*, for the operation of a subject called lightning, so popular morality also separates strength from expressions of strength, as if there were a neutral substratum behind the strong man, which was *free* to express strength or not to do so. But there is no such substratum; there is no "being" behind doing, effecting, becoming; "the doer" is merely a fiction added to the deed—the deed is everything. The popular mind in fact doubles the deed; when it sees the lightning flash, it is the deed of a deed: it posits the same event first as cause and then a second time as its effect. Scientists do no better when they say "force moves," "force causes," and the like— all its coolness, its freedom from emotion notwithstanding, our entire science still lies under the misleading influence of language and has not disposed of that little changeling, the "subject" (the atom, for example, is such a changeling, as is the Kantian "thing-in-itself"); no wonder if the submerged, darkly glowering emotions of vengefulness and hatred exploit this belief for their own ends and in fact maintain no belief more ardently than the belief that *the strong man is free* to be weak and the bird of prey to be a lamb— for thus they gain the right to make the bird of prey *accountable* for being a bird of prey.

When the oppressed, downtrodden, outraged exhort one another with the vengeful cunning of impotence: "let us be different from the evil, namely good! And he is good who does not outrage, who harms nobody, who does not attack, who does not requite, who leaves revenge to God, who keeps himself hidden as we do, who avoids evil and desires little from life, like us, the patient, humble, and just"—this, listened to calmly and without previous bias, really amounts to no more than: "we weak ones are, after all, weak; it would be good if we did nothing *for which we are not strong enough*"; but this dry matter of fact, this prudence of the lowest order which even insects possess (posing as dead, when in great danger, so as not to do "too much"), has, thanks to the counterfeit and self-deception of impotence, clad itself in the ostentatious garb of the virtue of quiet, calm resignation, just as if the weakness of the weak—that is to say, their *essence,* their effects, their sole ineluctable, irremovable reality—were a voluntary achievement, willed, chosen, a *deed,* a *meritorious* act. This type of man *needs* to believe in a neutral independent "subject," prompted by an instinct for self-preservation and self-affirmation in which every lie is sanctified. The subject (or, to use a more popular expression, the *soul*) has perhaps been believed in hitherto more firmly than anything else on earth because it makes possible to the majority of mortals, the weak and oppressed of every kind, the sublime self-deception that interprets weakness as freedom, and their being thus-and-thus as a *merit.*

14

Would anyone like to take a look into the secret of how *ideals are made* on earth? Who has the courage?— Very well! Here is a point we can see through into this dark workshop. But wait a moment or two, Mr. Rash and Curious: your eyes must first get used to this false iridescent light.— All right! Now speak! What is going on down there? Say what you see, man of the most perilous kind of inquisitiveness—now I am the one who is listening.—

—"I see nothing, but I hear the more. There is a soft, wary, malignant muttering and whispering coming from all the corners and nooks. It seems to me one is lying; a saccharine sweetness clings to every sound. Weakness is being lied into something *meritorious,* no doubt of it—so it is just as you said"—

—Go on!

—"and impotence which does not requite into 'goodness of heart'; anxious lowliness into 'humility'; subjection to those one hates into 'obedience' (that is, to one of whom they say he commands this subjection—they call him God). The inoffensiveness of the weak man, even the cowardice of which he has so much, his lingering at the door, his being ineluctably compelled to wait, here acquire flattering names, such as 'patience,' and are even called virtue itself; his inability for revenge is called unwillingness to revenge, perhaps even forgiveness ('for *they* know not what they do—we alone know what *they* do!'). They also speak of 'loving one's enemies'— and sweat as they do so."

—Go on!

—"They are miserable, no doubt of it, all these mutterers and nook counterfeiters, although they crouch warmly together—but they tell me their misery is a sign of being chosen by God; one beats the dogs one likes best; perhaps this misery is also a preparation, a testing, a schooling, perhaps it is even more—something that will one day be made good and recompensed with interest, with huge payments of gold, no! of happiness. This they call 'bliss.' "

—Go on!

—"Now they give me to understand that they are not merely better than the mighty, the lords of the earth whose spittle they have to lick (*not* from fear, not at all from fear! but because God has commanded them to obey the authorities)[1]—that they are not merely better but are also 'better off,' or at least will be better off someday. But enough! enough! I can't take any more. Bad air! Bad air! This workshop where *ideals are manufactured*—it seems to me it stinks of so many lies."

—No! Wait a moment! You have said nothing yet of the masterpiece of these black magicians, who make whiteness, milk, and innocence of every blackness—haven't you noticed their perfection

---

[1] Allusion to Romans 13:1–2.

of refinement, their boldest, subtlest, most ingenious, most mendacious artistic stroke? Attend to them! These cellar rodents full of
vengefulness and hatred—what have they made of revenge and hatred? Have you heard these words uttered? If you trusted simply to
their words, would you suspect you were among men of *ressentiment?* . . .

     —"I understand; I'll open my ears again (oh! oh! oh! and
close my nose). Now I can really hear what they have been saying
all along: 'We good men—*we are the just'*—what they desire they
call, not retaliation, but 'the triumph of *justice';* what they hate is
not their enemy, no! they hate 'injustice,' they hate 'godlessness';
what they believe in and hope for is not the hope of revenge, the
intoxication of sweet revenge (—'sweeter than honey' Homer
called it), but the victory of God, of the *just* God, over the godless;
what there is left for them to love on earth is not their brothers in
hatred but their 'brothers in love,' as they put it, all the good and
just on earth."

     —And what do they call that which serves to console them
for all the suffering of life—their phantasmagoria of anticipated
future bliss?

     —"What? Do I hear aright? They call that 'the Last Judg-
ment,' the coming of *their* kingdom, of the 'Kingdom of God'—
meanwhile, however, they live 'in faith,' 'in love,' 'in hope.' "

     —Enough! Enough!

15

    In faith in what? In love of what? In hope of what?— These
weak people—some day or other *they* too intend to be the strong,
there is no doubt of that, some day *their* "kingdom" too shall come
—they term it "the kingdom of God," of course, as aforesaid: for
one is so very humble in all things! To experience *that* one needs to
live a long time, beyond death—indeed one needs eternal life, so as
to be eternally indemnified in the "kingdom of God" for this earthly
life "in faith, in love, in hope." Indemnified for what? How indemnified?

    Dante, I think, committed a crude blunder when, with a terror-inspiring ingenuity, he placed above the gateway of his hell the inscription "I too was created by eternal love"—at any rate, there would be more justification for placing above the gateway to the Christian Paradise and its "eternal bliss" the inscription "I too was created by eternal *hate*"—provided a truth may be placed above the gateway to a lie! For *what* is it that constitutes the bliss of this Paradise?

We might even guess, but it is better to have it expressly described for us by an authority not to be underestimated in such matters, Thomas Aquinas, the great teacher and saint. *"Beati in regno coelesti,"* he says, meek as a lamb, *"videbunt poenas damnatorum,* **ut beatitudo illis magis complaceat."** [1] Or if one would like to hear it in a stronger key, perhaps from the mouth of a triumphant Church Father, adjuring his Christians to avoid the cruel pleasures of the public games—but why? "For the faith offers us much more"—he says, *De Spectaculis,* chs. 29f.—*"something much stronger;* thanks to the Redemption, quite other joys are at our command; in place of athletes we have our martyrs; if we crave blood, we have the blood of Christ . . . But think of what awaits us on the day of his return, the day of his triumph!"—and then he goes on, the enraptured visionary.[2] *"At enim supersunt alia spectacula, ille ultimus et per-*

---

[1] The blessed in the kingdom of heaven will see the punishments of the damned, *in order that their bliss be more delightful for them.*—To be precise, what we find in *Summa Theologiae,* III, *Supplementum,* Q. 94, Art. 1, is this: "In order that the bliss of the saints may be more delightful for them and that they may render more copious thanks to God for it, it is given to them to see perfectly the punishment of the damned." *Ut beatitudo sanctorum eis magis complaceat, et de ea uberiores gratias Deo agant, datur eis ut poenam impiorum perfecte intueantur.*

[2] Nietzsche quotes Tertullian in the original Latin. This footnote offers, first, an English translation, and then some discussion.

"Yes, and there are other sights: that last day of judgment, with its everlasting issues; that day unlooked for by the nations, the theme of their derision, when the world hoary with age, and all its many products, shall be consumed in one great flame! How vast a spectacle then bursts upon the eye! *What there excites my admiration? what my derision? Which sight gives me joy? which rouses me to exultation?*—as I see so many illustrious monarchs, whose reception into the heavens was publicly announced, groaning now in the lowest darkness with great Jove himself, and those, too, who bore witness of their exultation; governors of provinces, too, who persecuted the Christian name, in fires more fierce than those with which in the days of their pride they raged against the followers of Christ. What world's wise men besides,

petuus judicii dies, ille nationibus insperatus, ille derisus, cum tanta saeculi vetustas et tot ejus nativitates uno igne haurientur. Quae tunc spectaculi latitudo! **Quid admirer! Quid rideam! Ubi gaudeam! Ubi exultem,** *spectans tot et tantos* **reges,** *qui in coelum recepti nuntiabantur, cum ipso Jove et ipsis suis testibus in imis tenebris congemescentes! Item praesides"* (the provincial governors) *"persecutores dominici nominis saevioribus quam ipsi flammis saevierunt insultantibus contra Christianos liquescentes! Quos praeterea sapientes illos philosophos coram discipulis suis una conflagrantibus erubescentes, quibus nihil ad deum pertinere suadebant, quibus animas aut nullas aut non in pristina corpora redituras affirmabant! Etiam poëtas non ad Rhadamanti nec ad Minois, sed ad inopinati Christi tribunal palpitantes! Tunc magis tragoedi audiendi, magis*

---

the very philosophers, in fact, who taught their followers that God had no concern in aught that is sublunary, and were wont to assure them that either they had no souls, or that they would never return to the bodies which at death they had left, now covered with shame before the poor deluded ones, as one fire consumes them! Poets also, trembling not before the judgment-seat of Rhadamanthus or Minos, but of the unexpected Christ! I shall have a better opportunity then of hearing the tragedians, louder-voiced in their own calamity; of viewing the play-actors, much more 'dissolute' [another translation has "much lither of limb"] in the dissolving flame; of looking upon the charioteer, all glowing in his chariot of fire; of beholding the wrestlers, not in their gymnasia, but tossing in the fiery billows; unless even then I shall not care to attend to such ministers of sin, in my eager wish rather to fix a gaze *insatiable* on those whose fury vented itself against the Lord. 'This,' I shall say, 'this is that carpenter's or hireling's son, that Sabbath-breaker, that Samaritan and devil-possessed! This is He whom you purchased from Judas! [*Quaestuaria* means prostitute, not carpenter: see Nietzsche's parenthesis above.] This is He whom you struck with reed and fist, whom you contemptuously spat upon, to whom you gave gall and vinegar to drink! This is He whom His disciples secretly stole away, that it might be said He had risen again, or the gardener abstracted, that his lettuces might come to no harm from the crowds of visitants!' What quaestor or priest in his munificence will bestow on you the favour of seeing and *exulting in such things as these?* And yet even now we in a measure have them *by faith* in the picturings of imagination. But what are the things which eye has not seen, ear has not heard, and which have not so much as dimly dawned upon the human heart? Whatever they are, they are nobler, I believe, than circus, and both theatres, and every race-course." [Translation by the Rev. S. Thelwall.] There are two standard translations of Tertullian's *De Spectaculis.* One is by the Rev. S. Thelwall in *The Ante-Nicene Fathers: Translations of The Writings of The Fathers down to A.D. 325,* edited by the Rev. Alexander Roberts, D.D. and James Donaldson, LL.D., in volume III: *Latin Christianity: Its Founder, Tertullian* (American Reprint of the Edinburgh Edition, Grand Rapids, Mich., Wm. B. Eerd-

scilicet vocales" (in better voice, yet worse screamers) *"in sua propria calamitate; tunc histriones cognoscendi, solutiores multo per ignem; tunc spectandus auriga in flammea rota totus rubens, tunc xystici contemplandi non in gymnasiis, sed in igne jaculati, nisi quod ne tunc quidem illos velim vivos, ut qui malim ad eos potius conspectum* **insatiabilem** *conferre, qui in dominum desaevierunt. 'Hic est ille,' dicam, 'fabri aut quaestuariae filius' "* (what follows, and especially this term for the mother of Jesus, which is found in the Talmud, shows that from here on Tertullian is referring to the Jews), " *'sabbati destructor, Samarites et daemonium habens. Hic est, quem a Juda redemistis, hic est ille arundine et colaphis diverberatus, sputamentis dedecoratus, felle et aceto potatus. Hic est, quem clam discentes subripuerunt, ut resurrexisse dicatur vel hor-*

---

mans Publishing Company, 1957). The other translation is by Rudolph Arbesmann, O.S.A., Ph.D., Fordham University, in *The Fathers of the Church: A New Translation,* in the volume entitled *Tertullian: Disciplinary, Moral and Ascetical Works* (New York, Fathers of the Church, Inc., 1959, Imprimatur Francis Cardinal Spellman).

In the former edition we are told in a footnote to the title that although there has been some dispute as to whether the work was written before or after Tertullian's "lapse" from orthodoxy to Montanism, "a work so colourless that doctors can disagree about even its shading, must be regarded as practically orthodox. Exaggerated expressions are but the characteristics of the author's genius. We find the like in all writers of strongly marked individuality. Neander dates this treatise *circa* A.D. 197." And in a footnote to the last sentence quoted by Nietzsche, which concludes the last chapter of the treatise, we read: "This concluding chapter, which Gibbon delights to censure, because its fervid rhetoric so fearfully depicts the punishments of Christ's enemies, 'appears to Dr. Neander to contain a beautiful specimen of lively faith and Christian confidence.' "

In the latter edition we are informed that *"De Spectaculis* is one of Tertullian's most interesting and original works" (p. 38). And chapter 30, which Nietzsche quotes almost in its entirety, omitting only the first four lines, is introduced by a footnote that begins (and it continues in the same vein): "Tertullian gives here a colorful description of the millennium, picturing the feverish expectation of an early return of Christ . . ."

It is noteworthy that the Protestant edition finds the work "so colourless," while the Roman Catholic edition considers it "colorful"—and neither of them evinces any sensitivity to what outraged Nietzsche or Gibbon.

Edward Gibbon's comments are found in Chapter XV of *The History of The Decline and Fall of the Roman Empire:* "The condemnation of the wisest and most virtuous of the Pagans, on account of their ignorance or disbelief of the divine truth, seems to offend the reason and the humanity of the present age. But the primitive church, whose faith was of a much firmer consistence, delivered over, without hesitation, to eternal torture the far

tulanus detraxit, ne lactucae suae frequentia commeantium laede-
rentur.' Ut talia spectes, **ut talibus exultes,** *quis tibi praetor aut*
consul aut guaestor aut sacerdos de sua liberalitate praestabit? Et
tamen haec jam habemus quodammodo **per fidem** *spiritu imaginante*
repraesentata. Ceterum qualia illa sunt, quae nec oculus vidit nec
auris audivit nec in cor hominis ascenderunt?" (1 Cor. 2,9.) *"Credo*
circo et utraque cavea" (first and fourth rank or, according to others, the comic and tragic stage) *"et omni stadio gratiora."* —**Per**
fidem: thus is it written.

16

Let us conclude. The two *opposing* values "good and bad,"
"good and evil" have been engaged in a fearful struggle on earth
for thousands of years; and though the latter value has certainly
been on top for a long time, there are still places where the struggle
is as yet undecided. One might even say that it has risen ever higher
and thus become more and more profound and spiritual: so that
today there is perhaps no more decisive mark of a *"higher nature,"*
a more spiritual nature, than that of being divided in this sense and
a genuine battleground of these opposed values.[1]

The symbol of this struggle, inscribed in letters legible across
all human history, is "Rome against Judea, Judea against Rome":
—there has hitherto been no greater event than *this* struggle, *this*
question, *this* deadly contradiction. Rome felt the Jew to be something like anti-nature itself, its antipodal monstrosity as it were: in

---

greater part of the human species. . . . These rigid sentiments, which had
been unknown to the ancient world, appear to have infused a spirit of bitterness into a system of love and harmony. . . . The Christians, who, in this
world, found themselves oppressed by the power of the Pagans, were sometimes seduced by resentment and spiritual pride to delight in the prospect of
their future triumph. 'You are fond of spectacles,' exclaims the stern Tertullian; 'except the greatest of all spectacles, the last and eternal judgment of the
universe. How shall I admire, how laugh . . .' "

[1] This remark which recalls *Beyond Good and Evil,* section 200, is entirely
in keeping with the way in which the contrast of master and slave morality is
introduced in *Beyond Good and Evil,* section 260; and it ought not to be
overlooked. It sheds a good deal of light not only on this contrast but also
on Nietzsche's *amor fati,* his love of fate. Those who ignore all this material
are bound completely to misunderstand Nietzsche's moral philosophy.

Rome the Jew stood *"convicted* of hatred for the whole human race"; and rightly, provided one has a right to link the salvation and future of the human race with the unconditional dominance of aristocratic values, Roman values.

How, on the other hand, did the Jews feel about Rome? A thousand signs tell us; but it suffices to recall the Apocalypse of John, the most wanton of all literary outbursts that vengefulness has on its conscience. (One should not underestimate the profound consistency of the Christian instinct when it signed this book of hate with the name of the disciple of love, the same disciple to whom it attributed that amorous-enthusiastic Gospel: there is a piece of truth in this, however much literary counterfeiting might have been required to produce it.) For the Romans were the strong and noble, and nobody stronger and nobler has yet existed on earth or even been dreamed of: every remnant of them, every inscription gives delight, if only one divines *what* it was that was there at work. The Jews, on the contrary, were the priestly nation of *ressentiment par excellence,* in whom there dwelt an unequaled popular-moral genius: one only has to compare similarly gifted nations —the Chinese or the Germans, for instance—with the Jews, to sense which is of the first and which of the fifth rank.[2]

Which of them has won *for the present,* Rome or Judea? But there can be no doubt: consider to whom one bows down in Rome itself today, as if they were the epitome of all the highest values— and not only in Rome but over almost half the earth, everywhere that man has become tame or desires to become tame: *three Jews,* as is known, and *one Jewess* (Jesus of Nazareth, the fisherman Peter, the rug weaver Paul, and the mother of the aforementioned Jesus, named Mary). This is very remarkable: Rome has been defeated beyond all doubt.

There was, to be sure, in the Renaissance an uncanny and glittering reawakening of the classical ideal, of the noble mode of evaluating all things; Rome itself, oppressed by the new superimposed Judaized Rome that presented the aspect of an ecumenical

---

[2] Having said things that can easily be misconstrued as grist to the mill of the German anti-Semites, Nietzsche goes out of his way, as usual, to express his admiration for the Jews and his disdain for the Germans.

synagogue and was called the "church," stirred like one awakened from seeming death: but Judea immediately triumphed again, thanks to that thoroughly plebeian (German and English) *ressentiment* movement called the Reformation, and to that which was bound to arise from it, the restoration of the church—the restoration too of the ancient sepulchral repose of classical Rome.

With the French Revolution, Judea once again triumphed over the classical ideal, and this time in an even more profound and decisive sense: the last political *noblesse* in Europe, that of the *French* seventeenth and eighteenth century, collapsed beneath the popular instincts of *ressentiment*—greater rejoicing, more uproarious enthusiasm had never been heard on earth! To be sure, in the midst of it there occurred the most tremendous, the most unexpected thing: the ideal of antiquity itself stepped *incarnate* and in unheard-of splendor before the eyes and conscience of mankind—and once again, in opposition to the mendacious slogan of *ressentiment,* "supreme rights of the majority," in opposition to the will to the lowering, the abasement, the leveling and the decline and twilight of mankind, there sounded stronger, simpler, and more insistently than ever the terrible and rapturous counterslogan "supreme rights of the few"! Like a last signpost to the *other* path, Napoleon appeared, the most isolated and late-born man there has even been, and in him the problem of the *noble ideal as such* made flesh—one might well ponder *what* kind of problem it is: Napoleon, this synthesis of the *inhuman* and *superhuman*.

17

Was that the end of it? Had that greatest of all conflicts of ideals been placed *ad acta*[1] for all time? Or only adjourned, indefinitely adjourned?

Must the ancient fire not some day flare up much more terribly, after much longer preparation? More: must one not desire it with all one's might? even will it? even promote it?

Whoever begins at this point, like my readers, to reflect and

---

[1] Disposed of.

pursue his train of thought will not soon come to the end of it—
reason enough for me to come to an end, assuming it has long
since been abundantly clear what my *aim* is, what the aim of that
dangerous slogan is that is inscribed at the head of my last book
Beyond Good and Evil.— At least this does *not* mean "Beyond
Good and Bad."———

Note.[2] I take the opportunity provided by this treatise to express
publicly and formally a desire I have previously voiced only in occasional conversation with scholars; namely, that some philosophical faculty might advance *historical* studies *of morality* through a
series of academic prize-essays—perhaps this present book will
serve to provide a powerful impetus in this direction. In case this
idea should be implemented, I suggest the following question: it
deserves the attention of philologists and historians as well as that
of professional philosophers:

*"What light does linguistics, and especially the study of ety-
mology, throw on the history of the evolution of moral concepts?"*

On the other hand, it is equally necessary to engage the interest of physiologists and doctors in these problems (of the *value* of
existing evaluations); it may be left to academic philosophers to
act as advocates and mediators in this matter too, after they have
on the whole succeeded in the past in transforming the originally so
reserved and mistrustful relations between philosophy, physiology,
and medicine into the most amicable and fruitful exchange. Indeed,
every table of values, every "thou shalt" known to history or ethnology, requires first a *physiological* investigation and interpretation, rather than a psychological one; and every one of them needs
a critique on the part of medical science. The question: what is the
value of this or that table of values and "morals"? should be
viewed from the most divers perspectives; for the problem "value
for what?" cannot be examined too subtly. Something, for example, that possessed obvious value in relation to the longest possible
survival of a race (or to the enhancement of its power of adapta-

---

[2] *Anmerkung.*

tion to a particular climate or to the preservation of the greatest number) would by no means possess the same value if it were a question, for instance, of producing a stronger type. The well-being of the majority and the well-being of the few are opposite viewpoints of value: to consider the former *a priori* of higher value may be left to the naïveté of English biologists.— *All* the sciences have from now on to prepare the way for the future task of the philosophers: this task understood as the solution of the *problem of value*, the determination of the *order of rank among values*.

Second Essay

"Guilt," "Bad Conscience,"[1]
and the Like

1

To breed an animal *with the right to make promises*—is not this
the paradoxical task that nature has set itself in the case of man? is
it not the real problem regarding man?

That this problem has been solved to a large extent must seem
all the more remarkable to anyone who appreciates the strength of
the opposing force, that of *forgetfulness*. Forgetting is no mere *vis
inertiae*[2] as the superficial imagine; it is rather an active and in the
strictest sense positive faculty of repression,[3] that is responsible for
the fact that what we experience and absorb enters our consciousness as little while we are digesting it (one might call the process
"inpsychation") as does the thousandfold process, involved in physical nourishment—so-called "incorporation." To close the doors and
windows of consciousness for a time; to remain undisturbed by the
noise and struggle of our underworld of utility organs working with
and against one another; a little quietness, a little *tabula rasa*[4] of

---

[1] *Schlechtes Gewissen* is no technical term but simply the common German
equivalent of "bad conscience." Danto's translation "bad consciousness"
(*Nietzsche as Philosopher*, New York, Macmillan, 1965, pp. 164 and 180) is
simply wrong: *Gewissen*, like conscience, and unlike the French *conscience*,
cannot mean consciousness.

There are many mistranslations in Danto's *Nietzsche*. Another one,
though relatively unimportant, is of some interest and relevant to the *Genealogy*: *Schadenfreude*—a German word for which there is no English equivalent—is not quite "the wicked pleasure in the beholding of suffering"
(p. 181) or "in the sheer spectacle of suffering: in fights, executions, . . .
bullbaiting, cockfights, and the like" (p. 174). In such contexts the word is
utterly out of place: it signifies the petty, mischievous delight felt in the discomfiture of another human being.

[2] *Inertia.*

[3] *Positives Hemmungsvermögen.*

[4] Clean slate.

the consciousness, to make room for new things, above all for the nobler functions and functionaries, for regulation, foresight, pre-meditation (for our organism is an oligarchy)—that is the purpose of active forgetfulness, which is like a doorkeeper, a preserver of psychic order, repose, and etiquette: so that it will be immediately obvious how there could be no happiness, no cheerfulness, no hope, no pride, no *present,* without forgetfulness. The man in whom this apparatus of repression is damaged and ceases to function properly may be compared (and more than merely compared) with a dyspeptic—he cannot "have done" with anything.

Now this animal which needs to be forgetful, in which forget-ting represents a force, a form of *robust* health, has bred in itself an opposing faculty, a memory, with the aid of which forgetfulness is abrogated in certain cases—namely in those cases where promises are made. This involves no mere passive inability to rid oneself of an impression, no mere indigestion through a once-pledged word with which one cannot "have done," but an active *desire* not to rid oneself, a desire for the continuance of something desired once, a real *memory of the will*: so that between the original "I will," "I shall do this" and the actual discharge of the will, its *act,* a world of strange new things, circumstances, even acts of will may be inter-posed without breaking this long chain of will. But how many things this presupposes! To ordain the future in advance in this way, man must first have learned to distinguish necessary events from chance ones, to think causally, to see and anticipate distant eventualities as if they belonged to the present, to decide with cer-tainty what is the goal and what the means to it, and in general be able to calculate and compute. Man himself must first of all have become *calculable, regular, necessary,* even in his own image of himself, if he is to be able to stand security for *his own future,* which is what one who promises does!

2

This precisely is the long story of how *responsibility* origi-nated. The task of breeding an animal with the right to make prom-ises evidently embraces and presupposes as a preparatory task that one first *makes* men to a certain degree necessary, uniform, like among like, regular, and consequently calculable. The tremendous labor of that which I have called "morality of mores" (*Dawn,* sections 9, 14, 16)[1]—the labor performed by man upon himself during the greater part of the existence of the human race, his entire *prehistoric* labor, finds in this its meaning, its great justification, notwithstanding the severity, tyranny, stupidity, and idiocy involved in it: with the aid of the morality of mores and the social straitjacket, man was actually *made* calculable.

. If we place ourselves at the end of this tremendous process, where the tree at last brings forth fruit, where society and the morality of custom at last reveal *what* they have simply been the means to: then we discover that the ripest fruit is the *sovereign individual,* like only to himself, liberated again from morality of custom, autonomous and supramoral (for "autonomous" and "moral" are mutually exclusive),[2] in short, the man who has his own independent, protracted will and the *right to make promises*—and in him a proud consciousness, quivering in every muscle, of *what* has at length been achieved and become flesh in him, a consciousness of his own power and freedom, a sensation of mankind come to completion. This emancipated individual, with the actual *right* to make promises, this master of a *free* will, this sovereign man—how should he not be aware of his superiority over all those who lack the right to make promises and stand as their own guarantors, of how much trust, how much fear, how much reverence he arouses—he *"deserves"* all three—and of how this mastery over

---

[1] See also *Human, All-Too-Human,* section 96; *Mixed Opinions and Maxims,* section 89; and *The Dawn,* section 18, all of which are included in the present volume. *Dawn,* section 16, is included in *The Portable Nietzsche,* p. 76. The German phrase is *die Sittlichkeit der Sitte,* the morality of mores.

[2] The parenthetical statement is the contrary of Kant's view. When it was written, it must have struck most readers as paradoxical, but in the twentieth century it is apt to seem *less* paradoxical than Kant's view. *The Lonely Crowd* (by David Riesman, with Nathan Glazer and Reuel Denney; New Haven, Conn.: Yale University Press, 1950) has popularized a Nietzschean, non-Kantian conception of the autonomous individual, who is contrasted with the tradition-directed (Nietzsche's morality of mores), the inner-directed (Kant, for example), and the other-directed (Nietzsche's "last man").

himself also necessarily gives him mastery over circumstances, over nature, and over all more short-willed and unreliable creatures? The "free" man, the possessor of a protracted and unbreakable will, also possesses his *measure of value*: looking out upon others from himself, he honors or he despises; and just as he is bound to honor his peers, the strong and reliable (those with the *right* to make promises)—that is, all those who promise like sovereigns, reluctantly, rarely, slowly, who are chary of trusting, whose trust is a mark of *distinction*, who give their word as something that can be relied on because they know themselves strong enough to maintain it in the face of accidents, even "in the face of fate"—he is bound to reserve a kick for the feeble windbags who promise without the right to do so, and a rod for the liar who breaks his word even at the moment he utters it. The proud awareness of the extraordinary privilege of *responsibility*, the consciousness of this rare freedom, this power over oneself and over fate, has in his case penetrated to the profoundest depths and become instinct, the dominating instinct. What will he call this dominating instinct, supposing he feels the need to give it a name? The answer is beyond doubt: this sovereign man calls it his *conscience*.

3

His conscience?— It is easy to guess that the concept of "conscience" that we here encounter in its highest, almost astonishing, manifestation, has a long history and variety of forms behind it. To possess the right to stand security for oneself and to do so with pride, thus to possess also the *right to affirm oneself*—this, as has been said, is a ripe fruit, but also a *late* fruit: how long must this fruit have hung on the tree, unripe and sour! And for a much longer time nothing whatever was to be seen of any such fruit: no one could have promised its appearance, although everything in the tree was preparing for and growing toward it!

"How can one create a memory for the human animal? How can one impress something upon this partly obtuse, partly flighty mind, attuned only to the passing moment, in such a way that it will stay there?"

One can well believe that the answers and methods for solving this primeval problem were not precisely gentle; perhaps indeed there was nothing more fearful and uncanny in the whole prehistory of man than his *mnemotechnics*. "If something is to stay in the memory it must be burned in: only that which never ceases to *hurt* stays in the memory"—this is a main clause of the oldest (unhappily also the most enduring) psychology on earth. One might even say that wherever on earth solemnity, seriousness, mystery, and gloomy coloring still distinguish the life of man and a people, something of the terror that formerly attended all promises, pledges, and vows on earth is *still effective:* the past, the longest, deepest and sternest past, breathes upon us and rises up in us whenever we become "serious." Man could never do without blood, torture, and sacrifices when he felt the need to create a memory for himself; the most dreadful sacrifices and pledges (sacrifices of the first-born among them), the most repulsive mutilations (castration, for example), the cruelest rites of all the religious cults (and all religions are at the deepest level systems of cruelties)—all this has its origin in the instinct that realized that pain is the most powerful aid to mnemonics.

In a certain sense, the whole of asceticism belongs here: a few ideas are to be rendered inextinguishable, ever-present, unforgettable, "fixed," with the aim of hypnotising the entire nervous and intellectual system with these "fixed ideas"—and ascetic procedures and modes of life are means of freeing these ideas from the competition of all other ideas, so as to make them "unforgettable." The worse man's memory has been, the more fearful has been the appearance of his customs; the severity of the penal code provides an especially significant measure of the degree of effort needed to overcome forgetfulness and to impose a few primitive demands of social existence as *present realities* upon these slaves of momentary affect and desire.

We Germans certainly do not regard ourselves as a particularly cruel and hardhearted people, still less as a particularly frivolous one, living only for the day; but one has only to look at our former codes of punishments to understand what effort it costs on this earth to breed a "nation of thinkers" (which is to say, *the* nation in Europe in which one still finds today the maximum of trust, seriousness, lack of taste, and matter-of-factness—and with these qualities one has the right to breed every kind of European mandarin). These Germans have employed fearful means to acquire a memory, so as to master their basic mob-instinct and its brutal coarseness. Consider the old German punishments; for example, stoning (the sagas already have millstones drop on the head of the guilty), breaking on the wheel (the most characteristic invention and speciality of the German genius in the realm of punishment!), piercing with stakes, tearing apart or trampling by horses ("quartering"), boiling of the criminal in oil or wine (still employed in the fourteenth and fifteenth centuries), the popular flaying alive ("cutting straps"), cutting flesh from the chest, and also the practice of smearing the wrongdoer with honey and leaving him in the blazing sun for the flies. With the aid of such images and procedures one finally remembers five or six "I will not's," in regard to which one had given one's *promise* so as to participate in the advantages of society—and it was indeed with the aid of this kind of memory that one at last came "to reason"! Ah, reason, seriousness, mastery over the affects, the whole somber thing called reflection, all these prerogatives and showpieces of man: how dearly they have been bought! how much blood and cruelty lie at the bottom of all "good things"!

4

But how did that other "somber thing," the consciousness of guilt, the "bad conscience," come into the world?— And at this point we return to the genealogists of morals. To say it again—or haven't I said it yet?—they are worthless. A brief span of experience that is merely one's own, merely modern; no knowledge or will to knowledge of the past; even less of historical instinct, of that "second sight" needed here above all—and yet they undertake history of morality: it stands to reason that their results stay at a more than respectful distance from the truth. Have these genealogists of morals had even the remotest suspicion that, for example, the major moral concept *Schuld* [guilt] has its origin in the very material concept

Schulden [debts]?[1] Or that punishment, as requital, evolved quite independently of any presupposition concerning freedom or non-freedom of the will?—to such an extent, indeed, that a *high* degree of humanity had to be attained before the animal "man" began even to make the much more primitive distinctions between "intentional," "negligent," "accidental," "accountable," and their opposites and to take them into account when determining punishments. The idea, now so obvious, apparently so natural, even unavoidable, that had to serve as the explanation of how the sense of justice ever appeared on earth—"the criminal deserves punishment *because* he could have acted differently"—is in fact an extremely late and subtle form of human judgment and inference: whoever transposes it to the beginning is guilty of a crude misunderstanding of the psychology of more primitive mankind. Throughout the greater part of human history punishment was *not* imposed *because* one held the wrong-doer responsible for his deed, thus *not* on the presupposition that only the guilty one should be punished: rather, as parents still punish their children, from anger at some harm or injury, vented on the one who caused it—but this anger is held in check and modified by the idea that every injury has its *equivalent* and can actually be paid back, even if only through the *pain* of the culprit. And whence did this primeval, deeply rooted, perhaps by now ineradicable idea draw its power—this idea of an equivalence between injury and pain? I have already divulged it: in the contractual relationship between *creditor* and *debtor,* which is as old as the idea of "legal subjects" and in turn points back to the fundamental forms of buying, selling, barter, trade, and traffic.

---

[1] The German equivalent of "guilt" is *Schuld;* and the German for "debt(s)" is *Schuld(en)*. "Innocent" is *unschuldig;* "debtor" is *Schuldner;* and so forth. This obviously poses problems for an English translation of this essay; but once the point has been clearly stated, no misunderstandings need result. Nietzsche's claims obviously do not *depend* on the double meaning of a German word; nor are they weakened by the fact that in English there are two different words, one derived from an Anglo-Saxon root, the other from Latin.

5

When we contemplate these contractual relationships, to be sure, we feel considerable suspicion and repugnance toward those men of the past who created or permitted them. This was to be expected from what we have previously noted. It was here that *promises* were made; it was here that a memory had to be *made* for those who promised; it is here, one suspects, that we shall find a great deal of severity, cruelty, and pain. To inspire trust in his promise to repay, to provide a guarantee of the seriousness and sanctity of his promise, to impress repayment as a duty, an obligation upon his own conscience, the debtor made a contract with the creditor and pledged that if he should fail to repay he would substitute something else that he "possessed," something he had control over; for example, his body, his wife, his freedom, or even his life (or, given certain religious presuppositions, even his bliss after death, the salvation of his soul, ultimately his peace in the grave: thus it was in Egypt, where the debtor's corpse found no peace from the creditor even in the grave—and among the Egyptians such peace meant a great deal). Above all, however, the creditor could inflict every kind of indignity and torture upon the body of the debtor; for example, cut from it as much as seemed commensurate with the size of the debt—and everywhere and from early times one had exact evaluations, *legal* evaluations, of the individual limbs and parts of the body from this point of view, some of them going into horrible and minute detail. I consider it as an advance, as evidence of a freer, more generous, *more Roman* conception of law when the Twelve Tables of Rome decreed it a matter of indifference how much or how little the creditor cut off in such cases: *"si plus minusve secuerunt, ne fraude esto."* [1]

Let us be clear as to the logic of this form of compensation: it is strange enough. An equivalence is provided by the creditor's receiving, in place of a literal compensation for an injury (thus in place of money, land, possessions of any kind), a recompense in the

---

[1] If they have secured more or less, let that be no crime.

form of a kind of *pleasure*—the pleasure of being allowed to vent his power freely upon one who is powerless, the voluptuous pleasure *"de faire le mal pour le plaisir de le faire,"* [2] the enjoyment of violation. This enjoyment will be the greater the lower the creditor stands in the social order, and can easily appear to him as a most delicious morsel, indeed as a foretaste of higher rank. In "punishing" the debtor, the creditor participates in a *right of the masters:* at last he, too, may experience for once the exalted sensation of being allowed to despise and mistreat someone as "beneath him"— or at least, if the actual power and administration of punishment has already passed to the "authorities," to *see* him despised and mistreated. The compensation, then, consists in a warrant for and title to cruelty.——

6

It was in *this* sphere then, the sphere of legal obligations, that the moral conceptual world of "guilt," "conscience," "duty," "sacredness of duty" had its origin: its beginnings were, like the beginnings of everything great on earth, soaked in blood thoroughly and for a long time. And might one not add that, fundamentally, this world has never since lost a certain odor of blood and torture? (Not even in good old Kant: the categorical imperative smells of cruelty.) It was here, too, that that uncanny intertwining of the ideas "guilt and suffering" was first effected—and by now they may well be inseparable. To ask it again: to what extent can suffering balance debts or guilt? [3] To the extent that to *make* suffer was in the highest degree pleasurable, to the extent that the injured party exchanged for the loss he had sustained, including the displeasure caused by the loss, an extraordinary counterbalancing pleasure: that of *making* suffer—a genuine *festival,* something which, as aforesaid, was prized the more highly the more violently it contrasted with the rank and social standing of the creditor. This is offered only as a conjecture; for the depths of such subterranean things are difficult to fathom, besides being painful; and whoever clumsily interposes

---

[2] Of doing evil for the pleasure of doing it.

[3] "Debts or guilt": *"Schulden."*

the concept of "revenge" does not enhance his insight into the matter but further veils and darkens it (—for revenge merely leads us back to the same problem: "how can making suffer constitute a compensation?").

It seems to me that the delicacy and even more the tartuffery of tame domestic animals (which is to say modern men, which is to say us) resists a really vivid comprehension of the degree to which *cruelty* constituted the great festival pleasure of more primitive men and was indeed an ingredient of almost every one of their pleasures; and how naïvely, how innocently their thirst for cruelty manifested itself, how, as a matter of principle, they posited "disinterested malice" (or, in Spinoza's words, *sympathia malevolens*) as a *normal* quality of man—and thus as something to which the conscience cordially *says Yes!* A more profound eye might perceive enough of this oldest and most fundamental festival pleasure of man even in our time; in *Beyond Good and Evil,* section 229[4] (and earlier in *The Dawn,* sections 18, 77, 113)[5] I pointed cautiously to the ever-increasing spiritualization and "deification" of cruelty which permeates the entire history of higher culture (and in a significant sense actually constitutes it). In any event, it is not long since princely weddings and public festivals of the more magnificent kind were unthinkable without executions, torturings, or perhaps an auto-da-fé, and no noble household was without creatures upon whom one could heedlessly vent one's malice and cruel jokes. (Consider, for instance, Don Quixote at the court of the Duchess. Today we read *Don Quixote* with a bitter taste in our mouths, almost with a feeling of torment, and would thus seem very strange and incomprehensible to its author and his contemporaries: they read it with the clearest conscience in the world as the most cheerful of books, they laughed themselves almost to death over

---

[4] Nietzsche, as usual, furnishes a page reference to the first edition—in this instance, pp. 117ff., which would take us to the middle of section 194 and the following section(s); and German editors, down to Karl Schlechta, give the equivalent page reference. But 117 is plainly a misprint for 177, which takes us to section 229—beyond a doubt, the passage Nietzsche means.

[5] Section 18 is included in the present volume; section 113 is quoted and analyzed in Kaufmann's *Nietzsche,* Chapter 6, section II. Both repay reading in connection with the passage above, to avoid misunderstanding.

it). To see others suffer does one good, to make others suffer even more: this is a hard saying but an ancient, mighty, human, all-too-human principle to which even the apes might subscribe; for it has been said that in devising bizarre cruelties they anticipate man and are, as it were, his "prelude." Without cruelty there is no festival: thus the longest and most ancient part of human history teaches— and in punishment there is so much that is *festive!*—

7

With this idea, by the way, I am by no means concerned to furnish our pessimists with more grist for their discordant and creaking mills of life-satiety. On the contrary, let me declare expressly that in the days when mankind was not yet ashamed of its cruelty, life on earth was more cheerful than it is now that pessimists exist. The darkening of the sky above mankind has deepened in step with the increase in man's feeling of shame *at man.* The weary pessimistic glance, mistrust of the riddle of life, the icy No of disgust with life—these do not characterize the most *evil* epochs of the human race: rather do they first step into the light of day as the swamp weeds they are when the swamp to which they belong comes into being—I mean the morbid softening and moralization through which the animal "man" finally learns to be ashamed of all his instincts. On his way to becoming an "angel" (to employ no uglier word) man has evolved that queasy stomach and coated tongue through which not only the joy and innocence of the animal but life itself has become repugnant to him—so that he sometimes holds his nose in his own presence and, with Pope Innocent the Third, disapprovingly catalogues his own repellent aspects ("impure begetting, disgusting means of nutrition in his mother's womb, baseness of the matter out of which man evolves, hideous stink, secretion of saliva, urine, and filth").

Today, when suffering is always brought forward as the principal argument *against* existence, as the worst question mark, one does well to recall the ages in which the opposite opinion prevailed because men were unwilling to refrain from *making* suffer and saw in it an enchantment of the first order, a genuine seduction *to* life.

Perhaps in those days—the delicate may be comforted by this thought—pain did not hurt as much as it does now; at least that is the conclusion a doctor may arrive at who has treated Negroes (taken as representatives of prehistoric man—) for severe internal inflammations that would drive even the best constituted European to distraction—in the case of Negroes they do *not* do so. (The curve of human susceptibility to pain seems in fact to take an extraordinary and almost sudden drop as soon as one has passed the upper ten thousand or ten million of the top stratum of culture; and for my own part, I have no doubt that the combined suffering of all the animals ever subjected to the knife for scientific ends is utterly negligible compared with *one* painful night of a single hysterical bluestocking.) Perhaps the possibility may even be allowed that this joy in cruelty does not really have to have died out: if pain hurts more today, it simply requires a certain sublimation and subtilization, that is to say it has to appear translated into the imaginative and psychical and adorned with such innocent names that even the tenderest and most hypocritical conscience is not suspicious of them ("tragic pity" is one such name; *"les nostalgies de la croix"* [6] is another).

What really arouses indignation against suffering is not suffering as such but the senselessness of suffering: but neither for the Christian, who has interpreted a whole mysterious machinery of salvation into suffering, nor for the naïve man of more ancient times, who understood all suffering in relation to the spectator of it or the causer of it, was there any such thing as *senseless* suffering. So as to abolish hidden, undetected, unwitnessed suffering from the world and honestly to deny it, one was in the past virtually compelled to invent gods and genii of all the heights and depths, in short something that roams even in secret, hidden places, sees even in the dark, and will not easily let an interesting painful spectacle pass unnoticed. For it was with the aid of such inventions that life then knew how to work the trick which it has always known how to work, that of justifying itself, of justifying its "evil." Nowadays it might require other auxiliary inventions (for example, life as a

---

[6] The nostalgia of the cross.

riddle, life as an epistemological problem). "Every evil the sight of which edifies a god is justified": thus spoke the primitive logic of feeling—and was it, indeed, only primitive? The gods conceived of as the friends of *cruel* spectacles—oh how profoundly this ancient idea still permeates our European humanity! Merely consult Calvin and Luther. It is certain, at any rate, that the *Greeks* still knew of no tastier spice to offer their gods to season their happiness than the pleasures of cruelty. With what eyes do you think Homer made his gods look down upon the destinies of men? What was at bottom the ultimate meaning of Trojan Wars and other such tragic terrors? There can be no doubt whatever: they were intended as *festival plays* for the gods; and, insofar as the poet is in these matters of a more "godlike" disposition than other men, no doubt also as festival plays for the poets.

It was in the same way that the moral philosophers of Greece later imagined the eyes of God looking down upon the moral struggle, upon the heroism and self-torture of the virtuous: the "Herakles of duty" was on a stage and knew himself to be; virtue without a witness was something unthinkable for this nation of actors. Surely, that philosophers' invention, so bold and so fateful, which was then first devised for Europe, the invention of "free will," of the absolute spontaneity of man in good and in evil, was devised above all to furnish a right to the idea that the interest of the gods in man, in human virtue, *could never be exhausted*. There must never be any lack of real novelty, of really unprecedented tensions, complications, and catastrophies on the stage of the earth: the course of a completely deterministic world would have been predictable for the gods and they would have quickly grown weary of it—reason enough for those *friends of the gods,* the philosophers, not to inflict such a deterministic world on their gods! The entire mankind of antiquity is full of tender regard for "the spectator," as an essentially public, essentially visible world which cannot imagine happiness apart from spectacles and festivals.— And, as aforesaid, even in great *punishment* there is so much that is festive!

8

To return to our investigation: the feeling of guilt, of personal obligation, had its origin, as we saw, in the oldest and most primitive personal relationship, that between buyer and seller, creditor and debtor: it was here that one person first encountered another person, that one person first *measured himself* against another. No grade of civilization, however low, has yet been discovered in which something of this relationship has not been noticeable. Setting prices, determining values, contriving equivalences, exchanging—these preoccupied the earliest thinking of man to so great an extent that in a certain sense they constitute thinking *as such*: here it was that the oldest kind of astuteness developed; here likewise, we may suppose, did human pride, the feeling of superiority in relation to other animals, have its first beginnings. Perhaps our word "man" (*manas*) still expresses something of precisely *this* feeling of self-satisfaction: man designated himself as the creature that measures values, evaluates and measures, as the "valuating animal as such."

Buying and selling, together with their psychological appurtenances, are older even than the beginnings of any kind of social forms of organization and alliances: it was rather out of the most rudimentary form of personal legal rights that the budding sense of exchange, contract, guilt, right, obligation, settlement, first *transferred* itself to the coarsest and most elementary social complexes (in their relations with other similar complexes), together with the custom of comparing, measuring, and calculating power against power. The eye was now focused on this perspective; and with that blunt consistency characteristic of the thinking of primitive mankind, which is hard to set in motion but then proceeds inexorably in the same direction, one forthwith arrived at the great generalization, "everything has its price; *all* things can be paid for"—the oldest and naïvest moral canon of *justice,* the beginning of all "good-naturedness," all "fairness," all "good will," all "objectivity" on earth. Justice on this elementary level is the good will among parties of approximately equal power to come to terms with

one another, to reach an "understanding" by means of a settlement
—and to *compel* parties of lesser power to reach a settlement
among themselves.—

9

Still retaining the criteria of prehistory (this prehistory is in
any case present in all ages or may always reappear)[1]: the community, too, stands to its members in that same vital basic relation,
that of the creditor to his debtors. One lives in a community, one
enjoys the advantages of a communality (oh what advantages! we
sometimes underrate them today), one dwells protected, cared for,
in peace and trustfulness, without fear of certain injuries and hostile acts to which the man *outside,* the "man without peace," is
exposed—a German will understand the original connotations of
Elend [2]—since one has bound and pledged oneself to the community precisely with a view to injuries and hostile acts. What will
happen *if this pledge is broken?* The community, the disappointed
creditor, will get what repayment it can, one may depend on that.
The direct harm caused by the culprit is here a minor matter; quite
apart from this, the lawbreaker is above all a "breaker," a breaker
of his contract and his word *with the whole* in respect to all the
benefits and comforts of communal life of which he has hitherto
had a share. The lawbreaker is a debtor who has not merely failed
to make good the advantages and advance payments bestowed
upon him but has actually attacked his creditor: therefore he is not
only deprived henceforth of all these advantages and benefits, as is
fair—he is also reminded *what these benefits are really worth.* The
wrath of the disappointed creditor, the community, throws him
back again into the savage and outlaw state against which he has
hitherto been protected: it thrusts him away—and now every kind
of hostility may be vented upon him. "Punishment" at this level of
civilization is simply a copy, a *mimus,* of the normal attitude toward a hated, disarmed, prostrated enemy, who has lost not only
every right and protection, but all hope of quarter as well; it is thus

---

[1] A prophetic parenthesis.
[2] Misery. Originally, exile.

the rights of war and the victory celebration of the *vae victis!*[3] in all their mercilessness and cruelty—which explains why it is that war itself (including the warlike sacrificial cult) has provided all the *forms* that punishment has assumed throughout history.

10

As its power increases, a community ceases to take the individual's transgressions so seriously, because they can no longer be considered as dangerous and destructive to the whole as they were formerly: the malefactor is no longer "set beyond the pale of peace" and thrust out; universal anger may not be vented upon him as unrestrainedly as before—on the contrary, the whole from now on carefully defends the malefactor against this anger, especially that of those he has directly harmed, and takes him under its protection. A compromise with the anger of those directly injured by the criminal; an effort to localize the affair and to prevent it from causing any further, let alone a general, disturbance; attempts to discover equivalents and to settle the whole matter (*compositio*); above all, the increasingly definite will to treat every crime as in some sense *dischargeable,* and thus at least to a certain extent to *isolate* the criminal and his deed from one another—these traits become more and more clearly visible as the penal law evolves. As the power and self-confidence of a community increase, the penal law always becomes more moderate; every weakening or imperiling of the former brings with it a restoration of the harsher forms of the latter. The "creditor" always becomes more humane to the extent that he has grown richer; finally, how much injury he can endure without suffering from it becomes the actual *measure* of his wealth. It is not unthinkable that a society might attain such a *consciousness of power* that it could allow itself the noblest luxury possible to it—letting those who harm it go *unpunished.* "What are my parasites to me?" it might say. "May they live and prosper: I am strong enough for that!"

The justice which began with, "everything is dischargeable,

---

[3] Woe to the losers!

everything must be discharged," ends by winking and letting those incapable of discharging their debt go free: it ends, as does every good thing on earth, by *overcoming itself*.[1] This self-overcoming of justice: one knows the beautiful name it has given itself—*mercy;* it goes without saying that mercy remains the privilege of the most powerful man, or better, his—beyond the law.[2]

11

Here a word in repudiation of attempts that have lately been made to seek the origin of justice in quite a different sphere— namely in that of *ressentiment*. To the psychologists first of all, presuming they would like to study *ressentiment* close up for once, I would say: this plant blooms best today among anarchists and anti-Semites—where it has always bloomed, in hidden places, like the violet, though with a different odor. And as like must always produce like, it causes us no surprise to see a repetition in such circles of attempts often made before—see above, section 14—to sanctify

---

[1] *Sich selbst aufhebend.* And in the next sentence *Selbstaufhebung* has been translated as self-overcoming. Similarly, *aufzuheben* in the middle of section 13, below, and *aufgehoben* in section 8 of the third essay have been rendered "overcome." See also III, section 27, with note. *Aufheben* is a very troublesome word, though common in ordinary German. Literally, it means "pick up"; but it has two derivative meanings that are no less common: "cancel" and "preserve" or "keep." Something picked up is no longer there, but the point of picking it up may be to keep it. Hegel made much of this term; his use of it is explained and discussed in Walter Kaufmann, *Hegel* (Garden City, N.Y., Doubleday, 1965; Garden City, N.Y., Doubleday Anchor Books, 1966), section 34—and a comparison of Hegel and Nietzsche on this point may be found in Kaufmann's *Nietzsche,* Chapter 8, section II.

[2] The theme sounded here is one of the central motifs of Nietzsche's philosophy. Cf. *Dawn,* section 202: ". . . Let us eliminate the concept of *sin* from the world—and let us soon dispatch the concept of *punishment* after it! May these exiled monsters live somewhere else henceforth and not among men— if they insist on living and will not perish of disgust with themselves! . . . Shouldn't we be mature enough yet for the opposite view? Shouldn't we be able to say yet: every 'guilty' person is sick?— No, the hour for that has not yet come. As yet the physicians are lacking above all . . . As yet no thinker has had the courage of measuring the health of a society and of individuals according to how many parasites they can stand . . ." (See *The Portable Nietzsche,* pp. 85–88.) Cf. also *Zarathustra* II, "On the Tarantulas": *"That man be delivered from revenge,* that is for me the bridge to the highest hope . . ." (*ibid.,* p. 211). Many other pertinent passages are cited in Kaufmann, *Nietzsche,* Chapter 12, sections II and V.

revenge[1] under the name of *justice*[2]—as if justice were at bottom merely a further development of the feeling of being aggrieved—and to rehabilitate not only revenge but all *reactive* affects in general. To the latter as such I would be the last to raise any objection: in respect to the entire biological problem (in relation to which the value of these affects has hitherto been underrated) it even seems to me to constitute a *service*. All I draw attention to is the circumstance that it is the spirit of *ressentiment* itself out of which this new nuance of scientific fairness (for the benefit of hatred, envy, jealousy, mistrust, rancor, and revenge) proceeds. For this "scientific fairness" immediately ceases and gives way to accents of deadly enmity and prejudice once it is a question of dealing with another group of affects, affects that, it seems to me, are of even greater biological value than those reactive affects and consequently deserve even more to be *scientifically* evaluated and esteemed: namely, the truly *active* affects, such as lust for power, avarice, and the like. (E. Dühring:[3] *The Value of Life; A Course in Philosophy;* and, fundamentally, *passim.*)

So much against this tendency in general: as for Dühring's specific proposition that the home of justice is to be sought in the sphere of the reactive feelings, one is obliged for truth's sake to counter it with a blunt antithesis: the *last* sphere to be conquered by the spirit of justice is the sphere of the reactive feelings! When it really happens that the just man remains just even toward those who have harmed him (and not merely cold, temperate, remote, indifferent: being just is always a *positive* attitude), when the exalted, clear objectivity, as penetrating as it is mild, of the eye of justice and *judging* is not dimmed even under the assault of personal injury, derision, and calumny, this is a piece of perfection and supreme mastery on earth—something it would be prudent not to expect or to *believe* in too readily. On the average, a small dose

---

[1] *Rache.*

[2] *Gerechtigkeit.*

[3] Eugen Dühring (1833–1901), a prolific German philosopher and political economist, was among other things an impassioned patriot and anti-Semite and hated the cosmopolitan Goethe and the Greeks. He is remembered chiefly as the butt of polemical works by Karl Marx and Friedrich Engels and of scattered hostile remarks in Nietzsche's writings.

of aggression, malice, or insinuation certainly suffices to drive the blood into the eyes—and fairness out of the eyes—of even the most upright people. The active, aggressive, arrogant man is still a hundred steps closer to justice than the reactive man; for he has absolutely no need to take a false and prejudiced view of the object before him in the way the reactive man does and is bound to do. For that reason the aggressive man, as the stronger, nobler, more courageous, has in fact also had at all times a *freer* eye, a *better* conscience on his side: conversely, one can see who has the invention of the "bad conscience" on his conscience—the man of *ressentiment!*

Finally, one only has to look at history: in which sphere has the entire administration of law[4] hitherto been at home—also the need for law? In the sphere of reactive men, perhaps? By no means: rather in that of the active, strong, spontaneous, aggressive. From a historical point of view, law represents on earth—let it be said to the dismay of the above-named agitator (who himself once confessed: "the doctrine of revenge is the red thread of justice that runs through all my work and efforts")—the struggle *against* the reactive feelings, the war conducted against them on the part of the active and aggressive powers who employed some of their strength to impose measure and bounds upon the excesses of the reactive pathos and to compel it to come to terms. Wherever justice is practiced and maintained one sees a stronger power seeking a means of putting an end to the senseless raging of *ressentiment* among the weaker powers that stand under it (whether they be groups or individuals)—partly by taking the object of *ressentiment* out of the hands of revenge, partly by substituting for revenge the struggle against the enemies of peace and order, partly by devising and in some cases imposing settlements, partly by elevating certain equivalents for injuries into norms to which from then on *ressentiment* is once and for all directed. The most decisive act, however, that the supreme power performs and accomplishes against the predominance of grudges and rancor—it always takes this action as soon as it is in any way strong enough to do so—is the institution of *law*,[5] the imperative declaration of what in general counts as permitted,

---

[4] *Recht.*

[5] *Gesetz.*

as just,[6] in its eyes, and what counts as forbidden, as unjust:[7] once it has instituted the law, it treats violence and capricious acts on the part of individuals or entire groups as offenses against the law, as rebellion against the supreme power itself, and thus leads the feelings of its subjects away from the direct injury caused by such offenses; and in the long run it thus attains the reverse of that which is desired by all revenge that is fastened exclusively to the viewpoint of the person injured: from now on the eye is trained to an ever more *impersonal* evaluation of the deed, and this applies even to the eye of the injured person himself (although last of all, as remarked above).

"Just" and "unjust" exist, accordingly, only after the institution of the law (and *not*, as Dühring would have it, after the perpetration of the injury). To speak of just or unjust *in itself* is quite senseless; *in itself*, of course, no injury, assault, exploitation, destruction can be "unjust," since life operates *essentially,* that is in its basic functions, through injury, assault, exploitation, destruction and simply cannot be thought of at all without this character. One must indeed grant something even more unpalatable: that, from the highest biological standpoint, legal conditions can never be other than *exceptional conditions,* since they constitute a partial restriction of the will of life, which is bent upon power, and are subordinate to its total goal as a single means: namely, as a means of creating *greater* units of power. A legal order thought of as sovereign and universal, not as a means in the struggle between power-complexes but as a means of *preventing* all struggle in general— perhaps after the communistic cliché of Dühring, that every will must consider every other will its equal—would be a principle *hostile to life,* an agent of the dissolution and destruction of man, an attempt to assassinate the future of man, a sign of weariness, a secret path to nothingness.—

12

Yet a word on the origin and the purpose of punishment—two problems that are separate, or ought to be separate: unfortunately,

---

[6] *Recht.*

[7] *Unrecht.*

they are usually confounded. How have previous genealogists of morals set about solving these problems? Naïvely, as has always been their way: they seek out some "purpose" in punishment, for example, revenge or deterrence, then guilelessly place this purpose at the beginning as *causa fiendi*[1] of punishment, and—have done. The "purpose of law," however, is absolutely the last thing to employ in the history of the origin of law: on the contrary, there is for historiography of any kind no more important proposition than the one it took such effort to establish but which really *ought to be* established now: the cause of the origin of a thing and its eventual utility, its actual employment and place in a system of purposes, lie worlds apart; whatever exists, having somehow come into being, is again and again reinterpreted to new ends, taken over, transformed, and redirected by some power superior to it; all events in the organic world are a subduing, a *becoming master,* and all subduing and becoming master involves a fresh interpretation, an adaptation through which any previous "meaning" and "purpose" are necessarily obscured or even obliterated. However well one has understood the *utility* of any physiological organ (or of a legal institution, a social custom, a political usage, a form in art or in a religious cult), this means nothing regarding its origin: however uncomfortable and disagreeable this may sound to older ears—for one had always believed that to understand the demonstrable purpose, the utility of a thing, a form, or an institution, was also to understand the reason why it originated—the eye being made for seeing, the hand being made for grasping.

Thus one also imagined that punishment was devised for punishing. But purposes and utilities are only *signs* that a will to power has become master of something less powerful and imposed upon it the character of a function; and the entire history of a "thing," an organ, a custom can in this way be a continuous sign-chain of ever new interpretations and adaptations whose causes do not even have to be related to one another but, on the contrary, in some cases succeed and alternate with one another in a purely chance fashion. The "evolution" of a thing, a custom, an organ is thus by no means its *progressus* toward a goal, even less a logical *progressus* by the

---

[1] The cause of the origin.

shortest route and with the smallest expenditure of force—but a succession of more or less profound, more or less mutually independent processes of subduing, plus the resistances they encounter, the attempts at transformation for the purpose of defense and reaction, and the results of successful counteractions. The form is fluid, but the "meaning" is even more so.

The case is the same even within each individual organism: with every real growth in the whole, the "meaning" of the individual organs also changes; in certain circumstances their partial destruction, a reduction in their numbers (for example, through the disappearance of intermediary members) can be a sign of increasing strength and perfection. It is not too much to say that even a partial *diminution of utility,* an atrophying and degeneration, a loss of meaning and purposiveness—in short, death—is among the conditions of an actual *progressus,* which always appears in the shape of a will and way to *greater power* and is always carried through at the expense of numerous smaller powers. The magnitude of an "advance" can even be measured by the mass of things that had to be sacrificed to it; mankind in the mass sacrificed to the prosperity of a single *stronger* species of man—that *would* be an advance.

I emphasize this major point of historical method all the more because it is in fundamental opposition to the now prevalent instinct and taste which would rather be reconciled even to the absolute fortuitousness, even the mechanistic senselessness of all events than to the theory that in all events a *will to power* is operating. The democratic idiosyncrasy which opposes everything that dominates and wants to dominate, the modern *misarchism*[2] (to coin an ugly word for an ugly thing) has permeated the realm of the spirit and disguised itself in the most spiritual forms to such a degree that today it has forced its way, has acquired the *right* to force its way into the strictest, apparently most objective sciences; indeed, it seems to me to have already taken charge of all physiology and theory of life—to the detriment of life, as goes without saying, since it has robbed it of a fundamental concept, that of *activity*. Under the influence of the above-mentioned idiosyncracy, one

---

[2] Hatred of rule or government.

places instead "adaptation" in the foreground, that is to say, an activity of the second rank, a mere reactivity; indeed, life itself has been defined as a more and more efficient inner adaptation to external conditions (Herbert Spencer[3]). Thus the essence of life, its *will to power,* is ignored; one overlooks the essential priority of the spontaneous, aggressive, expansive, form-giving forces that give new interpretations and directions, although "adaptation" follows only after this; the dominant role of the highest functionaries within the organism itself in which the will to life appears active and form-giving is denied. One should recall what Huxley[4] reproached Spencer with—his "administrative nihilism": but it is a question of rather *more* than mere "administration."

13

To return to our subject, namely *punishment,* one must distinguish two aspects: on the one hand, that in it which is relatively *enduring,* the custom, the act, the "drama," a certain strict sequence of procedures; on the other, that in it which is *fluid,* the meaning, the purpose, the expectation associated with the performance of such procedures. In accordance with the previously developed major point of historical method, it is assumed without further ado that the procedure itself will be something older, earlier than its employment in punishment, that the latter is *projected* and interpreted *into* the procedure (which has long existed but been employed in another sense), in short, that the case is *not* as has hitherto been assumed by our naïve genealogists of law and morals, who have one and all thought of the procedure as *invented* for the purpose of punishing, just as one formerly thought of the hand as invented for the purpose of grasping.

As for the other element in punishment, the fluid element, its

---

[3] On Spencer, see the note in section 3 of the first essay, above.

[4] Thomas Henry Huxley (1825–95), the English biologist and writer, fought tirelessly for the acceptance of Darwinism. In 1869 he coined the word *agnosticism,* which Spencer took over from him. Aldous Huxley (1894–1963), the author of *Brave New World* (1932), and Julian Huxley (born 1897), the biologist, are T. H. Huxley's grandsons.

"meaning," in a very late condition of culture (for example, in modern Europe) the concept "punishment" possesses in fact not *one* meaning but a whole synthesis of "meanings": the previous history of punishment in general, the history of its employment for the most various purposes, finally crystallizes into a kind of unity that is hard to disentangle, hard to analyze and, as must be emphasized especially, totally *indefinable*. (Today it is impossible to say for certain *why* people are really punished: all concepts in which an entire process is semiotically concentrated elude definition; only that which has no history is definable.[1]) At an earlier stage, on the contrary, this synthesis of "meanings" can still be disentangled, as well as changed; one can still perceive how in each individual case the elements of the synthesis undergo a shift in value and rearrange themselves accordingly, so that now this, now that element comes to the fore and dominates at the expense of the others; and under certain circumstances one element (the purpose of deterrence perhaps) appears to overcome all the remaining elements.

To give at least an idea of how uncertain, how supplemental, how accidental "the meaning" of punishment is, and how one and the same procedure can be employed, interpreted, adapted to ends that differ fundamentally, I set down here the pattern that has emerged from consideration of relatively few chance instances I have noted. Punishment as a means of rendering harmless, of preventing further harm. Punishment as recompense to the injured party for the harm done, rendered in any form (even in that of a compensating affect). Punishment as the isolation of a disturbance of equilibrium, so as to guard against any further spread of the disturbance. Punishment as a means of inspiring fear of those who determine and execute the punishment. Punishment as a kind of repayment for the advantages the criminal has enjoyed hitherto (for example, when he is employed as a slave in the mines). Punishment as the expulsion of a degenerate element (in some cases, of an entire branch, as in Chinese law: thus as a means of preserving the purity of a race or maintaining a social type). Punishment as a festival, namely as the rape and mockery of a finally defeated enemy. Punishment as the making of a memory, whether for him

---

[1] A superb epigram that expresses a profound insight. Cf. *The Wanderer and His Shadow,* section 33, included in the present volume, pp. 159ff.

who suffers the punishment—so-called "improvement"—or for those who witness its execution. Punishment as payment of a fee stipulated by the power that protects the wrongdoer from the excesses of revenge. Punishment as a compromise with revenge in its natural state when the latter is still maintained and claimed as a privilege by powerful clans. Punishment as a declaration of war and a war measure against an enemy of peace, of the law, of order, of the authorities, whom, as a danger to the community, as one who has broken the contract that defines the conditions under which it exists, as a rebel, a traitor, and breaker of the peace, one opposes with the means of war.—

14

This list is certainly not complete; it is clear that punishment is overdetermined [1] by utilities of all kinds. All the more reason, then, for deducting from it a *supposed* utility that, to be sure, counts in the popular consciousness as the most essential one—belief in punishment, which for several reasons is tottering today, always finds its strongest support in this. Punishment is supposed to possess the value of awakening the *feeling of guilt* in the guilty person; one seeks in it the actual *instrumentum* of that psychical reaction called "bad conscience," "sting of conscience." Thus one misunderstands psychology and the reality of things even as they apply today: how much more as they applied during the greater part of man's history, his prehistory!

It is precisely among criminals and convicts that the sting of conscience is extremely rare; prisons and penitentiaries are *not* the kind of hotbed in which this species of gnawing worm is likely to flourish: all conscientious observers are agreed on that, in many cases unwillingly enough and contrary to their own inclinations. Generally speaking, punishment makes men hard and cold; it concentrates; it sharpens the feeling of alienation; it strengthens the power of resistance. If it happens that punishment destroys the vital energy and brings about a miserable prostration and self-abasement, such a result is certainly even less pleasant than the

---

[1] *Überladen.*

usual effects of punishment—characterized by dry and gloomy seriousness.

If we consider those millennia *before* the history of man, we may unhesitatingly assert that it was precisely through punishment that the development of the feeling of guilt was most powerfully *hindered*—at least in the victims upon whom the punitive force was vented. For we must not underrate the extent to which the sight of the judicial and executive procedures prevents the criminal from considering his deed, the type of his action *as such,* reprehensible: for he sees exactly the same kind of actions practiced in the service of justice and approved of and practiced with a good conscience: spying, deception, bribery, setting traps, the whole cunning and underhand art of police and prosecution, plus robbery, violence, defamation, imprisonment, torture, murder, practiced as a matter of principle and without even emotion to excuse them, which are pronounced characteristics of the various forms of punishment—all of them therefore actions which his judges in no way condemn and repudiate *as such,* but only when they are applied and directed to certain particular ends.

The "bad conscience," this most uncanny and most interesting plant of all our earthly vegetation, did *not* grow on this soil; indeed, during the greater part of the past the judges and punishers themselves were *not at all* conscious of dealing with a "guilty person." But with an instigator of harm, with an irresponsible piece of fate. And the person upon whom punishment subsequently descended, again like a piece of fate, suffered no "inward pain" other than that induced by the sudden appearance of something unforeseen, a dreadful natural event, a plunging, crushing rock that one cannot fight.

15

This fact once came insidiously into the mind of Spinoza (to the vexation of his interpreters, Kuno Fischer,[1] for example, who

---

[1] Kuno Fischer (1824–1907), professor at Heidelberg, made a great reputation with a ten-volume history of modern philosophy that consists of imposing monographs on selected modern philosophers. One of the volumes is devoted to Spinoza.

make a real *effort* to misunderstand him on this point), when one afternoon, teased by who knows what recollection, he mused on the question of what really remained to him of the famous *morsus conscientiae*[2]—he who had banished good and evil to the realm of human imagination and had wrathfully defended the honor of his "free" God against those blasphemers who asserted that God effected all things *sub ratione boni*[3] ("but that would mean making God subject to fate and would surely be the greatest of all absurdities"). The world, for Spinoza, had returned to that state of innocence in which it had lain before the invention of the bad conscience: what then had become of the *morsus conscientiae?*

"The opposite of *gaudium*," [4] he finally said to himself—"a sadness accompanied by the recollection of a past event that flouted all of our expectations." *Eth.III, propos. XVIII, schol. I. II.* Mischief-makers overtaken by punishments have for thousands of years felt in respect of their "transgressions" *just as Spinoza did:* "here something has unexpectedly gone wrong," *not:* "I ought not to have done that." They submitted to punishment as one submits to an illness or to a misfortune or to death, with that stout-hearted fatalism without rebellion through which the Russians, for example, still have an advantage over us Westerners in dealing with life.

If there existed any criticism of the deed in those days, it was prudence that criticized the deed: the actual *effect* of punishment must beyond question be sought above all in a heightening of prudence, in an extending of the memory, in a will henceforth to go to work more cautiously, mistrustfully, secretly, in the insight that one is definitely too weak for many things, in a kind of improvement in self-criticism. That which can in general be attained through punishment, in men and in animals, is an increase of fear, a heightening of prudence, mastery of the desires: thus punishment *tames* men, but it does not make them "better"—one might with more justice assert the opposite. ("Injury makes one prudent," says the proverb: insofar as it makes one prudent it also makes one bad. Fortunately, it frequently makes people stupid.)

---

[2] Sting of conscience.
[3] For a good reason.
[4] Joy.

16

At this point I can no longer avoid giving a first, provisional statement of my own hypothesis concerning the origin of the "bad conscience": it may sound rather strange and needs to be pondered, lived with, and slept on for a long time. I regard the bad conscience as the serious illness that man was bound to contract under the stress of the most fundamental change he ever experienced—that change which occurred when he found himself finally enclosed within the walls of society and of peace. The situation that faced sea animals when they were compelled to become land animals or perish was the same as that which faced these semi-animals, well adapted to the wilderness, to war, to prowling, to adventure: suddenly all their instincts were disvalued and "suspended." From now on they had to walk on their feet and "bear themselves" whereas hitherto they had been borne by the water: a dreadful heaviness lay upon them. They felt unable to cope with the simplest undertakings; in this new world they no longer possessed their former guides, their regulating, unconscious and infallible drives: they were reduced to thinking, inferring, reckoning, co-ordinating cause and effect, these unfortunate creatures; they were reduced to their "consciousness," their weakest and most fallible organ! I believe there has never been such a feeling of misery on earth, such a leaden discomfort— and at the same time the old instincts had not suddenly ceased to make their usual demands! Only it was hardly or rarely possible to humor them: as a rule they had to seek new and, as it were, subterranean gratifications.

All instincts that do not discharge themselves outwardly *turn inward*—this is what I call the *internalization*[1] of man: thus it was that man first developed what was later called his "soul." The entire inner world, originally as thin as if it were stretched between two membranes, expanded and extended itself, acquired depth, breadth, and height, in the same measure as outward discharge was *inhibited*. Those fearful bulwarks with which the political organiza-

---

[1] *Verinnerlichung.* Cf. Freud.

tion protected itself against the old instincts of freedom—punishments belong among these bulwarks—brought about that all those instincts of wild, free, prowling man turned backward *against man himself*. Hostility, cruelty, joy in persecuting, in attacking, in change, in destruction—all this turned against the possessors of such instincts: *that* is the origin of the "bad conscience."

The man who, from lack of external enemies and resistances and forcibly confined to the oppressive narrowness and punctiliousness of custom, impatiently lacerated, persecuted, gnawed at, assaulted, and maltreated himself; this animal that rubbed itself raw against the bars of its cage as one tried to "tame" it; this deprived creature, racked with homesickness for the wild, who had to turn himself into an adventure, a torture chamber, an uncertain and dangerous wilderness—this fool, this yearning and desperate prisoner became the inventor of the "bad conscience." But thus began the gravest and uncanniest illness, from which humanity has not yet recovered, man's suffering *of man, of himself*—the result of a forcible sundering from his animal past, as it were a leap and plunge into new surroundings and conditions of existence, a declaration of war against the old instincts upon which his strength, joy, and terribleness had rested hitherto.

Let us add at once that, on the other hand, the existence on earth of an animal soul turned against itself, taking sides against itself, was something so new, profound, unheard of, enigmatic, contradictory, *and pregnant with a future* that the aspect of the earth was essentially altered. Indeed, divine spectators were needed to do justice to the spectacle that thus began and the end of which is not yet in sight—a spectacle too subtle, too marvelous, too paradoxical to be played senselessly unobserved on some ludicrous planet! From now on, man is *included* among the most unexpected and exciting lucky throws in the dice game of Heraclitus' "great child," be he called Zeus or chance; he gives rise to an interest, a tension, a hope, almost a certainty, as if with him something were announcing and preparing itself, as if man were not a goal but only a way, an episode, a bridge, a great promise.—

17

Among the presuppositions of this hypothesis concerning the origin of the bad conscience is, first, that the change referred to was not a gradual or voluntary one and did not represent an organic adaptation to new conditions but a break, a leap, a compulsion, an ineluctable disaster which precluded all struggle and even all *ressentiment*. Secondly, however, that the welding of a hitherto unchecked and shapeless populace into a firm form was not only instituted by an act of violence but also carried to its conclusion by nothing but acts of violence—that the oldest "state" thus appeared as a fearful tyranny, as an oppressive and remorseless machine, and went on working until this raw material of people and semi-animals was at last not only thoroughly kneaded and pliant but also *formed*.

I employed the word "state": it is obvious what is meant—some pack of blond beasts of prey,[1] a conqueror and master race which, organized for war and with the ability to organize, unhesitatingly lays its terrible claws upon a populace perhaps tremendously superior in numbers but still formless and nomad. That is after all how the "state" began on earth: I think that sentimentalism which would have it begin with a "contract" has been disposed of. He who can command, he who is by nature "master," he who is violent in act and bearing—what has he to do with contracts! One does not reckon with such natures; they come like fate, without reason, consideration, or pretext; they appear as lightning appears, too terrible, too sudden, too convincing, too "different" even to be hated. Their work is an instinctive creation and imposition of forms; they are the most involuntary, unconscious artists there are —wherever they appear something new soon arises, a ruling structure that *lives,* in which parts and functions are delimited and co-

---

[1] *Irgendein Rudel blonder Raubtiere, eine Eroberer- und Herren-Rasse:* Francis Golffing, in his translation, spirits away both the blond beasts of prey and the master race by rendering these words "a pack of savages, a race of conquerors." Cf. section 11 of the first essay, above, with its three references to the *blonde Bestie,* and note 3 of section 11. See also Kaufmann's *Nietzsche,* Chapter 10, "The Master-Race."

ordinated, in which nothing whatever finds a place that has not first been assigned a "meaning" in relation to the whole. They do not know what guilt, responsibility, or consideration are, these born organizers; they exemplify that terrible artists' egoism that has the look of bronze and knows itself justified to all eternity in its "work," like a mother in her child. It is not in *them* that the "bad conscience" developed, that goes without saying—but it would not have developed *without them,* this ugly growth, it would be lacking if a tremendous quantity of freedom had not been expelled from the world, or at least from the visible world, and made as it were *latent* under their hammer blows and artists' violence. This *instinct for freedom* forcibly made latent—we have seen it already—this instinct for freedom pushed back and repressed, incarcerated within and finally able to discharge and vent itself only on itself: that, and that alone, is what the *bad conscience* is in its beginnings.

18

One should guard against thinking lightly of this phenomenon merely on account of its initial painfulness and ugliness. For fundamentally it is the same active force that is at work on a grander scale in those artists of violence and organizers who build states, and that here, internally, on a smaller and pettier scale, directed backward, in the "labyrinth of the breast," to use Goethe's expression, creates for itself a bad conscience and builds negative ideals —namely, the *instinct for freedom* (in my language: the will to power); only here the material upon which the form-giving and ravishing nature of this force vents itself is man himself, his whole ancient animal self—and *not,* as in that greater and more obvious phenomenon, some *other* man, *other* men. This secret self-ravishment, this artists' cruelty, this delight in imposing a form upon oneself as a hard, recalcitrant, suffering material and in burning a will, a critique, a contradiction, a contempt, a No into it, this uncanny, dreadfully joyous labor of a soul voluntarily at odds with itself that makes itself suffer out of joy in making suffer—eventually this entire *active* "bad conscience"—you will have guessed it—as the womb of all ideal and imaginative phenomena, also brought to light an abundance of strange new beauty and affirmation, and perhaps beauty itself.— After all, what would be "beautiful" if the contradiction had not first become conscious of itself, if the ugly had not first said to itself: "I am ugly"?

This hint will at least make less enigmatic the enigma of how contradictory concepts such as *selflessness, self-denial, self-sacrifice* can suggest an ideal, a kind of beauty; and one thing we know henceforth—I have no doubt of it—and that is the nature of the *delight* that the selfless man, the self-denier, the self-sacrificer feels from the first: this delight is tied to cruelty.

So much for the present about the origin of the moral value of the "unegoistic," about the soil from which this value grew: only the bad conscience, only the will to self-maltreatment provided the conditions for the *value* of the unegoistic.—

19

The bad conscience is an illness, there is no doubt about that, but an illness as pregnancy is an illness.[1] Let us seek out the conditions under which this illness has reached its most terrible and most sublime height; we shall see what it really was that thus entered the world. But for that one needs endurance—and first of all we must go back again to an earlier point of view.

The civil-law relationship between the debtor and his creditor, discussed above, has been interpreted in an, historically speaking, exceedingly remarkable and dubious manner into a relationship in which to us modern men it seems perhaps least to belong: namely into the relationship between the present generation and its ancestors.

Within the original tribal community—we are speaking of primeval times—the living generation always recognized a juridical duty toward earlier generations, and especially toward the earliest, which founded the tribe (and by no means a merely sentimental obligation: there are actually reasons for denying the existence of the latter for the greater part of human history). The conviction

---

[1] Cf. pp. 446ff. and 520f.

reigns that it is only through the sacrifices and accomplishments of the ancestors that the tribe *exists*—and that one has to *pay them back* with sacrifices and accomplishments: one thus recognizes a *debt* that constantly grows greater, since these forebears never cease, in their continued existence as powerful spirits, to accord the tribe new advantages and new strength. In vain, perhaps? But there is no "in vain" for these rude and "poor-souled" ages. What can one give them in return? Sacrifices (initially as food in the coarsest sense), feasts, music, honors; above all, obedience—for all customs, as works of the ancestors, are also their statutes and commands: can one ever give them enough? This suspicion remains and increases; from time to time it leads to a wholesale sacrifice, something tremendous in the way of repayment to the "creditor" (the notorious sacrifice of the first-born, for example; in any case blood, human blood).

The *fear* of the ancestor and his power, the consciousness of indebtedness to him, increases, according to this kind of logic, in exactly the same measure as the power of the tribe itself increases, as the tribe itself grows ever more victorious, independent, honored, and feared. By no means the other way round! Every step toward the decline of a tribe, every misfortune, every sign of degeneration, of coming disintegration always *diminishes* fear of the spirit of its founder and produces a meaner impression of his cunning, foresight, and present power. If one imagines this rude kind of logic carried to its end, then the ancestors of the *most powerful* tribes are bound eventually to grow to monstrous dimensions through the imagination of growing fear and to recede into the darkness of the divinely uncanny and unimaginable: in the end the ancestor must necessarily be transfigured into a *god*. Perhaps this is even the origin of gods, an origin therefore out of *fear!* . . . And whoever should feel obliged to add, "but out of piety also!" would hardly be right for the greater part of the existence of man, his prehistory. To be sure, he would be quite right for the *intermediate* age, in which the noble tribes developed—who indeed paid back their originators, their ancestors (heroes, gods) with interest all the qualities that had become palpable in themselves, the *noble* qualities. We shall take another look later at the ennoblement of the gods (which should not be confused with their becoming "holy"); let us first of all follow to its end the course of this whole development of the consciousness of guilt.

20

History shows that the consciousness of being in debt[1] to the deity did not by any means come to an end together with the organization of communities on the basis of blood relationship. Even as mankind inherited the concepts "good and bad" from the tribal nobility (along with its basic psychological propensity to set up orders of rank), it also inherited, along with the tribal and family divinities, the burden of still unpaid debts and of the desire to be relieved of them. (The transition is provided by those numerous slave and dependent populations who, whether through compulsion or through servility and mimicry, adapted themselves to their masters' cult of the gods: this inheritance then overflows from them in all directions.) The guilty feeling of indebtedness[2] to the divinity continued to grow for several millennia—always in the same measure as the concept of God and the feeling for divinity increased on earth and was carried to the heights. (The entire history of ethnic struggle, victory, reconciliation, fusion, everything that precedes the definitive ordering of rank of the different national elements in every great racial synthesis, is reflected in the confused genealogies of their gods, in the sagas of the gods' struggles, victories, and reconciliations; the advance toward universal empires is always also an advance toward universal divinities; despotism with its triumph over the independent nobility always prepares the way for some kind of monotheism.)

The advent of the Christian God, as the maximum god attained so far, was therefore accompanied by the maximum feeling of guilty indebtedness[3] on earth. Presuming we have gradually entered upon the *reverse* course, there is no small probability that with the irresistible decline of faith in the Christian God there is

---

[1] *Schulden zu haben.*

[2] *Das Schuldgefühl.*

[3] *Des Schuldgefühls.*

now also a considerable decline in mankind's feeling of guilt;[4] indeed, the prospect cannot be dismissed that the complete and definitive victory of atheism might free mankind of this whole feeling of guilty indebtedness[5] toward its origin, its *causa prima*.[6] Atheism and a kind of *second innocence*[7] belong together.—

21

So much for a first brief preliminary on the connection of the concepts "guilt" and "duty" with religious presuppositions: I have up to now deliberately ignored the moralization of these concepts (their pushing back into the conscience; more precisely, the involvement of the *bad* conscience with the concept of god); and at the end of the last section I even spoke as if this moralization had not taken place at all, and as if these concepts were now necessarily doomed since their presupposition, the faith in our "creditor," [1] in God, had disappeared. The reality is, to a fearful degree, otherwise.

The moralization of the concepts guilt and duty, their being pushed back into the *bad* conscience, actually involves an attempt to *reverse* the direction of the development described above, or at least to bring it to a halt: the *aim* now is to preclude pessimistically, once and for all, the prospect of a final discharge; the *aim* now is to make the glance recoil disconsolately from an iron impossibility; the *aim* now is to turn back the concepts "guilt" and "duty"—back against whom? There can be no doubt: against the "debtor" first of all, in whom from now on the bad conscience is firmly rooted, eating into him and spreading within him like a polyp, until at last the irredeemable debt gives rise to the conception of irredeemable penance, the idea that it cannot be discharged (*"eternal* punishment"). Finally, however, they are turned back against the "creditor," too: whether we think of the *causa prima* of

---

[4] *Schuldbewusstseins.*

[5] *Gefühl, Schulden . . . zu haben.*

[6] First cause.

[7] *Unschuld.*

[1] *Der Glaube an unsern "Gläubiger":* the creed in our "creditor"—or: that one credits our "creditor."

man, the beginning of the human race, its primal ancestor who is from now on burdened with a curse ("Adam," "original sin," "unfreedom of the will"), or of nature from whose womb mankind arose and into whom the principle of evil is projected from now on ("the diabolizing of nature"), or of existence in general, which is now considered *worthless as such* (nihilistic withdrawal from it, a desire for nothingness or a desire for its antithesis, for a different mode of being, Buddhism and the like)—suddenly we stand before the paradoxical and horrifying expedient that afforded temporary relief for tormented humanity, that stroke of genius on the part of Christianity: God himself sacrifices himself for the guilt of mankind, God himself makes payment to himself, God as the only being who can redeem man from what has become unredeemable for man himself—the creditor sacrifices himself for his debtor, out of *love* (can one credit that?), out of love for his debtor!—

22

You will have guessed *what* has really happened here, *beneath* all this: that will to self-tormenting, that repressed cruelty of the animal-man made inward and scared back into himself, the creature imprisoned in the "state" so as to be tamed, who invented the bad conscience in order to hurt himself after the *more natural* vent for this desire to hurt had been blocked—this man of the bad conscience has seized upon the presupposition of religion so as to drive his self-torture to its most gruesome pitch of severity and rigor. Guilt before *God:* this thought becomes an instrument of torture to him. He apprehends in "God" the ultimate antithesis of his own ineluctable animal instincts; he reinterprets these animal instincts themselves as a form of guilt before God (as hostility, rebellion, insurrection against the "Lord," the "father," the primal ancestor and origin of the world); he stretches himself upon the contradiction "God" and "Devil"; he ejects from himself all his denial of himself, of his nature, naturalness, and actuality, in the form of an affirmation, as something existent, corporeal, real, as God, as the holiness of God, as God the Judge, as God the Hangman, as the beyond, as eternity, as torment without end, as hell, as the immeasurability of punishment and guilt.

In this psychical cruelty there resides a madness of the will which is absolutely unexampled: the *will* of man to find himself guilty and reprehensible to a degree that can never be atoned for; his *will* to think himself punished without any possibility of the punishment becoming equal to the guilt; his *will* to infect and poison the fundamental ground of things with the problem of punishment and guilt so as to cut off once and for all his own exit from this labyrinth of "fixed ideas"; his *will* to erect an ideal—that of the "holy God"—and in the face of it to feel the palpable certainty of his own absolute unworthiness. Oh this insane, pathetic beast—man! What ideas he has, what unnaturalness, what paroxysms of nonsense, what *bestiality of thought* erupts as soon as he is prevented just a little from being a *beast in deed!*

All this is interesting, to excess, but also of a gloomy, black, unnerving sadness, so that one must forcibly forbid oneself to gaze too long into these abysses. Here is *sickness,* beyond any doubt, the most terrible sickness that has ever raged in man; and whoever can still bear to hear (but today one no longer has ears for this!) how in this night of torment and absurdity there has resounded the cry of *love,* the cry of the most nostalgic rapture, of redemption through *love,* will turn away, seized by invincible horror.— There is so much in man that is hideous!— Too long, the earth has been a madhouse!—

23

This should dispose once and for all of the question of how the "holy God" originated.

That the conception of gods *in itself* need not lead to the degradation of the imagination that we had to consider briefly, that there are *nobler* uses for the invention of gods than for the self-crucifixion and self-violation of man in which Europe over the past millennia achieved its distinctive mastery—that is fortunately revealed even by a mere glance at the *Greek gods,* those reflections of noble and autocratic men, in whom *the animal* in man felt deified and did *not* lacerate itself, did *not* rage against itself! For the longest time these Greeks used their gods precisely so as to ward off the "bad conscience," so as to be able to rejoice in their freedom of soul—the very opposite of the use to which Christianity put its God. They went *very far* in this direction, these splendid and lion-hearted children; and no less an authority than the Homeric Zeus himself occasionally gives them to understand that they are making things too easy for themselves. "Strange!" he says once—the case is that of Aegisthus, a *very* bad case—

> *Strange how these mortals so loudly complain of the gods!*
> We alone produce evil, *they say; yet themselves*
> *Make themselves wretched through folly, even counter to fate.*[1]

Yet one can see and hear how even this Olympian spectator and judge is far from holding a grudge against them or thinking ill of them on that account: "how *foolish* they are!" he thinks when he observes the misdeeds of mortals—and "foolishness," "folly," a little "disturbance in the head," this much even the Greeks of the strongest, bravest age conceded of themselves as the reason for much that was bad and calamitous—foolishness, *not* sin! do you grasp that?

Even this disturbance in the head, however, presented a problem: "how is it possible? how could it actually have happened to heads such as *we* have, we men of aristocratic descent, of the best society, happy, well-constituted, noble, and virtuous?"—thus noble Greeks asked themselves for centuries in the face of every incomprehensible atrocity or wantonness with which one of their kind had polluted himself. "He must have been deluded by a *god*," they concluded finally, shaking their heads . . . This expedient is *typical* of the Greeks . . . In this way the gods served in those days to justify man to a certain extent even in his wickedness, they served as the originators of evil—in those days they took upon themselves, not the punishment but, what is *nobler*, the guilt.[2]

---

[1] *Odyssey*, I, line 32ff.

[2] Cf. *Ecce Homo*, Chapter I, section 5, and Sartre's play *The Flies*, which was decisively influenced by Nietzsche, as I have shown in "Nietzsche Between Homer and Sartre: Five Treatments of the Orestes Story" (*Revue Internationale de Philosophie*, LXVII, 1964, pp. 50–73). See also my *Tragedy and Philosophy*, section 51.

24

I end up with three question marks; that seems plain. "What are you really doing, erecting an ideal or knocking one down?" I may perhaps be asked.

But have you ever asked yourselves sufficiently how much the erection of *every* ideal on earth has cost? How much reality has had to be misunderstood and slandered, how many lies have had to be sanctified, how many consciences disturbed, how much "God" sacrificed every time? If a temple is to be erected *a temple must be destroyed:* that is the law—let anyone who can show me a case in which it is not fulfilled!

We modern men are the heirs of the conscience-vivisection and self-torture[3] of millennia: this is what we have practiced longest, it is our distinctive art perhaps, and in any case our subtlety in which we have acquired a refined taste. Man has all too long had an "evil eye" for his natural inclinations, so that they have finally become inseparable from his "bad conscience." An attempt at the reverse would *in itself* be possible—but who is strong enough for it?—that is, to wed the bad conscience to all the *unnatural* inclinations, all those aspirations to the beyond, to that which runs counter to sense, instinct, nature, animal, in short all ideals hitherto, which are one and all hostile to life and ideals that slander the world. To whom should one turn today with *such* hopes and demands?

One would have precisely the *good* men against one; and, of course, the comfortable, the reconciled, the vain, the sentimental, the weary.

What gives greater offense, what separates one more fundamentally, than to reveal something of the severity and respect with which one treats oneself? And on the other hand—how accommodating, how friendly all the world is toward us as soon as we act as all the world does and "let ourselves go" like all the world!

---

[3] *Selbsttierquälerei: Tierquälerei* really means cruelty to animals or, literally, animal torture; hence Nietzsche's coinage suggests that this kind of self-torture involves mortification of the animal nature of man.

The attainment of this goal would require a *different* kind of spirit from that likely to appear in this present age: spirits strengthened by war and victory, for whom conquest, adventure, danger, and even pain have become needs; it would require habituation to the keen air of the heights, to winter journeys, to ice and mountains in every sense; it would require even a kind of sublime wickedness, an ultimate, supremely self-confident mischievousness in knowledge that goes with great health; it would require, in brief and alas, precisely this *great health!*

Is this even possible today?— But some day, in a stronger age than this decaying, self-doubting present, he must yet come to us, the *redeeming* man of great love and contempt, the creative spirit whose compelling strength will not let him rest in any aloofness or any beyond, whose isolation is misunderstood by the people as if it were flight *from* reality—while it is only his absorption, immersion, penetration *into* reality, so that, when he one day emerges again into the light, he may bring home the *redemption* of this reality: its redemption from the curse that the hitherto reigning ideal has laid upon it. This man of the future, who will redeem us not only from the hitherto reigning ideal but also from that which was bound to grow out of it, the great nausea, the will to nothingness, nihilism; this bell-stroke of noon and of the great decision that liberates the will again and restores its goal to the earth and his hope to man; this Antichrist and antinihilist; this victor over God and nothingness—*he must come one day.*—

25

But what am I saying? Enough! Enough! At this point it behooves me only to be silent; or I shall usurp that to which only one younger, "heavier with future," and stronger than I has a right— that to which only *Zarathustra* has a right, *Zarathustra the godless.*—

Third Essay
What Is the Meaning of Ascetic Ideals?

> Unconcerned, mocking, violent—thus
> wisdom wants *us:* she is a woman and
> always loves only a warrior.
>
> *Thus Spoke Zarathustra*[1]

1

What is the meaning of ascetic ideals?— In the case of artists they mean nothing or too many things; in the case of philosophers and scholars something like a sense and instinct for the most favorable preconditions of higher spirituality; in the case of women at best one *more* seductive charm, a touch of *morbidezza* in fair flesh, the angelic look of a plump pretty animal; in the case of the physiologically deformed and deranged (the *majority* of mortals) an attempt to see themselves as "too good" for this world, a saintly form of debauch, their chief weapon in the struggle against slow pain and boredom; in the case of priests the distinctive priestly faith, their best instrument of power, also the "supreme" license for power; in the case of saints, finally, a pretext for hibernation, their *novissima gloriae cupido,*[2] their repose in nothingness ("God"), their form of madness. *That* the ascetic ideal has meant so many things to man, however, is an expression of the basic fact of the human will, its *horror vacui.*[3] *it needs a goal*—and it will rather will *nothingness* than *not* will.— Am I understood? . . . Have I been understood?

---

[1] "On Reading and Writing" (*Portable Nietzsche,* p. 153).

[2] Newest lust for glory.

[3] Horror of a vacuum.

. . . *"Not at all, my dear sir!"*—Then let us start again, from the beginning.

2

What is the meaning of ascetic ideals?— Or, to take an individual case that I have often been asked about: what does it mean, for example, when an artist like Richard Wagner pays homage to chastity in his old age? In a certain sense, to be sure, he had always done this: but only in the very end in an ascetic sense. What is the meaning of this change of "sense," this radical reversal of sense?— for that is what it was: Wagner leaped over into his opposite. What does it mean when an artist leaps over into his opposite?

Here, if we are disposed to pause a moment at this question, we are at once reminded of what was perhaps the finest, strongest, happiest, *most courageous* period of Wagner's life: the period during which he was deeply concerned with the idea of Luther's wedding. Who knows upon what chance events it depended that instead of this wedding music we possess today *Die Meistersinger?* And how much of the former perhaps still echoes in the latter? But there can be no doubt that "Luther's Wedding" would also have involved a praise of chastity. And also a praise of sensuality, to be sure— and this would have seemed to be quite in order, quite "Wagnerian."

For there is no necessary antithesis between chastity and sensuality;[1] every good marriage, every genuine love affair, transcends this antithesis. Wagner would have done well, I think, to have brought this *pleasant* fact home once more to his Germans by means of a bold and beautiful Luther comedy, for there have always been and still are many slanderers of sensuality among the Germans; and perhaps Luther performed no greater service than to have had the courage of his *sensuality* (in those days it was called, delicately enough, "evangelical freedom"). But even in those cases in which this antithesis between chastity and sensuality really ex-

---

[1] This paragraph as well as section 3 was included with some revisions in *Nietzsche contra Wagner,* in the chapter "Wagner as the Apostle of Chastity" (*Portable Nietzsche,* pp. 673–75).

ists, there is fortunately no need for it to be a tragic antithesis. At least this holds good for all those well-constituted, joyful mortals who are far from regarding their unstable equilibrium between "animal and angel" as necessarily an argument against existence—the subtlest and brightest among them have even found in it, like Goethe and Hafiz, one *more* stimulus to life. It is precisely such "contradictions" that seduce one to existence . . . On the other hand, it is only too clear that when swine who have come to grief are finally induced to worship chastity—and there are such swine! —they will see and worship in it only their antithesis, the antithesis of failed swine—and one can imagine with what tragic zeal and grunting they will do so!—that embarrassing and superfluous antithesis which Richard Wagner at the end of his life unquestionably intended to set to music and put upon the stage. *But why?* as one might reasonably ask. For what were swine to him, what are they to us?—

3

This does not, of course, help us to avoid asking this other question, what that male (yet so unmanly) "country simpleton" was to him, that poor devil and nature boy Parsifal, whom he finally made into a Catholic by such captious means—what? was this Parsifal meant *seriously?* For one might be tempted to suppose the reverse, even to desire it—that the Wagnerian *Parsifal* was intended as a joke, as a kind of epilogue and satyr play with which the tragedian Wagner wanted to take leave of us, also of himself, above all *of tragedy* in a fitting manner worthy of himself, namely with an extravagance of wanton parody of the tragic itself, of the whole gruesome earthly seriousness and misery of his previous works, of the *crudest form,* overcome at long last, of the antinature of the ascetic ideal. This, to repeat, would have been worthy of a great tragedian, who, like every artist, arrives at the ultimate pinnacle of his greatness only when he comes to see himself and his art *beneath* him—when he knows how to *laugh* at himself. Is Wagner's *Parsifal* his secret laughter of superiority at himself, the triumph of his ultimate artist's freedom and artist's trans-

cendence? One could wish that it were, to repeat again; for what
would a *seriously-intended Parsifal* be? Must one really see in him
(as someone once put it to me) "the product of an insane hatred of
knowledge, spirit, and sensuality"? A curse on the senses and the
spirit in a *single* breath of hatred? An apostacy and return to morbid Christian and obscurantist ideals? And ultimately a self-
negation, a self-cancellation on the part of an artist who had
hitherto aimed with all the power of his will at the reverse, at the
highest spiritualization and sensualization of his art? And not of his
art only; of his life, too.

One should recall how enthusiastically Wagner at one time
followed in the footsteps of the philosopher Feuerbach:[1] Feuerbach's cry of "healthy sensuality"—that sounded in the thirties and
forties, to Wagner as to many other Germans (they called themselves the *"young* Germans"), like a cry of redemption. Did he at
last come to *learn otherwise?* For at least it seems that he finally
had the will to *teach otherwise.* And not only from the stage with
the trumpets of *Parsifal;* in the murky writings of his last years, as
unfree as they are perplexed, there are a hundred passages that
betray a secret wish and will, a despairing, unsure, unacknowl-
edged will to preach nothing other than reversion, conversion, denial, Christianity, medievalism, and to say to his disciples "it is no
good! seek salvation elsewhere!" Even the "blood of the Redeemer" is invoked in one place.—

4

In such a case as this, embarrassing in many ways, my view
is—and it is a *typical* case—that one does best to separate an artist
from his work, not taking him as seriously as his work. He is, after
all, only the precondition of his work, the womb, the soil, sometimes the dung and manure on which, out of which, it grows—and

---

[1] Ludwig Feuerbach (1804–1872) was the outstanding "Young" (left-wing)
Hegelian philosopher who tried to transform theology into anthropology. His
influence on Karl Marx was considerable, but Marx and Engels took sharp
issue with him. Feuerbach's book, *Das Wesen des Christentums* (1841) was
translated into English by George Eliot as *The Essence of Christianity*
(1853, 2nd ed., 1881), and is still considered a classic of humanism.

therefore in most cases something one must forget if one is to enjoy the work itself. Insight into the origin of a work concerns the physiologists and vivisectionists of the spirit; never the aesthetic man, the artist!

The poet and creator of *Parsifal* could no more be spared a deep, thorough, even frightful identification with and descent into medieval soul-conflicts, a hostile separation from all spiritual height, severity, and discipline, a kind of intellectual *perversity* (if I may be pardoned the word), than can a pregnant woman be spared the repellent and bizarre aspects of pregnancy—which, as aforesaid, must be *forgotten* if one is to enjoy the child.

One should guard against confusion through psychological *contiguity,* to use a British term,[1] a confusion to which an artist himself is only too prone: as if he himself were what he is able to represent, conceive, and express. The fact is that *if* he were it, he would not represent, conceive, and express it: a Homer would not have created an Achilles nor a Goethe a Faust if Homer had been an Achilles or Goethe a Faust. Whoever is completely and wholly an artist is to all eternity separated from the "real," the actual; on the other hand, one can understand how he may sometimes weary to the point of desperation of the eternal "unreality" and falsity of his innermost existence—and that then he may well attempt what is most forbidden him, to lay hold of actuality, for once actually to *be.* With what success? That is easy to guess.

It is the *typical velleity* of the artist: the same velleity to which the aged Wagner fell victim and for which he had to pay so high and fateful a price (it cost him those of his friends who were valuable). Finally, however, quite apart from this velleity, who would not wish for Wagner's own sake that he had taken leave of us and of his art *differently,* not with a *Parsifal* but in a more triumphant manner, more self-confident, more Wagnerian—less misleading, less ambiguous in relation to his over-all intentions, less Schopenhauerian, less nihilistic?

---

[1] Nietzsche uses the English term. The allusion is to David Hume.

5

What, then, is the meaning of ascetic ideals? In the case of an artist, as we see, *nothing whatever!* . . . Or so many things it amounts to nothing whatever!

Let us, first of all, eliminate the artists: they do not stand nearly independently enough in the world and *against* the world for their changing valuations to deserve attention *in themselves!* They have at all times been valets of some morality, philosophy, or religion; quite apart from the fact that they have unfortunately often been all-too-pliable courtiers of their own followers and patrons, and cunning flatterers of ancient or newly arrived powers. They always need at the very least protection, a prop, an established authority: artists never stand apart; standing alone is contrary to their deepest instincts.

Thus Richard Wagner, for example, used the philosopher Schopenhauer, when the latter's "time had come," as his herald and protection: who would regard it as even thinkable that he would have had the *courage* for the ascetic ideal without the prop provided by Schopenhauer's philosophy, without the authority of Schopenhauer which had gained *ascendancy* in Europe during the seventies? (Let us leave out of account whether in the *new* Germany an artist could have existed who lacked the milk of pious, *Reichs*-pious sentiments).

Here we have arrived at the more serious question: what does it mean when a genuine *philosopher* pays homage to the ascetic ideal, a genuinely independent spirit like Schopenhauer, a man and knight of a steely eye who had the courage to be himself, who knew how to stand alone without first waiting for heralds and signs from above?

Let us here consider straightaway the remarkable and for many kinds of men even fascinating attitude Schopenhauer adopted toward *art:* for it was obviously for the sake of this that Richard Wagner *initially* went over to Schopenhauer (persuaded, as one knows, by a poet, by Herwegh[1]), and did so to such an extent that

---

[1] Georg Herwegh, 1817–1875.

there exists a complete theoretical contradiction between his earlier and his later aesthetic creed—the former set down, for example, in *Opera and Drama,* the latter in the writings he published from 1870 onward. Specifically, he ruthlessly altered—and this is perhaps most astonishing—his judgment as to the value and status of *music:* what did he care that he had formerly made of music a means, a medium, a "woman" who required a goal, a man, in order to prosper—namely, drama! He grasped all at once that with the Schopenhauerian theory and innovation *more* could be done *in majorem musicae gloriam*[2]—namely, with the theory of the *sovereignty* of music as Schopenhauer conceived it: music set apart from all the other arts, the independent art as such, *not* offering images of phenomenality, as the other arts did, but speaking rather the language of the will itself, directly out of the "abyss" as its most authentic, elemental, nonderivative revelation. With this extraordinary rise in the value of music that appeared to follow from Schopenhauerian philosophy, the value of *the musician* himself all at once went up in an unheard-of manner, too: from now on he became an oracle, a priest, indeed more than a priest, a kind of mouthpiece of the "in itself" of things, a telephone from the beyond—henceforth he uttered not only music, this ventriloquist of God—he uttered metaphysics: no wonder he one day finally uttered *ascetic ideals.*

6

Schopenhauer made use of the Kantian version of the aesthetic problem—although he certainly did not view it with Kantian eyes. Kant thought he was honoring art when among the predicates of beauty he emphasized and gave prominence to those which establish the honor of knowledge: impersonality and universality. This is not the place to inquire whether this was essentially a mistake; all I wish to underline is that Kant, like all philosophers, instead of envisaging the aesthetic problem from the point of view of the artist (the creator), considered art and the beautiful purely from that of the "spectator," and unconsciously introduced the

---

[2] For the greater glory of music.

"spectator" into the concept "beautiful." It would not have been so bad if this "spectator" had at least been sufficiently familiar to the philosophers of beauty—namely, as a great *personal* fact and experience, as an abundance of vivid authentic experiences, desires, surprises, and delights in the realm of the beautiful! But I fear that the reverse has always been the case; and so they have offered us, from the beginning, definitions in which, as in Kant's famous definition of the beautiful, a lack of any refined first-hand experience reposes in the shape of a fat worm of error. "That is beautiful," said Kant,[1] "which gives us pleasure *without interest.*" Without interest! Compare with this definition one framed by a genuine "spectator" and artist—Stendhal, who once called the beautiful *une promesse de bonheur.*[2] At any rate he *rejected* and repudiated the one point about the aesthetic condition which Kant had stressed: *le désintéressement.* Who is right, Kant or Stendhal?

If our aestheticians never weary of asserting in Kant's favor that, under the spell of beauty, one can *even* view undraped female statues "without interest," one may laugh a little at their expense: the experiences of *artists* on this ticklish point are more "interesting," and Pygmalion was in any event *not* necessarily an "unaesthetic man." Let us think the more highly of the innocence of our aestheticians which is reflected in such arguments; let us, for example, credit it to the honor of Kant that he should expatiate on the peculiar properties of the sense of touch with the naïveté of a country parson!

And here we come back to Schopenhauer, who stood much closer to the arts than Kant and yet did not free himself from the spell of the Kantian definition: how did that happen? The circumstance is remarkable enough: he interpreted the term "without interest" in an extremely personal way, on the basis of one of his most regular experiences.

Of few things does Schopenhauer speak with greater assurance than he does of the effect of aesthetic contemplation: he says of it that it counteracts *sexual* "interestedness," like lupulin and camphor; he never wearied of glorifying *this* liberation from the

---

[1] *Critique of Judgment* (1790), sections 1–5.
[2] A promise of happiness.

"will" as the great merit and utility of the aesthetic condition. Indeed, one might be tempted to ask whether his basic conception of "will and representation," the thought that redemption from the "will" could be attained only through "representation," did not originate as a generalization from this sexual experience. (In all questions concerning Schopenhauer's philosophy, by the way, one should never forget that it was the conception of a young man of twenty-six; so that it partakes not only of the specific qualities of Schopenhauer, but also of the specific qualities of that period of life.) Listen, for instance, to one of the most explicit of the countless passages he has written in praise of the aesthetic condition (*World as Will and Representation,* I, p. 231 [3]); listen to the tone, the suffering, the happiness, the gratitude expressed in such words.

"This is the painless condition that Epicurus praised as the highest good and the condition of the gods; for a moment we are delivered from the vile urgency of the will; we celebrate the Sabbath of the penal servitude of volition; the wheel of Ixion stands still!"

What vehemence of diction! What images of torment and long despair! What an almost pathological antithesis between "a moment" and the usual "wheel of Ixion," "penal servitude of volition," and "vile urgency of the will!"— But even if Schopenhauer was a hundred times right in his own case, what insight does that give us into the nature of the beautiful? Schopenhauer described *one* effect of the beautiful, its calming effect on the will—but is this a regular effect? Stendhal, as we have seen, a no less sensual but more happily constituted person than Schopenhauer, emphasizes another effect of the beautiful: "the beautiful *promises* happiness"; to him the fact seems to be precisely that the beautiful *arouses the will* ("interestedness"). And could one not finally urge against Schopenhauer himself that he was quite wrong in thinking himself a Kantian in this matter, that he by no means understood the Kantian definition of the beautiful in a Kantian sense—that he, too, was pleased by the beautiful from an "interested" viewpoint, even from the very strongest, most personal interest: that of a tortured

---

[3] Ed. Julius Frauenstädt; i.e., Book III, section 38.

man who gains release from his torture?— And, to return to our first question, "what does it *mean* when a philosopher pays homage to the ascetic ideal?"—here we get at any rate a first indication: he wants *to gain release from a torture.*—

7

Let us not become gloomy as soon as we hear the word "torture": in this particular case there is plenty to offset and mitigate that word—even something to laugh at. Above all, we should not underestimate the fact that Schopenhauer, who treated sexuality as a personal enemy (including its tool, woman, that *"instrumentum diaboli"* [1]), *needed* enemies in order to keep in good spirits; that he loved bilious, black-green words, that he scolded for the sake of scolding, out of passion; that he would have become ill, become a *pessimist* (for he was not one, however much he desired it), if deprived of his enemies, of Hegel, of woman, of sensuality and the whole will to existence, to persistence. Without these, Schopenhauer would *not* have persisted, one may wager on that; he would have run away: but his enemies held him fast, his enemies seduced him ever again to existence; his anger was, just as in the case of the Cynics of antiquity, his balm, his refreshment, his reward, his specific against disgust, his *happiness*. So much in regard to what is most personal in the case of Schopenhauer; on the other hand, there is also something typical in him—and here we finally come back to our problem.

As long as there are philosophers on earth, and wherever there have been philosophers (from India to England, to take the antithetical poles of philosophical endowment), there unquestionably exists a peculiar philosophers' irritation at and rancor against sensuality: Schopenhauer is merely its most eloquent and, if one has ears for this, most ravishing and delightful expression. There also exists a peculiar philosophers' prejudice and affection in favor of the whole ascetic ideal; one should not overlook that. Both, to repeat, pertain to the type; if both are lacking in a philosopher,

---

[1] Instrument of the devil.

then—one can be sure of it—he is always only a "so-called" philosopher. What does that *mean?* For this fact has to be interpreted: *in itself* it just stands there, stupid to all eternity, like every "thing-in-itself."

Every animal—therefore *la bête philosophe*,[2] too—instinctively strives for an optimum of favorable conditions under which it can expend all its strength and achieve its maximal feeling of power; every animal abhors, just as instinctively and with a subtlety of discernment that is "higher than all reason," every kind of intrusion or hindrance that obstructs or could obstruct this path to the optimum (I am *not* speaking of its path to happiness, but its path to power, to action, to the most powerful activity, and in most cases actually its path to unhappiness). Thus the philosopher abhors *marriage,* together with that which might persuade to it—marriage being a hindrance and calamity on his path to the optimum. What great philosopher hitherto has been married? Heraclitus, Plato, Descartes, Spinoza, Leibniz, Kant, Schopenhauer—they were not; more, one cannot even *imagine* them married. A married philosopher belongs *in comedy,* that is my proposition—and as for that exception, Socrates[3]—the malicious Socrates, it would seem, married *ironically,* just to demonstrate *this* proposition.

Every philosopher would speak as Buddha did when he was told of the birth of a son: "Rahula has been born to me, a fetter has been forged for me" (Rahula here means "a little demon"); every "free spirit" would experience a thoughtful moment, supposing he had previously experienced a thoughtless one, of the kind that once came to the same Buddha—"narrow and oppressive," he thought to himself, "is life in a house, a place of impurity; freedom lies in leaving the house": "thinking thus, he left the house." Ascetic ideals reveal so many bridges to *independence* that a philosopher is bound to rejoice and clap his hands when he hears the story of all those resolute men who one day said No to all servitude and went into some *desert:* even supposing they were merely strong asses and quite the reverse of a strong spirit.

What, then, is the meaning of the ascetic ideal in the case of a

---

[2] The philosophical animal.

[3] Socrates appears in Aristophanes' comedy *The Clouds.*

philosopher? My answer is—you will have guessed it long ago: the philosopher sees in it an optimum condition for the highest and boldest spirituality and smiles—he does *not* deny "existence," he rather affirms *his* existence and *only* his existence, and this perhaps to the point at which he is not far from harboring the impious wish: *pereat mundus, fiat philosophia, fiat philosophus,* **fiam!** [4]—

8

As you see, they are not unbiased witnesses and judges of the *value* of the ascetic ideal, these philosophers! They think of *them-selves*—what is "the saint" to them! They think of what *they* can least do without: freedom from compulsion, disturbance, noise, from tasks, duties, worries; clear heads; the dance, leap, and flight of ideas; good air, thin, clear, open, dry, like the air of the heights through which all animal being becomes more spiritual and ac-quires wings; repose in all cellar regions; all dogs nicely chained up; no barking of hostility and shaggy-haired rancor; no gnawing worm of injured ambition; undemanding and obedient intestines, busy as windmills but distant; the heart remote, beyond, heavy with future, posthumous—all in all, they think of the ascetic ideal as the cheerful asceticism of an animal become fledged and divine, float-ing above life rather than in repose.

The three great slogans of the ascetic ideal are familiar: pov-erty, humility, chastity. Now take a close look at the lives of all the great, fruitful, inventive spirits: you will always encounter all three to a certain degree. *Not,* it goes without saying, as though these constituted their "virtues"—what has this kind of man to do with virtues!—but as the most appropriate and natural conditions of their *best* existence, their *fairest* fruitfulness. It is quite possible that their dominating spirituality had first to put a check on an unrestrained and irritable pride or a wanton sensuality, or that it perhaps had a hard job to maintain its will to the "desert" against a love of luxury and refinement or an excessive liberality of heart and hand. But it did it, precisely because it was the dominating

---

[4] Let the world perish, but let there be philosophy, the philosopher, *me!*

instinct whose demands prevailed against those of all the other instincts—it continues to do it; if it did not do it, it would not dominate. There is thus nothing of "virtue" in this.

The *desert,* incidentally, that I just mentioned, where the strong, independent spirits withdraw and become lonely—oh, how different it looks from the way educated people imagine a desert!—for in some cases they themselves are this desert, these educated people. And it is certain that no actor of the spirit could possibly endure life in it—for them it is not nearly romantic or Syrian enough, not nearly enough of a stage desert! To be sure, there is no lack of camels[1] in it; but that is where the similarity ends. A voluntary obscurity perhaps; an avoidance of oneself; a dislike of noise, honor, newspapers, influence; a modest job, an everyday job, something that conceals rather than exposes one; an occasional association with harmless, cheerful beasts and birds whose sight is refreshing; mountains for company, but not dead ones, mountains with *eyes* (that is, with lakes); perhaps even a room in a full, utterly commonplace hotel, where one is certain to go unrecognized and can talk to anyone with impunity—that is what "desert" means here: oh, it is lonely enough, believe me! When Heraclitus withdrew into the courtyards and colonnades of the great temple of Artemis, this was a worthier "desert," I admit: why do we *lack* such temples? (Perhaps we do *not* lack them: I just recall my most beautiful study—the Piazza di San Marco, in spring of course, and morning also, the time between ten and twelve.) That which Heraclitus avoided, however, is still the same as that which *we* shun today: the noise and democratic chatter of the Ephesians, their politics, their latest news of the "Empire" [2] (the Persian, you understand), their market business of "today"—for we philosophers need to be spared *one* thing above all: everything to do with "today." We reverence what is still, cold, noble, distant, past, and in general everything in the face of which the soul does not have to defend itself and wrap itself up—what one can speak to without speaking *aloud.*

One should listen to how a spirit sounds when it speaks: every

---

[1] Here used in the sense of silly asses, which is common in German.
[2] *Reich.*

spirit has its own sound and loves its own sound. That one, over there, for example, must be an agitator, that is to say, a hollow head, a hollow pot: whatever goes into him comes back out of him dull and thick, heavy with the echo of great emptiness. This fellow usually speaks hoarsely: has he perhaps *thought* himself hoarse? That might be possible—ask any physiologist—but whoever thinks in *words* thinks as an orator and not as a thinker (it shows that fundamentally he does not think facts, nor factually, but only in relation to facts; that he is really thinking of *himself* and his listeners). A third person speaks importunately, he comes too close to us, he breathes on us—involuntarily we close our mouths, although it is a book through which he is speaking to us: the sound of his style betrays the reason: he has no time to waste, he has little faith in himself, he must speak today or never. A spirit that is sure of itself, however, speaks softly; it seeks concealment, it keeps people waiting.

A philosopher may be recognized by the fact that he avoids three glittering and loud things: fame, princes, and women—which is not to say they do not come to him. He shuns light that is too bright: that is why he shuns his age and its "day." In this he is like a shadow: the lower his sun sinks the bigger he becomes. As for his "humility," he endures a certain dependence and eclipse, as he endures the darkness: more, he is afraid of being distracted by lightning, he shies away from the unprotected isolation of abandoned trees upon which any bad weather can vent its moods, any mood its bad weather. His "maternal" instinct, the secret love of that which is growing in him, directs him toward situations in which he is relieved of the necessity of thinking *of himself;* in the same sense in which the instinct of the *mother* in woman has hitherto generally kept woman in a dependent situation. Ultimately they ask for little enough, these philosophers: their motto is "he who possesses is possessed"—*not,* as I must say again and again, from virtue, from a laudable will to contentment and simplicity, but because their supreme lord demands this of them, prudently and inexorably: he is concerned with one thing alone, and assembles and saves up everything—time, energy, love, and interest—only for that one thing.

This kind of man does not like to be disturbed by enmities, nor by friendships; he easily forgets and easily despises. He thinks it in bad taste to play the martyr; "to *suffer* for truth"—he leaves that to the ambitious and the stage heroes of the spirit and to anyone else who has the time for it (the philosophers themselves have something to *do* for the truth). They use big words sparingly; it is said that they dislike the very word "truth": it sounds too grandiloquent.

As for the "chastity" of philosophers, finally, this type of spirit clearly has its fruitfulness somewhere else than in children; perhaps it also has the survival of its name elsewhere, its little immortality (philosophers in ancient India expressed themselves even more immodestly: "why should he desire progeny whose soul is the world?"). There is nothing in this of chastity from any kind of ascetic scruple or hatred of the senses, just as it is not chastity when an athlete or jockey abstains from women: it is rather the will of their dominating instinct, at least during their periods of great pregnancy. Every artist knows what a harmful effect intercourse has in states of great spiritual tension and preparation; those with the greatest power and the surest instincts do not need to learn this by experience, by unfortunate experience—their "maternal" instinct ruthlessly disposes of all other stores and accumulations of energy, of animal vigor, for the benefit of the evolving work: the greater energy then *uses up* the lesser.

Now let us interpret the case of Schopenhauer, discussed above, in the light of these remarks: the sight of the beautiful obviously had upon him the effect of releasing the *chief energy* of his nature (the energy of contemplation and penetration), so that this exploded and all at once became the master of his consciousness. This should by no means preclude the possibility that the sweetness and plenitude peculiar to the aesthetic state might be derived precisely from the ingredient of "sensuality" (just as the "idealism" of adolescent girls derives from this source)—so that sensuality is not overcome by the appearance of the aesthetic condition, as Schopenhauer believed, but only transfigured and no longer enters consciousness as sexual excitement. (I shall return to this point on another occasion, in connection with the still more delicate prob-

lems of the *physiology of aesthetics,*[3] which is practically un-
touched and unexplored so far.)

9

We have seen how a certain asceticism, a severe and cheerful
continence with the best will, belongs to the most favorable conditions of supreme spirituality, and is also among its most natural
consequences: hence it need be no matter for surprise that philosophers have always discussed the ascetic ideal with a certain fond-
ness. A serious examination of history actually reveals that the
bond between philosophy and the ascetic ideal is even much closer
and stronger. One might assert that it was only on the leading-
strings of this ideal that philosophy learned to take its first small
steps on earth—alas, so clumsily, so unwillingly, so ready to fall on
its face and lie on its belly, this timid little toddler and mollycoddle
with shaky legs!

Philosophy began as all good things begin: for a long time it
lacked the courage for itself; it was always looking round to see if
someone would come and help it; yet it was afraid of all who
looked at it. Draw up a list of the various propensities and virtues
of the philosopher—his bent to doubt, his bent to deny, his bent to
suspend judgment (his "ephectic" bent), his bent to analyze, his
bent to investigate, seek, dare, his bent to compare and balance,
his will to neutrality and objectivity, his will to every *"sine ira et
studio"*:[1] is it not clear that for the longest time all of them con-
travened the basic demands of morality and conscience (not to
speak of *reason* quite generally, which Luther liked to call "Mistress Clever, the clever whore")—that if a philosopher *had* been

---

[3] Nietzsche did not live to publish an essay on this subject, but see his next
two books, *The Case of Wagner* (p. 601f., below) and *Twilight of the Idols,*
"Skirmishes of an Untimely Man," section 8ff., 19ff., and 47ff. (*Portable
Nietzsche,* pp. 518ff.). See also *Nietzsche contra Wagner* (*ibid.*) and the
sections on "The Will to Power as Art" in *The Will to Power,* ed. Kaufmann
(New York, Random House, 1967).
[1] Without anger or affection; i.e., impartial(ity).

conscious of what he was, he would have been compelled to feel himself the embodiment of *"nitimur in vetitum"* [2]—and consequently *guarded* against "feeling himself," against becoming conscious of himself?

It is, to repeat, no different with all the good things of which we are proud today; measured even by the standards of the ancient Greeks, our entire modern way of life, insofar as it is not weakness but power and consciousness of power, has the appearance of sheer *hubris*[3] and godlessness: for the longest time it was precisely the reverse of those things we hold in honor today that had a good conscience on its side and God for its guardian. Our whole attitude toward nature, the way we violate her with the aid of machines and the heedless inventiveness of our technicians and engineers, is *hubris;* our attitude toward God as some alleged spider of purpose and morality behind the great captious web of causality, is *hubris* —we might say, with Charles the Bold when he opposed Louis XI, *"je combats l'universelle araignée"*;[4] our attitude toward *ourselves* is *hubris,* for we experiment with ourselves in a way we would never permit ourselves to experiment with animals and, carried away by curiosity, we cheerfully vivisect our souls: what is the "salvation" of the soul to us today? Afterward we cure ourselves: sickness is instructive, we have no doubt of that, even more instructive than health—*those who make sick* seem even more necessary to us today than any medicine men or "saviors." We violate ourselves nowadays, no doubt of it, we nutcrackers of the soul, ever questioning and questionable, as if life were nothing but cracking nuts; and thus we are bound to grow day-by-day more questionable, *worthier* of asking questions;[5] perhaps also worthier—of living?

All good things were formerly bad things; every original sin has turned into an original virtue. Marriage, for example, seemed for a long time a transgression against the rights of the community;

---

[2] We strive for the forbidden: *Ovid's Amores,* III, 4, 17. Cf. *Beyond Good and Evil,* section 227.

[3] Overweening pride—often ascribed to the heroes of Greek tragedies.

[4] I fight the universal spider.

[5] *Fragwürdiger,* würdiger *zu fragen.*

one had to make reparation for being so immodest as to claim a woman for oneself (hence, for example, the *jus primae noctis*,[6] which in Cambodia is still the prerogative of the priests, those guardians of all "hallowed customs"). The gentle, benevolent, conciliatory, and compassionate feelings—eventually so highly valued that they almost constitute "the eternal values"—were opposed for the longest time by self-contempt: one was ashamed of mildness as one is today ashamed of hardness (cf. *Beyond Good and Evil,* section 260). Submission to *law:* how the consciences of noble tribes all over the earth resisted the abandonment of vendetta and were loath to bow before the power of the law! "Law" was for a long time a *vetitum*,[7] an outrage, an innovation; it was characterized by violence—it *was* violence to which one submitted, feeling ashamed of oneself. Every smallest step on earth has been paid for by spiritual and physical torture: this whole point of view, "that not only every progressive step, no! every step, movement, and change has required its countless martyrs," sounds utterly strange to us today—I called attention to it in *The Dawn,* section 18.

"Nothing has been bought more dearly," I say there, "than the modicum of human reason and feeling of freedom that are now our pride. It is this pride, however, that makes it almost impossible for us today to empathize with that vast era of the 'morality of mores'[8] which preceded 'world history' as the truly decisive history that determined the character of mankind: when suffering was everywhere counted as a virtue, cruelty as a virtue, dissembling as a virtue, revenge as a virtue, slander of reason as a virtue, and when on the other hand well-being was counted as a danger, thirst for knowledge as a danger, peace as a danger, pity as a danger, being pitied as a disgrace, work as a disgrace, madness as divine, *change* as the very essence of immorality[9] and pregnant with disaster."

---

[6] The right of the first night.

[7] Something forbidden, or a prohibition.

[8] *Sittlichkeit der Sitte:* see Nietzsche's Preface, section 4.

[9] *Das Unsittliche . . . an sich: an sich* (in itself, the very essence of) and *überall* (everywhere) are not found in *The Dawn* but added by Nietzsche in the *Genealogy.* Where morality is identified with the traditional *mores* or customs, change is *eo ipso* immoral.

10

In the same book (section 42) it is explained under what valuation, what *oppression* of valuation, the earliest race of contemplative men had to live: when not feared, they were despised. Contemplation first appeared on earth in disguise, in ambiguous form, with an evil heart and often an anxious head: there is no doubt of that. The inactive, brooding, unwarlike element in the instincts of contemplative men long surrounded them with a profound mistrustfulness: the only way of dispelling it was to arouse a decided *fear* of oneself. And the ancient Brahmins, for instance, knew how to do this! The earliest philosophers knew how to endow their existence and appearance with a meaning, a basis and background, through which others might come to *fear* them: more closely considered, they did so from an even more fundamental need, namely, so as to fear and reverence themselves. For they found all the value judgments within them turned *against* them, they had to fight down every kind of suspicion and resistance against "the philosopher in them." As men of frightful ages, they did this by using frightful means: cruelty toward themselves, inventive self-castigation—this was the principal means these power-hungry hermits and innovators of ideas required to overcome the gods and tradition in themselves, so as to be able to *believe* in their own innovations. I recall the famous story of King Vishvamitra, who through millennia of self-torture acquired such a feeling of power and self-confidence that he endeavored to build a *new heaven*—the uncanny symbol of the most ancient and most recent experience of philosophers on earth: whoever has at some time built a "new heaven" has found the power to do so only in his *own hell*.

Let us compress the facts into a few brief formulas: to begin with, the philosophic spirit always had to use as a mask and cocoon the *previously established* types of the contemplative man—priest, sorcerer, soothsayer, and in any case a religious type—in order to be able to *exist at all: the ascetic ideal* for a long time served the philosopher as a form in which to appear, as a precondition of existence—he had to *represent* it so as to be able to be a philosopher; he had to *believe* in it in order to be able to represent it. The peculiar, withdrawn attitude of the philosopher, world-denying, hostile to life, suspicious of the senses, freed from sensuality, which has been maintained down to the most modern times and has become virtually the *philosopher's pose par excellence*—it is above all a result of the emergency conditions under which philosophy arose and survived at all; for the longest time philosophy would not have been *possible at all* on earth without ascetic wraps and cloak, without an ascetic self-misunderstanding. To put it vividly: the *ascetic priest* provided until the most modern times the repulsive and gloomy caterpillar form in which alone the philosopher could live and creep about.

Has all this really *altered?* Has that many-colored and dangerous winged creature, the "spirit" which this caterpillar concealed, really been unfettered at last and released into the light, thanks to a sunnier, warmer, brighter world? Is there sufficient pride, daring, courage, self-confidence available today, sufficient will of the spirit, will to responsibility, *freedom of will,* for "the philosopher" to be henceforth—*possible* on earth?—

11

Only now that we behold the *ascetic priest* do we seriously come to grips with our problem: what is the meaning of the ascetic ideal?—only now does it become "serious": we are now face to face with the actual *representative of seriousness.* "What is the meaning of all seriousness?"—this even more fundamental question may perhaps be trembling on our lips at this point: a question for physiologists, of course, but one which we must still avoid for the moment. The ascetic priest possessed in this ideal not only his faith but also his will, his power, his interest. His *right* to exist stands or falls with that ideal: no wonder we encounter here a terrible antagonist—supposing we are antagonists of that ideal—one who fights for his existence against those who deny that ideal.

On the other hand, it is inherently improbable that so interested an attitude toward our problem will benefit it: the ascetic priest will hardly provide the best defense of his ideal, just as a woman who tries to defend "woman as such" usually fails—and he certainly will not be the most objective judge of this controversy. Far from fearing he will confute us—this much is already obvious —we shall have to help him defend himself against us.

The idea at issue here is the *valuation* the ascetic priest places on our life: he juxtaposes it (along with what pertains to it: "nature," "world," the whole sphere of becoming and transitoriness) with a quite different mode of existence which it opposes and excludes, *unless* it turn against itself, *deny itself:* in that case, the case of the ascetic life, life counts as a bridge to that other mode of existence. The ascetic treats life as a wrong road on which one must finally walk back to the point where it begins, or as a mistake that is put right by deeds—that we *ought* to put right: for he *demands* that one go along with him; where he can he compels acceptance of *his* evaluation of existence.

What does this mean? So monstrous a mode of valuation stands inscribed in the history of mankind not as an exception and curiosity, but as one of the most widespread and enduring of all phenomena. Read from a distant star, the majuscule script of our earthly existence would perhaps lead to the conclusion that the earth was the distinctively *ascetic planet,* a nook of disgruntled, arrogant, and offensive creatures filled with a profound disgust at themselves, at the earth, at all life, who inflict as much pain on themselves as they possibly can out of pleasure in inflicting pain— which is probably their only pleasure. For consider how regularly and universally the ascetic priest appears in almost every age; he belongs to no one race; he prospers everywhere; he emerges from every class of society. Nor does he breed and propagate his mode of valuation through heredity: the opposite is the case—broadly speaking, a profound instinct rather forbids him to propagate. It must be a necessity of the first order that again and again promotes the growth and prosperity of this *life-inimical* species—it must indeed be in the *interest of life itself* that such a self-contradictory type does not die out. For an ascetic life is a self-contradiction: here rules a *ressentiment* without equal, that of an insatiable instinct and power-will that wants to become master not over something in life but over life itself, over its most profound, powerful,

and basic conditions; here an attempt is made to employ force to
block up the wells of force; here physiological well-being itself is
viewed askance, and especially the outward expression of this well-
being, beauty and joy; while pleasure is felt and *sought* in ill-
constitutedness, decay, pain, mischance, ugliness, voluntary deprivation, self-mortification, self-flagellation, self-sacrifice. All this is
in the highest degree paradoxical: we stand before a discord that
wants to be discordant, that *enjoys* itself in this suffering and even
grows more self-confident and triumphant the more its own presupposition, its physiological capacity for life, *decreases.* "Triumph in
the ultimate agony": the ascetic ideal has always fought under this
hyperbolic sign; in this enigma of seduction, in this image of torment and delight, it recognized its brightest light, its salvation, its
ultimate victory. *Crux, nux, lux*[1]—for the ascetic ideal these three
are one.—

12

Suppose such an incarnate will to contradiction and antinat-
uralness is induced to *philosophize:* upon what will it vent its innermost contrariness? Upon what is felt most certainly to be real
and actual: it will look for error precisely where the instinct of life
most unconditionally posits truth. It will, for example, like the ascetics of the Vedanta philosophy, downgrade physicality to an illusion; likewise pain, multiplicity, the entire conceptual antithesis
"subject" and "object"—errors, nothing but errors! To renounce
belief in one's ego, to deny one's own "reality"—what a triumph!
not merely over the senses, over appearance, but a much higher
kind of triumph, a violation and cruelty against *reason*—a voluptuous pleasure that reaches its height when the ascetic self-contempt
and self-mockery of reason declares: *"there is* a realm of truth and
being, but reason is *excluded* from it!"

---

[1] Cross, nut, light. In one of Nietzsche's notebooks we find this sketch for a
title:

Nux et Crux
A Philosophy for Good Teeth

(Erich Podach, *Ein Blick in Notizbücher Nietzsches,* Heidelberg, Wolfgang
Rothe, 1963, p. 163 and errata slip).

(Incidentally, even in the Kantian concept of the "intelligible character of things" something remains of this lascivious ascetic discord that loves to turn reason against reason: for "intelligible character" signifies in Kant that things are so constituted that the intellect comprehends just enough of them to know that for the intellect they are—*utterly incomprehensible.*)

But precisely because we seek knowledge, let us not be ungrateful to such resolute reversals of accustomed perspectives and valuations with which the spirit has, with apparent mischievousness and futility, raged against itself for so long: to see differently in this way for once, to *want* to see differently, is no small discipline and preparation of the intellect for its future "objectivity"—the latter understood not as "contemplation without interest" (which is a nonsensical absurdity), but as the ability *to control* one's Pro and Con and to dispose of them, so that one knows how to employ a *variety* of perspectives and affective interpretations in the service of knowledge.

Henceforth, my dear philosophers, let us be on guard against the dangerous old conceptual fiction that posited a "pure, will-less, painless, timeless knowing subject"; let us guard against the snares of such contradictory concepts as "pure reason," "absolute spirituality," "knowledge in itself": these always demand that we should think of an eye that is completely unthinkable, an eye turned in no particular direction, in which the active and interpreting forces, through which alone seeing becomes seeing *something,* are supposed to be lacking; these always demand of the eye an absurdity and a nonsense. There is *only* a perspective seeing, *only* a perspective "knowing"; and the *more* affects we allow to speak about one thing, the *more* eyes, different eyes, we can use to observe one thing, the more complete will our "concept" of this thing, our "objectivity," be.[1] But to eliminate the will altogether, to suspend each and every affect, supposing we were capable of this—what would that mean but to *castrate* the intellect?—

_____

[1] This passage throws a great deal of light on Nietzsche's perspectivism and on his style and philosophical method.

13

But let us return to our problem. It will be immediately obvious that such a self-contradiction as the ascetic appears to represent, "life *against* life," is, physiologically considered and not merely psychologically, a simple absurdity. It can only be *apparent;* it must be a kind of provisional formulation, an interpretation and psychological misunderstanding of something whose real nature could not for a long time be understood or described *as it really was*—a mere word inserted into an old *gap* in human knowledge. Let us replace it with a brief formulation of the facts of the matter: *the ascetic ideal springs from the protective instinct of a degenerating life* which tries by all means to sustain itself and to fight for its existence; it indicates a partial physiological obstruction and exhaustion against which the deepest instincts of life, which have remained intact, continually struggle with new expedients and devices. The ascetic ideal is such an expedient; the case is therefore the opposite of what those who reverence this ideal believe: life wrestles in it and through it with death and *against* death; the ascetic ideal is an artifice for the *preservation* of life.

That this ideal acquired such power and ruled over men as imperiously as we find it in history, especially wherever the civilization and taming of man has been carried through, expresses a great fact: the *sickliness* of the type of man we have had hitherto, or at least of the tamed man, and the physiological struggle of man against death (more precisely: against disgust with life, against exhaustion, against the desire for the "end"). The ascetic priest is the incarnate desire to be different, to be in a different place, and indeed this desire at its greatest extreme, its distinctive fervor and passion; but precisely this power of his desire is the chain that holds him captive so that he becomes a tool for the creation of more favorable conditions for being here and being man—it is precisely this *power* that enables him to persuade to existence the whole herd of the ill-constituted, disgruntled, underprivileged, unfortunate, and all who suffer of themselves, by instinctively going before them as their shepherd. You will see my point: this ascetic priest, this apparent enemy of life, this *denier*—precisely he is among the greatest *conserving* and yes-creating[1] forces of life.

Where does it come from, this sickliness? For man is more sick, uncertain, changeable, indeterminate than any other animal, there is no doubt of that—he is *the* sick animal: how has that come about? Certainly he has also dared more, done more new things, braved more and challenged fate more than all the other animals put together: he, the great experimenter with himself, discontented and insatiable, wrestling with animals, nature, and gods for ultimate dominion—he, still unvanquished, eternally directed toward the future, whose own restless energies never leave him in peace, so that his future digs like a spur into the flesh of every present—how should such a courageous and richly endowed animal not also be the most imperiled, the most chronically and profoundly sick of all sick animals?

Man has often had enough; there are actual epidemics of having had enough (as around 1348, at the time of the dance of death); but even this nausea, this weariness, this disgust with himself—all this bursts from him with such violence that it at once becomes a new fetter. The No he says to life brings to light, as if by magic, an abundance of tender Yeses; even when he *wounds* himself, this master of destruction, of self-destruction—the very wound itself afterward compels him *to live*.—

14

The more normal sickliness becomes among men—and we cannot deny its normality—the higher should be the honor accorded the rare cases of great power of soul and body, man's *lucky hits;* the more we should protect the well-constituted from the worst kind of air, the air of the sickroom. Is this done?

The sick represent the greatest danger for the healthy; it is *not*

---

[1] *Dieser Verneinende . . . und Ja-schaffende:* cf. Goethe, *Faust,* lines 1335ff., where Mephistopheles calls himself: "The spirit that negates [*verneint*]" and "part of that force which would / Do evil evermore, and yet creates the good." In the next paragraph, the portrait of "the great experimenter" brings to mind Goethe's Faust.

the strongest but the weakest who spell disaster for the strong. Is this known?

Broadly speaking, it is not fear of man that we should desire to see diminished; for this fear compels the strong to be strong, and occasionally terrible—it *maintains* the well-constituted type of man. What is to be feared, what has a more calamitous effect than any other calamity, is that man should inspire not profound fear but profound *nausea;* also not great fear but great *pity.* Suppose these two were one day to unite, they would inevitably beget one of the uncanniest monsters: the "last will" of man, his will to nothingness, nihilism. And indeed a great deal points to this union. Whoever can smell not only with his nose but also with his eyes and ears, scents almost everywhere he goes today something like the air of madhouses and hospitals—I am speaking, of course, of the cultural domain, of every kind of "Europe" on this earth. The *sick* are man's greatest danger; *not* the evil, *not* the "beasts of prey." Those who are failures from the start, downtrodden, crushed—it is they, the *weakest,* who must undermine life among men, who call into question and poison most dangerously our trust in life, in man, and in ourselves. Where does one not encounter that veiled glance which burdens one with a profound sadness, that inward-turned glance of the born failure which betrays how such a man speaks to himself—that glance which is a sigh! "If only I were someone else," sighs this glance: "but there is no hope of that. I am who I am: how could I ever get free of myself? And yet—I *am sick of myself!*"

It is on such soil, on swampy ground, that every weed, every poisonous plant grows, always so small, so hidden, so false, so saccharine. Here the worms of vengefulness and rancor swarm; here the air stinks of secrets and concealment; here the web of the most malicious of all conspiracies is being spun constantly—the conspiracy of the suffering against the well-constituted and victorious, here the aspect of the victorious is *hated.* And what mendaciousness is employed to disguise that this hatred is hatred! What a display of grand words and postures, what an art of "honest" calumny! These failures: what noble eloquence flows from their lips! How much sugary, slimy, humble submissiveness swims in their eyes! What do they really want? At least to *represent* justice, love, wisdom, superiority—that is the ambition of the "lowest," the sick. And how skillfull such an ambition makes them! Admire above all the forger's skill with which the stamp of virtue, even the ring, the golden-sounding ring of virtue, is here counterfeited. They monopolize virtue, these weak, hopelessly sick people, there is no doubt of it: "we alone are the good and just," they say, "we alone are *homines bonae voluntatis*." [1] They walk among us as embodied reproaches, as warnings to us—as if health, well-constitutedness, strength, pride, and the sense of power were in themselves necessarily vicious things for which one must pay some day, and pay bitterly: how ready they themselves are at bottom to *make* one pay; how they crave to be *hangmen*. There is among them an abundance of the vengeful disguised as judges, who constantly bear the word "justice" in their mouths like poisonous spittle, always with pursed lips, always ready to spit upon all who are not discontented but go their way in good spirits. Nor is there lacking among them that most disgusting species of the vain, the mendacious failures whose aim is to appear as "beautiful souls" and who bring to market their deformed sensuality, wrapped up in verses and other swaddling clothes, as "purity of heart": the species of moral masturbaters and "self-gratifiers." The will of the weak to represent *some* form of superiority, their instinct for devious paths to tyranny over the healthy—where can it not be discovered, this will to power of the weakest!

The sick woman especially: no one can excel her in the wiles to dominate, oppress, and tyrannize. The sick woman spares nothing, living or dead; she will dig up the most deeply buried things (the Bogos say: "woman is a hyena").

Examine the background of every family, every organization, every commonwealth: everywhere the struggle of the sick against the healthy—a silent struggle as a rule, with petty poisons, with pinpricks, with sly long-suffering expressions, but occasionally also with that invalid's Phariseeism of *loud* gestures that likes best to pose as "noble indignation." This hoarse, indignant barking of sick

---

[1] Men of good will.

dogs, this rabid mendaciousness and rage of "noble" Pharisees, penetrates even the hallowed halls of science (I again remind readers who have ears for such things of that Berlin apostle of revenge, Eugen Dühring, who employs moral mumbo-jumbo more indecently and repulsively than anyone else in Germany today: Dühring, the foremost moral bigmouth today—unexcelled even among his own ilk, the anti-Semites).

They are all men of *ressentiment*, physiologically unfortunate and worm-eaten, a whole tremulous realm of subterranean revenge, inexhaustible and insatiable in outbursts against the fortunate and happy[2] and in masquerades of revenge and pretexts for revenge: when would they achieve the ultimate, subtlest, sublimest triumph of revenge? Undoubtedly if they succeeded in *poisoning the consciences* of the fortunate with their own misery, with all misery, so that one day the fortunate began to be ashamed of their good fortune and perhaps said one to another: "it is disgraceful to be fortunate: *there is too much misery!*"

But no greater or more calamitous misunderstanding is possible than for the happy, well-constituted, powerful in soul and body, to begin to doubt their *right to happiness* in this fashion. Away with this "inverted world"! Away with this shameful emasculation of feeling! That the sick should *not* make the healthy sick—and this is what such an emasculation would involve—should surely be our supreme concern on earth; but this requires above all that the healthy should be *segregated* from the sick, guarded even from the sight of the sick, that they may not confound themselves with the sick. Or is it their task, perhaps, to be nurses or physicians?[3]

But no worse misunderstanding and denial of *their* task can be imagined: the higher *ought* not to degrade itself to the status of an

---

2 "Fortunate and happy": *die Glücklichen*. In the next sentence the word is rendered "the fortunate," and *Glück* as "good fortune"; but in the next paragraph "happy" and "happiness" have been used, as Nietzsche evidently means both.

3 Cf. Goethe's letter to Frau von Stein, June 8, 1787: "Also, I must say myself, I think it true that humanity will triumph eventually, only I fear that at the same time the world will become a large hospital and each will become the other's humane nurse." In a letter to Rée, April 17, 1877, Nietzsche writes, "each the other's 'humane nurse.'"

instrument of the lower, the pathos of distance *ought* to keep their tasks eternally separate! Their right to exist, the privilege of the full-toned bell over the false and cracked, is a thousand times greater: they alone are our *warranty* for the future, they alone are *liable* for the future of man. The sick can never have the ability or obligation to do what *they* can do, what *they* ought to do: but if they are to be able to do what *they* alone ought to do, how can they at the same time be physicians, consolers, and "saviors" of the sick?

And therefore let us have fresh air! fresh air! and keep clear of the madhouses and hospitals of culture! And therefore let us have good company, *our* company! Or solitude, if it must be! But away from the sickening fumes of inner corruption and the hidden rot of disease! . . . So that we may, at least for a while yet, guard ourselves, my friends, against the two worst contagions that may be reserved just for us—against the *great nausea at man!* against *great pity for man!* [4]

15

If one has grasped in all its profundity—and I insist that precisely this matter requires *profound* apprehension and comprehension—how it cannot be the task of the healthy to nurse the sick and to make them well, then one has also grasped one further necessity—the necessity of doctors and nurses *who are themselves sick;* and now we understand the meaning of the ascetic priest and grasp it with both hands.

We must count the ascetic priest as the predestined savior, shepherd, and advocate of the sick herd: only thus can we understand his tremendous historical mission. *Dominion over the suffering* is his kingdom, that is where his instinct directs him, here he possesses his distinctive art, his mastery, his kind of happiness. He

---

[4] The dangers of the great nausea and the great pity are among the central motifs of *Thus Spoke Zarathustra*. The theme of nausea is introduced in the chapter "On the Rabble" in Part Two and is encountered again and again in later chapters. Another chapter in Part Two bears the title "On the Pitying," and the whole of Part Four, which bears a motto from that chapter, is cast in the form of a story: having overcome his nausea at the end of Part Three, Zarathustra's final temptation is pity.

must be sick himself, he must be profoundly related to the sick—
how else would they understand each other?—but he must also be
strong, master of himself even more than of others, with his will to
power intact, so as to be both trusted and feared by the sick, so as
to be their support, resistance, prop, compulsion, taskmaster, tyrant, and god. He has to defend his herd—against whom? Against
the healthy, of course, and also against envy of the healthy; he
must be the natural opponent *and despiser* of all rude, stormy, unbridled, hard, violent beast-of-prey health and might. The priest is
the first form of the more *delicate* animal that despises more readily than it hates. He will not be spared war with the beasts of prey,
a war of cunning (of the "spirit") rather than one of force, as goes
without saying; to fight it he will under certain circumstances need
to evolve a virtually new type of preying animal out of himself, or
at least he will need to *represent* it—a new kind of animal ferocity
in which the polar bear, the supple, cold, and patient tiger, and not
least the fox seem to be joined in a unity at once enticing and
terrifying. If need compels him, he will walk among the other
beasts of prey with bearlike seriousness and feigned superiority,
venerable, prudent, and cold, as the herald and mouthpiece of
more mysterious powers, determined to sow this soil with misery,
discord, and self-contradiction wherever he can and, only too certain of his art, to dominate the *suffering* at all times. He brings
salves and balm with him, no doubt; but before he can act as a
physician he first has to wound; when he then stills the pain of the
wound *he at the same time infects the wound*—for that is what he
knows to do best of all, this sorcerer and animal-tamer, in whose
presence everything healthy necessarily grows sick, and everything
sick tame.

Indeed, he defends his sick herd well enough, this strange
shepherd—he also defends it against itself, against the baseness,
spite, malice, and whatever else is natural to the ailing and sick and
smolders within the herd itself; he fights with cunning and severity
and in secret against anarchy and ever-threatening disintegration
within the herd, in which the most dangerous of all explosives, *ressentiment,* is constantly accumulating. So to detonate this explosive
that it does not blow up herd and herdsman is his essential art, as it

is his supreme utility; if one wanted to express the value of the priestly existence in the briefest formula it would be: the priest *alters the direction* of *ressentiment*.

For every sufferer instinctively seeks a cause for his suffering; more exactly, an agent; still more specifically, a *guilty* agent who is susceptible to suffering—in short, some living thing upon which he can, on some pretext or other, vent his affects, actually or in effigy: for the venting of his affects represents the greatest attempt on the part of the suffering to win relief, *anaesthesia*—the narcotic he cannot help desiring to deaden pain of any kind. This alone, I surmise, constitutes the actual physiological cause of *ressentiment,* vengefulness, and the like: a desire to *deaden pain by means of affects.* This cause is usually sought, quite wrongly in my view, in defensive retaliation, a mere reactive protective measure, a "reflex movement" set off by sudden injury or peril, such as even a beheaded frog still makes to shake off a corrosive acid. But the difference is fundamental: in the one case, the desire is to prevent any further injury, in the other it is to *deaden,* by means of a more violent emotion of any kind, a tormenting, secret pain that is becoming unendurable, and to drive it out of consciousness at least for the moment: for that one requires an affect, as savage an affect as possible, and, in order to excite that, any pretext at all. "Someone or other must be to blame for my feeling ill"—this kind of reasoning is common to all the sick, and is indeed held the more firmly the more the real cause of their feeling ill, the physiological cause, remains hidden. (It may perhaps lie in some disease of the *nervus sympathicus,* or in an excessive secretion of bile, or in a deficiency of potassium sulphate and phosphate in the blood, or in an obstruction in the abdomen which impedes the blood circulation, or in degeneration of the ovaries, and the like).

The suffering are one and all dreadfully eager and inventive in discovering occasions for painful affects; they enjoy being mistrustful and dwelling on nasty deeds and imaginary slights; they scour the entrails of their past and present for obscure and questionable occurrences that offer them the opportunity to revel in tormenting suspicions and to intoxicate themselves with the poison of their own malice: they tear open their oldest wounds, they bleed from long-healed scars, they make evildoers out of their friends, wives, children, and whoever else stands closest to them.[1] "I suffer: some-one must be to blame for it"—thus thinks every sickly sheep. But his shepherd, the ascetic priest, tells him: "Quite so, my sheep! someone must be to blame for it: but you yourself are this some-one, you alone are to blame for it—*you alone are to blame for yourself!*"—This is brazen and false enough: but one thing at least is achieved by it, the direction of *ressentiment* is *altered*.

16

You will guess what, according to my idea, the curative in-stinct of life has at least *attempted* through the ascetic priest, and why it required for a time the tyranny of such paradoxical and paralogical concepts as "guilt," "sin," "sinfulness," "depravity," "damnation": to render the sick to a certain degree *harmless,* to work the self-destruction of the incurable, to direct the *ressenti-ment* of the less severely afflicted sternly back upon themselves ("one thing is needful")—and in this way to *exploit* the bad in-stincts of all sufferers for the purpose of self-discipline, self-surveil-lance, and self-overcoming.

It goes without saying that a "medication" of this kind, a mere affect medication, cannot possibly bring about a real cure of sick-ness in a physiological sense; we may not even suppose that the instinct of life contemplates or intends any sort of cure. A kind of concentration and organization of the sick on one side (the word "church" is the most popular name for it), a kind of provisional safeguarding of the more healthily constituted, the more fully

---

[1] The most striking illustration of this sentence is found in Dostoevsky's *Notes from Underground*—and on February 23, 1887, not quite nine months before the publication of the *Genealogy,* Nietzsche wrote Overbeck about his accidental discovery of Dostoevsky in a bookstore, where he had chanced upon a French translation of that work: "my joy was extraordinary" (*Portable Nietzsche*, pp. 454f.). In 1888 he wrote in section 45 of *Twilight of the Idols:* "The testimony of Dostoevsky is relevant to this problem—Dos-toevsky, the only psychologist, incidentally, from whom I had something to learn; he ranks among the most beautiful strokes of fortune in my life, even more than my discovery of Stendhal. . . ." (*ibid.,* p. 549; cf. also pp. 601 and 603). See also note 8, section 24, below.

achieved, on the other, and the creation of a *chasm* between healthy and sick—for a long time that was all! And it was much! *very much!*

(It is plain that in this essay I proceed on a presupposition that I do not first have to demonstrate to readers of the kind I need: that man's "sinfulness" is not a fact, but merely the interpretation of a fact, namely of physiological depression—the latter viewed in a religio-moral perspective that is no longer binding on us.— That someone *feels* "guilty" or "sinful" is no proof that he is right, any more than a man is healthy merely because he feels healthy. Recall the famous witch trials: the most acute and humane judges were in no doubt as to the guilt of the accused; the "witches" *themselves did not doubt it*—and yet there was no guilt. — To express this presupposition in a more general form: I consider even "psychological pain" to be not a fact but only an interpretation—a causal interpretation—of facts that have hitherto defied exact formulation—too vague to be scientifically serious—a fat word replacing a very thin question mark. When someone cannot get over a "psychological pain," that is *not* the fault of his "psyche" but, to speak crudely, more probably even that of his belly (speaking crudely, to repeat, which does not mean that I want to be heard crudely or understood crudely—). A strong and well-constituted man digests his experiences (his deeds and misdeeds included) as he digests his meals, even when he has to swallow some tough morsels. If he cannot get over an experience and have done with it, this kind of indigestion is as much physiological as is the other—and often in fact merely a consequence of the other.— With such a conception one can, between ourselves, still be the sternest opponent of all materialism.—)

17

But is he really a *physician,* this ascetic priest?—We have seen why it is hardly permissible to call him a physician, however much he enjoys feeling like a "savior" and letting himself be reverenced as a "savior." He combats only the suffering itself, the discomfiture of the sufferer, *not* its cause, *not* the real sickness: this must be our most fundamental objection to priestly medication.

But if one adopts the only perspective known to the priest, it is not easy to set bounds to one's admiration of how much he has seen, sought, and found under this perspective. The *alleviation* of suffering, "consolation" of every kind—here lies his genius; how inventively he has gone about his task of consolation, how boldly and unscrupulously he has selected the means for it! Christianity in particular may be called a great treasure house of ingenious means of consolation: it offers such a collection of refreshments, palliatives, and narcotics; it risks so much that is most dangerous and audacious; it has displayed such refinement and subtlety, such southern subtlety, in guessing what stimulant affects will overcome, at least for a time, the deep depression, the leaden exhaustion, the black melancholy of the physiologically inhibited. For we may generalize: the main concern of all great religions has been to fight a certain weariness and heaviness grown to epidemic proportions.

One may assume in advance the probability that from time to time and in certain parts of the earth a *feeling of physiological inhibition* is almost bound to seize on large masses of people, though, owing to their lack of physiological knowledge, they do not diagnose it as such: its "cause" and remedy are sought and tested only in the psychological-moral domain (this is my most general formula for what is usually called a *"religion"*). Such a feeling of inhibition can have the most various origins: perhaps it may arise from the crossing of races too different from one another (or of classes—classes always also express differences of origin and race: European *"Weltschmerz,"* [1] the "pessimism" of the nineteenth century, is essentially the result of an absurdly precipitate mixing of classes); or from an injudicious emigration—a race introduced into a climate for which its powers of adaptation are inadequate (the case of the Indians in India); or from the aftereffects of age and exhaustion in the race (Parisian pessimism from 1850 onward); or from an incorrect diet (the alcoholism of the Middle Ages; the absurdity of the *vegetarians* who, to be sure, can invoke

---

[1] Sentimental sorrow over the world's woes.

the authority of Squire Christopher in Shakespeare);[2] or from degeneration of the blood, malaria, syphilis, and the like (German depression after the Thirty Years' War, which infected half of Germany with vile diseases and thus prepared the ground for German servility, German pusillanimity). In every such case a grand *struggle against the feeling of displeasure* is attempted; let us briefly examine its principal forms and methods. (I here ignore altogether, as seems reasonable, *the philosophers'* struggle against this feeling, which is usually waged at the same time: it is interesting enough but too absurd, too practically ineffective, too much the work of web-spinners and idlers—as when pain is proved to be an error, in the naïve supposition that pain is *bound* to vanish as soon as the error in it is recognized; but behold! it refuses to vanish . . .)

This dominating sense of displeasure is combatted, *first*,[3] by means that reduce the feeling of life in general to its lowest point. If possible, will and desire are abolished altogether; all that produces affects and "blood" is avoided (abstinence from salt: the hygienic regimen of the fakirs); no love; no hate; indifference; no revenge; no wealth; no work; one begs; if possible, no women, or as little as possible; in spiritual matters, Pascal's principle *il faut s'abêtir*"[4] is applied. The result, expressed in moral-psychological terms, is "selflessness," "sanctification"; in physiological terms: hypnotization—the attempt to win for man an approximation to what in certain animals is *hibernation,* in many tropical plants *estivation,* the minimum metabolism at which life will still subsist without really entering consciousness. An astonishing amount of human energy has been expended to this end—has it been in vain?

---

[2] Nietzsche uses the English word "vegetarians." The reference to *Junker Christoph,* who is mentioned once more later in this section, is presumably intended to allude to *The Taming of the Shrew.* "She eat no meat today, nor none shall eat" (IV. 2, line 200) is, of course, said by Petruchio, and in the accepted version of the play Christopher Sly, the drunken tinker who is made to believe that he is a lord, appears only in the "Induction" (or Prologue) and in one subsequent comment. But in *The Taming of A* (sic) *Shrew* (1594), which slightly antedates the accepted version and is attributed to Shakespeare by a few scholars, the characters introduced in the Induction make comments from time to time throughout the play.

[3] The *second* strategy is introduced at the beginning of section 18.

[4] One must make oneself stupid: in the famous passage in the *Pensées* in which Pascal's wager is found.

There can be no doubt that these *sportsmen*[5] of "sanctity" who proliferate in almost all ages and all peoples have in fact discovered a real release from that which they combated with such rigorous *training: in countless cases they have really freed* themselves from that profound physiological depression by means of their system of hypnotics, which thus counts among the most universal facts of ethnology. Nor is there any ground for considering this program of starving the body and the desires as necessarily a symptom of lunacy (as a certain clumsy kind of beef-eating "free spirits" and Squire Christopher are wont to do). But it is certainly capable of opening the way to all kinds of spiritual disturbances, to "an inner light" for instance, as with the Hesychasts of Mount Athos,[6] to auditory and visual hallucinations, to voluptuous inundations and ecstasies of sensuality (the case of St. Theresa). It goes without saying that the interpretation which those subject to these states have placed upon them has always been as enthusiastic and false as possible; but we should not overlook the note of utterly convinced gratitude that finds expression in the very *will* to offer that kind of interpretation. The supreme state, *redemption* itself, total hypnotization and repose at last achieved, is always accounted the mystery as such for whose expression even the supreme symbols are inadequate, as entry and return into the ground of things, as liberation from all illusion, as "knowledge," as "truth," as "being," as release from all purpose, all desire, all action, as a state beyond even good and evil. "Good and evil," says the Buddhist—"both are fetters: the Perfect One became master over both"; "what is done and what is not done," says the believer of the Vedanta, "give him no pain; as a sage, he shakes good and evil from himself; no deed can harm his kingdom; he has gone beyond both good and evil": this idea is common to all of India, Hindu and Buddhist. (Neither in the Indian nor in the Christian conception is this "redemption" *attainable* through virtue, through moral improvement, however highly they may esteem the value of virtue

---

[5] Nietzsche uses the English word; also "training" later in the same sentence and in some later passages.

[6] A sect of mystics that originated among the monks on Mount Athos in the fourteenth century.

as a means of hypnotization: one should remember this—here they are true to the facts. To have remained *true* in this may perhaps be regarded as the finest piece of realism in the three great religions, which are in other respects so steeped in moralization. "For the man of knowledge there are no duties."

"Redemption cannot be attained through an *increase* in virtue; for redemption consists in being one with Brahma, in whom no increase in perfection is possible; nor through a *decrease* in faults: for Brahma, with whom to be one constitutes redemption, is eternally pure." These are passages from the commentary of Shankara, quoted by the first European *expert* in Indian philosophy, my friend Paul Deussen.[7]) Let us therefore honor "redemption" as it appears in the great religions. But it is not easy for us to take seriously the high valuation placed on *deep sleep* by these people, so weary of life that they are too weary even to dream—deep sleep, that is, as an entry into Brahma, as an *achieved unio mystica* with God.

"When he is completely asleep"—it says in the oldest and most venerable "scripture"—"and perfectly at rest, so that he no longer dreams, then, dearly beloved, he is united with What Is, he has entered into himself—embraced by the cognitive self, he is no longer conscious of what is without or within. Over this bridge come neither day nor night, nor death, nor suffering, nor good works, nor evil works."

"In deep sleep," say the faithful of this deepest of the three great religions, "the soul rises out of the body, enters into the supreme light and thus steps forth in its real form: there it is the supreme spirit itself that walks about, joking and playing and amusing itself, whether with women or with carriages or with friends; there it thinks no more of this appendage of a body to which the *prana* (the breath of life) is harnessed like a beast to a cart."

Nonetheless, we must bear in mind here, as in the case of

---

[7] Paul Deussen (1845–1919) translated sixty Upanishads into German, wrote pioneering works on the Vedanta and on Indian philosophy generally, as well as a multi-volume history of philosophy—and *Erinnerungen an Friedrich Nietzsche* (Leipzig, Brockhaus, 1901: "Reminiscences of Friedrich Nietzsche").

"redemption," that, although it is arrayed in Oriental exaggeration, what is expressed is merely the same appraisal as that of the clear, cool, Hellenically cool, but suffering Epicurus: the hypnotic sense of nothingness, the repose of deepest sleep, in short *absence of suffering*—sufferers and those profoundly depressed will count this as the supreme good, as the value of values; they are *bound* to accord it a positive value, to experience it as *the* positive as such. (According to the same logic of feeling, all pessimistic religions call nothingness *God.*)

18

Much more common than this hypnotic muting of all sensitivity, of the capacity to feel pain—which presupposes rare energy and above all courage, contempt for opinion, "intellectual stoicism"—is a different *training* against states of depression which is at any rate easier: *mechanical activity*. It is beyond doubt that this regimen alleviates an existence of suffering to a not inconsiderable degree: this fact is today called, somewhat dishonestly, "the blessings of work." The alleviation consists in this, that the interest of the sufferer is directed entirely away from his suffering—that activity, and nothing but activity, enters consciousness, and there is consequently little room left in it for suffering: for the chamber of human consciousness is *small!*

Mechanical activity and what goes with it—such as absolute regularity, punctilious and unthinking obedience, a mode of life fixed once and for all, fully occupied time, a certain permission, indeed training for "impersonality," for self-forgetfulness, for *"incuria sui"* [1]—: how thoroughly, how subtly the ascetic priest has known how to employ them in the struggle against pain! When he was dealing with sufferers of the lower classes, with work-slaves or prisoners (or with women—who are mostly both at once, work-slaves and prisoners), he required hardly more than a little ingenuity in name-changing and rebaptizing to make them see benefits and a relative happiness in things they formerly hated: the slave's

---

[1] Lack of care of self.

discontent with his lot was at any rate *not* invented by the priest.

An even more highly valued means of combating depression is the prescribing of a *petty pleasure* that is easily attainable and can be made into a regular event; this medication is often employed in association with the previous one. The most common form in which pleasure is thus prescribed as a curative is that of the pleasure of *giving* pleasure (doing good, giving, relieving, helping, encouraging, consoling, praising, rewarding); by prescribing "love of the neighbor," the ascetic priest prescribes fundamentally an excitement of the strongest, most life-affirming drive, even if in the most cautious doses— namely, of the *will to power*. The happiness of "slight superiority," involved in all doing good, being useful, helping, and rewarding, is the most effective means of consolation for the physiologically inhibited, and widely employed by them when they are well advised: otherwise they hurt one another, obedient, of course, to the same basic instinct.

When one looks for the beginnings of Christianity in the Roman world, one finds associations for mutual aid, associations for the poor, for the sick, for burial, evolved among the lowest strata of society, in which this major remedy for depression, petty pleasure produced by mutual helpfulness, was consciously employed: perhaps this was something new in those days, a real discovery? The "will to mutual aid," to the formation of a herd, to "community," to "congregation," called up in this way is bound to lead to fresh and far more fundamental outbursts of that will to power which it has, even if only to a small extent, aroused: the *formation of a herd* is a significant victory and advance in the struggle against depression. With the growth of the community, a new interest grows for the individual, too, and often lifts him above the most personal element in his discontent, his aversion to *himself* (Geulincx's *"despectio sui"*).[2] All the sick and sickly instinctively strive after a herd organization as a means of shaking off their dull displeasure and feeling of weakness: the ascetic priest divines this instinct and furthers it; wherever there are herds, it is the instinct of weakness that has willed the herd and the prudence of the priest

---

[2] Self-contempt. Arnold Geulincx (1624–1669) was a Belgian philosopher.

that has organized it. For one should not overlook this fact: the strong are as naturally inclined to *separate* as the weak are to *congregate;* if the former unite together, it is only with the aim of an aggressive collective action and collective satisfaction of their will to power, and with much resistance from the individual conscience; the latter, on the contrary, *enjoy* precisely this coming together— their instinct is just as much satisfied by this as the instinct of the born "masters" (that is, the solitary, beast-of-prey species of man) is fundamentally irritated and disquieted by organization. The whole of history teaches that every oligarchy conceals the lust for *tyranny;* every oligarchy constantly trembles with the tension each member feels in maintaining control over this lust. (So it was in *Greece,* for insance: Plato bears witness to it in a hundred passages—and he knew his own kind—*and* himself . . .)

19

The means employed by the ascetic priest that we have discovered up to now—the general muting of the feeling of life, mechanical activity, the petty pleasure, above all "love of one's neighbor," herd organization, the awakening of the communal feeling of power through which the individual's discontent with himself is drowned in his pleasure in the prosperity of the community—these are, by modern standards, his *innocent* means in the struggle with displeasure; let us now turn to the more interesting means, the "guilty" ones. They all involve one thing: some kind of an *orgy of feeling*—employed as the most effective means of deadening dull, paralyzing, protracted pain; hence priestly inventiveness in thinking through this single question—*"how* can one produce an orgy of feeling?"—has been virtually inexhaustible.

This sounds harsh; obviously it would sound more pleasant and be more ingratiating if I said: "the ascetic priest has at all times made use of the *enthusiasm* that lies in all strong affects." But why stroke the effeminate ears of our modern weaklings? Why should *we* give way even one step to their tartuffery of words? For us psychologists this would constitute a tartuffery in *deed,* quite apart from the fact that it would nauseate us. For if a psychologist today has *good taste* (others might say, integrity) it consists in resistance to the shamefully *moralized* way of speaking which has gradually made all modern judgments of men and things slimy.[1] One should not deceive oneself in this matter: the most distinctive feature of modern souls and modern books is not lying but their inveterate *innocence* in moralistic mendaciousness. To have to rediscover this "innocence" everywhere—this constitutes perhaps the most disgusting job among all the precarious tasks a psychologist has to tackle today; it is a part of *our* great danger—it is a path that may lead precisely *us* toward great nausea.

I have no doubt for *what* sole *purpose* modern books (if they last, which we fortunately have little reason to fear, and if there will one day be a posterity with a more severe, harder, *healthier* taste)—for what purpose *everything* modern will serve this posterity: as an emetic—and that on account of its moral mawkishness and falseness, its innermost feminism that likes to call itself "idealism" and at any rate believes it is idealism. Our educated people of today, our "good people," do not tell lies—that is true; but that is *not* to their credit! A real lie, a genuine, resolute, "honest" lie (on whose value one should consult Plato) would be something far too severe and potent for them: it would demand of them what one *may* not demand of them, that they should open their eyes to themselves, that they should know how to distinguish "true" and "false" in themselves. All they are capable of is a *dishonest* lie; whoever today accounts himself a "good man" is utterly incapable of confronting any matter except with *dishonest mendaciousness*—a mendaciousness that is abysmal but innocent, truehearted, blue-

---

[1] Here as much as anywhere Freud is Nietzsche's great heir who did more than anyone else to change the style of the twentieth century. Freud's insistence on using the term "sexual" rather than "erotic" is a case in point; so is his stubborn insistence on the crucial importance of sexual factors. This was indeed influenced by the time and place in which he lived, as his critics have long claimed—but not in the sense intended by them: rather, he fought against the slimy idealism of the age. And he was quick to suspect, not without reason, that erstwhile followers who developed more ingratiating variations on his theories were guilty of "tartuffery in *deed*" and not merely in words. He seems to have felt—and this is at any rate one of Nietzsche's central motifs—that a cleansing of the atmosphere and a radical change in tone were indispensable presuppositions of major scientific advances in psychology.

eyed, and virtuous. These "good men"—they are one and all moralized to the very depths and ruined and botched to all eternity as far as honesty is concerned: who among them could endure a single *truth* "about man"? Or, put more palpably: who among them could stand a *true* biography?

A couple of pointers: Lord Byron wrote a number of very personal things about himself, but Thomas Moore was "too good" for them: he burned his friend's papers.[2] Dr. Gwinner, Schopenhauer's executor, is said to have done the same:[3] for Schopenhauer, too, had written a few things about himself and perhaps against himself (*eis heauton*[4]). The solid American, Thayer, Beethoven's biographer, suddenly called a halt to his work: at some point or other in this venerable and naïve life he could no longer take it.[5]

Moral: what prudent man would write a single honest word about himself today?—he would have to be a member of the Order of Holy Foolhardiness to do so. We are promised an autobiography of Richard Wagner: who doubts that it will be a *prudent* autobiography?

Let us finally mention that ludicrous horror aroused in Germany by the Catholic priest Janssen with his incomparably artless and innocuous picture of the Reformation movement. What would happen if someone were to describe this movement *differently,* if a real psychologist were to describe a real Luther, not with the moralistic simplicity of a country parson, not with the sickly and discreet bashfulness of a Protestant historian, but, say, with the

---

[2] Thomas Moore (1779–1852) was an Irish poet. A brief account of the episode mentioned here may be found in the article on Moore in the Encyclopaedia Britannica, 11th ed.

[3] Wilhelm von Gwinner (1825–1917) was a German jurist and civil servant (Stadtgerichtsrat in Frankfurt a. M., and later Konsistorialpräsident). As Schopenhauer's executor, he did indeed destroy his autobiographical papers —and then published three biographical studies of Schopenhauer: *Arthur Schopenhauer aus persönlichem Umgang dargestellt* (1862: "A. S. as seen at first hand"), *Schopenhauer und seine Freunde* (1863: "S. and his friends"), and *Schopenhauers Leben* (1878: "S.'s life").

[4] About, or against, himself.

[5] The most scholarly edition of the *Life of Beethoven* by Alexander Wheelock Thayer (1817–1897) is that revised and edited by Elliot Forbes (2 volumes, Princeton, N.J., Princeton University Press, 1964).

intrepidity of a Taine, out of *strength of soul* and not out of a prudent indulgence toward strength? [6] (The Germans, incidentally, have finally produced a beautiful example of the classical type of the latter—they may well claim him as one of their own and be proud of him: Leopold Ranke,[7] that born classical *advocatus* of every *causa fortior*,[8] that most prudent of all prudent "realists.")

20

But my point will have been taken—there is reason enough, is there not, for us psychologists nowadays to be unable to shake off a certain mistrust *of ourselves*.

Probably, we, too, are still "too good" for our job; probably, we, too, are still victims of and prey to this moralized contemporary taste and ill with it, however much we think we despise it— probably it infects even *us*. What was the warning that diplomat gave his colleagues? "Let us above all mistrust our first impulses, gentlemen!" he said; *"they are almost always good."*— Thus should every psychologist, too, address his colleagues today.

And with that we return to our problem, which in fact demands a certain severity of us, especially a certain mistrust of "first impulses." *The ascetic ideal employed to produce orgies of feeling* —whoever recalls the preceding essay will anticipate from these nine words the essence of what is now to be shown. To wrench the human soul from its moorings, to immerse it in terrors, ice, flames, and raptures to such an extent that it is liberated from all petty displeasure, gloom, and depression as by a flash of lightning: what paths lead to *this* goal? And which of them do so most surely?

Fundamentally, every great affect has this power, provided it explodes suddenly: anger, fear, voluptuousness, revenge, hope, triumph, despair, cruelty; and the ascetic priest has indeed pressed into his service indiscriminately the *whole* pack of savage hounds in man and let loose now this one and now that, always with the

---

[6] Again, it was Freud who did more than anyone else to change the tone and standards of biography—including discussions of Luther.

[7] Perhaps the most renowned German historian of his time (1795–1886).

[8] Stronger cause.

same end in view: to awaken men from their slow melancholy, to hunt away, if only for a time, their dull pain and lingering misery, and always under cover of a religious interpretation and "justification." Every such orgy of feeling has to be *paid* for afterward, that goes without saying—it makes the sick sicker; and that is why this kind of cure for pain is, by modern standards, "guilty." Yet, to be fair, one must insist all the more that it was employed *with a good conscience,* that the ascetic priest prescribed it in the profoundest faith in its utility, indeed indispensability—and even that he was often almost shattered by the misery he had caused; one must also add that the violent physiological revenge taken by such excesses, including even mental disturbances, does not really confute the sense of this kind of medication, which, as has been shown above, does *not* aim at curing the sickness but at combating the depression by relieving and deadening its displeasure. This is one way of attaining that end.

The chief trick the ascetic priest permitted himself for making the human soul resound with heart-rending, ecstatic music of all kinds was, as everyone knows, the exploitation of the *sense of guilt*. Its origin has been briefly suggested in the preceding essay—as a piece of animal psychology, no more: there we encountered the sense of guilt in its raw state, so to speak. It was only in the hands of the priest, that artist in guilt feelings, that it achieved form—oh, what a form! "Sin"—for this is the priestly name for the animal's "bad conscience" (cruelty directed backward)—has been the greatest event so far in the history of the sick soul: we possess in it the most dangerous and fateful artifice of religious interpretation. Man, suffering from himself in some way or other but in any case physiologically like an animal shut up in a cage, uncertain why or wherefore, thirsting for reasons—reasons relieve—thirsting, too, for remedies and narcotics, at last takes counsel with one who knows hidden things, too—and behold! he receives a hint, he receives from his sorcerer, the ascetic priest, the *first* hint as to the "cause" of his suffering: he must seek it in *himself,* in some *guilt,* in a piece of the past, he must understand his suffering as a *punishment*.

He has heard, he has understood, this unfortunate: from now

on he is like a hen imprisoned by a chalk line. He can no longer get out of this chalk circle: the invalid has been transformed into "the sinner."

For two millennia now we have been condemned to the sight of this new type of invalid, "the sinner"—shall it always be so?— everywhere one looks there is the hypnotic gaze of the sinner, always fixed on the same object (on "guilt" as the *sole* cause of suffering); everywhere the bad conscience, that "abominable beast," as Luther called it; everywhere the past regurgitated, the fact distorted, the "jaundiced eye" for all action; everywhere the *will* to misunderstand suffering made the content of life, the reinterpretation of suffering as feelings of guilt, fear, and punishment; everywhere the scourge, the hair shirt, the starving body, contrition; everywhere the sinner breaking himself on the cruel wheel of a restless, morbidly lascivious conscience; everywhere dumb torment, extreme fear, the agony of the tortured heart, convulsions of an unknown happiness, the cry for "redemption." The old depression, heaviness, and weariness were indeed *overcome* through this system of procedures; life again became *very* interesting: awake, everlastingly awake, sleepless, glowing, charred, spent and yet not weary—thus was the man, "the sinner," initiated into *this* mystery. This ancient mighty sorcerer in his struggle with displeasure, the ascetic priest—he had obviously won, *his* kingdom had come: one no longer protested *against* pain, one *thirsted* for pain; *"more* pain! *more* pain!" the desire of his disciples and initiates has cried for centuries. Every painful orgy of feeling, everything that shattered, bowled over, crushed, enraptured, transported; the secrets of the torture chamber, the inventiveness of hell itself—all were henceforth discovered, divined, and exploited, all stood in the service of the sorcerer, all served henceforward to promote the victory of his ideal, the ascetic ideal.— "My kingdom is not of *this* world"—he continued to say, as before: but did he still have the right to say it?

Goethe claimed there were only thirty-six tragic situations: one could guess from that, if one did not know it anyway, that Goethe was no ascetic priest. He—knows more.—

21

It would be pointless to indulge in criticism of *this* kind of priestly medication, the "guilty" kind. Who would want to maintain that such orgies of feeling as the ascetic priest prescribed for his sick people (under the holiest names, as goes without saying, and convinced of the holiness of his ends) ever *benefited* any of them? At least we should be clear on the meaning of the word "benefit." If one intends it to convey that such a system of treatment has *improved* men, I shall not argue: only I should have to add what "improved" signifies to me—the same thing as "tamed," "weakened," "discouraged," "made refined," "made effete," "emasculated" (thus almost the same thing as *harmed*.) But when such a system is chiefly applied to the sick, distressed, and depressed, it invariably makes them *sicker,* even if it does "improve" them; one need only ask psychiatrists[1] what happens to patients who are methodically subjected to the torments of repentance, states of contrition, and fits of redemption. One should also consult history: wherever the ascetic priest has prevailed with this treatment, sickness has spread in depth and breadth with astonishing speed. What has always constituted its "success"? A shattered nervous system added to any existing illness—and this on the largest as on the smallest scale, in individuals as in masses.

In the wake of repentance and redemption *training* we find tremendous epileptic epidemics, the greatest known to history, such as the St. Vitus' and St. John's dances of the Middle Ages; as another aftereffect we encounter terrible paralyses and protracted states of depression, which sometimes transform the temperament of a people or a city (Geneva, Basel) once and for all into its opposite; here we may also include the witch-hunt hysteria, something related to somnambulism (there were eight great epidemic outbreaks of this between 1564 and 1605 alone); we also find in its wake those death-seeking mass deliria whose dreadful cry *"evviva la morte!"* [2] was heard all over Europe, interspersed now

---

[1] *Irrenärzte:* we probably ought to think of physicians working in lunatic asylums, as psychiatrists in the twentieth-century sense did not exist in 1887.

[2] Long live death!

with voluptuous idiosyncrasies, now with rages of destruction; and the same alternation of affects, accompanied by the same intermissions and somersaults, is to be observed even today whenever the ascetic doctrine of sin again achieves a grand success. (The religious neurosis *appears* as a form of evil; there is no doubt about that. What is it? *Quaeritur*.[3]) Broadly speaking, the ascetic ideal and its sublimely moral cult, this most ingenious, unscrupulous, and dangerous systematization of all the means for producing orgies of feeling under the cover of holy intentions, has inscribed itself in a fearful and unforgettable way in the entire history of man—and unfortunately *not only* in his history.

I know of hardly anything else that has had so destructive an effect upon the *health* and racial strength of Europeans as this ideal; one may without any exaggeration call it *the true calamity* in the history of European health. The only thing that can be compared with its influence is the specifically Teutonic influence: I mean the alcoholic poisoning of Europe, which has hitherto gone strictly in step with the political and racial hegemony of the Teutons (wherever they infused their blood they also infused their vice).— Third in line would be syphilis—*magno sed proxima intervallo*.[4]

22

The ascetic priest has ruined psychical health wherever he has come to power; consequently he has also ruined taste *in artibus et litteris*[1]—he is still ruining it. "Consequently?" I hope I shall be granted this "consequently"; at any rate, I don't want to bother to prove it. Just one pointer: it concerns the basic book of Christian literature, its model, its "book in itself." Even in the midst of Graeco-Roman splendor, which was also a splendor of books, in the face of an ancient literary world that had not yet eroded and been ruined, at a time when one could still read some books for whose possession one would nowadays exchange half of some national literatures, the simplicity and vanity of Christian agitators—

---

[3] That is the question.
[4] After a great interval, though next.
[1] In arts and letters.

they are called Church Fathers—had the temerity to declare: "*we, too,* have a classical literature, *we have no need of that of the Greeks";* and saying this they pointed proudly to books of legends, letters of apostles, and apologetic tracts, rather as the English "Salvation Army" today employs similar literature in its struggle against Shakespeare and other "pagans."

I do not like the "New Testament," that should be plain; I find it almost disturbing that my taste in regard to this most highly esteemed and overestimated work should be so singular (I have the taste of two millennia *against* me): but there it is! "Here I stand, I cannot do otherwise" [2]— I have the courage of my bad taste. The *Old* Testament—that is something else again: all honor to the Old Testament! I find in it great human beings, a heroic landscape, and something of the very rarest quality in the world, the incomparable naïveté of the *strong heart;* what is more, I find a people. In the New one, on the other hand, I find nothing but petty sectarianism, mere rococo of the soul, mere involutions, nooks, queer things, the air of the conventicle, not to forget an occasional whiff of bucolic mawkishness that belongs to the epoch (*and* to the Roman province) and is not so much Jewish as Hellenistic. Humility and self-importance cheek-by-jowl; a garrulousness of feeling that almost stupefies; impassioned vehemence, not passion; embarrassing gesticulation; it is plain that there is no trace of good breeding. How can one make such a fuss about one's little lapses as these pious little men do! Who gives a damn? Certainly not God. Finally, they even want "the crown of eternal life," these little provincial people; but for what? to what purpose? Presumption can go no further. An "immortal" Peter: who could stand him? Their ambition is laughable: people of *that* sort regurgitating their most private affairs, their stupidities, sorrows, and petty worries, as if the Heart of Being were obliged to concern itself with them; they never grow tired of involving God himself in even the pettiest troubles they have got themselves into. And the appalling taste of this perpetual familiarity with God! This Jewish and not merely Jewish obtrusiveness of pawing and nuzzling God!

---

[2] Luther's famous words at the Diet of Worms.

There are despised little "pagan nations" in eastern Asia from whom these first Christians could have learned something important, some *tact* in reverence; as Christian missionaries witness, these nations do not even utter the name of their god. This seems to me delicate enough; it is certainly too delicate not only for "*first*" Christians: to see the full contrast, one should recall Luther, for instance, that "most eloquent" and presumptuous peasant Germany has ever produced, and the tone he preferred when conversing with God. Luther's attack on the mediating saints of the church (and especially on "the devil's sow, the pope") was, beyond any doubt, fundamentally the attack of a lout who could not stomach the *good etiquette* of the church, that reverential etiquette of the hieratic taste which permits only the more initiated and silent into the holy of holies and closes it to louts. Here of all places the louts were to be kept from raising their voices; but Luther, the peasant, wanted it altogether different: this arrangement was not *German* enough for him: he wanted above all to speak directly, to speak himself, to speak "informally" with his God.— Well, he did it.

It is easy to see that the ascetic ideal has never and nowhere been a school of good taste, even less of good manners—at best it was a school of hieratic manners: that is because its very nature includes something that is the deadly enemy of all good manners—lack of moderation, dislike of moderation; it itself is a "*non plus ultra.*" [3]

23

The ascetic ideal has not only ruined health and taste, it has also ruined a third, fourth, fifth, sixth thing as well—I beware of enumerating everything (I'd never finish). It is my purpose here to bring to light, not what this ideal has *done,* but simply what it *means;* what it indicates; what lies hidden behind it, beneath it, in it; of what it is the provisional, indistinct expression, overlaid with question marks and misunderstandings. And it is only in pursuit of

---

[3] Ultimate extreme.

this end that I could not spare my readers a glance at its monstrous and calamitous effects, to prepare them for the ultimate and most terrifying aspect of the question concerning the meaning of this ideal. What is the meaning of the *power* of this ideal, the monstrous nature of its power? Why has it been allowed to flourish to this extent? Why has it not rather been resisted? The ascetic ideal expresses a will: *where* is the opposing will that might express an *opposing ideal*? The ascetic ideal has a *goal*—this goal is so universal that all the other interests of human existence seem, when compared with it, petty and narrow; it interprets epochs, nations, and men inexorably with a view to this one goal; it permits no other interpretation, no other goal; it rejects, denies, affirms, and sanctions solely from the point of view of *its* interpretation (and has there ever been a system of interpretation more thoroughly thought through?); it submits to no power, it believes in its own predominance over every other power, in its absolute *superiority of rank* over every other power—it believes that no power exists on earth that does not first have to receive a meaning, a right to exist, a value, as a tool of the ascetic ideal, as a way and means to *its* goal, to *one* goal.— Where is the match of this closed system of will, goal, and interpretation? Why has it not found its match?— Where is the *other "one* goal"?

But they tell me it is *not* lacking, it has not merely waged a long and successful fight against this ideal, it has already conquered this ideal in all important respects: all of modern *science*[1] is supposed to bear witness to that—modern science which, as a genuine philosophy of reality, clearly believes in itself alone, clearly possesses the courage for itself and the will to itself, and has up to now survived well enough without God, the beyond, and the virtues of denial. Such noisy agitators' chatter, however, does not impress me: these trumpeters of reality are bad musicians, their voices obviously do *not* come from the depths, the abyss of the scientific

---

[1] *Wissenschaft* does not refer only, or primarily, to the natural sciences, and when Nietzsche refers to scholars later in this section he is by no means changing the subject. It seems best to call attention to this while using "science" to translate *Wissenschaft*. Cf. Part Six, "We Scholars" (*Wir Gelehrten,* sections 204–13) in *Beyond Good and Evil,* p. 309f., above.

conscience does *not* speak through them—for today the scientific conscience is an abyss—the word "science" in the mouths of such trumpeters is simply an indecency, an abuse, and a piece of impudence. The truth is precisely the opposite of what is asserted here: science today has absolutely *no* belief in itself, let alone an ideal above it—and where it still inspires passion, love, ardor, and *suffering* at all, it is not the opposite of the ascetic ideal but rather *the latest and noblest form of it*. Does that sound strange to you?

Today there are plenty of modest and worthy laborers[2] among scholars, too, who are happy in their little nooks; and because they are happy there, they sometimes demand rather immodestly that one ought to be content with things today, generally—especially in the domain of science, where so much that is useful remains to be done. I am not denying that; the last thing I want is to destroy the pleasure these honest workers take in their craft: for I approve of their work. But that one works rigorously in the sciences and that there are contented workers certainly does *not* prove that science as a whole possesses a goal, a will, an ideal, or the passion of a great faith. The opposite is the case, to repeat: where it is not the latest expression of the ascetic ideal—and the exceptions are too rare, noble, and atypical to refute the general proposition—science today is a *hiding place* for every kind of discontent, disbelief, gnawing worm, *despectio sui,* bad conscience—it is the unrest of the *lack* of ideals, the suffering from the *lack* of any great love, the discontent in the face of involuntary contentment.

Oh, what does science not conceal today! how much, at any rate, is it *meant* to conceal! The proficiency of our finest scholars, their heedless industry, their heads smoking day and night, their very craftsmanship—how often the real meaning of all this lies in the desire to keep something hidden from oneself! Science as a means of self-narcosis: *do you have experience of that?*

Whoever associates with scholars knows that one occasionally wounds them to the marrow with some harmless word; one incenses one's scholarly friends just when one means to honor them,

[2] *Braves und bescheidnes Arbeitervolk:* the following remarks about these laborers (where the English text speaks of "workers" the original again has *Arbeiter*) should be compared with *Beyond Good and Evil,* section 211.

one can drive them beside themselves merely because one has been too coarse to realize with whom one was really dealing—with *sufferers* who refuse to admit to themselves what they are, with drugged and heedless men who fear only one thing: *regaining consciousness*.—

24

And now look, on the other hand, at those rarer cases of which I spoke, the last idealists left among philosophers and scholars: are they perhaps the desired *opponents* of the ascetic ideal, the *counteridealists*? Indeed, they *believe* they are, these "unbelievers" (for that is what they are, one and all); they are so serious on this point, so passionate about it in word and gesture, that the faith[1] that they are opponents of this ideal seems to be the last remnant of faith they have left—but does this mean that their faith is *true?*

We "men of knowledge" have gradually come to mistrust believers of all kinds; our mistrust has gradually brought us to make inferences the reverse of those of former days: wherever the strength of a faith is very prominently displayed, we infer a certain weakness of demonstrability, even the *improbability* of what is believed. We, too, do not deny that faith "makes blessed": that is precisely *why* we deny that faith *proves* anything—a strong faith that makes blessed raises suspicion against that which is believed; it does not establish "truth," it establishes a certain probability—of *deception*. What is the situation in the present case?

These Nay-sayers and outsiders of today who are unconditional on one point[2]—their insistence on intellectual cleanliness; these hard, severe, abstinent, heroic spirits who constitute the

---

[1] In German there is a single word for belief and faith, *Glaube*. To believe is *glauben;* unbelievers, *Ungläubige*. In the translation, "faith" is called for rather than belief; for Nietzsche emphasizes the unconditional and religious character of the faith he discusses.

The ideas expressed here are developed further in *The Antichrist*, sections 50ff. (*Portable Nietzsche*, pp. 631ff.)

See also Kaufmann's *Nietzsche*, Chapter 12, section III (about ten pages on "Faith versus Reason"). Most of the relevant passages, from the *Dawn* on, are cited there.

[2] This unconditional attitude, this refusal to question one point, is what seems objectionable to Nietzsche.

honor of our age; all these pale atheists, anti-Christians,[3] immoralists, nihilists; these skeptics, ephectics,[4] *hectics* of the spirit (they are all hectics in some sense or other); these last idealists of knowledge in whom alone the intellectual conscience dwells and is incarnate today[5]—they certainly believe they are as completely liber-

---

[3] *Antichristen* could also mean Antichrists; and when Nietzsche, a year later, entitled one of his last books *Der Antichrist* he plainly meant *The Antichrist:* the content of that book makes that clear, nor can there be any doubt about his wish at that time to be as provocative as possible. In the last sentence of section 5 of the Preface, which Nietzsche had added to the new edition of *The Birth of Tragedy* in 1886, the year before, the grammatical form no less than the meaning makes it clear that "the Antichrist" is meant. The enumeration in the text above raises the question whether the critique Nietzsche offers is not applicable to himself: after all, he had also called himself an immoralist both in *Beyond Good and Evil,* section 32, and in the Preface added to the new edition of *The Dawn* (section 4); and in *Ecce Homo,* the following year, he several times called himself "the first immoralist." Nevertheless, the plural in the text above and the whole "feel" of the passage make "anti-Christians" the more plausible reading. For all that, the points just mentioned color the tone: the men he speaks of are plainly very close to him.

[4] In section 9 above, Nietzsche explained the "ephectic bent": it is the propensity to suspend judgment. The primary denotation of the next word, "hectics," is consumptive.

[5] This, from Nietzsche, is high praise indeed. Cf., e.g., *The Gay Science,* section 2: *"The Intellectual Conscience.— . . . By far the most lack an intellectual conscience . . .* I mean: *by far the most* do not find it contemptible to believe this or that and to live according to it, *without* first having become conscious of the last and surest reasons pro and con, and without even taking the trouble to consider such reasons afterward; the most gifted men and the most noble women still belong to these 'by far the most.' Yet what is good-heartedness, refinement, and genius to me, when the human being who has these virtues tolerates slack feelings in his faith and judgments, and when the demand for certainty is not to him the inmost craving and the deepest need—that which distinguishes the higher from the lower men. . . . *Not to question,* not to tremble with the craving and the joy of questioning . . . that is what I feel to be *contemptible . . ."*
  Nietzsche never renounced these views. See, e.g., one of his very last works, *The Antichrist* (section 50; *Portable Nietzsche,* p. 632): "At every step one has to wrestle for truth; one has had to surrender for it almost everything to which the heart, to which our love, our trust in life, cling otherwise. That requires greatness of soul: the service of truth is the hardest service. What does it mean, after all, to have *integrity* in matters of the spirit? That one is severe against one's heart, that one despises 'beautiful sentiments,' that one makes of every Yes and No a matter of conscience. Faith makes blessed: consequently it lies."
  Nietzsche's objection to those "in whom alone the intellectual conscience dwells and is incarnate today" is that there is "one point" they refuse to question; that there is one "beautiful sentiment" they still permit themselves. As Nietzsche puts it a few lines later: "they still have faith in truth."

ated from the ascetic ideal as possible, these "free, *very* free spirits"; and yet, to disclose to them what they themselves cannot see—for they are too close to themselves: this ideal is precisely *their* ideal, too; they themselves embody it today and perhaps they alone; they themselves are its most spiritualized product, its most advanced front-line troops and scouts, its most captious, tender, intangible form of seduction—if I have guessed any riddles, I wish that *this* proposition might show it!— They are far from being *free* spirits: *for they still have faith in truth.*

When the Christian crusaders in the Orient encountered the invincible order of Assassins,[6] that order of free spirits *par excellence,* whose lowest ranks followed a rule of obedience the like of which no order of monks ever attained, they obtained in some way or other a hint concerning that symbol and watchword reserved for the highest ranks alone as their *secretum*: "Nothing is true, everything is permitted."— Very well, *that* was *freedom* of spirit; in *that* way the faith in truth itself was *abrogated.*[7]

Has any European, any Christian free spirit ever strayed into this proposition and into its labyrinthine consequences? has one of them ever known the Minotaur of this cave *from experience?*— I doubt it;[8] more, I know better: nothing is more foreign to these

---

[6] An Islamic sect, founded in the eleventh century. "As for the initiated, they knew the worthlessness of positive religion and morality; they believed in nothing . . ." (Encyclopaedia Britannica, 11th ed.)

[7] The striking slogan is plainly neither Nietzsche's coinage nor his motto. It is a quotation on which he comments, contrasting it with the unquestioning faith in the truth that characterizes so many so-called free spirits.

[8] The Assassins' slogan is often mistaken for Nietzsche's coinage and derived from Dostoevsky; e.g., by Danto: it "must surely be a paraphrase of the Russian novelist he so admired" (*op. cit.,* p. 193).

In Dostoevsky's *Brothers Karamazov* we encounter the idea that, if mankind lost the belief in God and immortality, "everything would be permitted." But what matters to Nietzsche in this section is the first half of his quotation, "nothing is true," which has no parallel in Dostoevsky. Moreover, the quotation from *The Brothers* is not particularly profound: it "works" in its context in the novel but expresses no great insight, taken by itself.

Incidentally, Nietzsche never read *The Brothers* (originally serialized in Russia in 1879–80); and this novel was not translated into French until 1888, in a mutilated version. On March 7, 1887, Nietzsche wrote Gast that he had read, first, *L'Esprit souterrain* (translated, 1886: *Notes from Underground*); then *La maison des morts* (tr., 1886: *The House of the Dead*); finally, *Humiliés et offensés* (tr., 1884: *The Injured and the Insulted*—the

men who are unconditional about *one* thing, these *so-called* "free spirits," than freedom and liberation in this sense; in no respect are they more rigidly bound;[9] it is precisely in their faith in truth that they are more rigid and unconditional than anyone. I know all this from too close up perhaps:[10] that venerable philosopher's abstinence to which such a faith commits one; that intellectual stoicism which ultimately refuses not only to affirm but also to deny; that *desire* to halt before the factual, the *factum brutum;* that fatalism of *"petits faits"* (*ce petit faitalisme*,[11] as I call it) through which French scholarship nowadays tries to establish a sort of moral superiority over German scholarship; that general renunciation of all interpretation (of forcing, adjusting, abbreviating, omitting, padding, inventing, falsifying, and whatever else is of the *essence* of interpreting)—all this expresses, broadly speaking, as much ascetic virtue as any denial of sensuality (it is at bottom only a particular mode of this denial). That which *constrains* these men, however, this unconditional will to truth, is *faith in the ascetic ideal itself,* even if as an unconscious imperative—don't be deceived about that —it is the faith in a *metaphysical* value, the absolute value of *truth,* sanctioned and guaranteed by this ideal alone (it stands or falls with this ideal).

Strictly speaking, there is no such thing as science "without any presuppositions"; this thought does not bear thinking through,

---

first of Dostoevsky's novels to be translated into French). On October 14, 1888, Nietzsche wrote Gast: "The French have produced a stage version of Dostoevsky's main novel." This was *Le Crime et le châtiment* (tr., 1884: *Crime and Punishment*). Cf. F. W. J. Hemmings, *The Russian Novel in France, 1884–1914* (New York, Oxford University Press, 1950), especially p. 241. See also the note on section 15 above.

Finally, see section 602 of *The Will to Power,* probably written in 1884: ". . . 'Everything is false! Everything is permitted!' . . ."

[9] Nietzsche returns to his objection.

[10] Is Nietzsche here referring to himself? Without ruling out the possibility that he also had some first-hand experience of the attitude he goes on to describe—at least as a possibility—I find the portrait very different from him. On the other hand, "that intellectual stoicism which ultimately refuses not only to affirm but also to deny"—and not only this trait—seems as close to Nietzsche's best friend, Franz Overbeck (professor of church history at Basel, and an unbeliever), as it seems remote from Nietzsche's own spirit.

[11] The pun is less felicitous in English: small facts (the small factalism, as I call it).

it is paralogical: a philosophy, a "faith," must always be there first of all, so that science can acquire from it a direction, a meaning, a limit, a method, a *right* to exist. (Whoever has the opposite notion, whoever tries, for example, to place philosophy "on a strictly scientific basis," first needs to stand not only philosophy but truth itself *on its head*—the grossest violation of decency possible in relation to two such venerable females!) There is no doubt of it—and here I cite the fifth book of my *Gay Science* (section 344[12]):

"The truthful man, in the audacious and ultimate sense presupposed by the faith in science, *thereby affirms another world* than that of life, nature, and history; and insofar as he affirms this 'other world,' does this not mean that he has to deny its antithesis, this world, *our* world? . . . It is still a *metaphysical faith* that underlies our faith in science—and we men of knowledge of today, we godless men and anti-metaphysicians, we, too, still derive *our* flame from the fire ignited by a faith millennia old, the Christian faith, which was also Plato's, that God is truth, that truth is *divine.*—But what if this belief is becoming more and more unbelievable, if nothing turns out to be divine any longer unless it be error, blindness, lies—if God himself turns out to be our *longest lie?*"

At this point it is necessary to pause and take careful stock. Science itself henceforth *requires* justification (which is not to say that there is any such justification).[13] Consider on this question both the earliest and most recent philosophers: they are all oblivious of how much the will to truth itself first requires justification; here there is a lacuna in every philosophy—how did this come about? Because the ascetic ideal has hitherto *dominated* all philosophy, because truth was posited as being, as God, as the highest court of appeal—because truth was not *permitted* to be a problem

---

12 In the following quotation, the three dots mark Nietzsche's omission of a few words (about one line) from the text he quotes. Most of section 344 will be found in the *Portable Nietzsche,* pp. 448–50. See also Kaufmann's *Nietzsche,* Chapter 12, section III.

13 Neither is it to say that no justification is possible. The point is that the problem has to be considered in all seriousness. Even as it is naïve to suppose that we *know* what is good and what is evil—and it is Nietzsche's intent to show us how problematic morality is—it is also naïve to overlook that the justification of science poses a problem.

at all. Is this "permitted" understood?— From the moment faith in the God of the ascetic ideal is denied, a *new problem arises:* that of the *value* of truth.

The will to truth requires a critique—let us thus define our own task—the value of truth must for once be experimentally *called into question.*[14]

(Whoever feels that this has been stated too briefly should read the section of the *Gay Science* entitled "To What Extent We, Too, Are Still Pious" (section 344), or preferably the entire fifth book of that work, as well as the Preface to *The Dawn.*)

25

No! Don't come to me with science when I ask for the natural antagonist of the ascetic ideal, when I demand: "where is the opposing will expressing the *opposing ideal?*" Science is not nearly self-reliant enough to be that; it first requires in every respect an ideal of value, a value-creating power, in the *service* of which it could *believe* in itself—it never creates values. Its relation to the ascetic ideal is by no means essentially antagonistic; it might even be said to represent the driving force in the latter's inner development. It opposes and fights, on closer inspection, not the ideal itself but only its exteriors, its guise and masquerade, its temporary dogmatic hardening and stiffening, and by denying what is exoteric in this ideal, it liberates what life is in it. This pair, science and the ascetic ideal, both rest on the same foundation—I have already indicated it: on the same overestimation of truth (more exactly: on the same belief that truth is inestimable and cannot be criticized). Therefore they are *necessarily* allies, so that if they are to be fought they can only be fought and called in question together. A depreciation of the ascetic ideal unavoidably involves a depreciation of science: one must keep one's eyes and ears open to this fact!

(*Art*—to say it in advance, for I shall some day return to this subject at greater length—art, in which precisely the *lie* is sanctified and the *will to deception* has a good conscience, is much more

---

[14] This is the conclusion to which Nietzsche has been working up.

fundamentally opposed to the ascetic ideal than is science: this was instinctively sensed by Plato, the greatest enemy of art Europe has yet produced. Plato versus Homer: that is the complete, the genuine antagonism—there the sincerest advocate of the "beyond," the great slanderer of life; here the instinctive deifier, the *golden* nature.[1] To place himself in the service of the ascetic ideal is therefore the most distinctive *corruption* of an artist that is at all possible; unhappily, also one of the most common forms of corruption, for nothing is more easily corrupted than an artist.)

Physiologically, too, science rests on the same foundation as the ascetic ideal: a certain *impoverishment of life* is a presupposition of both of them—the affects grown cool, the tempo of life slowed down, dialectics in place of instinct, seriousness imprinted on faces and gestures (seriousness, the most unmistakable sign of a labored metabolism, of struggling, laborious life). Observe the ages in the history of people when the scholar steps into the foreground: they are ages of exhaustion, often of evening and decline; overflowing energy, certainty of life and of the *future,* are things of the past. A predominance of mandarins always means something is wrong; so do the advent of democracy, international courts in place of war, equal rights for women, the religion of pity, and whatever other symptoms of declining life there are. (Science posed as a problem; what is the meaning of science?—cf. the Preface[2] to *The Birth of Tragedy.*)

---

[1] We return to a problem posed in Nietzsche's first book, *The Birth of Tragedy:* the relation of art and science. There it was the contrast of tragedy and Socratism that served as a point of departure; here "Plato versus Homer" sums up the problem. Nietzsche still finds Socratism and the unquestioned faith in a life devoted to scientific inquiry problematic. But he is as far as ever from contempt for the life of inquiry: after all, was not this the life he himself chose, clinging to it in spite of his doctors' advice to read and write less?

Here we should recall the symbol of the "artistic Socrates" that Nietzsche introduced near the end of section 14 of *The Birth.* He clearly does not cast his lot with either Plato or Homer. He is a philosopher *and* a poet—in his *concerns* much more a philosopher, but in his loving transfiguration of the language closer to the poets—and he does not denigrate this world in favor of another. He wants to celebrate this world, though, like Homer, he is anything but blind to its suffering. And not only *The Birth of Tragedy* is relevant to Nietzsche's theme here; *The Gay Science* is, too; e.g., section 327, which will be found in this volume.

[2] Added in 1886 to the new edition.

No! this "modern science"—let us face this fact!—is the *best* ally the ascetic ideal has at present, and precisely because it is the most unconscious, involuntary, hidden, and subterranean ally! They have played the same game up to now, the "poor in spirit" and the scientific opponents of this ideal (one should not think, by the way, that they are their opposites, the *rich* in spirit perhaps— they are *not;* I have called them the hectics[3] of the spirit). As for the famous *victories* of the latter, they undoubtedly are victories— but over what? The ascetic ideal has decidedly not been conquered: if anything, it became stronger, which is to say, more elusive, more spiritual, more captious, as science remorselessly detached and broke off wall upon wall, external additions that had coarsened its appearance. Does anyone really believe that the defeat of theological astronomy represented a defeat for that ideal?

Has man perhaps become *less desirous* of a transcendent solution to the riddle of his existence, now that this existence appears more arbitrary, beggarly, and dispensable in the *visible* order of things? Has the self-belittlement of man, his *will* to self-belittlement, not progressed irresistibly since Copernicus? Alas, the faith in the dignity and uniqueness of man, in his irreplaceability in the great chain of being,[4] is a thing of the past—he has become an *animal,* literally and without reservation or qualification, he who was, according to his old faith, almost God ("child of God," "God-man").

Since Copernicus, man seems to have got himself on an inclined plane—now he is slipping faster and faster away from the center into—what? into nothingness? into a *"penetrating* sense of his nothingness"?[5] Very well! hasn't this been the straightest route to—the *old* ideal?

All science (and by no means only astronomy, on the humiliating and degrading effect of which Kant made the noteworthy confession: "it destroys my importance" . . .), all science, natural as well as *unnatural*—which is what I call the self-critique of knowledge—has at present the object of dissuading man from his

---

[3] Section 24 above.

[4] *Rangabfolge der Wesen.*

[5] Here Nietzsche makes use of material included in section 1 of the posthumous edition of *The Will to Power.*

former respect for himself, as if this had been nothing but a piece of bizarre conceit. One might even say that its own pride, its own austere form of stoical ataraxy, consists in sustaining this hard-won *self-contempt* of man as his ultimate and most serious claim to self-respect (and quite rightly, indeed: for he that despises is always one who "has not forgotten how to respect" . . .) Is this really to *work against* the ascetic ideal? Does one still seriously believe (as theologians imagined for a while) that Kant's *victory* over the dogmatic concepts of theology ("God," "soul," "freedom," "immortality") damaged that ideal?—it being no concern of ours for the present whether Kant ever had any intention of doing such a thing. What is certain is that, since Kant, transcendentalists of every kind have once more won the day—they have been emancipated from the theologians: what joy!— Kant showed them a secret path by which they may, on their own initiative and with all scientific respectability, from now on follow their "heart's desire."

In the same vein: who could hold it against the agnostics if, as votaries of the unknown and mysterious as such, they now worship the *question mark itself* as God? (Xaver Doudan[6] once spoke of the *ravages* worked by *"l'habitude d'admirer l'inintelligible au lieu de rester tout simplement dans l'inconnu"*;[7] he thought the ancients had avoided this.) Presuming that everything man "knows" does not merely fail to satisfy his desires but rather contradicts them and produces a sense of horror, what a divine way out to have the right to seek the responsibility for this not in "desire" but in "knowledge"!

"There is no knowledge: *consequently*—there is a God": what a new *elegantia syllogismi!* [8] what a *triumph* for the ascetic ideal!—

---

6 Ximénès Doudan (1800–1872), a French critic, contributed to the *Journal des Débats* and was the author of the posthumously published *Mélanges et lettres* (1876–77; Mixed writings and letters), *Lettres* (1879; Letters), and *Pensées et fragments, suivis des révolutions du goût* (1881; Thoughts and fragments, and the revolutions of taste).

7 The habit of admiring the unintelligible instead of staying quite simply in the unknown.

8 Elegance of the syllogism.

26

Or does modern historiography perhaps display an attitude more assured of life and ideals? Its noblest claim nowadays is that it is a mirror; it rejects all teleology; it no longer wishes to "prove" anything; it disdains to play the judge and considers this a sign of good taste—it affirms as little as it denies; it ascertains, it "describes" . . . All this is to a high degree ascetic; but at the same time it is to an even higher degree *nihilistic,* let us not deceive ourselves about that! One observes a sad, stern, but resolute glance —an eye that looks far, the way a lonely Arctic explorer looks far (so as not to look within, perhaps? so as not to look back? . . .) Here is snow; here life has grown silent; the last crows whose cries are audible here are called "wherefore?," "in vain!," *"nada!"*— here nothing will grow or prosper any longer, or at the most Petersburg metapolitics and Tolstoian "pity."

As for that other type of historian, an even more "modern" type perhaps, a hedonist and voluptuary who flirts both with life and with the ascetic ideal, who employs the word "artist" as a glove and has today taken sole lease of the praise of contemplation: oh how these sweetish and clever fellows make one long even for ascetics and winter landscapes! No! the devil take this type of "contemplative"! I would even prefer to wander through the gloomy, gray, cold fog with those historical nihilists! Indeed, if I *had* to choose I might even opt for some completely unhistorical, antihistorical person (such as Dühring, whose voice today intoxicates in Germany a hitherto shy and unavowed species of "beautiful soul," the *species anarchistica* within the educated proletariat).

The "contemplatives" are a hundred times worse: I know of nothing that excites such disgust as this kind of "objective" armchair scholar, this kind of scented voluptuary of history, half parson, half satyr, perfume by Renan,[1] who betrays immediately with

---

[1] Ernest Renan (1823–1892), a prolific French scholar and writer, is remembered chiefly for his immensely successful *Life of Jesus,* published in June 1863. Before November 1863, 60,000 copies were in circulation. This was his first volume on the *Origins of Christianity,* followed shortly by

the high falsetto of his applause what he lacks, *where* he lacks it,
where in this case the Fates have applied their cruel shears with,
alas, such surgical skill! This offends my taste; also my patience.
let him have patience with such sights who has nothing to lose by
them—such a sight arouses my ire, such "spectators" dispose me
against the "spectacle" more than the spectacle itself (the spectacle
of history, you understand); I fall unawares into an Anacreontic
mood. Nature, which gave the bull his horns and the lion his
chasm' odontōn,[2] why did nature give me my foot? . . . To kick,
Holy Anacreon! and not only for running away; for kicking to
pieces these rotten armchairs, this cowardly contemplativeness, this
lascivious historical eunuchism, this flirting with ascetic ideals, this
justice-tartuffery of impotence!

All honor to the ascetic ideal *insofar as it is honest!* so long
as it believes in itself and does not play tricks on us! But I do not
like all these coquettish bedbugs with their insatiable ambition to
smell out the infinite, until at last the infinite smells of bedbugs; I do
not like these whited sepulchers who impersonate life; I do not like
these weary and played-out people who wrap themselves in wisdom
and look "objective"; I do not like these agitators dressed up as
heroes who wear the magic cap of ideals on their straw heads; I do
not like these ambitious artists who like to pose as ascetics and
priests but who are at bottom only tragic buffoons; and I also do not
like these latest speculators in idealism, the anti-Semites, who today
roll their eyes in a Christian-Aryan-bourgeois manner and exhaust
one's patience by trying to rouse up all the horned-beast elements in
the people by a brazen abuse of the cheapest of all agitator's tricks,
moral attitudinizing (that *no* kind of swindle fails to succeed in

---

The Apostles (1866) and *St. Paul* (1869). In 1876 the fourth volume appeared, Renan's *Antichrist*, which dealt with the reign of Nero; and by 1881
two more volumes came out, *The Christian Church* and *Marcus Aurelius*.
Renan published many other works as well.

Nietzsche's references to him are uniformly hostile: see *Beyond Good
and Evil*, section 48; *Twilight*, "Skirmishes," sections 2 and 6 (*Portable
Nietzsche*, pp. 513f. and 516); and *Antichrist*, sections 17, 29, 31, and 32
(*ibid.*, pp. 584, 600, and 604).

2 "Nature gave horns to the bull . . . to the lion a chasm of teeth" is what
Anacreon, the Greek lyrical poet who flourished in 540 B.C., wrote in one
of his odes (number 24).

Germany today is connected with the undeniable and palpable stagnation of the German spirit; and the cause of that I seek in a too exclusive diet of newspapers, politics, beer, and Wagnerian music, together with the presuppositions of such a diet: first, national constriction and vanity, the strong but narrow principle *"Deutschland, Deutschland über alles,"* and then the *paralysis agitans*[3] of "modern ideas").

Europe is rich and inventive today above all in means of excitation; it seems to need nothing as much as it needs stimulants and brandy: hence also the tremendous amount of forgery in ideals, this most potent brandy of the spirit; hence also the repulsive, ill-smelling, mendacious, pseudo-alcoholic air everywhere. I should like to know how many shiploads of sham idealism, heroic trappings and grand-word-rattles, how many tons of sugared sympathy-spirits (distillers: *la religion de la souffrance*[4]), how many "noble-indignation" stilts for the aid of the spiritually flatfooted, how many *comedians* of the Christian-moral ideal would have to be exported from Europe today before its air would begin to smell fresh again.

With this overproduction there is obviously a new opening for *trade* here; there is obviously a "business" to be made out of little ideal-idols and the "idealists" who go with them: don't let this opportunity slip! Who has the courage for it?—we have in our *hands* the means to "idealize" the whole earth!

But why am I speaking of courage: only one thing is needed here, the hand, an uninhibited, a very uninhibited hand.—

27

Enough! Enough! Let us leave these curiosities and complexities of the most modern spirit, which provoke as much laughter as chagrin: *our* problem, the problem of the *meaning* of the ascetic ideal, can dispense with them: what has this problem to do with yesterday or today! I shall probe these things more thoroughly and severely in another connection (under the title "On the History of

---

[3] Shaking palsy, *alias* Parkinson's disease.
[4] The religion of suffering.

European Nihilism"; it will be contained in a work in progress: *The Will to Power: Attempt at a Revaluation of All Values*[1]). All I have been concerned to indicate here is this: in the most spiritual sphere, too, the ascetic ideal has at present only *one* kind of real enemy capable of *harming* it: the comedians of this ideal— for they arouse mistrust of it. Everywhere else that the spirit is strong, mighty, and at work without counterfeit today, it does without ideals of any kind—the popular expression for this abstinence is "atheism"—*except for its will to truth*. But this will, this *remnant* of an ideal, is, if you will believe me, this ideal itself in its strictest, most spiritual formulation, esoteric through and through, with all external additions abolished, and thus not so much its remnant as its *kernel*. Unconditional honest atheism (and *its* is the only air we breathe, we more spiritual men of this age!) is therefore *not* the antithesis of that ideal, as it appears to be; it is rather only one of the latest phases of its evolution, one of its terminal forms and inner consequences—it is the awe-inspiring *catastrophe* of two thousand years of training in truthfulness that finally forbids itself the *lie involved in belief in God*.

(The same evolutionary course in India, completely independent of ours, should prove something: the same ideal leads to the same conclusion; the decisive point is reached five centuries before the beginning of the European calendar, with Buddha; more exactly, with the Sankhya philosophy, subsequently popularized by Buddha and made into a religion.)

What, in all strictness, has really *conquered* the Christian God? The answer may be found in my *Gay Science* (section 357): "Christian morality itself, the concept of truthfulness taken more and more strictly, the confessional subtlety of the Christian conscience translated and sublimated into the scientific conscience, into intellectual cleanliness at any price. To view nature as if it were a proof of the goodness and providence of a God; to interpret

---

[1] Nietzsche never finished this work nor any part of it. But many of his notes were published posthumously under the title *The Will to Power: Attempt at a Revaluation of All Values* (1st ed., 1901; 2nd, radically revised ed., 1906), and the second chapter of this collection was entitled "On the History of European Nihilism." (English edition with commentary by Walter Kaufmann, New York, Random House, 1967.)

history to the glory of a divine reason, as the perpetual witness to a moral world order and moral intentions; to interpret one's own experiences, as pious men long interpreted them, as if everything were preordained, everything a sign, everything sent for the salvation of the soul—that now belongs to the *past,* that has the conscience *against* it, that seems to every more sensitive conscience indecent, dishonest, mendacious, feminism, weakness, cowardice: it is this rigor if anything that makes us *good Europeans* and the heirs of Europe's longest and bravest self-overcoming."

All great things bring about their own destruction through an act of self-overcoming:[2] thus the law of life will have it, the law of the necessity of "self-overcoming" in the nature of life—the lawgiver himself eventually receives the call: *"patere legem, quam ipse tulisti."* [3] In this way Christianity *as a dogma* was destroyed by its own morality; in the same way Christianity *as morality* must now perish, too: we stand on the threshold of *this* event. After Christian truthfulness has drawn one inference after another, it must end by drawing its *most striking inference,* its inference *against* itself; this will happen, however, when it poses the question *"what is the meaning of all will to truth?"*

And here I again touch on my problem, on our problem, my *unknown* friends (for as yet I *know* of no friend): what meaning would *our* whole being possess if it were not this, that in us the will to truth becomes conscious of itself as a *problem?*

As the will to truth thus gains self-consciousness—there can be no doubt of that—morality will gradually *perish* now: this is the great spectacle in a hundred acts reserved for the next two centuries in Europe—the most terrible, most questionable, and perhaps also the most hopeful of all spectacles.—

---

[2] *Selbstaufhebung:* cf. the end of section 10 in the second essay, above. Two lines above the footnoted reference and also in the line below it, "self-overcoming" is used to render *Selbstüberwindung.*

[3] Submit to the law you yourself proposed.

28

Apart from the ascetic ideal, man, the human *animal,* had no meaning so far. His existence on earth contained no goal; "why man at all?"—was a question without an answer; the *will* for man and earth was lacking; behind every great human destiny there sounded as a refrain a yet greater "in vain!" *This* is precisely what the ascetic ideal means: that something was *lacking,* that man was surrounded by a fearful *void*—he did not know how to justify, to account for, to affirm himself; he *suffered* from the problem of his meaning. He also suffered otherwise, he was in the main a sickly animal: but his problem was *not* suffering itself, but that there was no answer to the crying question, "*why* do I suffer?"

Man, the bravest of animals and the one most accustomed to suffering, does *not* repudiate suffering as such; he *desires* it, he even seeks it out, provided he is shown a *meaning* for it, a *purpose* of suffering. The meaninglessness of suffering, *not* suffering itself, was the curse that lay over mankind so far—*and the ascetic ideal offered man meaning!* It was the only meaning offered so far; any meaning is better than none at all; the ascetic ideal was in every sense the *"faute de mieux" par excellence* so far. In it, suffering was *interpreted;* the tremendous void seemed to have been filled; the door was closed to any kind of suicidal nihilism. This interpretation—there is no doubt of it—brought fresh suffering with it, deeper, more inward, more poisonous, more life-destructive suffering: it placed all suffering under the perspective of *guilt.*

But all this notwithstanding—man was *saved* thereby, he possessed a meaning, he was henceforth no longer like a leaf in the wind, a plaything of nonsense—the "sense-less"—he could now *will* something; no matter at first to what end, why, with what he willed: *the will itself was saved.*

We can no longer conceal from ourselves *what* is expressed by all that willing which has taken its direction from the ascetic ideal: this hatred of the human, and even more of the animal, and more still of the material, this horror of the senses, of reason itself, this fear of happiness and beauty, this longing to get away from all

appearance, change, becoming, death, wishing, from longing itself
—all this means—let us dare to grasp it—*a will to nothingness,* an
aversion[1] to life, a rebellion against the most fundamental presuppositions of life; but it is and remains a *will!* . . . And, to repeat
in conclusion what I said at the beginning: man would rather will
nothingness than *not* will.[2]—

---

[1] *Widerwillen.*

[2] *Lieber will noch der Mensch* das Nichts *wollen, als* nicht *wollen* . . .

The
CASE of
WAGNER

A Musicians' Problem

———◆———

FOR
Lilli Seligsohn

CONTENTS

TRANSLATOR'S INTRODUCTION   *603*
The Case of Wagner   *609*

FROM NIETZSCHE'S CORRESPONDENCE ABOUT
The Case of Wagner   *649*

INDEX TO *The Case of Wagner*   *831*

Translator's Introduction

Although it is well known that Nietzsche and Wagner were friends for a while and then broke with each other, this essay has not received the attention it deserves. In English it has so far been available only in the old eighteen-volume edition of the *Collected Works.* An earlier version, done for the same collection, was discarded.

This is not the place to review the relation of the two men in detail, or to discuss and evaluate the literature on the subject. A rapid sketch of the background of this book must suffice.

Wagner, born in 1813—the same year as Nietzsche's father, as well as Verdi and Kierkegaard—was the only great genius whom Nietzsche ever knew intimately. The friendship was never even remotely symmetrical: apart from the difference in age, Nietzsche was still a student in November 1868 when, at twenty-four, he first met Wagner who, at fifty-five, had completed the bulk of his work. That winter Nietzsche was appointed to a chair of classical philology at the University of Basel, in Switzerland, within easy reach of Tribschen, also in Switzerland, where Wagner was then living. For Wagner, who had many detractors, it was nice to have a brilliant young professor as an ally; and when *The Birth of Tragedy* appeared, he wrote Nietzsche: "I have never yet read anything more beautiful than your book." What he liked best was, of course, the worst part of the book, the lengthy last part with its effusive appreciation of Wagner. Nor did he have anything but praise for those stylistic qualities which Nietzsche himself later criticized in his preface to the edition of 1886. Such imitation of his own manner and such acceptance of his image of himself at face value were the tribute Wagner exacted. Indeed, he asked for revisions in the endings of *The Birth* and, a little later, of the third "Untimely Meditation" on *Schopenhauer as Educator;* and he was displeased that in the second "meditation," *On the Use and Disadvantage of History for Life,* there was no explicit reference to him. He had no sense of Nietzsche's distinctive genius and mission: the younger man was to be his apostle—and a friend who could be asked to do the master's Christmas shopping and to help with other such chores.

No doubt there were many factors that helped to maintain the friendship for almost ten years. Not the least of these was a common enthusiasm for Schopenhauer, who had only recently begun to gain recognition as a major philospher. But as far as Nietzsche was concerned, the major consideration was surely that, for all his faults and foibles, Wagner was a great artist and incomparably more fascinating than anybody else Nietzsche knew. To be close personally to such a man, to be able to listen to him discoursing freely about his work and ideas, to belong to the master's inner circle—all that was not merely a privilege but seemed the best thing that had ever happened to the young professor. Not only was he able to try out his own ideas on a man of genius; he had found a second home. Nietzsche's father had died in 1849, before the boy was five, and his mother's narrow piety and lack of education had made his own home quite devoid of intellectual stimulation. Nietzsche had several good friends his own age, and some of these shared his enthusaism for Wagner—notably Erwin Rohde, the classical philologist, and Gustav Krug, who had tried to convert his friends to Wagner in the early eighteen-sixties.[1]

That Wagner was demanding and irritable, and that many of his emphatic opinions were very dubious, was obvious but seemed a small price for the benefits of such a friendship. Even Ernest Newman, who yields to none in his admiration and enthusiasm for Wagner, while he lacks any solid first-hand knowledge of Nietzsche and, on the basis of the "masterly epitome of Nietzsche's thinking"[2] written by one of the worst Nazi hacks, gives a thoroughly

---

[1] See Frederick R. Love's monograph on *Young Nietzsche and the Wagnerian Experience* (Chapel Hill, University of North Carolina Press, 1963). Love's most original contribution is that he shows how "the record of Nietzsche's compositions clearly provides a basis for modifying the widely held view of the philosopher as a passionate devotee of Wagnerian music" (p. viii). He also argues that "Wagner's music remained for Nietzsche an unsolved problem from first to last, a problem that was temporarily suppressed during the period of his closest association with the composer" (p. 80), and that "Nietzsche's infatuation with Wagnerian music . . . may indeed be regarded as an aberration" (p. 82). In other words, in 1878 Nietzsche did not break faith with himself, as the Wagnerians have claimed, but began to find himself.

[2] Ernest Newman, *The Life of Richard Wagner* (New York, Alfred A. Knopf), vol. IV, p. 335. The reference is to Alfred Bäumler's notorious

misleading picture of Nietzsche, speaks of Wagner's "insatiable lust for domination," admits that he wanted to be "an undisputed dictator," [3] and describes how Wagner "worked himself into a paroxysm over Bismarck's tolerance towards the Jews." [4] In short, to come fully into his own, Nietzsche had to break with Wagner.

As long as he lived at Tribschen, a lonely genius, Wagner's impassioned faith in the superiority of the Germans and the inferiority of other peoples, especially the French and the Jews, could perhaps be decently ignored; but when Wagner came to terms with the new German Empire and set up a great cultural center in Bayreuth, the time for a clear stand was at hand—and Nietzsche dissociated himself from what Bayreuth symbolized.[5] Two further factors contributed to the break.

Nietzsche did not take Christianity lightly. His father, whose memory he revered, had been a minister; so had both of his grandfathers; and his mother was a devout Christian. The significance of Schopenhauer for Nietzsche and Wagner had been tied to Schopenhauer's frank atheism. In January 1878, when Wagner sent Nietzsche his *Parsifal,* with a humorous and friendly inscription, this opera struck Nietzsche as shameless: Wagner was exploiting Christianity for theatrical effect, and the self-styled modern Aeschylus was celebrating the anti-Greek ideal of what Wagner himself called "pure foolishness." But what sealed the break was not even *Parsifal,* nor Nietzsche's reaction to Wagner. It was rather Nietzsche's emergence into independence and Wagner's reaction to that.

In May 1878 Nietzsche sent Wagner his own new book, *Human, All-Too-Human,* with a motto from Descartes and a dedication to Voltaire. He was done with silence in the face of anti-French outbursts. He had developed from Schopenhauer to Voltaire, and from romantic essays to aphorisms influenced by French models. He repudiated nationalism emphatically and proposed the ideal of the "good European." All this was much more unforgivable in Wagner's eyes than even *Parsifal* had been in Nietzsche's, and in

---

Nietzsche, der Philosoph und Politiker (1931), which led the Nazis to call Bäumler to Berlin as Professor of Philosophy.

[3] *Ibid.,* p. 297.

[4] *Ibid.,* p. 598.

[5] Newman is thus more right than he himself realizes when he admits that the break was precipitated "not by Wagner's art, but by Bayreuth" (p. 525).

August of that year Wagner attacked his erstwhile friend in the *Bayreuther Blätter*.

In 1874, when he was still working on the fourth "meditation," a eulogy of Wagner, Nietzsche had also jotted down in his notebooks a great many critical observations. *The Birth* had appeared in 1872, the first "meditation" in 1873, the second and third both in 1874, but the fourth gave Nietzsche a great deal of trouble and was not published until 1876. In *Human, All-Too-Human* (1878) Wagner's name does not appear—it is found in the preface added to the new edition of 1886—but the chapter on the souls of artists and writers contains observations and reflections prompted by Wagner. With this book Nietzsche came into his own.

In his later works Wagner is occasionally mentioned, but it was not until 1888, when his inhibitions had decreased drastically, that he published a small volume devoted entirely to "The Case of Wagner." That this book on Wagner troubled him, too, is evident even from its form: there is a postscript of considerable length, then a second postscript, and finally an epilogue.

Wagner was dead by then, and the problem that confronted Nietzsche was in part similar to that which Heine had resolved when he had published one of his best books, *Ludwig Börne* (1840), after Börne's death. The book had been greeted by a storm of indignation, but much later Thomas Mann was to say that of Heine's "works I have long loved the book on Börne most. . . . His psychology of the Nazarene type anticipates Nietzsche. . . . And incidentally this book contains the most superb German prose before Nietzsche. Incidentally? Ah, only those who understand the blissfully distracted smile with which he answered his friends when they warned him, presenting to him the human, personal, political offensiveness of the book, 'But isn't it expressed beautifully?'— only those comprehend what a memorable phenomenon this artist Jew has been among Germans!" [6]

After the storm broke in 1888, Nietzsche, who had meanwhile completed *Twilight of the Idols* and *The Antichrist,* divided his time between *Ecce Homo* and his final effort, *Nietzsche contra Wagner,* which he finished Christmas 1888, only a few days before

---

[6] Thomas Mann, "Notiz über Heine" (1908) in *Rede und Antwort* (1922: speech and response—an early collection of his non-fiction), p. 382.

his total collapse. This last book consists of passages "selected . . . from my older writings—some go back all the way to 1877—perhaps clarified here and there, above all, shortened." [7] The book was designed to show that *The Case of Wagner* had not been inspired by sudden malice, and that Nietzsche had long taken similar stands. Nietzsche sometimes wrote in relative haste, though the difference between the books he prepared for publication and the notes others published after his death remains very considerable. *Nietzsche contra Wagner* is perhaps his most beautiful book, and those seeking a commentary to *The Case of Wagner* would surely have been referred to the later, still briefer book, had they asked the author.

The present commentary consists of three parts: the translator's introduction, a number of footnotes to the translation, and a selection of pertinent passages from Nietzsche's correspondence of 1888. A weightier commentary does not seem necessary—and would not be in the spirit of this very short and elegant work.

W. K.

---

[7] Preface. A complete translation is included in *The Portable Nietzsche*, ed. and tr. by Walter Kaufmann.

THE
CASE OF WAGNER

———◆———

Turinese Letter of May 1888

ridendo dicere severum[1]—

---

[1] "Through what is laughable say what is somber." A variation of Horace's *ridentem dicere verum, quid vetat* ("What forbids us to tell the truth, laughing?") *Satires* I.24.

Preface

I have granted myself some small relief. It is not merely pure malice when I praise Bizet in this essay at the expense of Wagner. Interspersed with many jokes, I bring up a matter that is no joke. To turn my back on Wagner was for me a fate; to like anything at all again after that, a triumph. Perhaps nobody was more dangerously attached to—grown together with—Wagnerizing; nobody tried harder to resist it; nobody was happier to be rid of it. A long story! — You want a word for it?— If I were a moralist, who knows what I might call it? Perhaps self-overcoming.— But the philosopher has no love for moralists. Neither does he love pretty words.

What does a philosopher demand of himself first and last? To overcome his time in himself, to become "timeless." With what must he therefore engage in the hardest combat? With whatever marks him as the child of his time. Well, then! I am, no less than Wagner, a child of this time; that is, a decadent: but I comprehended this, I resisted it. The philosopher in me resisted.

Nothing has preoccupied me more profoundly than the problem of decadence—I had reasons. "Good and evil" is merely a variation of that problem. Once one has developed a keen eye for the symptoms of decline, one understands morality, too—one understands what is hiding under its most sacred names and value formulas: impoverished life, the will to the end, the great weariness. Morality negates life.

For such a task I required a special self-discipline: to take sides against everything sick in me, including Wagner, including Schopenhauer, including all of modern "humaneness."— A profound estrangement, cold, sobering up—against everything that is of this time, everything timely—and most desirable of all, the eye of Zarathustra, an eye that beholds the whole fact of man at a tremendous distance—below. For such a goal—what sacrifice wouldn't be fitting? what "self-overcoming"? what "self-denial"?

My greatest experience was a recovery. Wagner is merely one of my sicknesses.

Not that I wish to be ungrateful to this sickness. When in this essay I assert the proposition that Wagner is harmful, I wish no less to assert for whom he is nevertheless indispensable—for the philosopher. Others may be able to get along without Wagner; but the philosopher is not free to do without Wagner. He has to be the bad conscience of his time:[1] for that he needs to understand it best. But confronted with the labyrinth of the modern soul, where could he find a guide more initiated, a more eloquent prophet of the soul, than Wagner? Through Wagner modernity speaks most intimately, concealing neither its good nor its evil—having forgotten all sense of shame. And conversely: one has almost completed an account of the value of what is modern once one has gained clarity about what is good and evil in Wagner.

I understand perfectly when a musician says today: "I hate Wagner, but I can no longer endure any other music." But I'd also understand a philosopher who would declare: "Wagner sums up modernity. There is no way out, one must first become a Wagnerian."

---

[1] Cf. *Beyond Good and Evil,* section 212.

1

Yesterday I heard—would you believe it?—Bizet's master-piece, for the twentieth time. Again I stayed there with tender devotion; again I did not run away. This triumph over my impatience surprises me. How such a work makes one perfect! One becomes a "masterpiece" oneself.

Really, every time I heard *Carmen* I seemed to myself more of a philosopher, a better philosopher, than I generally consider myself: so patient do I become, so happy, so Indian, so settled.— To sit five hours: the first stage of holiness!

May I say that the tone of Bizet's orchestra is almost the only one I can still endure? That other orchestral tone which is now the fashion, Wagner's, brutal, artificial, and "innocent" at the same time—thus it speaks all at once to the three senses of the modern soul—how harmful for me is this Wagnerian orchestral tone! I call it *sirocco*. I break out into a disagreeable sweat. *My* good weather is gone.

This music seems perfect to me. It approaches lightly, supplely, politely. It is pleasant, it does not *sweat*. "What is good is light; whatever is divine moves on tender feet": first principle of my aesthetics. This music is evil, subtly fatalistic: at the same time it remains popular—its subtlety belongs to a race, not to an individual. It is rich. It is precise. It builds, organizes, finishes: thus it constitutes the opposite of the polyp in music, the "infinite melody." Have more painful tragic accents ever been heard on the stage? How are they achieved? Without grimaces. Without counterfeit. Without the *lie* of the great style.

Finally, this music treats the listener as intelligent, as if himself a musician—and is in this respect, too, the counterpart of Wagner, who was, whatever else he was, at any rate the most *impolite* genius in the world (Wagner treats us as if——he says something so often—till one despairs—till one believes it).

Once more: I become a better human being when this Bizet speaks to me. Also a better musician, a better *listener*. Is it even possible to listen better?— I actually bury my ears under this music to hear its causes. It seems to me I experience its genesis—I tremble before dangers that accompany some strange risk; I am delighted by strokes of good fortune of which Bizet is innocent.— And, oddly, deep down I don't think of it, or don't know how much I think about it. For entirely different thoughts are meanwhile running through my head.

Has it been noticed that music liberates the spirit? gives wings to thought? that one becomes more of a philosopher the more one becomes a musician?— The gray sky of abstraction rent as if by lightning; the light strong enough for the filigree of things; the great problems near enough to grasp; the world surveyed as from a mountain.— I have just defined the pathos of philosophy.— And unexpectedly answers drop into my lap, a little hail of ice and wisdom, of *solved* problems.— Where am I?— Bizet makes me fertile. Whatever is good makes me fertile. I have no other gratitude, nor do I have any other *proof* for what is good.

2

This work, too, redeems; Wagner is not the only "redeemer." With this work one takes leave of the *damp* north, of all the steam of the Wagnerian ideal. Even the plot spells redemption from that. From Mérimée it still has the logic in passion, the shortest line, the *harsh* necessity; above all, it has what goes with the torrid zone: the dryness of the air, the *limpidezza*[1] in the air. In every respect, the climate is changed. Another sensuality, another sensibility speaks here, another cheerfulness. This music is cheerful, but not in a French or German way. Its cheerfulness is African; fate hangs over it; its happiness is brief, sudden, without pardon. I envy Bizet for having had the courage for this sensibility which had hitherto had no language in the cultivated music of Europe—for this more southern, brown, burnt sensibility.— How the yellow afternoons of its happiness do us good! We look into the distance as we listen: did we ever find the sea smoother?— And how soothingly the Moorish dance speaks to us? How even our insatiability for once gets to know satiety in this lascivious melancholy!

Finally, love—love translated back into nature. Not the love of a "higher virgin"! No Senta-sentimentality![2] But love as *fatum*,

---

[1] Limpidity, clarity
[2] Senta is the heroine of Wagner's *Flying Dutchman*.

as fatality, cynical, innocent, cruel—and precisely in this a piece of
nature. That love which is war in its means, and at bottom the
deadly hatred of the sexes!— I know no case where the tragic joke
that constitutes the essence of love is expressed so strictly, translated with equal terror into a formula, as in Don José's last cry,
which concludes the work:

> "Yes. I *have killed her,*
> I—*my adored Carmen!*"

Such a conception of love (the only one worthy of a philosopher)
is rare: it raises a work of art above thousands.[3] For on the average, artists do what all the world does, even worse—they misunderstand love. Wagner, too, misunderstood it. They believe one
becomes selfless in love because one desires the advantage of another human being, often against one's own advantage. But in return for that they want to *possess* the other person.—Even God
does not constitute an exception at this point. He is far from thinking, "What is it to you if I love you?" [4]—he becomes terrible when
one does not love him in return. *L'amour*—this saying remains true
among gods and men—*est de tous les sentiments le plus égoïste, et
par conséquent, lorsqu'il est blessé, le moins généreux.* (B. Constant.)[5]

3

You begin to see how much this music improves me?— *Il faut
méditerraniser la musique:*[1] I have reasons for this formula (*Beyond Good and Evil,* Aph. 255). The return to nature, health,

---

[3] Compare Nietzsche's admiration for Shakespeare's characterization of
Brutus in Julius Caesar (discussed with quotations in Kaufmann's *Nietzsche*—see Index, under Brutus), and Oscar Wilde's *Ballad of Reading Gaol*
(1898): "For all men kill the thing they love . . ."

[4] Goethe, *Wahrheit und Dichtung,* Book 14; cf. *Wilhelm Meisters Lehrjahre,*
IV.9 (*Theatralische Sendung,* VI.4), where the wording is ever so slightly
different. In his autobiography Goethe links these words with Spinoza's famous dictum: "Whoever loves God cannot will that God should love him in
return" (*Ethics,* V.19).

[5] "Love is of all sentiments the most egoistic, and, as a consequence, when
it is wounded, the least generous."

[1] "Music should be Mediterranianized."

cheerfulness, youth, *virtue!*— And yet I was one of the most corrupted Wagnerians.— I was capable of taking Wagner seriously.— Ah, this old magician, how much he imposed upon us! The first thing his art offers us is a magnifying glass: one looks through it, one does not trust one's own eyes—everything looks big, *even Wagner.*— What a clever rattlesnake! It has filled our whole life with its rattling about "devotion," about "loyalty," about "purity"; and with its praise of chastity it withdrew from the corrupted world.— And we believed it in all these things.—

But you do not hear me? You, too, prefer Wagner's problem to Bizet's? I, too, do not underestimate it; it has its peculiar magic. The problem of redemption is certainly a venerable problem. There is nothing about which Wagner has thought more deeply than redemption: his opera is the opera of redemption. Somebody or other always wants to be redeemed in his work: sometimes a little male, sometimes a little female—this is *his* problem.— And how richly he varies his leitmotif! What rare, what profound dodges! Who if not Wagner would teach us that innocence prefers to redeem interesting sinners? (The case in *Tannhäuser.*) Or that even the Wandering Jew is redeemed, settles down, when he marries? (The case in *The Flying Dutchman.*) Or that old corrupted females prefer to be redeemed by chaste youths? (The case of Kundry.[2]) Or that beautiful maidens like best to be redeemed by a knight who is a Wagnerian? (The case in *Die Meistersinger.*) Or that married women, too, enjoy being redeemed by a knight? (The case of Isolde.) Or that "the old God," after having compromised himself morally in every respect, is finally redeemed by a free spirit and immoralist? (The case in the *Ring.*) Do admire this final profundity above all! Do you understand it? I—beware of understanding it.

That yet other lessons may be learned from the works just named I'd sooner demonstrate than deny. That a Wagnerian ballet may drive one to despair—and virtue! (Again the case of *Tannhäuser.*) That it may have the direst consequences if one doesn't go to bed at the right time. (Once more the case of *Lohengrin.*) That one should never know too precisely whom exactly one has married. (For the third time, the case of *Lohengrin.*)

---

[2] In *Parsifal.*

Tristan and Isolde glorifies the perfect spouse who in a certain case has only the single question: "But why didn't you tell me this before? Nothing simpler than that!" Answer:

> *"That I may not tell you;*
> *and what you ask*
> *you may never know."*

Lohengrin contains a solemn excommunication of inquiry and questioning. Wagner thus represents the Christian concept, "you ought to and must *believe.*" It is a crime against what is highest and holiest to be scientific.

The Flying Dutchman preaches the sublime doctrine that woman makes even the most restless man stable; in Wagnerian terms, she "redeems" him. Here we permit ourselves a question. Supposing this were true, would it also be desirable?

What becomes of the "Wandering Jew" [3] whom a woman adores and makes stable? He merely ceases to be eternal; he gets married, he is of no further concern to us.

Translated into reality: the danger for artists, for geniuses—and who else is the "Wandering Jew"?—is woman: adoring women confront them with corruption. Hardly any of them have character enough not to be corrupted—or "redeemed"—when they find themselves treated like gods: soon they condescend to the level of the women.— Man is a coward, confronted with the Eternal-Feminine [4]—and the females know it.— In many cases of feminine love, perhaps including the most famous ones above all, love is merely a more refined form of parasitism, a form of nestling down in another soul, sometimes even in the flesh of another—alas, always decidedly at the expense of "the host"!

One knows Goethe's fate in moraline-sour, old-maidish Germany. He always seemed offensive to Germans; he had honest admirers only among Jewesses. Schiller, the "noble" Schiller, who lambasted the ears of the Germans with big words—*he* was after their hearts. What did they hold against Goethe? The "mount of

---

[3] In German, literally the "Eternal Jew."

[4] Goethe's *Faust* ends: "The Eternal-Feminine / Lures us to perfection." But the classical representative of the attitude toward marriage expressed in the sentences about the "Wandering Jew" was nevertheless Goethe.

Venus"; and that he had written *Venetian Epigrams*. Klopstock[5] already felt called upon to deliver a moral sermon to him; there was a time when Herder[6] liked to use the word "Priapus" whenever he spoke of Goethe. Even *Wilhelm Meister* was considered merely a symptom of decline, "going to the dogs" as far as morals go. Niebuhr,[7] for example, was enraged by the "menagerie of tame animals" and the "worthlessness" of the hero, and finally he broke out into the lament, fit to be sung by Biterolf:[8] "Nothing could easily make a more painful impression than a great spirit who deprives himself of his wings and seeks virtuosity in something much inferior, *renouncing what is higher.*"— Above all, however, the higher virgins were indignant: all the petty courts, every kind of "Wartburg"[9] in Germany crossed themselves against Goethe, against the "unclean spirit" in Goethe.

This is the story Wagner put into music. He *redeems* Goethe, that goes without saying; but in such a way that at the same time he himself sides shrewdly with the higher virgin. Goethe is saved: a prayer saves him, a higher virgin *lures him to perfection.*

What Goethe might have thought of Wagner?— Goethe once asked himself what danger threatened all romantics: the fatality of romanticism. His answer was: "suffocating of the rumination of moral and religious absurdities." In brief: *Parsifal.*

The philosopher adds an epilogue to this: *Holiness*—perhaps

---

[5] Friedrich Gottlieb Klopstock (1724–1803), twenty-five years older than Goethe, was the most renowned German poet of his generation.

[6] Johann Gottfried von Herder (1744–1803) studied under Kant and became one of Germany's most influential writers. His major works include the first great collection of folk poetry, *Stimmen der Völker in Liedern* (voices of peoples in songs), 1778–79, and *Ideen zur Philosophie der Geschichte der Menschheit* (ideas on the philosophy of the history of humanity), 1784–91. He was a friend of, and major influence on, the young Goethe, and in 1776 he became general superintendent and court preacher in Weimar.

[7] Barthold Georg Niebuhr (1776–1831) was a statesman and historian. "Niebuhr's *Roman History* counts among epoch-making histories both as marking an era in the study of its special subject and for its momentous influence on the general conception of history" (*Encyclopaedia Britannica*, 11th ed., vol. XIX, p. 668).

[8] Biterolf is one of the knights in Wagner's *Tannhäuser*.

[9] Luther translated the Bible on the Wartburg, and on one of the walls tourists are shown an inkspot which originated, according to tradition, when Luther threw his inkwell at the devil who had appeared to him.

the last thing the people and women still get to see of higher values, the horizon of the ideal for all who are by nature myopic. But among philosophers this is, like every horizon, a mere case of lack of understanding, a sort of shutting the gate at the point where *their* world only begins—*their* danger, their ideal, their desideratum.— To say it more politely: *la philosophie ne suffit pas au grand nombre. Il lui faut la sainteté.*—[10]

4

I shall still relate the story of the *Ring*. It belongs here. It, too, is a story of redemption: only this time it is Wagner who is redeemed.—

Half his life, Wagner believed in the Revolution as much as ever a Frenchman believed in it. He searched for it in the runic writing of myth, he believed that in Siegfried he had found the typical revolutionary.

"Whence comes all misfortune in the world?" Wagner asked himself. From "old contracts," he answered, like all revolutionary ideologists. In plain: from customs, laws, moralities, institutions, from everything on which the old world, the old society rests. "How can one rid the world of misfortune? How can one abolish the old society?" Only by declaring war against "contracts" (tradition, morality). *That is what Siegfried does.* He starts early, very early: his very genesis is a declaration of war against morality—he comes into this world through adultery, through incest.— It is not the saga but Wagner who invented this radical trait; at this point he revised the saga.

Siegfried continues as he has begun: he merely follows his first impulse, he overthrows everything traditional, all reverence, all *fear*. Whatever displeases him he stabs to death. Without the least respect, he tackles old deities. But his main enterprise aims *to emancipate woman*—"to redeem Brunhilde."— Siegfried and Brunhilde; the sacrament of free love; the rise of the golden age; the twilight of the gods for the old morality—*all ill has been abolished*.

For a long time, Wagner's ship followed *this* course gaily. No

---

[10] "Philosophy is not suited for the masses. What they need is holiness."

doubt, this was where Wagner sought his highest goal.— What happened? A misfortune. The ship struck a reef; Wagner was stuck. The reef was Schopenhauer's philosophy; Wagner was stranded on a *contrary* world view. What had he transposed into music? Optimism. Wagner was ashamed. Even an optimism for which Schopenhauer had coined an evil epithet—*infamous*[1] optimism. He was ashamed a second time. He reflected for a long while, his situation seemed desperate.— Finally, a way out dawned on him: the reef on which he was shipwrecked—what if he interpreted it as the *goal,* as the secret intent, as the true significance of his voyage? To be shipwrecked *here*—that was a goal, too. *Bene navigavi, cum naufragium feci.*[2]

So he translated the *Ring* into Schopenhauer's terms. Everything goes wrong, everything perishes, the new world is as bad as the old: the *nothing,* the Indian Circe beckons.

Brunhilde was initially supposed to take her farewell with a song in honor of free love, putting off the world with the hope for a socialist utopia in which "all turns out well"—but now gets something else to do. She has to study Schopenhauer first; she has to transpose the fourth book of *The World as Will and Representation* into verse. *Wagner was redeemed.*

In all seriousness, this *was* a redemption. The benefit Schopenhauer conferred on Wagner is immeasurable. Only the *philosopher of decadence* gave to the artist of decadence—*himself.*

5

To *the artist of decadence:* there we have the crucial words. And here my seriousness begins. I am far from looking on guilelessly while this decadent corrupts our health—and music as well. Is Wagner a human being at all? Isn't he rather a sickness? He makes sick whatever he touches—*he has made music sick—*

A typical decadent who has a sense of necessity in his corrupted taste, who claims it as a higher taste, who knows how to get his corruption accepted as law, as progress, as fulfillment.

And he is not resisted. His seductive force increases tremen-

---

[1] *Ruchlos.*
[2] "When I suffer shipwreck, I have navigated well."

dously, smoke clouds of incense surround him, the misunderstandings about him parade as "gospel"—he hasn't by any means converted only the *poor in spirit*.

I feel the urge to open the windows a little. Air! More air!—[1]

That people in Germany should deceive themselves about Wagner does not surprise me. The opposite would surprise me. The
Germans have constructed a Wagner for themselves whom they
can revere: they have never been psychologists; their gratitude consists in misunderstanding. But that people in Paris, too, deceive
themselves about Wagner, though there they are hardly anything
anymore except psychologists! And in St. Petersburg, where they
guess things that aren't guessed even in Paris! How closely related
Wagner must be to the whole of European decadence to avoid being experienced by them as a decadent. He belongs to it: he is its
protagonist, its greatest name.— One honors oneself when raising
him to the clouds.

For that one does not resist him, this itself is a sign of decadence. The instincts are weakened. What one ought to shun is
found attractive. One puts to one's lips what drives one yet faster
into the abyss.

Is an example desired? One only need observe the regimen
that those suffering from anemia or gout or diabetes prescribe for
themselves. Definition of a vegetarian: one who requires a corrob-
orant diet. To sense that what is harmful is harmful, to be *able* to
forbid oneself something harmful, is a sign of youth and vitality.
The exhausted are *attracted* by what is harmful: the vegetarian by
vegetables.[2] Sickness itself can be a stimulant to life: only one has
to be healthy enough for this stimulant.[3]

---

[1] *Luft! Mehr Luft!* Goethe's last words are said to have been: *Licht! Mehr
Licht!* "Light! More light!"

[2] Wagner was a doctrinaire vegetarian, and Nietzsche's brother-in-law, Bernhard Förster, copied Wagner's vegetarianism along with his anti-Semitic
ideology; so did Hitler. Nietzsche wrote his mother about Förster: "For my
personal taste such an agitator is something impossible for closer acquaintance. . . . Vegetarianism, as Dr. Förster wants it, makes such natures only
still more petulant" (*Briefe an Mutter und Schwester* [letters to mother and
sister, Leipzig, 1909] no. 409; for further quotations from letters about
Förster see Kaufmann's *Nietzsche,* Chapter 1, section III).

[3] For parallel passages in Nietzsche's other works, see the last three pages
of Chapter 4, section I, in Kaufmann's *Nietzsche*.

Wagner increases exhaustion: that is why he attracts the weak and exhausted. Oh, the rattlesnake-happiness of the old master when he always saw precisely "the little children" coming unto him! [4]

I place this perspective at the outset: Wagner's art is sick. The problems he presents on the stage—all of them problems of hysterics—the convulsive nature of his affects, his overexcited sensibility, his taste that required ever stronger spices, his instability which he dressed up as principles, not least of all the choice of his heroes and heroines—consider them as physiological types (a pathological gallery)!—all of this taken together represents a profile of sickness that permits no further doubt. *Wagner est une névrose.*[5] Perhaps nothing is better known today, at least nothing has been better studied, than the Protean character of degeneration that here conceals itself in the chrysalis of art and artist. Our physicians and physiologists confront their most interesting case in Wagner, at least a very complete case. Precisely because nothing is more modern than this total sickness, this lateness and overexcitement of the nervous mechanism, Wagner is *the modern artist par excellence,* the Cagliostro of modernity. In his art all that the modern world requires most urgently is mixed in the most seductive manner: the three great *stimulantia* of the exhausted—the *brutal,* the *artificial,* and the *innocent* (idiotic).[6]

Wagner represents a great corruption of music. He has guessed that it is a means to excite weary nerves—and with that he has made music sick. His inventiveness is not inconsiderable in the art of goading again those who are weariest, calling back into life those who are half dead. He is a master of hypnotic tricks, he manages to throw down the strongest like bulls. Wagner's *success*—his success with nerves and consequently women—has turned the whole world of ambitious musicians into disciples of his secret art. And not only the ambitious, the *clever,* too.— Only sick music makes money today; our big theaters subsist on Wagner.

---

[4] Allusion to Matthew 19:14, Mark 10:14, Luke 18:16.

[5] "Wagner is a neurosis."

[6] The words "idiot" and "idiotic" occur frequently in Nietzsche's writings—after his discovery of Dostoevsky early in 1887. See Kaufmann's *Nietzsche,* Chapter 12, note 2, where the relevant passages are cited.

6

I permit myself some exhilaration again. Suppose it were the case that Wagner's *success* became incarnate, took human form and, dressed up as a philanthropic music scholar, mixed with young artists. How do you suppose he would talk?

My friends, he would say, let us have a few words among ourselves. It is easier to write bad music than good. What if it were more profitable, too? more effective, persuasive, inspiring, reliable—*Wagnerian?*—*Pulchrum est paucorum hominum.*[1] Bad enough. We understand Latin; perhaps we also understand our own advantage. What is beautiful has a fly in its ointment: we know that. Why, then, have beauty? Why not rather that which is great, sublime, gigantic—that which moves *masses?*— Once more: it is easier to be gigantic than to be beautiful; we know that.

We know the masses, we know the theater. The best among those who sit there—German youths, horned Siegfrieds, and other Wagnerians—require the sublime, the profound, the overwhelming. That much we are capable of. And the others who also sit there—the culture *crétins,* the petty snobs, the eternally feminine, those with a happy digestion, in sum, the *people*—also require the sublime, the profound, the overwhelming. They all have the same logic. "Whoever throws us is strong; whoever elevates us is divine; whoever leads us to have intimations is profound."— Let us make up our minds, honored musicians: we want to throw them, we want to elevate them, we want to lead them to have intimations. That much we are capable of.

Regarding the matter of inducing intimations: this is the point of departure for our concept of "style." Above all, no thought! Nothing is more compromising than a thought. Rather the state preceding thought, the throng of yet unborn thoughts, the promise of future thoughts, the world as it was before God created it—a recrudescence of chaos.— Chaos induces intimations.

To speak in the language of the master: infinity, but without melody.

Secondly, as far as throwing people is concerned, this really

---

[1] "What is beautiful belongs to the few."

belongs partly in physiology. Let us study the instruments above all. Some of them persuade even the intestines (they *open* the gates, as Handel put it); others bewitch the marrow of the spine. The color of the tone is decisive; what it is that resounds is almost a matter of indifference. This is the point to refine. Why squander ourselves? Regarding the tone, let us be characteristic to the point of folly. People will give credit to our spirit if our tones seem to pose many riddles. Let us agitate the nerves, let us slay them, let us handle lightning and thunder—that will throw them.—

Above all, however, *passion* throws people.— Let us reach an understanding about passion. Nothing is cheaper than passion. One can dispense with all the virtues of counterpoint, one need not have learned a thing—passion is one ability we always have. Beauty is difficult: beware of beaufy!— And *melody!* Slander, my friends, let us slander, if we are at all serious about our ideal, let us slander melody! Nothing is more dangerous than a beautiful melody. Nothing corrupts taste more surely. We are lost, my friends, once beautiful melodies are loved again!—

Principle: melody is immoral. *Proof:* Palestrina. *Practical application: Parsifal.* The lack of melody even sanctifies.—

And this is the definition of passion. Passion—or the gymnastics of what is ugly on the rope of enharmonics.— Let us dare, my friends, to be ugly. Wagner has dared it. Let us dauntlessly roll in front of us the mud of the most contrary harmonies. Let us not spare our hands. Only thus will we become *natural.*

A final bit of advice! Perhaps it includes everything else. *Let us be idealists!* This is, if not the cleverest thing we can do at least the wisest. To elevate[2] men one has to be sublime[3] oneself. Let us walk on clouds, let us harangue the infinite, let us surround ourselves with symbols! *Sursum! Bumbum!*—there is no better advice. The "swelled bosom" shall be our argument, the beautiful sentiment our advocate. Virtue prevails even over counterpoint. "Whoever makes us better cannot fail to be good himself": thus mankind has always inferred. So let us improve mankind! [4] Thus one be-

---

2 *Erheben.*

3 *Erhaben.*

4 Nietzsche's next book, *Twilight of the Idols,* contains a chapter with the sarcastic title, "The 'Improvers' of Mankind."

comes good (thus one even becomes a "classic" [5]—Schiller became a "classic"). The hunt for low excitement of the senses, for so-called beauty, has enervated the Italians: let us remain German! Even Mozart's attitude to music was—as Wagner said to comfort *us*—at bottom frivolous.

Let us never admit that music "serves recreation"; that it "exhilarates"; that it "gives pleasure." *Let us never give pleasure!* We are lost as soon as art is again thought of hedonistically.— That is bad eighteenth century.— Nothing on the other hand should be more advisable than a dose of—*hypocrisy, sit venia verbo.*[6] That lends dignity.— And let us choose the hour when it is decent to look black, to heave sighs publicly, to heave Christian sighs, to make an exhibition of great Christian pity. "Man is corrupt: who redeems him? *what redeems him?"*— Let us not answer. Let us be cautious. Let us resist our ambition which would found religions. But nobody may doubt that *we* redeem him, that *our* music alone saves.— (Wagner's essay, *Religion and Art.*)

7

Enough! Enough! My cheerful strokes, I fear, may have revealed sinister reality all too clearly—the picture of a decay of art, a decay of the artists as well. The latter, the decay of a character, could perhaps find preliminary expression in this formula: the musician now becomes an actor, his art develops more and more as a talent to *lie*. I shall have an opportunity (in a chapter of my main work, entitled "Toward a Physiology of Art" [1]) to show in more detail how this over-all change of art into histrionics is no less an expression of physiological degeneration (more precisely, a form of hystericism) than every single corruption and infirmity of the art inaugurated by Wagner: for example, the visual restlessness which requires one continually to change one's position. One doesn't understand a thing about Wagner as long as one finds in him merely an arbitrary play of nature, a whim, an accident. He was no

---

[5] *Klassiker,* a term pre-eminently associated with Goethe and Schiller.

[6] "May this word be forgiven."

[1] This was not actually written, but notes for it were included in the posthumously published *Will to Power,* in Book 3, Part 4.

"fragmentary," "hapless," or "contradictory" genius, as people have said. Wagner was something *perfect,* a typical decadent in whom there is no trace of "free will" and in whom every feature is necessary. If anything in Wagner is interesting it is the logic with which a physiological defect makes move upon move and takes step upon step as practice and procedure, as innovation in principles, as a crisis in taste.

For the present I merely dwell on the question of *style.*— What is the sign of every *literary decadence?* That life no longer dwells in the whole. The word becomes sovereign and leaps out of the sentence, the sentence reaches out and obscures the meaning of the page, the page gains life at the expense of the whole—the whole is no longer a whole.[2] But this is the simile of every style of *decadence*: every time, the anarchy of atoms, disgregation of the will, "freedom of the individual," to use moral terms—expanded into a political theory, "*equal* rights for all." Life, *equal* vitality, the vibration and exuberance of life pushed back into the smallest forms; the rest, *poor* in life. Everywhere paralysis, arduousness, torpidity *or* hostility and chaos: both more and more obvious the higher one ascends in forms of organization. The whole no longer lives at all: it is composite, calculated, artificial, and artifact.—

Wagner begins from a hallucination—not of sounds but of gestures. Then he seeks the sign language of sounds for them. If one would admire him, one should watch him at work at this point: how he separates, how he gains small units, how he animates these, severs them, and makes them visible. But this exhausts his strength: the rest is no good. How wretched, how embarrassed, how amateurish is his manner of "development," his attempt to at least interlard what has not grown out of each other. His manners recall those of the *frères* de Goncourt,[3] who are quite generally pertinent to Wagner's style: one feels a kind of compassion for so much distress. That Wagner disguised as a principle his incapacity

---

[2] To those who know Nietzsche's own books only superficially, this may seem to be a perfect description of *his* style. But see the second paragraph of his preface to *The Case of Wagner,* and Kaufmann's *Nietzsche,* Chapter 2, section I.

[3] Cf. *Twilight of the Idols* (in *Portable Nietzsche*), p. 517 ("Skirmishes of an Untimely Man," section 7).

for giving organic form, that he establishes a "dramatic style" where we merely establish his incapacity for any style whatever, this is in line with a bold habit that accompanied Wagner through his whole life: he posits a principle where he lacks a capacity (— very different in this respect, incidentally, from the old Kant who preferred another boldness: wherever he lacked a principle he posited a special human capacity).[4]

Once more: Wagner is admirable and gracious only in the invention of what is smallest, in spinning out the details. Here one is entirely justified in proclaiming him a master of the first rank, as our greatest *miniaturist* in music who crowds into the smallest space an infinity of sense and sweetness. His wealth of colors, of half shadows, of the secrecies of dying light spoils one to such an extent that afterward almost all other musicians seem too robust.

If one would believe me one should have to derive the highest conception of Wagner not from what is liked about him today. That has been invented to persuade the masses; from that we recoil as from an all too impudent fresco.[5] Of what concern to *us* is the *agaçant*[6] brutality of the *Tannhäuser* Overture. Or the circus of *Walküre?* Whatever of Wagner's music has become popular also apart from the theater shows dubious taste and corrupts taste. The *Tannhäuser* March I suspect of *bonhommerie;*[7] the overture of *The Flying Dutchman* is noise about nothing;[8] the *Lohengrin* Prelude furnished the first example, only too insidious, only too successful, of hypnotism by means of music (—I do not like whatever music has no ambition beyond persuasion of the nerves). But quite apart from the *magnétiseur*[9] and fresco-painter Wagner, there is another Wagner who lays aside small gems: our greatest melancholiac in music, full of glances, tendernesses, and comforting words in which nobody has anticipated him, the master in tones of a heavy-hearted and drowsy happiness.

---

[4] Cf. *Beyond Good and Evil,* section 11.

[5] *Einem allzufrechen Affresko.*

[6] *Provocative.*

[7] *Biedermännerei.*

[8] *Ein Lärm um nichts.* The German version of Shakespeare's *Much Ado About Nothing* is entitled *Viel Lärmen um Nichts.*

[9] Hypnotist.

A lexicon of Wagner's most intimate words, all of them short things of five to fifteen measures, all of it music *nobody knows.*— Wagner had the virtue of decadents: pity.

8

"Very good. But how *can* one lose a taste for this decadent if one does not happen to be a musician, if one does not happen to be a decadent oneself?"

On the contrary, how can one *fail* to do it? Just try it.— You do not know who Wagner is: a first-rate actor. Is a more profound, a *weightier* effect to be found in the theater? Just look at these youths —rigid, pale, breathless! These are the Wagnerians: they understand nothing about music—and yet Wagner becomes master over them.— Wagner's art has the pressure of a hundred atmospheres: stoop! what else can one do?

The actor Wagner is a tyrant; his pathos topples every taste, every resistance.— Who equals the persuasive power of these gestures? Who else envisages gestures with such assurance, so clearly from the start? The way Wagner's pathos holds its breath, refuses to let go an extreme feeling, achieves a terrifying *duration* of states when even a moment threatens to strangle us—

Was Wagner a musician at all? At any rate, there was something else that he was more: namely, an incomparable *histrio,*[1] the greatest mime, the most amazing genius of the theater ever among Germans, our *scenic artist par excellence.* He belongs elsewhere, not in the history of music: one should not confuse him with the genuine masters of that. Wagner *and* Beethoven—that is blasphemy and really wrongs even Wagner.— As a musician, too, he was only what he was in general: he *became* a musician, he *became* a poet because the tyrant within him, his actor's genius, compelled him. One cannot begin to figure out Wagner until one figures out his dominant instinct.

Wagner was *not* a musician by instinct. He showed this by abandoning all lawfulness and, more precisely, all style in music in order to turn it into what he required, theatrical rhetoric, a means of expression, of underscoring gestures, of suggestion, of the psy-

---

[1] Actor.

chologically picturesque. Here we may consider Wagner an inventor and innovator of the first rank—*he has increased music's capacity for language to the point of making it immeasurable:* he is the Victor Hugo of music as language. Always presupposing that one first allows that under certain circumstances music may be not music but language, instrument, *ancilla*[2] *dramaturgica.* Wagner's music, if not shielded by theater taste, which is a very tolerant taste, is simply bad music, perhaps the worst ever made. When a musician can no longer count up to three he becomes "dramatic," he becomes "Wagnerian."

Wagner almost discovered how much magic is still possible with music that has been dissolved and, as it were, made *elementary.* His consciousness of that is downright uncanny, no less than his instinctive realization that he simply did not require the higher lawfulness, *style.* What is elementary is *sufficient*—sound, movement, color, in brief the sensuousness of music. Wagner never calculates as a musician, from some sort of musician's conscience: what he wants is effect, nothing but effect. And he knows those on whom he wants to achieve his effects.— At this point he is as free from qualms as Schiller was, as every man of the theater is, and he also has the same contempt for the world which he prostrates at his feet.— One is an actor by virtue of being ahead of the rest of mankind in one insight: what is meant to have the effect of truth must not be true. The proposition was formulated by Talma;[3] it contains the whole psychology of the actor; it also contains—we need not doubt it—his morality. Wagner's music is never true.

But *it is taken for true;* and thus it is in order.

As long as we are still childlike, and Wagnerians as well, we consider Wagner himself rich, even as a paragon of a squanderer, even as the owner of huge estates in the realm of sound. He is admired for what young Frenchmen admire in Victor Hugo, "the royal largesse." Later one comes to admire both of them for the opposite reasons: as masters and models of economy, as *shrewd* hosts. Nobody equals their talent for presenting a princely table at modest expense.

The Wagnerian, with his believer's stomach, actually feels

---

[2] Handmaiden.

[3] François Joseph Talma (1763–1826) was a celebrated French actor.

sated by the fare his master's magic evokes for him. The rest of us, demanding *substance* above all else, in books as well as in music, are scarcely taken care of by merely "represented" tables and hence are much worse off. To say it plainly: Wagner does not give us enough to chew on. His *recitativo*—little meat, rather more bone, and a lot of broth—I have called *"alla genovese"*—without the least intention of flattering the Genoese, but rather the *older recitativo,* the *recitativo secco*.[4]

Finally, as far as the Wagnerian "leitmotif" is concerned, I lack all culinary understanding for that. If pressed, I might possibly concede it the status of an ideal toothpick, as an opportunity to get rid of *remainders* of food. There remain the "arias" of Wagner.— And now I shall not say another word.

9

In projecting his plot, too, Wagner is above all an actor. What he envisages first is a scene whose effectiveness is absolutely safe, a genuine *actio** with an *hautrelief* of gestures, a scene that *throws* people—this he thinks through in depth, and from this he then derives the characters. All the rest follows from this, in accordance with a technical economy that has no reasons for being subtle. It is *not* the public of Corneille of whom Wagner has to be considerate, but mere nineteenth century. About "the one thing needful" Wagner would think approximately the way any other actor today thinks about it: a series of strong scenes, one stronger than the other—and in between much *shrewd* stupidity. To begin with, he tries to guarantee the effectiveness of his work to himself; he starts with the third act; he *proves* his work to himself by means of its ultimate effect. With such a sense of the theater for one's guide, one

---

[4] Dry.

* [Nietzsche's] *Note.* It has been a real misfortune for aesthetics that the word *drama* has always been translated "action" [*Handlung*]. It is not Wagner alone who errs at this point, the error is world-wide and extends even to the philologists who ought to know better. Ancient drama aimed at scenes of great *pathos*—it precluded action (moving it *before* the beginning or *behind* the scene). The word *drama* is of Doric origin, and according to Doric usage it means "event," "story"—both words in the hieratic sense. The most ancient drama represented the legend of the place, the "holy story" on which the foundation of the cult rested (not a doing but a happening: *dran* in Doric actually does not mean "do").

is in no danger of unexpectedly creating a drama. Drama requires *rigorous* logic: but what did Wagner ever care about logic? To say it once more: it was *not* the public of Corneille of whom Wagner had to be considerate—but mere Germans.

We know which technical problem requires all of the dramatist's powers and often makes him sweat blood: making the *knot* necessary, and the resolution as well, so both will be possible in one way only while giving the impression of freedom (the principle of the least exertion of energy). That, however, leads Wagner least of all to sweat blood; it is certain that he exerted the least energy on the knot and its resolution. Take any of Wagner's "knots" and examine it under the microscope—and you'll have to laugh, I promise you. Nothing is more amusing than the knot of *Tristan,* unless it is the knot of the *Meistersinger.*

Wagner is *no* dramatist; don't be imposed upon! He loved the word "drama"—that's all; he always loved pretty words. The word "drama" in his writings is nevertheless a mere misunderstanding (and a bit of shrewdness: Wagner always affected superiority over the word "opera")—much the way the word "spirit" in the New Testament is a mere misunderstanding.

For one thing, he was not enough of a psychologist for drama; instinctively, he avoided psychological motivation—how? by always putting idiosyncrasy in its place.— Very modern, isn't it? Very Parisian. Very *decadent.*

Incidentally, the *knots* that Wagner really could resolve with the aid of dramatic inventions were of an entirely different nature. I offer an example. Assume a case in which Wagner requires a female voice. An entire act *without* a female voice—impossible! But none of the "heroines" are free at the moment. What does Wagner do? He emancipates the oldest woman of the world, Erda: "Come up, old grandmother! You have to sing." Erda sings. Wagner's purpose is realized. Immediately he abolishes the old lady again. "Why ever did you come? Beat it. Go on sleeping."— *In summa:* a scene full of mythological shivers which gives Wagnerians *intimations.*—

"But the *content* of the Wagnerian texts! their mythic content! their eternal content!"— Question: how can we test this content, this eternal content?— The chemist replies: translate Wagner into reality, into the modern—let us be even crueler—into the bourgeois! What becomes of Wagner then?— Among ourselves, I have tried it. Nothing is more entertaining, nothing to be recommended more highly for walks, than retelling Wagner in *more youthful* proportions: for example, Parsifal as a candidate for a theological degree, with secondary school education (the latter being indispensable for *pure foolishness*). What surprises one encounters in the process! Would you believe it? All of Wagner's heroines, without exception, as soon as they are stripped of their heroic skin, become almost indistinguishable from Madame Bovary! And conversely one understands that Flaubert *could have* translated his heroine into Scandinavian or Carthaginian terms and then offered her, mythologized, to Wagner as a libretto. Indeed, transposed into hugeness, Wagner does not seem to have been interested in any problems except those which now preoccupy the little decadents of Paris. Always five steps from the hospital. All of them entirely modern, entirely *metropolitan* problems. Don't doubt it.

Have you ever noticed (it belongs with this association of ideas) that Wagner's heroines never have children?— They *can't*.— The despair with which Wagner tackled the problem of having Siegfried born at all shows *how* modern his feelings were at this point.— Siegfried "emancipates woman"—but without any hope of progeny.— One fact, finally, which leaves us dumfounded: Parsifal is the father of Lohengrin. How did he do it?— Must one remember at this point that "chastity works *miracles*"?—

Wagnerus dixit princeps in castitate auctoritas.[1]

10

Incidentally, a word about Wagner's writings: they offer, among other things, a course in *shrewdness*. The system of procedures that Wagner handles is applicable to a hundred other cases: let him who has ears hear. Perhaps I shall be entitled to public gratitude if I formulate the three most valuable procedures with some precision.

Everything Wagner can *not* do is reprehensible.

There is much else Wagner could do: but he doesn't want to, from rigorism in principle.

Everything Wagner *can* do, nobody will be able to do after

---

[1] "Said by Wagner, the foremost authority on chastity."

him, nobody has done before him, nobody *shall* do after him.—
Wagner is divine.

These three propositions are the quintessence of Wagner's literature; the rest is—mere "literature."

Not every music so far has required a literature: one ought to
look for a sufficient reason here. Is it that Wagner's music is too
difficult to understand? Or is he afraid of the opposite, that it might
be understood too easily—that one will *not* find it *difficult enough*
to understand?

As a matter of fact, he repeated a single proposition all his life
long: that his music did not mean mere music. But more. But infinitely more.— *"Not mere* music"—no musician would say that. To
say it once more, Wagner was unable to create from a totality; he
had no choice, he had to make patchwork, "motifs," gestures, formulas, doing things double and even a hundredfold—he remained
an orator even as a musician—he therefore had to move his "it
means" into the foreground as a matter of principle. "Music is always a mere means": that was his theory, that above all the only
practice open to him. But no musician would think that way.

Wagner required literature to persuade all the world to take
his music seriously, to take it as profound "because its *meaning
was infinite*"; he was his life long the commentator of the "idea."—
What is the meaning of Elsa? But there is no doubt about that:
Elsa is "the unconscious *spirit of the people*" (—"realizing this, I
necessarily became a complete revolutionary").

Let us remember that Wagner was young at the time Hegel
and Schelling seduced men's spirits; that he guessed, that he
grasped with his very hands the only thing the Germans take seriously—"the idea," which is to say, something that is obscure, uncertain, full of intimations; that among Germans clarity is an objection, logic a refutation. Harshly, Schopenhauer accused the epoch
of Hegel and Schelling of dishonesty—harshly, also wrongly: he
himself, the old pessimistic counterfeiter,[1] was not a whit more
"honest" than his more famous contemporaries. Let us keep morals out of this: Hegel is a *taste*.— And not merely a German but a

---

[1] This is one of many passages in which Nietzsche uses this term in exactly
the same sense in which André Gide (1869–1951) later used it, in 1926, as
the title of his greatest novel: *Les Faux-monnayeurs*. Gide had earlier used
another Nietzschean term in another book title: *The Immoralist* (1902).

European taste.— A taste Wagner comprehended—to which he felt equal—which he immortalized.— He merely applied it to music—he invented a style for himself charged with "infinite meaning"—he became the *heir of Hegel*.— Music as "idea."—

And how Wagner was understood!— The same human type that raved about Hegel, today raves about Wagner; in his school they even *write* Hegelian.— Above all, German youths understood him. The two words "infinite" and "meaning" were really sufficient: they induced a state of incomparable well-being in young men. It was not with his music that Wagner conquered them, it was with the "idea"—it is the enigmatic character of his art, its playing hide-and-seek behind a hundred symbols, its polychromy of the ideal that leads and lures these youths to Wagner; it is Wagner's genius for shaping clouds, his whirling, hurling, and twirling through the air, his everywhere and nowhere—the very same means by which Hegel formerly seduced and lured them!

In the midst of Wagner's multiplicity, abundance, and arbitrariness they feel as if justified in their own eyes—"redeemed." Trembling, they hear how the *great symbols* approach from foggy distances to resound in his art with muted thunder; they are not impatient when at times things are gray, gruesome, and cold. After all, they are, without exception, like Wagner himself, *related* to such bad weather, German weather! Wotan is their god: but Wotan is the god of bad weather.

They are quite right, these German youths, considering what they are like: how *could* they miss what we others, *we halcyons,* miss in Wagner—*la gaya scienza;*[2] light feet, wit, fire, grace; the great logic; the dance of the stars; the exuberant spirituality; the southern shivers of light; the *smooth* sea—perfection.—

11

I have explained where Wagner belongs—*not* in the history of music. What does he signify nevertheless in that history? *The emer-*

---

[2] These three words form the subtitle of Nietzsche's book, *Die Fröhliche Wissenschaft* (the gay science; 1882), translated into English under the title *Joyful Wisdom*. The concept of "gay science" goes back to the fourteenth century, when it was used to refer to the art of the troubadours. Cf. also *Beyond Good and Evil,* end of section 260.

gence of the actor in music: a capital event that invites thought, perhaps also fear. In a formula: "Wagner and Liszt."

Never yet has the integrity of musicians, their "authenticity," been put to the test so dangerously. One can grasp it with one's very hands: great success, success with the masses no longer sides with those who are authentic—one has to be an actor to achieve that.

Victor Hugo and Richard Wagner—they signify the same thing: in declining cultures, wherever the decision comes to rest with the masses, authenticity becomes superfluous, disadvantageous, a liability. Only the actor still arouses *great* enthusiasm.

Thus the *golden age* dawns for the actor—for him and for everything related to his kind. Wagner marches with drums and pipes at the head of all artists of delivery, of presentation, of virtuosity; the conductors, machinists, and stage singers were the first he convinced. Not to forget the orchestra musicians—these he "redeemed" from boredom.

The movement Wagner created even reaches over into the field of knowledge: gradually, relevant sciences emerge from centuries of scholasticism. To give an example, I single out for special commendation the merits of *Riemann*[1] regarding rhythmics: he was the first to establish the validity of the central concept of punctuation for music, too (unfortunately, he used an ugly term, *Phrasierung* [phrasing]).

All of these are, as I own gratefully, the best among Wagner's admirers, those most deserving of our respect—they are simply right to admire Wagner. They share the same instinct, they recognize in him the highest representative of their type, they feel changed into a power, even a great power, ever since he kindled them with his own ardor. For here, if anywhere, Wagner's influence has really been *beneficial*. Never yet has so much been thought, desired, and worked in this area. Wagner has given all of these artists a new conscience. What they now demand of themselves, *get* from themselves, they never demanded of themselves before Wagner came along—formerly, they were too modest. A new spirit pre-

---

[1] Karl Wilhelm Julius Hugo Riemann (1849–1919; pseudonym, Hugibert Ries) wrote extensively on musical theory and published a musical dictionary that went into many editions.

vails in the theater since Wagner's spirit prevails there: one demands what is most difficult, one censures severely, one praises rarely—what is good, even excellent, is considered the rule. Taste is no longer required; not even a voice. Wagner is sung only with a ruined voice: the effect is "dramatic." Even talent is precluded. *Espressivo* at any cost, as demanded by the Wagnerian ideal, the ideal of decadence, does not get along well with talent. It merely requires *virtue*—meaning training, automatism, "self-denial." Neither taste, nor voice, nor talent: Wagner's stage requires one thing only—*Teutons!*— Definition of the Teuton: obedience and long legs.—

It is full of profound significance that the arrival of Wagner coincides in time with the arrival of the *"Reich":* both events prove the very same thing: obedience and long legs.— Never has obedience been better, never has commanding. Wagnerian conductors in particular are worthy of an age that posterity will call one day, with awed respect, *the classical age of war.* Wagner understood how to command; in this, too, he was the great teacher. He commanded as the inexorable will to himself, as lifelong self-discipline: Wagner who furnishes perhaps the greatest example of self-violation in the history of art (—even Alfieri,[2] otherwise his closest relative, stands surpassed. Note by a Turinese).

12

The insight that our actors are more deserving of admiration than ever does not imply that they are any less dangerous.— But who could still doubt what I want—what are the *three demands* for which my wrath, my concern, my love of art has this time opened my mouth?

> *That the theater should not lord it over the arts.*
> *That the actor should not seduce those who are authentic.*
> *That music should not become an art of lying.*

FRIEDRICH NIETZSCHE

---

[2] Count Vittorio Alfieri (1749–1803), a dramatist, spent much of his life in Turin.

Postscript

The seriousness of the last words permits me to publish at this point a few sentences from an as yet unprinted essay. At least they should leave no room for doubt about my seriousness in this matter. This essay bears the title: *The Price We Are Paying for Wagner*.

One pays heavily for being one of Wagner's disciples. An obscure recognition of this fact is still encountered even today. Wagner's success, his *triumph*, has not eradicated it. But formerly it was strong, it was terrible, it was like a dark hatred—through almost three quarters of Wagner's life. The resistance he encountered among us Germans cannot be esteemed too highly or honored too much. He was resisted like a sickness—not with reasons—one does not refute a sickness—but with inhibition, mistrust, vexation, and disgust, with a gloomy seriousness, as if he represented some great creeping danger. Our honored aestheticians have compromised themselves when, coming from three schools of German philosophy, they waged an absurd war against Wagner's principles with "if" and "for"—as if he cared about principles, even his own!

The Germans themselves had reason enough in their instincts to rule out any "if" and "for." An instinct is weakened when it rationalizes itself: for *by* rationalizing itself it weakens itself. If there are any signs that, in spite of the total character of European decadence, the German character still possesses some degree of health, some instinctive sense for what is harmful and dangerous, this *dim* resistance to Wagner is the sign I should like least to see underestimated. It does us honor, it even permits a hope: France would not have that much health any more. The Germans, the *delayers par excellence* in history, are today the most retarded civilized nation in Europe:[1] this has its advantages—by the same token they are relatively the *youngest*.

One pays heavily for being one of Wagner's disciples. Only

---

[1] *Das zurückgebliebenste Kulturvolk Europas.* For the conception of the Germans as "delayers" (*Verzögerer*), cf. *The Antichrist*, section 61, written a few months after *The Case of Wagner* (*Portable Nietzsche*, p. 653ff.) and the chapter on *The Case of Wagner* in *Ecce Homo*.

quite recently have the Germans shed a kind of fear of him—the itch *to be rid of him* they felt at every opportunity.*

It is a curious matter, still remembered, which revealed this old feeling once more at the very end, quite unexpectedly. It happened at Wagner's funeral: the first German Wagner Association, that of Munich, placed a wreath on his grave, with an inscription that immediately became famous. It read: "Redemption for the redeemer!" Everybody admired the lofty inspiration that had dictated this inscription; also the taste that distinguished Wagner's admirers. But many (strangely enough!) made the same small correction: "Redemption *from* the redeemer!"— One heaved a sigh of relief.—

One pays heavily for being one of Wagner's disciples. Let us take the measure of this discipleship by considering its cultural effects. Whom did his movement bring to the fore? What did it breed and multiply?— Above all, the presumption of the layman, the art-idiot. That kind now organizes associations, wants its "taste" to prevail, wants to play the judge even in *rebus musicis et musicantibus*.[2] Secondly: an ever growing indifference against all severe, noble, conscientious training in the service of art; all this is to be replaced by faith in genius or, to speak plainly, by impudent dilettantism (—the formula for this is to be found in the *Meistersinger*). Thirdly and worst of all: *theatrocracy*—the nonsense of a faith in the *precedence* of the theater, in the right of the theater to *lord it* over the arts, over art.—

But one should tell the Wagnerians a hundred times to their faces *what* the theater is: always only *beneath* art, always only something secondary, something made cruder, something twisted

---

* [Nietzsche's] *Note.* Was Wagner a German at all? There are some reasons for this question. It is difficult to find any German trait in him. Being a great learner, he learned to imitate much that was German—that's all. His own nature *contradicts* that which has hitherto been felt to be German— not to speak of a German musician.— His father was an actor by the name of Geyer. A Geyer [vulture] is practically an Adler [eagle].— What has hitherto circulated as "Wagner's Life" is *fable convenue* [a myth that has gained acceptance], if not worse. I confess my mistrust of every point attested to only by Wagner himself. He did not have pride enough for any truth about himself; nobody was less proud. Entirely like Victor Hugo, he remained faithful to himself in biographical questions, too—he remained an actor. [See the letters of August 1888, printed below. W. K.]

[2] Of music and musicians.

tendentiously, mendaciously, for the sake of the masses. Wagner, too, did not change anything in this respect: Bayreuth is large-scale opera—and not even *good* opera.— The theater is a form of demolatry[3] in matters of taste; the theater is a revolt of the masses,[4] a plebiscite *against* good taste.— *This is precisely what is proved by the case of Wagner:* he won the crowd, he corrupted taste, he spoiled even our taste for opera!—[5]

One pays heavily for being one of Wagner's disciples. What does it do to the spirit? *Does Wagner liberate the spirit?*— He is distinguished by every ambiguity, every double sense, everything quite generally that persuades those who are uncertain without making them aware *of what* they have been persuaded. Thus Wagner is a seducer on a large scale. There is nothing weary, nothing decrepit, nothing fatal and hostile to life in matters of the spirit that his art does not secretly safeguard: it is the blackest obscurantism that he conceals in the ideal's shrouds of light. He flatters every nihilistic (Buddhistic) instinct and disguises it in music; he flatters everything Christian, every religious expression of decadence. Open your ears: everything that ever grew on the soil of *impoverished* life, all of the counterfeiting of transcendence and beyond,[6] has found its most sublime advocate in Wagner's art—*not* by means of formulas: Wagner is too shrewd for formulas—but by means of a persuasion of sensuousness which in turn makes the spirit weary and worn-out. Music as Circe.

---

[3] Worship of the people, or of the masses. Cf. Aristotle's disparagement of "spectacle" in his *Poetics* (end of Chapter 6) and, above all, Plato's *Laws,* 700—the passage in which he introduces the term *theatrocracy,* here taken up by Nietzsche.

[4] *Ein Massen-Aufstand:* the phrase is here introduced in the very same sense in which Ortega y Gasset (1883–1955) gave it world-wide currency when he made it the title of his best known book in 1930. Nietzsche's influence on Oretga was very great.

[5] *Er verdarb den Geschmack, er verdarb selbst für die Oper unsren Geschmack!— "Verderben"* can mean "spoil" as well as "corrupt."

If *verdarb* were taken to mean "corrupted" in both places, the meaning of the second part of the sentence would be puzzling: "he corrupted our taste even for opera." Why *"even* for opera"? One would expect Nietzsche to say that Wagner corrupted not only musical taste, and taste for opera above all, but also taste in general. So Nietzsche presumably means: he corrupted taste and spoiled even our taste for opera.

[6] *Die ganze Falschmünzerei der Transcendenz und des Jenseits.* See section 10, footnote 1, above.

His last work is in this respect his greatest masterpiece. In the art of seduction, *Parsifal* will always retain its rank—as *the stroke of genius* in seduction.— I admire this work; I wish I had written it myself; failing that, *I understand it.*— Wagner never had better inspirations than in the end. Here the cunning in his alliance of beauty and sickness goes so far that, as it were, it casts a shadow over Wagner's earlier art—which now seems too bright, too healthy. Do you understand this? Health, brightness having the effect of a shadow? almost of an *objection?*— To such an extent have we become *pure fools.*— Never was there a greater master in dim, hieratic aromas—never was there a man equally expert in all *small* infinities, all that trembles and is effusive, all the feminisms from the *idioticon*[7] of happiness!— Drink, O my friends, the philters of this art! Nowhere will you find a more agreeable way of enervating your spirit, of forgetting your manhood under a rosebush.— Ah, this old magician! This Klingsor[8] of all Klingsors! How he thus wages war against *us!* us, the free spirits! How he indulges every cowardice of the modern soul with the tones of magic maidens!— Never before has there been such a *deadly hatred* of the search for knowledge!— One has to be a cynic in order not to be seduced here; one has to be able to bite in order not to worship here. Well then, you old seducer, the cynic warns you— *cave canem.*—[9]

One pays heavily for being one of Wagner's disciples. I observe those youths who have been exposed to his infection for a long time. The first, relatively innocent effect is the corruption of taste. Wagner has the same effect as continual consumption of alcohol: blunting, and obstructing the stomach with phlegm. Specific effect: degeneration of the sense of rhythm. In the end the Wagnerian calls rhythmic what I myself call, using a Greek proverb, "moving the swamps." Considerably more dangerous is the corruption of concepts. The youth becomes a moon-calf—an "idealist." He has gone beyond science; in this way he has reached the master's level. And he poses as a philosopher; he writes *Bayreuther Blätter;*[10] he

---

[7] A dictionary confined to a particular dialect.

[8] Magician in *Parsifal.*

[9] Beware of the dog! Greek *kynikos* (cynical) means literally "doglike."

[10] Literally, leaves, leaflets, or papers from Bayreuth: the monthly organ of the Wagner Societies to which Wagner himself contributed copiously.

solves all problems in the name of the father, the son, and the holy master.[11] What is uncanniest, however, is the corruption of the nerves. Let anyone walk through a city: everywhere he will hear how instruments are ravished in a solemn rage—interspersed with a savage howling. What's going on?— The youths are worshiping Wagner.— Bayreuth rhymes on institute for cold-water therapy.[12] — Typical telegram from Bayreuth: *bereits bereut* [already rued].—

Wagner is bad for youths; he is calamitous for women. What is a female Wagnerian, medically speaking?— It seems to me, a doctor can't confront young women too seriously with this alternative for the conscience: one or the other.— But they have already made their choice. One cannot serve two masters when the name of one is Wagner. Wagner has redeemed woman; in return, woman has built Bayreuth for him. All sacrifice, all devotion: one has nothing that one would not give to him. Woman impoverishes herself for the benefit of the master, she becomes touching, she stands naked before him.— The female Wagnerian—the most charming ambiguity that exists today; she *embodies* the cause of Wagner—in her sign his cause triumphs.— Ah, this old robber! He robs our youths, he even robs our women and drags them into his den.— Ah, this old Minotaur! The price we have had to pay for him! Every year trains of the most beautiful maidens and youths are led into his labyrinth, so that he may devour them—every year all of Europe intones the words, "off to Crete! off to Crete!" [13]

Second Postscript

My letter, it seems, is open to a misunderstanding. On certain faces the lines of gratitude appear; I even hear a modest exultation. I

---

[11] *Und des heiligen Meisters* instead of *und des heiligen Geistes.* In English, unlike German, "master" does not sound much like "spirit" or "ghost."

[12] In German this does not rhyme either: *Bayreuth reimt sich auf Kaltwasserheilanstalt.*

[13] See the letter to Gast, August 24, 1888, below.

should prefer to be understood in this matter—as in many others. — But since a new animal plays havoc in the vineyards of the German spirit, the *Reich*-worm, the famous *Rhinoxera,*[1] not a word I write is understood any more. Even the *Kreuzzeitung*[2] testifies to that, not to speak of the *Literarische Zentralblatt.*[3]— I have given the Germans the most profound books they have—reason enough for the Germans not to understand a single word.—

When in *this* essay I declare war upon Wagner—and incidentally upon a German "taste"—when I use harsh words against the cretinism of Bayreuth, the last thing I want to do is start a celebration for any *other* musicians. *Other* musicians don't count compared to Wagner. Things are bad generally. Decay is universal. The sickness goes deep. If Wagner nevertheless gives his name to the *ruin of music,* as Bernini did to the ruin of sculpture, he is certainly not its cause. He merely accelerated its tempo—to be sure, in such a manner that one stands horrified before this almost sudden downward motion, abyss-ward. He had the naïveté of decadence: this was his superiority. He believed in it, he did not stop before any of the logical implications of decadence. The others *hesitate*—that is what differentiates them. Nothing else.

---

[1] Nietzsche's coinage. No previous German or English edition attempts an explanation. The similarity of the word to "rhinoceros" makes the name sound like that of a real animal; but Greek *rhinos,* which can either mean skin or be the genitive of *rhis* (nose), does not seem relevant. Douglas E. Wilson has called my attention to *Phylloxera,* the plant lice that attack European grape vines, and I have found that in 1881 there actually was an international convention about means to combat this vine pest. Nietzsche's *Rhinoxera* might thus be translated Rhinepest. The Rhine is a symbol of German nationalism and central in Wagner's *Ring.*

None of this should be taken too seriously, any more than similar coinages in *Zarathustra.* But it helps to explain why Christian Morgenstern (1871–1914) placed a motto from Nietzsche at the head of his delightful *Galgenlieder* (Gallow Songs: three are included in *Twenty German Poets: A Bilingual Edition,* ed. and tr. Walter Kaufmann, New York, The Modern Library): these songs abound in similar coinages.

[2] A prominent right-wing newspaper; cf. *Ecce Homo,* Chapter III, end of section 1: "Is it credible that the *Nationalzeitung*—a Prussian newspaper, to explain this to my foreign readers—I myself read, if I may say so, only the *Journal des Débats*—should in all seriousness have understood the book [*Beyond Good and Evil*] as a 'sign of the times,' as the true and proper *Junker* philosophy for which the *Kreuzzeitung* merely lacked the courage?"

[3] A weekly survey of scholarly publications, founded in 1850.

What Wagner has in common with "the others"—I'll enumerate it: the decline of the power to organize; the misuse of traditional means without the capacity to furnish any *justification,* any for-the-sake-of; the counterfeiting[4] in the imitation of big forms for which nobody today is strong, proud, self-assured, *healthy* enough; excessive liveliness in the smallest parts; excitement at any price; cunning as the expression of *impoverished* life; more and more nerves in place of flesh.— I know only one musician who is still capable today of creating an overture that is *of one piece:* and nobody knows him.[5]

Those famous today do not write "better" music than Wagner but merely less decisive music, more indifferent music—more indifferent because what is merely half is dated by *the presence of what is whole.* But Wagner was whole; but Wagner was the whole corruption; but Wagner was courage, the will, *conviction* in corruption—what does Johannes Brahms matter now?— His good fortune was a German misunderstanding: he was taken for Wagner's antagonist—an antagonist was *needed.*— That does not make for *necessary* music, that makes, above all, for too much music.— If one is not rich one should have pride enough for poverty.

The sympathy Brahms inspires undeniably at certain points, quite aside from this party interest, party misunderstanding, long seemed enigmatic to me—until finally I discovered, almost by accident, that he affects a certain type of man. His is the melancholy of incapacity; he does *not* create out of an abundance, he *languishes* for abundance. If we discount what he imitates, what he borrows from great old or exotic-modern styles—he is a master of imitation—what remains as specifically his is *yearning.*— This is felt by all who are full of yearning and dissatisfaction of any kind. He is too little a person, too little a center.— This is understood by those who are "impersonal," those on the periphery—and they love him for that. In particular, he is the musician for a certain type of dissatisfied women. Fifty steps more, and you have got the female Wagnerian—just as fifty steps beyond Brahms you encounter Wagner—the female Wagnerian, a type that is more incisive, more

---

[4] See section 10, note 1.

[5] Nietzsche's young friend and disciple, Heinrich Köselitz, alias Peter Gast. See the letter of August 9, 1888, below.

interesting, and above all *more charming*. Brahms is touching as long as he is secretly enraptured or mourns for himself—in this he is "modern"; he becomes cold and of no further concern to us as soon as he becomes *the heir* of the classical composers.— People like to call Brahms the *heir* of Beethoven: I know no more cautious euphemism.—

Everything in music today that lays claim to a "great style" *either* deceives us *or* deceives itself. This alternative gives enough food for thought; for it includes some casuistry about the value of these two cases. "Deceives *us*": most people's instinct protests against this—they don't want to be deceived—but I myself should still prefer even this type to the other ("deceives *itself*"). This is *my* taste.—

To make this easier to understand, for the benefit of the "poor in spirit": Brahms—*or* Wagner.— Brahms is *no* actor.— A goodly portion of the *other* musicians may be subsumed in the concept of Brahms.—

I waste no words on the clever apes of Wagner, Goldmark, for example: with the *Queen of Sheba*[6] one belongs in a zoo—one can make an exhibit of oneself.— What can be done well today, what can be masterly, is only what is small. Here alone integrity is still possible.—

Nothing, however, can cure music *in* what counts, *from* what counts, from the fatality of being an expression of the physiological contradiction—of being *modern*. The best instruction, the most conscientious training, intimacy on principle, even isolation in the company of the old masters—all this remains merely palliative—to speak more precisely, illusory—for one no longer has the presupposition in one's body, whether this be the strong race of a Handel or whether it be the overflowing animal vitality of a Rossini.— Not everybody has a *right* to every teacher: that applies to whole ages.—

To be sure, the possibility cannot be excluded that somewhere in Europe there are still *remnants* of stronger generations, of typically untimely human beings: if so, one could still hope for a *belated*

---

6 The first and best-known opera (1875) by Karl Goldmark (1830–1915), a Jewish composer who was born in Hungary and died in Vienna.

beauty and perfection in music, too, from that quarter. What we can still experience at best are exceptions. From the *rule* that corruption is on top, that corruption is fatalistic, no god can save music.

Epilogue

Let us recover our breath in the end by getting away for a moment from the narrow world to which every question about the worth of *persons* condemns the spirit. A philosopher feels the need to wash his hands after having dealt so long with "The Case of Wagner."—

I offer my conception of what is *modern.*— In its measure of strength every age also possesses a measure for what virtues are permitted and forbidden to it. Either it has the virtues of *ascending* life: then it will resist from the profoundest depths the virtues of declining life. Or the age itself represents declining life: then it also requires the virtues of decline, then it hates everything that justifies itself solely out of abundance, out of the overflowing riches of strength. Aesthetics is tied indissolubly to these biological presuppositions: there is an aesthetics of *decadence,* and there is a *classical* aesthetics—the "beautiful in itself" [1] is a figment of the imagination, like all of idealism.—

In the narrower sphere of so-called moral values one cannot find a greater contrast than that between a *master morality* [2] and the morality of *Christian* value concepts: the latter developed on soil that was morbid through and through (the Gospels present us with precisely the same physiological types that Dostoevsky's novels describe),[3] master morality ("Roman," "pagan," "classical," "Renaissance") is, conversely, the sign language of what has turned out well, of *ascending* life, of the will to power as the principle of life. Master morality *affirms* as instinctively as Christian morality *negates* ("God," "beyond," "self-denial"—all of them negations). The former gives to things out of its own abundance—it transfigures, it beautifies the world and *makes it more rational*— the latter impoverishes, pales and makes uglier the value of things, it *negates* the world. "World" is a Christian term of abuse.—

---

[1] *"Schönes an sich"* might also be rendered in this context as "inherently beautiful" or "absolutely" or "unconditionally beautiful."

[2] See *Beyond Good and Evil,* section 260.

[3] Cf. *The Antichrist* (in *Portable Nietzsche*), pp. 585, 601, and 603, including the translator's footnotes; also Kaufmann, *Nietzsche,* Chapter 12, section I.

These opposite forms in the optics of value are *both* necessary: they are ways of seeing, immune to reasons and refutations. One cannot refute Christianity; one cannot refute a disease of the eye. That pessimism was fought like a philosophy, was the height of scholarly idiocy. The concepts "true" and "untrue" have, as it seems to me, no meaning in optics.—

What alone should be resisted is that falseness, that deceitfulness of instinct which *refuses* to experience these opposites as opposites—as Wagner, for example, refused, being no mean master of such falsehoods. To make eyes at master morality, at *noble* morality (Icelandic saga is almost its most important document) while mouthing the counterdoctrine, that of the "gospel of the lowly," of the *need* for redemption!—

I admire, incidentally, the modesty of the Christians who go to Bayreuth. I myself wouldn't be able to endure certain words out of the mouth of a Wagner. There are concepts which do *not* belong in Bayreuth.—

What? A version of Christianity adapted for female Wagnerians, perhaps *by* female Wagnerians—for Wagner was in his old days by all means *feminini generis*? To say it once more, the Christians of today are too modest for my taste.—

If Wagner was a Christian, then Liszt was perhaps a church father! [4]— The need for *redemption,* the quintessence of all Christian needs, has nothing to do with such buffoons: it is the most honest expression of decadence, it is the most convinced, most painful affirmation of decadence in the form of sublime symbols and practices. The Christian wants to be *rid* of himself. *Le moi est toujours haïssable.*[5]

Noble morality, master morality, conversely, is rooted in a triumphant Yes said to *oneself*—it is self-affirmation, self-glorification of life; it also requires sublime symbols and practices, but only because "its heart is too full." All of *beautiful,* all of *great*

---

[4] Franz Liszt (1811–86) was the father of Cosima (1837–1930), Wagner's second wife. This is not the first allusion to Cosima in this work; cf. Kaufmann, *Nietzsche* (1950), pp. 28–31; (1956), pp. 38–41; i.e., Chapter 1, section II. Liszt had retired to Rome in 1861, joined the Franciscan order in 1865—and eventually joined the Wagners in Bayreuth, where he died in 1886.

[5] "The ego is always hateful." Cf. *Nietzsche contra Wagner* (in *Portable Nietzsche*), p. 671.

art belongs here: the essence of both is gratitude. On the other hand, one cannot dissociate from it an instinctive aversion *against* decadents, scorn for their symbolism, even horror: such feelings almost prove it. Noble Romans experienced Christianity as *foeda superstitio*:[6] I recall how the last German of noble taste, how Goethe experienced the cross.[7]

One looks in vain for more valuable, more *necessary* opposites.—*

But such falseness as that of Bayreuth is no exception today. We are all familiar with the unaesthetic concept of the Christian *Junker*. Such *innocence* among opposites, such a "good conscience" in a lie is actually *modern par excellence,* it almost defines modernity. Biologically, modern man represents a *contradiction of values;* he sits between two chairs, he says Yes and No in the same breath. Is it any wonder that precisely in our times falsehood itself has become flesh and even genius? that *Wagner* "dwelled among us"? It was not without reason that I called Wagner the Cagliostro of modernity.—

But all of us have, unconsciously, involuntarily in our bodies values, words, formulas, moralities of *opposite* descent—we are, physiologically considered, *false.*— *A diagnosis of the modern soul* —where would it begin? With a resolute incision into this instinctive contradiction, with the isolation of its opposite values, with the vivisection of the *most instructive* case.— The case of Wagner is for the philosopher a *windfall*—this essay is inspired, as you hear, by gratitude.—

---

[6] "An abominable superstition."

[7] See Goethe's *Venetian Epigrams,* cited in section 3 above; especially:
> Much there is I can stand, and most things not easy to suffer
> I bear with quiet resolve, just as a god commands it.
> Only a few I find as repugnant as snakes and poison—
> These four: tobacco smoke, bedbugs, garlic, and †.

For other examples see Kaufmann, *Twenty German Poets,* pp. 28–33; for Nietzsche on Goethe, *Twilight of the Idols* (in *Portable Nietzsche*), pp. 553–55.

* [Nietzsche's] *Note.* The opposition between *"noble* morality" and "Christian morality" was first explained in my *Genealogy of Morals:* perhaps there is no more decisive turning point in the history of our understanding of religion and morality. This book, my touchstone for what belongs to me, has the good fortune of being accessible only to the most high-minded and severe spirits: the *rest* lack ears for it. One must have one's passion in things where nobody else today has it.—

FROM Nietzsche's Correspondence

About *The Case of Wagner*[1]

LETTER TO GAST:
SILS MARIA, *July 17, 1888*

. . . Dear friend, do you recall that in Turin I wrote a little pamphlet? Now we are printing it; and you are requested most urgently to help. Naumann[2] already has your address. The title is:

The Case of Wagner
A Musicians' Problem
By
FRIEDRICH NIETZSCHE.

It is something *amusing* with a *fond* of almost too much seriousness.— Could you get hold of Wagner's coll. writings? I'd like to have a few references, to be able to quote exactly, with the numbers of volumes and pages. (1) In the text of the *Ring* there is a variant of Brünnhilde's last aria that is entirely Buddhistic: I only need the numbers of volume and page, *not* the words. (2) How does this passage in *Tristan* go *literally:*

> *The awful deep mysterious ground,*
> *Who will proclaim it to the world?*

Is this right?

3) In one of his last writings Wagner once said—*in italics* if I remember it right—that "chastity works *miracles.*" Here I'd like the exact wording.

For the rest I ask you to offer every kind of objection, of criticism of wording and taste. There are many bold things in this little fabrication.— Procedure with printer's proofs as usual. About appearance, paper, etc., Naumann and I have already reached agreement. The manuscript will be in his hands July 19. . . .

---

[1] For editions of Nietzsche's letters, see the Bibliography in my *Nietzsche* (3rd ed., 1968), p. 484ff.
[2] The publisher.

FROM GAST'S LETTER
TO NIETZSCHE, *July 31, 1888*

. . . In the *score,* which arrived recently from Venice, Marke's[3] question is:

> *The* unfathomably *deep*
> *mysterious ground, etc.*

The text in the *Collected Edition,* if I am not mistaken, is

> *The unfathomable*
> *awfully deep*
> *mysterious ground.*

It was some such entirely insane piling up of words.——

Instead of Brunhilde Wagner says *Brünnhilde* (pp. 11 and 12). . . .

LETTER TO GAST:
SILS MARIA, *August 9, 1888*

Dear Friend,

In the first lines of the *Preface* I had changed the words "many jokes" to read "a hundred jokes." Looking back, the word "hundred" here seems to me too strong; I suggest that in your revision you restore the original "many."

Today an incredibly beautiful day, colors of the south!

Your friend
NIETZSCHE.

POSTCARD TO GAST:
SILS MARIA, *August 9, 1888*

Dear Friend,

There are still *postscripts* to my "letter" of which proofs must be read; I am sorry. A lot of pepper and salt; in the *second* postscript I take the problem by the horns in amplified form (I shan't easily find another opportunity to speak of these matters *again;* the

---

[3] The name of the King in *Tristan and Isolde.*

form chosen this time allows me many "liberties"). Among other things, a judgment of the dead also for Brahms. At one point I even permitted myself to allude to *you*—in a form that will have your consent, I hope.

Just now I have instructed Naumann to send you the printer's proofs I corrected last, making quite a few changes, for a final *revision*.

With the utmost gratitude,

Your friend

N.

LETTER TO GAST:
SILS MARIA, *August 11, 1888*

. . . The strongest passages are really in the "postscripts"; at one point I even have doubts whether I have not gone too far (*not* in the facts but in speaking of the facts). Perhaps we better *omit* the note[4] (in which something is suggested about Wagner's descent) and instead leave larger spaces between the *major subdivisions* of the "postscript." . . .[5]

FROM GAST'S LETTER
TO NIETZSCHE, *August 11, 1888*

. . . "Redemption for the redeemer" (p. 42, line 8 [6]) are the final words of Wagner's *Parsifal*. Whether the Wagner Association in Munich was the first in Germany I have not been able to confirm, though I have looked in lots of places: but perhaps you don't mean it chronologically?— "Everybody" on p. 42, line 12,[7] you might change to "But many also made."

What you mean by saying "Bayreuth rhymes on institute for cold-water therapy" (p. 46, line 8 from bottom[8]) is not immedi-

---

[4] See the letter of August 18, note 10, below.
[5] To avoid leaving a gap on the printed page.
[6] First Postscript, see p. 638, line 7.
[7] In the sentence with the parenthesis "(strangely enough!)" just a few lines later. Nietzsche accepted this suggestion.
[8] First Postscript, penultimate paragraph.

ately clear to the reader. Neither is "she stands naked before him" (p. 47, line 7 [9]). . . .

LETTER TO GAST:
SILS MARIA, *August 18, 1888*

Dear friend,

delighted with your letter, just received.— Regarding the *note*,[10] I have made up my mind to retain it *in its entirety* (except for a more cautious nuance in the question of descent). For in a kind of epilogue I return with great force to Wagner's falseness: so every hint in this direction becomes valuable. (This epilogue I have *reworked* several times. What you will receive from the printer is *still not* the right version. But send it to me, corrected!)—

I do mean the *Venetian Epigrams* (and *not* the *Roman Elegies*). It is a historical fact (as I have learned from Hehn's book[11]) that *they* gave the greatest offense. . . .

LETTER TO GAST:
SILS MARIA, *August 24, 1888*

Dear friend, I am just mailing the epilogue to Naumann with the request that it be sent to you once more for a *final revision*. It seemed useful to me to say a few things more clearly (it seemed a finesse to shield *Christianity* against Wagner). Also, the very last sentence is stronger now—also more cheerful.

"Off to Crete!" is a famous chorus in *La Belle Hélène*.[12] This I am telling you from malice because you "instructed" me about the final words of *Parsifal*. These "last words" of Wagner had after all been my leitmotif. . . .

---

[9] *Ibid.*, last paragraph. Nietzsche ignored these last two criticisms.

[10] Nietzsche's footnote to the first Postscript, p. 638, in which he insinuates that Wagner's father may have been a Jew, Adler being a Jewish name. The point here depends on Wagner's inveterate and vocal anti-Semitism.

[11] Victor Hehn, *Gedanken über Goethe* (reflections on Goethe), 1887. The reference is to section 3.

[12] By Jacques Offenbach. The words "Off to Crete!" conclude the (first) Postscript.

FROM GAST'S LETTER TO
NIETZSCHE, *September 11, 1888*

. . . I did not know that "Off to Crete!" comes from *La Belle Hélène*. When I took the liberty of indicating the source of the words "Redemption for the redeemer," I was misled by your expression which leads one to suppose that you accord the honor of invention to the presiding officers of the Wagner Association of Munich. . . .

FROM NIETZSCHE'S LETTER
TO OVERBECK, *October 18, 1888*

It is surprising how easily one can learn from this essay about the *degree* of my heterodoxy which actually does not leave a single stone standing on another. Against the *Germans* I here advance on all fronts: you'll have no occasion for complaints about "ambiguity." This utterly irresponsible race which has on its conscience all the great disasters of civilization and at all *decisive* moments of history had something "else" on its mind (the Reformation at the time of the Renaissance; Kantian philosophy precisely when a *scientific* way of thinking had just been attained with some trouble in England and France; "Wars of Liberation" when Napoleon appeared, the only man so far who was strong enough to turn Europe into a political and *economic unit*), now has "the *Reich*" on its mind—this recrudescence of petty state politics and cultural atomism—at a moment when the great *question of values* is posed for the first time. There has never been a more important moment in history: but *who might be aware of that?*

ECCE HOMO

———◆———

FOR
Barklie McKee Henry
1902–1966

CONTENTS

EDITOR'S INTRODUCTION   *657*

A NOTE ON THE PUBLICATION OF *Ecce Homo*   *666*

NIETZSCHE'S PREFACE   *673*

Why I Am So Wise   *678*
Why I Am So Clever   *692*
Why I Write Such Good Books   *715*
   The Birth of Tragedy   *726*
   The Untimely Ones   *732*
   Human, All-Too-Human   *739*
   Dawn   *746*
   The Gay Science   *749*
   Thus Spoke Zarathustra   *751*
   Beyond Good and Evil   *766*
   Genealogy of Morals   *768*
   Twilight of the Idols   *770*
   The Case of Wagner   *773*
Why I Am a Destiny   *782*

APPENDIX: *Variants from Nietzsche's Drafts*   *793*

INDEX TO *Ecce Homo*   *835*

Editor's Introduction

1

Ecce Homo is one of the treasures of world literature. Written in 1888 and first published in 1908, it has been largely ignored or misunderstood. Yet it is Nietzsche's own interpretation of his development, his works, and his significance; and we should gladly trade the whole vast literature on Nietzsche for this one small book. Who would not rather have Shakespeare on Shakespeare, including the poet's own reflections on his plays and poems, than the exegeses and conjectures of thousands of critics and professors?

Socrates said in the *Apology* that the poets are among the worst interpreters of their own works: they create without understanding, on the wings of inspiration; but when they discuss their works they rely on their uninspired reason and falter. But *Ecce Homo* is clearly not the work of a pedant whose genius has quit him. It is itself a work of art and marks one of the high points of German prose.

There are those who like Nietzsche's early works best—especially *The Birth of Tragedy* and the "untimely" meditation on historiography; but they are few by now and no longer a force to reckon with. Others have always preferred the aphoristic works in which Nietzsche emerged as Germany's greatest master of prose. By far the larger number of his readers have most admired *Zarathustra*. And the rest, including the greater part of the Anglo-American philosophers who take him seriously at all, have little doubt that *Beyond Good and Evil* and the *Genealogy of Morals* are his finest books. I am assuredly in a minority—perhaps of one—when I confess that I love best the five books Nietzsche wrote during his last productive year, 1888—not least because they are such brilliant works of art.

The Case of Wagner, The Twilight of the Idols, The Antichrist, and *Ecce Homo* present a crescendo without equal in prose. Then comes the final work, *Nietzsche contra Wagner,* Nietzsche's briefest and most beautiful book—a selection of passages from his earlier works, admittedly very slightly revised and improved in a few places—an attempt to approximate perfection. The preface to that book was dated Christmas 1888. A few days later, during the first week of January, he collapsed on the street, recovered sufficient lucidity to dispatch a few mad but strangely beautiful letters[1] —and then darkness closed in and extinguished passion and intelligence. He suffered and thought no more. He had burnt himself out.

Was the vegetating body that survived another decade and more, until August 1900, still the poet and philosopher, artist and Antichrist? Socrates gently ridiculed disciples who thought that the body that remained after his death would still be Socrates. But reproductions of portraits of Nietzsche in the eighteen-nineties, commissioned by his sister who let his mustache grow as he himself never had, who clad him in white robes and fancied his vacant stare—portraits that show no glimpse of Nietzsche's vanished spirit —these appear with his books to this day.

Of Nietzsche's last works, none has proved harder to understand than *Ecce Homo*. The self-portrait is not naturalistic; hence, it was widely felt, it is clearly insane and to be disregarded. This prevalent view is doubly false. The lack of naturalism is not proof of insanity but a triumph of style—of a piece with the best paintings of that time. And even if what might be interpreted as signs of madness do occasionally flicker in a passage, that does not mean that the portrait can therefore be ignored. In both respects Nietzsche should be compared with Van Gogh.

Ecce Homo does not fit any ordinary conception of philosophers. It is not only remote from the world of professorial or donnish philosophy, from tomes and articles, footnotes and jargon—in brief, from the modern image. It is equally far from the popular notion of the wise man: serene, past passion, temperate, and Apollinian. But this is plainly part of Nietzsche's point: to offer a new image—a philosopher who is not an Alexandrian academician, nor an Apollinian sage, but Dionysian.

While Van Gogh, having fled his native north, burnt himself

---

[1] See, e.g., *Portable Nietzsche* (New York, Viking, 1954), pp. 684–87.

out in southern France, creating an incredible number of works without any public recognition, fighting time till 1890, when madness could no longer be held off and he shot himself, Nietzsche spent himself with comparable passion just a few miles further east, writing feverishly—not even pausing, as in keeping with his own ideas he ought to have done, to take his life before his spirit quit it. Freud used to say of him that "he had a more penetrating knowledge of himself than any other man who ever lived or was ever likely to live";[2] yet Nietzsche was not aware of his impending madness and therefore, unable to forestall it.

In his first book Nietzsche had traced the "birth of tragedy" to the creative fusion of the Apollinian and the Dionysian, and the death of tragedy to the imperious rationalism for which he found the most impressive symbol in Socrates. Then he had found a rebirth of tragedy in Wagner's work and had looked forward to the advent of an "artistic Socrates"—Nietzsche himself. The critical passion, the revolt against hallowed pieties, the demand for clarity, and the fusion of life and thought need not always remain opposed to the spirit of art and need not inspire such confidence in the unaided reason that one's heir would proceed to proscribe all tragedy, as Plato did; rather, all this might be merged with a vision of the world that would be closer to Sophocles, and with a poetic temperament partaking more of Pindar than of Plato, more of Dionysus than Apollo. *Ecce Homo* is the *Apology* of this "artistic Socrates."

Plato's Socrates had claimed in his *Apology* that he was the wisest of men, not because he was so wise but because his fellow men were so stupid, especially those who were considered the wisest—for they thought they knew what in fact they did not know. And Socrates, accused of impiety and corrupting the youth of Athens, argued that he was actually the city's greatest benefactor and deserving of the highest honors. Thus, *Ecce Homo* could have been entitled "Variations on a Theme by Socrates." That would have been an artistic title, but out of the question for a writer who had just finished *The Antichrist*. *Ecce Homo*—the words Pilate had, according to John (19:5), spoken of Jesus: "Behold the man!"—

---

[2] Ernest Jones, *The Life and Work of Sigmund Freud*, Vol. II, (New York, Basic Books, 1953), p. 344.

seemed more to the point. But that point was not to suggest any close similarity between himself and Jesus; more nearly the opposite. *Here* is a man! Here is a new, a different image of humanity: not a saint or holy man any more than a traditional sage, but a *modern* version.

In the text Nietzsche said he wished to prevent any mischievous use of himself—*dass man Unfug mit mir treibt*. Our knowledge that two months after finishing the first draft of the book, and less than four weeks after he had gone over the whole work once more, he became insane gives the book a tragic dimension that is heightened almost intolerably if we bear in mind how he failed to prevent the mischief he feared. The first section of the Preface ends: "Above all, do not mistake me for someone else!" He underlined this cry—but soon his sister imposed her exceedingly unsubtle notion of hero and prophet on a mindless invalid—and in her sign he triumphed.

That was but the beginning. Far worse mischief followed. Nietzsche's voice was drowned out as misinterpretations that he had explicitly repudiated with much wit and malice were accepted and repeated, and repeated and accepted, until most readers knew what to expect before they read Nietzsche, and so read nothing but what they had long expected.

2

What of Nietzsche's comments on his own works? Can his interpretations really be taken seriously?

The very question smacks of an obscene revaluation of all values, through which, soon after the book was written, everything was turned upside down. Nietzsche's sister had mocked her brother's claims to fame, but then, switching to his cause after her husband's suicide, she took private lessons in Nietzsche's philosophy from Rudolf Steiner, a Goethe scholar who later became famous as the founder of anthroposophy. Soon Steiner gave her up as simply incapable of understanding Nietzsche. Meanwhile she became her brother's official exegete and biographer, tampered with his letters —and was taken seriously by almost everyone. And who was *not* taken seriously? Even the most unscrupulous Nazi interpretations were taken seriously not only inside Germany, but by a host of foreign scholars who did not bother to check Nazi quotations.

Earlier, Ernst Bertram had frankly subtitled his interpretation "Attempt at a Mythology": but who checked *his* quotations? And whose Nietzsche image, except the sister's, was taken more seriously from 1918, when Bertram's *Nietzsche* appeared, until 1933 when Hitler broke out? Or who checked Jaspers' quotations *in their context?* (The English translation of his *Nietzsche* omits all source references, as Bertram had done.)

It would be pointless to rescue from their imminent oblivion many lesser figures who have also associated their names with Nietzsche's, writing about him without having read carefully the works they discuss, or editing him by selecting passages from hopeless mistranslations that these professors lacked the German or the patience to check. Yet such publications are taken seriously and used as the basis for many discussions in colleges and universities.

While some of Nietzsche's self-interpretations are much less persuasive than others, all of them have several inestimable advantages over almost everything that passes as serious literature about him: he did not discuss any of his works without having read them carefully, more than once; indeed, he did not discuss any without knowing all of them, in the sequence in which they were written—and, of course, in the original. He also knew all of his letters, as well as his unpublished fragments and notes. And he wrote about his *oeuvre* with singular penetration, wit, and style.

Let us be specific: Do his comments on *The Birth of Tragedy* make sense? Very little written on that book is as illuminating, and most discussions of the book are dated by Nietzsche's own discussion, which long antedates them.

Yet *Ecce Homo* has its faults. It contains all too many references to *Zarathustra*—most of them embarrassing—and the numerous long quotations from that book are almost rendered pointless by *Zarathustra*'s great posthumous success: the quotations were intended for readers who did not know that book. And although Nietzsche has often been linked with German nationalism, his remarks about the Germans are open to criticism for being too extreme in stressing what he finds abominable.

We return to the question of naturalism. Nietzsche's portrait of the Germans is not meant to be objective. It partakes more nearly of the spirit of George Grosz, who, after World War I, entitled a collection of his graphic attacks on his countrymen, *Ecce Homo*. But we also hear the anguished cry of one who sees—foresees—himself mistaken for a writer he is not: for an apostle of military power and empire, a nationalist, and even a racist. In order to define himself emphatically, Nietzsche underlines (too often) and shrieks—to no avail. Those who construe the overman in evolutionary terms he calls "oxen"—in vain. Respected professors *still* write books in which Nietzsche's ethics is presented as "evolutionary."

The break with Wagner? Nietzsche's picture is stylized, not false. There is, of course, hindsight in it; but readers of Sartre should know, if they have not learned it firsthand from Nietzsche himself, that an act is one event, and the way we interpret it afterward and relate ourselves to it is another. Looking back on the year in which he resigned from the university, published *Human, All-Too-Human* with a dedication to Voltaire—turning from German romanticism to the French enlightenment, and from Wagner to independence—he felt, more clearly than he had felt it at the time, that this had been his Rubicon, the turning point in his life. Can one deny that it was?

For all that, is Wagner represented in a Manichaean spirit, as the force of evil, as a dragon? On the contrary, the portrait is imbued with gratitude and love—with *amor fati,* love of fate. *There is no "if only" in this autobiography, and there are no excuses.* A man who was in physical agony much of his adult life and warned by his doctors not to read or write much lest he strain his half-blind eyes, does not once complain. He is thankful for his illness and tells us how it made his life better.

The philosophical and religious literature of the world does not contain many sayings that equal the wisdom and nobility of *Zarathustra*'s challenge: "If you have an enemy, do not requite him evil with good, for that would put him to shame. Rather prove that he did you some good." [3] In *Ecce Homo* Nietzsche embodies

---

[3] Part One, "On the Adder's Bite" (*Portable Nietzsche*, p. 180).

this attitude, this triumph over *ressentiment*. Instead of bearing a grudge toward the world that treated him so cruelly, instead of succumbing to the rancor of sickness, he relates the story of his life and work in a spirit of gratitude—and goes out of his way to pay his respects to Paul Rée and Lou Salomé,[4] with whom he had fallen out.

Ecce Homo, "Dionysus versus the Crucified": the contrast with the Jesus of the Gospels is central. The Jesus of the Gospels— who, Nietzsche argued in *The Antichrist,* is different in this respect from the historic Jesus—is far from being above resentment: not only does he obsessively slander his enemies, he stands opposed to this world and this life, and neither takes nor teaches any joy in small pleasures and beauties. The strange emphasis on little things, material factors generally thought beneath the notice of philosophers and sages, that distinguishes the first two chapters of *Ecce Homo* has to be seen in this light, too. This theme was picked up by Camus, also with an anti-Christian pathos, but restrained by lyricism and his distinctive charm. Nietzsche, like Socrates who was said to look like a satyr, disdains charm and embraces irony and sarcasm: he is not ingratiating, but wants to give offense. Is there no resentment in that?

In the case of Socrates, Nietzsche emphasized the element of rancor in his sarcasm—what he called *Bosheit,* malice. And in that case many did not wish to see Socrates in this light and, because Socrates was felt to be ideal, tranquil, the perfect sage, took offense at Nietzsche's portrait. Only the safe distance of more than twenty centuries could make the hero of the *Apology* look saintly. No doubt, those who had *heard* his apology, felt what Nietzsche saw— and had smarted under it for years. After all, what Socrates boasted of was perfectly true: he had taken pleasure in engaging men of reputation in the marketplace to humiliate them before the crowd that gathered—often (assuming, as is surely fair, that Plato did not

---

[4] Both are discussed briefly in my *Nietzsche: Philosopher, Psychologist, Antichrist* (1950; 2nd rev. ed., 1956; 3rd rev. ed., 1968). Chapter 1, section III. For a much more comprehensive treatment that embodies a vast amount of original research, see Rudolph Binion's *Frau Lou* (Princeton, N.J.: Princeton University Press, 1968).

mean to slander Socrates) by using clever debater's tricks. He had a wicked sense of humor and found all this very funny; those he bested certainly did not.

Goethe, too, possessed not only the serenity of *amor fati*[5] but also an Olympian malice. But even if Nietzsche is in noble company, was there not after all resentment in him, even in *Ecce Homo?* It is a matter of what Nietzsche called in *The Gay Science* "giving style to one's character." The negative feelings, he taught, should not be suppressed, much less extirpated; they should be sublimated. And in *Ecce Homo* he discusses how he was both a No-saying and a Yes-saying spirit. The negative feelings are not vented on individuals or directed against life or the world; they are mobilized in the service of life and creativity against obstructions, movements, causes.

Ultimate nobility must rise above rancor and must yet be capable of echoing Voltaire's cry, *écrasez l'infâme*.[6] Resentment is reprehensible, but so is the failure to engage in the fight against infamy. It is only when the infamy to be crushed turns out to be Christianity that most readers recoil. But Nietzsche's attack, of course, depends on his conception of Christianity and—as he himself insists—cannot be understood at all except as a part of his campaign against resentment.

Indeed, this attack seems to me much more successfully stylized than Nietzsche's denunciations of the Germans. Since World War II the Germans may seem fair game, but Nietzsche's indictments are sometimes stained by his own wounds: in more than one passage he falls short of his own standards, and resentment clings to him like a leech.

Nietzsche's ties to the pre-Christian world are stronger than is usually supposed, though this should not surprise us in a classical philologist who, even in his teens, nourished his spirit and emotions on Greek literature and thought. This is not the place for a lengthy survey of classical inspirations, but in addition to Socrates' *Apology* we must mention Aristotle's portrait of the great-souled man in the *Nicomachean Ethics*. It is a commonplace that Aristotle's eth-

---

[5] Cf. p. 714, note 4.
[6] Crush the infamy.

ics was based in large measure on the morality of Athenian gentlemen, and that the man described in this passage represents not
merely Aristotle's ideal but a type very much admired in Athens. It
has not been widely noticed—and for all I know, I may have been
the first to point this out some years ago—that Aristotle's portrait
was probably inspired in part by Socrates' *Apology*. In any case,
both left their mark on *Ecce Homo*.

"A person is thought to be great-souled if he claims much and
deserves much." Aristotle's words—antithetical as they are to the
Christian influence on modern morality—represent *one* of the leitmotifs of *Ecce Homo*. "He does not bear a grudge" represents another. That he does not speak evil "even of his enemies, except
when he deliberately intends to give offense," is a third. But Aristotle's whole portrait is relevant.[7] And to Nietzsche's central contrast of the New Testament and the Greeks, Greek tragedy, Thucydides, and the *Iliad* are relevant, too. And so is Greek comedy;
so are the satyrs, the companions of Dionysus; so are Greek laughter and Socratic irony. It should not be assumed that the chapter
titles of *Ecce Homo* are devoid of all humor. Neither, of course, is
Nietzsche *only* speaking in jest when he explains, "Why I Write
Such Good Books"—any more than George Bernard Shaw was
only jesting when he spoke in a similar vein.

Looking for a pre-Christian, Greek symbol that he might oppose to "the Crucified," Nietzsche found Dionysus. His "Dionysus" is neither the god of the ancient Dionysian festivals nor the
god Nietzsche had played off against Apollo in *The Birth of Tragedy*, although he does, of course, bear some of the features of
both. In the later works of Nietzsche, "Dionysus" is no longer the
spirit of unrestrained passion, but the symbol of the affirmation of
life with all its suffering and terror. "The problem," Nietzsche explained in a note that was later included in the posthumous *Will to
Power* (section 1052), "is that of the meaning of suffering: whether
a Christian meaning or a tragic meaning. . . . The tragic man
affirms even the harshest suffering." And *Ecce Homo* is, not least
of all, Nietzsche's final affirmation of his own cruel life.

[7] *Nicomachean Ethics*, IV.3. Most of the description is quoted in my
Nietzsche, Chapter 12, section VI; much of it also in my note on *Beyond
Good and Evil*, section 212, p. 328 above.

A Note on the Publication of Ecce Homo

Many who have never carefully read any of Nietzsche's works have read *about* two German editions of the works that elicited some sensational but uninformed comments in print. The first was Karl Schlechta's edition of all of Nietzsche's books and a selection from his notes, fragments, and letters, in three volumes. But Schlechta simply reprinted the previously published versions of *Ecce Homo* and need not be considered here.

The second was Erich F. Podach's book, *Friedrich Nietzsches Werke des Zusammenbruchs* (1961),[1] which offered texts of *Nietzsche contra Wagner, The Antichrist, Ecce Homo,* and the so-called *Dionysus Dithyrambs* that were said to supersede all previous editions. I have shown elsewhere[2] how ill-founded Podach's strident claims are. Here we need only consider his handling of *Ecce Homo.* He aims to show that "The hitherto familiar *Ecce Homo* does not exist" (p. 208). This sensational charge has to be met here, even if some readers should prefer to skim the next six paragraphs.

Podach prints the manuscript with Nietzsche's editorial directions, such as requests to insert or move passages; he reproduces alternative versions of the same passages, including pages that had been pasted over; and he admits that he has "not indicated where whole sections in the manuscript sent to the printer are crossed out. Here some of the texts show plainly that they are variants or preliminary versions, while in other cases [very few] it cannot be decided whether N or Gast [Nietzsche's young friend who helped him with editorial chores and proofs] has deleted them" (p. 408).

In fact, *Ecce Homo* was begun October 15, 1888, on Nie-

---

[1] "The Works of Friedrich Nietzsche's Collapse" (or, literally, "Friedrich Nietzsche's Works of the Collapse"), Heidelberg, Wolfgang Rothe, 1961.

[2] "Nietzsche in the Light of His Suppressed Manuscripts," *Journal of the History of Philosophy,* II (October 1964), 205–25. This is included in the revised third edition of my *Nietzsche* (1968).

tzsche's forty-fourth birthday, and finished November 4. A few days later Nietzsche sent the manuscript to his publisher, Naumann; but on November 20 he mentioned some additions in a letter to Georg Brandes, the Danish critic who was the first to lecture on Nietzsche at a university (Copenhagen); and then he also mentioned additions to Naumann. On a postcard, November 27, he asked Naumann to return "the second part of the MS . . . because I still want to insert some things," and explained that he meant "the whole second half of the MS, beginning with the section entitled *Thus Spoke Zarathustra.*' I assume that this won't delay the printing for even a moment as I shall send back the MS immediately." On December 1 he acknowledged receipt of the second half but requested the return of the whole MS, including the additions: "I want to give you a MS as good as the last one, at the risk that I have to be a copier for another week." On December 3 Naumann replied that he was returning the MS, but "copying it once more I do not consider necessary; I merely should especially recommend that you read the proofs carefully although I shall make a point of doing likewise." This shows plainly how wrong Podach's claims are: *the publisher found the manuscript finished, clear, and printable.*

Nor did Nietzsche keep it long. On December 6, he telegraphed Naumann: "MS back. Everything reworked [*umgearbeitet*]." And on the eighth, Nietzsche wrote Gast: "I sent *Ecce Homo* back to C. G. Naumann day before yesterday after laying it once more on the gold scales from the first to the last word to set my conscience finally at rest."

All this information was given by Professor Raoul Richter in his long postscript to the first edition of 1908, and Richter also described the manuscript: "The manuscript is written clearly and cleanly from beginning to end, so that even every untrained person can read it quickly on the whole, without trouble. Changes have been made either by striking things out (with pencil or ink) or by pasting things over. In both cases the editor [Richter] has copied the original version in order to help provide a basis for a later critical edition. For that, ample use would also have to be made of the drafts and variants found in the three octavo notebooks

(. . .)[3] and some separate sheets. Nietzsche's corrections in the manuscript have been entered with scrupulous exactness; where, owing to lack of space, some additions had to be written in miniature script, they are little graphic masterpieces: so readable is every letter, and so exactly is the bracket of insertion drawn above the line . . . Slips that affect the spelling or grammar are very rare and probably rarer than in the average manuscript submitted to a printer" (p. 146).

Neither Richter's probity nor the authenticity of the letters I have cited, and of any number of others that corroborate them, has ever been questioned. Podach simply ignores all of this. Still, two departures of his version from the traditional ones ought to be mentioned here. First, he omits section 7 of the second chapter, which contains Nietzsche's well-known poem that is sometimes called "Venice," sometimes "Gondola Song." Podach prints this section under the title "Intermezzo," after the second section of *Nietzsche contra Wagner*. This is understandable, for that is where it appeared in the unpublished first printing of the latter book (1889; I have a copy of that), though not in any published version. But on December 20 Nietzsche sent his publisher a postcard: "I have sent you a single sheet with the title 'Intermezzo,' with the request to insert it in *N. contra W*. Now let us rather insert it in *Ecce,* for which it was intended originally[!]—in the *second* chapter (Why I am so clever), as *section 5* [*sic*]. The following numbers will have to be changed accordingly. The title 'Intermezzo,' of course, goes." Two days later Nietzsche wrote Gast similarly. But a few days later he received proofs of *Nietzsche contra Wagner* that naturally still included this section, and he did not delete it but made some slight corrections in it. Richter printed it in his edition of *Ecce Homo,* with the corrections Nietzsche had made in the proofs. Podach mentions none of this but says simply that Gast, "for his own glory and the enhancement of *Ecce Homo,* embodied the 'Intermezzo' printed in *Nietzsche contra Wagner* in the manuscript" (p. 188; cf. also p. 201). While this is in keeping with the tenor of Podach's book, it seems sensible to me to include this

---

[3] Identified in parentheses by their Archive numbers.

section in *Ecce Homo,* in keeping with all previous editions except Podach's.

Finally, at the end of *Ecce Homo,* Podach prints a three-page poem entitled "Ruhm und Ewigkeit" (fame and eternity). Here he follows Richter's edition, while all subsequent editions have omitted the poem. This did not involve any suppression, although Podach is very scornful of all who have omitted it at this point: the poem has usually been included in the so-called *Dionysus Dithyrambs* and is readily available in volumes containing Nietzsche's poems. Podach considers it important—it is not clear why or for what—that Nietzsche wanted to conclude all of his last works with poems. But as a matter of fact, the last two books he saw through the press, *The Case of Wagner* and *The Twilight of the Idols,* did not end with poems; neither did *The Antichrist;* and as for *Nietzsche contra Wagner* and *Ecce Homo,* in his last communications to his publisher, Nietzsche asked Naumann January 1, 1889, to return one final poem, and January 2, 1889, to return both. That he did not want them published in their present form at the end of these books seems clear; that he would have revised them, if he had not collapsed on January 3, is possible. But it is no less possible and actually more likely, I think, that he realized that the books would be better without these poems.

After Nietzsche's collapse, his family decided not to publish any further books by him. *The Twilight of the Idols* did appear, as scheduled, in January 1889, but the three books written after that were held up. In 1891 the fourth part of *Thus Spoke Zarathustra* was printed, together with the *Dionysus Dithyrambs*—and published in 1892. By 1895 there was sufficient interest in Nietzsche to include both *The Antichrist* and *Nietzsche contra Wagner* in volume VIII of a new edition of Nietzsche's works. But *Ecce Homo* was held back, perhaps partly because it might compromise Nietzsche, partly because his sister found it useful to quote from Nietzsche's self-interpretations when she wrote prefaces for new editions of his books. As long as she knew *Ecce Homo* and the public did not, her biographies of her brother as well as her occasional journalistic pieces had a special authority.

Finally, in 1908 the book appeared in an expensive limited

edition of 1250 copies. It was not brought out by a publisher who had been previously associated with Nietzsche, but by the Insel Verlag; and the title, binding, and ornaments had all been designed by Henry van de Velde in the *Jugendstil* of that time. There is no English word for that style: one uses the French phrase *art nouveau*. Nietzsche, who had written Gast, November 26, 1888, that he wanted *Ecce* to be designed just like *Twilight*—that is, very simply, with clear print and wide margins and nothing to distract the eye from the text—would surely have found the book hideous. But Richter's postscript was dignified and informative.

Two years later, in 1910, *Ecce Homo* was included in the new volume XV of Nietzsche's works, which along with volume XVI (1911) contained a greatly enlarged and entirely remodeled version of the *Will to Power* and replaced the old volume XV (1901), which had contained the first edition of the *Will to Power*. Many libraries acquired only volume XVI, adding it to their old sets: as a result, many sets of the so-called Grossoktav edition[4] of Nietzsche's works lack *Ecce Homo*. But henceforth *Ecce* was included in editions of the works and no longer hard to come by. And all editions of the book, except for Podach's, followed the first edition, except that they omitted the poem at the end.

The present translation follows the standard editions, but the notes and Appendix also offer previously untranslated variants and passages from drafts, along with other information and comments not previously found in any edition in any language. In a way, all this apparatus weighs down a book written with light feet; but *Ecce* is not easily accessible, and on a first or second reading the commentary may prove helpful. The form in which it is offered should make it easy to reread *Ecce Homo* straight through, without any editorial interruptions.

Perhaps one or another reader of the book will react in a manner similar to "Napoleon's surprise when he came to see Goethe: it shows what people had associated with the 'German spirit' for centuries. *'Voilà un homme!'* "[5]

---

[4] The various editions of Nietzsche's works are discussed in the Bibliography of my *Nietzsche* (3rd ed., 1968).

[5] *Beyond Good and Evil*, section 209.

ECCE HOMO

———◀●▶———

How One Becomes What One Is

Preface

1

Seeing that before long I must confront humanity with the most difficult demand ever made of it, it seems indispensable to me to say *who I am*. Really, one should know it, for I have not left myself "without testimony." But the disproportion between the greatness of my task and the *smallness* of my contemporaries has found expression in the fact that one has neither heard nor even seen me. I live on my own credit; it is perhaps a mere prejudice that I live.

I only need to speak with one of the "educated" who come to the Upper Engadine[1] for the summer, and I am convinced that I do *not* live.

Under these circumstances I have a duty against which my habits, even more the pride of my instincts, revolt at bottom—namely, to say: *Hear me! For I am such and such a person. Above all, do not mistake me for someone else.*

2

I am, for example, by no means a bogey, or a moralistic monster—I am actually the very opposite of the type of man who so far has been revered as virtuous. Between ourselves, it seems to me that precisely this is part of my pride. I am a disciple of the philosopher Dionysus; I should prefer to be even a satyr to being a saint. But one should really read this essay. Perhaps I have succeeded; perhaps this essay had no other meaning than to give expression to this contrast in a cheerful and philanthropic manner.

The last thing *I* should promise would be to "improve" mankind.[2] No new idols are erected by me; let the old ones learn what

---

[1] The Alpine valley in Switzerland where Nietzsche spent almost every summer from 1879 to 1888.
[2] Cf. the chapter "The 'Improvers' of Mankind" in *Twilight of the Idols*.

feet of clay mean. *Overthrowing idols* (my word for "ideals")—that comes closer to being part of my craft. One has deprived reality of its value, its meaning, its truthfulness, to precisely the extent to which one has mendaciously invented an ideal world.

The "true world" and the "apparent world"—that means: the mendaciously invented world and reality.

The *lie* of the ideal has so far been the curse on reality; on account of it, mankind itself has become mendacious and false down to its most fundamental instincts—to the point of worshipping the *opposite* values of those which alone would guarantee its health, its future, the lofty *right* to its future.

3

Those who can breathe the air of my writings know that it is an air of the heights, a *strong* air. One must be made for it. Otherwise there is no small danger that one may catch cold in it. The ice is near, the solitude tremendous—but how calmly all things lie in the light! How freely one breathes! How much one feels *beneath* oneself!

Philosophy, as I have so far understood and lived it, means living voluntarily among ice and high mountains—seeking out everything strange and questionable in existence, everything so far placed under a ban by morality. Long experience, acquired in the course of such wanderings *in what is forbidden,* taught me to regard the causes that so far have prompted moralizing and idealizing in a very different light from what may seem desirable: the *hidden* history of the philosophers, the psychology of the great names, came to light for me.

How much truth does a spirit *endure,* how much truth does it *dare?* More and more that became for me the real measure of value. Error (faith in the ideal) is not blindness, error is *cowardice.*

Every attainment, every step forward in knowledge, *follows* from courage, from hardness against oneself, from cleanliness in relation to oneself.

I do not refute ideals, I merely put on gloves before them.

Nitimur in vetitum.[3] in this sign my philosophy will triumph one day, for what one has forbidden so far as a matter of principle has always been—truth alone.

4

Among my writings my *Zarathustra* stands to my mind by itself. With that I have given mankind the greatest present that has ever been made to it so far. This book, with a voice bridging centuries, is not only the highest book there is, the book that is truly characterized by the air of the heights—the whole fact of man lies *beneath* it at a tremendous distance—it is also the *deepest,* born out of the innermost wealth of truth, an inexhaustible well to which no pail descends without coming up again filled with gold and goodness. Here no "prophet" is speaking, none of those gruesome hybrids of sickness and will to power whom people call founders of religions. Above all, one must *hear* aright the tone that comes from this mouth, the halcyon tone, lest one should do wretched injustice to the meaning of its wisdom.

"It is the stillest words that bring on the storm. Thoughts that come on doves' feet guide the world." [4]

> The figs are falling from the trees; they are good and sweet; and, as they fall, their red skin bursts. I am a north wind to ripe figs.
>
> Thus, like figs, these teachings fall to you, my friends: now consume their juice and their sweet meat. It is fall around us, and pure sky and afternoon.[5]

It is no fanatic that speaks here; this is not "preaching"; no *faith* is demanded here: from an infinite abundance of light and depth of happiness falls drop upon drop, word upon word: the tempo of these speeches is a tender adagio. Such things reach only

---

[3] "We strive for the forbidden": Ovid, *Amores,* III, 4, 17. Cf. *Beyond Good and Evil,* section 227.

[4] *Thus Spoke Zarathustra,* Second Part, last chapter: *The Portable Nietzsche,* tr. Walter Kaufmann (New York, Viking, 1954), p. 258.

[5] *Ibid.,* second chapter.

the most select. It is a privilege without equal to be a listener here. Nobody is free to have ears for Zarathustra.

Is not Zarathustra in view of all this a *seducer?*— But what does he himself say, as he returns again for the first time to his solitude? Precisely the opposite of everything that any "sage," "saint," "world-redeemer," or any other decadent would say in such a case.— Not only does he speak differently, he also *is* different.—

Now I go alone, my disciples, You, too, go now, alone. Thus I want it.

Go away from me and resist Zarathustra! And even better: be ashamed of him! Perhaps he deceived you.

The man of knowledge must not only love his enemies, he must also be able to hate his friends.

One repays a teacher badly if one always remains nothing but a pupil. And why do you not want to pluck at my wreath?

You revere me; but what if your reverence *tumbles* one day? Beware lest a statue slay you.

You say that you believe in Zarathustra? But what matters Zarathustra? You are my believers—but what matter all believers?

You had not yet sought yourselves; and you found me. Thus do all believers; therefore all faith amounts to so little.

Now I bid you lose me and find yourselves; and only *when you have all denied me* will I return to you.[6]

Friedrich Nietzsche

---

[6] *Ibid.,* First Part, last chapter.

On this perfect day, when everything is ripening and not only the grape turns brown, the eye of the sun just fell upon my life: I looked back, I looked forward, and never saw so many and such good things at once. It was not for nothing that I buried my forty-fourth year today; I had the *right* to bury it; whatever was life in it has been saved, is immortal. The first book of the *Revaluation of All Values,*[1] the *Songs of Zarathustra,*[2] the *Twilight of the Idols,* my attempt to philosophize with a hammer[3]—all presents of this year, indeed of its last quarter! *How could I fail to be grateful to my whole life?—*and so I tell my life to myself.

---

[1] *The Antichrist.*

[2] Published, after Nietzsche's collapse, under the title *Dionysus Dithyrambs,* in the same volume with *Zarathustra IV.*

[3] This image is explained in the preface of *Twilight:* ". . . idols, which are here touched with a hammer as with a tuning fork."

Why I Am So Wise

1

The good fortune of my existence, its uniqueness perhaps, lies in its fatality: I am, to express it in the form of a riddle, already dead as my father, while as my mother I am still living and becoming old. This dual descent, as it were, both from the highest and the lowest rung on the ladder of life, at the same time a *decadent* and a *beginning*—this, if anything, explains that neutrality, that freedom from all partiality in relation to the total problem of life, that perhaps distinguishes me. I have a subtler sense of smell for the signs of ascent and decline than any other human being before me; I am the teacher *par excellence* for this—I know both, I am both.

My father died at the age of thirty-six: he was delicate, kind, and morbid, as a being that is destined merely to pass by—more a gracious memory of life than life itself. In the same year in which his life went downward, mine, too, went downward: at thirty-six, I reached the lowest point of my vitality—I still lived, but without being able to see three steps ahead. Then—it was 1879—I retired from my professorship at Basel, spent the summer in St. Moritz like a shadow, and the next winter, than which not one in my life has been poorer in sunshine, in Naumburg *as* a shadow. This was my minimum: the *Wanderer and His Shadow* originated at this time. Doubtless, I then knew about shadows.

The following winter, my first one in Genoa, that sweetening and spiritualization which is almost inseparably connected with an extreme poverty of blood and muscle, produced *The Dawn*. The perfect brightness and cheerfulness, even exuberance of the spirit, reflected in this work, is compatible in my case not only with the most profound physiological weakness, but even with an excess of pain. In the midst of the torments that go with an uninterrupted three-day migraine, accompanied by laborious vomiting of phlegm, I possessed a dialectician's clarity *par excellence* and thought through with very cold blood matters for which under healthier circumstances I am not mountain-climber, not subtle, not *cold* enough. My readers know perhaps in what way I consider dialectic as a symptom of decadence; for example in the most famous case, the case of Socrates.

All pathological disturbances of the intellect, even that half-numb state that follows fever, have remained entirely foreign to me to this day; and I had to do research to find out about their nature and frequency. My blood moves slowly. Nobody has ever discovered any fever in me. A physician who treated me for some time as if my nerves were sick finally said: "It's not your nerves, it is rather I that am nervous." There is altogether no sign of any local degeneration; no organically conditioned stomach complaint, however profound the weakness of my gastric system may be as a consequence of over-all exhaustion. My eye trouble, too, though at times dangerously close to blindness, is only a consequence and not a cause: with every increase in vitality my ability to see has also increased again.

A long, all too long, series of years signifies recovery for me; unfortunately it also signifies relapse, decay, the periodicity of a kind of decadence. Need I say after all this that in questions of decadence I am *experienced?* I have spelled them forward and backward. Even that filigree art of grasping and comprehending in general, those fingers for *nuances,* that psychology of "looking around the corner," and whatever else is characteristic of me, was learned only then, is the true present of those days in which everything in me became subtler—observation itself as well as all organs of observation. Looking from the perspective of the sick toward *healthier* concepts and values and, conversely, looking again from the fullness and self-assurance of a *rich* life down into the secret work of the instinct of decadence—in this I have had the longest training, my truest experience; if in anything, I became master in *this.* Now I know how, have the know-how, to *reverse perspectives:* the first reason why a "revaluation of values" is perhaps possible for me alone.

2

Apart from the fact that I am a decadent, I am also the opposite. My proof for this is, among other things, that I have always instinctively chosen the *right* means against wretched states; while the decadent typically chooses means that are disadvantageous for him. As *summa summarum,*[1] I was healthy; as an angle, as a specialty, I was a decadent. The energy to choose absolute solitude and leave the life to which I had become accustomed; the insistence on not allowing myself any longer to be cared for, waited on, and *doctored*—that betrayed an absolute instinctive certainty about *what* was needed above all at that time. I took myself in hand, I made myself healthy again: the condition for this—every physiologist would admit that—is *that one be healthy at bottom.* A typically morbid being cannot become healthy, much less make itself healthy. For a typically healthy person, conversely, being sick can even become an energetic *stimulus* for life, for living *more.* This, in fact, is how that long period of sickness appears to me *now:* as it were, I discovered life anew, including myself; I tasted all good and even little things, as others cannot easily taste them—I turned my will to health, to *life,* into a philosophy.

For it should be noted: it was during the years of my lowest vitality that I *ceased* to be a pessimist; the instinct of self-restoration *forbade* me a philosophy of poverty and discouragement.

What is it, fundamentally, that allows us to recognize *who has turned out well?* That a well-turned-out person pleases our senses, that he is carved from wood that is hard, delicate, and at the same time smells good. He has a taste only for what is good for him; his pleasure, his delight cease where the measure of what is good for him is transgressed. He guesses what remedies avail against what is harmful; he exploits bad accidents to his advantage; what does not kill him makes him stronger.[2] Instinctively, he collects from everything he sees, hears, lives through, *his* sum: he is a principle of selection, he discards much. He is always in his own company,

---

[1] Over-all.

[2] Cf. *Twilight,* Chapter I, section 8 (*Portable Nietzsche,* p. 467).

whether he associates with books, human beings, or landscapes: he honors by *choosing*, by *admitting*, by *trusting*. He reacts slowly to all kinds of stimuli, with that slowness which long caution and deliberate pride have bred in him: he examines the stimulus that approaches him, he is far from meeting it halfway. He believes neither in "misfortune" nor in "guilt": he comes to terms with himself, with others; he knows how to *forget*—he is strong enough; hence everything *must* turn out for his best.

Well then, I am the *opposite* of a decadent, for I have just described *myself*.

3

This *dual* series of experiences, this access to apparently separate worlds, is repeated in my nature in every respect: I am a *Doppelgänger*, I have a "second" face in addition to the first. *And* perhaps also a third.

Even by virtue of my descent, I am granted an eye beyond all merely local, merely nationally conditioned perspectives; it is not difficult for me to be a "good European." On the other hand, I am perhaps more German than present-day Germans, mere citizens of the German *Reich*, could possibly be—I, the last *anti-political* German. And yet my ancestors were Polish noblemen: I have many racial instincts in my body from that source—who knows? In the end perhaps even the *liberum veto*.[1]

When I consider how often I am addressed as a Pole when I travel, even by Poles themselves, and how rarely I am taken for a German, it might seem that I have been merely externally *sprinkled* with what is German. Yet my mother, Franziska Oehler, is at any rate something very German; ditto, my grandmother on my father's side, Erdmuthe Krause. The latter lived all her youth in the middle

---

[1] Unrestricted veto—one of the traditional privileges of the members of the Polish Diet.

During the Nazi period, one of Nietzsche's relatives, Max Oehler, a retired major, went to great lengths to prove that Nietzsche had been racially pure: "Nietzsches angebliche polnische Herkunft" (N's alleged Polish descent) in *Ostdeutsche Monatshefte*, 18 (1938), 679–82, and *Nietzsches Ahnentafel* (N's pedigree), Weimar, 1938.

of good old Weimar, not without some connection with the circle of Goethe. Her brother, the professor of theology Krause in Königsberg, was called to Weimar as general superintendent after Herder's death. It is not impossible that her mother, my great-grandmother, is mentioned in the diary of the young Goethe under the name of "Muthgen." Her second marriage was with the superintendent Nietzsche in Eilenburg; and in the great war year of 1813, on the day that Napoleon entered Eilenburg with his general staff, on the tenth of October, she gave birth. As a Saxon, she was a great admirer of Napoleon; it could be that I still am, too. My father, born in 1813, died in 1849. Before he accepted the pastor's position in the parish of Röcken, not far from Lützen, he lived for a few years in the castle of Altenburg and taught the four princesses there. His pupils are now the Queen of Hanover, the Grand Duchess Constantine, the Grand Duchess of Altenburg, and the Princess Therese of Saxe-Altenburg. He was full of deep reverence for the Prussian king Frederick William IV, from whom he had also received his pastoral position; the events of 1848 grieved him beyond all measure. I myself, born on the birthday of the above named king, on the fifteenth of October, received, as fitting, the Hohenzollern name *Friedrich* Wilhelm. There was at least one advantage to the choice of this day: my birthday was a holiday throughout my childhood.

I consider it a great privilege to have had such a father: it even seems to me that this explains whatever else I have of privileges—*not* including life, the great Yes to life. Above all, that it requires no resolve on my part, but merely biding my time, to enter quite involuntarily into a world of lofty and delicate things: I am at home there, my inmost passion becomes free only there. That I have almost paid with my life for this privilege is certainly no unfair trade.

In order to understand anything at all of my *Zarathustra* one must perhaps be similarly conditioned as I am—with one foot *beyond* life.

4

I have never understood the art of predisposing people against me—this, too, I owe to my incomparable father—even when it seemed highly desirable to me. However un-Christian this may seem, I am not even predisposed against myself. You can turn my life this way and that, you will rarely find traces, and actually only once, that anybody felt ill will toward me—but perhaps rather too many traces of *good* will.

Even my experiences with people with whom everybody has bad experiences bear witness, without exception, in their favor: I tame every bear, I make even buffoons behave themselves. During the seven years that I taught Greek in the senior class in the *Pädagogium* in Basel, I never had occasion to punish anyone; the laziest boys worked hard. I am always equal to accidents; I have to be unprepared to be master of myself. Let the instrument be what it may, let it be as out of tune as only the instrument "man" can be—I should have to be sick if I should not succeed in getting out of it something worth hearing. And how often have I been told by the "instruments" themselves that they had never heard themselves like that.— Most beautifully perhaps by Heinrich von Stein,[1] who died so unpardonably young. Once, after he had courteously requested permission, he appeared for three days in Sils Maria, explaining to everybody that he had *not* come to see the Engadine. This excellent human being, who had walked into the Wagnerian morass with all the impetuous simplicity of a Prussian Junker (and in addition even into that of Dühring![2]), acted during these three days like one transformed by a tempest of freedom, like one who has suddenly been lifted to his own height and acquired wings. I always said to him that this was due to the good air up here, that this happened to everybody, that one was not for nothing six thousand feet above Bayreuth[3]—but he would not believe me.

---

[1] For Nietzsche's relation to this young man, see my note on the "Aftersong" that concludes *Beyond Good and Evil*, p. 429 above.

[2] See my note in *Genealogy* II, section 11, p. 510 above.

[3] The capital of the Wagner cult. Stein admired Wagner as well as Nietzsche.

If, in spite of that, some small and great misdemeanors have been committed against me, "the will" cannot be blamed for this, least of all any *ill* will: sooner could I complain, as I have already suggested, of the good will that has done no small mischief in my life. My experiences entitle me to be quite generally suspicious of the so-called "selfless" drives, of all "neighbor love" that is ready to give advice and go into action. It always seems a weakness to me, a particular case of being incapable of resisting stimuli: *pity* is considered a virtue only among decadents. I reproach those who are full of pity for easily losing a sense of shame, of respect, of sensitivity for distances; before you know it, pity begins to smell of the mob and becomes scarcely distinguishable from bad manners—and sometimes pitying hands can interfere in a downright destructive manner in a great destiny, in the growing solitude of one wounded, in a privileged right to heavy guilt.

The overcoming of pity I count among the *noble* virtues: as "Zarathustra's temptation" I invented a situation in which a great cry of distress reaches him, as pity tries to attack him like a final sin that would entice him away from *himself.*[4] To remain the master at this point, to keep the eminence of one's task undefiled by the many lower and more myopic impulses that are at work in so-called selfless actions, that is the test, perhaps the ultimate test, which a Zarathustra must pass—his real *proof* of strength.

5

At another point as well, I am merely my father once more and, as it were, his continued life after an all-too-early death. Like everyone who has never lived among his equals and who finds the concept of "retaliation" as inaccessible as, say, the concept of "equal rights," I forbid myself all countermeasures, all protective measures, and, as is only fair, also any defense, any "justification," in cases when some small or *very great* folly is perpetrated against me. My kind of retaliation consists in following up the stupidity as fast as possible with some good sense: that way one may actually

---

[4] *Zarathustra IV,* Chapter 2.

catch up with it.[1] Metaphorically speaking, I send a box of confections to get rid of a painful story.

One needs only to do me some wrong, I "repay" it—you may be sure of that: soon I find an opportunity for expressing my gratitude to the "evil-doer" (at times even for his evil deed)—or to *ask* him for something, which can be more obliging than giving something.

It also seems to me that the rudest word, the rudest letter are still more benign, more decent than silence. Those who remain silent are almost always lacking in delicacy and courtesy of the heart. Silence is an objection; swallowing things leads of necessity to a bad character—it even upsets the stomach. All who remain silent are dyspeptic.

You see, I don't want rudeness to be underestimated: it is by far the *most humane* form of contradiction and, in the midst of effeminacy, one of our foremost virtues.

If one is rich enough for this, it is even a good fortune to be in the wrong. A god who would come to earth must not *do* anything except wrong: not to take the punishment upon oneself but the *guilt* would be divine.[2]

6

Freedom from *ressentiment,* enlightenment about *ressentiment*—who knows how much I am ultimately indebted, in this respect also, to my protracted sickness! This problem is far from simple: one must have experienced it from strength as well as from weakness. If anything at all must be adduced against being sick and being weak, it is that man's really remedial instinct, his *fighting*

---

[1] Cf. the chapter "On The Adder's Bite" in *Zarathustra I:* "If you have an enemy, do not requite him evil with good, for that would put him to shame. Rather prove that he did you some good. And rather be angry than put to shame. . . ."

[2] Cf. *ibid.,* "Would that you might invent for me the love that bears not only all punishment but also all guilt!" This theme is developed in Sartre's *Flies.* For Nietzsche's immense influence on *The Flies,* see my article on "Nietzsche Between Homer and Sartre" in *Revue internationale de philosophie,* 1964.

instinct[1] wears out. One cannot get rid of anything, one cannot get over anything, one cannot repel anything—everything hurts. Men and things obtrude too closely; experiences strike one too deeply; memory becomes a festering wound. Sickness itself *is* a kind of *ressentiment*.

Against all this the sick person has only one great remedy: I call it *Russian fatalism,* that fatalism without revolt which is exemplified by a Russian soldier who, finding a campaign too strenuous, finally lies down in the snow. No longer to accept anything at all, no longer to take anything, no longer to absorb anything—to cease reacting altogether.

This fatalism is not always merely the courage to die; it can also preserve life under the most perilous conditions by reducing the metabolism, slowing it down, as a kind of will to hibernate. Carrying this logic a few steps further, we arrive at the fakir who sleeps for weeks in a grave.

Because one would use oneself up too quickly if one reacted in *any* way, one does not react at all any more: this is the logic. Nothing burns one up faster than the affects of *ressentiment*. Anger, pathological vulnerability, impotent lust for revenge, thirst for revenge, poison-mixing in any sense—no reaction could be more disadvantageous for the exhausted: such affects involve a rapid consumption of nervous energy, a pathological increase of harmful excretions—for example, of the gall bladder into the stomach. *Ressentiment* is what is forbidden *par excellence* for the sick —it is their specific evil—unfortunately also their most natural inclination.

This was comprehended by that profound physiologist, the Buddha. His "religion" should rather be called a kind of *hygiene,* lest it be confused with such pitiable phenomena as Christianity: its effectiveness was made conditional on the victory over *ressentiment*. To liberate the soul from this is the first step toward recovery. "Not by enmity is enmity ended; by friendliness is enmity ended": these words stand at the beginning of the doctrine of the

---

[1] *Wehr- und Waffen-Instinkt* (emphasized in the original) alludes to Luther's famous hymn, "A mighty fortress is our God, a good defense and weapons [*ein' gute Wehr und Waffen*]."

Buddha.[2] It is *not* morality that speaks thus; thus speaks physiology.

Born of weakness, *ressentiment* is most harmful for the weak themselves. Conversely, given a rich nature, it is a *superfluous* feeling; mastering this feeling is virtually what proves riches. Whoever knows how seriously my philosophy has pursued the fight against vengefulness and rancor, even into the doctrine of "free will" [3]— the fight against Christianity is merely a special case of this—will understand why I am making such a point of my own behavior, my *instinctive sureness* in practice. During periods of decadence I forbade myself such feelings as harmful; as soon as my vitality was rich and proud enough again, I forbade myself such feelings as *beneath* me. I displayed the "Russian fatalism" I mentioned by tenaciously clinging for years to all but intolerable situations, places, apartments, and society, merely because they happened to be given by accident: it was better than changing them, than *feeling* that they could be changed—than rebelling against them.

Any attempt to disturb me in this fatalism, to awaken me by force, used to annoy me mortally—and it actually was mortally dangerous every time.

Accepting oneself as if fated, not wishing oneself "different" —that is in such cases *great reason* itself.

7

War[1] is another matter. I am warlike by nature. Attacking is one of my instincts. Being *able* to be an enemy, *being* an enemy— perhaps that presupposes a strong nature; in any case, it belongs to every strong nature. It needs objects of resistance; hence it *looks*

---

[2] Cf. *The Dhammapada*, tr. Max Müller: "Hatred does not cease by hatred at any time: hatred ceases by love" (Chapter 1). Given the original context, Nietzsche's comments are not at all far-fetched.

[3] Cf. *Twilight*, "The Four Great Errors," section 7 (*Portable Nietzsche*, pp. 499ff.). Nietzsche's attack on Christianity cannot be understood apart from the point made in the sentence above.

[1] This section throws a great deal of light on some of Nietzsche's other writings—especially the chapter "On War and Warriors" in *Zarathustra I*. Cf. also below, "Human, All-Too-Human," section 1, and "Dawn," section 1.

for what resists: the *aggressive* pathos belongs just as necessarily to strength as vengefulness and rancor belong to weakness. Woman, for example, is vengeful: that is due to her weakness, as much as is her susceptibility to the distress of others.

The strength of those who attack can be measured in a way by the opposition they require: every growth is indicated by the search for a mighty opponent—or problem; for a warlike philosopher challenges problems, too, to single combat. The task is *not* simply to master what happens to resist, but what requires us to stake all our strength, suppleness, and fighting skill—opponents that are our *equals*.

Equality before the enemy: the first presupposition of an *honest* duel. Where one feels contempt, one *cannot* wage war; where one commands, where one sees something beneath oneself, one has no business waging war.

My practice of war can be summed up in four propositions. First: I only attack causes that are victorious; I may even wait until they become victorious.[2]

Second: I only attack causes against which I would not find allies, so that I stand alone—so that I compromise myself alone.— I have never taken a step publicly that did not compromise me: that is *my* criterion of doing right.

Third: I never attack persons; I merely avail myself of the person as of a strong magnifying glass that allows one to make visible a general but creeping and elusive calamity. Thus I attacked David Strauss—more precisely, the *success* of a senile book with the "cultured" people in Germany: I caught this culture in the act.

Thus I attacked Wagner—more precisely, the falseness, the half-couth instincts of our "culture" which mistakes the subtle for the rich, and the late for the great.

Fourth: I only attack things when every personal quarrel is excluded, when any background of bad experiences is lacking. On the contrary, attack is in my case a proof of good will, sometimes

---

2 Nietzsche's first great polemic was directed against the tremendous success of David Friedrich Strauss' book, *The Old Faith and The New,* and he broke with Wagner only after Wagner had returned to Germany and triumphed in Bayreuth.

even of gratitude. I honor, I distinguish by associating my name with that of a cause or a person: pro or con—that makes no difference to me at this point. When I wage war against Christianity I am entitled to this because I have never experienced misfortunes and frustrations from that quarter—the most serious Christians have always been well disposed toward me. I myself, an opponent of Christianity *de rigueur*,[3] am far from blaming individuals for the calamity of millennia.

8

May I still venture to sketch one final trait of my nature that causes me no little difficulties in my contacts with other men? My instinct for cleanliness is characterized by a perfectly uncanny sensitivity so that the proximity or—what am I saying?—the inmost parts, the "entrails" of every soul are physiologically perceived by me—*smelled*.

This sensitivity furnishes me with psychological antennae with which I feel and get a hold of every secret: the abundant *hidden* dirt at the bottom of many a character—perhaps the result of bad blood, but glossed over by education—enters my consciousness almost at the first contact. If my observation has not deceived me, such characters who offend my sense of cleanliness also sense from their side the reserve of my disgust—and this does not make them smell any better.

As has always been my wont—extreme cleanliness in relation to me is the presupposition of my existence; I perish under unclean conditions—I constantly swim and bathe and splash, as it were, in water—in some perfectly transparent and resplendent element. Hence association with people imposes no mean test on my patience: my humanity does *not* consist in feeling with men how they are, but in *enduring* that I feel with them.[1]

My humanity is a constant self-overcoming.

But I need *solitude*—which is to say, recovery, return to myself, the breath of a free, light, playful air.

[3] In accordance with good manners.

[1] Nietzsche's critique of pity should be considered in this light.

My whole *Zarathustra* is a dithyramb on solitude or, if I have been understood, on *cleanliness*.—Fortunately not on *pure foolishness*.[2]—. Those who have eyes for colors will compare it to a diamond.— *Nausea* over man, over the "rabble," was always my greatest danger.— Do you want to hear the words in which Zarathustra speaks of the *redemption* from nausea?

What was it that happened to me? How did I redeem myself from nausea? Who rejuvenated my sight? How did I fly to the height where no more rabble sits by the well? Was it my nausea itself that created wings for me and water-divining powers? Verily, I had to fly to the highest spheres that I might find the fount of pleasure again.

Oh, I found it, my brothers! Here, in the highest spheres the fount of pleasure wells up for me! And here is a life of which the rabble does not drink.

You flow for me almost too violently, fountain of pleasure. And often you empty the cup again by wanting to fill it. And I must still learn to approach you more modestly: all too violently my heart still flows toward you—my heart, upon which my summer burns, short, hot, melancholy, overblissful: how my summer heart craves your coolness!

Gone is the hesitant gloom of my spring! Gone the snowflakes of my malice in June![3] Summer have I become entirely, and summer noon! A summer in the highest spheres with cold wells and blissful silence: oh, come, my friends, that the silence may become still more blissful!

For this is *our* height and our home: we live here too high and steep for all the unclean and their thirst. Cast your pure eyes into the well of my pleasure, friends! How should that make it muddy? It shall laugh back at you in its own purity.

On the tree, Future, we build our nest; and in our solitude eagles shall bring us nourishment in their beaks. Verily, no nourishment that the unclean might share: they would think

---

[2] Wagner himself had characterized his Parsifal as the pure fool.

[3] This long passage is quoted from the chapter "On The Rabble" in *Zarathustra II*. But in *Zarathustra*, Nietzsche had "the malice of my snowflakes in June!"

they were devouring fire, and they would burn their mouths. Verily, we keep no homes here for the unclean: our pleasure would be an ice cave to their bodies and their spirits.

And we want to live over them like strong winds, neighbors of the eagles, neighbors of the snow, neighbors of the sun: thus live strong winds. And like a wind I yet want to blow among them one day, and with my spirit take away the breath of their spirit: thus my future wills it.

Verily, a strong wind is Zarathustra for all who are low; and this counsel I give to all his enemies and all who spit and spew: Beware of spitting *against* the wind! . . .

Why I Am So Clever

1

Why do I know a few things *more?* Why am I altogether so clever? I have never reflected on questions that are none—I have not wasted myself.

Really *religious* difficulties, for example, I don't know from experience. It has escaped me altogether in what way I was supposed to be "sinful." Likewise, I lack any reliable criterion for recognizing the bite of conscience: according to what one *hears* about it, the bite of conscience does not seem respectable to me.

I do not want to leave an action in the lurch *afterward;*[1] I should prefer to exclude the bad result, the *consequences,* from the question of value as a matter of principle. Faced with a bad result, one loses all too easily the *right* perspective for what one has done: the bite of conscience seems to me a kind of *"evil eye."* To hold in honor in one's heart even more what has failed, *because* it failed— that would go better with my morality.

"God," "immortality of the soul," "redemption," "beyond"— without exception, concepts to which I never devoted any attention, or time; not even as a child. Perhaps I have never been childlike enough for them?

I do not by any means know atheism as a result; even less as an event: it is a matter of course with me, from instinct. I am too inquisitive, too *questionable,* too exuberant to stand for any gross answer.[2] God is a gross answer, an indelicacy against us thinkers—

---

[1] Cf. *Twilight,* Chapter I, section 10: "Not to perpetrate cowardice against one's own acts! Not to leave them in the lurch afterwards! The bite of conscience is indecent." And *The Will to Power,* section 234: *"The bite of conscience:* a sign that the character is no match for the deed." Also Sartre's *The Flies* and Walter Kaufmann, "Nietzsche Between Homer and Sartre," *Revue internationale de philosophie,* 1964.

[2] *Ich bin zu neugierig, zu* fragwürdig, *zu übermütig, um mir eine faustgrobe Antwort gefallen zu lassen.* Nietzsche's atheism is not a "result"; it is a cor-

at bottom merely a gross prohibition for us: you shall not think!

I am much more interested in a question on which the "salvation of humanity" depends far more than on any theologians' curio: the question of *nutrition*. For ordinary use, one may formulate it thus: "how do *you,* among all people, have to eat to attain your maximum of strength, of *virtu* in the Renaissance style, of moraline-free[3] virtue?"

My experiences in this matter are as bad as possible; I am amazed how late I heard this question, how late I learned "reason" from these experiences. Only the complete worthlessness of our German education—its "idealism"—explains to me to some extent why at precisely this point I was backward to the point of holiness. This "education" which teaches one from the start to ignore *realities* and to pursue so-called "ideal" goals—a "classical education," for example—as if it were not hopeless from the start to unite "classical" and "German" into a single concept! More, it is amusing: only imagine a "classically educated" man with a Leipzig dialect! [4]

Indeed, till I reached a very mature age I always ate *badly:* morally speaking, "impersonally," "selflessly," "altruistically"—for the benefit of cooks and other fellow Christians. By means of Leipzig *cuisine,* for example, I very earnestly denied my "will to life" at the time when I first read Schopenhauer (1865). To upset one's stomach for the sake of inadequate nutrition—this problem seemed to me to be solved incredibly well by the aforementioned

---

rolary of his commitment to question every conviction, including his own convictions.

In a sense, of course, he does know atheism "as an event"; namely, as a cultural event which he designated with the words, "God is dead" (*Gay Science,* section 125; *Zarathustra,* Prologue, section 2: *Portable Nietzsche,* pp. 95f., 124). What he means above is that he did not experience the loss of faith in God as an event in his own life: he did not pass through any crisis of faith. Cf. *Genealogy* III, section 27, and Kaufmann's *Nietzsche,* Chapter 3, section I.

[3] The coinage of a man who neither smoked nor drank coffee. Cf. *Antichrist,* section 2 (*Portable Nietzsche,* p. 570).

[4] Leipzig, about a hundred miles south-southwest of Berlin, is one of the two major cities of Saxony and renowned for its exceptionally broad dialect. It is also the seat of a university at which Nietzsche studied classical philology.

cuisine. (It is said that 1866 brought about a change in this respect.)[5] But German cuisine quite generally—what doesn't it have on its conscience! Soup *before* the meal (in Venetian cookbooks of the sixteenth century this is still called *alla tedesca*);[6] overcooked meats, vegetables cooked with fat and flour; the degeneration of pastries and puddings into paperweights! Add to this the virtually bestial prandial drinking habits of the ancient, and by no means only the *ancient* Germans, and you will understand the origin of the *German spirit*—from distressed intestines.

The German spirit is an indigestion: it does not finish with anything.

But *English* diet, too—which is, compared to the German and even to the French, a kind of "return to nature," meaning to cannibalism—is profoundly at odds with my instincts: it seems to me that it gives the spirit *heavy* feet—the feet of English women.

The best *cuisine* is that of *Piedmont.*[7]

Alcohol is bad for me: a single glass of wine or beer in one day is quite sufficient to turn my life into a vale of misery—the people of Munich are my antipodes. Assuming that I did not comprehend this until rather late, I really *experienced* it from childhood. As a boy I believed that drinking wine was, like smoking, to begin with merely a vanity of young men, and later on a bad habit. Perhaps this *harsh* judgment should be blamed in part on the wine of Naumburg.[8] To believe that wine *exhilarates* I should have to be a Christian—believing what is for me an absurdity. Strangely enough, in spite of this extreme vulnerability to *small,* strongly diluted doses of alcohol, I almost become a sailor when it is a matter of *strong* doses. Even as a boy, my fortitude appeared at that point. Writing a long Latin essay in a single night, and copying it over, too, with the ambition in my pen to emulate my model, Sallust, in

---

[5] In June 1866, during the war with Austria, the Prussians marched into Saxony and occupied Dresden (the capital).

[6] After the German manner.

[7] The north-westernmost province of Italy, which borders on France and Switzerland. Its biggest city is Turin, where Nietzsche lived for two months in the spring of 1888, and again from September 21, 1888, until his collapse in January, 1889.

[8] The city, thirty miles southwest of Leipzig, where Nietzsche had grown up.

severity and compactness, and to pour some grog of the heaviest caliber over my Latin—even when I was a student at the venerable Schulpforta,[9] that did not in any way disagree with my physiology, nor perhaps with that of Sallust—however it disagreed with the venerable Schulpforta.

Later, around the middle of life, to be sure, I decided more and more strictly *against* all "spirits": I, an opponent of vegetarianism from experience, just like Richard Wagner, who converted me, cannot advise all *more spiritual* natures earnestly enough to abstain entirely from alcohol. *Water* is sufficient.

I prefer towns in which opportunities abound for dipping from running wells (Nizza, Turin, Sils); a small glass accompanies me like a dog.[10] *In vino veritas:*[11] it seems that here, too, I am at odds with all the world about the concept of "truth"—in my case, the spirit moves over water.[12]

A few more hints from my morality. A hearty meal is easier to digest than one that is too small. That the stomach as a whole becomes active is the first presupposition of a good digestion. One has to know the size of one's stomach. For the same reason one should be warned against those long-drawn-out meals which I call interrupted sacrificial feasts—those at a *table d'hôte*.

No meals between meals, no coffee: coffee spreads darkness. *Tea* is wholesome only in the morning. A little, but strong: tea is very unwholesome and sicklies one o'er the whole day if it is too weak by a single degree. Everybody has his own measure, often between the narrowest and most delicate limits. In a climate that is very *agaçant*,[13] tea is not advisable for a beginning: one should begin an hour earlier with a cup of thick, oil-less cocoa.

Sit as little as possible; give no credence to any thought that

---

[9] Perhaps the most famous boarding school in Germany.

[10] This is surely the meaning intended, although *ein kleines Glas läuft mir nach wie ein Hund* means literally: a small glass runs after me like a dog. This sentence has been adduced—very unreasonably—as evidence that Nietzsche was suffering from hallucinations and no longer sane when he wrote *Ecce Homo.*

[11] In wine there is truth.

[12] Allusion to Genesis 1.2.

[13] Provocative.

was not born outdoors while one moved about freely—in which the muscles are not celebrating a feast, too. All prejudices[14] come from the intestines.

The sedentary life—as I have said once before[15]—is the real *sin* against the holy spirit.

2

The question of *place* and *climate* is most closely related to the question of nutrition. Nobody is free to live everywhere; and whoever has to solve great problems that challenge all his strength actually has a very restricted choice in this matter. The influence of climate on our *metabolism,* its retardation, its acceleration, goes so far that a mistaken choice of place and climate can not only estrange a man from his task but can actually keep it from him: he never gets to see it. His animal *vigor* has never become great enough for him to attain that freedom which overflows into the most spiritual regions and allows one to recognize: *this* only I can do.

The slightest sluggishness of the intestines is entirely sufficient, once it has become a bad habit, to turn a genius into something mediocre, something "German." The German climate alone is enough to discourage strong, even inherently heroic, intestines. The *tempo* of the metabolism is strictly proportionate to the mobility or lameness of the spirit's *feet;* the "spirit" itself is after all merely an aspect of this metabolism. List the places where men with *esprit*[1] are living or have lived, where wit, subtlety, and malice belonged to happiness, where genius found its home almost of necessity: all of them have excellent dry air. Paris, Provence, Florence, Jerusalem, Athens—these names prove something: genius *depends* on dry air, on clear skies—that is, on a rapid metabolism, on the possibility of drawing again and again on great, even tre-

---

14 *Vorurteile. Vorteile* (advantages) in Karl Schlechta's edition is a misprint.

15 *Twilight,* Chapter I, section 34 (*Portable Nietzsche,* p. 471).

1 *Geistreiche Menschen. Geistreich,* literally rich in spirit, means ingenious, witty, intelligent, bright.

mendous quantities of strength. I know of a case in which a spirit of generous predisposition, destined for greatness, became, merely because he lacked any delicate instinct for climate, narrow, withdrawn, a peevish specialist. And I myself might ultimately have become just such a case, if my sickness had not forced me to see reason, to reflect on reason in reality. Now that the effects of climate and weather are familiar to me from long experience and I take readings from myself as from a very subtle and reliable instrument—and even during a short journey, say, from Turin to Milan, my system registers the change in the humidity—I reflect with horror on the *dismal* fact that my life, except for the last ten years, the years when my life was in peril, was spent entirely in the wrong places that were nothing short of *forbidden* to me. Naumburg, Schulpforta, the province of Thuringia quite generally, Leipzig, Basel, Venice—so many disastrous places for my physiology.

Altogether, I have no welcome memories whatever from my whole childhood and youth; but it would be folly to drag in socalled "moral" reasons, such as the undeniable lack of adequate company: for this lack persists today as it has always persisted, without preventing me from being cheerful and brave. Rather it was the ignorance *in physiologicis*—that damned "idealism"—that was the real calamity in my life, totally superfluous and stupid, something of which nothing good ever grew, for which there is no compensation, no counterbalance. The consequences of this "idealism" provide my explanation of all blunders, all great instinctual aberrations and "modesties" that led me away from the *task* of my life; for example, that I became a philologist—why not at least a physician or something else that opens one's eyes?

During my Basel period [2] my whole spiritual diet, including the way I divided up my day, was a completely senseless abuse of extraordinary resources, without any new supply to cover this consumption in any way, without even any thought about consumption and replenishment. Any refined self-concern, any protection by some commanding instinct was lacking; I simply posited myself as

---

[2] The ten years when Nietzsche was a professor of classical philology at the University of Basel, Switzerland.

equal to any nobody; it was a "selflessness," an oblivion of all distance between myself and others that I shall never forgive myself. When I was close to the end, *because* I was close to the end, I began to reflect on this fundamental unreason of my life—this "idealism." Only my sickness brought me to reason.

3

The choice of nutrition; the choice of climate and place: the third point at which one must not commit a blunder at any price is the choice of *one's own kind of recreation*. Here, too, depending on the degree to which a spirit is *sui generis*,[1] the limits of what is permitted to him, that is, profitable for him, are narrow, quite narrow. In my case, every kind of reading belongs among my recreations—hence among the things that liberate me from myself, that allow me to walk about in strange sciences and souls—that I no longer take seriously. Reading is precisely my recreation from my own seriousness. During periods when I am hard at work you will not find me surrounded by books: I'd beware of letting anyone near me talk, much less think. And that is what reading would mean.

Has it been noted that in that profound tension to which pregnancy condemns the spirit, and at bottom the whole organism, chance and any kind of stimulus from the outside have too vehement an effect and strike[2] too deep? One must avoid chance and outside stimuli as much as possible; a kind of walling oneself in belongs among the foremost instinctive precautions of spiritual pregnancy. Should I permit an *alien* thought to scale the wall secretly?— And that is what reading would mean.

The periods of work and fertility are followed by periods of recreation: come to me, pleasant, brilliant, clever books!

Will it be German books?

I must count back half a year before catching myself with a book in my hand. What was it?— A superb study by Victor Bro-

---

[1] Unique.
[2] *"Einschlägt"* (placed in quotes by Nietzsche) suggests lightning.

chard, *Les Sceptiques Grecs*,[3] in which my *Laertiana*[4] are also put to good use. The skeptics, the only honorable type among the equivocal, quinquivocal tribe of philosophers!

Otherwise I almost always seek refuge with the same books—actually, a small number—books *proved to me*. Perhaps it is not my way to read much, or diverse things: a reading room makes me sick. Nor is it my way to love much, or diverse things. Caution, even hostility against new books comes closer to my instincts than "tolerance," *"largeur du coeur,"* [5] and other "neighbor love." [6]

It is a small number of old Frenchmen to whom I return again and again: I believe only in French culture[7] and consider everything else in Europe today that calls itself "culture" a misunderstanding—not to speak of German culture.

The few cases of high culture that I have encountered in Germany have all been of French origin, especially Frau Cosima Wagner, by far the first voice in matters of taste that I have ever heard.

The fact that I do not read but *love* Pascal, as the most instructive victim of Christianity, murdered slowly, first physically, then psychologically—the whole logic of this most gruesome form of inhuman cruelty; that I have in my spirit—who knows? perhaps also in my body—something of Montaigne's sportiveness; that my artist's taste vindicates the names of Molière, Corneille, and Racine, not without fury, against a wild genius like Shakespeare—all that does not preclude in the end that I find even the most recent Frenchmen charming company. I do not see from what century of the past one could dredge up such inquisitive and at the same time such delicate psychologists as in contemporary Paris: tentatively—for their number is far from small—I name Messieurs Paul Bourget, Pierre Loti, Gyp, Meilhac, Anatole France, Jules Lemaître, or,

---

[3] The Greek skeptics.

[4] Nietzsche's early philological studies of Diogenes Laertius: *De Laertii Diogenis fontibus* (On Diogenes Laertius' sources, 1868 and 1869) and *Beiträge zur Quellenkunde und Kritik des Laertius Diogenes* (contributions to the critique and the study of the sources of Diogenes Laertius, 1870).

[5] Largeness of heart.

[6] Nietzsche had corrected printer's proofs and given his *imprimatur* up to this point in the book, before he collapsed.

[7] The word here rendered several times as "culture" is *Bildung*.

to single out one of the strong race, a genuine Latin toward whom I
am especially well disposed, Guy de Maupassant.[8] Between ourselves, I prefer *this* generation even to their great teachers who,
without exception, have been corrupted by German philosophy
(M. Taine, for example, by Hegel, to whom he owes his misunderstanding of great men and ages). As far as Germany extends, she
corrupts culture. Only the war[9] "redeemed" the spirit in France.

Stendhal, one of the most beautiful accidents of my life—for
whatever marks an epoch in it came my way by accident, never
through someone's recommendation—is truly invaluable with his
anticipatory psychologist's eye, with his knack for the facts which
is reminiscent of the greatest of factual men (*ex ungue Napole-
onem*),[10] and finally not least as an *honest* atheist—a species that
is rare in France and almost impossible to find—with all due respect for *Prosper Mérimée*.[11]

Perhaps I am even envious of Stendhal? He took away from
me the best atheistical joke that precisely I might have made:
"God's only excuse is that he does not exist."

---

[8] Paul Bourget (1852–1935), a critic and novelist, wrote, among other things,
Essais de psychologie contemporaine, of which the first volume (1883) contains a chapter *"Théorie de la décadence."* On the question of Bourget's influence on Nietzsche see the first footnote in Chapter 2 of my *Nietzsche*.

Pierre Loti was the pen name of Louis Marie Julien Viaud (1850–1923)
who wrote, e.g., *Pêcheur d'Islande* (the Iceland fisherman; 1886).

Gyp was the pen name of Sibylle Gabrielle Marie Antoinette Riqueti de
Mirabeau, Comtesse de Martel de Janville (1850–1932), a very prolific
writer.

Henri Meilhac (1831–1897) was a dramatist and collaborated with
Ludovic Halévy (1834–1908) on a large number of operettas, farces, and
comedies, including librettos for Offenbach; e.g., *La Belle Hélène* (1864).

Anatole France was the pen name of Jacques Anatole Thibault (1844–
1924), generally regarded as one of the leading French writers of his time.

François Élie Jules Lemaître (1853–1914) was a critic and dramatist.

Guy de Maupassant (1850–1893), though also a poet and novelist, is
remembered chiefly for his magnificent short stories. He died in an insane
asylum.

[9] The Franco-Prussian War of 1870–71.

[10] From the claw (you can tell) Napoleon. Nietzsche's variation of *ex ungue
leonem* (from the claw, a lion).

[11] Novelist, essayist, and archaeologist (1803–1870), now best remembered
for his *Carmen* (1847), which became the basis of the libretto for Georges
Bizet's opera.

I myself have said somewhere: what has been the greatest objection to existence so far? *God*.[12]

4

The highest concept of the lyrical poet was given to me by *Heinrich Heine*. I seek in vain in all the realms of history for an equally sweet and passionate music. He possessed that divine malice without which I cannot imagine perfection: I estimate the value of men, of races, according to the necessity by which they cannot conceive the god apart from the satyr.

And how he handles his German! One day it will be said that Heine and I have been by far the foremost artists of the German language—at an incalculable distance from everything mere Germans have done with it.[1]

I must be profoundly related to *Byron's* Manfred: all these abysses I found in myself; at the age of thirteen I was ripe for this work. I have no word, only a glance, for those who dare to pronounce the word "Faust" in the presence of Manfred.[2] The Germans are *incapable* of any notion of greatness; proof: Schumann. Simply from fury against this sugary Saxon, I composed a counter-overture for *Manfred* of which Hans von Bülow said that he had

---

[12] *Twilight*, "The Four Great Errors," section 8 (*Portable Nietzsche*, p. 501).

[1] *Ecce Homo* was published in 1908. The same year Thomas Mann penned a "Note on Heine" (*Notiz über Heine*) in which he said: "Of his works I have long loved the book on Börne most. . . . His psychology of the Nazarene type anticipates Nietzsche. . . . And incidentally no German prose prior to Nietzsche's matches its genius" (*Rede und Antwort* [speech and reply], 1922, p. 382). Nietzsche's reference to "mere Germans" makes a point of the fact that Heine was a Jew (and very widely resented), and Nietzsche took himself to be of Polish descent.

[2] Nietzsche neither emphasizes book titles nor usually places them in quotes after the German manner; but the comparison Nietzsche intends is presumably between the two heroes, Faust and Manfred. Nietzsche's tremendous admiration for Goethe was not primarily based on *Faust*. Cf. *Portable Nietzsche*, pp. 69f. and 553ff., and for further quotations Kaufmann's *Nietzsche*, the final pages of Chapter 4.

never seen anything like it on paper, and he called it rape of Euterpe.[3]

When I seek my ultimate formula for *Shakespeare,* I always find only this: he conceived of the type of Caesar. That sort of thing cannot be guessed: one either is it, or one is not. The great poet dips *only* from his own reality—up to the point where afterward he cannot endure his work any longer.

When I have looked into my *Zarathustra,* I walk up and down in my room for half an hour, unable to master an unbearable fit of sobbing.

I know no more heart-rending reading than Shakespeare: what must a man have suffered to have such a need of being a buffoon! [4]

Is Hamlet *understood?* Not doubt, *certainty* is what drives one insane.[5]— But one must be profound, an abyss, a philosopher to feel that way.— We are all *afraid* of truth.

And let me confess it: I feel instinctively sure and certain that Lord Bacon was the originator, the self-tormentor[6] of this uncanniest kind of literature: what is the pitiable chatter of American flat- and muddle-heads to *me?* But the strength required for the vision of the most powerful reality is not only compatible with the most powerful strength for action, for monstrous action, for crime—it even presupposes it.[7]

We are very far from knowing enough about Lord Bacon, the first realist in every great sense of that word, to know everything he did, wanted, and experienced in himself.

---

[3] The muse of music. Bülow (1830–1894) was a pianist and conductor. In 1857 he married Cosima Liszt, who later left him for Richard Wagner, whom she married in 1870.

[4] A hint for readers of *Ecce Homo.*

[5] Cf. *The Birth of Tragedy,* end of section 7.

[6] *Selbsttierquäler:* literally, self-animal-tormentor. Incidentally, Freud believed that the Earl of Oxford had written "Shakespeare's" plays.

[7] Presumably Nietzsche means that he has been persuaded not by American Baconians but by considerations of his own. Bacon was Lord Chancellor, and the "crime" to which he pleaded guilty in 1621 was bribery. He explained: "I was the justest judge that was in England these fifty years; but it was the justest censure in Parliament that was these two hundred years." In accordance with the general practice of the age, he said, he had accepted gifts from litigants; but his judgment had never been swayed by a bribe.

And damn it, my dear critics! Suppose I had published my *Zarathustra* under another name—for example, that of Richard Wagner—the acuteness of two thousand years would not have been sufficient for anyone to guess that the author of *Human, All-Too-Human* is the visionary of *Zarathustra*.

5

Speaking of the recreations of my life, I must say a word to express my gratitude for what has been by far the most profound and cordial recreation of my life. Beyond a doubt, that was my intimate relationship with Richard Wagner. I'd let go cheap the whole rest of my human relationships; I should not want to give away out of my life at any price the days of Tribschen[1]—days of trust, of cheerfulness, of sublime accidents, of *profound* moments.

I do not know what experiences others have had with Wagner: *our* sky was never darkened by a single cloud.

And with that I return once more to France—I have no reasons but merely a contemptuous corner of the mouth for Wagnerians *et hoc genus omne*[2] who think they are honoring Wagner by finding him similar to *themselves*.

The way I am, so alien in my deepest instincts to everything German that the mere proximity of a German retards my digestion, the first contact with Wagner was also the first deep breath of my life: I experienced, I revered him as a *foreign* land, as an antithesis, as an incarnate protest against all "German virtues."

We who were children in the swamp air of the fifties are of necessity pessimists concerning the concept "German"; we simply cannot be anything but revolutionaries—we shall not come to terms with any state of affairs in which the *bigot*[3] is at the top. It is a matter of total indifference to me whether today he dons different

---

[1] The place in Switzerland where Wagner had lived and Nietzsche had often visited him.

[2] And all that tribe. Wagner *was* a Francophobe and Teutomaniac, but Nietzsche insists that he was very different indeed from his nationalist followers.

[3] *Mucker.*

colors, clothing himself in scarlet and putting on a hussar's uniform.[4]

Well then! Wagner was a revolutionary—he ran away from the Germans.[5]

As an *artist* one has no home in Europe, except Paris: the *délicatesse* in all five artistic senses that is presupposed by Wagner's art, the fingers for *nuances,* the psychological morbidity are found only in Paris. Nowhere else does one have this passion in questions of form, this seriousness in *mise en scène*[6]—which is Parisian seriousness *par excellence.* In Germany people simply lack any notion of the tremendous ambition that lives in the soul of a Parisian artist. Germans are good-natured—Wagner was anything but good-natured.

But I have long said adequately (in *Beyond Good and Evil,* section 256)[7] where Wagner belongs and who are his closest relatives: the late French romantics, that high-flying and yet rousing manner of artists like Delacroix, like Berlioz, with a characteristic *fond*[8] of sickness, of incurability—all of them fanatics of *expression,* virtuosos through and through.

Who was the first *intelligent* adherent of Wagner anywhere? Charles Baudelaire, who was also the first to understand Delacroix —that typical decadent in whom a whole tribe of artists recognized themselves—and perhaps he was also the last.[9]

What did I never forgive Wagner? That he *condescended* to the Germans—that he became *reichsdeutsch.*[10]

As far as Germany extends, she corrupts culture.[11]

---

[4] The allusion is primarily to Kaiser Wilhelm II, who had ascended to the throne in June 1888, but is also aimed at the German *Reich* in which Wagner had become a national—and nationalist—hero.

[5] During the time of their friendship Wagner was quite literally living in voluntary exile in Switzerland.

[6] Staging.

[7] Pp. 256f. in the MS is a slip.

[8] Core.

[9] That is, the last *intelligent* adherent of Wagner.

[10] That is, made common cause with the new German Empire.

[11] Quoting section 3 above.

6

All things considered, I could not have endured my youth without Wagner's music. For I was *condemned* to Germans. If one wants to rid oneself of an unbearable pressure, one needs hashish. Well then, I needed Wagner. Wagner is the antitoxin against everything German *par excellence*—a toxin, a poison, that I don't deny.

From the moment when there was a piano score of *Tristan*—my compliments, Herr von Bülow—I was a Wagnerian.[1] Wagner's

---

[1] This would take us back to the spring of 1861 when Nietzsche was sixteen. Indeed, the text of one of Nietzsche's own compositions, dated June 1861, "included an unmistakable token of the proximity of *Tristan und Isolde:* 'Wild wogt der Wahn, wo durch bewegt, das Wunder wollend mein Gemüth? [*sic*]' " (Frederick R. Love, *Young Nietzsche and the Wagnerian Experience,* Chapel Hill, N. C., University of North Carolina Press, 1963, p. 22; reviewed by Walter Kaufmann in *Journal of the History of Philosophy,* October 1965, pp. 284–86). The quoted passage reads like a parody of Wagner and makes little sense: "Wildly illusion surges, whereby moves the wonder wishing my bosom?"

Nevertheless, Love, making use of unpublished materials, including Nietzsche's compositions, argues convincingly that Nietzsche never was "a passionate devotee of Wagnerian music" (p. viii). He finds "nothing whatever Wagnerian" in Nietzsche's songs between 1862 and 1865 (p. 28); he cites a letter of the winter 1865–66 in which Nietzsche, then a student, wrote, "Three things are my recreations, but rare recreations, my Schopenhauer, Schumann's music, finally long walks"; and he cites a list Nietzsche made around the same time of his musical favorites: Schumann, Beethoven, and Schubert are most prominent, "two choral works by Bach are mentioned, 'ein paar' [a couple of] Lieder of Brahms, and of Wagner only the early opera *Tannhäuser,* listed indiscriminately next to a work by Meyerbeer" (p. 35).

Love argues further: "As for Wagner's music, it can be stated unequivocally that *Die Meistersinger* was the only one of the mature works which Nietzsche acquired fully on his own and the one which he knew best from actual performance" (p. 63). *Tristan* he heard only twice, in June 1872, in Munich, where "Hans von Bülow gave the European musical public its second chance to experience a production of *Tristan*" (p. 64). Love thinks that *Tristan* "became for Nietzsche the permanent symbol of his unforgettable Tribschen experience" because "Wagner himself must have opened his mind to the deeper meaning of his most radical work" (p. 65).

Love fails to note that Nietzsche's tribute to von Bülow in the text above evidently conflates two events: the one in 1861 to which Nietzsche alludes, and the other in 1872. Love also refers to (p. 69) but does not quote von Bülow's scathing letter to Nietzsche about one of Nietzsche's compositions. It is noteworthy that Nietzsche cites this letter in section 4 above, humor-

older works I deemed beneath myself—still too vulgar, too "German."

But to this day I am still looking for a work that equals the dangerous fascination and the gruesome[2] and sweet infinity of *Tristan*—and look in all the arts in vain. All the strangenesses of Leonardo da Vinci emerge from their spell at the first note of *Tristan*. This work is emphatically Wagner's *non plus ultra;* with the *Meistersinger* and the *Ring* he recuperated[3] from it. Becoming healthier—is a retrogression, given a nature like Wagner's.

I take it for a good fortune of the first order that I lived at the right time and among Germans, of all peoples, so that I was *ripe* for this work: that is how far the psychologist's inquisitiveness extends in my case. The world is poor for anyone who has never been sick enough for this "voluptuousness of hell": it is permitted, it is almost imperative, to employ a formula of the mystics at this point.

I think I know better than anyone else of what tremendous things Wagner is capable—the fifty worlds of alien ecstasies for which no one besides him had wings; and given the way I am, strong enough to turn even what is most questionable and dangerous to my advantage and thus to become stronger, I call Wagner the great benefactor of my life. That in which we are related—that

---

ously, without any trace of *ressentiment,* and that he goes out of his way in the text above to voice his gratitude to von Bülow.

Regarding Nietzsche's relationship to Wagner's music, Love is surely right in not regarding Nietzsche's break with Wagner as an act of self-betrayal (as many Wagnerians have done), concluding instead that "Nietzsche's infatuation with Wagnerian music . . . may indeed be regarded as an aberration" from his own line. But again it is noteworthy that Nietzsche makes a point of speaking of Wagner without *ressentiment* and with gratitude; and it is obviously possible to have *more opportunities* to hear *Die Meistersinger* and even, whether this is true in Nietzsche's case or not, to know and in some sense like this opera especially well, while yet considering *Tristan* "Wagner's *non plus ultra.*"

Nietzsche's judgments in *Ecce Homo* are plainly highly stylized: he loves Wagner—in spite of his Teutonomania, in spite of his ideas and his self-image, in spite of everything that eventually endeared him to his countrymen; he loves Wagner as the ultimate in decadence, as a kind of apotheosis of *French* romanticism, as fascinatingly sick—and *Tristan* fits into that picture a thousand times better than *Die Meistersinger.*

[2] *Schauerlich:* etymologically, what makes one shudder.

[3] *Er erholte sich.* Above, *Erholung* has been rendered several times as recreation.

we have suffered more profoundly, also from each other, than men of this century are capable of suffering—will link our names again and again, eternally; and as certainly as Wagner is merely a misunderstanding among Germans, just as certainly I am and always shall be.

Two centuries of psychological and artistic discipline must come first, my dear Teutons!— But with that one does not catch up.

7

I shall say another word for the most select ears: what I really want from music. That it be cheerful and profound like an afternoon in October. That it be individual, frolicsome, tender, a sweet small woman full of beastliness and charm.

I shall never admit that a German *could* know what music is. Those who are called German composers—the greatest above all —are *foreigners:* Slavs, Croats, Italians, Dutchmen—or Jews; otherwise, Germans of the strong race, *extinct* Germans, like Heinrich Schütz, Bach, and Handel. I myself am still enough of a Pole to surrender the rest of music for Chopin, excepting, for three reasons, Wagner's Siegfried Idyll, perhaps also a few things by Liszt, who surpasses all other musicians in his noble orchestral accents, and, finally, everything that grew beyond the Alps—*this* side.[1]

I should not know how to get along without Rossini; even less, without my own south in music, the music of my Venetian *maëstro Pietro Gasti.*[2] And when I say beyond the Alps, I really

---

[1] Nietzsche spent his summers in Switzerland, his winters in Italy, and wrote *Ecce Homo* in Turin.

[2] Heinrich Köselitz, a young composer who vastly admired Nietzsche, helped him prepare copies of his manuscripts for the printer, read proofs for him, and assisted him very devotedly. Nietzsche called him Peter Gast, and this became his pen name when he later became one of the editors of Nietzsche's works. His opera, "The Lion of Venice," never made a reputation for him as a composer, but Nietzsche's letters to Gast (1908) made him famous. His own letters to Nietzsche (2 vols., 1923–24) are much less interesting and not at all widely known. The passage in the text is plainly inspired by gratitude and to that extent offers a clue to some of Nietzsche's other judgments in *Ecce Homo:* he is often more concerned with his own attitudes and their fittingness, their style, than with their literal content.

merely say Venice. When I seek another word for music, I always find only the word Venice. I do not know how to distinguish between tears and music—I do not know how to think of happiness, of the *south,* without shudders of timidity.

> *At the bridge I stood*
> *lately in the brown night.*
> *From afar came a song:*
> *as a golden drop it welled*
> *over the quivering surface.*
> *Gondolas, lights, and music—*
> *drunken it swam out into the twilight.*
>
> *My soul, a stringed instrument,*
> *sang to itself, invisibly touched,*
> *a secret gondola song,*
> *quivering with iridescent happiness.*
> *—Did anyone listen to it?*

8

In all these matters—in the choice of nutrition, of place and climate, of recreation—an instinct of self-preservation issues its commandments, and it gains its most unambiguous expression as an instinct of *self-defense.* Not to see many things, not to hear many things, not to permit many things to come close—first imperative of prudence, first proof that one is no mere accident but a necessity. The usual word for this instinct of self-defense is *taste.* It commands us not only to say No when Yes would be "selfless" but also to say *No as rarely as possible.* To detach oneself, to separate oneself from anything that would make it necessary to keep saying No. The reason in this is that when defensive expenditures, be they ever so small, become the rule and a habit, they entail an extraordinary and entirely superfluous impoverishment. Our *great* expenses are composed of the most frequent small ones. Warding off, not letting things come close, involves an expenditure—let nobody deceive himself about this—energy *wasted* on negative ends. Merely through the constant need to ward off, one can become weak enough to be unable to defend oneself any longer.

Suppose I stepped out of my house and found, instead of quiet, aristocratic Turin, a small German town: my instinct would have to cast up a barrier to push back everything that would assail it from this pinched and flattened, cowardly world. Or I found a German big city—this built-up vice where nothing grows, where everything, good or bad, is imported. Wouldn't this compel me to become a *hedgehog?*

But having quills is a waste, even a double luxury when one can choose not to have quills but *open* hands.

Another counsel of prudence and self-defense is to *react as rarely as possible,* and to avoid situations and relationships that would condemn one to suspend, as it were, one's "freedom" and initiative and to become a mere reagent. As a parable I choose association with books. Scholars who at bottom do little nowadays but thumb books—philologists, at a moderate estimate, about 200 a day—ultimately lose entirely their capacity to think for themselves. When they don't thumb, they don't think. They *respond* to a stimulus (a thought they have read) whenever they think—in the end, they do nothing but react. Scholars spend all of their energies on saying Yes and No, on criticism of what others have thought—they themselves no longer think.

The instinct of self-defense has become worn-out in them; otherwise they would resist books. The scholar—a decadent.

I have seen this with my own eyes: gifted natures with a generous and free disposition, "read to ruin" in their thirties—merely matches that one has to strike to make them emit sparks—"thoughts."

Early in the morning, when day breaks, when all is fresh, in the dawn of one's strength—to *read a book* at such a time is simply depraved!

9

At this point the real answer to the question, *how one becomes what one is,* can no longer be avoided. And thus I touch on the masterpiece of the art of self-preservation—of *selfishness.*

For let us assume that the task, the destiny, the fate of the task transcends the average very significantly: in that case, nothing could be more dangerous than catching sight of oneself *with* this task. To become what one is, one must not have the faintest notion *what* one is. From this point of view even the *blunders* of life have their own meaning and value—the occasional side roads and wrong roads, the delays, "modesties," seriousness wasted on tasks that are remote from *the* task. All this can express a great prudence, even the supreme prudence: where *nosce te ipsum*[1] would be the recipe for ruin,[2] forgetting oneself, *misunderstanding* oneself, making oneself smaller, narrower, mediocre, become reason itself. Morally speaking: neighbor love, living for others, and other things *can* be a protective measure for preserving the hardest self-concern. This is the exception where, against my wont and conviction, I side with the "selfless" drives: here they work in the service of *self-love, of self-discipline.*[3]

The whole surface of consciousness—consciousness *is* a surface[4]—must be kept clear of all great imperatives. Beware even of every great word, every great pose! So many dangers that the instinct comes too soon to "understand itself"———. Meanwhile the organizing "idea" that is destined to rule keeps growing deep down —it begins to command; slowly it leads us *back* from side roads and wrong roads; it prepares *single* qualities and fitnesses that will one day prove to be indispensable as means toward a whole—one by one, it trains all *subservient* capacities before giving any hint of the dominant task, "goal," "aim," or "meaning."

Considered in this way, my life is simply wonderful. For the task of a *revaluation of all values* more capacities may have been needed than have ever dwelt together in a single individual—above all, even contrary capacities that had to be kept from disturbing, destroying one another. An order of rank among these capacities; distance; the art of separating without setting against one another; to mix nothing, to "reconcile" nothing; a tremendous variety that is nevertheless the opposite of chaos—this was the precondition, the long, secret work and artistry of my instinct. Its *higher protection*

---

[1] Know thyself.

[2] *Untergang.*

[3] *Selbstsucht, Selbstzucht.*

[4] This anti-Cartesian epigram anticipates Freud.

manifested itself to such a high degree that I never even suspected what was growing in me—and one day all my capacities, suddenly ripe, *leaped forth* in their ultimate perfection.[5] I cannot remember that I ever tried hard [6]—no trace of *struggle* can be demonstrated in my life; I am the opposite of a heroic nature. "Willing" something, "striving" [7] for something, envisaging a "purpose," a "wish"—I know none of this from experience. At this very moment I still look upon my future—an *ample* future!—as upon calm seas: there is no ripple of desire. I do not want in the least that anything should become different than it is; I myself do not want to become different.

But that is how I have always lived. I had no wishes. A man over forty-four who can say that he never strove[8] for *honors,* for *women,* for *money!*

Thus it happened, for example, that one day I was a university professor—no such idea had ever entered my mind, for I was barely twenty-four years old. Thus it happened two years earlier that one day I was suddenly a philologist—insofar as my *first* philological essay, my beginning in every sense, was requested by my teacher, Ritschl, for publication in his *Rheinisches Museum.*[9] (*Ritschl*—I say it with reverence—the only scholar of genius on whom I have laid eyes to this day. He was characterized by that agreeable corruption which distinguishes us Thuringians and which makes even Germans sympathetic: even to reach truth, we still prefer furtive paths. These words are not meant to underestimate my close compatriot, the *clever* Leopold von Ranke———.)[10]

---

[5] An allusion to the birth of Pallas Athene who was said to have sprung, fully armed, from the head of Zeus.

[6] *Dass ich mich je bemüht hätte.* Deliberately or not, Nietzsche pictures himself as the antithesis of Goethe's Faust who speaks of his ardent *Bemühn* in the first sentence of his first speech (line 357); and Faust's redemption after his death is explained by the angels in two of the most famous lines of German literature: "Who ever strives with all his power,/ We are allowed to save"; *Wer immer strebend sich bemüht,/ Den können wir erlösen* (lines 11936–37).

[7] *Streben:* see the preceding note.

[8] *Dass er sich nie . . . bemüht hat!*

[9] One of the leading professional journals.

[10] The great historian (1795–1886) was born in Wiehe, in Thuringia,

10

One will ask me why on earth I've been relating all these small things which are generally considered matters of complete indifference: I only harm myself, the more so if I am destined to represent great tasks. Answer: these small things—nutrition, place, climate, recreation, the whole casuistry of selfishness—are inconceivably more important than everything one has taken to be important so far. Precisely here one must begin to *relearn*. What mankind has so far considered seriously have not even been realities but mere imaginings—more strictly speaking, *lies* prompted by the bad instincts of sick natures that were harmful in the most profound sense —all these concepts, "God," "soul," "virtue," "sin," "beyond," "truth," "eternal life."— But the greatness of human nature, its "divinity," was sought in them.— All the problems of politics, of social organization, and of education have been falsified through and through because one mistook the most harmful men for great men—because one learned to despise "little" things, which means the basic concerns of life itself.[1]

When I now compare myself with the men who have so far

---

roughly thirty miles west of Röcken (near Lützen), where Nietzsche was born. And Ranke, like Nietzsche, got his secondary school education at Schulpforta.

[1] Podach (*Friedrich Nietzsches Werke*, 1961) reproduces a photograph of section 10 (plate XV) and points out that the spiral scribble used to delete the following passage at this point was characteristic of Nietzsche's sister and never employed by him (p. 408; cf. also pp. 245f.).

"Our present culture is ambiguous in the highest degree.— The German emperor making a pact with the pope, as if the pope were not the representative of deadly hostility to life!— What is being built today will no longer stand in three years.— When I measure myself against my *ability*, not to speak of what will come after me, a collapse, a construction without equal, then I more than any other mortal have a claim to the epithet of greatness."

In the first edition of *Ecce Homo* (1908) this paragraph was printed in a footnote in Raoul Richter's postscript (pp. 147f.) and introduced with the following comment: "There are only two passages of any length where the peculiarity of the crossing out and Peter Gast's testimony, based on his recollection, make it merely *probable* that the deletion was Nietzsche's own." The other passage will be found at the end of the discussion of "The Case of Wagner," below.

been honored as the *first,* the difference is palpable. I do not even count these so-called "first" men among men in general: for me they are the refuse of humanity, monsters of sickness and vengeful instincts; they are inhuman, disastrous, at bottom incurable, and revenge themselves on life.

I want to be their opposite: it is my privilege to have the subtlest sensitivity for all signs of healthy instincts. There is no pathological trait in me; even in periods of severe sickness I never became pathological; in vain would one seek for a trait of fanaticism in my character. There is not a moment in my life to which one could point to convict me of a presumptuous and pathetic[2] posture. The pathos of poses does *not* belong to greatness; whoever needs poses at all is *false.*— Beware of all picturesque men!

Life was easy for me—easiest when it made the hardest demands on me. Whoever saw me during the seventy days this fall when, without interruption, I did several things of the first rank the like of which nobody will do after me—or impose on me[3]—with a

---

[2] *Pathetisch* in German is closer in meaning to bombastic than it is to pitiful. The word is readily associated with an actor's style and with highly idealistic passages in drama—in Schiller's plays, for example—where big words are used freely and a laugh would puncture the whole effect. The same consideration applies to *Pathos* in the next sentence.

One may wonder whether this whole paragraph is starkly ironical or, on the contrary, totally lacking in self-awareness. Without denying that both alternatives contain a grain of truth, one may insist that Nietzsche's central point is important. He never lost the ability to laugh, and his self-image was the very antithesis of his sister's later image of him which, at her bidding, was translated into pictures and sculptures that she commissioned and for which she posed her brother who was by then a helpless invalid.

Finally, if we take seriously Nietzsche's words, "not a moment in my life"—as distinguished from "not a line in this book"—he is incontestably right. Consider how Dr. Paneth, one of Freud's friends, described Nietzsche of whom he saw a great deal in Nizza from December 26, 1883, until March 26, 1884: "There is not a trace of false pathos or the prophet's pose in him, as I had rather feared after his last work. Instead his manner is completely inoffensive and natural. . . . He told me, but without the least affectation or conceit, that he always felt himself to have a task . . ." For further quotations from his letters and some discussion, see Walter Kaufmann, *From Shakespeare to Existentialism* (Garden City, N.Y., Doubleday Anchor Books, 1960) pp. 323f.

[3] *Die kein Mensch mir nachmacht—oder vormacht* . . . If Nietzsche meant —and this possibility cannot be ruled out—"or has done before me," the text ought to read: *oder mir vorgemacht hat.*

responsibility for all millennia after me, will not have noticed any trace of tension in me; but rather an overflowing freshness and cheerfulness. I never ate with more pleasant feelings; I never slept better.

I do not know any other way of associating with great tasks than *play:* as a sign of greatness, this is an essential presupposition. The least compulsion, a gloomy mien, or any harsh tone in the throat are all objections to a man; how much more against his work!— One must not have any nerves.— *Suffering* from solitude is also an objection—I have suffered only from "multitudes."

At an absurdly early age, at seven, I already knew that no human word would ever reach me: has anyone ever seen me saddened on that account?

To this day I still have the same affability for everyone; I even treat with special respect those who are lowliest: in all of this there is not one grain of arrogance or secret contempt. If I despise a man, he *guesses* that I despise him: by my mere existence I outrage everything that has bad blood in its veins.

My formula for greatness in a human being is *amor fati:*[4] that one wants nothing to be different, not forward, not backward, not in all eternity. Not merely bear what is necessary, still less conceal it—all idealism is mendaciousness in the face of what is necessary—but *love* it.

---

[4] Love of fate. It should be noted how *Ecce Homo* exemplifies this attitude. As long as one overlooks this, as well as the fact that Nietzsche's life for the preceding decade, and more, had been troubled by continued ill health and excruciating physical pain, and that his books were, without exception, totally "unsuccessful," one does not begin to understand *Ecce Homo.*

Why I Write Such Good Books

1

I am one thing, my writings are another matter.— Before I discuss them, one by one, let me touch on the question of their being understood or *not* understood. I'll do it as casually as decency permits; for the time for this question certainly hasn't come yet. The time for me hasn't come yet: some are born posthumously.

Some day institutions will be needed in which men live and teach as I conceive of living and teaching; it might even happen that a few chairs will then be set aside for the interpretation of *Zarathustra*. But it would contradict my character entirely if I expected ears and hands for my truths today: that today one doesn't hear me and doesn't accept my ideas is not only understandable, it even seems right to me. I don't want to be confounded with others —not even by myself.

To repeat, one cannot find many traces of ill will in my life; and of literary ill will, too, I could scarcely relate a single case. But only too many of pure foolishness!

To me it seems one of the rarest distinctions that a man can accord himself if he takes one of my books into his hands—I even suppose that he first takes off his shoes,[1] not to speak of boots.

When Dr. Heinrich von Stein once complained very honestly that he didn't understand a word of my *Zarathustra*, I told him that this was perfectly in order: having understood six sentences from it—that is, to have really experienced them—would raise one to a higher level of existence than "modern" men could attain. Given this feeling of distance, how could I possibly wish to be read by those "moderns" whom I know!

My triumph is precisely the opposite of Schopenhauer's: I say, *"non legor, non legar."* [2]

---

[1] Allusion to Exodus 3:5.

[2] I am not read, I *will* not be read.

Not that I should like to underestimate the pleasure I have felt on several occasions at the *innocence* of people who said No to my writings. Only this past summer, at a time when I may have upset the balance of the whole rest of literature with my weighty, too weighty, literature, a professor from the University of Berlin suggested very amiably that I ought to try another form: nobody read such things.

In the last analysis, it was not Germany but Switzerland that produced the two extreme cases. An essay by Dr. V. Widmann in the *Bund,* about *Beyond Good and Evil,* under the title "Nietzsche's Dangerous Book," and a comprehensive report about my books in general by Karl Spitteler,[3] also in the *Bund,* represent a maximum in my life—I refrain from saying, of what.

The latter treated my *Zarathustra,* for example, as an advanced exercise in style, and expressed the wish that later on I might provide some content as well. Dr. Widmann expressed his respect for the courage I had shown in my attempt to abolish all decent feelings.[4]

---

[3] J. V. Widmann (1842–1911) published his review in the *Berner Bund* on September 16–17, 1888. In the *Encyclopedia of Poetry and Poetics,* ed. Alex Preminger (Princeton, N. J., Princeton University Press, 1965), Henri de Ziègler, former President of the University of Geneva, says of him in the article on "Swiss Poetry" (p. 830): "A fascinating grace of expression—rare in German-Swiss literature—distinguishes the anachronistic verse-idylls of Spitteler's friend J. V. Widmann."

Carl Spitteler (1845–1924) published the "comprehensive report," mentioned in the text, in the New Year's Supplement, 1888, of the *Bund.* On November 8, 1888, he published a very favorable review of *The Case of Wagner* in the *Bund.* This book he also reviewed in *Basler Nachrichten.* Nietzsche was so pleased with Spitteler's reaction to *The Case of Wagner* that he asked him to publish, with a preface, the passages from Nietzsche's earlier books that Nietzsche *then* decided—even before Spitteler had had time to decline—to publish himself: *Nietzsche contra Wagner.* In 1908 Spitteler published a small fifty-page pamphlet, *Meine Beziehungen zu Nietzsche* (my relations—or contacts—with Nietzsche; Munich, *Süddeutsche Monatshefte*). In Peter Gast's notes on Nietzsche's letters to him, February 26, 1888, and December 16, 1888, Gast took issue with Spitteler (*Friedrich Nietzsches Briefe an Peter Gast,* Leipzig, 1908, pp. 503, 517f.). In 1919 Spitteler received the Nobel Prize for literature.

See also note 4 below.

[4] At this point Nietzsche himself deleted the following passage in his MS: "Not that there was any lack of 'good will' in either case; even less, of intelligence. Indeed, I consider Herr Spitteler one of the most welcome and refined of all who write criticism today; his work on the French drama— not published yet—may be of the first rank. That much more do I seek

As the petty spite of accident would have it, every sentence in this latter piece was, with a consistency I admired, some truth stood on its head: one really had to do no more than "revalue all values" in order to hit the nail on the head about me in a truly remarkable manner—instead of hitting my head with a nail.— That makes an explanation only more desirable.

Ultimately, nobody can get more out of things, including books, than he already knows. For what one lacks access to from experience one will have no ear. Now let us imagine an extreme case: that a book speaks of nothing but events that lie altogether beyond the possibility of any frequent or even rare experience— that it is the first language for a new series of experiences. In that case, simply nothing will be heard, but there will be the acoustic illusion that where nothing is heard, nothing is there.

This is, in the end, my average experience and, if you will, the originality of my experience. Whoever thought he had understood something of me, had made up something out of me after his own image—not uncommonly an antithesis to me; for example, an "idealist"—and whoever had understood nothing of me, denied that I need be considered at all.

The word "overman," as the designation of a type of supreme achievement, as opposed to "modern" men, to "good" men, to Christians and other nihilists—a word that in the mouth of a Zarathustra, the annihilator of morality, becomes a very pensive word —has been understood almost everywhere with the utmost innocence in the sense of those very values whose opposite Zarathustra was meant to represent—that is, as an "idealistic" type of a higher kind of man, half "saint," half "genius."

Other scholarly oxen have suspected me of Darwinism on that account. Even the "hero worship" of that unconscious and involuntary conterfeiter, Carlyle, which I have repudiated so maliciously, has been read into it. Those to whom I said in confidence that they should sooner look even for a Cesare Borgia than for a Parsifal, did not believe their own ears.[5]

---

some explanation" (see Podach, *Friedrich Nietzsches Werke,* p. 249; and for Nietzsche's instructions to delete these sentences, p. 250).

[5] All of Nietzsche's references to Cesare Borgia are discussed in Kaufmann's *Nietzsche,* Chapter 7, section III.

That I feel no curiosity at all about reviews of my books, especially in newspapers, should be forgiven me. My friends and my publishers know this and do not speak to me about such things. In one particular case I once did get to see all the sins that had been committed against one of my books—it was *Beyond Good and Evil*—and I could make a pretty report about that. Would you believe it? The *Nationalzeitung*—a Prussian newspaper, as I might explain for the benefit of my foreign readers—I myself read, if I may say so, only the *Journal des Débats*—actually managed to understand the book as a "sign of the times," as the real and genuine Junker philosophy for which the *Kreuzzeitung*[6] merely lacked the courage.

2

This was said for the benefit of Germans; for everywhere else I have readers—nothing but first-rate intellects and proven characters, trained in high positions and duties; I even have real geniuses among my readers. In Vienna, in St. Petersburg, in Stockholm, in Copenhagen, in Paris, in New York—everywhere I have been discovered; but not in the shallows of Europe, Germany.[1]

And let me confess that my nonreaders delight me even more—those who have never heard my name, nor the word "philosophy." But wherever I go, here in Turin, for example, everybody's face lights up and looks pleased at my sight. What has flattered me most so far is that old costermonger women won't relax until they have found their sweetest grapes for me. That is the extent to which one should be a philosopher.

It is not for nothing that the Poles are called the Frenchmen among the Slavs. A charming Russian woman would not doubt for

---

[6] An ultra-right newspaper.

[1] In a discarded draft for this passage we find the following (Podach, pp. 254f.): "Whoever reads me in Germany today has first *de-Germanized* himself thoroughly, as I have done: my formula is known, 'to be a good German means to de-Germanize oneself'; or he is—no small distinction among Germans—of Jewish descent.— Jews among Germans are always the higher race—more refined, spiritual, kind.— *L'adorable* Heine, they say in Paris."

a moment where I belong. I cannot be solemn, at most I become embarrassed.

To think German, to feel German—I can do anything, but not that.

My old teacher, Ritschl, actually claimed that I planned even my philological essays like a Parisian *romancier*—absurdly exciting. Even in Paris they are amazed by *"tout mes audaces et finesses"*—this is M. Taine's expression.[2] I fear that even into the highest forms of the dithyramb one finds in my case some admixture of that salt which never loses its savor and becomes flat—"German"—namely, *esprit*.— I cannot do otherwise. God help me! Amen.[3]

All of us know, some even know from experience, which animal has long ears. Well then, I dare assert that I have the smallest ears. This is of no small interest to women—it seems to me that they may feel I understand them better.— I am the *anti-ass par excellence* and thus a world-historical monster—I am, in Greek, and not only in Greek, the *Antichrist*.

3

I have some notion of my privileges as a writer; in a few instances I have been told, too, how getting used to my writings "spoils" one's taste. One simply can no longer endure other books, least of all philosophical works. It is a distinction without equal to enter this noble and delicate world—one must not by any means be a German; it is after all a distinction one must have earned. But whoever is related to me in the height of his aspirations will experience veritable ecstasies of learning; for I come from heights that no bird ever reached in its flight, I know abysses into which no foot ever strayed. I have been told that it is impossible to put down one of my books—that I even disturb nightly rest.

Altogether, there is no prouder and at the same time subtler

---

[2] "All my audacities and finesses." Nietzsche's correspondence with Hippolyte Taine has been published in *Friedrich Nietzsches Gesammelte Briefe,* vol. III, Berlin and Leipzig, Schuster & Loeffler, 1905.

[3] Luther's famous words at the Diet of Worms.

type of book: here and there they achieve the highest thing achievable on earth, cynicism; they have to be conquered with the most delicate fingers as well as the bravest fists. Every frailty of the soul excludes one once and for all, even every kind of dyspepsia: one must not have any nerves, one needs a cheerful digestion. Not only the poverty, also the nook air of a soul excludes one; even more, any cowardice, uncleanliness, secret vengefulness in the entrails: a single word from me drives all his bad instincts into a man's face. My acquaintances include several guinea pigs who illustrate for me different reactions to my writings—different in a very instructive manner. Those who want no part of the contents, my so-called friends, for example, become "impersonal": they congratulate me for having got "that far" again—and find some progress in the greater cheerfulness of the tone.

Utterly depraved "spirits," "beautiful souls," being mendacious through and through, simply do not know where they are with these books—hence they consider them *beneath* themselves, the beautiful consistency of all "beautiful souls." The oxen among my acquaintances—mere Germans, if I may say so—suggest that one cannot always agree with my opinions, but at times— This I have been told even about *Zarathustra*.

All "feminism," too—also in men—closes the door: it will never permit entrance into this labyrinth of audacious insights. One must never have spared oneself, one must have acquired hardness as a habit to be cheerful and in good spirits in the midst of nothing but hard truths. When I imagine a perfect reader, he always turns into a monster of courage and curiosity; moreover, supple, cunning, cautious; a born adventurer and discoverer. In the end, I could not say better to whom alone I am speaking at bottom than Zarathustra said it: to whom alone will he relate his riddle?

"To you, the bold searchers, researchers, and whoever embarks with cunning sails on terrible seas—to you, drunk with riddles, glad of the twilight, whose soul flutes lure astray to every whirlpool, because you do not want to grope along a thread with cowardly hand; and where you can *guess,* you hate to *deduce*." [1]

---

[1] Part III, "On the Vision and the Riddle," section 1.

4

This is also the point for a general remark about my art of style. To communicate a state, an inward tension of pathos, by means of signs, including the tempo of these signs—that is the meaning of every style;[1] and considering that the multiplicity of inward states is exceptionally large in my case, I have many stylistic possibilities—the most multifarious art of style that has ever been at the disposal of one man. *Good* is any style that really communicates an inward state, that makes no mistake about the signs, the tempo of the signs, the gestures—all the laws about long periods are concerned with the art of gestures.[2] Here my instinct is infallible.

Good style *in itself*—a pure folly, mere "idealism," on a level with the "beautiful in itself," the "good in itself," the "thing in itself."

Always presupposing that there are ears—that there are those capable and worthy of the same pathos, that there is no lack of those to whom one *may* communicate oneself.— My *Zarathustra,* for example, is still looking for those—alas, it will have to keep looking for a long time yet!— One must be worthy of hearing him.

And until then there will be nobody to understand the art that has been squandered here: nobody ever was in a position to squander more new, unheard-of artistic devices that had actually been created only for this purpose. That this was possible in German, of all languages, remained to be shown: I myself would have rejected any such notion most unhesitatingly before. Before me, it was not known what could be done with the German language—what could be done with language in general. The art of the *great* rhythm, the *great* style of long periods to express a tremendous up and down of sublime, of superhuman passion, was discovered only by me; with a dithyramb like the last one in the third part of *Zarathustra,* enti-

---

[1] For the importance of tempo, cf. *Beyond Good and Evil,* sections 27, 28, and 246.

[2] See *ibid.,* section 247. This sentence suggests some of the difficulties faced by a translator of Nietzsche.

tled "The Seven Seals," I soared a thousand miles beyond what was
called poetry hitherto.

5

That a psychologist without equal speaks from my writings, is
perhaps the first insight reached by a good reader—a reader as I
deserve him, who reads me the way good old philologists read their
Horace. Those propositions on which all the world is really agreed
—not to speak of the world's common run of philosophers, the
moralists and other hollow pots, cabbage heads[1]—appear in my
books as naïve blunders: for example, the belief that "unegoistic"
and "egoistic" are opposites, while the ego itself is really only a
"higher swindle," an "ideal."— There are neither egoistic nor unegoistic acts: both concepts are psychological absurdities. Or the
proposition: "man strives for happiness."— Or the proposition:
"happiness is the reward of virtue."— Or the proposition: "pleasure and displeasure are opposites."— The Circe of humanity, morality, has falsified all *psychologica* through and through—*moralizing* them—down to that gruesome nonsense that love is supposed
to be something "unegoistic."— One has to sit firmly upon *oneself*,
one must stand bravely on one's own two legs, otherwise one is
simply *incapable* of loving. Ultimately, women know that only too
well: they don't give a damn about selfless, merely objective men.

May I here venture the surmise that I *know* women? That is
part of my Dionysian dowry. Who knows? Perhaps I am the first
psychologist of the eternally feminine. They all love me—an old
story—not counting *abortive* females, the "emancipated" who lack
the stuff for children.— Fortunately, I am not willing to be torn to
pieces: the perfect woman tears to pieces when she loves.— I know
these charming maenads.— Ah, what a dangerous, creeping, subterranean little beast of prey she is! And yet so agreeable!— A little
woman who pursues her revenge would run over fate itself.—
Woman is indescribably more evil than man; also cleverer: good
nature is in a woman a form of degeneration.— In all so-called

---

[1] *Den Allerwelts-Philosophen, den Moralisten und andren Hohltöpfen,
Kohlköpfen.*

"beautiful souls" something is physiologically askew at bottom; I do not say everything, else I should become medi-cynical. The fight for equal rights is actually a symptom of a disease: every physician knows that.— Woman, the more she is a woman, resists rights in general hand and foot: after all, the state of nature, the eternal war between the sexes, gives her by far the first rank.

Has my definition of love been heard? It is the only one worthy of a philosopher. Love—in its means, war; at bottom, the deadly hatred of the sexes.

Has my answer been heard to the question how one *cures* a woman—"redeems" her? One gives her a child. Woman needs children, a man is for her always only a means: thus spoke *Zarathustra*.

"Emancipation of women"—that is the instinctive hatred of the abortive[2] woman, who is incapable of giving birth, against the woman who is turned out well [3]—the fight against the "man" is always a mere means, pretext, tactic. By raising themselves higher, as "woman in herself," as the "higher woman," as a female "idealist," they want to lower the level of the general rank of woman; and there is no surer means for that than higher education, slacks, and political voting-cattle rights. At bottom, the emancipated are anarchists in the world of the "eternally feminine," the underprivileged whose most fundamental instinct is revenge.

One whole species of the most malignant "idealism"—which, incidentally, is also encountered among men; for example, in Henrik Ibsen, this typical old virgin—aims to *poison* the good conscience, what is natural in sexual love.[4]

And lest I leave any doubt about my very decent and strict views in these matters, let me still cite a proposition against vice from my moral code: I use the word "vice" in my fight against

---

[2] *Missraten.*

[3] *Wohlgeraten.*

[4] It seems plain that Nietzsche did not know most of Ibsen's plays. Cf. my edition of *The Will to Power* (New York, Random House, 1967), sections 86 (including my long note) and 747, and for some parallels between Ibsen and Nietzsche also my Preface to *Beyond Good and Evil*, p. 187f., above, as well as note 37 on p. 330f. Nietzsche would have loved *The Wild Duck*.

every kind of antinature or, if you prefer pretty words, idealism.
The proposition reads: "The preaching of chastity amounts to a
public incitement to antinature. Every kind of contempt for sex,
every impurification of it by means of the concept 'impure,' is the
crime *par excellence* against life—is the real sin against the holy
spirit of life."

6

To give an idea of me as a psychologist, I choose a curious bit
of psychology from *Beyond Good and Evil;* incidentally, I forbid
any surmise about whom I am describing in this passage:[1]

The genius of the heart, as that great concealed one possesses it, the tempter god and born pied piper of consciences
whose voice knows how to descend into the netherworld of every soul; who does not say a word or cast a glance in which
there is no consideration and ulterior enticement; whose mastery includes the knowledge of how to seem—not what he is
but what is to those who follow him one *more* constraint to
press ever closer to him in order to follow him even more inwardly and thoroughly—the genius of the heart who silences
all that is loud and self-satisfied, teaching it to listen; who
smooths rough souls and lets them taste a new desire—to lie
still as a mirror, that the deep sky may mirror itself in them—
the genius of the heart who teaches the doltish and rash hand
to hesitate and reach out more delicately; who guesses the concealed and forgotten treasure, the drop of graciousness and
sweet spirituality under dim and thick ice, and is a divining rod
for every grain of gold that has long lain buried in the dungeon
of much mud and sand; the genius of the heart from whose
touch everyone walks away richer, not having received grace
and surprised, not as blessed and oppressed by alien goods, but

---

[1] Section 295. In a footnote for that section (in my translation of *Beyond
Good and Evil*) I have brought together materials that show how much this
portrait owes to Socrates; also how Nietzsche came to see *himself* this way.
"I forbid any surmise . . ." surely suggests that the description seems to
Nietzsche to fit himself.

richer in himself, newer to himself than before, broken open, blown at and sounded out by a thawing wind, perhaps more unsure, tenderer, more fragile, more broken, but full of hopes that as yet have no name, full of new will and currents, full of new dissatisfaction and undertows . . .

The Birth of Tragedy

1

To be fair to *The Birth of Tragedy* (1872), one has to forget a few things. Its effect and fascination were due to what was wrong with it—its practical application to Wagnerism, as if that were a symptom of *ascent*. In this respect, this essay was an event in the life of Wagner: it was only from that moment on that Wagner's name elicited high hopes. People still remind me of this today, sometimes even in the context of *Parsifal*—how I am the one who has it on his conscience that such a high opinion of the *cultural value* of this movement gained prevalence.

Several times I saw this book cited as "The Re-Birth of Tragedy Out of the Spirit of Music": what people had ears for was only a new formula for the art, the intentions, the task of *Wagner*—and what was really valuable in the essay was ignored. "Hellenism and Pessimism" would have been a less ambiguous title—suggesting the first instruction about how the Greeks got over their pessimism, how they *overcame* it.

Precisely their tragedies prove that the Greeks were *not* pessimists: Schopenhauer went wrong at this point, as he went wrong everywhere.

Taken up with some degree of neutrality, *The Birth of Tragedy* looks quite untimely: one would never dream that it was begun amid the thunder of the battle of Wörth. Before the walls of Metz, in cold September nights, while on duty as a medical orderly, I thought through these problems. One might sooner believe that the essay was fifty years older.[1] It is indifferent toward politics—"un-German," to use the language of the present time—it smells offensively Hegelian, and the cadaverous perfume of Schopenhauer sticks

---

[1] That would take us back to the time of Hegel, 1820.

only to a few formulas. An "idea" [2]—the antithesis[3] of the Diony-sian and the Apollinian—translated into the realm of metaphysics; history itself as the development of this "idea"; in tragedy this an-tithesis is sublimated [4] into a unity; and in this perspective things that had never before faced each other are suddenly juxtaposed, used to illuminate each other, and comprehended [5]—opera, for example, and the revolution.

The two decisive innovations of the book are, first, its under-standing of the Dionysian phenomenon among the Greeks: for the first time, a psychological analysis of this phenomenon is offered, and it is considered as one root of the whole of Greek art. Sec-ondly, there is the understanding of Socratism: Socrates is recog-nized for the first time as an instrument of Greek disintegration, as a typical decadent. "Rationality" *against* instinct. "Rationality" at any price as a dangerous force that undermines life.[6]

Profound, hostile silence about Christianity throughout the book. That is neither Apollinian nor Dionysian; it negates all aes-thetic values—the only values recognized in *The Birth of Tragedy:* it is nihilistic in the most profound sense, while in the Dionysian symbol the ultimate limit of affirmation is attained. There is one allusion to Christian priests as a "vicious kind of dwarfs" who are "subterranean." [7]

2

This beginning is exceedingly strange. I had discovered the only parable and parallel in history for my own inmost experience

---

[2] *Idee:* one of the key terms of Hegel's philosophy.

[3] *Gegensatz:* the word Hegel generally uses where English translations have "antithesis."

[4] *Aufgehoben:* a term Hegel liked especially because in ordinary German it can mean canceled, preserved, and lifted up. For this whole passage, cf. Kaufmann's *Nietzsche,* Chapter 13, section I, including note 7.

[5] *Begriffen:* another term Hegel used frequently.

[6] For a comprehensive discussion of Nietzsche's complex attitude toward Socrates and its development from *The Birth of Tragedy* to *Ecce Homo,* see Kaufmann's *Nietzsche,* Chapter 13.

[7] At the end of section 24. But the quotation is inexact, and the interpreta-tion—that priests were meant—is questionable.

—and thus became the first to comprehend the wonderful phenomenon of the Dionysian. At the same time my discovery that Socrates was a decadent proved unequivocally how little the sureness of my psychological grasp would be endangered by any moral idiosyncrasy: seeing morality itself as a symptom of decadence is an innovation and a singularity of the first rank in the history of knowledge. How high had I jumped with these two insights above the wretched and shallow chatter about optimism versus pessimism!

I was the first to see[1] the real opposition: the degenerating instinct that turns against life with subterranean vengefulness (Christianity, the philosophy of Schopenhauer, in a certain sense already the philosophy of Plato, and all of idealism as typical forms) versus a formula for the highest affirmation, born of fullness, of overfullness, a Yes-saying without reservation, even to suffering, even to guilt, even to everything that is questionable and strange in existence.

This ultimate, most joyous, most wantonly extravagant Yes to life represents not only the highest insight but also the *deepest,* that which is most strictly confirmed and born out by truth and science. Nothing in existence may be subtracted, nothing is dispensable— those aspects of existence which Christians and other nihilists repudiate are actually on an infinitely higher level in the order of rank among values than that which the instinct of decadence could approve and call good.[2] To comprehend this requires courage and, as a condition of that, an excess of strength: for precisely as far as courage may venture forward, precisely according to that measure of strength one approaches the truth. Knowledge, saying Yes to reality, is just as necessary for the strong as cowardice and the flight from reality—as the "ideal" is for the weak, who are inspired by weakness.

They are not free to know: the decadents *need* the lie—it is one of the conditions of their preservation.

Whoever does not merely comprehend the word "Dionysian"

---

[1] Except for the context, this could well mean: First I saw . . .

[2] *Gutheissen, gut heissen.*

but comprehends *himself* in the word "Dionysian" needs no refutation of Plato or Christianity or Schopenhauer—he *smells the decay.*

3

How I had thus found the concept of the "tragic" and at long last knowledge of the psychology of tragedy, I have explained most recently in *Twilight of the Idols,* p. 139:[1]

"Saying Yes to life even in its strangest and hardest problems; the will to life rejoicing over its own inexhaustibility even in the very sacrifice of its highest types—that is what I called Dionysian, that is what I understood as[2] the bridge to the psychology of the tragic poet. Not in order to get rid of terror and pity, not in order to purge oneself of a dangerous affect by its vehement discharge—Aristotle misunderstood [3] it that way—but in order to be oneself the eternal joy of becoming, beyond all terror and pity—that joy which includes even joy in destroying."

In this sense I have the right to understand myself as the first *tragic philosopher*—that is, the most extreme opposite and antipode of a pessimistic philosopher. Before me this transposition of the Dionysian into a philosophical pathos did not exist: *tragic wisdom* was lacking; I have looked in vain for signs of it even among the *great* Greeks in philosophy, those of the two centuries *before* Socrates.[4] I retained some doubt in the case of *Heraclitus,* in whose proximity I feel altogether warmer and better than anywhere else. The affirmation of passing away *and destroying,* which is the decisive feature of a Dionysian philosophy; saying Yes to opposition and war; *becoming,* along with a radical repudiation of the very concept of *being*—all this is clearly more closely related to me than anything else thought to date. The doctrine of the "eternal recurrence," that is, of the unconditional and infinitely repeated circular

---

[1] In the final section of the book (*Portable Nietzsche,* pp. 562f.).

[2] In *Twilight:* guessed to be.

[3] In *Twilight:* understood. Nietzsche is referring to Aristotle's conception of catharsis (*Poetics* 6, 1449b).

[4] Nietzsche's extremely high valuation of the pre-Socratics was taken up by Karl Jaspers and Martin Heidegger.

course of all things—this doctrine of Zarathustra *might* in the end
have been taught already by Heraclitus. At least the Stoa has traces
of it, and the Stoics inherited almost all of their principal notions
from Heraclitus.

4

A tremendous hope speaks out of this essay. In the end I lack
all reason to renounce the hope for a Dionysian future of music.
Let us look ahead a century; let us suppose that my attempt to
assassinate two millennia of antinature and desecration of man were
to succeed. That new party of life which would tackle the greatest
of all tasks, the attempt to raise humanity higher, including the
relentless destruction of everything that was degenerating and
parasitical, would again make possible that excess of life on earth
from which the Dionysian state, too, would have to awaken again.
I promise a tragic age: the highest art in saying Yes to life, tragedy,
will be reborn when humanity has weathered the consciousness of
the hardest but most necessary wars *without suffering from it.*

A psychologist might still add that what I heard as a young
man listening to Wagnerian music really had nothing to do with
Wagner; that when I described Dionysian music I described what *I*
had heard—that instinctively I had to transpose and transfigure
everything into the new spirit that I carried in me. The proof of
that, *as strong as any proof can be,* is my essay on *Wagner in Bayreuth:* in all psychologically decisive places I alone am discussed—
and one need not hesitate to put down my name or the word "Zarathustra" where the text has the word "Wagner." The entire picture of the dithyrambic artist is a picture of the pre-existent poet of
Zarathustra, sketched with abysmal profundity and without touching even for a moment the Wagnerian reality. Wagner himself had
some notion of that; he did not recognize himself in this essay.

Similarly, "the idea of Bayreuth" was transformed into something that should not puzzle those who know my *Zarathustra:* into
that great noon at which the most elect consecrate themselves for
the greatest of all tasks. Who could say? The vision of a feast that I
shall yet live to see.

The pathos of the first pages is world-historical; the glance spoken of on the seventh page is Zarathustra's distinctive glance; Wagner, Bayreuth, the whole wretched German pettiness are a cloud in which an infinite mirage of the future is reflected. Even psychologically all decisive traits of my own nature are projected into Wagner's—the close proximity of the brightest and the most calamitous forces, the will to power as no man ever possessed it,[5] the ruthless courage in matters of the spirit, the unlimited power to learn without damage to the will to act. Everything in this essay points to the future: the impending return of the Greek spirit, the necessity of counter-Alexanders who will retie the Gordian knot of Greek culture.

Listen to the world-historical accent with which the concept of the tragic attitude is introduced at the end of section 4: this essay is full of world-historical accents. This is the strangest "objectivity" possible: the absolute certainty about what I am was projected on some accidental reality—the truth about me spoke from some gruesome depth. At the beginning of section 9 the *style* of *Zarathustra* is described with incisive certainty and anticipated; and no more magnificent expression could be found for the *event* of *Zarathustra,* the act of a tremendous purification and consecration of humanity, than was found in section 6.[6]

---

[5] This striking confession of the philosopher of the will to power has been ignored although, quite apart from its human and psychological interest, it helps to illuminate his conception of the will to power.

[6] All these references are to *Richard Wagner in Bayreuth,* and that is the book discussed in the last four paragraphs of this section. Nietzsche, as usual, furnishes page references—which Karl Schlechta, in his edition of the works, misconstrues as referring to *The Birth of Tragedy:* whoever looks up Schlechta's page references won't find any of the passages discussed by Nietzsche.

The Untimely Ones[1]

1

The four Untimely Ones are certainly warlike. They prove that I was no Jack the Dreamer, that I take pleasure in fencing—perhaps also that I am dangerously quick at the draw. The *first* attack (1873) was directed against German "culture"[2] on which I looked down even then with ruthless contempt. Without meaning, without substance, without aim: mere "public opinion." There is no more malignant misunderstanding than to believe that the great military success[3] of the Germans proved anything in favor of this "culture"—or, of all things, *its* triumph over France.

The *second* Untimely One (1874) brings to light what is dangerous and gnaws at and poisons life in our kind of traffic with science and scholarship[4]—how life is made sick by this dehumanized and mechanical grinding of gears, the "impersonality" of the laborer, the false economy of the "division of labor." The aim is lost, genuine culture—and the means, the modern traffic with science, *barbarized*. In this essay the "historical sense" of which this century is proud was recognized for the first time as a disease, as a typical symptom of decay.

---

[1] *Die Unzeitgemässen:* the four essays in question were published as *Unzeitgemässe Betrachtungen* (untimely meditations), one by one, with separate titles: *David Strauss, The Confessor and Writer; On the Use and Disadvantage of History for Life; Schopenhauer as Educator;* and *Richard Wagner in Bayreuth.*

[2] *Bildung* has no exact equivalent in English: *Bild* means picture or image; *bilden,* to shape or form, but also to educate; *ungebildet,* uneducated, uncultured. In this section, *Bildung* has been rendered by "culture" (in quotes), *Kultur* by culture (without quotes).

[3] In the Franco-Prussian War of 1870–71.

[4] Science and scholarship: *Wissenschaft.* After this, science has been used to render *Wissenschaft,* but it should be kept in mind that the reference is not primarily to the natural sciences. Cf. *Beyond Good and Evil,* Part Six ("We Scholars," sections 204–13): the concept of the laborer is used similarly in section 211. See also *Genealogy,* III, sections 23ff.

In the *third* and *fourth* Untimely Ones, two images of the hardest self-love, self-discipline[5] are put up against all this, as pointers to a higher concept of culture, to restore the concept of culture—untimely types *par excellence,* full of sovereign contempt for everything around them that was called "Empire," "culture," [6] "Christianity," "Bismarck," "success"—Schopenhauer and Wagner *or,* in one word, Nietzsche.

2

Of these four attempts at assassination the first had an extraordinary success. The noise it evoked was in every sense splendid. I had touched the sore spot of a victorious nation—that its victory was *not* a cultural event but perhaps, perhaps something altogether different.

The response came from all sides and by no means only from the old friends of David Strauss whom I had made ridiculous as a type of the German "cultural" philistine and *satisfait,*[1] in short as the author of his beer-hall gospel of *The Old and the New Faith* (the word *Bildungsphilister* has survived in the German language from my essay).[2] These old friends, Württembergers and Swabians whom I had wounded deeply when I found their prodigy, Strauss, funny, replied in such a foursquare and rude manner that I could not have asked for more; the replies from Prussia were more prudent—they had more Prussian, Berlin blue in them. It was a news-

---

[5] *Selbstsucht, Selbstzucht.* On the former, see the chapter "On the Three Evils" in *Zarathustra III* (*Portable Nietzsche,* pp. 298ff., especially 302): the word used there is also *Selbstsucht.* Cf. also Aristotle's *Nicomachean Ethics,* 1169a: "the good man ought to be a lover of self since he will then act nobly, and so both benefit himself and aid his fellows; but the bad man ought not to be a lover of self, since he will follow his base passions, and so injure both himself and his neighbours" (trans. Rackham, Loeb Classical Library).

[6] *"Reich," "Bildung"* . . .

[1] *Smug.*

[2] The word had actually been used earlier by Gustav Teichmüller (1832–1888), a professor at Basel from 1868 to 1871; but Nietzsche's claim (*ist von meiner Schrift her in der Sprache übriggeblieben*) is literally true. For all that, he would hardly have said this if he had remembered that the coinage was Teichmüller's.

paper in Leipzig, the notorious *Grenzboten,* that became most indecent; I found it difficult to restrain the indignant Baselers from
taking action. The only ones who decided unconditionally in my
favor were a few old gentlemen, from mixed and in part undiscov-
erable motives. Ewald in Göttingen was among them;[3] he suggested
my attempt had been fatal for Strauss. Also the old Hegelian,
Bruno Bauer,[4] who was henceforth one of my most attentive readers. During his last years he liked to refer to me; for example, by
giving Herr von Treitschke, the Prussian historiographer, a hint
whom he might ask for some information about the concept of
culture which had escaped him. Nothing written about this essay
and its author was more thought-provoking or longer than what an
old disciple of the philosopher von Baader[5] said, a Professor
Hoffmann in Würzburg.[6] On the basis of this essay he predicted a
great destiny for me—bringing about a kind of crisis and ultimate

---

[3] Heinrich Ewald (1803–1875), a very eminent Old Testament scholar and
orientalist, was one of the celebrated "Göttingen Seven" who in 1837 were
expelled from the university because they had signed a liberal manifesto; he
went to Tübingen, but returned to Göttingen in 1848—and was pensioned
off in 1867 because he refused to swear an oath of allegiance to the king
of Prussia.

[4] Bruno Bauer (1809–82) started out as a right-wing, conservative Hegelian
and became a professor of theology at Bonn in 1839. In 1840 and 1841 he
published two volumes of New Testament criticism, and in 1842 he was
deprived of the right to teach. Now he was accounted a "Young" or left-wing
Hegelian, and he has been called "the most radical of the New Testament
critics of his age." He attacked David Friedrich Strauss's ideas about the
origins of Christianity and emphasized Hellenistic influences. Albert Schweitzer praised him highly in his *Geschichte der Leben Jesu Forschung* (Tübingen 1921, p. 161; *The Quest of the Historical Jesus*) for having assembled
the most brilliant and complete summary of the difficulties presented by the
life of Jesus. Marx's and Engels' attacks on Bauer, as "St. Bruno," written in
1845/46, are included in *Die Deutsche Ideologie* (published posthumously
in 1932; The German Ideology). Bauer's ideas are also discussed by Karl
Löwith in *Von Hegel bis Nietzsche* (Europa Verlag, Zürich and New York
1941; *From Hegel to Nietzsche,* Holt, Rinehart and Winston, New York
1964).

[5] Franz Xaver von Baader (1765–1841), who became a professor at Munich
in 1826, influenced Schelling and other romantics.

[6] Franz Hoffmann, *Philosophische Schriften,* vol. V (Erlangen, 1878), pp.
410–47. See also J. Haefner, *Leben und Schaffen des Würzburger Philoso-
phen F. K. Hoffmann* (The life and work of the Würzburg philosopher
F. K. Hoffmann; dissertation, 1941, 112 pp.).

decision in the problem of atheism whose most instinctive and relentless type he divined in me. It was atheism that led me to Schopenhauer.

Nothing was heard as well or experienced as bitterly as an extraordinarily strong and courageous plea by the usually mild Karl Hillebrand, this last *humane* German who knew how to write. His piece was read in the *Augsburger Zeitung;* today it can be read, in a somewhat more cautious form, in his collected essays.[7] Here the essay was considered as an event, a turning point, a first self-examination, the very best sign, as a real *return* of German seriousness and German passion in matters of the spirit. Hillebrand was full of high praise for the form of the essay, for its mature taste, for its perfect tact in distinguishing between the person and the issue: he designated it as the best polemical essay written in German—in the art of polemics which is so dangerous and inadvisable for Germans. Saying Yes unconditionally, even sharpening the points I had dared to make against the galloping slovenliness of the German language[8] (today they play the purists and can no longer form a sentence), with equal contempt for the "foremost writers" of this nation, he concluded with an expression of his admiration for my *courage*—that "supreme courage which prefers charges precisely against the favorites of a people."

The aftereffects of this essay upon my life are virtually inestimable. Nobody so far has picked quarrels with me; in Germany I am treated with gloomy caution: for years I have made use of an unconditional freedom of speech for which nobody today, least of all in the *Reich,* has sufficient liberty. My paradise lies "in the shadow of my sword."

At bottom, I had put into practise one of Stendhal's maxims:

---

[7] Karl Hillebrand, "Einiges über den Verfall der deutschen Sprache und der deutschen Gesinnung" (some thoughts about the decay of the German language and the German mind) in *Zeiten, Völker und Menschen* (periods, peoples, and persons), vol. II (Berlin, 1875; 2nd ed., Strassburg, 1892), pp. 291–310. Hillebrand also reviewed Nietzsche's second and third "untimely meditations": "Über Wissen und historischen Sinn" (on knowledge and the historical sense) and "Schopenhauer und das deutsche Publikum" (Schopenhauer and the German public), *ibid.,* pp. 311-38 and 353–66.

[8] *Sprach-Verlumpung in Deutschland.*

he advises men to make their entry into society with a *duel*. And how I had picked my opponent! the foremost German free spirit!

Indeed, an altogether new type of free spirit thus gained his first expression: to this day nothing is more foreign and less related to me than the whole European and American species of *libres penseurs*.[9] I am much more profoundly at odds with them, as incorrigible blockheads and buffoons of "modern ideas," than with any of their opponents. They also want in their own way to "improve" mankind, in their own image; against what I am, what I *want*, they would wage an irreconcilable war if they understood me: all of them still believe in the "ideal."— I am the first *immoralist*.

3

That the two Untimely Ones distinguished by the names of Schopenhauer and Wagner contribute much to the understanding of, or even to the formulation of the proper psychological questions about, these two cases, I should not wish to assert—excepting, as seems fair, some details. Thus, for example, the elementary fact in Wagner's character is already designated with a profound sureness of instinct as an actor's talent that merely explicates itself in his means and intentions.

What I was fundamentally trying to do in these essays was something altogether different from psychology: an unequaled problem of education, a new concept of self-discipline, self-defense to the point of hardness, a way to greatness and world-historical tasks was seeking its first expression. Broadly speaking, I caught hold of two famous and as yet altogether undiagnosed types, as one catches hold of an opportunity, in order to say something, in order to have at hand a few more formulas, signs, means of language. This is really suggested with a perfectly uncanny sagacity near the end of section 7 in the third Untimely One. Plato employed Socrates in this fashion, as a [sign language for Plato].[1]

---

[9] Cf. *Beyond Good and Evil,* Part Two, "The Free Spirit," especially section 44.

[1] The words placed in brackets are not in Nietzsche's hand and were added

Now that I am looking back from a certain distance upon the conditions of which these essays bear witness, I do not wish to deny that at bottom they speak only of me. The essay *Wagner in Bayreuth* is a vision of my future, while in *Schopenhauer as Educator* my innermost history, my *becoming,* is inscribed. Above all, my promise!

What I am today, where I am today—at a height where I speak no longer with words but with lightning bolts—ah, how remote from this I still was at that time!— But I beheld the land—I did not deceive myself for a moment about the way, the sea, the danger—and success. The great calm in promising, this happy gaze into a future that is not to remain a mere promise!

Here every word is experienced, is deep, is inward; what is most painful is not lacking: there are words in it that are virtually bloodthirsty. But a wind of the great freedom blows over everything; even wounds do not have the effect of objections.

How I understand the philosopher—as a terrible explosive, endangering everything—how my concept of the philosopher is worlds removed from any concept that would include even a Kant, not to speak of academic "ruminants" and other professors of philosophy—this essay gives inestimable information about that, although at bottom it is admittedly not "Schopenhauer as Educator" that speaks here, but his opposite, "Nietzsche as Educator."

Considering that in those days I practiced the scholar's craft, and perhaps *knew* something about this craft, the harsh psychology of the scholar that suddenly emerges in this essay is of some significance: it expresses the *feeling of distance,*[2] the profound assurance

---

by a German editor—presumably Gast. What Nietzsche claims may sound farfetched, but actually the *first* section of *Schopenhauer as Educator* makes this point very plainly. The question is raised how we can realize our true self, and the prescription is that we should ask ourselves: "What have you really loved till now?" For "your true self does not lie deeply concealed within you but immeasurably high above you, or at least above what you usually take for your ego. Your real educators, those who formed you, reveal to you what is the true primary meaning and fundamental substance of your being . . ." The meditation on Schopenhauer is thus introduced as Nietzsche's attempt to discover his own true self; and Nietzsche's praise not only of Schopenhauer's honesty but also—of all things—of his "cheerfulness" (in section 2) points in the same direction.

[2] Cf. the *pathos of distance* in section 257 of *Beyond Good and Evil.*

about what could be my *task* and what could only be means, *en-tr'acte,* and minor works. It shows my prudence that I was many things and in many places in order to be able to become one thing —to be able to attain one thing. I *had* to be a scholar, too, for some time.[3]

---

[3] Cf. *ibid.,* section 211: "It may be necessary for the education of a genuine philosopher that he himself has also once stood on all these steps on which his servants, the scientific laborers of philosophy, remain standing . . ."

Human, All-Too-Human
With Two Sequels

1

Human, All-Too-Human is the monument of a crisis. It is subtitled "A Book for *Free* Spirits": almost every sentence marks some victory—here I liberated myself from what in my nature did not belong to me. Idealism, for example; the title means: "where *you* see ideal things, *I* see what is—human, alas, all-too-human!"—I know man better.

The term "free spirit" here is not to be understood in any other sense; it means a spirit that has *become free*,[1] that has again taken possession of itself. The tone, the voice, is completely changed: you will find the book clever, cool, perhaps hard and mocking. A certain spirituality of noble *taste* seems to be fighting continually against a more passionate current in order to stay afloat. In this connection it makes sense that it was actually the hundredth anniversary of the death of *Voltaire* that the book pleaded, as it were, as an excuse for coming out in 1878.[2] For Voltaire was above all, in contrast to all who wrote after him, a *grandseigneur*[3] of the spirit—like me.— The name of Voltaire on one of my essays —that really meant progress—*toward me*.

On closer inspection you discover a merciless spirit that knows all the hideouts where the ideal is at home—where it has its secret dungeons and, as it were, its ultimate safety. With a torch whose light never wavers, an incisive light is thrown into this *underworld* of the ideal. This is war, but war without powder and smoke, without warlike poses, without pathos and strained limbs:[4] all that

---

[1] Cf. *Twilight*, section 49 (*Portable Nietzsche*, p. 554).

[2] The first edition bore the following dedication: "To the memory of Voltaire, in commemoration of his death, May 30, 1878."

[3] Nobleman.

[4] Cf. section 7 of the first chapter, above; also the first footnote for that section.

would still be "idealism." One error after another is coolly placed
on ice; the ideal is not refuted—it *freezes* to death.— Here, for
example, "the genius" freezes to death; at the next corner, "the
saint"; under a huge icicle, "the hero"; in the end, "faith," so-
called "conviction"; "pity" also cools down considerably—and almost everywhere "the thing in itself" freezes to death.

2

The beginnings of this book belong right in the midst of the
first *Bayreuther Festspiele;*[1] a profound alienation from everything
that surrounded me there is one of its preconditions. Whoever has
any notion of the visions I had encountered even before that, may
guess how I felt when one day I woke up in Bayreuth. As if I were
dreaming!

Wherever was I? There was nothing I recognized; I scarcely
recognized Wagner. In vain did I leaf through my memories. Tribschen—a distant isle of the blessed: not a trace of any similarity.
The incomparable days when the foundation stone was laid, the
small group of people that had belonged, had celebrated, and did
not need first to acquire fingers for delicate matters—not a trace of
any similarity. *What had happened?*— Wagner had been translated
into German! The Wagnerian had become master over Wagner.—
German art. The *German* master. *German* beer.

We others, who know only too well to what subtle artists and
what cosmopolitanism of taste Wagner's art speaks, exclusively,
were beside ourselves when we found Wagner again, draped with
German "virtues."

I think I know the Wagnerians; I have experienced three generations, beginning with the late Brendel [2] who confounded Wagner
and Hegel, down to the "idealists" of the *Bayreuther Blätter*[3] who

---

[1] The Wagner opera festivals at Bayreuth.

[2] Karl Franz Brendel (1811–1868) was editor of the *Neue Zeitschrift für
Musik* (new journal for music), 1845–1868, and of *Anregungen für Kunst,
Leben und Wissenschaft* (stimulations for art, life and science), 1856–61.
He became a champion of Wagner in 1851.

[3] Wagner's new periodical.

confound Wagner and themselves—I have heard every kind of confession of "beautiful souls" about Wagner. A kingdom for one sensible word!— In truth, a hair-raising company! Nohl, Pohl, *Kohl*— droll with charm, *in infinitum!* [4] Not a single abortion is missing among them, not even the anti-Semite.— Poor Wagner! Where had he landed!— If he had at least entered into swine! [5] But to descend among Germans!

Really, for the instruction of posterity one ought to stuff a genuine Bayreuther or, better yet, preserve him in spirits, for spirits are lacking—with the label: that is how the "spirit" looked on which the *Reich* was founded.

Enough; in the midst of it I left for a couple of weeks,[6] very suddenly, although a charming Parisienne tried to console me; the

---

[4] Karl Friedrich Ludwig Nohl (1831–1885) was a professor of music at the universities of Munich and Heidelberg, a prolific writer, especially on Mozart and Beethoven, and a dedicated Wagnerian. His publications include *R. Wagners Bedeutung für die nationale Kunst* (R. Wagner's significance for national art; Vienna, 1883) and *Das moderne Musikdrama* (the modern music drama; Vienna, 1884).

Richard Pohl (1826–1896) became co-editor (with Brendel) of *Anregungen für Kunst, Leben und Wissenschaft,* in 1857. A Wagnerian since 1846, he was sometimes called "the oldest Wagnerian."

Kohl, emphasized by Nietzsche, means drivel or twaddle as well as cabbage, and "drivel" is clearly the primary meaning intended here ("droll" represents an attempt to capture something of the spirit of the passage). This does not preclude the possibility that there may also have been some individual with this unfortunate name; e.g., a young man named Otto Kohl was a member of a small circle of philology students to which Nietzsche and Erwin Rohde had belonged in Leipzig.

A superseded draft for this section contains two short passages worth quoting here: "Typical was the old Kaiser [i.e., Wilhelm I] who applauded with his hands while saying loudly to his adjutant, Count Lehndorf: 'Hideous! hideous!' [*scheusslich! scheusslich!*]" And: "In the music of Wagner, which persuaded by means of its secret sexuality, one found a bond for a society in which everybody pursued his own *plaisirs* [pleasures]. The rest and, if you will, also the innocence of the matter, its 'idealists' were the idiots, the Nohl, Pohl, *Kohl*—the latter, known to me, the *genius loci* [minor local deity] in Bayreuth . . ." (Podach, *Friedrich Nietzsches Werke,* 1961, p. 276).

[5] Luke 8:33.

[6] Podach's vitriolic attack on Nietzsche's account of his break with Wagner, and on *Ecce Homo* generally, is often out of touch with the facts—as when he says of Nietzsche's sister, ignoring these words: "After all, it was scarcely feasible to blow down the story in *Ecce Homo* like a house of cards, by stating that her brother, in spite of financial difficulties, had soon returned to Bayreuth . . ." (p. 196).

only excuse I offered Wagner was a fatalistic telegram. In Klingenbrunn, a small town concealed in the woods of the *Böhmerwald,* I
dragged around my melancholy and contempt for Germans like a
disease—and from time to time I'd write a sentence into my note-
book, under the general title "The Plowshare"—*hard psychologica*
that can perhaps still be found in *Human, All-Too-Human.*

3

What reached a decision in me at that time was not a break
with Wagner: I noted a total aberration of my instincts of which
particular blunders, whether Wagner or the professorship at Basel,
were mere symptoms. I was overcome by *impatience* with myself; I
saw that it was high time for me to recall and reflect on myself. All
at once it became clear to me in a terrifying way how much time I
had already wasted—how useless and arbitrary my whole existence
as a philologist appeared in relation to my task. I felt ashamed of
this *false* modesty.

Ten years lay behind me in which the nourishment of my
spirit had really come to a stop; I had not learned anything new that
was useful; I had forgotten an absurd amount for the sake of dusty
scholarly gewgaws. Crawling scrupulously with bad eyes through
ancient metrists—that's what I had come to!— It stirred my compassion to see myself utterly emaciated, utterly starved: my knowledge simply failed to include *realities,* and my "idealities" were
not worth a damn.

A truly burning thirst took hold of me: henceforth I really
pursued nothing *more*[1] than physiology, medicine, and natural
sciences—and I did not return even to properly historical studies
until my *task* compelled me to, imperiously. It was then, too, that
I first guessed how an activity chosen in defiance of one's instincts,
a so-called "vocation" for which one does not have the least vocation, is related to the need for *deadening* the feeling of desolation

---

[1] . . . *nichts mehr getrieben als* . . . : if the accent falls on *nichts,* the
meaning is "pursued nothing any more except," which is palpably false as a
matter of biographical fact. If the accent falls on *mehr,* the meaning is that
suggested above, which may still be considered a rhetorical exaggeration.

and hunger by means of a narcotic art—for example, Wagnerian art.

Looking about me cautiously, I have discovered that a large number of young men experience the same distress: one antinatural step virtually compels the second. In Germany, in the *Reich*— to speak unambiguously—all too many are condemned to choose vocations too early, and then to waste away under a burden they can no longer shake off.— These people require Wagner as an *opiate:* they forget themselves, they are rid of themselves for a moment.— What am I saying? For *five or six hours!*

4

It was then that my instinct made its inexorable decision against any longer yielding, going along, and confounding myself. Any kind of life, the most unfavorable conditions, sickness, poverty—anything seemed preferable to that unseemly "selflessness" into which I had got myself originally in ignorance and *youth* and in which I had got stuck later on from inertia and so-called "sense of duty." [1]

Here it happened in a manner that I cannot admire sufficiently that, precisely at the right time, my father's *wicked* heritage came to my aid—at bottom, predestination to an early death. [2] Sickness *detached me slowly:* it spared me any break, any violent and offensive step. Thus I did not lose any good will and actually gained not a little. My sickness also gave me the right to change all my habits completely; it permitted, it *commanded* me to forget; it bestowed on me the necessity of lying still, of leisure, of waiting and being patient.— But that means, of thinking.— My eyes alone put an end to all bookwormishness—in brief, philology: I was delivered from the "book"; for years I did not read a thing—the greatest benefit I ever conferred on myself.— That nethermost self which had, as it

---

[1] This splendid sentence illuminates Nietzsche's ideas about "self-love" and "selflessness."

[2] Nietzsche collapsed a few weeks after writing this. This paragraph illustrates beautifully what Nietzsche says about *amor fati,* freedom from *ressentiment,* and saying Yes even to suffering.

were, been buried and grown silent under the continual pressure of having to listen to other selves (and that is after all what reading means) awakened slowly, shyly, dubiously—but eventually it spoke again. Never have I felt happier with myself than in the sickest and most painful periods of my life: one only need look at *The Dawn* or perhaps *The Wanderer and His Shadow* to comprehend what this "return to myself" meant—a supreme kind of recovery. —The other kind merely followed from this.

5

Human, All-Too-Human, this monument of rigorous self-discipline with which I put a sudden end to all my infections with "higher swindle," "idealism," "beautiful feelings," and other effeminacies, was written in the main in Sorrento; it was finished and received its final form during a winter in Basel, under conditions incomparably less favorable than those in Sorrento. Ultimately, Herr *Peter Gast,* who was then studying at the University of Basel and very devoted to me, has this book on his conscience. I dictated, my head bandaged and in pain; he wrote and also corrected: fundamentally, he was really the writer while I was merely the author.

When the book was finally finished and in my hands—a profound surprise for one so seriously ill—I also sent two copies, among others, to Bayreuth. By a miraculously meaningful coincidence, I received at the very same time a beautiful copy of the text of *Parsifal,* with Wagner's inscription for me, "for his dear friend, Friedrich Nietzsche, Richard Wagner, Church Councilor."— This crossing of the two books—I felt as if I heard an ominous sound— as if two swords had crossed.— At any rate, both of us felt that way; for both of us remained silent.— Around that time the first *Bayreuther Blätter* appeared: I understood for *what* it was high time.— Incredible! Wagner had become pious.

6

How I thought about myself at this time (1876), with what tremendous sureness I got hold of my task and its world-historical aspect—the whole book bears witness to that, above all a very explicit passage. Only, with my instinctive cunning, I avoided the little word "I" once again and bathed in world-historical glory—not Schopenhauer or Wagner this time but one of my friends, the excellent Dr. Paul Rée—fortunately far too refined a creature to—[1]

Others were less refined: I have always recognized who among my readers was hopeless—for example, the typical German professor—because on the basis of this passage they thought they had to understand the whole book as higher Réealism.— In fact, the contents contradicted five or six propositions of my friend—a point discussed in the Preface to my *Genealogy of Morals*.

The passage reads: "What is after all the main proposition that one of the boldest and coldest thinkers, the author of the book *On the Origin of Moral Feelings* [read: Nietzsche, the first *immoralist*] has reached on the basis of his incisive and penetrating analyses of human activity? 'The moral man is no closer to the intelligible world than the physical man—for there is no intelligible world . . .' This proposition, grown hard and sharp under the hammer blow of historical insight [read: *revaluation of all values*], may perhaps one day, in some future—1890!—serve as the ax swung against the 'metaphysical need' of mankind—but whether that will be more of a blessing or a curse for mankind, who could say? But in any case as a proposition of immense consequences, fruitful and terrible at the same time, looking into the world with that Janus face which all great insights share . . ." [2]

---

[1] Presumably: to have misunderstood and taken this literally.

[2] In the various German editions of *Ecce Homo* this quotation is not printed in quotation marks, and Nietzsche's insertions are placed in parentheses rather than brackets; nor is there any reference to the source of the quotation: *Human, All-Too-Human*, section 37. As a result, it is left unclear what exactly is quoted and what is not. Of course, "—1890!—" is also an insertion not found in the text of 1878. Nietzsche's other deviations from the original text are so slight that they are not worth listing here, except that the quotation from Rée's book originally read as follows: "The moral man," says he, "is no closer to the intelligible (metaphysical) world than the physical man." The next six words were not quoted in *Human, All-Too-Human*.

Dawn
Thoughts About Morality as a Prejudice

1

With this book my campaign against morality begins. Not that it smells in the least of powder: you will smell far different and much lovelier scents in it, assuming your nostrils have some sensitivity. Neither big nor small guns: if the effect of the book is negative, its means are anything but that—these means from which the effect issues like an inference, not like a cannon shot. If one takes leave of the book with a cautious reserve about everything that has so far attained honor and even worship under the name of morality, this in no way contradicts the fact that the whole book contains no negative word, no attack, no spite—that it lies in the sun, round, happy, like some sea animal basking among rocks.

Ultimately, I myself was this sea animal: almost every sentence in this book was first thought, *caught* among that jumble of rocks near Genoa where I was alone and still had secrets with the sea. Even now, whenever I accidentally touch this book, almost every sentence turns for me into a net that again brings up from the depths something incomparable: its entire skin trembles with tender thrills of memory. The art that distinguishes it is not inconsiderable when it comes to fixing to some extent things that easily flit by, noiselessly—moments I call divine lizards—but not with the cruelty of that young Greek god who simply speared the poor little lizard, though, to be sure, with something pointed—a pen.

"There are so many dawns that have not yet glowed"—this Indian inscription marks the opening of this book. Where does its author seek that new morning, that as yet undiscovered tender red that marks the beginning of another day—ah, a whole series, a whole world of new days? In a *revaluation of all values,* in a liberation from all moral values, in saying Yes to and having confidence in all that has hitherto been forbidden, despised, and damned. This

Yes-saying book pours out its light, its love, its tenderness upon ever so many wicked things; it gives back to them their "soul," a good conscience, the lofty right and privilege of existence. Morality is not attacked, it is merely no longer in the picture.

This book closes with an "Or?"—it is the only book that closes with an "Or?"

2

My task of preparing a moment of the highest self-examination for humanity, a *great noon* when it looks back and far forward, when it emerges from the dominion of accidents and priests and for the first time poses, *as a whole,* the question of Why? and For What?—this task follows of necessity from the insight that humanity is *not* all by itself on the right way, that it is by no means governed divinely, that, on the contrary, it has been precisely among its holiest value concepts that the instinct of denial, corruption, and decadence has ruled seductively. The question concerning the origin of moral values is for me a question of the very first rank because it is crucial for the future of humanity. The demand that we should believe that everything is really in the best of hands, that a book, the Bible, offers us definitive assurances about the divine governance and wisdom in the destiny of man, is—translated back into reality—the will to suppress the truth about the pitiable opposite of all this; namely, that humanity has so far been in the *worst* of hands and that it has been governed by the underprivileged, the craftily vengeful, the so-called "saints," these slanderers of the world and violators of man.

The decisive symptom that shows how the priest (including those *crypto*-priests, the philosophers) has become master quite generally and not only within a certain religious community, and that the morality of decadence, the will to the end has become accepted as morality itself, is the fact that what is unegoistic is everywhere assigned absolute value while what is egoistic is met with hostility. Whoever is at odds with me about that is to my mind *infected.*— But all the world is at odds with me.

For a physiologist such a juxtaposition of values simply leaves no doubt. When the least organ in an organism fails, however slightly, to enforce with complete assurance its self-preservation, its "egoism," restitution of its energies—the whole degenerates. The physiologist demands *excision* of the degenerating part; he denies all solidarity with what degenerates; he is worlds removed from pity for it. But the priest desires precisely the degeneration of the whole, of humanity: for that reason, he *conserves* what degenerates —at this price he rules.

When seriousness is deflected from the self-preservation and the enhancement of the strength of the body—*that is, of life*— when anemia is construed as an ideal, and contempt for the body as "salvation of the soul"—what else is this if not a *recipe* for decadence?

The loss of the center of gravity, resistance to the natural instincts—in one word, "selflessness"—that is what was hitherto called *morality*.— With the *Dawn* I first took up the fight against the morality that would unself man.[1]

---

[1] *Die Entselbstungs-Moral: Entselbstung* is Nietzsche's coinage; "unself" is inspired by Lady Macbeth's "unsex me."

The Gay Science
("la gaya scienza")

The *Dawn* is a Yes-saying book, deep but bright and gracious. The same is true also and in the highest degree of the *gaya scienza:* in almost every sentence profundity and high spirits go tenderly hand in hand. Some verses that express my gratitude for the most wonderful month of January I ever experienced—this whole book was its present—reveals sufficiently from what depths this "science" emerged to gaiety:

> *With a flaming spear you parted*
> *All its ice until my soul*
> *Hurries roaring toward the ocean*
> *Of its highest hope and goal:*
>
> *Ever healthier and brighter,*
> *In most loving constraint, free—*
> *Thus it praises your great wonders,*
> *Fairest month of January!* [1]

What is here called "highest hope"—who could have any doubt about that when he sees the diamond beauty of the first words of *Zarathustra* flashing at the end of the fourth book?— Or when at the end of the third book he reads the granite words in which a destiny finds for the first time a formula for itself, for *all* time? [2]

---

[1] *Der du mit dem Flammenspeere*
  Meiner Seele Eis zerteilt,
  Dass sie brausend nun zum Meere
  Ihrer höchsten Hoffnung eilt:

  Heller stets und stets gesunder,
  Frei im liebevollsten Muss—
  Also preist sie deine Wunder,
  Schönster Januarius!

[2] The last three aphorisms of Book III, numbered 273–75, are included in this volume.

The "Songs of Prince Free-as-a-Bird," [3] written for the most part in Sicily, are quite emphatically reminiscent of the Provençal concept of *gaya scienza*—that unity of *singer, knight,* and *free spirit* which distinguishes the wonderful early culture of the Provençals from all equivocal cultures. The very last poem above all, "To the Mistral," [4] an exuberant dancing song in which, if I may say so, one dances right over morality, is a perfect Provençalism.

---

[3] An appendix of poems, added along with Book V (sections 343–83) to the second edition, in 1887. *Vogelfrei,* rendered literally above, also means: declared an outlaw whom anybody may shoot at sight.

[4] This poem is included in my *Twenty German Poets: A Bilingual Edition* (New York, Modern Library, 1963).

Thus Spoke Zarathustra
A Book for All and None

1

Now I shall relate the history of *Zarathustra*. The fundamental conception of this work, the idea of the eternal recurrence, this highest formula of affirmation that is at all attainable, belongs in August 1881: it was penned on a sheet with the notation underneath, "6000 feet beyond man and time." That day I was walking through the woods along the lake of Silvaplana; at a powerful pyramidal rock not far from Surlei I stopped.[1] It was then that this idea came to me.

If I reckon back a few months from this day, I find as an omen a sudden and profoundly decisive change in my taste, especially in music. Perhaps the whole of *Zarathustra* may be reckoned as music; certainly a rebirth of the art of *hearing* was among its preconditions. In a small mountain spa not far from Vicenza, Recoaro, where I spent the spring of 1881, I discovered together with my maestro and friend, Peter Gast, who was also "reborn," that the phoenix of music flew past us with lighter and more brilliant feathers than it had ever displayed before. But if I reckon forward from that day to the sudden birth that occurred in February 1883 under the most improbable circumstances—the *finale* from which I have quoted a few sentences in the Preface was finished exactly in that sacred hour in which Richard Wagner died in Venice—we get eighteen months for the pregnancy. This figure of precisely eighteen months might suggest, at least to Buddhists, that I am really a female elephant.

---

[1] Clearly, the rock is not the one on the Chasté, a peninsula in the Silser See, on which a tablet with the text of the "Drunken Song" from *Zarathustra IV* (section 12) has been fastened. A photograph of the right rock illustrates a small booklet of 44 pages put out by and entitled *Nietzsche-Haus in Sils-Maria.*

My *gaya scienza* belongs in the interval and contains a hundred signs of the proximity of something incomparable; in the end it even offers the beginning of *Zarathustra,* and in the penultimate section of the fourth book the basic idea of *Zarathustra.*[2]

Something else also belongs in this interval: that *Hymn to Life* (for mixed choir and orchestra) whose score was published two years ago by E. W. Fritzsch in Leipzig—a scarcely trivial symptom of my condition during that year when the Yes-saying pathos *par excellence,* which I call the tragic pathos, was alive in me to the highest degree. The time will come when it will be sung in my memory.[3]

The text, to say this expressly because a misunderstanding has gained currency, is not by me: it is the amazing inspiration of a young Russian woman who was my friend at that time, Miss Lou von Salomé.[4] Whoever can find any meaning at all in the last words

---

[2] Section 341 (*Portable Nietzsche,* pp. 101f.). The idea meant is that of the eternal recurrence.

[3] The manuscript sent to the printer (*Druckmanuskript*) was preserved in the Nietzsche Archive and characterized as follows by Hans Joachim Mette: "Autograph composition for a solo voice with piano accompaniment,* written in August/September 1882, based on a stanza of the poem *Prayer to Life* by Lou Salomé: this very Lied was reworked by Peter Gast, who also took into account the second stanza, which Nietzsche presumably communicated to him—and was turned, in the summer of 1887, into a *Hymn to Life: Composition for Mixed Choir and Orchestra* and published by him under this title over Nietzsche's name, in the form of a first edition, E 39 (cf. *Friedrich Nietzsches Gesammelte Briefe,* III.2, 2nd ed., 1919, pp. 366–68); music sheet written upon on both sides." Mette's footnote reads: "*The melody had been found already in 1873/74 for the *Hymn to Friendship*" (*Der Literarische Nachlass Friedrich Nietzsches,* Hadl, Leipzig 1932, pp. 12f.; the same report was included a year later in the first volume of Nietzsche's *Werke und Briefe: Historisch-Kritische Gesamtausgabe; Werke,* vol. I, Munich, Beck, 1933).

Cf. Podach, *Ein Blick in Notizbücher Nietzsches* (a glance into Nietzsche's notebooks; Heidelberg, Wolfgang Rothe, 1963), p. 132: ". . . Gast had reworked the score so often that it . . . really was his. Nietzsche knew this very well and suggested that the composer's name should appear on the title page. A correspondence on this point ensued, not only with Gast who protested modestly but also with the publisher . . ."

See also Frederick R. Love, *Young Nietzsche and the Wagnerian Experience* (Chapel Hill, N.C., University of North Carolina Press, 1963).

[4] In the MS, Nietzsche's sister crossed out the last eleven words of this sentence, but they were printed nevertheless in 1908, and in all subsequent editions (cf. Podach, *Friedrich Nietzsches Werke,* pp. 200 and 285).

of this poem will guess why I preferred and admired it: they attain greatness. Pain is *not* considered an objection to life: "If you have no more happiness to give me, well then! *you still have suffering.*" Perhaps my music, too, attains greatness at this point. (Last note of the A-clarinet, c flat, not c: misprint.)

The following winter I stayed in that charming quiet bay of Rapallo which, not far from Genoa, is cut out between Chiavari and the foothills of Portofino. My health could have been better; the winter was cold and excessively rainy; my small *albergo,*[5] situated right at the sea so that the high sea made it impossible to sleep at night, was in just about every way the opposite of what one might wish for. In spite of this and almost in order to prove my proposition that everything decisive comes into being "in spite of," it was that winter and under these unfavorable circumstances that my *Zarathustra* came into being.

Mornings I would walk in a southerly direction on the splendid road to Zoagli, going up past pines with a magnificent view of the sea; in the afternoon, whenever my health permitted it, I walked around the whole bay from Santa Margherita all the way to Portofino. This place and this scenery came even closer to my heart because of the great love that Emperor Frederick III felt for them; by chance, I was in this coastal region again in the fall of 1886 when he visited this small forgotten world of bliss for the last time.[6]

---

[5] Hotel.

[6] Nietzsche originally wrote, "the unforgettable German Emperor" but then crossed out three words (Podach, p. 286). When the first Emperor of the Second *Reich,* Wilhelm I, had died at ninety-one on March 9, 1888, his much more liberal son, Friedrich III, had succeeded him; but Friedrich died of cancer after a hundred days, June 15, and was succeeded by his son, the last German Kaiser, Wilhelm II. It has often been surmised that European history might have taken a different turn if Friedrich III had lived longer.

On June 20 Nietzsche had written Gast: "The death of Kaiser Friedrich has moved me: in the end he was a small glimmering light of *free* thought, the last hope for Germany. Now the rule of *Stöcker* begins: I project the consequence and already *know* that now my *Will to Power* will be confiscated in Germany first of all."

Hofprediger (Court Chaplain) Stöcker was the leading German anti-Semite of that period. *The Will to Power* was then no more than a project for which Niezsche had accumulated a great deal of material, and the work now known under this striking title is merely a posthumously published col-

— It was on these two walks that the whole of *Zarathustra I* occurred to me,[7] and especially Zarathustra himself as a type: rather, he *overtook me*.[8]

2

To understand this type, one must first become clear about his physiological presupposition: this is what I call the *great health*. I don't know how I could explain this concept better, more *personally*, than I have done it in one of the last sections of the fifth book of my *gaya scienza*.[1]

Being new, nameless, self-evident, we premature births of an as yet unproven future, we need for a new goal also a new means—namely, a new health, stronger, more seasoned, tougher, more audacious, and gayer than any previous health. Whoever has a soul that craves to have experienced the whole range of values and desiderata to date, and to have sailed around all the coasts of this ideal "mediterranean"; whoever wants to know from the adventures of his own most authentic experience how a discoverer and conqueror of the ideal feels, and also an artist, a saint, a legislator, a sage, a scholar, a pious man,[2] and one who stands divinely apart in the old style—needs one thing above everything else: the *great health*—that one does not merely have but also acquires continually, and must acquire because one gives it up again and again, and must give it up.

And now, after we have long been on our way in this manner, we argonauts of the ideal, with more daring perhaps

---

lection of many of Nietzsche's most interesting notes. Still, this letter shows —along with a lot of other evidence—how the title was *not* meant, and how thoroughly Nietzsche's intentions and spirit differed from those of the last Kaiser.

[7] *Fiel mir . . . ein.*

[8] *Überfiel mich.*

[1] The last section but one, number 382.

[2] At this point, the original text of 1887 still had "a soothsayer" in addition to the others enumerated above.

than is prudent, and have suffered shipwreck and damage often enough, but are, to repeat it, healthier than one likes to permit us, dangerously healthy, ever again healthy—it will seem to us as if, as a reward, we now confronted an as yet undiscovered country whose boundaries nobody has surveyed yet, something beyond all the lands and nooks of the ideal so far, a world so overrich in what is beautiful, strange, questionable, terrible, and divine that our curiosity as well as our craving to possess it has got beside itself—alas, now nothing will sate us any more!

After such vistas and with such a burning hunger in our conscience and science,[3] how could we still be satisfied with *present-day man?* It may be too bad but it is inevitable that we find it difficult to remain serious when we look at his worthiest goals and hopes, and perhaps we do not even bother to look any more.

Another ideal runs ahead of us, a strange, tempting, dangerous ideal to which we should not wish to persuade anybody because we do not readily concede *the right to it* to anyone: the ideal of a spirit who plays naïvely—that is, not deliberately but from overflowing power and abundance—with all that was hitherto called holy, good, untouchable, divine; for whom those supreme things that the people naturally accept as their value standards, signify danger, decay, debasement, or at least recreation, blindness, and temporary self-oblivion; the ideal of a human, superhuman well-being and benevolence[4] that will often appear *inhuman*—for example, when it confronts all earthly seriousness so far, all solemnity in gesture, word, tone, eye, morality, and task so far, as if it were their most incarnate and involuntary parody—and in spite of all of this, it is perhaps only with him that *great seriousness* really begins, that the real question mark is posed for the first time, that the destiny of the soul changes, the hand moves forward, the tragedy *begins.*[5]

---

[3] *In Wissen und Gewissen.*

[4] *Wohlseins und Wohlwollens.*

[5] The last aphorism of Book IV, which concluded the first edition of *The*

3

Has anyone at the end of the nineteenth century a clear idea of what poets of strong ages have called *inspiration?* If not, I will describe it.— If one had the slightest residue of superstition left in one's system, one could hardly reject altogether the idea that one is merely incarnation, merely mouthpiece, merely a medium of overpowering forces. The concept of revelation—in the sense that suddenly, with indescribable certainty and subtlety, something becomes *visible,* audible, something that shakes one to the last depths and throws one down—that merely describes the facts. One hears, one does not seek; one accepts, one does not ask who gives; like lightning, a thought flashes up, with necessity, without hesitation regarding its form—I never had any choice.

A rapture whose tremendous tension occasionally discharges itself in a flood of tears—now the pace quickens involuntarily, now it becomes slow; one is altogether beside oneself, with the distinct consciousness of subtle shudders and of one's skin creeping[1] down to one's toes; a depth of happiness in which even what is most painful and gloomy does not seem something opposite but rather conditioned, provoked, a *necessary* color in such a superabundance of light; an instinct for rhythmic relationships that arches over wide spaces of forms—length, the need for a rhythm with wide arches,[2] is almost the measure of the force of inspiration, a kind of compensation for its pressure and tension.

Everything happens involuntarily in the highest degree but as in a gale of a feeling of freedom, of absoluteness, of power, of

---

Gay Science, had been entitled *Incipit tragoedia* (the tragedy begins) and was reused as the first section of the Prologue of *Zarathustra.*

The reference to "parody" in the sentence above is a reminder that Nietzsche's occasional pathos in *Zarathustra* and *Ecce Homo* is not devoid of irony: cf. the opening paragraph of section 4 of "Why I Am So Clever."

[1] "One's skin creeping": *Überrieselungen* conjures up a slightly different image—as if water trickled over us.

[2] "Arches over" and "wide arches" are in the original *überspannt* and *weit-gespannt,* and the word for tension at the end of the sentence and also a little earlier is *Spannung.*

divinity.— The involuntariness of image and metaphor is strangest of all; one no longer has any notion of what is an image or a metaphor: everything offers itself as the nearest, most obvious, simplest expression. It actually seems, to allude to something Zarathustra says, as if the things themselves approached and offered themselves as metaphors ("Here all things come caressingly to your discourse and flatter you; for they want to ride on your back. On every metaphor you ride to every truth. . . . Here the words and word-shrines of all being open up before you; here all being wishes to become word, all becoming wishes to learn from you how to speak").[3]

This is *my* experience of inspiration; I do not doubt that one has to go back thousands of years in order to find anyone who could say to me, "it is mine as well." [4]

4

Afterwards I was sick for a few weeks in Genoa. Then came a melancholy spring in Rome where I put up with life—it was not easy. Fundamentally, this most indecent place on earth for the poet of *Zarathustra* distressed me exceedingly, and I had not chosen it voluntarily. I wanted to go to *Aquila,*[1] Rome's counterconcept, founded from hostility against Rome, as I shall one day found a place, in[2] memory of an atheist and enemy of the church *comme il faut,*[3] one of those most closely related to me, the great Hohenstaufen Emperor Frederick II.[4] But some fatality was at work: I had to

---

[3] *Zarathustra III,* "The Return Home." The German editions do not have the three dots inserted above to mark Nietzsche's omission of almost one page; and instead of "you" (twice) after the three dots, *Zarathustra* has "me."

[4] This conclusion is criticized by Kaufmann, *Critique of Religion and Philosophy* (New York, Harper, 1958; Garden City, N.Y., Doubleday Anchor Books, 1961), section 75.

[1] A town 50 miles northeast of Rome, 2360 feet above sea level, founded as a bulwark against the power of the papacy by Conrad, son of Emperor Frederick II, about 1250, the year Frederick II died.

[2] Reading *zur* (in) where the German editions have *die* (the). The German reading makes no sense and presumably represents an error due to haste.

[3] As he should be.

[4] Cf. *Beyond Good and Evil,* section 200.

go back again.[5] In the end I resigned myself to the Piazza Barberini, after my exertions to go to an *anti-Christian* environment had wearied me. I fear that in order to avoid bad odors as far as possible I once inquired at the Palazzo del Quirinale itself [6] whether they did not have a quiet room for a philosopher.

It was on a *loggia* high above that Piazza, from which one has a fine view of Rome and hears the *fontana* splashing far below, that the loneliest song was written that has ever been written, the "Night Song." [7] Around that time a melody of indescribable melancholy was always about me, and I found its refrain in the words, "dead from immortality."

That summer, back home at the holy spot where the first lightning of the *Zarathustra* idea had flashed for me, I found *Zarathustra II*. Ten days sufficed; in no case, neither for the first nor for the third and last,[8] did I require more. The next winter, under the halcyon sky of Nizza, which then shone into my life for the first time, I found *Zarathustra III*—and was finished. Scarcely a year for the whole of it.

Many concealed spots and heights in the landscape around Nizza are hallowed for me by unforgettable moments; that decisive passage which bears the title "On Old and New Tablets" [9] was composed on the most onerous ascent from the station to the marvelous Moorish eyrie, Eza—the suppleness of my muscles has always been greatest when my creative energies were flowing most abundantly. The *body* is inspired; let us keep the "soul" out of it.—

---

[5] Here the following words in the MS were deleted, I do not know by whom —but Nietzsche himself might well have struck them out on rereading them: "In Rome I had the experience that *Parsifal* was praised to my face: twice I had attacks of laughter at that" (Podach, p. 289).

[6] Before 1870 this had been a papal residence; since 1870 it was the residence of the king of Italy. One of Nietzsche's last letters (December 31, 1888, to Gast) ends: "My address I do not know any more: let us suppose that at first it may be the *Palazzo del Quirinale*. N."

[7] The ninth chapter of *Zarathustra II*.

[8] Nietzsche had published only Parts I, II, and III, at first separately and then, in 1887, also in one volume. Part IV, written in Nizza and Mentone the next winter (early in 1885) was printed privately in 1885 (only forty copies), and only seven copies were distributed among close friends.

[9] The twelfth chapter of *Zarathustra III*.

Often one could have seen me dance; in those days I could walk in the mountains for seven or eight hours without a trace of weariness. I slept well, I laughed much—my vigor and patience were perfect.

5

Except for these ten-day works, the years during and above all *after* my *Zarathustra* were marked by distress without equal. One pays dearly for immortality: one has to die several times while still alive.

There is something I call the *rancune*[1] of what is great: everything great—a work, a deed—is no sooner accomplished than it turns *against* the man who did it. By doing it, he has become *weak;* he no longer endures his deed, he can no longer face it. Something one was never permitted to will lies *behind* one, something in which the knot in the destiny of humanity is tied—and now one labors *under* it!— It almost crushes one.— The *rancune* of what is great.

Then there is the gruesome silence one hears all around one. Solitude has seven skins; nothing penetrates them any more. One comes to men, one greets friends—more desolation, no eye offers a greeting. At best, a kind of revolt. Such revolts I experienced, very different in degree but from almost everybody who was close to me. It seems nothing offends more deeply than suddenly letting others feel a distance;[2] those *noble* natures who do not know how to live without reverence are rare.

Thirdly, there is the absurd sensitivity of the skin to small stings, a kind of helplessness against everything small.[3] This seems

---

[1] Rancor.

[2] Cf. the "pathos of distance," *Beyond Good and Evil,* section 257; also above, "The Untimely Ones," section 3, the last paragraph.

[3] In a discarded draft we find the following passage: "The psychologist still adds that there are no conditions in which one's defenselessness and lack of protection are greater. If there are any means at all for destroying [*umzu-bringen*] men who *are destinies,* the instinct of poisonous flies discerns these means. For one who has greatness there is no fight with the small: hence the small become masters" (Podach, pp. 291f.). Cf. also "The Flies of the Market Place" in *Zarathustra I* and, of course, Sartre's *The Flies.*

to me to be due to the tremendous squandering of all defensive energies which is a presupposition of every *creative* deed, every deed that issues from one's most authentic, inmost, nethermost regions. Our *small* defensive capacities are thus, as it were, suspended; no energy is left for them.

I still dare to hint that one digests less well, does not like to move, is all too susceptible to feeling chills as well as mistrust— mistrust that is in many instances merely an etiological blunder. In such a state I once sensed the proximity of a herd of cows even before I saw it, merely because milder and more philanthropic thoughts came back to me: *they* had warmth.

6

This work stands altogether apart. Leaving aside the poets: perhaps nothing has ever been done from an equal excess of strength. My concept of the "Dionysian" here became a *supreme deed;* measured against that, all the rest of human activity seems poor and relative. That a Goethe, a Shakespeare, would be unable to breathe even for a moment in this tremendous passion and height, that Dante is, compared with Zarathustra, merely a believer and not one who first *creates* truth, a *world-governing* spirit, a destiny—that the poets of the Veda are priests and not even worthy of tying the shoelaces of a Zarathustra—that is the least thing and gives no idea of the distance, of the *azure* solitude in which this work lives. Zarathustra possesses an eternal right to say: "I draw circles around me and sacred boundaries; fewer and fewer men climb with me on ever higher mountains: I am building a mountain range out of ever more sacred mountains." [1]

Let anyone add up the spirit and good nature of all great souls: [2] all of them together would not be capable of producing even one of Zarathustra's discourses. The ladder on which he ascends and descends [3] is tremendous; he has seen further, willed fur-

---

[1] *Zarathustra III,* "On Old and New Tablets," section 19.
[2] Cf. Aristotle's conception of *megalopsychia,* cited in the Editor's Introduction, section 2.
[3] Genesis 28:12.

ther, been *capable* further than any other human being. In every word he contradicts, this most Yes-saying of all spirits; in him all opposites are blended into a new unity. The highest and the lowest energies of human nature, what is sweetest, most frivolous, and most terrible wells forth from one fount with immortal assurance. Till then one does not know what is height, what depth; one knows even less what truth is. There is no moment in this revelation of truth that has been anticipated or guessed by even *one* of the greatest. There is no wisdom, no investigation of the soul, no art of speech before Zarathustra; what is nearest and most everyday, here speaks of unheard-of things. Epigrams trembling with passion, eloquence become music, lightning bolts hurled forward into hitherto unfathomed futures. The most powerful capacity for metaphors that has existed so far is poor and mere child's play compared with this return of language to the nature of imagery.

And how Zarathustra descends and says to everyone what is most good-natured! How gently he handles even his antagonists, the priests, and suffers of them *with* them!— Here man has been overcome at every moment; the concept of the "overman" has here become the greatest reality—whatever was so far considered great in man lies beneath him at an infinite distance. The halcyon, the light feet, the omnipresence of malice and exuberance, and whatever else is typical of the type of Zarathustra—none of this has ever before been dreamed of as essential to greatness. Precisely in this width of space and this accessibility for what is contradictory, Zarathustra experiences himself as the *supreme type of all beings;* and once one hears how he defines this, one will refrain from seeking any metaphor for it.[4]

"The soul that has the longest ladder and reaches down deepest—the most comprehensive soul, which can run and stray and roam farthest within itself; the most necessary soul that plunges joyously into chance; the soul that, having being, dives into becoming; the soul that *has,* but *wants* to want and will; the soul that flees itself and catches up with itself in the widest circles; the wisest soul that folly exhorts most sweetly; the soul that loves itself most, in

---

[4] *Nach seinem Gleichnis zu suchen.* This makes little sense; Nietzsche probably meant: *nach seinesgleichen zu suchen,* i.e.: seeking his equal.

which all things have their sweep and countersweep and ebb and flood——" [5]

But that is the concept of Dionysus himself.— Another consideration leads to the very same result. The psychological problem in the type of Zarathustra is how he that says No and *does* No to an unheard-of degree, to everything to which one has so far said Yes, can nevertheless be the opposite of a No-saying spirit; how the spirit who bears the heaviest fate, a fatality of a task, can nevertheless be the lightest and most transcendent—Zarathustra is a dancer —how he that has the hardest, most terrible insight into reality, that has thought the "most abysmal idea," nevertheless does not consider it an objection to existence, not even to its eternal recurrence—but rather one reason more for being himself the eternal Yes to all things, "the tremendous, unbounded saying Yes and Amen." [6]— "Into all abysses I still carry the blessings of my saying Yes."— *But this is the concept of Dionysus once again.*

7

What language will such a spirit speak when he speaks to himself? The language of the *dithyramb*. I am the inventor of the dithyramb. Listen to how Zarathustra speaks to himself before sunrise: such emerald happiness, such divine tenderness did not have a tongue before me. Even the deepest melancholy of such a Dionysus still turns into a dithyramb. To give some indication of this, I choose the "Night Song," the immortal lament at being condemned by the overabundance of light and power, by his sun-nature, not to love.

Night has come; now all fountains speak more loudly. And my soul, too, is a fountain.

---

[5] "On Old and New Tablets," section 19. The first dash, after "deepest," is not found in the original but has been inserted above to mark Nietzsche's omission of the words: "how should the most parasites not sit on that?" And where Nietzsche has a double dash, Zarathustra concludes: "oh, how should the highest soul not have the worst parasites?"

[6] Cf. *Zarathustra III,* the last chapter, which is entitled "The Seven Seals (Or: The Yes and Amen Song)."

Night has come; only now all the songs of lovers awaken. And my soul, too, is the song of a lover.

Something unstilled, unstillable is within me; it wants to be voiced. A craving for love is within me; it speaks the language of love.

Light am I; ah, that I were night! But this is my loneliness that I am girt with light. Ah, that I were dark and nocturnal! How I would suck at the breasts of light! And even you would I bless, you little sparkling stars and glowworms up there, and be overjoyed with your gifts of light.

But I live in my own light; I drink back into myself the flames that break out of me. I do not know the happiness of those who receive; and I have often dreamed that even stealing must be more blessed than receiving. This is my poverty, that my hand never rests from giving; this is my envy, that I see waiting eyes and the lit-up nights of longing. Oh, wretchedness of all givers! Oh, darkening of my sun! Oh, craving to crave! Oh, ravenous hunger in satiation!

They receive from me, but do I touch their souls? There is a cleft between giving and receiving; and the narrowest cleft is the last to be bridged. A hunger grows out of my beauty: I should like to hurt those for whom I shine; I should like to rob those to whom I give; thus do I hunger for malice. To withdraw my hand when the other hand already reaches out to it; to linger like the waterfall, which lingers even while it plunges: thus do I hunger for malice. Such revenge my fullness plots: such spite wells up out of my loneliness. My happiness in giving died in giving; my virtue tired of itself in its overflow.

The danger of those who always give is that they lose their sense of shame; and the heart and hand of those who always mete out become callous from always meting out. My eye no longer wells over at the shame of those who beg; my hand has grown too hard for the trembling of filled hands. Where have the tears of my eyes gone and the down of my heart? Oh, the loneliness of all givers! Oh, the taciturnity of all who shine!

Many suns revolve in the void: to all that is dark they

speak with their light—to me they are silent. Oh, this is the enmity of the light against what shines: merciless it moves in its orbit. Unjust in its heart against all that shines, cold against suns—thus moves every sun.

The suns fly like a storm in their orbits: that is their motion. They follow their inexorable will: that is their coldness.

Oh, it is only you, you dark ones, you nocturnal ones, who create warmth out of that which shines. It is only you who drink milk and refreshment out of the udders of light.

Alas, ice is all around me, my hand is burned by the ice. Alas, thirst is within me that languishes after your thirst.

Night has come: alas, that I must be light! And thirst for the nocturnal! And loneliness!

Night has come: now my craving breaks out of me like a well; to speak I crave.

Night has come; now all fountains speak more loudly. And my soul, too, is a fountain.

Night has come; now all the songs of lovers awaken. And my soul, too, is the song of a lover.

8

Nothing like this has ever been written, felt, or *suffered:* thus suffers a god, a Dionysus. The answer to such a dithyramb of solar solitude in the light would be Ariadne.— Who besides me knows what Ariadne is!— For all such riddles nobody so far had any solution; I doubt that anybody even saw any riddles here.

Zarathustra once defines, quite strictly, his task—it is mine, too—and there is no mistaking his meaning: he says Yes to the point of justifying, of redeeming even all of the past.

"I walk among men as among the fragments of the future— that future which I envisage. And this is all my creating and striving, that I create and carry together into One what is fragment and riddle and dreadful accident. And how could I bear to be a man if man were not also a creator and guesser of riddles and redeemer of accidents? *To redeem those who lived in the past* and to turn every 'it was' into a 'thus I willed it'—that alone should I call redemption." [1]

In another passage he defines as strictly as possible what alone "man" can be for him—*not* an object of love or, worse, pity—Zarathustra has mastered the *great nausea* over man, too: man is for him an un-form, a material, an ugly stone that needs a sculptor.

"Willing no more and *esteeming* no more and *creating* no more—oh, that this great weariness might always remain far from me! In knowledge, too, I feel only my will's joy in begetting and becoming; and if there is innocence in my knowledge, it is because the *will to beget* is in it. Away from God and gods this will has lured me; what could one create if gods—were there?

"But my fervent will to create impels me ever again toward man; thus is the hammer impelled toward the stone. O men, in the stone an image is sleeping, the image of images! Alas, that it has to sleep in the hardest, ugliest stone! *Now my hammer rages cruelly against its prison.* Pieces of rock rain from the stone: what is that to me? I want to perfect it; for a shadow came to me—the stillest and lightest of all things once came to me. The beauty of the overman came to me as a shadow. O my brothers, what are gods to me now?" [2]

I stress a final point: the verse in italics furnishes the occasion. Among the conditions for a *Dionysian* task are, in a decisive way, the hardness of the hammer, the *joy even in destroying.* The imperative, "become hard!" the most fundamental certainty *that all creators are hard,* [3] is the distinctive mark of a Dionysian nature.

---

[1] *Zarathustra II,* "On Redemption." The lines after the phrase in italics should be compared with "Human, All-Too-Human," section 4, above: *Ecce Homo* voices Nietzsche's own *amor fati.*

[2] *Zarathustra II,* "Upon the Blessed Isles."

[3] *Zarathustra III,* "On Old and New Tablets," 29, as quoted at the end of *Twilight (Portable Nietzsche,* pp. 326 and 563). *Zarathustra:* "For creators are hard." *Twilight:* "For all creators are hard." And "Become hard!" is emphasized in *Zarathustra* but not in *Twilight.*

Beyond Good and Evil
Prelude to a Philosophy of the Future

1

The task for the years that followed now was indicated as clearly as possible. After the Yes-saying part of my task had been solved, the turn had come for the No-saying, *No-doing* part: the revaluation of our values so far, the great war—conjuring up a day of decision. This included the slow search for those related to me, those who, prompted by strength, would offer me their hands for *destroying*.

From this moment forward all my writings are fish hooks: perhaps I know how to fish as well as anyone?— If nothing was caught, I am not to blame. *There were no fish.*

2

This book (1886) is in all essentials a *critique of modernity*, not excluding the modern sciences, modern arts, and even modern politics, along with pointers to a contrary type that is as little modern as possible—a noble, Yes-saying type. In the latter sense, the book is a school for the *gentilhomme*,[1] taking this concept in a more spiritual and radical sense than has ever been done. One has to have guts merely to endure it; one must never have learned how to be afraid.

All those things of which our age is proud are experienced as contradictions to this type, almost as bad manners; our famous "objectivity," for example; "pity for all that suffers"; the "historical sense" with its submission to foreign tastes, groveling on its belly before *petits faits*,[2] and "being scientific."

When you consider that this book followed *after Zarathustra*,

---

[1] Nobleman, gentleman.
[2] Small facts.

you may perhaps also guess the dietetic regimen to which it owes its origin. The eye that had been spoiled by the tremendous need for seeing *far*—Zarathustra is even more far-sighted than the Tsar —is here forced to focus on what lies nearest, the age, the around-us. In every respect, above all also in the form, you will find the same *deliberate* turning away from the instincts that had made possible a Zarathustra. The refinement in form, in intention, in the art of *silence* is in the foreground; psychology is practiced with admitted hardness and cruelty—the book is devoid of any good-natured word.

All this is a recuperation: who would guess after all *what* sort of recuperation such a squandering of good-naturedness as Zarathustra represents makes necessary?

Theologically speaking—listen closely, for I rarely speak as a theologian—it was God himself who at the end of his days' work lay down as a serpent under the tree of knowledge: thus he recuperated from being God.— He had made everything too beautiful.[3] — The devil is merely the leisure of God on that seventh day.

---

[3] Or: too beautifully.

Genealogy of Morals
A Polemic

Regarding expression, intention, and the art of surprise, the three inquiries which constitute this *Genealogy* are perhaps uncannier than anything else written so far. Dionysus is, as is known, also the god of darkness.

Every time a beginning that is *calculated* to mislead: cool, scientific, even ironic, deliberately foreground, deliberately holding off. Gradually more unrest; sporadic lightning; very disagreeable truths are heard grumbling in the distance—until eventually a *tempo feroce* is attained in which everything rushes ahead in a tremendous tension. In the end, in the midst of perfectly gruesome detonations, a *new* truth becomes visible every time among thick clouds.

The truth of the *first* inquiry is the birth of Christianity: the birth of Christianity out of the spirit of *ressentiment,* not, as people may believe, out of the "spirit"—a countermovement by its very nature, the great rebellion against the dominion of *noble* values.

The *second* inquiry offers the psychology of the *conscience*—which is not, as people may believe, "the voice of God in man": it is the instinct of cruelty that turns back after it can no longer discharge itself externally. Cruelty is here exposed for the first time as one of the most ancient and basic substrata of culture that simply cannot be imagined away.

The *third* inquiry offers the answer to the question whence the ascetic ideal, the priests' ideal, derives its tremendous *power* although it is the *harmful* ideal *par excellence,* a will to the end, an ideal of decadence. Answer: not, as people may believe, because God is at work behind the priests but *faute de mieux*[1]—because it was the only ideal so far, because it had no rival. "For man would

---

[1] Lacking something better.

rather will even nothingness than *not* will." [2]— Above all, a *counterideal* was lacking—*until Zarathustra.*

I have been understood. Three decisive preliminary studies by a psychologist for a revaluation of all values.— This book contains the first psychology of the priest.

---

[2] An almost but not quite exact quotation of the last words of the book, found also—again a little differently—near the end of the first section of the third inquiry.

Twilight of the Idols
How One Philosophizes with a Hammer[1]

1

This essay of less than 150 pages,[2] cheerful and ominous in tone, a demon that laughs—the work of so few days that I hesitate to mention how many, is an exception among books: there is none richer in substance, more independent, more subversive[3]—more evil. If you want a quick idea how before me everything stood on its head,[4] begin with this essay. What is called *idol* on the title page is simply what has been called truth so far. *Twilight of the Idols*—that is: the old truth is approaching its end.

2

There is no reality, no "ideality" that is not touched in this essay (touched: what a cautious euphemism!). Not only *eternal* idols, also the youngest which are therefore feeblest on account of their age. "Modern ideas," for example. A great wind blows among the trees, and everywhere fruit fall down—truths. The squandering of an all-too-rich autumn: one stumbles over truths, one steps on and kills a few—there are too many.

But what we get hold of is no longer anything questionable but rather decisions. I am the first to hold in my hands the measure for "truths"; I am the first who is *able* to decide. Just as if a second

---

[1] For the meaning of this famous phrase, see the Preface to the book: ". . . not just idols of the age, but eternal idols, which are here touched with a hammer as with a tuning fork: there are . . . none more hollow."

[2] *Portable Nietzsche,* pp. 465–563.

[3] *Umwerfenderes:* literally, more overthrowing.

[4] Nietzsche's revaluation, like Marx's correction of Hegel, represents an attempt to put things right-side up again. Yet Nietzsche and Marx have usually been misrepresented as if they had boasted that *they* had stood everything on its head.

consciousness had grown in me; just as if "the will" had kindled a light for itself in me so that it might see the inclined plane, the *askew* path[5] on which it went down so far.— The *askew* path— people called it the way to "truth."

It is all over with all "darkling aspiration"; precisely the *good* man was least aware of the right way.[6]— And in all seriousness: nobody before me knew the right way, the way *up;* it is only beginning with me that there are hopes again, tasks, ways that can be prescribed for culture—*I am he that brings these glad tidings.*— And thus I am also a destiny.—

3

Immediately upon finishing this work, without losing even one day, I attacked the tremendous task of the *Revaluation,*[1] with a sovereign feeling of pride that was incomparable, certain at every moment of my immortality, engraving sign upon sign on bronze tablets with the sureness of a destiny. The Preface was written on September 3, 1888: when I stepped outdoors the morning after, I saw the most beautiful day that the Upper Engadine ever showed me—transparent, the colors glowing, including all opposites, everything that lies between ice and south.

It was only on September 20 that I left Sils Maria, detained by floods—in the end by far the only guest of this wonderful place on which my gratitude wants to bestow an immortal name. After a journey with incidents, including some danger to my life in Como, which was flooded—I got there only late at night—I reached Turin on the afternoon of the 21st—my *proven* place, my residence from now on. I took the same apartment I had occupied in the spring, Via Carlo Alberto 6, fourth floor, opposite the imposing Palazzo

---

[5] Here six words have been used to render *die schiefe Bahn;* in the next sentence, only three words. The ordinary German reader would assume at first that an inclined plane was meant; then, coming to the second occurrence of *schiefe,* emphasized by Nietzsche, he would interpret it as askew, crooked.

[6] Allusion to Goethe's *Faust,* lines 328f.

[1] That is, *The Antichrist,* which Nietzsche conceived as the first of the four parts of the *Revaluation of All Values.* Cf. the Preface (*Portable Nietzsche,* pp. 568f.).

Carignano in which Vittorio Emanuele[2] was born, with a view of the Piazza Carlo Alberto and of the hills beyond. Without hesitation and without permitting myself to be distracted for a moment, I went back to work: only the final quarter of the work remained to be done. On the 30th of September, great victory; seventh day; the leisure of a god walking along the Po river.[3] On the same day I wrote the Preface for *Twilight of the Idols:* [4] correcting the printer's proofs of that book had been my recreation in September.

Never have I experienced such an autumn, nor considered anything of the sort possible on earth—a Claude Lorrain[5] projected into the infinite, every day of the same indomitable perfection.

---

[2] Born 1820, King of Sardinia 1849–1861, the first King of Italy from 1861 until his death in 1878.

[3] *Müssiggang eines Gottes am Po entlang.*

[4] When he wrote the Preface he still intended to call the book *Müssiggang eines Psychologen* (a psychologist's leisure). A letter from Peter Gast (cited in *Portable Nietzsche,* p. 464), asking for a less unassuming title, changed Nietzsche's mind. The book appeared with the new title in January 1889, a few days after Nietzsche's collapse. *The Case of Wagner,* on the other hand, had appeared in the fall of 1888: with respect to these two books, Nietzsche does not adhere to the chronological order. *The Antichrist,* which is not reviewed here by Nietzsche, and *Nietzsche contra Wagner,* which was composed after *Ecce Homo,* were first published in 1895.

[5] French painter (1600–1682). His real name was Claude Gelée (also spelled Gellée), but he is remembered as Claude Lorrain.

The Case of Wagner
A Musician's Problem

1

To do justice to this essay, one has to suffer of the fate of music as of an open wound.— Of *what* do I suffer when I suffer of the fate of music? That music has been done out of its world-transfiguring, Yes-saying character, so that it is music of decadence and no longer the flute of Dionysus.

Assuming, however, that a reader experiences the cause of music in this way as his own cause, as the history of his own sufferings, he will find this essay full of consideration and exceedingly mild. To be cheerful in such cases, genially mocking oneself, too—*ridendo dicere severum*[1] when the *verum dicere* would justify any amount of hardness—is humanity itself. Does anyone really doubt that I, as the old artillerist I am,[2] could easily bring up my *heavy* guns against Wagner?— Everything decisive in this matter I held back—I have loved Wagner.

Ultimately, an attack on a subtler "unknown one," whom nobody else is likely to guess, is part of the meaning and way of my task—oh, I can uncover "unknown ones" who are in an altogether different category from a Cagliostro[3] of music—even more, to be sure, an attack on the German nation which is becoming ever lazier

---

[1] The motto of the book: "Through what is laughable say what is somber"— a variation of Horace's *ridentem dicere verum, quid vetat* (what forbids us to tell the truth, laughing?), *Satires* I.24.

[2] Nietzsche had done his compulsory military service with an artillery regiment, beginning in October 1867; but his actual service was cut short by an accident in which he was hurt, and he was bedridden and then convalescing until his discharge in October 1868. During the Franco-Prussian War of 1870–71, he was a Swiss subject, being a Swiss professor, but volunteered and served briefly as a medical orderly—for less than a month. Sick with dysentery and diphtheria, he was discharged.

[3] An impostor or charlatan, after Count Alessandro di Cagliostro (1743–1795; really Giuseppe Balsamo).

and more impoverished in its instincts, ever more *honest,* and
which continues with an enviable appetite to feed on opposites,
gobbling down without any digestive troubles "faith" as well as
scientific manners,[4] "Christian love" as well as anti-Semitism, the
will to power (to the *Reich*) as well as the *évangile des humbles.*[5]
— Such a failure to take sides among opposites! Such neutrality
and "selflessness" of the stomach! This sense of justice of the German palate that finds all causes just and accords all equal rights[6]—
that finds everything tasty.— Beyond a doubt, the Germans are
idealists.

When I visited Germany last, I found the German taste exert-
ing itself to concede equal rights to Wagner and to the *Trumpeter
of Säkkingen;*[7] I myself witnessed how a Liszt Society was founded
in Leipzig, for the cultivation and propagation of insidious[8] church
music, ostensibly in honor of one of the most genuine and German
musicians—German in the old sense of that word, no mere *Reichs-
deutscher*—the old master Heinrich Schütz.— Beyond a doubt, the
Germans are idealists.[9]

---

[4] *Wissenschaftlichkeit.*

[5] Gospel of the humble.

[6] *. . . Gaumens, der allem gleiche Rechte gibt . . .*

[7] An immensely popular epic poem by Josef Viktor Scheffel (1826–1886)
that had gone through about 140 editions by 1886. In an earlier draft for this
passage Nietzsche had considered pairing "Goethe and Scheffel" the way the
will to power and the gospel of the humble are paired above (see Podach,
Friedrich Nietzsches Werke, p. 309).

Richard M. Meyer says of Scheffel in *Die deutsche Literatur des Neun-
zehnten Jahrhunderts* (German literature of the nineteenth century, Berlin,
Bondi, 1900): "No poet of our time has been glorified with so many monuments, memorial stones, and memorial tablets"; also, *"The Trumpeter of Säkkingen* (1854) belongs among those books which have made popularity
unpopular among us" (pp. 523, 528).

[8] *Listiger.* Franz Liszt (1811–1886), the composer and pianist—and father
of Cosima, then Wagner's widow—was born in Raiding, Hungary; retired to
Rome in 1861 and joined the Franciscan order in 1865; he died in Bayreuth
in 1886.

[9] In the sense made popular by Schelling and Hegel: men who seek syn-
theses of opposites.

2

But here nothing shall keep me from becoming blunt and telling the Germans a few hard truths: *who else would do it?*

I speak of their indecency *in historicis*. Not only have the German historians utterly lost the *great perspective* for the course and the values of culture; nor are they merely, without exception, buffoons of politics (or the church)—but they have actually *proscribed* this great perspective. One must first be "German" and have "race," then one can decide about all values and disvalues *in historicis*—one *determines* them.

"German" has become an argument, *Deutschland, Deutschland über alles*[1] a principle; the Teutons represent the "moral world order" in history—the carriers of freedom versus the *imperium Romanum,* and the restoration of morality and the "categorical imperative" [2] versus the eighteenth century.— There is now a historiography that is *reichsdeutsch;* there is even, I fear, an anti-Semitic one—there is a *court* historiography, and Herr von Treitschke is not ashamed—[3]

Recently an idiotic[4] judgment *in historicis,* a proposition of the fortunately late aesthetic Swabian, Vischer,[5] was repeated in one German newspaper after another, as a "truth" to which every German has to say Yes: "The Renaissance *and* the Reformation—

---

[1] "Germany, Germany above everything": the beginning of the German national anthem.

[2] The unconditional and universal imperative that Kant considered the core of morality.

[3] For Nietzsche's thoughts on Heinrich von Treitschke (1834–1896) and the German historians of that time see also *Beyond Good and Evil,* section 251, along with my long footnote (22). None of this kept Ernest Barker, an eminent British scholar, from publishing a tract on *Nietzsche and Treitschke: The Worship of Power in Modern Germany,* Oxford Pamphlets, Number 20, London, Oxford University Press, 1914; 4th impression, 1914!

[4] The words "idiot" and "idiotic" figure prominently in Nietzsche's writings, beginning in 1887: see Kaufmann's *Nietzsche,* Chapter 12, note 2.

[5] Friedrich Theodor Vischer (1807–1887) wrote *Aesthetik,* 6 volumes (1846–57); also a parody of Goethe's *Faust II,* entitled *Faust: Der Tragödie dritter Teil* (i.e., Faust III; 1862, under the pseudonym Mystifizinski), and a very popular novel, *Auch Einer* (another one; 1879).

only the two together make a whole: the aesthetic rebirth *and* the moral rebirth."

When I read such sentences, my patience is exhausted and I feel the itch, I even consider it a duty, to tell the Germans for once how many things they have on their conscience by now.[6] *All great crimes against culture for four centuries they have on their conscience.*— And the reason is always the same: their innermost *cowardice* before reality, which is also cowardice before the truth; their untruthfulness which has become instinctive with them; their "idealism."

The Germans did Europe out of the harvest, the meaning, of the last *great* age, the age of the Renaissance, at a moment when a higher order of values, the noble ones, those that say Yes to life, those that guarantee the future, had triumphed at the seat of the opposite values, those of *decline—even in the very instincts of those who were sitting there*. Luther, this calamity of a monk, restored the church and, what is a thousand times worse, Christianity, at the very moment *when it was vanquished.*— Christianity, this denial of the will to life become religion!— Luther, an impossible monk who, on account of his own "impossibility," attacked the church and—consequently—restored it.— The Catholics would have good reasons to celebrate Luther festivals, to write Luther plays.— Luther—and the "moral rebirth"! To hell with psychology! [7]— Beyond a doubt, the Germans are idealists.

Twice, when an honest, unequivocal, perfectly scientific way of thinking had just been attained with tremendous fortitude and self-overcoming, the Germans managed to find devious paths to the old "ideal," reconciliations of truth and "ideal"—at bottom, formulas for a right to repudiate science, a right to *lie*. Leibniz and Kant—these two greatest brake shoes of intellectual integrity in Europe!

---

[6] The remainder of this section is quite similar to *The Antichrist*, section 61 (*Portable Nietzsche*, pp. 653ff.).

[7] *Zum Teufel mit aller Psychologie:* presumably, Nietzsche means that those who associate Luther with a "moral rebirth" have no regard whatever for psychology. Cf. *The Antichrist*, section 39 (*Portable Nietzsche*, p. 613), *The Will to Power*, section 192, and Kaufmann's *Nietzsche*, Chapter 12, section II.

Finally, when on the bridge between two centuries of decadence, a *force majeure*[8] of genius and will became visible, strong enough to create a unity out of Europe, a political and *economic* unity for the sake of a world government—the Germans with their "Wars of Liberation" did Europe out of the meaning, the miracle of meaning in the existence of Napoleon; hence they have on their conscience all that followed, that is with us today—this most *anticultural* sickness and unreason there is, nationalism, this *névrose nationale*[9] with which Europe is sick, this perpetuation of European particularism, of *petty* politics:[10] they have deprived Europe itself of its meaning, of its reason—they have driven it into a dead-end street.[11]— Does anyone besides me know the way out of this dead-end street?— A task that is great enough to *unite* nations again?

3

And in the end, why should I not voice my suspicion? In my case, too, the Germans will try everything to bring forth from a tremendous destiny—a mouse. So far they have compromised themselves in my case; I doubt that they will do any better in the future.— Ah, how I wish I were a *bad* prophet in this case!— My natural readers and listeners are even now Russians, Scandinavians, and Frenchmen—will it always be that way?

In the history of the quest for knowledge the Germans are inscribed with nothing but ambiguous names; they have always brought forth only "unconscious" counterfeiters (Fichte, Schelling, Schopenhauer, Hegel, and Schleiermacher deserve this epithet as well as Kant and Leibniz: they are all mere veil makers):[1] they shall never enjoy the honor that the first *honest* spirit in the history

---

[8] Superior force.

[9] National neurosis.

[10] *Der Kleinstaaterei Europas, der* kleinen *Politik.*

[11] *Sie haben Europa selbst um seinen Sinn, um seine* Vernunft—*sie haben es in eine Sackgasse gebracht.*

[1] The name of Schleiermacher (1768–1834), the leading Protestant theologian of the German romantic movement, means literally veil maker.

of the spirit, the spirit in whom truth comes to judgment over the counterfeiting of four millennia, should be counted one with the German spirit.

The "German spirit" is for me bad air: I breathe with difficulty near the by now instinctive uncleanliness *in psychologicis* which every word, every facial expression of a German betrays. They have never gone through a seventeenth century of hard self-examination, like the French—a La Rochefoucauld and a Descartes are a hundred times superior in honesty to the foremost Germans—to this day they have not had a psychologist. But psychology is almost the measure of the *cleanliness* or *uncleanliness* of a race.

And if one is not even cleanly, how should one have *depth?* It is with Germans almost as it is with women: one never fathoms their depths; they don't have any, that is all. They aren't even shallow.[2]— What is called "deep" in Germany is precisely this instinctive uncleanliness in relation to oneself of which I have just spoken: one does not *want* to gain clarity about oneself. Might I not propose the word "German" as an international coinage for this psychological depravity?— At this very moment, for example, the German Kaiser calls it his "Christian duty" to liberate the slaves in Africa: among us other Europeans this would then simply be called "German."

Have the Germans produced even one book that has depth? They even lack the *idea* of depth in a book. I have met scholars who considered Kant deep; at the Prussian court, I fear, Herr von Treitschke is considered deep. And when I occasionally praise Stendhal as a deep psychologist, I have encountered professors at German universities who asked me to spell his name.

4

And why should I not go all the way? I like to make a clean sweep of things. It is part of my ambition to be considered a de-

---

[2] Nietzsche here uses one of the "Maxims and Arrows" (number 27) from *Twilight* and applies it to the Germans. The last sentence is crossed out in the MS—presumably not by Nietzsche, and therefore printed in the German editions.

spiser of the Germans *par excellence.* My mistrust of the German character I expressed even when I was twenty-six (in the third Untimely One, section 6)[1]—the Germans seem impossible to me. When I imagine a type of man that antagonizes all my instincts, it always turns into a German.[2]

The first point on which I "try the reins" is to see whether a man has a feeling for distance in his system, whether he sees rank, degree,[3] order between man and man everywhere, whether he makes *distinctions:* with that one is a *gentilhomme;* otherwise one belongs hopelessly in the broad-minded—ah, so good-natured— concept of canaille. But the Germans are canaille—ah, they are so good-natured.— One lowers oneself when one associates with Germans: the German puts others on a par.— Except for my association with a few artists, above all with Richard Wagner, I have not spent one good hour with a German.[4]—

If the most profound spirit of all millennia appeared among Germans, some savioress of the capitol [5] would suppose that her very unbeautiful soul deserved at least equal consideration.— I cannot endure this race among whom one is always in bad company, that has no fingers for nuances—alas, I am a nuance—that has no *esprit* in its feet and does not even know how to walk.— The Germans ultimately have no feet at all, they have only legs.— The Germans have no idea how vulgar they are; but that is the superlative of vulgarity—they are not even *ashamed* of being merely Germans.— They join in every discussion; they consider

---

[1] Just before the middle of the section: ". . . Certainly, one who has to live among Germans suffers badly from the notorious grayness of their life and senses, their crudity, their dullness and doltishness, their clumsiness in delicate relationships, and even more their envy and a certain slyness and uncleanliness in their character; one is pained and offended by their deeply rooted pleasure in the false and inauthentic . . ." *Schopenhauer as Educator* was written and published in 1874, the year Nietzsche turned thirty. And he was twenty-seven when his first book appeared. Thus "twenty-six" in the text is an error; but it is noteworthy how early he attributed "uncleanliness" to the Germans.

[2] There is no period in the MS, which continued: "—or an anti-Semite." These words were struck out, presumably not by Nietzsche.

[3] Cf. Ulysses' great speech in Shakespeare's *Troilus and Cressida,* Act I, scene 3, about "degree."

[4] See Appendix, section 3.

[5] That is, some goose.

themselves decisive; I fear they have reached a decision even about me.

My whole life is the demonstration *de rigueur*[6] of these propositions. In vain do I seek among them for some sign of tact, of *délicatesse* in relation to me. From Jews, yes; never yet from Germans.

It is part of my nature to be gentle and benevolent toward everybody—I have the *right* not to make distinctions—but that does not prevent me from keeping my eyes open. I except no one, least of all my friends; in the end I hope that this has not diminished my humanity in relation to them. There are five or six things that have always been a point of honor with me.— Nevertheless it is true that almost every letter that has reached me for years now strikes me as a piece of cynicism: there is more cynicism in being kind to me than in any hatred.

I tell every one of my friends to his face that he has never considered it worth while to *study* any of my writings: I infer from the smallest signs that they do not even know what is in them. As for my *Zarathustra:* who among my friends saw more in it than an impermissible but fortunately utterly inconsequential presumption?

Ten years—and nobody in Germany has felt bound in conscience to defend my name against the absurd silence under which it lies buried: it was a foreigner, a Dane, who first possessed sufficient refinement of instinct *and courage* for this, who felt outraged by my alleged friends.— At what German university would it be possible today to have lectures on my philosophy, such as were given last spring in Copenhagen by Dr. Georg Brandes who thus proved himself once again as a psychologist?

I myself have never suffered from all this; what is *necessary* does not hurt me; *amor fati*[7] is my inmost nature. But this does not preclude my love of irony, even world-historical irony. And thus I have sent into the world, about two years before the shattering lightning bolt of the *Revaluation* that will make the earth convulse —*The Case of Wagner:* let the Germans commit one more immortal blunder in relation to me that will stand in all eternity. There is

---

[6] According to strict form.

[7] Cf. the conclusion of Chapter 2, above.

barely enough time left for that.— Has it been accomplished?—
Most delightfully, my dear Teutons! My compliments! [8]

---

[8] According to Podach (p. 410) the following passage (*ibid.*, p. 315) is crossed out in the MS with a colored pencil, meaning that it was deleted by the printer: "Just now, lest my friends be left out, an old friend writes me that she is now *laughing* at me.— And that at a moment when an indescribable responsibility weighs on me—when no word can be delicate and no eye respectful enough towards me. For I bear the destiny of humanity on my shoulders."

Raoul Richter included this passage in a footnote to his postscript to the first edition of *Ecce Homo* (1908) but said he considered it *"probable* that the deletion was Nietzsche's own" (p. 147). Cf. note 1 to Chapter 2, section 10, above.

The reference to the *Revaluation,* in the text, should be compared with section 3 of "Twilight of the Idols," above: Nietzsche is speaking of his forthcoming book. He is not implying that the earth will be convulsed by his revelation of new values; as he explains in the first section of "Beyond Good and Evil," above, the revaluation is a "No-saying"—a critique of faith and morals. This point is developed further on the following pages.

Why I Am a Destiny

1

I know my fate. One day my name will be associated with the memory of something tremendous—a crisis without equal on earth, the most profound collision of conscience, a decision that was conjured up *against* everything that had been believed, demanded, hallowed so far. I am no man, I am dynamite.[1]— Yet for all that, there is nothing in me of a founder of a religion—religions are affairs of the rabble; I find it necessary to wash my hands after I have come into contact with religious people.— I *want* no "believers"; I think I am too malicious to believe in myself; I never speak to masses.— I have a terrible fear that one day I will be pronounced *holy:* you will guess why I publish this book *before;* it shall prevent people from doing mischief with me.[2]

I do not want to be a holy man; sooner even a buffoon.— Perhaps I am a buffoon.— Yet in spite of that—or rather *not* in spite of it, because so far nobody has been more mendacious than holy men—the truth speaks out of me.— But my truth is *terrible;* for so far one has called *lies* truth.

Revaluation of all values: that is my formula for an act of supreme self-examination on the part of humanity, become flesh and genius in me. It is my fate that I have to be the first *decent* human being; that I know myself to stand in opposition to the mendaciousness of millennia.— I was the first to *discover* the truth by being the first to experience lies as lies—smelling them out.— My genius is in my nostrils.

---

[1] This had been said of Nietzsche in the *Berner Bund,* in J. V. Widmann's review of *Beyond Good and Evil*, September 16–17, 1886. The passage is quoted at length in Nietzsche's letter to Malwida von Meysenbug, September 24, 1886 (*Werke,* ed. Karl Schlechta, vol. III, p. 1245).

[2] But *Ecce Homo* was not published until 1908, and at Nietzsche's funeral in 1900 Peter Gast proclaimed: "Holy be thy name to all coming generations." Even after it was published, *Ecce Homo* failed to prevent far worse mischief.

I contradict as has never been contradicted before and am nevertheless the opposite of a No-saying spirit. I am a bringer of glad tidings like no one before me; I know tasks of such elevation that any notion of them has been lacking so far; only beginning with me are there hopes again. For all that, I am necessarily also the man of calamity. For when truth enters into a fight with the lies of millennia, we shall have upheavals, a convulsion of earthquakes, a moving of mountains and valleys, the like of which has never been dreamed of. The concept of politics will have merged entirely with a war of spirits; all power structures of the old society will have been exploded—all of them are based on lies: there will be wars the like of which have never yet been seen on earth. It is only beginning with me that the earth knows *great politics*.

2

You want a formula for such a destiny *become man?* That is to be found in my *Zarathustra:*

"And whoever wants to be[1] a creator in good and evil, must first be an annihilator and break values. Thus the highest evil belongs to the greatest goodness: but this is—being creative."

I am by far the most terrible human being that has existed so far; this does not preclude the possibility that I shall be the most beneficial. I know the pleasure in destroying to a degree that accords with my powers to destroy—in both respects I obey my Dionysian nature which does not know how to separate doing No from saying Yes. I am the first immoralist: that makes me the annihilator *par excellence*.

3

I have not been asked, as I should have been asked, what the name of Zarathustra means in my mouth, the mouth of the first immoralist: for what constitutes the tremendous historical uniqueness of that Persian is just the opposite of this. Zarathustra was the first to consider the fight of good and evil the very wheel in the

---

[1] In *Zarathustra II*, "On Self-Overcoming," the text reads "must be"; and "evil" is followed by "verily."

machinery of things: the transposition of morality into the meta-physical realm, as a force, cause, and end in itself, is *his* work. But this question itself is at bottom its own answer. Zarathustra created this most calamitous error, morality; consequently, he must also be the first to recognize it. Not only has he more experience in this matter, for a longer time, than any other thinker—after all, the whole of history is the refutation by experiment of the principle of the so-called "moral world order"—what is more important is that Zarathustra is more truthful than any other thinker. His doctrine, and his alone, posits truthfulness as the highest virtue; this means the opposite of the cowardice of the "idealist" who flees from real-ity; Zarathustra has more intestinal fortitude than all other thinkers taken together. To speak the truth and to *shoot well with arrows,* that is Persian virtue.[2]— Am I understood?— The self-overcoming of morality, out of truthfulness; the self-overcoming of the moral-ist, into his opposite—into me—that is what the name of Zarathus-tra means in my mouth.

4

Fundamentally, my term *immoralist* involves two negations. For one, I negate a type of man that has so far been considered supreme: the good, the benevolent, the beneficent. And then I ne-gate a type of morality that has become prevalent and predominant as morality itself—the morality of decadence or, more concretely, *Christian* morality. It would be permissible to consider the second contradiction the more decisive one, since I take the overestimation of goodness and benevolence on a large scale for a consequence of decadence, for a symptom of weakness, irreconcilable with an ascending, Yes-saying life: negating *and destroying* are conditions of saying Yes.[1]

---

[2] Cf. *Zarathustra I,* "On the Thousand and One Goals": ". . . 'To speak the truth and to handle bow and arrow well'—that seemed both dear and diffi-cult to the people who gave me my name . . ."

[1] Although Nietzsche associates this with Dionysus, cf. also Jer. 1:10: "See, I have this day set thee over the nations and over the kingdoms, to root out, and to pull down, and to destroy, and to throw down, to build and to plant." But Jeremiah felt no pleasure in destruction.

Let me tarry over the psychology of the good human being. To estimate what a type of man is worth, one must calculate the price paid for his preservation—one must know the conditions of his existence. The condition of the existence of the good is the *lie:* put differently, not *wanting* to see at any price how reality is constituted fundamentally—namely, not in such a way as to elicit benevolent instincts at all times, and even less in such a way as to tolerate at all times the interference of those who are myopically good-natured. To consider distress of all kinds as an objection, as something that must be abolished, is the *niaiserie*[2] *par excellence* and, on a large scale, a veritable disaster in its consequences, a nemesis[3] of stupidity—almost as stupid as would be the desire to abolish bad weather—say, from pity for poor people.

In the great economy of the whole, the terrible aspects of reality (in affects, in desires, in the will to power) are to an incalculable degree more necessary than that form of petty happiness which people call "goodness"; one actually has to be quite lenient to accord the latter any place at all, considering that it presupposes an instinctive mendaciousness. I shall have a major occasion to demonstrate how the historical consequences of *optimism,* this abortion of the *homines optimi,*[4] have been uncanny beyond measure. Zarathustra, who was the first to grasp that the optimist is just as decadent as the pessimist, and perhaps more harmful, says: *"Good men never speak the truth."* [5]

"False coasts and assurances the good have taught you; in the lies of the good you were hatched and huddled. Everything has been made fraudulent and has been twisted through and through by the good." [6]

Fortunately, the world has not been designed with a view to such instincts that only good-natured herd animals could find their narrow happiness in it: to demand that all should become "good

---

[2] Folly, stupidity, silliness.

[3] *Schicksal.*

[4] Best men.

[5] Quoted from *Zarathustra III,* "On Old and New Tablets," section 7. There are no quotation marks in the German text.

[6] *Ibid.,* section 28. Again, no quotation marks.

human beings," herd animals, blue-eyed, benevolent, "beautiful
souls"—or as Mr. Herbert Spencer[7] would have it, altruistic—
would deprive existence of its *great* character and would castrate
men and reduce them to the level of desiccated Chinese stagnation.
— *And this has been attempted!*— *Precisely this has been called
morality*.

In this sense, Zarathustra calls the good, now "the last
men,"[8] now the "beginning of the end"; above all, he considers
them the most harmful type of man because they prevail at the
expense of *truth* and at the expense of the *future*.[9]

"The good are unable to *create*; they are always the beginning
of the end; they crucify him who writes new values on new tablets;
they sacrifice the future to *themselves*—they sacrifice all man's future.

"The good have always been the beginning of the end."

"And whatever harm those do who slander the world, the
harm done by the good is the most harmful harm."[10]

5

Zarathustra, the first psychologist of the good, is—consequently—a friend of the evil. When a decadent type of man ascended to the rank of the highest type, this could only happen at
the expense of its countertype, the type of man that is strong and
sure of life. When the herd animal is irradiated by the glory of the
purest virtue, the exceptional man must have been devaluated into
evil. When mendaciousness at any price monopolizes the word
"truth" for its perspective, the really truthful man is bound to be
branded with the worst names. Zarathustra leaves no doubt at this

---

[7] English philosopher (1820–1903).

[8] In the "Prologue," section 5. Indeed, that section, along with the whole
Prologue, may be the best commentary on the above section—though it
would be more accurate to say that the above is a commentary on *Zarathustra*.

[9] Those who want to abolish all hardships because they themselves are not
up to them are like sick people who wish to abolish rain, no matter what the
consequences might be to others and to the earth generally. Cf. Nietzsche's
own remark about "bad weather" above.

[10] Both quotations are from section 26 of "On Old and New Tablets"; but
the second quotation occurs earlier in that section.

point: he says that it was his insight precisely into the good, the "best," that made him shudder at man in general; that it was from *this* aversion that he grew wings "to soar off into distant futures"; he does not conceal the fact that *his* type of man, a relatively superhuman type, is superhuman precisely in its relation to the *good* —that the good and the just would call his overman *devil*.

"You highest men whom my eyes have seen, this is my doubt about you and my secret laughter: I guess that you would call my overman—devil."

"What is great is so alien to your souls that the overman would be terrifying to you in his goodness." [1]

It is here and nowhere else that one must make a start to comprehend what Zarathustra wants: this type of man that he conceives, conceives reality *as it is,* being strong enough to do so; this type is not estranged or removed from reality but is reality itself and exemplifies all that is terrible and questionable in it—*only in that way can man attain greatness.*

6

There is yet another sense, however, in which I have chosen the word *immoralist* as a symbol and badge of honor for myself; I am proud of having this word which distinguishes me from the whole of humanity. Nobody yet has felt *Christian* morality to be *beneath* him: that requires a height, a view of distances, a hitherto altogether unheard-of psychological depth and profundity. Christian morality has been the Circe of all thinkers so far—they stood in her service.— Who before me climbed into the caverns from which the poisonous fumes of this type of ideal—slander of the world—are rising? Who even dared to suspect that they are caverns? Who among philosophers was a *psychologist* at all before me, and not rather the opposite, a "higher swindler" and "idealist"? There was no psychology at all before me.— To be the first here may be a curse; it is at any rate a destiny: *for one is also the first to despise.— Nausea* at man is my danger.

---

[1] All three quotations, beginning with "to soar off . . ." come from *Zarathustra II,* "On Human Prudence."

7

Have I been understood?— What defines me, what sets me apart from the whole rest of humanity is that I *uncovered* Christian morality. That is why I needed a word that had the meaning of a provocation for everybody. That they did not open their eyes earlier at this point, I regard as the greatest uncleanliness that humanity has on its conscience; as self-deception become instinctive; as a fundamental will *not* to see any event, any causality, any reality; as counterfeiting *in psychologicis* to the point of criminality. Blindness to Christianity is the crime *par excellence*—the crime against life.

The millennia, the nations, the first and the last, the philosophers and old women—excepting five, six moments in history, and me as the seventh—at this point all of them are worthy of each other. The Christian has so far been *the* "moral being"—a matchless curiosity—and *as* the "moral being" he was more absurd, mendacious, vain, frivolous, and more disadvantageous for himself than even the greatest despiser of humanity could imagine in his dreams. Christian morality—the most malignant form of the will to lie, the real Circe of humanity—that which *corrupted* humanity. It is *not* error as error that horrifies me at this sight—not the lack, for thousands of years, of "good will," discipline, decency, courage in matters of the spirit, revealed by its victory: it is the lack of nature, it is the utterly gruesome fact that *antinature* itself received the highest honors as morality and was fixed over humanity as law and categorical imperative.— To blunder to such an extent, not as individuals, not as a people, but as humanity!— That one taught men to despise the very first instincts of life; that one mendaciously invented a "soul," a "spirit" to ruin the body; that one taught men to experience the presupposition of life, sexuality, as something unclean; that one looks for the evil principle in what is most profoundly necessary for growth, in *severe* self-love[1] (this very word

---

[1] *Selbstsucht:* the word is pejorative, like "selfishness." Cf. note 5, section 1 of "The Untimely Ones," above; also the beginning of section 4 on "Human, All-Too-Human."

constitutes slander); that, conversely, one regards the typical signs of decline and contradiction of the instincts, the "selfless," the loss of a center of gravity, "depersonalization" and "neighbor love" (*addiction* to the neighbor) as the *higher* value—what am I saying?—the *absolute* value!

What? Is humanity itself decadent? Was it always?— What is certain is that it has been *taught* only decadence values as supreme values. The morality that would un-self man is the morality of decline *par excellence*—the fact, "I am declining," transposed into the imperative, "all of you *ought* to decline"—and not only into the imperative.— This only morality that has been taught so far, that of un-selfing, reveals a will to the end; fundamentally, it negates life.

This would still leave open the possibility that not humanity is degenerating but only that parasitical type of man—that of the *priest*—which has used morality to raise itself mendaciously to the position of determining human values—finding in Christian morality the means to come to *power*.— Indeed, this is *my* insight: the teachers, the leaders of humanity, theologians all of them, were also, all of them, decadents: *hence* the revaluation of all values into hostility to life,[2] *hence* morality—

Definition of morality: Morality—the idiosyncrasy of decadents, with the ulterior motive of revenging oneself against life—successfully. I attach value to this definition.

8

Have I been understood?— I have not said one word here that I did not say five years ago through the mouth of Zarathustra.

The uncovering of Christian morality is an event without parallel, a real catastrophe. He that is enlightened about that, is a *force majeure,* a destiny—he breaks the history of mankind in two. One lives before him, or one lives after him.

The lightning bolt of truth struck precisely what was highest

---

[2] Nietzsche's revaluation is meant to undo the damage done by a previous revaluation: values have been stood on their head and are now to be turned right-side up again.

so far: let.whoever comprehends *what* has here been destroyed see whether anything is left in his hands. Everything that has hitherto been called "truth" has been recognized as the most harmful, insidious, and subterranean form of lie; the holy pretext of "improving" mankind, as the ruse for sucking the blood of life itself. Morality as vampirism.

Whoever uncovers morality also uncovers the disvalue of all values that are and have been believed; he no longer sees anything venerable in the most venerated types of man, even in those pronounced holy; he considers them the most calamitous type of abortion—calamitous because they exerted such fascination.

The concept of "God" invented as a counterconcept of life—everything harmful, poisonous, slanderous, the whole hostility unto death against life synthesized in this concept in a gruesome unity! The concept of the "beyond," the "true world" invented in order to devaluate the only world there is[1]—in order to retain no goal, no reason, no task for our earthly reality! The concept of the "soul," the "spirit," finally even *"immortal* soul," invented in order to despise the body,[2] to make it sick, "holy"; to oppose with a ghastly levity everything that deserves to be taken seriously in life, the questions of nourishment, abode, spiritual diet, treatment of the sick, cleanliness, and weather.[3]

In place of health, the "salvation of the soul"—that is, a *folie circulaire*[4] between penitential convulsions and hysteria about redemption. The concept of "sin" invented along with the torture instrument that belongs with it, the concept of "free will," in order to confuse the instincts, to make mistrust of the instincts second nature. In the concept of the "selfless," the "self-denier," the distinctive sign of decadence, feeling attracted by what is harmful, being unable to find any longer what profits one, self-destruction is turned into the sign of value itself, into "duty," into "holiness," into what is "divine" in man. Finally—this is what is most terrible of all—the concept of the *good* man signifies that one sides

---

[1] Cf. *Twilight,* Chapters III and IV.
[2] Cf. *Zarathustra I,* "On The Despisers of the Body."
[3] Cf. "Why I am So Clever," above.
[4] Manic-depressive insanity.

with all that is weak, sick, failure, suffering of itself—all that ought to perish: the principle of selection is crossed [5]—an ideal is fabricated from the contradiction against the proud and well-turned-out human being who says Yes, who is sure of the future, who guarantees the future—and he is now called *evil*.— And all this was believed, *as morality!— Ecrasez l'infâme!* [6]——

9

Have I been understood?— *Dionysus versus the Crucified*.—[1]

---

[5] Cf. *The Antichrist*, section 7.

[6] Voltaire's motto—crush the infamy—in his fight against the church.

[1] The best commentary is section 1052 of *The Will to Power*.

APPENDIX

---◆---

Variants from Nietzsche's Drafts

1

Part of a discarded draft for section 3 of "Why I Am So Clever" (Podach, *Friedrich Nietzsches Werke*, pp. 236f.):

Emerson with his essays has been a good friend and cheered me up even in black periods: he contains so much skepsis, so many "possibilities" that even virtue achieves esprit in his writings. A unique case! Even as a boy I enjoyed listening to him. *Tristram Shandy* also belongs to my earliest favorites; how I experienced Sterne may be seen from a very pensive passage in *Human, All-Too-Human* [Part II, section 113]. Perhaps it was for related reasons that I preferred Lichtenberg[1] among German books, while the "idealist" Schiller was more than I could swallow even when I was thirteen.— I don't want to forget Abbé Galiani,[2] this most profound buffoon that ever lived.

Of *all* books, one of my strongest impressions is that exuberant Provençal, Petronius, who composed the last *Satura Menippea*.[3] Such sovereign freedom from "morality," from "seriousness," from his own sublime taste; such subtlety in his mixture of vulgar and "educated" Latin; such indomitable good spirits that leap with grace and malice over all anomalies of the ancient "soul"

[1] Georg Christoph Lichtenberg (1742–1799), professor of physics at Göttingen, was perhaps the greatest German aphorist and satirist of his century.

[2] A writer (1728–1787) often mentioned by Nietzsche. See my note (6) in *Beyond Good and Evil*, section 26, p. 228 above.

[3] The relevant information has been put most succinctly by William Arrowsmith, in his Introduction to his own translation of *The Satyricon of Petronius* (Ann Arbor, Mich., University of Michigan Press, 1959), p. x: "Formally . . . the *Satyricon* . . . belongs to that genre we call Menippean satire, the curious blending of prose with verse and philosophy with realism invented by the Cynic philosopher Menippus of Gadara [third century B.C.] and continued by his Roman disciple, Varro [116–27 B.C.]." The identity and dates of Petronius have been disputed, but he probably committed suicide when Nero was Emperor. Cf. *Beyond*, section 28, p. 231 above.

—I could not name any book that makes an equally liberating impression on me: the effect is Dionysian. In cases in which I find it necessary to recuperate quickly from a base impression—for example, because for the sake of my critique of Christianity I had to breathe all too long the swampy air of the apostle Paul—a few pages of Petronius suffice me as a *heroic* remedy, and immediately I am well again.

2

Part of a discarded draft for section 3 of "Why I Write Such Good Books" (Podach, *Friedrich Nietzsches Werke,* pp. 251f.):

My writings are difficult; I hope this is not considered an objection? To understand the most *abbreviated* language ever spoken by a philosopher—and also the one poorest in formulas, most alive, most artistic—one must follow the *opposite* procedure of that generally required by philosophical literature. Usually, one must *condense,* or upset one's digestion; I have to be diluted, liquefied, mixed with water, else one upsets one's digestion.

Silence is as much of an instinct with me as is garrulity with our dear philosophers. I am *brief;* my readers themselves must become long and comprehensive in order to bring up and together all that I have thought, and thought deep down.

On the other hand, there are prerequisites for "understanding" here, which very few can satisfy: one must be able to see a problem in its proper place—that is, in the context of the other problems that *belong with it;* and for this one must have at one's finger tips the topography of various nooks and the difficult areas of whole sciences and above all of philosophy.

Finally, I speak only of what I have lived through, not merely of what I have thought through; the opposition of thinking and life is lacking in my case. My "theory" grows from my "practice"—oh, from a practice that is not by any means harmless or unproblematic!

3

In his postscript to the first edition, 1908, Raoul Richter said: "A page that, according to information received from Frau Förster-Nietzsche, was mailed to Paraguay, with a notation regarding its insertion in *Ecce Homo,* survives in a copy and contains invective against his brother-in-law and friends, but has been excluded from publication here as something not belonging to the authentic Nietzsche. This is presumably one of those violent outpourings of which several have been found in the Förster papers, some of them long destroyed, with uninhibited attacks on Bismarck, the Kaiser, and others. The fact alone that an addition to *Ecce Homo* was sent to South America [where the sister and brother-in-law were then living], instead of being sent to the publisher in Leipzig, shows that this is presumably a page that belongs to the first days of the collapse. Possibly, a similar but no longer extant note sent to the publisher was also intended for *Ecce.*" Podach's criticism of Richter for not publishing this note (*Friedrich Nietzsches Werke*, pp. 198f.) seems highly unreasonable; but the text (p. 314) deserves inclusion in this Appendix. Nietzsche's notation read: "To be inserted in the chapter 'The Case of Wagner,' section 4, after the words: 'Except for my association with a few artists, above all with Richard Wagner, I have not spent one good hour with a German' " (*ibid.*, p. 410). The text itself reads:

Shall I here divulge my "German" experiences?—Förster: long legs, blue eyes, blond (straw head!), a "racial German" who with poison and gall attacks everything that guarantees spirit and future: Judaism, vivisection, etc.—but for his sake my sister left those nearest her[1] and plunged into a world full of dangers and evil accidents.

Köselitz:[2] Saxon, weak, at times awkward, immovable, an embodiment of the law of gravity—but his music is of the first rank and runs on light feet.

Overbeck[3] dried up, become sour, subject to his wife, hands me,

---

[1] *Ihre "Nächsten"*: The word used in the Bible for neighbor.

[2] Heinrich Köselitz was the real name of Peter Gast.

[3] Franz Overbeck was professor of church history at Basel, but an unbeliever. For accounts of Förster, Gast, and Overbeck see Kaufmann's *Nietzsche*, Chapter 1, sections I and III, or—for a much fuller account, in German—Podach's *Gestalten um Nietzsche* (figures around Nietzsche; Weimar, Lichtenstein, 1932).

like Mime,[4] the poisoned draft of doubt and mistrust of myself—but he shows how he is full of good will toward me and worried about me and calls himself my "indulgent friend."

Look at them—these are three German types! Canaille!

And if the most profound spirit of all millennia appeared among Germans

4

All of the paragraphs in this section come from three discarded drafts for the attack on the Germans in the chapter "The Case of Wagner." (a) and (b) constitute the beginning and end of the same draft (Podach, *Friedrich Nietzsches Werke*, p. 316); (c) comes from another attempt (*ibid.*, p. 317); (d) from the last (*ibid.*, pp. 318f.).

(a)

And from what side did all *great* obstructions, all calamities in my life emanate? Always from Germans. The damnable German anti-Semitism, this poisonous boil of *névrose nationale*, has intruded into my existence almost ruinously during that decisive time when not my destiny but the destiny of humanity was at issue. And I owe it to the same element that my *Zarathustra* entered this world as *indecent* literature—its publisher being an anti-Semite. In vain do I look for some sign of tact, of *délicatesse*, in relation to me: from Jews, yes; never yet from Germans.

(b)

The Germans are by far the worst experience of my life; for sixteen years now one has left me in the lurch, not only concerning my philosophy but also in regard to my honor. What respect can I have for the Germans when even my friends cannot discriminate between me and a liar like Richard Wagner? In one extreme case, one even straddles the fence between me and anti-Semitic canaille. — And this at a moment when an indescribable responsibility weighs on me—[1]

---

[4] In Wagner's *Ring*.

[1] The passage ends like the one cited in the final footnote for that chapter, above. The "extreme case" is presumably that of Nietzsche's sister.

(c)

It seems to be that association with Germans even corrupts one's character. I lose all mistrust; I feel how the fungus of neighbor-love spreads in me—it has even happened, to my profound humiliation, that I have become *good-natured*. Is it possible to sink any lower?— For with me, malice belongs to happiness—I am no good when I am not malicious[2]—I find no small justification of existence in provoking tremendous stupidities against me.

(d)

I am *solitude* become man.[3]— That no word ever reached me, forced me to reach myself.— I should not be possible without a countertype of race, without Germans, without *these* Germans, without Bismarck, without 1848, without "Wars of Liberation," without Kant, even without Luther.— The great crimes committed against culture by the Germans are justified in a *higher* economy of culture.— I want nothing differently, not backward either—I was not permitted to want anything differently.— *Amor fati.*— Even Christianity becomes necessary: only the highest form, the most dangerous, the one that was most seductive in its No to life, provokes its highest affirmation—me.— What in the end are these two millennia? Our most instructive experiment, a vivisection of life itself.— Merely two millennia!—

5

For a time, Nietzsche thought of concluding *Ecce Homo* with two sections that are included in a table of contents reproduced photographically by Podach (*Friedrich Nietzsches Werke,* plate XIV); but then he wrote on a separate sheet (*ibid.*, p. 332): "The section *Declaration of War* is to be omitted— Also *The Hammer Speaks.*" The latter he moved to the end of *Twilight* (*Portable Nietzsche,* p. 563); the former is lost, except for the following paragraph on a sheet with the notation: "At the end, after the Declaration of War" (*ibid.*, p. 332).

---

[2] *Ich tauge Nichts, wenn ich nicht boshaft bin.* "Malice": *Bosheit.*
[3] *Ich bin die* Einsamkeit *als Mensch.*

Final Consideration

If we could dispense with wars, so much the better. I can imagine more profitable uses for the twelve billion now paid annually for the armed peace we have in Europe; there are other means of winning respect for physiology than field hospitals.— Good; *very good even:* since the old God is abolished, I am prepared *to rule the world—*

Bibliographical Note

Nietzsche's works are generally cited by section numbers, as these are the same in all editions.

Thus Spoke Zarathustra, Twilight of the Idols, and *Nietzsche contra Wagner* are not composed of consecutively numbered sections; but they are available in a single volume, along with *The Antichrist* and selections from Nietzsche's other books, from his notes, and from his letters: *The Portable Nietzsche,* selected and translated, with an introduction, prefaces, and notes, by Walter Kaufmann, The Viking Press, New York, 1954. Page numbers refer to this volume.

Walter Kaufmann, *Nietzsche: Philosopher, Psychologist, Antichrist* was originally published by the Princeton University Press in 1950. The pagination of the revised paperback edition, published by Meridian Books, New York, 1956, was different, and that of the third revised and greatly enlarged edition (Princeton University Press and Random House, Vintage Books, 1968) is different again. The book is therefore cited not by pages but by chapters and sections. The third edition contains a comprehensive Bibliography that includes Nietzsche's books, collected editions, material not included in these, his correspondence in German, English translations, and works about Nietzsche by over a hundred authors.

INDEX
The Birth of Tragedy

All numbers refer to sections, not to pages. **RW** refers to the Preface to Richard Wagner; **SC**, to the Attempt at a Self-Criticism; **TI**, to the Translator's Introduction; **n** to the Translator's Notes. For references to Nietzsche's works, see Nietzsche.

A

Achilles, 3, 5, 15
Adam, 18
Admetus, 8
Aeschylus, **TI**1, **TI**2, 4**n**, 7, 9–12, 14, 15, 19, 25; *Prometheus,* 9
Aesopian fable, 14
aesthetics, **SC**5, 1, 5, 6, 8, 16, 19, 21, 22, 24; aesthetic listener, 22, 23; as justifying the world, 5, 24
Agathon, 14
Alexandrian, 18**n**, 17–20, 23
Alcestis, 8
Alcibiades, 13
Amenophis III, 9**n**
Amphion, 19
Anaxagoras, 12
Antichrist, **SC**5. *See also* Christianity
Antigone, 4, 4**n**
antimorality, *see* morality
Apollinian, **TI**1, **TI**3, **TI**3**n**, **SC**3**n**, 1, 4, 4**n**, 5, 6, *passim;* art of sculpture, 1; and arts, 1, 2, 5, 22, 24; culture, 3, 4; epos, 6; illusion, 21, 24; and music, 5; tragedy, *see* tragedy, Apollinian; will, 9
Apollo, **TI**3, 1–5, 8, 9, 10, 14, 16, 21, 24; the shining one, 1, 1**n**
appearance(s), **SC**5, 1, 1**n**, 3–9, 12, 15, 15**n**, 24; mere appearance of mere appearance, 4
Archilochus, 5, 5**n**, 6
Argonauts, 15**n**
Aristophanes, 11**n**, 13, 17; Aristophanean Euripides, 11; Aristophanic comedy, *see* comedy; *Frogs,* 11
Aristotle, **TI**1, **TI**2, 2, 6, 7, 12**n**, 14, 14**n**, 18**n**, 22

Arnim, Achim von, 6**n**
Arnold, Matthew, **TI**3, **TI**3**n**
art, artist(s), **TI**3, **SC**1, **SC**2, **SC**5, **SC**6, **SC**7, 6, 15, *passim;* art of metaphysical comfort, **SC**7 (*see also* metaphysical comfort); artist god, **SC**5; artistic meaning of world, **SC**5; Doric, 2, 4; Greek, **SC**1; impulses of nature, 2; naïve, 3, 4; objective artist, 5; Olympian middle world of, 3; plastic, 1, 5, 16, 22; relation of art and science, **TI**1, **SC**2; Socratic attitude to, 14; subjective artist, 5; degenerate art (entartete Kunst), 16**n**. *See also* Apollinian and Dionysian
Aryans, 9, 9**n**
Asia Minor, 1
Atlas, 9
Atridae, 3

B

Babylon, 1
Bacchants, 8; Bacchic choruses, 1
Bach, Johann Sebastian, 19
barbaric, the, 4
beauty, **SC**4, **SC**5, 3, 4, 12, 16, 18, 19, 21, 25; "beautiful forms," 16, 16**n**
Beethoven, Ludwig van, **RW,** 1, 1**n**, 6, 16, 19, 22, 25**n**; symphonies, 6
beyond good and evil, **SC**5, **SC**5**n**, 3**n**
Brentano, Clemens, 6**n**
Brinton, Crane, **TI**3
Brünnhilde, 24
Buddhism, 7; Buddhistic culture, 18, 18**n**; Buddhistic negation of the will, **TI**3, 7; Indian, 21

C

Cadmus, 12
Campbell, Joseph, 1n
Cambridge school, TI2
catharsis, 22
Cassandra, 4, 4n, 5n
character representation, 17
cheerfulness, Alexandrian, 17, 19;
    Greek, SC1, SC4, 9, 11, 15, 17, 20,
    23
chorus, SC4, 7, 8, 8n, 10, 11, 12, 14;
    Bacchic, 1; destruction of, 14; and
    Euripides, 11; ideal spectator, 7, 8,
    8n; in New Comedy, 11n; popular,
    7; satyr, 7, 8
Christianity, Christians, SC3n, SC5,
    SC7, 11, 24n; life's nausea, SC5
comedy, SC4, 10, 11, 11n; Aristoph-
    anic, 13; New Attic, 11, 14, 17.
    See also Euripides
contemplation, 5, 5n
contradiction, 5
Cornford, F. M., TI2
critic(s), 22
cross, death, and tomb, 19n
cruelty, TI3, 2, 7
culture, 18, 20, 22, 23; Alexandrian,
    18, 18n, 19, 20; Apollinian, 3, 4;
    Buddhistic, 18, 18n; German, 20;
    Greek, 20; Indian (Brahmanic),
    18n; lie of, 8; Olympian, 10; of
    the opera, 19; theoretical, 18, 19;
    tragic, 18
Cyclops, 14
Cynic writers, 14

D

daimonion of Socrates, 13
dance, 1, 9
Dante, 15n, 19
Delos, 25
Demeter, 10
dénouements, 17
Descartes, René, 12
deus ex machina, 17, 18
dialogue, 9
Dionysian, TI1–3, SC1–7, 1, 2, 4,
    4n, 5–7, passim; Antichrist, SC5;
    and art, 5, 10, 16, 17; festivals,
    TI3, SC3n, 2, 4; mask, 9; music,
    1, 2, 5–7, 16, 16n, 17, 19, 21, 24;
    power, 2; spirit, 20; and tragedy,
    7, 8, 12, 14, 21, 22

Dionysus, TI3, SC3, SC6, 3–5, 8, 8n,
    10, 12, 16, 19, 21, 24, 25; suffer-
    ing of, 10
Dodds, E. R., TI3
Doric: art, 2, 4; state, 4; view, 4
drama, dramatists, 8, 11, 12, 14, 21,
    24
dramatic dithyramb, 4, 5, 7, 8, 8n;
    New Attic Dithyramb, 17, 19
Dräseke, Johannes, TI2, TI2n
dreams, 1–6, 8, 10, 12, 14
Dürer, Albrecht, 20

E

Eckermann, Johann Peter, TI3, 18
ego, 5, 5n
Egyptians, 9, 9n; Egyptian priests, 17
Eleusinian mysteries, 1
Eliot, T. S.; "Love Song of J. Alfred
    Prufrock," 22n; The Waste Land,
    21n
Else, Gerald F., TI2
empirical existence (reality), 4, 5, 7
Epicurus, SC4; Epicureans, SC1
epos, 10; Apollinian, 6; dramatized,
    12
epopts, 10, 10n
Etruscans, 3
Euripides, TI1, TI3, 5, 10, 11, 11n,
    12–14, 14n, 17, 18; Aristophanean,
    11; and comedy, 11; as thinker,
    11; Euripidean prologue, 12
Europe, Europeans, SC1, SC6
evil, 9; individuation as cause of, 10
excess, 4
existence, see life
existentialism, TI3, 7n, 15n

F

fall of man, myth of, 9
Faust, see Goethe
Fiji Islands, 15n
fire, 9
Florence, 19
folk: folk-diseases, 1; philosophy, 4;
    songs, 4, 6; wisdom, 3
France, 23, 23n
Franco-Prussian War, SC1
Freud, Sigmund, 7n

G

Gellert, Christian Fürchtegott, 14

genius, 5, 6, 8, 15; German, 16; non-genius, 5
George, Stefan, SC3n
German(s), TI2, TI3, SC3, RW, 7, 23; character, 23, 24; culture, 20; genius, 16; Germany, TI1, SC6n, 18n; Middle Ages, 1; music, *see* music; philosophy, 19; rebirth of the German myth, 23; Reformation, 23; Reich, SC6, 23n; songs, 24; spirit, SC6, 19, 20, 23n, 24
Gervinus, G. G., 21, 21n, 22
Glasenapp, Helmuth von, 1n
God, SC3, SC5n, SC7, 12, 15n
god(s), TI3, SC4, 3, 5, 7–10, 14, 15n, 20, 21; as necessity for Greek life, 3; Delphic, 2, 4; demigod, 3
Goethe, Johann Wolfgang von, TI3, SC3n, SC5n, SC6n, 2n, 7, 9, 11n, 12, 18, 18n, 20, 22; *Faust*, SC7, 4n, 8n, 9n, 13n, 16n, 18, 18n, 19n, 21n; "Generalbeichte," 18n; "Grabschrift," 11n; *Nausikaa*, 12
Golffing, Francis, 8n
Gorgon's head, 2
Graeculus, 11, 23, 23n
Greece, Greek(s), *passim;* art, SC1; culture, TI3, 20; language, 6; longing, TI3; philosophers, 17; poets, 17; problem, SC6; state, 23; theater, 8. *See also* cheerfulness

H

Hades, 11
Hamlet, 5n, 7, 17; and Dionysian man, 7
Handel, George Frederick, 25n
harmony, 2
Harrison, Jane, TI2
Haydn, Franz Joseph, 25n
healthy-mindedness, 1
Hegel, G. W. F., TI1, TI3, 7n
Heidegger, Martin, TI1
Heine, Heinrich, SC5n
Helen, 3, 18n
Hellenism, *passim*
Herakles, TI2, 10, 19, 19n
Heraclitus, 11, 19, 24
hero(es), 16, 17; tragic, 11, 21, 22, 24
Hesiod, TI2
historiography, 20
Homer, TI3n, 2, 3, 5, 6, 8, 10, 13, 15, 19; *Iliad,* TI3; *Odyssey,* 3n

I

Ibsen, Henrik: *Peer Gynt,* 9n
ideal, 19; idealism, 7; Idealistic philosophers, SC5
illusion, 1, 1n, 3, 4, 7, 15, 18, 19; Apollinian, 21, 24; mirror of, 5; transfiguring, 25
image(s), 5, 6, 8, 10, 12, 14, 16, 21, 24; image sparks, 6; myth as, 23; pure contemplation of, 5
India, SC1, 20; Indian Buddhism, 21
individuation, 9, 10, 16, 22, 24, 25. *See also principium individuationis*
insight, *passim;* tragic, 15
instinct(s), 13, 15, 22, *passim;* political, 21
interest, devoid of, 5, 5n
intoxication, 1, 2
Iphigenia, 20
Isolde, 21, 22

J

Jack the Dreamer, 7
Jahn, Otto, 19, 19n
Jaspers, Karl, 15n
John, St., 1
journalist, 22; the paper slave of the day, 20
justice, Aeschylean, 9; poetic, 22; eternal, 25

K

Kant, Immanuel, TI2, SC6, 18, 19
Kierkegaard, Søren, 15n, 19n
Knaben Wunderhorn, Des, 6, 6n
Knight, A. H. J., TI3, TI3n
knowledge, 2–4, 7, 9, 12, 13, 15, 15n, 17, 18, 23; "knowledge is virtue," 12, 14; "know thyself," 4; pure knowing, 5; self-knowledge, 4, 9
Kurvenal, 21

L

Lamiae, 18
laughter, SC7
Lessing, Gotthold Ephraim, TI3, 11, 15, 15n
life, SC5, SC6, 3, 7, 7n, 17, 18, 20, 23; and music, 16; perspective of, SC2, SC4; seriousness of, RW
linguistic microscopist, 20
listener, aesthetic, 22, 23

logic, 13–15
Lohengrin, 19n, 22
Lucian, 10
Lucretius, 1
Luther, Martin, TI2, 23
Lycurgus, 12
Lycambes, daughters of, 5
Lynceus, 15, 15n
lyric, lyrist, 5, 6. *See also* poetry

M

madness, SC4
Maenads, 5
man, 25, *passim;* Aeschylean, *passim*
  (*see also* Aeschylus); Alexandrian,
  18, 19; Apollinian, *see* Apollinian;
  of culture, 8; Dionysian, *see* Dionysian; Hellenic, *passim;* Homeric,
  3; modern, 18; mythless, 23; primitive, 19; Renaissance, 19; in song
  and dance, 1; theoretical, 15, 17,
  18, 19
Mann, Thomas, 3n, 20n
mask, 5n, 9, 10, 12; Prometheus as
  Dionysian mask, 9
māyā, 1, 1n, 2, 18
measure, 4
Meier (Meyer), Bruno, TI2
melody, 16, 19, 21; as primary and
  universal, 6
Memnon's Column, 9; in Ibsen's
  Peer Gynt, 9n
Menander, 11
Mephistopheles, 4n, 18
metaphor, 8
metaphysics, SC5, SC7, 4, 9, 16, 21,
  23; and art, RW, 24; artist's, SC7;
  metaphysical comfort, 7, 8, 17, 18;
  of music (Schopenhauer), 5
Mette, Hans Joachim, 15n
Meyer, Bruno, *see* Meier
Michelangelo Buonarroti, 22n
microscopist, linguistic, 20
Midas, 3
Middle Ages, German, 1
Milton, John, 15n
Moira, 3, 9
Moore, Charles, 1n
Morgan, George A., Jr., TI3n
morality, antimorality, SC4, SC5, 3,
  13, 14, 23, 24
Mothers of Being, 16, 16n
Mozart, Wolfgang Amadeus, 16n,
  19n, 25n

Murray, Gilbert, TI2
music, SC1, SC3, SC6, 1, 2, 5, 6, 10,
  12, 14–17, 19–25; Apollinian, 5;
  choric, 12; Dionysian, *see* Dionysian; German, SC6, SC7, 19, 23;
  as language of the will, 16; life
  and, 16; metaphysics of, 5; musical dissonance, 24, 25; musical
  mood, 5; musical tragedy, 21, 22,
  24; New Dithyrambic, 17; operatic, 19; as symbolic dream image,
  5; Wagner's, TI2, 16; words in, 6,
  19, 21
myth(s), 9, 10, 15, 16, 17, 18, 22,
  passim; as image, 23; rebirth of
  German, 23; tragic, 16, 21, 22, 24,
  25

N

naïve, naïveté, 2, 2n, 3, 4, 6, 9, 13,
  14, 17–19; Homeric naïveté, 3
Napoleon, 18
naturalism, 7
nature, 1–4, 6–10, 15–17, 19; art as
  metaphysical supplement of, 24;
  wisdom as crime against, 9
nausea, 7, 19
Nazis, TI3n, 16n
neuroses of health, SC4
New Attic Dithyramb, 17, 19
Newman, Ernest, TI3
Nietzsche: Works: "Attempt at a
  Self-Criticism," TI3, 18n; *Beyond
  Good and Evil,* SC5n, 16n; *Case
  of Wagner,* TI1, 9n; *David Friedrich Strauss, the Confessor and
  Writer,* 15n, 23n; *Ecce Homo,*
  TI3, 24n; *Gay Science,* 15n, 16n;
  Nietzsche contra Wagner, 15n,
  16n; *Socrates und die griechische
  Tragödie: Ursprüngliche Fassung
  der Geburt der Tragödie aus dem
  Geiste der Music* (original version
  of *The Birth of Tragedy*), 15n;
  Twilight of the Idols, SC3n, 1n;
  The Wanderer and His Shadow,
  16n; *Werke, Grossoktav* edition,
  18n
novel, the, 14
nous, the, 12, 12n
Now, the, SC7

O

Oceanides, chorus of the, 7

Odysseus, 11
Oedipus, 3, 4, 9, 10
Oehler, Richard, TI3, TI3n
Olympians, Olympus, 3, 6, 7, 9, 10, 15n
Omphale, 19, 19n
opera, 8, 16, 19
Ophelia, 7
optimism, SC4, SC7, 7n, 14, 15, 18, 19, 24; theoretical optimist, 15
orchestra, 8, 8n
Orestes, 3
Orpheus, 12, 19
Ovid: Heroïdes, 19n

P

pain, SC4, 2; Greek relation to, SC4; primordial, 5
Palestrina, Giovanni Pierluigi da, 19
Pan, 11
"pasquinader," TI, TIn
passions, SC3n, SC5, 5
Pentheus, 12
Pericles, SC4, 13
Persia, Persians, 9, 21
pessimism, SC1, SC4, SC5, SC7, 9, 10, 15
Phidias, 13, 18n
Philemon, 11
philology, SC3; of the future, TI2
philosophy, 14; German, 19; Idealistic philosophers, SC5
Pindar, 6, 13
Plato, TI2, TI3, SC4, 10, 12–14, 18n; Platonic Socrates, 15
Podach, Erich, TI3, TI3n
poetry, poets, TI3, SC3, 1, 5–9, 12, 14, 17, 19; epic poet, 5, 22; Greek poets, 17; lyric poetry, 5, 6, 8; sphere of, 8
political instincts, drives, 21
porcupines, Schopenhauer's parable, 22, 22n
Praxiteles, 18n
primal unity, 4–6
primordial being, 17, 22
principium individuationis, 1, 1n, 2, 4, 16, 21, 22. See also individuation
Prometheus, RW, 3, 4, 7, 9–11
public, the, see listener; spectator
Pythagoras, 11
Pythia, 13

R

Radhakrishnan, S., 1n
Raphael, 4
rationality, SC4
reality, SC7, 1, 4, 7, 8, 12, 14, 21, 24; dream-reality, 1; idyllic, 19; waking, 4
recitative, 19
religions, 15, 18; death of, 10; myth as prerequisite of, 18
resignationism, SC6
Rilke, Rainer Maria, TI1
Ritschl, Friedrich, TI2, 19n
Rohde, Erwin, TI2, 19n
romance, romantic, romanticism, SC6, SC7, 3, 23; romantic love in comedy, 11n
Rome, 21
Rousseau, Jean-Jacques, Emile, 3

S

Sacaea, Babylonian, 1, 1n, 2
Sachs, Hans, 1
sacrilege, 9
Sartre, Jean-Paul, 7n, 15n
satyr, SC4, 2, 7, 8; satyr chorus, 7, 8
Schiller, Friedrich, TI3, SC2n, 1n, 2n, 3, 5, 7, 8, 19, 20, 22; Bride of Messina, 7; insight into tragedy, 7, 8
Schlegel, A. W., 7, 7n, 8
Schopenhauer, Arthur, TI2, TI3, SC5, SC6, 1, 5, 5n, 6, 7n, 8n, 16, 18, 19, 19n, 20, 22
science, scientific, SC1, SC2, SC4, 14–18, 23; problem of, SC2; relation of art and science, TI1, SC2
sculptor god, 1
self-abnegation, 2, 5
Semitic character, 9, 9n
sensuality, 2, 3; of Dionysian festivals, 2
Shakespeare, William, 2, 7n, 17, 22; Hamlet, 7, 7n
Silenus, 3, 4, 7, 24
sin, origin of, 9, 10
slave class as necessity of Alexandrian culture, 18
Socrates, TI3, SC1, 12–20, 23, 24; Socratic man, TI2, 20, 23; Socratism, SC1, 12–15, 19, 23; artistic Socrates, TI3, 14, 15n; music-practicing, 15, 15n, 17

song(s), **TI**3, **SC**1; German, 24; nature of, 5; operatic singer, 19

Sophocles, **TI**1, **TI**2, 4**n**, 7, 9, 11–14, 17; *Oedipus at Colonus,* 3**n**, 9, 17; *Trachiniae,* 19**n**

sophrosune, 15, 15**n**

Sparta, 4

spectator, 12, 17, 21; ideal, 7, 8, 8**n**; on the stage, 11

Spengler, Oswald, **TI**3**n**, **SC**5**n**

Sphinx, 9; riddle of, 4, 9

stilo rappresentativo, 19

sub specie aeterni, 23, 23**n**

sub specie saeculi, 23, 23**n**

suffering, **TI**3, **SC**3**n**, 3, 4, 7–9, 10, 18, 20; of Dionysus, 10

symbolic faculties, 2

T

Tannhäuser, 19**n**

Tartarus, 10

Terpander, 6, 6**n**

terror, 1, 2, 3

theater, Greek, 8

Thucydides, **SC**4, 18**n**

Tiberius, 11

Tiresias, 12

Titan(s), 3, 4, 9, 10, 21

tone(s), 2, 6; tone-painting, 17

tragedy, **TI**1, **TI**3, **SC**1, **SC**4, **SC**6, 2, 5, 7–17, 19–22; Apollinian, 8, 9, 12, 22; Attic, 1, 1**n**, 4, 8; birth of, **TI**3, 7; character representation in, 17; death of, **TI**3, 11, 14, 23; Dionysian, *see* Dionysian; as flattering art, 14; musical, 21, 22, 24; mystery doctrine of, 10, 21; origins of, **SC**4, 5, 7, 8, 12; rebirth of, 16, 19–22; Schiller's insight into, 7, 8; theme of, 10;

tragic insight, 15; tragic myth, 22, 24, 25

Tristan, 21

truth, **SC**1, 1, 7, 8, 10, 12, 14, 15, 15**n**, 19; excess as, 4

U

unity, primal, 4, 5, 6

utilitarianism, **SC**4

V

Vergil, 19

Vitus, St., 1

W

Wagner, Richard, **TI**1, **TI**2, **SC**2, **SC**3, **SC**5, 1**n**, 7, 9**n**, 16, 16**n**, 19, 19**n**, 20**n**, 23**n**, 25**n**

Wilamowitz-Moellendorff, Ulrich, **TI**2, 4**n**, 18**n**; Wilamops, **TI**2

will, 3, 5, 6, 16, 17, 18, 19, 21, 22; Apollinian, 9; Buddhistic negation of the, 7; Hellenic, 1, 3, 17; music as language of, 16; negation of, 7, 7**n**; will to decline, **SC**5, **SC**5**n**; will to power, **SC**6**n**

Winckelmann, Johann Joachim, **TI**3, 20

wisdom, 9, 18

Wörth, battle of, **SC**1

Wotan, 24

Z

Zagreus, 10

Zarathustra, **SC**7

Zeus, 10

Zimmer, Heinrich, 1**n**

INDEX

Seventy-five Aphorisms

Arabic figures refer to sections, not pages. The following abbreviations have been employed:

D: *Dawn;* **GS:** *Gay Science;* **H:** *Human, All-Too-Human;* **MM:** *Mixed Opinions and Maxims;* **S:** *The Wanderer and His Shadow.*

For references to Nietzsche's works, see Nietzsche.

A

aphorisms, **MM**168, **GS**381
artists, **H**136, **MM**206
asceticism, **GS**327n; Christian, **H**136, **H**137, **H**142, **H**143, **H**144. *See also* holy man

B

Bach, Johann Sebastian, **MM**298
bad, **GS**273; bad arguments, **S**302; bad manners, **MM**130
Beethoven, Ludwig van, **MM**298
benevolence, **H**96
Bible, the, **H**143
books, honest, **MM**145
Buddha, **GS**108, **GS**142; Buddhists, **H**144

C

chance, **GS**258
Christianity, Christians, **H**143, **H**144, **GS**130, **GS**142; founder of, **H**144. *See also* asceticism, Christian
community, **H**45, **H**96, **D**18. *See also* society
convictions, **S**317, **S**317n

criticism, **MM**168
crowd, the, **GS**173
cruelty, **D**18

D

dance, **GS**381
death, **S**322, **S**333
depth, **GS**173, **GS**381
dog, **GS**312
dreams, **S**194, **GS**232
duty, **MM**404, **D**112

E

Eckhart, Meister, **GS**292, **GS**292n
egoistic/unegoistic, **H**92, **H**96
Empedocles, **MM**408n
end and goal, **S**204
Epicurus, **MM**408, **MM**408n
equality, **S**263
eternal aliveness, **MM**408
Europe, **GS**316
evil, **H**45, **H**96, **H**136. *See also* good
experiences, **S**203, **S**297, **S**298

F

fear, **S**3

forgetfulness, **H**92
fraternity, **S**263
freedom, **GS**275; freedom of the will, **D**112

G

gay science, *see* science
German virtue, **MM**298, **D**231
Gibraltar, **GS**316
goal, **S**204
God, **H**92, **H**137, **H**143, **GS**108, **GS**129, **GS**292, **GS**381; son of, **H**144
god(s), **H**45, **D**18
Goethe, Johann Wolfgang von, **M**298, **MM**408, **MM**408n
good, **H**45, **H**96
gratitude, **H**92
greatness, **GS**325
Greek(s), **H**45, **H**96; Greek philosopher, **H**144

H

Hades, journey to, **MM**408
Handel, George Frederick, **MM**298
Hardenberg, Friedrich von (pseud. Novalis), *see* Novalis
harming neighbor, **H**96
Heraclitus, **MM**408n
holy man, *see* Christian asceticism; holy man of India, **H**144
Homer, **H**45
honor, **S**33

I

immoral, immorality, **H**96
individual vs. society, **MM**89
intellect, **GS**327
intelligibility, **GS**381

J

justice, **H**92, **GS**292

K

knowledge, **GS**231, **GS**381

L

laughter, **GS**200
law, **H**96
liberty, **S**263
life, **GS**121
love, **S**301, **S**301n
Luther, Martin, **GS**129

M

master, love of, **MM**341
masters and slaves, **H**45n
mediators, **GS**228
misunderstanding, **MM**346, **GS**381
Montaigne, Michel Eyquiem de, **MM**408, **MM**408n
morality, morals, **H**45n, **H**137, **MM**89, **GS**292; being moral, **H**96; morality of custom, **D**18; morality of voluntary suffering, **D**18; most moral man, **D**18; slave morality, **H**45n. *See also* mores
mores, **H**96, **MM**89, **D**18
Mozart, Wolfgang Amadeus, **MM**298

N

need, **GS**205
Newton, Sir Isaac, **GS**381
Nietzsche, understanding of, **GS**381; works: *The Antichrist*, **S**317n; *Beyond Good and Evil*, **H**45n, **H**96n, **GS**121n; *The Dawn*, **D**18n; *On the Genealogy of Morals*, **H**45n, **H**96n, **D**231n, **GS**327n
Novalis, **H**142, **H**142n

O

Odysseus, **MM**408
old, regard for, **H**96
opinions, **MM**325, **S**317, **S**333
original, **MM**200

P

pain, **GS**312
Pascal, Blaise, **MM**408, **MM**408n
philosopher(s), **H**137, **GS**332, **GS**381;

Greek, **H**144; philosophers' error, **MM**201

pity, **H**45, **H**96, **D**18

Plato, **MM**408; theory of ideas, **S**33n

power and rights, **D**112

prayer to man, **MM**258

prophets, **GS**316

punishment, **S**33, **S**323, **D**236

R

rationality *ex post facto*, **D**1

readers, **MM**130, **MM**137, **MM**145

religion, **H**142. *See also* asceticism

remorse, **S**323

revenge, **S**33

rights, *see* duty

Rousseau, Jean Jacques, **MM**408, **MM**408n

S

schadenfroh, **GS**200, **GS**200n, **GS**-332n

schlecht/schlicht, **D**231, **D**231n

scholars versus artists, **MM**206

Schopenhauer, Arthur, **H**143n, **MM**408

science, **H**136, **H**144, **MM**206, **GS**381; gay science, **GS**327, **GS**327n

self-preservation, **S**33

Sermon on the Mount, **H**137

shame, **GS**273–275, **GS**381

siding against oneself, **MM**309

skepticism, **GS**51

society, **MM**89. *See also* community

Socrates, **MM**408n

spernere se sperni, **H**137, **H**137n

Spinoza, Baruch, **MM**408, **MM**408n

suffering, **D**18, **GS**325, **GS**325n

T

taking leave, **S**307

"taking the matter seriously," **GS**327

thinkers, thinking, **GS**322, **GS**327. *See also* philosophers, scholars

Thucydides, **H**92

tourists, **S**202

tradition, **H**96

Trojan, **H**45

truth, sense of, **GS**51

U

unegoistic, *see* egoistic

V

victory, great, **GS**163

virtue(s), **MM**405, **GS**292; German, **D**231

W

Wagner, Richard; Nietzsche's relationship to, **MM**341, **MM**341n; Wagner circle, **GS**325n

"whoever is not for me, is against me," **S**208

will, freedom of, **D**112

will to power, **D**18n

wise men, **S**298, **GS**129

Wittgenstein, Ludwig, *Philosophical Investigations*, **S**33n

Z

Zarathustra, **GS**381

INDEX
Beyond Good and Evil

Figures refer to sections, not to pages. **NP** refers to Nietzsche's Preface; **TP** to the translator's Preface; **n** to the translator's notes; **A** to the Aftersong at the end of this book. For references to Nietzsche's works, see Nietzsche.

A

actors, 7, 9, 97, 205
admiration, 118
Aeschylus, 224
affability, 93
affect, 13**n**, 85, 117, 187, 192, 198, 258, 260, 284; will as, 19, 19**n**, 36
Alcibiades, 200
"all too human," **TP, NP,** 204, 271
America, 44
anarchists, 188, 202; anarchism, 248
Anglomania, 253
Antichrist, 256
anti-Semitism, 248**n**, 251. See also Jews
Apollo, 295**n**
Aquinas, Thomas, 13**n**, 19**n**
Ariadne, 295, 295**n**
aristocracies, 258, 259; faith of, 260; aristocratic: feeling, 58; morals, 46; society, 257, 262; spirit, 239; values, 32
Aristophanes, 28, 231, 232; Aristophanean derision, 223
Aristotle, **TP,** 211**n**, 212**n**, 239**n**, 287**n**; Aristotelianism of morals, 198; Aristotelian presuppositions, 188
art(s), 33, 59, 188, 198, 223, 224, 240, 246, 255, 256, 260, 291; artists, 11, 31, 59, 110, 137, 188, 192, 200, 204, 209, 210, 213, 225, 240, 269, 287
asceticism, 61; ascetics, 229
Asia (Asiatic), **NP,** 52, 56, 188, 208, 238

atheism, 53, 209
Atkins, Samuel D., 27**n**
atomism, 12, 12**n**, 17
Augustine, 12**n**, 50, 200
Austria, 251, 251**n**

B

Bacon, Francis, 252
bad, the, 190, 260. *See also* beyond good and evil; evil
Baldwin, James Mark, 13**n**, 19**n**
Balzac, Honoré de, 204, 256
Bayle, Pierre, 28
Beethoven, Ludwig van, 245, 256
Being, lap of, 2
Benebelungen, 251**n**
Bentham, Jeremy, 228
Berkeley, George, 36
Berlin wit and sand, 244
Bertram, Ernst, 200**n**, 250**n**
Beyle, Henri, 39, 254, 256
beyond good and evil, **TP,** 40**n**, 44, 56, 153, 241**n**, 250**n**, 255, 260. *See also* evil; good
Bible, **TP,** 28, 52, 247, 263
bieder; Biederkeit, 244
Bismarck, Otto von, 241**n**, 251**n**, 254**n**
Bizet, Georges, 254
"blood," concept of, 213, 213**n**
Borgia, Cesare, 197, 197**n**
Boscovich, Ruggiero Giuseppe, 12, 12**n**
Bradley, F. H., **TP**
Brahmins, 61
Brandes, Georg, **TP, NPn**

breeding, 262
Bruno, Giordano, 25
Buddha, 56; Buddhism, 61, 202
Burckhardt, Jacob, **TP**
Butler, Samuel, 264n
Byron, Lord, 245, 269

C

Caesar, Julius, 200; Caesarian cultivator, 207
Cagliostro, Alessandro, 194, 205
cant, 228
Carlyle, Thomas, 252
Catholicism, 48; Catholics, 251n;
Roman catholicity, 46; anti-Cath-
olicism, 256
Catiline, Lucius Sergius, 194
causa sui, 15, 21
cause and effect, 21, 47
Celts, 48
certainty, 1, 10; "immediate," 16,
17, 34; uncertainty, 1
Chimaera, 190n
China, 32; Chinese, 267, 296; Mozart's Chinese touches, 245
Christianity (Christian, Christians),
NP, 11, 12, 46, 48, 49, 52, 54,
56, 61, 62, 104, 104n, 168, 188,
189, 191, 200, 202, 203, 210, 223,
229, 252, 256, 261, 263; Christian-
ecclesiastical pressure of millennia,
NP; spiritual men of, 62. *See also*
religion
Cicero, 13n, 19n, 247.
Circe, 208, 229
cleanliness, 74, 74n, 271, 284
cogito, "I think," "it thinks," 16, 17,
54
cognition, 192
Comte, Auguste, 48
conscience, 98, 208, 208n; good, 214,
291; and science, 45, 45n
cooking, 234
Copernicus, Nicholas, 12
Cornford, F. M., **TP**
corruption, 258, 269
Corsica, 208
costume(s), 223; lie-costumes, 208
Cowan, Marianne, **TP,** 1n, 204n,
205n, 208n, 260n, 289n

criminal, 109–10; criminals, punishment of, 201
Cromwell, Oliver, 46
cruelty in higher culture, 229; in religion, 55; in tragedy, 229
cultivation (cultivate), **NPn,** 61, 203,
213, 239, 262, 263; Caesarian cultivator, 207; of new ruling class in
Europe, 251; of tyrants, 242;
species-cultivating, 4
culture, evolution of higher, 257
cynicism, 26

D

danger, dangerous, dangers, 28, 29,
39, 40, 42, 44, 45, 62, 103, 195,
198, 201, 205, 207, 208, 212, 220,
224, 228, 238, 239, 242, 245, 282;
as mother of morals, 262; dangerous maybes, 2; undangerous, 260
Dante Alighieri, **TP,** 236
Danto, Arthur C., 56n
Darwin, Charles, 253; Darwinists,
14
Davenant, Sir William, 294n
deception, 2, 9, 31, 34, 36, 264
Delacroix, Ferdinand Victor Eugène,
256
democracy, democratic, democrats,
NP, 202–204, 210, 238n, 239; democratic bourgeoisie, 254; democratic enlightenment, **NP;** democratic taste, 44; Europe's democratic movement, 242; splinter
wills in, 208
Demosthenes, 247
Descartes, René, 2n, 54, 191
devil, 129
Diderot, Denis, 28
Dionysiokolakes, Dionysus, 7, 7n,
295, 295n
discipline, 188, 203, 219, 225, 252,
262; critical, 210; of science, 230
disappointment, 99
disinterest, 220; disinterested knowledge, 207
distance, pathos of, 257
dogmatism, dogmatists, dogmatizing,
NP, 43, 43n, 211
Don Quixote, 25n

Dostoevsky, Feodor Mikhailovich, **TP**

dreams, 193

drives, 6, 23, 36, 158, 189, 201

Dühring, Eugen, 204, 204n

dumpf, 241n

duty, 226

E

ego, 16, 17

Egypt, **NP,** 28

Elector of Brandenburg, 251n

Electra, 209n

Empedocles, 204

England, **TP,** 208, 228, 251n, 252, 253, 253n

English, **TP, TPn,** 4n, 8n, 189, 224, 228, 251–54, 294; nobility, 251; women, **TP**

enthusiasm, 288

Epicurus, 7, 7n; Epicurean, 200; god, 62; philosophy, 61; spirit, 62; Epicureanism, 270

d'Épinay, Mme, 26n, 222

equality, 30, 201, 259; "equal before God," 62; of rights, 44, 212, 219, 238, 265

Eros, 168

Eternal-Feminine/Masculine, 236

eternal recurrence, 56, 56n

Europe, **TPn, NP,** 10–12, 44, 47, 52, 62, 186, 189, 199, 202, 208, 209, 212, 222, 224, 228, 231, 232, 239, 241, 242, 244, 245, 251, 254, 256, 260, 263, 293; what Europe owes to the Jews, 250

European(s), 62, 188, 200, 201, 202, 209, 214, 223, 224, 242, 245, 253, 254, 259, 267; "evolving European," 242; good Europeans, **NP, NPn,** 241, 243, 254; morality, 203; music, 255; problem, 251; races, 62; spirit, 188, 253; soul, 254, 256; theism, 53

evil, 39, 195, 201, 250n, 260; good and, 149, 153, 202, 241n, 250n, 255, 260. *See also* beyond good and evil; good and evil

existentialism, **TP,** 21n, 43n

exploitation, 259

F

faculties, Kant's concept of, 11

faith, 1n, 2, 36, 46, 55, 58, 180, 186, 191, 202, 203, 205, 223, 231, 239, 241, 250n, 264, 269, 287; in opposite values, 2; of former times, 10; of governesses, 34, 34n; of aristocrats, 260; Christian, 46

falseness, falsification, 4, 34, 59, 191, 230

familiarity, 182

fatherlandishness, 241, 245, 254, 256

fear, 192, 209, 229, 232, 239, 269; in religion, 49, 59; of eternal misunderstanding, 268; of the neighbor, 201, 201n

Fichte, Johann Gottlieb, 244

Flaubert, Gustave, 218

Florentine, 223

Förster, Bernhard, **TP**

France, 48, 208, 210, 218, 241n, 253, 254, 256, 258; "France of taste," 254

French, **TP,** 4n, 48, 209, 244, 248, 254, 256; character, 254; "French ideas," 253; anti-French stupidity, 251

French Revolution, 38, 46, 191, 239, 244, 245, 258

Frederick II (medieval German emperor), 200, 200n; Frederick II (the Great), 209, 209n; Frederickianism, 209

Frederick William I, 209n

Freud, Sigmund, **TP,** 68n, 189n, 289n, 231n

friends, friendship, **TP,** 27, 40, 195, 217, 260, 268, 283

G

Galiani, Abbé Ferdinand, 26, 26n, 222, 228, 270, 288

gāngāsrotagati, 27, 27n

Ganges River, 27n

Gast, Peter, **TPn,** 8n

Gemüt, gemütlich, 244n

genius, 248, 274, 274n; of the heart, 295; "of the species," 268

Geoffrin, Marie-Thérèse, 26n
German, Germans, **TP**, **NP**, 11, 28,
  56, 58, 126, 126n, 192, 193, 204,
  209, 239, 240, 245–48, 250n, 251,
  252, 254, 255, 256; honesty, 244;
  music, 255; "profundity of," 244;
  skepticism, 209; soul, 48, 240, 244;
  spirit, 11, 209, 251–53; taste, 28,
  39, 244, 254; Germanomania, 251
Germany, **TP**, 28, 47, 58, 204, 208,
  209, 210, 214n, 247, 251, 254
Gillispie, Charles C., 12n
God, 10, 21, 26, 34n, 37, 50, 53, 55,
  56n, 57–60, 101, 121, 129, 150,
  164, 186, 188, 191, 198, 199, 202,
  203, 205, 205n, 207, 219, 223, 237,
  244, 248, 295; "equal before," 62;
  love of, 67
god(s), 2, 7, 40, 44, 46, 55, 56n,
  62, 65a, 66, 80, 144, 188, 202n,
  218, 227, 262, 264, 269, 294, 295,
  295n; on the cross, 46
Goethe, Johann Wolfgang von, 28,
  198, 198n, 209, 209n, 231n, 232n,
  236, 238n, 241n, 244, 244n, 252,
  256, 266, 286, 295n; *Faust,* 244n,
  286n; *Werther,* 245
Gogol, Nikolai Vasilievich, 269
good, the, **NPn**, 23, 35n, 39, 43, 135,
  148, 190, 191, 194, 202, 204, 223,
  250n, 260, 261, 268; common, 43;
  good will, 208
good conscience, 291, definition of,
  214
good and evil, 4, 147, 147n, 149, 159,
  198, 201, 202, 207, 209, 250n, 260;
  "good" and "wicked" drives, 23
good taste, 224
gratitude, 49, 49n, 58, 62, 74, 74n,
  207, 260
Great Britain, *see* England
great men, 269; man who strives for
  the great, 273
greatness, concept of, 212
greatness of soul, 212; Aristotle's
  portrait of, 212n
Greece, 7, 49, 260
Greek(s), 28, 30, 49, 52, 121, 238,
  248, 248n, 267; philosophy, 20;
  polis, 262
Grossoktav edition, 65an, 269n
Gundolf, Friedrich, 200n

Guyon, Jeanne-Marie Bouvier de, 50,
  50n

H

Hafiz, 198
Hamlet, 62n, 208, 208n, 270, 270n
Hampshire, Stuart N., 12n
happiness, 103, 193, 198, 212, 279
Harpies, 282
Hartmann, Eduard von, 204, 204n
Hauptstück, 1n
Hegel, Georg Wilhelm Friedrich,
  TP, 43n, 204, 204n, 210, 211, 244,
  252, 252n, 254; Hegelianism, **TP**
Heine, Heinrich, 254, 256
Helvétius, Claude Adrien, 228, 228n
Heraclitus, 204
Hercules (constellation), 243
herd, 191, 199, 201–03, 212, 228,
  242; instincts, 201, 202
heredity, 264
hermit, 289
"higher men," 61, 62, 72, 173, 182,
  212, 221, 228, 256, 269, 274, 286
historical sense, 204, 224
Hobbes, Thomas, 252, 294, 294n
Homer, 224, 228, 238; *Iliad,* 191n,
  258n, 260n
honesty, 26, 31, 34, 227, 230, 250n,
  284n; German, 244
Horace, *Odes,* 251n; *Epistles,* 264n
Hugo, Victor, 254, 254n
Hume, David, 209n, 252

I

Ibsen, Henrik, **TP**, 213n; *An Enemy
  of the People,* **TP**, 213n
immoral, immorality, 6, 32, 95, 201,
  221, 226, 228, 259
independence, 29, 41
Indian(s), 20, 30, 52; Wars, 208
Indo-Germanic peoples, 20
Innocent XII, 50n
Inquisition, 50n
insanity and nationality, 256
instinct(s), 3, 10, 13, 22, 26, 36, 44,
  55, 58, 59, 62, 83, 145, 189, 191,
  201, 202, 206, 207, 209, 212, 218,
  224, 233, 238, 239, 251, 258; of
  cleanliness, 271; of obedience, 199;

for rank, 263; religious, 53, 58; instinctive activities, 3
intimacy, 167
irony, 212
Italians, 247, 251
Italy, 208

J

Jack the Dreamer, 208n
Japanese, 229
Jaspers, Karl, 40n, 250n
Java, 258
Jean Paul, *see* Richter, J. P. F.
Jesuitism, Jesuits, **NP**, 48, 206
Jesus, 164, 269
Jews, Jewish, **TP, TPn,** 52, 164, 195, 248, 248n, 250n, 251, 251n; Jewess, **TPn;** "Wandering Jew," 251
Joyce, James, 208n, 253n
judgments, 4, 4n, 11, 32, 43, 191, 205, 219; synthetic *a priori,* 11
justice, 9, 201, 213, 262, 265

K

Kant, Immanuel, 1n, 4n, 5, 11, 54, 187, 188, 209n, 210, 210n, 211, 211n, 220n, 252; the great Chinese of Königsberg, 210; table of categories, 11, 44
Kantorowicz, Ernst, 200n
Kierkegaard, Soren, **TP,** 40n
kindness, 184
Kleist, Heinrich von, 269
knowledge, 2, 6, 25, 26, 64, 65, 71, 101, 152, 171, 191, 192, 204, 205, 208 210, 229, 231, 253, 270; about love, 269; absolute, 16; and cognition, 192; "disinterested," 207; self-, 32, 231, 281; will to, 24
Kotzebue, August Friedrich Ferdinand von, 244, 244n
Kundry, 47
kūrmagati, 27, 27n

L

laisser aller, 188
Lamarck, Jean-Baptiste, 213n, 264n
Lambert, Anne-Thérèse de, 235

last man, 225n
laughter, 223, 294, 294n
Leibniz, Gottfried Wilhelm von, 207
leisure, 189
Leopardi, Giacomo, 269
Lessing, Gotthold Ephraim, **TP,** 28; *Emilia Galotti,* 274n
Levy, Oscar, **TP**
literature, French, 254; German, 246
Locke, John, 20, 252, 252n
love, 142; of God, 67; as passion, 260, 269; self-, 287n; sexual, 114; Christians' love of men, 104
Luther, Martin, 46, 50; Luther's Bible, 247
lying, 180, 183, 192

M

Macbeth, 229n
Machiavelli, Niccolò, 28, 28n; *The Prince,* 28
McTaggart, J. M. E., **TP**
madness, 156
Magnus, L. A., **A**
man, enhancement of, 257
mandūkagati, 27, 27n
Manu's laws, 260n
Marianus, Doctor, 286n
Marlowe, Christopher, 209n
marriage, 123
Marschner, Heinrich, 245
mask(s), **NP,** 4, 5, 25, 30n, 40, 40n, 47, 204, 221, 225, 230, 270, 278, 289
master(s), 6, 46, 198, 202, 204, 207, 212, 230, 241, 241n, 246, 261, 293; master and slave morality, 40n, 212n, 260, 260n, 261
mediocrity, 201, 206, 218, 242, 262; truths of mediocre minds, 253
Mendelssohn, Felix, 245, 248n
Mephistopheles, 209n, 244
metaphysicians, metaphysics, metaphysical, 2, 6, 16, 21, 229, 230; faith of, 2; "need," 12
Methodism, 252
Michelet, Jules, 209
Mill, John Stuart, 253
Molière, 11
Molinos, Miguel, 50n
Montaigne, Michel Eyquem de, 208

"monumentalistic" historiography, 200n

Moore, G. E., **TP**

morality, moral, morals, 4–6, 9, 23, 25, 26, 32, 34, 39, 46, 47, 55, 56, 64, 95, 108, 143, 164, 186–203, 204, 208, 211, 212, 215–18, 221, 223, 228, 250, 252, 254, 255, 257, 260, 262, 291; aristocratic, 46; definition of, 19; extra-moral period, 32; higher, 202; of mediocrity, 262; of self-denial, 33; moral judgments, 219; pre-moral period, 32; rational foundation of, 186; as timidity, 198, 201

Moses, 60n

Mozart, Wolfgang Amadeus, 245

Münchhausen, Baron, 21

Musarion edition, 65an, 186n, 227n, 294n

music, 106, 239, 254; French, 254; German, 245, 255. *See also* Wagner

Muslims, 20, 30

Musset, Alfred de, 269

mysticism, mystics, 5, 11, 40, 50, 50n, 204, 220

N

Napoleon, 199, 209, 232, 244, 244n, 245, 256; Napoleonic tempo, 254; Napoleon's mother, 239

Naumann, C. G., **TP**

nausea, 203, 203n, 224, 263, 269, 270, 282

Nausicaa, 96

Nazis, 251n, 264n

Necker, Mme, 26n

New Testament, 52, 212n, 260n, 287n. *See also* Bible; Old Testament

niaiserie, 3, 3n; *allemande*, 11; *religieuse*, 48

Nietzsche: Works: *The Antichrist*, **NPn**, 208n, 210n, 260n; *The Birth of Tragedy*, 208n, 240n, 295n; *The Case of Wagner*, 240n; *The Dawn*, 195n, 201n, 284n; *Ecce Homo*, 209n, 221n, 227n, 251n, 295n; editions, **TP**, 65an *see also* Gross-

oktav edition; Musarion edition); *Friedrich Nietzsches Briefe an Mutter und Schwester*, **TP**; *Friedrich Nietzsches Briefe an Peter Gast*, **TP**; *Friedrich Nietzsches Briefwechsel mit Franz Overbeck*, **TP**; *Friedrich Nietzsches Gesammelte Briefe*, **An**; *The Gay Science* (*Die fröhliche Wissenschaft*), 209n, 260n, 294n, 295n; *Genealogy of Morals*, 54n, 260n; *Human, All-Too-Human*, **TPn**, **NPn**, 195n, 260n, 294n; *Nietzsche contra Wagner*, 240n, 254n, 269, 269n, 270n; *Schopenhauer as Educator*, 227n; *Thus Spoke Zarathustra*, **TP**, 26n, 41n, 56n, 202n, 225n, 269n, 285n, 294n, 295n, "To the Mistral: A Dancing Song," **An**; *Twilight of the Idols*, 21n, 209n, 260n, 295n; "Untimely Meditation," 200n; *Werke in drei Bänden*, **TP** (*see also* Schlechta); *The Will to Power*, 260n

noble, nobility, 49, 61, 62, 190, 201, 206, 212, 212n, 213, 224; posterity, 38; signs of, 272; what is noble, 257–96.

O

obedience, 187, 188, 199

Odysseus, 96, 230

Oedipus, 1, 230

Oehler, Richard, 251n

Ogden, C. K., 4n

Old Testament, 52. *See also* Bible; New Testament

opposite(s), 2, 9, 47, 56, 58, 200, 212; men, 44; values, 2, 274n

Orient, the, 46

Oriental(s), 50, 238

Overbeck, Franz, **TP**

Ovid, 227n

P

Paneth, Doctor, **TPn**

Pascal, Blaise, 45, 46, 62, 229

Passmore, John, 34n

pathos of distance, 257
Pericles, 238
Persians, 30
perspective, 10, 11, 34, 188, 201, 250n; for Plato, NP; frog perspective, 2
Petronius, 28
Pharisaism, 135
philosophy, philosophers, TP, NP, 1–23, 25, 26, 34, 39, 47, 54, 56, 59, 61, 62, 186, 190, 191, 204, 205, 207–213, 220, 225, 228, 229, 241, 252, 262, 269, 289, 292–95; drive to knowledge in, 6; English, 252; German, 11, 20; good philosophers, 39, 39n; Greek, 20; Indian, 20; martyrdom of the philosopher, 25; new species of philosophers, 42–44, 61, 203, 210, 211; philosophers of the dangerous, 2; philosophical concepts, 20; philosophical laborers versus philosophers, 211
Phoenicians, 229; Phoenicianism, 46
physics, 14
physiology, 15
pia fraus, 105, 105n
pity, 29, 30, 62, 82, 171, 199, 201, 202, 204, 206, 222, 225, 239, 260, 269, 293; saint's, 271
Plato, Platonism, TP, NP, 7, 7n, 14, 28, 105n, 106, 190, 190n, 191, 204, 211n, 284n; Theaetetus, 295n
"plebs," 264, 287
Podach, E. F., TP, 9n
Poe, Edgar Allan, 269
poets, 161, 188, 269
Poles, 251n
positivism, 10, 204, 210
possession, 194
praise, 122, 170, 283; self-praise, 204, 204n
Praxiteles, 224n
prejudice(s), 1–23, 32, 34, 44, 199, 224, 242, 274n; moral, 23
pride, 9, 11, 21, 43, 46, 58, 73a, 111, 186, 211, 213, 229, 230, 270
Protagoras, 4n
Protestant(s), Protestantism, 48, 50, 58
Provençal knight-poets, 260

Prussia(n), 209, 254n; "pluck," 244; stupidity, 251
psychology, 23, 45, 47, 196, 218, 222, 229, 269, 270
punishing, 201, 201n
Puritanism, 61, 188, 216, 228, 229

Q

Quietism, 50n

R

races, 48, 61, 188, 189, 200, 208, 224, 242, 244, 251, 252, 256, 262; European, 62; Latin, 48, 256; Nazi race views, 251n; problem of, 264, 264n; spirit of, 48
rank, order of, 30, 39n, 52n, 59, 61, 194, 203, 204, 206, 212, 213, 219, 221, 224, 228, 257, 260, 263, 265, 268, 270, 285, 287, 294
Raphael, 224n; "Raphael without hands," 274, 274n
reality, 36
religion, 45–62, 198, 202, 205, 206, 216, 222, 229, 293; as sovereign, 62; for education and cultivation, 61; religious cruelty, 55; religious neurosis, 47. See also Christianity
Renan, Ernest, 48
reputation, 92
resentment, 49n, 58n, 73An
rhetoric, 247
Richter, Johann Paul Friedrich, 244, 244n, 245
Rilke, Rainer Maria, 201n
Roland, Mme, 233
Roman(s), 50n, 201, 229, 248, 248n; logic, 48; Rome, 46, 256
romanticism, 245, 250, 256
rhyme and rhythm, 188
Roosevelt, F. D., 201n
Ross, W. D., 34n
Rousseau, Jean-Jacques, 245
Russell, Bertrand, TP
Russia, 208, 227; Russian(s), 208, 208n; Russian Empire, 251
Ryle, Gilbert, 34n

S

Sabbath, 189

Saccheti, Franco, 147

sacrifice(s), 55, 220, 229, 229n, 230, 265; Christian faith as a, 46

Sainte-Beuve, Charles-Augustin de, 48

Saint-Évremond, Charles de, 224

saints, 30, 47, 50, 51, 271

Salis, Frl. von, TP

Salvation Army, 47, 252

Sand, George, 233

Sand, Karl Ludwig, 244, 244n

Sartre, Jean-Paul, TP, 21n, 109n, 203n

Schelling, Friedrich Wilhelm Joseph von, 11, 252

Schiller, Johann Christophe Friedrich von, 245; *Die Piccolomini,* 237n; "Shakepeare's Shadow," 239n; *Wilhelm Tell,* 229n

Schlechta, Karl, TP, 65n, 99n, 186n, 237n, 269n, 270n

Schlosser, Rat, 266

Schmeitzner, Ernst, TP, 5n

scholars, 39, 45, 58, 137, 204–14, 220, 239, 250n, 287; German, 58, 244; interests of, 6

Schopenhauer, Arthur, TP, 16, 19, 36, 47, 56, 186, 186n, 204, 204n, 227, 252, 252n, 254, 256; Schopenhauerian "genius of the species," 268

Schumann, Robert, 245

science, scientists, NP, 6, 14, 21, 23, 26, 127, 192, 198, 204, 205, 210, 230, 237; and conscience, problem of, 45, 45n; "being scientific," 208, 232; nature's conformity to law, 22; "science of morals," 186; scientific average man, 206; scientific men, 80, 211, 270

self-love, 287n

self-preservation, 13

semi-barbarism, 224

sensuality, 120, 155

sexual love, 114; sexuality, 75

Shakespeare, William, 224; "Shakespeare's Shadow," 239n. *See also* *Hamlet; Macbeth*

shame, 40, 65, 167, 231, 295

Shaw, George Bernard, 253n, 264n; *Major Barbara,* 202n

Shelley, Percy Bysshe, 245

siao-sin, 267

Siegfried, 256

Sipo Matador, 258

skepticism, skeptics, 46, 48, 54, 208, 208n, 209, 209n, 210, 211

slave(s), slavery, 44, 46, 50, 188, 195, 207, 225, 239, 242, 257, 258, 260, 261; slave morality, 212n, 260, 260n, 261; slave rebellion in morals, 195, 195n

socialists, 202, 203, 251n, 256

Socrates, NP, 80, 190, 191, 202, 208, 212, 295n; Socratism, 190

solitude, 44, 61

soul, 12, 19, 20, 30–32, 44, 45, 47, 52, 54, 58, 61, 62, 79, 188, 193, 203, 204, 207, 212, 225, 240, 245, 252, 254, 256, 257, 260, 263, 264, 268, 269, 271, 276, 291; democratic instincts of, 22; French, 253; German, 48, 240, 244; immortal, 10, 12; in true love, 142, 142n; "modern," 224; noble, 265, 287; soul superstition, NP

Spain, 208

Spaniards, 229

Spencer, Herbert, 253

Spinoza, Baruch, 5, 13, 13n, 25, 198, 205n, 211n

spirit(s), TPn, NP, 6, 46, 48, 52, 56–58, 74, 75, 87, 90, 122, 184, 186, 193, 199, 201, 203, 204, 207, 209, 210, 214, 216, 218–20, 223–25, 229, 230, 235, 238, 239, 241, 252–254, 263, 264n, 274, 285, 286, 288; "basic will of the," 229, 230; Epicurean, 62; free, 24–44, 61, 87, 105, 188, 203, 211, 213, 227, 230, 250n, 270; German 11, 209, 251–253; objective, 207–208

spiritual, spirituality, spiritualization, NPn, 26, 45, 57, 61, 188, 194, 198, 201, 209, 213, 227, 229, 252; spiritual *fatum,* 231; spiritual haughtiness, 270; malice spiritualized, 219; spiritual Germanization, 254

Staël, Mme de, 209n, 232, 233
Stände, 257n
Stefan George Circle, 200n
Stein, Heinrich von, **A, An**
Stendhal, *see* Beyle
Stoa, Stoicism, Stoics, 8, 9, 188, 189, 198, 207, 227
style, tempo of, 28
sublimation, 58, 189, 189n, 209
suffering 62, 202, 225, 229, 251, 270, 284n, 293
suicide, 157
superstition, **NP**, 32, 47; of logicians, 17
Swabians, 244
Sybel, Heinrich von, 251, 251n
sympathy, 284, 284n
synthesis, 256

T

Tacitus, 195
Taine, Hippolyte, 254
talent, 130, 151
Tartuffery, 5, 24, 228, 249
Täusche-Volk, 244
teleology, 13, 14
tempo, 27, 27n, 28, 28n, 246, 246n
Teutonic stupidity, 251
theology, 204
thinking, concept of, 16, 17, 19, 213
Tiberius, 55
tragedy, 229, 239, 239n; sense of the tragic, 155
translations, 28
Treitschke, Henrich von, 251, 251n
truth, truthfulness, **NP**, 1–5, 9–11, 16, 25, 34, 35, 39, 43–45, 48, 59, 81, 128, 134, 166, 177, 202, 210, 211, 220, 229, 230–32, 261, 264; mediocre, 253

U

untruth, 1, 3; as a condition of life, 4; the will to, 24, 59
Ural-Altaic languages, 20
utilitarianism, utilitarians, utility, 174, 188, 196, 191, 201, 204, 206, 225, 228, 260, 261

V

Vaihinger, Hans, 4n
values(s), 1, 2, 4, 32, 34, 43, 46, 62, 186, 191, 203, 206, 208, 211, 212, 250n, 253, 260 261, 268, 274n; aristocratic, 32; Christian value judgments, 189; inversion of, 195; one's own, 261; of a soul, 263; value-creating, 260, 285n
vanity, 143, 176, 261
Vedanta, **NP**, 54
Venice, 262
Versuch, Versucher, Versuchung, 42n, 210n
Vinci, Leonardo da, 200
virtues, 30, 39, 132, 199, 201, 207, 208, 212–39, 241, 249, 251, 260, 262, 262n, 288; four virtues, 284, 284n
Voltaire, 26, 28, 35, 224; Voltairian bitterness, 216

W

Wagner, Richard, 41n, 47, 203n, 240, 244, 245, 254, 254n, 256, **A**; *Meistersinger,* 240; *Nietzsche contra Wagner,* 269n; *Parsifal,* 256, *Tristan and Isolde,* 229; Wagnerienne, 229, "Wagnerize," 254
war, 273
Wars of Liberation, 244
Weber, Karl Maria von, 245
Wesen, 45n
Whither and For What of man, the, 211
will, 1, 19, 21, 24, 36, 44, 47, 51, 61, 62, 117, 188, 201, 203, 208, 209, 211, 212, 229, 230, 239, 242; as affect, 19, 19n, 36; freedom of, 18, 19, 21, 44, 53, 208, 213; sickness of, 208; will to stupidity, 107; will to the denial of life, 259; "unfree will," 21; will to untruth, 24, 59
will to power, 22, 23, 40n, 44, 51, 186, 198, 211, 227, 241n, 257, 259, 294n; exploitation as a consequence of, 259; life as, 13, 36; of

the spirit, 229, 230; spiritual, 9
Winkel, 41n
Wittgenstein, Ludwig. 28n
woman, women, **TP**, 84–86, 114–15,
 127, 131, 139, 144–45, 147–48,
 194, 204, 207, 231–39, 261, 269
Wotan, 260

Y

Yeats, William Butler, 253n
youth, 31, 44, 260

Z

Zimmern, Helen, **TP, A**

INDEX

On the Genealogy of Morals

Arabic figures refer to sections, not to pages. Roman numerals refer to the three essays that comprise the *Genealogy*. **E** refers to the editor's Introduction, **P** to Nietzsche's Preface, **n** to the editor's notes. For references to Nietzsche's works, see Nietzsche.

A

Achilles, III 4

activity, mechanical, III 18, III 19

Adam, II 21

adaptation, II 12

aesthetic contemplation, III 6; physiology of aesthetics, III 8

Aegisthus, II 23

affect(s), II 3, III 15, III 16, III 19, III 20, III 21

agathos, I 5

agnosticism, II 12n; agnostics, III 25

alcoholism, German, III 21

alienation, II 14

amor fati, E4, E 4n, I 16n

Anacreon, III 26, III 26n

anarchism, I 5; anarchists, II 11; species anarchistica, III 26. *See also* nihilism

ancestors, fear of, II 19

anolbos, I 10, ¶ 10n

Antichrist, III 24, III 24n

anti-Semites, II 11, III 14, III 26; anti-Semitism, E3, I 5n

aphorisms, E1, E3, P8

Apocalypse of John, I 16

Aquinas, Thomas, I 15, I 15n

Arabian nobility, I 11

Arbesman, Rudolph, I 15n

Aristophanes, *The Clouds,* III 7n

Aristotle, I 5n

art, III 6, III 25, III 25n; artists, II 17, II 18, III 1–6, III 8, III 26

Artemis, temple of, III 8

Aryan, I 5, III 26; pre-Aryan populace, I 11

ascetic ideals, E3, I 6, II 3, III, *passim;* ascetic priests, *see* priests

Asia, III 22

Assassins, Order of, III 24, III 24n

astronomy, III 25

atheism, II 20, III 27

Athenians, I 11, I 11n

aufheben, II 10n, III 27n

autonomous, individual, II 2, II 2n

B

bad conscience, *see* conscience

barbarians, I 11

Barker, Ernest, **E** 3n

beasts of prey, I 11, III 14, III 15, III 18; birds of prey, I 13

beauty, Kant's concept of, III 6

Beethoven, Ludwig van, III 19, III 19n

Beyle, Henri, *see* Stendhal

beyond good and evil, I 12, III 17

Binion, Rudolph, T4n

biography, honest, III 19

birds of prey, *see* beasts of prey

Bismark, Otto von, I 5n

Black Beast, I 11n

blond beast(s), I 11, I 11n, II 17, II 17n

Bogos, III 14

bonus, I 5, I 5n

bourgeois morality, *see* morality

Brahma, Brahmins, I 6, III 10, III 17

British, *see* England

Buber, Martin, E3

Buckle, Henry Thomas, I 4, I 4n

Buddha, III 7, III 27; Buddhist (-ism), P5, I 6, II 21, III 17

buyer-seller, creditor-debtor, relationship, II 4, II 4n, II 5, II 7, II 8, II 9, II 19, II 21. *See also* creditor, debt

Byron Lord, III 19

common, I 3, I 4, I 10; common man, I 5, I 10

community, II 9, II 10, II 13, III 9, III 18, III 19; as creditor, II 9; "commune," inclination for, I 5; tribal community, II 19

conscience, II 2, II 3, II 5, II 6, II 11, II 14, II 21, II 24, III 27; bad conscience, E4, II 1n, II 4, II 11, II 14–19, II 21–24, III 20, III 23; intellectual, III 24n; *morus conscientiae,* II 15

consciousness, II 1, II 16; bad, II 1n; of power, II 10

consolation, III 17

contempt, I 10

Copernicus, Nicholas, III 25

creditor(s), II 4–6, II 8–10, II 19, II 21, II 21n

crime, treatment of, II 10; criminal, II 14

cruelty, II 5–7, II 9, II 18, III 19, III 20; as a festival, II 6, II 7; cruelty of man turned inward, II 22, III 10, III 20

culture, I 11

Cynics, III 7

C

Calvin, John, II 7

Cambodia, III 9

Camus, Albert, E3

candidus, I 5n

categorical imperative, P3, II 6

Catholics, III 3

Celts, I 5

Charles the Bold, III 9

chastity, III 2, III 8

child, E4

Chinese, I 12, I 16; Chinese law, II 13

Christian (-ity), E3, I 1, I 9, I 12, I 15n, I 16, II 7, II 20, II 21, II 23, III 3, III 17, III 18, III 22, III 24, III 26, III 27; anti-Christians, III 24, III 24n; Christian paradise, I 15

Christopher, Squire, III 17, III 17n

church, I 9, I 16, III 16, III 22; Church Father(s), I 15, III 22

D

Dante Alighieri, I 15

Danto, Arthur C., P8n, I 11n, II 1n, III 24n

Darwin, Charles, P7; Darwinism, II 2n

debt, to ancestors, II 19; to the deity, II 20, II 21; debtor, II 4, II 4n, II 5, II 8, II 9, II 19, II 21. *See also* buyer-seller, creditor-debtor relationship

deed, I 13

deilos, deilaios, I 5, I 10, I 10n

democracy, I 5, III 25; democratic idiosyncrasy, II 12

Demosthenes, I 11n

Denny, Reuel, II 2n

depression, III 17, III 18, III 20

Descartes, René, III 7

deterministic world, II 7

Deussen, Paul, III 17, III 17n

devil, II 22

diabolizing of nature, II 21
Diet of Worms, III 22
Dionysian drama, **P**7; Dionysian vision, **E**4; Dionysus, **E**4
Donaldson, James, I 15**n**
Don Quixote, II 6
Dostoevsky, Feodor Mikhailovich, III 15**n**, III 24**n**
Doudan, Ximénès, III 25, III 25**n**
Dühring, Eugen, II 11, II 11**n**, III 14, III 26
duty, II 6, II 8, II 21. *See also* guilt
dystichein, I 10, I 10**n**

E

egoistic/unegoistic, I 2, I 3, II 18
Egyptians, II 5
Eliot, George III 3**n**
Else, Gerald F., *Aristotle's Poetics: The Argument,* I 5**n**
enemy (-ies), I 10, I 11
Engels, Friedrich, II 11**n**, III 3**n**
England, III 7; English, **E**3, **P**4, **P**7, I 16; English biologists, I 17; English psychologists, I 1–3; English "Salvation Army," III 22
Ephesians, III 8
Epicurus, III 6, III 17
esthlos and *kakos,* I 5, I 5**n**
eu prattein, I 10, I 10**n**
Europe (-ans), **P**5, I 2, I 5, I 11, I 12, I 16, I 17, II 3, II 7, II 13, II 23, III 5, III 14, III 21, III 24, III 25, III 26, III 27; European health, *see* health; European mandarin, II 3; European *Weltschmerz,* III 17; "good European," **E**3
evangelical freedom, III 2
"everything has its price," II 8
evil, **P**3, **P**4, **P**6, I, II 7, II 15, II 20, II 23, III 13**n**, III 14, III 17, III 21; "the Evil One," I 10
"evolution" of a thing, II 12

F

failures, III 14
fairness, II 8; scientific, II 11
faith, III 24, III 24**n**; in opposite values, **E**4

Fates, III 26
Faust, **P**3**n**, III 4, III 13**n**
fear, of ancestors, II 19; of man, III 14; of oneself, III 10
feelings, *see* affects
Feuerbach, Ludwig, III 3, III 3**n**
Fin-Gal, I 5
Fischer, Kuno, II 15, II 15**n**
Forbes, Elliot, III 19**n**
forgetfulness, II 1, II 3; forgetting, I 2, I 3
France, French, **E**3, I 16; French Revolution, I 16; French scholarship, III 24
Frauenstädt, Julius, III 6**n**
freedom of the will, III 10; free will, II 1, II 2, II 4, II 7; instinct for freedom, II 17, II 18; evangelical freedom, III 2
Freud, Sigmund, **E**3, II 16**n**, III 19**n**, III 20**n**

G

Gast, Peter, **E**2, III 24**n**
gay science, **P**7
gennaios, I 10, I 10**n**
German(s), **E**3, I 11, I 16, I 16**n**, II 3, II 9, III 2, III 3, III 17, III 19; German alcoholism, III 21; German nationalism, I 11**n**; punishments, II 3, German scholarship, III 24; Germany, I 5, III 5, III 14, III 17, III 19, III 22, III 26
Geulincx, Arnold, III 18, III 18**n**
Gibbon, Edward, I 15**n**
Gide, André, **E**3
Glazer, Nathan, II 2**n**
God, **P**3, I 6–8, I 13–15, I 15**n**, II 7, II 15, II 20–24, III 1, III 8, III 17, III 22–25, III 27; God on the cross, I 8; the Lord, I 15**n**, II 22; Kingdom of God, I 15, I 15**n**
god(s), II 7, II 19, II 20, II 21, II 23, III 6, III 10, III 15; godlessness, I 14; Greek, II 23; the godlike, I 5
Goethe, Johann Wolfgang von, **P**3**n**, II 11**n**, II 18, III 2, III 4, III 14**n**, III 20; *Faust,* III 13**n**
Golffing, Francis, I 11**n**, II 17**n**
Gomme, A. W., I 11**n**

good, **E4**, **P3**, **P4**, **P6**, I 4, I 5, I 5**n**, II 3, II 7, II 15, II 20, III 13**n**, III 17; good men, I 11, II 24, III 19; "good one," I 10; doing good, III 18; good-naturedness, II 8; good will, II 8

Goths, I 5, I 11, I 11**n**

Greek(s), **E3**, I 5, I 5**n**, I 10, I 11**n**, II 7, II 17, II 23, III 9, III 22; Greece, III 18; Greek gods, II 23; Greek philosophers, II 7; Greek nobility, *see* nobility; Greek trage-dies, III 9**n**

guilt(y), **E4**, II 4, II 4**n**, II 6, II 8, II 14, II 17, II 20, II 21, II 23, II 23**n**, III 16, III 19–21, III 28; before God, II 22

Gwinner, Dr. Wilhelm von, III 19

H

Hafiz, III 2

happiness, I 10; right to, of the healthy, III 14

hatred, I 14, III 14

health(y), II 24, III 14–16, III 21–23; European health, III 21

Hegel, Georg Wilhelm Friedrich, **E2**, **E3**, II 10**n**, III 7; Hegelian, III 3**n**

Heidegger, Martin, **E2**, **E3**

Hemmings, F. W. J., III 24**n**

Heraclitus, II 16, III 7, III 8

Herakles of duty, II 7

herd, I 9, III 13, III 15, III 18, III 19; herd instinct, I 2

Herwegh, Georg, III 5, III 5**n**

Hesiod, I 11

Hesychasts of Mount Athos, III 17, III 17**n**

historiography, modern, III 26; his-torical spirit, I 2

Homer, I 5**n**, I 11, I 11**n**, I 14, II 7, II 23**n**, III 4; Homeric heroes, I 11; Plato vs. Homer, III 25, III 25**n**

Horace, *Satires,* I 5**n**

hubris, III 9, III 9**n**

Hume, David, III 4**n**

humility, III 8

Huxley, Aldous; *Brave New World,*

I 11**n**, II 12**n**; Julian, II 12**n**; Thomas Henry, II 12, II 12**n**

I

Idealism, III 19, III 19**n**; ideals, II 24. *See also* ascetic ideals

impotence, I 10, I 13, II 4; priestly impotence, I 7

impure, *see* pure

India (Indians), III 7, III 8, III 17, III 27

injustice, I 14. *See also* justice

innocence, III 19; second, II 20

Innocent III, pope, II 7

inpsychation, II 1, II 1**n**

instinct(s), II 2, II 7, II 16; animal, II 22; for freedom, II 17, II 18; historical, II 4

intellectuals, British: attitude of to-ward Nietzsche, **E3**

internalization of man, II 16, II 16**n**

Israel, *see* Jews

Italian, **E3**; Italy, I 5

Ixion, wheel of, III 6

J

Janssen, Johannes, III 19

Jaspers, Karl, **E3**

Jesus of Nazareth, I 8, I 16; Christ, I 15, I 15**n**; "Redeemer," I 8

Jews, **E3**, I 5**n**, I 7, I 8, I 9, I 15, I 15**n**, I 16, I 16**n**, III 22. *See also* anti-Semites

John, Apocalypse of, I 16

Jove, I 15, I 15**n**

Judas, I 15, I 15**n**

Judea, *see* Jews

jus primae noctis, III 9

justice, **P4**, I 14, II 4, II 8, II 10, II 11, II 14, III 14; *ressentiment* as origin of, *see* ressentiment

K

kakos, see *esthlos*

Kant, Immanuel, **P3**, **P5**, II 2**n**, II 6, III 6, III 7, III 25; anti-Kantian, **P3**; Kantian, I 13, III 6, III 12

kingdom of heaven, I 15, I 15**n**

L

language, Nietzsche's, E3; origin of, II 2

La Rochefoucauld, Francois Duc de, P5

Latin, E3

law, II 5, II 6, II 10, II 11, III 9; Chinese II 13; penal, II 10; purpose of, II 12; Twelve Tables of Rome, II 5; lawbreaker, II 9; legal obligations, II 5–6

Leibniz, Gottfried Wilhelm von, E3, III 7

lies, lying, III 19

life, III 13; aversion to, III 28; curative instinct of, III 16; life-inimical species, III 11

Loeb and Leopold, E1

Louis XI, III 9

love, II 22; of one's enemies, I 14; of one's neighbor III 19

Luther, Martin, II 7, III 2, III 19, III 19n, III 20, III 22, III 22n; Luther's wedding, III 2

M

malefactor, II 10. *See also* crime

Malraux, André, E3

malus, melas, I 5

man, I 6, I 11, I 12, II 1, II 3, II 4, II 6–8, II 16, II 28, III 28; aggressive, II 11; common, I 5, I 10; European, I 12; good, I 14, III 19; higher, I 2, I 11; internalization of, II 16, II 16n; last, II 2n; man as animal with right to make promises, II 1, II 2; man of the future, II 24; reactive, II 11; redeeming II 24; sickly, *see* sickness; stronger species of, II 12; overman, I 11n

Mann, Thomas, E3

marriage, III 7, III 9

Marx, Karl, II 11n, III 3n

Mary, I 16

mask, P6, III 10

master(s), I 5, I 7, I 9, I 13, II 12, II 17, III 18; right of, in punishing, *see* punishment; master race, I 5; master and slave morality, *see* morality

mechanical activity, III 18, III 19

memory, II 1, II 3, II 5, II 13; mnemotechnics, II 3. *See also* forgetfulness

Mephistopheles, III 13n

mercy, II 10, II 10n

Middle Ages, III 17, III 21

Minos, I 15, I 15n

Minotaur, III 24

Mirabeau, Victor de Riquetti, Marquis de, I 10, I 10n

Mistress Clever, III 9

Mitchell, Silas Weir, I 6, I 6n

mochtēros, I 10, I 10n

Montanism, I 15n

Moore, Thomas, III 19, III 19n

morality, P3ff; bourgeois, E3; Christian, E3; of custom, P4, II 2, III 9; etymology of, I 17; master and slave, E1, E4; of mores, II 2, II 2n, III 9; slave revolt in, E3, I 7, I 10, I 11; moral prejudices, P2

music, III 5; Wagnerian, III 26

N

Napoleon Bonaparte, I 16

nausea, II 24, III 14, III 14n

Nazis, I 11n

Neander, Dr., I 15n

Negroes, I 11n, II 7

New/Old Testament, III 22

Nietzsche: works: *The Antichrist,* III 24n, III 26n; *Beyond Good and Evil,* E3, E4, P8n, I 7, I 16n, I 17, II 6, III 9, III 9n, III 9n, III 23n, III 24n, III 26n; *The Birth of Tragedy,* III 8n, III 24n, III 25, III 25n; *The Case of Wagner,* III 8n; *The Dawn,* P4, P8n, I 4, II 2, II 2n, II 6, II 10n, III 9, III 9n, III 10, III 24, III 24n; *Ecce Homo,* E4; I 24n; *The Gay Science,* E2, E3, III 24, III 24n, III 25n, III 27; *Human, All-Too-Human,* E1, P2, P4, II 2n; *Nietzsche contra Wagner,* III 2n, III 8n; *Thus Spoke Zarathustra,* E4, P8, I 11n, I 12n, II 10n, III 14n; *Twilight of the*

Idols, I 11n, III 8n, III 15n, III 26n; *The Wanderer and His Shadow,* **P4,** II 13n; *The Will to Power,* **E2, P8,** III 3n, III 24n, III 25, III 27, III 27n; "Zur Geschichte der Theognideischen Spruchsammlung," I 5n

nihilism, **P5,** I 12, II 24, III 14, III 27; administrative, II 12, III 26, "On the History of European Nihilism," III 27, III 27n. *See also* nothingness

Nirvana, I 6

noble, nobility, **P4,** I 2, I 4, I 5, I 7–11, I 16, II 19, II 20, II 23, III 9; noble indignations, III 14; noble man, I 10, I 11

nothingness, I 6, II 24, III 1, III 14, III 17, III 25, and *passim;* will to, III 28. *See also* nihilism

O

objectivity, II 8, III 12, III 26, and *passim*

obligations, legal, *see* law

oïzyros, I 10, I 10n

Old Testament vs. New, III 22

oligarchy, III 18

orgies of feeling, III 19, III 20, III 21

original sin, II 21, III 9

Orwell, George, (*1984*), I 11n

Overbeck, Franz, III 15n, III 24n

overman, I 11n

P

pagans, I 15n

pain, II 4, II 5, II 7, III 11, III 19, III 20; psychological, III 16

paradise, Christian, *see* Christian

Parsifal, III 3, III 4

Pascal, Blaise, III 17, III 17n

pathos of distance, I 2

Paul, St., I 16

Pericles, I 11

Persian Empires, III 8

perspective(s), III 12, III 12n, III 17

pessimism, mass, III 17

Peter, St., I 16, III 22

petty pleasure, as cure for depression, III 18, III 19

Pharisees, III 14

philologists, I 17

philosophers, **P2, P5,** I 15, I 15n, I 17, II 7, III 1, III 7n, III 8–10, III 12, III 17, III 24; Greek moral, II 7; Indian, III 8, III 17, III 17n; and marriage, III 7; philosophy, III 5, III 9, III 10, III 24; Sankhya philosophy, III 27; "spectators" of beauty, III 6

physiological inhibition, III 17

pity, **P5, P6,** III 14, III 14n, III 25; Tolstoian, III 26; tragic, II 7

Plato, **P5,** I 1, III 7, III 18, III 19, III 24; Plato vs. Homer, III 25, III 25n

plebeianism, I 4

Podach, Erich, III 11n

ponēros, I 10, I 10n

poverty, III 8

pregnancy image, **E4,** II 16, 19

pride, II 8

priests (-ly), I 6, III 1, III 9, III 10; artist in guilt feelings, III 20; ascetic priests, III 10, III 11, III 13, III 15, III 17–22, III 26; impotence in, I 7

promises, II 3, II 5

punishment, **P4,** II 3–5, II 7, II 9, II 10, II 10n, II 12–16, II 22, III 20; as festival, II 6, II 7, II 13; eternal, II 21, II 22; revenge as purpose of, II 12; right of masters in, II 5

pure/impure, I 6; pure reason, III 12

Pygmalion, III 6

R

Rahula, III 7

rank, order of, **P3,** I 2; order of rank among values, I 17

Ranke, Leopold von, III 19, III 19n

reading, **P8, P8n**

reality, redemption of, II 24

reason, II 3, III 8, III 12

redemption, III 17, III 20, and *passim;* through love, II 22; of reality, II 24

Rée, Dr. Paul, **P4, P7**

Reformation, I 16, III 19
religion, III 17; and guilt, II 20, II 21; religious cults, II 3; religious neurosis, III 21. *See also* Christianity; God; priests
Renaissance, I 16
Renan, Ernest, III 26, III 26n
responsibility, origins of, II 2
ressentiment, E3, I 10, I 11, I 13, I 14, I 16, II 11, II 17, III 11, III 14–16; not origin of justice, II 11
revenge, I 7, I 8, I 14, II 6, II 10n, II 11, III 9, III 14, III 20; as purpose of punishment, II 12
Rhadamanthus, I 15n
rhathymia, I 11
Riesman, David, II 2n
Rilke, Rainer Maria, E3
Roberts, Alexander, I 15n
Rome, Roman, I 5, I 11n, I 15, I 16, III 18; nobility, I 11; values, I 16; Twelve Tables of Rome, II 5
Russians, II 15

S

sacrifices, II 19
St. John's dance, III 21
St. Thomas, I 15, I 15n
St. Vitus dance, III 21
saints, III 1
Salvation Army, British, III 22
sanctity, III 17
Sankhya philosophy, III 27
Sartre, Jean-Paul, E3, II 23n
Schadenfreude, II 1n
Scheler, Max, E3
Schlechta, Karl, II 6n
scholars, III 23–24; Nietzsche "scholars," E3
Schopenhauer, Arthur, P5, III 4–7, III 19, III 19n
science, I 13, III 23–25, III 23n
Selbstaufhebung, II 10n, III 27n
Selbsttierquälerei, II 24n
Selbstüberwindung, III 27n
self-overcoming, II 10, II 10n, III 27
self-sacrifice, P5, II 18, III 11
self-torture, II 24, III 10
sensuality, III 2, III 3, III 6–8, III 10, III 24

seriousness, III 11
Shakespeare, William, I 11n, III 17, III 17n, III 22; *Taming of the Shrew,* III 17n
shame, II 7
Shankara, III 17
Shaw, George Bernard, E3
sickness, sickliness, I 11, I 12, II 22, III 9, III 13, III 14, III 16–18; III 20, III 21, III 28; brain-sickness, I 2; the sick, III 14, III 15, III 18
sin, sinfulness, sinners, III 16, III 20, III 21; original sin, II 21, III 9
slave revolt in morality, E3, I 7, I 10, I 11
Slavic, I 5
sleep, deep, III 17
slimy, III 19, III 19n
socialists, I 5
Socrates, III 7, III 7n; artistic Socrates, III 25n
soul, I 13, II 16; salvation of, III 9
spectator, III 6
Spencer, Herbert, I 3, I 3n, II 12
Spinoza, Baruch, P5, II 6, II 15, II 15n, III 7
spirit(s), I 2, III 8, III 10, III 15, III 27; free spirits, I 9, III 24, III 24n; historical, I 2
state, beginning of, II 17
Stendhal, III 6, III 15n
strong, the, I 13, III 14, III 18
suffering, II 6, II 7, III 9, III 11, III 15, III 17, III 18, III 20, III 23, III 28; pleasure in causing suffering, II 5, II 6; religion of, III 26
sympathia malevolens, II 6
syphilis, III 21

T

Taine, Hippolyte, III 19
Tertullian, I 15n
Teutons, I 11n; Teutonic influence, III 21
Thayer, Alexander Wheelock, III 19, III 19n
Thebes, I 11
Thelwall, S., I 15n
Theognis, I 5, I 5n
theology, theologians, III 25

Theresa, St., III 17

Thirty Years' War, I 4, III 17

tlēmōn, I, 10, I 10n

Tolstoian pity, III 26

torture, III 7; self-torture, II 24, III 10

tragedies, III 9n

Trojan Wars, II 7; Troy, I 11

truth, III 8, III 24, III 24n; the truthful, I 5; will to, III 27

U

United States, E3

utility, I 2, I 3, II 14; utility and origins of things, II 12

V

values, P6, I 2, I 7, I 8, I 17; inversion of, I 7, I 10; order of rank among, *See* order of rank; value judgments, III 10; value of values, P6, I 17

Vandals, I 11, I 11n

Vedanta philosophy, III 12, III 17, III 17n

vegetarians, III 17, III 17n

vengefulness, *see* revenge

vetitum, III 9, III 9n

Vikings, I 11

Virchow, Rudolf, I 5, I 5n

Vishramitra, King, III 10

Voss, Johann Heinrich, E3

W

Wagner, Richard, E3, III 2, III 2n, III 3, III 4, III 5, III 19; Wag-

nerian music, III 26; *Opera and Drama,* III 5; *Parsifal,* III 3–4

war, II 9

warrior(s), I 5, I 7, III 1

weak, I 10, I 13, I 14, III 14, III 18

Weber, Max, E3

Weir-Mitchell isolation cure, I 6, I 6n

Weltschmerz, III 17, III 17n

will: to community, III 18; free, II 2, III 10; to guilt and punishment, II 22; last will of man, III 14; of life, II 11; to nothingness, III 14, III 28; and representation, III 6; to truth, III 27

will to power, II 12, II 18, III 18; of the weak, III 14

Will to Power, The, III 27, III 27n

witch trials, III 16; witch-hunt hysteria, III 21

woman, women, III 1, III 8, III 11, III 14, III 18

World War I and II, E3

X

xymphora, I 10, I 10n

Y

Yeats, William Butler, E3

Z

Zarathustra, II 25

Zeus, II 16; Homeric Zeus, II 23

INDEX

The Case of Wagner

Figures refer to sections, not to pages. **TI** refers to the translator's Introduction; **P** to Nietzsche's Preface; **PS**1 to Postscript 1; **PS**2 to Postscript 2; **E** to the Epilogue; **L** to the letters that follow *The Case of Wagner;* **n** to the translator's notes. For references to Nietzsche's works, see Nietzsche.

A

actor(s), emergence of, in music, 11, 12; Wagner as, *see* Wagner
Aeschylus, **TI**
aesthetics, **E**
Alfieri, Count Vittorio, 11, **11n**
anti-Semitism, Wagner's, **Ln**
Aristotle, **PS1n**
ascending life, **E**

B

Beethoven, Ludwig van, 8, **PS2**
Bernini, Giovanni Lorenzo, **PS2**
Bismarck, Otto von, **TI**
Biterolf, 3
Bizet, Georges, **P**, 1, 3; *Carmen,* 1, 2
Börne, Ludwig, **TI**
Brahms, Johannes, **PS2**, **L**
Brunhilde, 4; Brünnhilde, **L**
Brutus, Marcus Junius, **2n**
Buddhism, **L**

C

Cagliostro, Alessandro, 5, **E**
"The Case of Wagner," **PS1**, **E**
Christian (Christianity), **TI**, 3, 6, **PS1**, **E**, **L**; concept, 3; Junker; **E**; morality, **E**, **En**
Circe, **PS1**; Indian, 4
Constant, Benjamin, 2
"contracts," Wagner's war against, 4
Corneille, Pierre, 9
counterfeit, counterfeiter, counterfeiting, 1, 10, **10n**, **PS1**, **PS2**

D

decadence, decadent, *passim;* artist of decadence, 4, 5; literary deca-dence, 7; problem of, **P**; virtue of decadents, 7
Descartes, René, **TI**
Dostoevsky, Feodor, **5n**, **E**
drama, definition of, 9, **9n**

E

Elsa, 10
England, **L**
Erda, 9
Europe, 1, 2; "good European," **TI**

F

Flaubert, Gustave, 9
Flying Dutchman, The, **2n**, 3, 7
Förster, Bernhard, **5n**
France, **PS1**, **L**
"free will," 7
French (Frenchmen), **TI**, 2, 4, 8

G

Gast, Peter, *see* Köselitz, Heinrich
gaya scienza, 10, **10n**
German (Germans), **TI**, 2, 3, 5, 6, 8, 9, 10, **PS1**, **PS2**, **E**, 4; character, **PS1**; delayers par excellence, **PS1**, **PS1n**; Empire, **TI**; philosophy, **PS1**; spirit, **PS2**; "taste," 10, **PS2**; youth, 10. *See also* Wagnerians
Geyer, Ludwig (Wagner's father), **PS1n**
Gide, André, **10n**
God, 2, **2n**, **E**; "the old God," 3
Goethe, Johann Wolfgang von, 2, 3, **3n**, **5n**, **6n**, **E**, **En**; "Priapus," 3
Goldmark, Karl, **PS2**, **PS2n**; *Queen of Sheba,* **PS2**, **PS2n**
Goncourt, Frères de, 7

H

Handel, George Frederick, 6, **PS**2
Hegel, G. W. F., 10
Hehn, Victor, **L**, **Ln**
Heine, Heinrich, **TI**
Herder, Johann Gottfried von, 3, **3n**
Hitler, Adolf, **5n**
holiness, 3, **3n**
Horace, (motto on title page)
Hugo, Victor, 8, 11, **PS**1n

I

Icelandic saga, **E**
"the idea," 10
"idiot," "idiotic," **5n**
intimations, 6, 9
Isolde, 3
Italians, 6

J

Jews, Jewesses, **TI**, 3, **3n**, **L**; the
  "Wandering Jew," 3, **3n**
Journal des Débats, **PS**2n

K

Kant, Immanuel, **3n**, 7, **L**
Kierkegaard, Søren, **TI**
Klingsor, **PS**1
Klopstock, Friedrich, 3, **3n**
"knots," Wagner's, 9
Köselitz, Heinrich (pseud. Peter
  Gast), **PS**2n, **L**
Kreuzzeitung, **PS**2, **PS**2n
Krug, Gustav, **TI**
Kundry, 3

L

Liszt, Franz, 11, **E**, **En**
Literarische Zentralblatt, **PS**2, **PS**2n
Lohengrin, 9; *Lohengrin,* 3, 7
love, 2, **2n**, 3, 4, 12; free love, 4; of
  a "higher virgin," 2
Love, Frederick R., **TI**n
Luther, Martin, **3n**

M

Mann, Thomas, **TI**, **TI**n
Marke, **L**
master morality, **E**
Meistersinger, Die, 3, 9, **PS**1, **PS**1n
melody, 6
Mérimée, Prosper, 2
modern, modernity, **P**, 1, 5, **PS**2, **E**;
  the Cagliostro of modernity, 5
morality, morals, **P**, 3, 4, 10, **E**; actor

morality, 8; master morality, **E**;
  noble morality, **E**, **En**
Morgenstern, Christian, **PS**2n
"mount of Venus," 3
Mozart, Wolfgang Amadeus, 6
music, 1–8, 10, 11, **PS**1, **PS**2; "emergence of actor in," 11

N

Napoleon, **L**
National Zeitung, **PS**2n
Naumann, C. G., **L**, **Ln**
Nazi(s), **TI**, **TI**n
Newman, Ernest, **TI**, **TI**n
Niebuhr, Barthold Georg, 3, **3n**
Nietzsche: Works: *The Antichrist,* **TI**;
  Beyond Good and Evil, **Pn**, 3, 7;
  The Birth of Tragedy, **TI**; *Ecce
  Homo,* **TI**, **PS**1n, **PS**2n; *Fröhliche
  Wissenschaft* (*The Gay Science*),
  10n; *Genealogy of Morals,* **En**;
  Human, All-Too-Human, **TI**;
  Nietzsche contra Wagner, **TI**, **E**;
  *The Price We Are Paying for
  Wagner,* **PS**1; *Schopenhauer as
  Educator,* **TI**; *Thus Spoke Zara-
  thustra,* **PS**2n; *Twilight of the
  Idols,* **TI**, **6n**, **7n**, **En**; *On the Use
  and Disadvantage of History for
  Life,* **TI**; *The Will to Power,* **7n**
noble morality, **E**, **En**

O

Offenbach, Jacques, **L**
"Off to Crete," **PS**1, **L**, **Ln**
optimism, infamous, 4
Ortega y Gasset, José, **PS**1n

P

Palestrina, Giovanni Pierluigi da, 6
Parsifal, 9; *Parsifal,* **TI**, 3, **3n**, 6,
  PS1, **L**
passion, definition of, 6
philosopher(s), philosophy, **P**, 1, 2,
  3, **3n**, **PS**1, **E**; pathos of, 1
Plato, **PS**1n
plot, Wagner's projection of, 9
"Priapus," 3
Proteus, 5

R

redemption, redeemed, 2, 3, 4, 11,
  PS1, **E**; "Redemption for the re-
  deemer," **PS**1, **L**
Reformation, **L**

Reich, 11, **PS2**, L
Renaissance, **E, L**
Revolution, Wagner's belief in, 4
Rhine River, **PS2n**
Rhinoxera, **PS2, PS2n**
Riemann, Karl Wilhelm, 11, 11**n**
Ries, Hugibert (pseud.), *see* Riemann, K. W.
Ring (*Der Ring des Nibelungen*), 3, 4, **PS2**, L
Rohde, Erwin, **TI**
romanticism, fatality of, 3
Rossini, Gioachino Antonio, **PS2**

S

Schelling, Friedrich Wilhelm Joseph von, 10
Schiller, Friedrich, 3, 6, 6**n**, 8
Schopenhauer, Arthur, **TI, P**, 4, 10; philosopher of decadence, 4
Senta, 2, 2**n**
Shakespeare, William, 2**n**, 7**n**
Siegfried, 9; as typical revolutionary, 4
Spinoza, Baruch, 2**n**
spirit, 3, 6, 10, 11, **PS1n, PS2**; most high-minded and severe spirits, **En**; "poor in spirit," 5, **PS2**
stimulantia of the exhausted, 5
style, 7

T

Talma, François Joseph, 8
Tannhäuser, 3, 3**n**, 7
taste, Wagner's corruption of, **PS1**
Teuton, definition of, 11
theatrocracy, **PS1**

Tristan, 9
Tristan and Isolde, 3, **L**

V

vegetarian, definition of, 5; vegetarianism, 5**n**
Verdi, Giuseppe, **TI**
Voltaire (François Marie Arouet), **TI**

W

Wagner, Cosima, **En**
Wagner, Richard, *passim;* as actor, 8, 9, **PS1**; anti-Semitism of, **Ln**; content of Wagner's operas, 9; as corrupter of taste, **PS1**; as dramatist, 2, 9; as German, **PS1**; influence of, 11; literary style, 7; as musician, 8, 9, 10, **PS1**; as revolutionist, 4; resistance to, **PS1**; Wagner Association(s), **PS1, L;** "Wagner is a neurosis," 5**n;** Wagner's heroines, 9; Wagner's writings, 6, 10. Operas and *dramatis personae* are listed individually
Wagnerians, 6, 8, 9, **PS1**; female, **PS1, PS2, E**
Walküre, 7
Wartburg, 3, 3**n**
"Wars of Liberation," **L**
Wilde, Oscar, 2**n**
woman, women, 3, 4; women Wagnerians, **PS1, PS2, E**
Wotan, 10

Z

Zarathustra, **P**

INDEX

Ecce Homo

Arabic numerals refer to sections, not to pages.
The following abbreviations have been used:

I:	Why I Am So Wise
II:	Why I Am So Clever
III:	Why I Write Such Good Books
IV:	Why I Am a Destiny
BT:	Birth of Tragedy
U:	Untimely Ones
H:	Human, All-Too-Human
D:	Dawn
GS:	Gay Science
Z:	Thus Spoke Zarathustra
B:	Beyond Good and Evil
GM:	Genealogy of Morals
T:	Twilight of the Idols
W:	The Case of Wagner
A:	Appendix
E:	Editor's Introduction
NP:	Note on the Publication of *Ecce Homo*
P:	Nietzsche's Preface
n:	Editor's notes

For reference to Nietzsche's works, see Nietzsche: works.

A

affect(s), **BT3**, **BT3n**; of *ressentiment*, I 6

Africa, **W3**

air of the heights, **P3**, **P4**

alcohol, II 1

Alexandrian academician, **E1**; counter-Alexanders, **BT4**

alienation, **H2**

Alps, II 7, II 7n

Altenburg: castle of, I 3; Grand Duchess of, I 3

amor fati, **E2**, II 10, II 10n, **H4n**, **Z8n**, **W4**, **W4n**, **A4**

Antichrist, *see* Nietzsche's works; anti-Christian, *see* Christianity

antinature (-al), III 5, **BT3**, **H3**, **IV** 7

anti-Semite, **H2**, **Z1n**, **W1**, **W4n**, **A4**; anti-Semitic historiography, **W2**. *See also* Jews; Judaism

Apollo, **E1**, **E2**; Apollinian, **E1**, **BT1**
Aquila, **Z4**, **Z4n**
Ariadne, **Z8**
Aristotle, **E2**, **BT3**, **BT3n**, **U1n**, **Z6n**; *Nicomachean Ethics,* **E2**, **E2n**, **U1n**; *Poetics,* **BT3n**
Arrowsmith, William, **A1n**
art nouveau, **NP**
artist(s), **II 5**, **Z2**
atheism, **II 1**, **II 1n**, **II 3**; Nietzsche's atheism, *see* Nietzsche
Athens, **E1**, **E2**, **II 2**
Augsburger Zeitung, **U2**
Austria, **II 1n**

B

Baader, Franz Xaver von, **U2**, **U2n**
Bach, Johann Sebastian, **II 6n**, **II 7**
Bacon, Lord, **II 4**, **II 4n**; American Baconians, **II 4n**
Balsamo, Giuseppe, *see* Cagliostro
Barker, Ernest, **W2n**
Basel, **I 1**, **II 2**, **II 2n**, **H3**, **A3n**; Pädagogium, **I 4**; University, **H5**; Baselers, **U2**
Basler Nachrichten, **III 1n**
Baudelaire, Charles, **II 5**
Bauer, Bruno, **U2**, **U2n**
Bayreuth, **I 4**, **I 4n**, **I 7n**, **BT4**, **H2**, **H2n**, **H5**, **W1n**
Bayreuther Blätter, **H2**, **H5**, **H5n**
Bayreuther Festspiele, **H2**, **H2n**
bearing a grudge, **E2**
beast of prey, **III 5**
becoming, **BT3**; becoming what one is, **II 9**, **U3**
Beethoven, Ludwig van, **II 6n**, **H2n**
being, **BT3**
Berlin, **U2**; University of, **III 1**
Berlioz, Hector, **II 5**
Berner Bund, **III 1n**, **IV 1n**
Bertram, Ernst, **E2**
Beyle, Henri, *see* Stendhal
"beyond," concept of, **II 10**, **Z1**, **IV 8**
Bible, **D2**, **A3n**
Bildungsphilister, **U2**, **U2n**
Binion, Rudolph, **E2n**
birth of tragedy, *see* tragedy
Bismarck, Otto von, **U1**, **A3**, **A4**
Bizet, Georges, **II 3n**

Böhmerwald, **H2**
books, **II 8**, **W3**; Nietzsche's reactions to, **III 3**, **III 5**. *See also* reading
Borgia, Cesare, **III 1**, **III 1n**
Börne, Ludwig, **II 4n**
Bosheit, **E2**
Bourget, Paul, **II 3**, **II 3n**
Brahms, Johannes, **II 6n**
Brandes, Georg, **NP**, **W4**
Brendel, Karl Franz, **H2**, **H2n**
Brochard, Victor, **II 3**
Buddha, **I 6**; Buddhists, **Z1**; *The Dhammapada,* **I 6n**
Bülow, Hans von, **II 4**, **II 4n**, **II 6**, **II 6n**
Byron, Lord; *Manfred,* **II 4**

C

Cagliostro, Count Allesandro di, **W1**, **W1n**
Camus, Albert, **E2**
Carlyle, Thomas, **III 1**
Carmen, **II 3n**
categorical imperative, *see* Kant
catharsis, Aristotle's concept of, **BT3**, **BT3n**
Catholics, **W2**
Chasté, **Z1n**
Chiavari, **Z1**
Chinese stagnation, **IV 4**
Chopin, Frederic, **II 7**
Christianity, Christian(s), **E2**, **I 6**, **I 6n**, **I 7**, **II 1**, **II 3**, **III 1**, **BT1**, **BT2**, **U1**, **Z4**, **GM**, **W2**, **W3**, **IV 7**, **A1**, **A4**; Christian love, **W1**; morality, **IV 4**, **IV 6–8**; anti-Christian, **Z4**. *See also* God; priests
church, **W2**
cleanliness/uncleanliness, **I 8**, **IV 8**, **W3**
climate, **II 2**, **II 8**, **II 10**
coffee, **II 1**
Como, **T3**
Conrad, V, **Z4n**
conscience, **II 1**, **II 1n**, **III 5**, **III 6**, **Z2**, **GM**; bite of, **II 1**, **II 1n**; good, **D1**
consciousness, **II 9**, **II 9n**
Constantine, Grand Duchess, **I 3**

conviction, **H**1
Copenhagen, **NP**, III 2, **W**4
Corneille, Pierre, II 3
cowardice, **BT**2
creating, creators, **Z**8, **Z**8n; aftermath of creative deed, **Z**5, **Z**5n
cruelty, **GM**
culture, **U**1, **U**2, **GS**, **GM**, **W**2, **A**4; French II 3; German, *see also* German culture

D

dance, dancing, **GS**, **Z**4, **Z**6
Dante Alighieri, **Z**6
darkling aspiration, **T**2, **T**2n
Darwinism, III 1
Da Vinci, Leonardo, II 6
decadence, decadent(s), I 1, I 2, I 4, I 6, II 5, II 8, **BT**1, **BT**2, **D**2, **GM**, **W**1, **W**2, IV 4, IV 5, IV 7, IV 8; decay, **U**1; Nietzsche as a decadent, I 2
decisions, **T**2
defense, I 5; defenselessness of creator, **Z**5, **Z**5n; self-defense, II 8, **U**3
degree(s), **W**4, **W**4n
Delacroix, Ferdinand Victor Eugene, II 5
depersonalization, IV 7
depth, German, **W**3
Descartes, René, **W**3
destiny, II 9, **D**2, **Z**5n, **Z**6, **T**2, IV 1–9
destroying, **BT**3, **Z**8, **B**1, IV 2, IV 4, IV 4n
"Deutschland, Deutscland über Alles," **W**2
Dhammapada, see Buddha
dialectic I 1
Diet of Worms, III 2n
Diogenes Laertius, II 3n
Dionysus, **E**1, **E**2, **P**2, **Z**6, **Z**7, **GM**, **W**1, IV 4n; Dionysian, **E**1, III 5, **BT**1–4, **Z**6, **Z**7, **Z**8, IV 2, **A**1; Dionysus vs. the Crucified, IV 9, IV 9n
displeasure, *see* pleasure
distance(s), I 4, II 4, II 9, III 1, **U**3,
Z5, **Z**6, **W**4, IV 6; pathos of, **U**3n, **Z**5n
distinctions, making, **W**4
distress, IV 4
dithyramb(-ic), **BT**3, **Z**7
doubt, II 4
Dresden, II 1n
Dühring, Eugen, I 4, I 4n
duty, II 4, **H**4, IV 8

E

education, German, II 1
egoistic/unegoistic, III 5, **D**2
Eilenburg, I 3
Emerson, Ralph Waldo, **A**1
enemy(-ies), **E**2, **P**4, I 5n, I 7, I 8; enmity, I 6, I 6n
Engadine, *see* Upper Engadine
English diet, II 1; English women, II 1
equal rights, I 5, III 5, **W**1
error, **P**3, IV 7
esprit, III 2
eternal life, II 10
eternal recurrence, II 10, **BT**3, **Z**1, **Z**1n, **Z**6
eternally feminine, III 5
ethics, Aristotle's, **E**2
Europe, II 3, II 5, III 2, **W**2, **A**5
European(s), **U**2, **W**3; European history, **Z**1n; good European, I 3
Euterpe, rape of, II 4, II 4n
évangelie des humbles, **W**1, **W**1n
evil, IV 2, IV 3, IV 5–8; speaking evil, **E**2
Ewald, Heinrich, **U**2, **U**2n
Exodus, III 1, III 1n
Eza, near Nizza, **Z**4

F

faith, **P**4, **H**1, **W**1
fatalism, *see* Russian fatalism
Faust, *see* Goethe: *Faust*
feelings, **E**2, **H**5. See also affects; *ressentiment*
feminism, III 3
Fichte, Johann Gottlieb, **W**3
flies, **Z**5, **Z**5n
Florence, II 2

foolishness, I 8

forbidden, the, **P3**, **P3n**

Förster, Bernhard (Nietzsche's brother-in-law), **A3**, **A3n**

Förster-Nietzsche, Elisabeth (Nietzsche's sister), **NP**, **E1**, **E2**, II 10**n**, **H2n**, **Z1n**, **A3**, **A4n**

France, II 3, II 5, U1. *See also* French

France, Anatole, II 3, II 3**n**

Franco-Prussian War, II 3, II 3**n**, **U1n**, **W1n**

Frederick II, **Z4**, **Z4n**

Frederick III, **Z1**, **Z1n**

Frederick William IV, I 3

freedom, II 8; free spirit, *see* spirit; free will, *see* will

French, **E2**, II 1, II 3, **W3**; drama, III 1**n**; romantics, II 5, II 6**n**

Freud, Sigmund, **E1**, II 4**n**, II 9**n**, II 10**n**

Fritzsch, E. W., **Z1**, **Z1n**

G

Galiani, Abbé Ferdinand, **A1**

Gast, Peter, **NP**, II 7**n**, II 10**n**, III 1**n**, **U3n**, **H5**, **Z1**, **Z1n**, **Z4n**, **T3n**, IV 1**n**, **A3**, **A3n**; Pietro Gasti, II 7, II 7**n**

gaya scienza, **GS**, **Z1**, **Z2**. *See also* Nietzsche's works: *The Gay Science*

Gelée, Claude, *see* Lorrain, Claude

Genesis, II 1**n**, **Z6**

genius, II 2, III 1, **H1**, **W2**; of the heart, III 6

Genoa, I 1, **D1**, **Z1**, **Z4**

gentilhomme, **B2**, **W4**. *See also* noble

German(s), **E2**, I 3, II 1, II 1**n**, II 2, II 4–6, II 8, II 9, III 2, III 2**n**, III 3, III 4, **BT3**, **U1**, **U2**, **H2**, **H6**, **W1–4**, **A3**, **A4**; anti-Semitism, **A4** (*see also* anti-Semitism); books, II 3, **A1**; composers, II 7 (*see also* Wagner); culture, I 7, II 3, **U1**, **U1n**, **U2**; education II 1; emperor, II 10**n**; Kaiser, **A3**, **W3**; language, **U2**; nationalism, **E2**; philosophy, *see* philosophy; prose, **E1**; *Reich*, I 3, II 5, II 5**n**, **U1**, **U2**, **H2**, **H3**,

Z1n, **W1**, **W2**; spirit, *see* spirit; taste, **W1**; uncleanliness, **W3**; virtues, II 5, **H2**; Wars of Liberation, **W2**, **A4** (*see also* Franco-Prussian War); un-German, **BT1**

Germany, **E1**, **E2**, I 7, II 3, II 5, III 1, III 2, III 2**n**, **U2**, **H3**, **Z1n**, **W1**, **W2**, **W2n**, **W4**

giving and receiving, **Z7**

God, I 6**n**, II 1, II 1**n**, II 3, II 10, III 2, III 3, **B2**, **GM**, IV 8, **A5**

god(s), **E2**, II 4, **Z8**, **D1**; god of darkness, *see* Dionysus

Goethe, Johann Wolfgang von, **E2**, **NP**, I 3, II 4**n**, **Z6**, **W1n**; *Faust*, II 4, II 4**n**, II 9**n**, **T2n**, **W2n**

good, IV 2–5; as beginning of the end, IV 4; good men, III 1, **T2**, IV 4, IV 8

gospel of the humble, **W1**, **W1n**

Göttingen, **U2**, **U2n**, **A1n**; Göttingen Seven, **U2n**

greatness, II 10, **Z5**, **Z5n**, **Z6**

Greeks(s), **E2**, III 2, **BT1**, **BT3**, **D1**; comedy, **E2**; pessimism, **BT1**; tragedy, *see* tragedy

Grenzboten, **U2**

Grossoktav edition of Nietzsche's works, **NP**

Grosz, George, **E2**

guilt, I 2, I 5, I 5**n**, **BT2**

Gyp (pseudonym of Sibylle de Mirabeau), II 3, II 3**n**

H

Haefner, J., **U2n**

Halévy, Ludovic, III 3**n**

Hamlet, II 4

Handel, George Frederick, II 7

Hanover, Queen of, I 3

happiness, III 5, **Z1**, IV 4

hatred, I 6**n**

health, healthy, I 2, II 6, II 10, **Z2**, IV 8. *See also* sickness

Hegel, G. W. F., II 3, **BT1n**, **H2**, **T1n**, **W1n**, **W3**; Hegelian, **BT1**, **U2**

Heidegger, Martin, **BT3n**

height, I 8, III 3, **U3**, **Z6**, IV 6

Heine, Heinrich, II 4, II 4**n**, III 2**n**

"Hellenism and Pessimism," **BT1**

Heraclitus, **BT3**

herd, the, IV 4, IV 5; mob, I 4; rabble, I 8, IV 1

Herder, Johann Gottfried von, I 3

hero, **H1**

higher man, III 1; higher swindle, **H5**

Hillebrand, Karl, **U2**, **U2n**

historians, German, **W2**; historical sense, **U1**, **BT2**; *historicis*, **W2**; historiography, **E1**, **W2**

Hitler, Adolf, **E2**

Hoffmann, Franz, **U2**, **U2n**

holiness, IV 8; holy, IV 1, IV 1n, IV 8

Homer, I 5n; *Iliad*, **E2**

Horace, III 5; *Satires*, **W1n**

"How One Philosophizes with a Hammer," **T**, **Tn**

human nature, divinity of, II 10

humanity, **D2**, IV 7. *See also* man

Hymn to Friendship, **Z1n**

Hymn to Life, **Z1**, **Z1n**

I

Ibsen, Henrik, III 5, III 5n

idea(s), II 9, **BT1**, **BT1n**; modern, **T2**

ideal(s), idealists, **P2**, **P3**, III 1, III 5, **BT2**, **U2**, **H1**, **H2**, **H2n**, **Z2**, **GM**, **W1**, **W2**, IV 3, IV 6, IV 8; idealism, II 1, II 2, II 10, III 4, III 5, **BT2**, **H1**, **H5**, **W2**; idealities, **H3**, **T2**. *See also* idols

idiot, idiotic, **W2**, **W2n**

idols, **P2**, **T1–3**. *See also* ideals

immoralist(s), IV 2–4, IV 6

immortality, **Z5**; Nietzsche's, **T3**; of the soul, II 1

Insel Verlag, **NP**

inspiration, **Z3**

instinct(s), I 6, I 6n, **BT1**, **BT2**, IV 8; of cruelty, **GM**; German, **W1**, IV 7; Nietzsche's, **H3–4**

irony, **W4**

Italy, II 7n; king of, **Z4n**, **T3**, **T3n**

J

Jack the Dreamer, **U1**

Jaspers, Karl, **E2**, **BT3n**

Jeremiah, IV **4n**

Jerusalem, II 2

Jesus, **E1**, **E2**; the crucified, IV 9

Jews, II 7, III 2n, **W4**, **A4**. *See also* anti-Semite; Judaism

John, St., **E1**

Jones, Ernest, **E1n**

Journal des Débats, III 1

Judaism, **A3**. *See also* anti-Semite; Jews

Jugendstil, **NP**

Junker philosophy, III 1

justice, German sense of, **W1**

justification, I 5

K

Kant, Immanuel, **U3**, **W2**, **W2n**, **W3**, **A4**; categorical imperative, **W2**, **W2n**, IV 7

Klingenbrunn, **H2**

"know thyself," II 9, II **9n**

knowledge, **BT2**; will to beget, **Z8**

Kohl, Otto, **H2n**

Königsberg, I 3

Köselitz, Heinrich, *see* Gast

Krause, Erdmuthe, I 3, Krause, Professor, I 3

Kreuzzeitung, III 1, III 1n

L

La Rochefoucauld, Duc François de, **W3**

Latin, **A1**

Lehndorf, Count, **H2n**

Leibniz, Gottfried Wilhelm von, **W2**, **W3**

Leipzig, II 1, II 1n, II 2, **U2 H2n**, **Z1**, **W1**, **A1**

Lemaître, Jules, II 3, II 3n

liberum veto, I 3, I 3n

libre penseurs, American, **U2**

Lichtenberg, Georg Christoph, **A1**, **A1n**

lie, the, IV 4, IV 8, **BT2**; lies, II 10, IV 1. *See also* truth

life, III 5, **BT3**, **D2**; hostility to, IV 7, IV 8; little things of, II 10; sedentary, II 1; Yes to, I 3, **BT2**, **BT3**. *See also* Yes-saying

Liszt, Franz, II 7, **W1n;** Liszt So-
ciety, **W1**
little things of life, *see* life
Lorrain, Claude (pseud. of Claude
Gelée), **T3, T3n**
Loti, Pierre (pseud. of Louis Marie
Julien Viaud), II 3, II 3n
love, I 5n, I 6n, III 5, **U3n, Z7;**
Christian, **W1;** of fate, *see amor
fati;* neighbor love, I 4, II 3, II
3n, II 9, IV 7, **A4;** self-love, II 9,
U1, U1n, H4n, IV 7; sexual, III 5
Love, Frederick R., II 6n, **Z1n**
Luke, **H2n**
Luther, Martin, I 6n, III 2n, **W2,
W2n, A4**
Lützen, I 4, II 9n

M

Macbeth, Lady, **D2n**
malice, **E2,** I 8n, II 4, **Z6 A1, A4,
A4n**
man, decadent IV 5; exceptional IV
5; good, *see* good men, higher, III
1; holy, IV 8; last, IV 4; moral
H6, H6n; present-day, **Z2;** truth-
ful, IV 5; Zarathustra's feeling for,
Z8. *See also* overman
Mann, Thomas, II 4n
Marx, Karl, **T1n**
master(s), I 1, I 4, **D2, Z5n**
Maupassant, Guy de, II 3, II 3n
Meilhac, Henri, II 3, II 3n
Menippus of Gadara, **A1n**
Mentone, **Z4n**
Mérimée, Prosper, II 3, II 3n
metabolism, II 2
metaphysical need, **H6**
Mette, H. J., **Z1n**
Metz, **BT**1
Meyer, Richard M., **W1n**
Meyerbeer, Giacomo, II 6n
Meysenbug, Malwida von, IV 1n
Milan, II 2
Mime, **A3**
Mirabeau, Sibylle de, *see* Gyp
misfortune, I 2
mistrust, **Z5**
Molière, II 3
Montaigne, Michel Eyquem de, II 3

morality, **E2, P3,** I 6, II 9, III 5, **BT2,
H6, D1, D2, GS,** IV 3, **A1;** Chris-
tian, IV 4–8; moral man, **H6,
H6n;** moral world order, **W2,** III
5, IV 3; Nietzsche's, II 1
Mozart, Wolfgang Amadeus, **H2n**
Müller, Max, I 6n
Munich, II 1; University of, **H2n**
music, II 7, **BT3, W1–4;** church, **W1;**
Gast's, **A3;** Nietzsche's taste in, II
7, **Z1;** Wagner's, II 6, II 6n, **BT3**
Mystifizinski, *see* Vischer

N

Napoleon I, **NP,** I 3, II 3, II 3n, **W2**
nationalism, **W2;** German **E2.** *See
also* névrose nationale
Nationalzeitung, III 1
Naumann, C. G., **NP**
Naumburg, I 1, II 1, II 1n, II 2
nausea, I 8, IV 6
Nazarene type, II 4n
Nazi interpretations of Nietzsche, **E2**
Nero, **A1n**
névrose nationale, **W2, W2n, A4**
Neue Zeitschrift für Musik, **H2n**
New Testament, **E2**
New York, III 2
niaiserie, IV 4, IV 4n
Nice, *see* Nizza
Nietzsche: autobiographical details
I 1, and *passim;* ancestors, I 3;
atheism, II 1, II 1n, II 3, **U2;** Basel
period, II 2, II 2n, **H3;** brother-
in-law, *see* Förster, Bernhard; ca-
pacities, II 9; decadence, *see* de-
cadence; diet, III 1; father, I 1,
I 3, I 4, I 5, **H4;** formula for great-
ness, II 10, II 10n; Freud on, **E1,
E1n;** as immoralist, **U2, H6;** inter-
pretations of, **E2;** military service,
W1n; mother, *see* Oehler, Fran-
zisca; musical compositions, II 6,
II 6n; portraits of, **E1;** psychological make-up, I 4, I 5; as psychologist, III 5, III 6; recreations, *see*
recreation; self-evaluation, II 10,
II 10n, III, **A2;** sickness, I 1,
I 6, II 1, II 10, II 10n, **H4, H4n,
H5, Z1n, W1n;** sister, *see* Förster-

Nietzsche, Elisabeth; spiritual diet, II 2; on style, III 4; taste in reading, II 3, III 5; as tragic philosopher, **BT**3; as Wagnerian, II 6, II 6n, H5 (*see also* Wagner); his own will to power, **BT**4, **BT**4n

Nietzsche: works: *The Antichrist*, E1–2, **NP**, **P**4n, II 1n, III 2, T3n, W2n IV 8n; *Beyond Good and Evil*, E1, E2n, **NP**, P3n, II 5, III 1, III 4n, III 5n, III 6, U1n, U2n, U3n, Z4n, Z5n, W2n, IV 1n, A1n; *The Birth of Tragedy*, E1, E2, **BT**3n; *The Case of Wagner*, E1, **NP**, III 1n, T3n, A3, A4; *David Strauss, the Confessor and Writer*, U1n; *The Dawn*, I 1, I 7n, H4, **GS**; *Dionysus Dithyrambs*, **NP**, P5n; "Drunken Song," Z1n; *Ecce Homo* (editions), **NP**; (variants), A1–5; "The Flies of the Market Place," Z5n; *The Gay Science*, E2, II 1n; *On the Genealogy of Morals*, E1, II 1n, U1n, H6; *Human, All-Too-Human*, E2, I 7n, II 4, H6n, IV 7n, A1; "Intermezzo," **NP**; *Laertiana*, II 3, II 3n; "Maxims and Arrows" (in *Twilight*), W3n; *Müssiggang eines Psychologen* (projected title), T3n; *Nietzsche contra Wagner*, E1, **NP**, III 1n, T3n; "Night Song" (in *Zarathustra*), Z4, Z4n, Z7; "On Human Prudence" (in *Zarathustra*), IV 5n; "On the Adder's Bite" (in *Zarathustra*), E2n, I 5n; "On Old and New Tablets" (in *Zarathustra*), Z4, Z4n, Z6, Z6n, IV 4n; "On Redemption" (in *Zarathustra*), Z8n; "On Self-Overcoming" (in *Zarathustra*), IV 2n; "On the Thousand and One Goals" (in *Zarathustra*), IV 4; *On the Use and Disadvantage of History for Life*, U1n; poems, **NP**; "The Plowshare," H2; "Ruhm und Ewigkeit," **NP**; *Schopenhauer as Educator*, U1n, U3, U3n, W4n; "The Seven Seals (or: The Yes and Amen Song)" (in *Zarathustra*), Z6n; "Songs of Prince Free-as-a-Bird."

GS, GSn; *Thus Spoke Zarathustra*, E1–2, **NP**, **P**4, **P**4n, I 3, I 4, I 4n, I 5n, I 7n, I 8, I 8n, II 1n, II 4, III 1, III 3–5, **BT**4, U1n, **GS**, B2, **GM**, W4, IV 2, IV 2n, IV 3–5, IV 4n, IV 5n, IV 8, IV 8n, A4; "To the Mistral," **GS**, **GSn;** *The Twilight of the Idols*, E1, **NP**, P2n, **P**4, **P**4n, P5, P5n, I 2n, I 6n, II 1n, II 3n, III 3n, **BT**3, **BT**3n, H1n, Z7, Z8n, W3n, IV 8n, A5; "The Untimely Ones" (*Untimely Meditations*), U1n, Z5n, W4, W4n, IV 7n; "Upon the Blessed Isles," Z8n (in *Zarathustra*), "Venice" ("Gondola Song"), **NP**, II 7; *Richard Wagner in Bayreuth*, **BT**4, **BT**4n, U1n, U3; *The Wanderer and His Shadow*, I 1, H4; *The Will to Power*, E2, **NP**, II 1n, III 5n, Z1n, W2n, IV 9n; *Werke und Briefe*, Z1n; "Why I Am So Clever" (in *Ecce Homo*), **NP**; "Why I Write Such Good Books" (in *Ecce Homo*), E2; *Zarathustra*, see *Thus Spoke Zarathustra*

nihilists, III 1, **BT**2

Nizza (Nice), II 1, II 10n, Z4, Z4n

noble, nobility, E2, Z5; nobleman, H1, B2n; noble values, *see* values; noble virtues, *see* virtues. *See also* gentilhomme

No-doing, **B**1

Nohl, Karl Friedrich Ludwig, H2, H2n

No-saying, *see* Yes-saying

nothingness, **GM**

nutrition, II 1–3, II 8, II 10, IV 8

O

objectivity, **B**2

Oehler, Franziska (Nietzsche's mother), I 1, I 3

Oehler, Max, I 3n

Offenbach, Jacques, III 3n

opera, **BT**1. *See also* Wagner

optimism, **BT**2, IV 4

Overbeck, Franz, A3, A3n

overman, E2, III 1, Z6, Z8, IV 5

Ovid; *Amores,* **P**3n
Oxford, Earl of, II 4n

P

Pädagogium in Basel, I 4
pain, *see* suffering
Palazzo Carignano, **T**3
Palazzo del Quirinale, **Z**4, **Z**4n
Pallas Athene, II 9n
Paneth, Josef, II 10n
Paraguay, **A**3
Paris, II 2, II 3, II 5, III 2, III 2n
Pascal, Blaise, II 3
pathos, II 10, II 10n, III 4, **BT**3; aggressive, I 7; of distance, **U**3n, **Z**5n; Yes-saying, **Z**1; *pathetisch,* II 10n
Paul, St., **A**1
Persian virtues, IV 3, IV 3n
perspective(s), I 1, I 3, II 1, **BT**1, **W**2, IV 5
pessimism (-ist), **BT**2, IV 4; Greek, **BT**1; pessimistic philosopher, **BT**3
Petronius, **A**1, **A**1n
philologists, II 8
philosophy, philosophers, **E**1, **E**2, **P**3, II 3, II 4, III 2, III 5, **BT**2, **BT**3, **U**3, **U**3n, **D**2, **W**4, IV 6, IV 7, **A**1n, **A**2; Anglo-American, **E**1; German, **E**2, II 3; Junker, III 1; "How One Philosophizes with a a Hammer," **T**, **T**1n; Stoics, **BT**3; tragic philosophers, **BT**3
Piazza Barberini, **Z**4
Piazza Carlo Alberto, **T**3
Piedmont, II 1
Pilate, **E**1
Pindar, **E**1
pity, I 4, I 8n, **BT**3, **H**1, **D**2, **B**2
place, question of, II 2, II 8, II 10
Plato, **E**1, **E**2, **BT**2, **U**3; *Apology,* **E**1, **E**2
pleasure/displeasure, III 5
Po River, **T**3
Podach, Erich F., **E**3, **E**3n, II 10n, III 1n, III 2n, **H**2n, **Z**1n, **Z**4n, **Z**5n, **W**1n, **W**4n, A *passim*
poets, Socrates on, **E**1
Pohl, Richard, **H**2, **H**2n

Poles, I 3, I 7; "Frenchmen among the Slavs," III 2; Polish Diet, I 3n
politics, **W**2, IV 1
pope, II 10n
Portofino, **Z**1
prejudices, II 1, II 1n, **D**1, **D**2
pre-Socratics, **BT**3n
priests, **BT**1, **D**2, **Z**6, **GM**, IV 7
prophet, Nietzsche no, **P**4
Provence, II 2; Provençals, Provençalism, **GS**, **A**1
prudence, II 8, II 9
Prussian(s), II 1n, **U**2; king of, **U**2n; court, **W**3
psychology, **W**2, **W**2n, **W**3, IV 6; *psychologicis,* IV 7; Nietzsche as psychologist, *see* Nietzsche
punishment, I 5, I 5n

R

race, **W**2, **A**4; cleanliness/uncleanliness of, **W**3
Racine, Jean Baptiste, II 3
rank, order of, II 9, **BT**2
Ranke, Leopold von, II 9, II 9n
Rapallo, bay of, **Z**1
rationalism, **E**1; rationality, **BT**1
reader, reading, II 3, II 8, III 5, **H**4; readers of Nietzsche, III 2, **A**1, **W**3; Nietzsche's reading, **A**1
reality (-ies), **P**2, II 1, II 2, II 4, II 10, **H**3, **D**2, **T**2, **W**2, IV 3, IV 4, IV 5; saying Yes to, **BT**2
realization of true self, **U**3n
receiving, *see* giving
Recoaro, **Z**1
recreation(s), II 8, II 10; Nietzsche's, II 3–6, II 6n
redemption, II 1, **Z**8, **Z**8n, IV 8
Rée, Dr. Paul, **E**2, **H**6, **H**6n; Réealism, **H**6
Reformation, **W**2
Reich, see German
religion, **P**4, II 1, IV 1. *See also* Buddha; Christianity; Judaism; priests
Renaissance, II 1, **W**2
repayment of wrong, I 5
ressentiment, **E**2, I 6, II 6n, **H**4n, **GM**

retaliation, I 5
revaluation of values, *see* values
revenge, III 5; vengefulness, I 7
Richter, Raoul, E3, II 10n, W4n, A3
Ritschl, Friedrich, II 9, III 2
Röcken, I 3, II 9n
Rohde, Erwin, H2n
Rome, Z4, Z4n, W1n
Rossini, Gioacchino Antonio, II 7
rudeness, I 5
Russians, III 2, W3; Russian fatal-
    ism, I 6

S

sage, E1, P4
saint(s), P2, P4, III 1, H1, D2, Z2
St. Moritz, I 1
St. Petersburg, III 2
Sallust, II 1
Salomé, Lou, E2, Z1, Z1n
salvation of the soul, D2, IV 8
Santa Margherita, Z1
Sartre, Jean-Paul, E2; *The Flies,* I
    5n, II 1n, Z5n
satyr(s), E2, P2, II 4
Schlechta, Karl, II 1n, BT4n
science, U1, U1n, GS, Z2, B2, W2;
    scientific manners, W1
Selbstsucht, Selbstzucht, U1n
Selbsttierquäler, II 4n
self-defense, instinct of, II 8, U3
self-denier, IV 8
self-discipline, II 9, U1, U1n, U3, H5
selfishness, II 9, II 10, IV 7n
selfless, selflessness, II 2, H4, H4n,
    D2, IV 7, IV 8; selfless drives, I 4,
    II 9; German selflessness, W1
self-love, *see* love
self-preservation, instinct of, II 8, II
    9, D2
seriousness, D2, A1; great, Z2; Pari-
    sian, II 5
sex, III 5, H2n, IV 7
Shakespeare, William, E1, II 3, II 4,
    II 4n, Z6, W4n; *Troilus and Cres-
    sida,* W4n
Shaw, George Bernard, E2
Sicily, GS
sickness, P4, I 6, II 5, II 10, W2, IV

8; Nietzsche's sickness, *see* Nietz-
    sche
silence, I 5, B2, A1
Sils Maria, I 4, II 1, T3; *Nietzsche
    Haus,* Z1n
Silser See, Z1n
Silvaplana, lake of, Z1
sin, II 10, III 5, IV 8
small, the, Z5, Z5n; little things, II
    10; small facts, B2
Socrates, E1, E2, I 1, III 6n, BT1,
    BT1n, BT2, BT3, U3; *Apology,*
    E2; pre-Socratics, BT3n
solitude, I 2, I 8, II 10, Z5, Z6, A4,
    A4n
Sophocles, E1
Sorrento, H5
soul, II 10, III 2, III 6, D1, Z2, IV 7,
    IV 8; A1; beautiful souls, III 3, III
    5, H2, IV 4; great souls, Z6, Z6n
Spencer, Herbert, IV 4, IV 4n
spirit(s), P3, II 1, II 2, II 3, III 3,
    BT3, U2, H2, Z6, GM, W3, IV
    1, IV 7, IV 8; free, U2, H1, G3;
    German, E3, II 1, U2, W3; Yes-
    and-No saying, E2, Z6
spiritual diet, IV 8
Spitteler, Carl, III 1, III 1n
Stein, Heinrich von, I 4, I 4n, III 1
Steiner, Rudolf, E2
Stendhal, II 3, U2, W3
Sterne, Laurence, A1
Stoa, Stoics, BT3
Stöcker, Hofprediger, Z1n
Stockholm, III 2
Strauss, David Friedrich, I 7, I 7n,
    U1n, U2
strength, BT2, D2; the strong, BT2
style, Nietzsche's, III 4
success, U2
suffering, E2, BT2, H4n, Z1, IV 8;
    from multitudes, II 10
Surlei, rock, Z1, Z1n
Swabians, U2
Switzerland, II 5n, II 7n, III 1

T

Taine, Hippolyte, II 3, III 2, III 2n
taste, II 8; H1; German, W1
tea, II 1

Teichmüller, Gustav, **U2n**
tempo, III 4, III 4n
Teutons, II 6, **W2**, **W4**. *See also* Germans; Germany
Therese, Princess of Saxe-Altenburg, I 3
Thibault, Jacques Anatole, *see* France, Anatole
"thing in itself, the," **H1**
Thucydides, **E2**
Thuringia, II 2, II 2n
tragedy, **E1**, **E2**, **BT3**; birth, death, and rebirth, of, **E1**; Greek, **E2**, **BT1**; tragic pathos, **Z1**; tragic philosopher, **BT3**. *See also* Nietzsche: works: *The Birth of Tragedy*
Treitschke, Heinrich von, **U2**, **W2**, **W2n**, **W3**
Tribschen, II 5, II 5n, II 6n, **H2**
Tristram Shandy, **A1**
Trumpeter of Sakkingen, **W1**, **W1n**
truth(s), **P3**, II 1, II 1n, II 4, II 10, III 2, **BT2**, **D2**, **Z3**, **Z6**, **GM**, **T1**, **T1n**, **T2**, **W2**, IV 1, IV 3–5, IV 8; true world, **P2**
Tsar, the, **B2**
Tübingen, **U2n**
Turin, II 1, II 1n, II 2, II 7n, II 8, III 2, **T3**

U

Ulysses, Shakespeare's, **W4n**
uncleanliness, German, **W3**, **W4n**
unegoistic, *see* egoistic
Upper Engadine, **P1**, **P1n**, I 4, **T3**

V

value(s), II 1, **BT1**, **Z2**, **W2**, IV 7; noble, **GM**; revaluation of, **E2**, I 1, II 9, III 1, **H6**, **D1**, **B1**, **GM**, **T3**, **T3n**, **W4**, **W4n**, IV 1, IV 7, IV 7n
Van Gogh, Vincent, **E1**
Varro, **A1n**
Veda, **Z6**
vegetarianism, II 1
Velde, Henry van de, **E3**

Venetian cookbook, II 1
Venice, II 2, II 7, **Z1**
Viaud, Louis Marie Julien, *see* Loti
"vice," III 5
Vicenza, **Z1**
Vienna, III 2
virtues, I 5, II 10, **A1**; German, II 5, **H2**; noble, I 4; Persian, IV 3, IV 3n
Vischer, Friedrich Theodor, **W2**, **W2n**
Vittorio Emanuele, **T3**, **T3n**
vivisection, **A3**
vocation, **H3**
Voltaire, **E2**, **H1**, **H1n**, IV 8n

W

Wagner, Cosima, II 3, II 4n, **W1n**
Wagner, Richard, **E1**, **E2**, I 4n, I 7, I 7n, I 8n, II 1, II 4, II 4n, II 5, II 5n, II 6, **BT1**, **BT4**, **U1**, **U3**, **H2**, **H2n**, **H3**, **H5**, **H6**, **Z1**, **W1–4**, **A3**, **A4**; music, *see* music; Wagnerian morass, **I** 4; Wagnerism, **BT1**; Works: *Die Meistersinger,* II 6, II 6n; *Parsifal,* I 8n, III 1, **BT1**, **H5**, **Z4n**; *Ring,* II 6, **A3n**; "Siegfried Idyll," II 7; *Tannhäuser,* II 6n; *Tristan und Isolde,* II 6, II 6n
war, **I** 7, I 7n, III 5, **BT3**, **H1**, **B**, **A5**
"Wars of Liberation," **W2**, **A4**
weak, weakness, **BT2**, IV 4, IV 8
Weimar, I 3
well-turned person, the, **P2n**
Widmann, J. V., III 1, III 1n, IV 1n
Wiehe, II 9n
Wilhelm I, **H2n**, **Z1n**; Wilhelm II, II 5n, **Z1n**
will, I 4, **T2**, **W2**; free will, I 6, I 6n, IV 8; will to create, **Z8**; to the end, **D2**, **GM**; good will, IV 7; will to lie, IV 7; to life, II 1, **BT3**; will to power, **BT4**, **BT4n**, **W1**, **W1n**, IV 4; hybrids of sickness and, **P4**; Nietzsche's own will to power, **BT4**, **BT4n**
woman, women, I 7, II 1, III 2, III 5, **W3**
World War I, **E2**; World War II, **E2**

Wörth, Battle of, **BT**1
Württembergers, **U**2
Würzburg, **U**2

Y

Yes-saying, **E**2, **BT**2, **BT**3, **U**2, **H**4n,
   D1, **Z**6, **B**1, **B**2, **W**1, **W**2, **IV** 1, **IV**
   2, **IV** 4, **IV** 8, **A**4; *Dawn* as a Yes-
saying book, **GS**; pathos; *see*
pathos; Yes and Amen, **Z**6, **Z**6n

Z

Zeus, II 9n
Ziègler, Henri de, III 1n
Zoagli, road to, **Z**1

Commentary

MARTIN HEIDEGGER

ALBERT CAMUS

GILLES DELEUZE

MARTIN HEIDEGGER

[The] word *nihilism* came into vogue through Turgeniev as a name for the notion that only what is perceptible to our senses, that is, only beings that one experiences oneself, only these and nothing else are real and have being. Therefore, anything grounded on tradition, authority, or any other definitive value is negated. Usually, however, the name *positivism* is used to designate this point of view.

For Nietzsche, though, the word *nihilism* means something substantially "more." Nietzsche speaks about "European nihilism." He does not mean the positivism that arose in the mid-nineteenth century and spread throughout Europe. "European" has a historical significance here, and means as much as "Western" in the sense of Western history. Nietzsche uses *nihilism* as the name for the historical movement that he was the first to recognize and that already governed the previous century while defining the century to come, the movement whose essential interpretation he concentrates in the terse sentence: "God is dead." That is to say, the "Christian God" has lost His power over beings and over the determination of man. "Christian God" also stands for the "transcendent" in general in its various meanings—for "ideals" and "norms," "principles" and "rules," "ends" and "values," which are set *above* the being, in order to give being as a whole a purpose, an order, and—as it is succintly expressed—"meaning." Nihilism is that historical process whereby the dominance of the "transcendent" becomes null and void, so that all being loses its worth and meaning. Nihilism is the history of the being itself, through which the death of the Christian God comes slowly but inexorably to light. It may be that this God will continue to be believed in, and that His world will be taken as "real," "effectual," and "determinative." This history resembles the process in which the light of a star that has been extinguished for millennia still gleams, but in its gleaming nonetheless remains a mere "appearance." For Nietzsche, therefore, nihilism is in no way some kind of viewpoint "put forward" by somebody, nor is it an arbitrary historical "given," among many others, that can be historically documented. Nihilism is, rather, that event of long duration in which the truth of being as a whole is essentially transformed and driven toward an end that such truth has determined.

The truth of being as a whole has long been called *metaphysics*. Every era, every human epoch, is sustained by some metaphysics and is placed thereby in a definite relation to being as a whole and also to itself. The end of metaphysics discloses itself as the collapse of the reign of the transcendent and the "ideal" that sprang from it. But the end of metaphysics does not mean the cessation of history. It is the *beginning* of a serious concern with that "event": "God is dead." That beginning is already under way. Nietzsche himself understood his philosophy as an introduction to the beginning of a new age. He envisioned the coming century—that is, the current, twentieth century—as the start of an era whose upheavals could not be compared to anything previously known. Although the scenery of the world theater might remain the same for a time, the play in performance would already be a different one. The fact that earlier aims now disappear and former values are devalued is no longer experienced as sheer annihilation and deplored as wasteful and wrong, but is rather greeted as a liberation, touted as an irrevocable gain, and perceived as a *fulfillment*.

"Nihilism" is the increasingly dominant truth that all prior aims of being have become superfluous. But with this transformation of the erstwhile relation to ruling values, nihilism has also perfected itself for the free and genuine task of a *new* valuation. Such nihilism, which is in itself perfected and is decisive for the future, may be characterized as "classical nihilism." Nietzsche describes his own "metaphysics" with this name and conceives it to be *the* counterstroke to all preceding metaphysics. The name *nihilism* thus loses the purely nihilistic sense in which it means a destruction and annihilation of previous values, the mere negation of beings and the futility of human history.

"Nihilism," thought now in its classic sense, calls for freedom *from* values as freedom *for* a *revaluation* of all (such) values. Nietzsche uses the expression "revaluation of all values hitherto" alongside the key word *nihilism* as another *major rubric* by which he assigns his own fundamental metaphysical position its definite place within the history of Western metaphysics.

From the rubric "revaluation of values," we expect that altered values will be posited in place of earlier ones. But for Nietzsche "revaluation" means that the very "place" for previous values disappears, not merely that the values themselves fall away. This implies that the nature and direction of valuation, and the definition of the essence of value are transformed. The revaluation thinks Being for the first time as value. With it, metaphysics begins to be value thinking. In accordance with this transformation, prior values do not merely succumb to devaluation but, above all, the *need* for values in their former shape and in their previous place—that is to say, their place in the transcendent—is uprooted. The uprooting of past needs most assuredly takes place by cultivating the growing ignorance of past values and by obliterating history through a revision of its basic traits. "Revaluation of prior values" is primarily the metamorphosis of all valuation heretofore and the "breeding" of a new need for values.

If such revaluation of all prior values is not only to be carried out but is also to be grounded, then it has need of a "new principle"; that is, the establishment of a basis for defining beings as a whole in a new, authoritative way. But if the interpretation of beings as a whole cannot issue from a transcendent that is posited "over" them from the outset, then the new values and their standard of measure can only be drawn from the realm of beings themselves. Thus beings themselves require a new interpretation through which their basic character may be defined in a way that will make it fit to serve as a "principle" for the inscription of a new table of values and as a standard of measure for suitably ranking such values.

If the essence of metaphysics consists in grounding the truth of being as a whole, then the revaluation of all values, as a grounding of the principle for a new valuation, is itself metaphysics. What Nietzsche perceives and posits as the basic character of being as a whole is what he calls the "will to power." That concept does not merely delimit *what* a being in its Being *is:* Nietzsche's phrase, "will to power," which has in many ways become familiar, contains his interpretation of the *essence of power.* Every power is a power only as long as it is more power; that is to say, an increase in power. Power can maintain itself in itself, that is, in its essence, only if it overtakes and overcomes the power level it has already attained—*overpowering* is the expression we use. As soon as power stalls at a certain power level, it immediately becomes powerless. "Will to power" does not mean simply the "romantic" yearning and quest for power by those who have no power; rather, "will to power" means the accruing of power by power for its own overpowering.

"Will to power" is a single name for the basic character of beings and for the essence of power. Nietzsche often substitutes "force" for "will to power" in a way that is easily misunderstood. His conception of the basic character of beings as will to power is not the contrivance or whim of a fantast who has strayed off of chase chimeras. It is the fundamental experience of a *thinker;* that is, of one of those individuals who have no choice but to find words for what a being *is* in the history of its Being. Every being, insofar as it *is,* and is *as* it is, is "will to power." The phrase names that from which all valuation proceeds and to which it returns. However, as we have said, the new valuation is not a "revaluation of all prior values" merely in that it supplants all earlier values with power, the uppermost value, but first and foremost because power and *only power* posits values, validates them, and makes decisions about the possible justifications of a valuation. If all being is will to power, then only what is fulfilled in its essence by power "has" value or "is" a value. But power is power only as enhancement of power. To the extent that it is truly power, alone determining all beings, power does not recognize the worth or value of anything outside of itself. That is why will to power as a principle for the new valuation tolerates no end outside of being as a whole. Now, because all beings as will to power—that is, as incessant self-overpowering—must be *a continual "becoming,"* and because such "becoming" cannot move "toward an end" *outside* its own "farther and farther," but is ceaselessly caught up in the cyclical increase of power to which it reverts, then being as a whole too, as this power-conforming becoming, must itself always recur again and bring back the same.

Hence, the basic character of beings as will to power is also defined as "the eternal recurrence of the same." The latter constitutes yet another major rubric in Nietzsche's metaphysics and, moreover, implies something essential: *only* through the adequately conceived essence of will to power can it become clear why the Being of beings as a whole must be eternal recurrence of the same. The reverse holds as well: only through the essence of the eternal recurrence of the same can the innermost core of will to power and its necessity be grasped. The phrase "will to power" tells *what* beings are in their "essence" (in their constitution). The phrase "eternal recurrence of the same" tells *how* beings of such an essence must as a whole be.

It remains for us to observe what is decisive here; namely, that Nietzsche had to think the eternal recurrence of the same *before* the will to power. The most essential thought is thought first.

When Nietzsche himself insists that Being, as "life," is in essence "*becoming*," he does not intend the roughly defined concept of "becoming" to mean either an endless, continual progression to some unknown goal, nor is he thinking about the confused turmoil and tumult of unrestrained drives. The vague and hackneyed term *becoming* signifies the overpowering of power, as the essence of power, which powerfully and continually returns to itself in its own way.

At the same time, the eternal recurrence of the same offers the keenest interpretation of "classical nihilism," which absolutely obliterates any end above and beyond beings. For such nihilism, the words "God is dead" suggest the impotence not only of the Christian God but of every transcendent element under which men might want to shelter themselves. And that impotence signifies the collapse of the old order.

With the revaluation of all past values, an unrestricted challenge has been issued to men: that unconditionally from, through, and over themselves, they raise "new standards" under which the accommodation of being as a whole to a new order must be effected. Because the "transcendent," the "beyond," and "heaven" have been abolished, only the "earth" remains. The new order must therefore be the absolute dominance of pure power over the earth through man—not through any arbitrary kind of man, and certainly not through the humanity that has heretofore lived under the old values. Through what kind of man, then?

With nihilism—that is to say, with the revaluation of all prior values among beings as will to power and in light of the eternal recurrence of the same—it becomes necessary to posit a new essence for man. But, because "God is dead," only man himself can grant man his measure and center, the "*type*," the "model" of a certain kind of man who has assigned the task of a revaluation of all values to the individual power of his will to power and who is prepared to embark on the absolute domination of the globe. Classical nihilism, which as the revaluation of all values hitherto understands beings as will to power and can admit eternal recurrence of the same as the sole "end," must take man himself—that is, man as he has been until now—out of and "over" himself and must fashion as his measure the figure of the "Overman."

From Nietzsche's point of view, the Overman is not meant to be a mere amplification of prior man, but the most unequivocally singular form of human existence that, as absolute will to power, is brought to power in every man to some degree and that thereby grants him his membership in being as a whole—that is, in will to power—and that shows him to be a true "being," close to reality and "life." The Overman simply leaves the man of traditional values behind, *overtakes* him, and transfers the justification for all laws and the positing of all values to the empowering of power. An act or accomplishment is valid as such only to the extent that it serves to equip, nurture, and enhance will to power.

The five main rubrics we have mentioned—"nihilism," "revaluation of all values hitherto," "will to power," "eternal recurrence of the same," and "Overman"—each portrays Nietzsche's metaphysics from just *one* perspective, although in each case it is a perspective that defines the whole. Thus Nietzsche's metaphysics is grasped only when what is named in these five headings can be thought—that is, essentially experienced—in its primordial and heretofore merely intimated conjunction. We can learn what "nihilism" in Nietzsche's sense is only if we also comprehend, in their contexts, "revaluation of all values hitherto," "will to power," "eternal recurrence of the same," and "Overman." By starting from an adequate comprehension of nihilism and working in the opposite direction, we can also acquire knowledge about the essence of revaluation, the essence of will to power, the essence of the eternal recurrence of the same, and the essence of the Overman. But to have such knowledge is to stand within the moment that the history of Being has opened up for our age.

The necessity of having to think the essence of "nihilism" in the context of the "revaluation of all values," "will to power," "eternal recurrence of the same," and the "Overman" lets us readily surmise that the essence of nihilism is in itself manifold, multileveled, and multifarious.

The word *nihilism* therefore permits many applications. It can be mis-used as an empty slogan or epithet that both repels and discredits and that conceals the user's own thoughtlessness from him. But we can also ex-perience the full burden of what the name says when uttered in *Nietz-sche's* sense. Here it means to think the history of Western metaphysics as the ground of our own history; that is, of future decisions. Finally, we can ponder more essentially what Nietzsche was thinking in using this word if we grasp his "classical nihilism" as *that* nihilism *whose "classi-cism" consists in the fact that it must unwittingly put itself on extreme guard against knowledge of its innermost essence.* Classical nihilism, then, discloses itself as the fulfillment of nihilism, whereby it considers itself exempt from the necessity of thinking about the very thing that constitutes its essence: the *nihil,* the nothing—as the veil that conceals the truth of the Being of beings.

From *Nihilism,* vol. 5, edited by David Farrell Krell, translated by Frank A. Capuzzi, originally published as part of *Nietzsche, Zweiter Band* (1961)

ALBERT CAMUS

With Nietzsche, nihilism seems to become prophetic. But we can draw no conclusions from Nietzsche, except the base and mediocre cruelty that he hated with all his strength, unless we give first place in his work—well ahead of the prophet—to the diagnostician. The provisional, methodical, strategic character of his thought cannot be doubted for a moment. With him, nihilism becomes conscious for the first time. Diag-nosticians have this in common with prophets—they think and operate in terms of the future. Nietzsche never thought except in terms of an apoc-alypse to come, not in order to extol it, for he guessed the sordid and cal-culating aspect that this apocalypse would finally assume, but in order to avoid it and to transform it into a renaissance. He recognized nihilism for what it was and examined it like a clinical fact.

He said of himself that he was the first complete nihilist of Europe. Not by choice, but by condition, and because he was too great to refuse the heritage of his time. He diagnosed in himself, and in others, the in-ability to believe and the disappearance of the primitive foundation of all faith—namely the belief in life. The "Can one live as a rebel?" became

with him "Can one live, believing in nothing?" His reply is in the affirmative. Yes, if one creates a system out of absence of faith, if one accepts
the final consequences of nihilism, and if, on emerging into the desert
and putting one's confidence in what is going to come, one feels, with the
same primitive instinct, both pain and joy.

[. . .]

Nietzsche's philosophy, undoubtedly, revolves around the problem
of rebellion. More precisely, it begins by being a rebellion. But we sense
the change of position that Nietzsche makes. With him, rebellion begins
at "God is dead" which is assumed as an established fact; then rebellion
hinges on everything that aims at falsely replacing the vanished deity and
reflects dishonour on a world which undoubtedly has no direction but
which remains the only proving-ground of the gods.

Contrary to the opinion of certain of his Christian critics, Nietzsche
did not form a project to kill God. He found Him dead in the soul of his
contemporaries. He was the first to understand the immense importance
of the event and to decide that this rebellion among men could not lead
to a renaissance unless it were controlled and directed. Any other attitude
towards it, whether it were regret or complacency, must lead to the apocalypse. Thus Nietzsche did not formulate a philosophy of rebellion, but
constructed a philosophy on rebellion.

[. . .]

In Nietzsche's mind, the only problem was to see that the human
spirit bowed proudly to the inevitable. We know, however, his posterity
and the kind of politics that were to be authorized by the man who
claimed to be the last anti-political German. He dreamed of tyrants who
were artists. But tyranny comes more naturally than art to mediocre men.
"Rather Cesare Borgia than Parsifal," he exlaimed. He begat both Caesar
and Borgia, but devoid of the distinction of feeling which he attributed to
the great men of the Renaissance. As a result of his insistence that the individual should bow before the eternity of the species and should sub-
merge himself in the great cycle of time, race has been turned into a
special aspect of the species and the individual has been made to bow before this sordid god. The life of which he spoke with such fear and trembling has been degraded to a sort of biology for domestic use. Finally a
race of vulgar overlords, with a blundering desire for power, adopted, in

his name, the "anti-semitic deformity" on which he never ceased to pour scorn.

In the history of intelligence, with the exception of Marx, Nietzsche's adventure has no equivalent: we shall never finish making reparation for the injustice done to him. Of course history records other philosophies that have been misconstrued and betrayed. But up to the time of Nietzsche and national socialism, it was quite without parallel that a process of thought—brilliantly illuminated by the nobility and by the sufferings of an exceptional mind—should have been demonstrated to the eyes of the world by a parade of lies and by the hideous accumulation of corpses from concentration camps. The doctrine of the superman led to the methodical creation of submen—a fact that doubtless should be denounced but which also demands interpretation. If the final result of the great movement of rebellion in the nineteenth and twentieth centuries was to be this ruthless bondage then surely rebellion should be rejected and Nietzsche's desperate cry to his contemporaries taken up: "My conscience and yours are no longer the same conscience."

From "Metaphysical Rebellion," in *The Rebel,* translated by Anthony Bower (1951)

GILLES DELEUZE

The eternal return is as badly misunderstood as the will to power. Every time we understand the eternal return as the return of a particular arrangement of things after all the other arrangements have been realised, every time we interpret the eternal return as the return of the identical or the same, we replace Nietzsche's thought with childish hypotheses. No one extended the critique of all forms of identity further than Nietzsche. On two occasions in *Zarathustra* Nietzsche explicitly denies that the eternal return is a circle which makes the same return. The eternal return is the strict opposite of this since it cannot be separated from a selection, from a double selection. Firstly, there is the selection of willing or of thought which constitutes Nietzsche's ethics: only will that of which one also wills the eternal return (to eliminate all half-willing, everything which can only be willed with the proviso "once, only once"). Secondly, there is the selection of being which constitutes Nietzsche's ontology: only that which *becomes* in the fullest sense of the word can return, is fit to return. Only action and affirmation return: becoming has being and only becoming has being. That which is opposed to becoming, the same or the identical, strictly speaking, *is* not. The negative as the lowest degree of power, the reactive as the lowest degree of force, do not return because they are the opposite of becoming and only becoming has being. We can thus see how the eternal return is linked, not to a repetition of the same, but on the contrary, to a transmutation. It is the moment or the eternity of becoming which eliminates all that resists it. It releases, indeed it creates, the purely active and pure affirmation. And this is the sole content of the Overman; he is the joint product of the will to power and the eternal return, Dionysus and Ariadne. This is why Nietzsche says that the will to power is not wanting, coveting or seeking power, but only "giving" or "creating."

But the difficulty of Nietzsche depends less on conceptual analysis than on practical evaluations which evoke a whole atmosphere, all kinds of emotional dispositions in the reader. Like Spinoza, Nietzsche always maintained that there is the deepest relationship between concept and affect. Conceptual analyses are indispensable and Nietzsche takes them further than anyone else. But they will always be ineffective if the reader grasps them in an atmosphere which is not that of Nietzsche. As long as the reader persists in: 1) seeing the Nietzschean "slave" as someone who finds himself dominated by a master, and deserves to be; 2) understanding the will to power as a will which wants and seeks power; 3) conceiving the eternal return as the tedious return of the same; 4) imagining the Overman as a given master race—no positive relationship between Nietzsche and his reader will be possible. Nietzsche will appear a nihilist, or worse, a fascist and at best as an obscure and terrifying prophet. Nietzsche knew this, he knew the fate that lay in store for him, he who gave Zarathustra an "ape" or "buffoon" as a double, foretelling that Zarathustra would be confused with his ape (a prophet, a fascist or a madman . . .). This is why a book about Nietzsche must try hard to correct the practical or emotional misunderstanding as well as re-establishing the conceptual analysis.

And it is indeed true that Nietzsche diagnosed nihilism as the movement which carries history forward. No one has analysed the concept of nihilism better than he did, he invented the concept. But it is important to see that he defined it in terms of the triumph of reactive forces or the negative in the will to power. To nihilism he opposed transmutation, that is the becoming which is simultaneously the only action of force and the only affirmation of power, the transhistoric element of man, the Overman (and not the superman). The Overman is the focal point, where the reactive (*ressentiment* and bad conscience) is conquered, and where the negative gives way to affirmation. Nietzsche remains inseparable, at every moment, from the forces of the future, from the forces yet to come that his prayers invoke, that his thought outlines, that his art prefigures. He not only diagnoses, as Kafka put it, the diabolical forces already knocking at the door, but he exorcises them by raising the last Power capable of struggling with them, against them, and of ousting them both within us and outside us. A Nietzschean "aphorism" is not a mere fragment, a morsel of thought: it is a proposition which only makes sense in relation to the state of forces that it expresses, and which changes sense, which must change sense, according to the new forces which it is "capable" (has the power) of attracting.

And without doubt this is the most important point of Nietzsche's philosophy: the radical transformation of the image of thought that we create for ourselves. Nietzsche snatches thought from the element of truth and falsity. He turns it into an interpretation and an evaluation, interpretation of forces, evaluation of power.—It is a thought-movement, not merely in the sense that Nietzsche wants to reconcile thought and concrete movement, but in the sense that thought itself must produce movements, bursts of extraordinary speed and slowness (here again we can see the role of the aphorism, with its variable speeds and its "projectile-like" movement). As a result philosophy has a new relationship to the arts of movement: theatre, dance and music. Nietzsche was never satisfied with the discourse or the dissertation (*logos*) as an expression of philosophical thought, although he wrote the finest dissertations—notably the *Genealogy of Morals,* to which all modern ethnology owes an inexhaustible "debt." But a book like *Zarathustra* can only be read as a modern opera and seen and heard as such. It is not that Nietzsche produces a philosophical opera or a piece of allegorical theatre, but he creates a piece of theatre or an opera which directly expresses thought

as experience and movement. And when Nietzsche says that the Overman resembles a Borgia rather than a Parsifal, or that he is a member of
both the order of Jesuits and the Prussian officer corps, it would be
wrong to see these as protofascist statements, since they are the remarks
of a director indicating how the Overman should be "played" (rather like
Kierkegaard saying that the knight of the faith is like a bourgeois in his
Sunday best).—To think is to create: this is Nietzsche's greatest lesson.
To think, to cast the dice . . . : this was already the sense of the eternal return.

From *Nietzsche and Philosophy,* translated by Hugh Tomlinson (1983)

Reading Group Guide

1. Nietzsche remains one of the most influential philosophers of our time. As Walter Kaufmann notes, "No other philosopher since Plato and Aristotle, with the exception of Kant and Hegel, has influenced so many widely different thinkers and writers so profoundly." What are some of the main aspects of Nietzsche's influence, and what are some of the factors that account for his tremendous and enduring influence?

2. One of Nietzsche's major themes is the idea of "the eternal recurrence." What do you think Nietzsche was attempting to do with this idea? What does he seem to mean by it? What are its implications?

3. As Peter Gay notes, Nietzsche has been one of the most persistently misunderstood writers in the history of Western thought. What are some of the misunderstandings that have attended his work? Are some thinkers more easily misappropriated than others?

4. Nietzsche's style is particularly iconoclastic and unique; as Walter Kaufmann notes, "Nietzsche clearly wanted to be read with a delighted awareness of nuances of style and thought." Discuss how Nietzsche's style—which often condenses complex ideas into seemingly simple phrases—works to inform your reading or understanding of his thought. Is Nietzsche's style inseparable from his meaning?

5. One of Nietzsche's favorite devices is the aphorism. Why is this form significant for Nietzsche? What does he accomplish by writing in this way? Can all of his writing be said to be in some way aphoristic?

6. For Nietzsche, the most important philosophy is always "untimely," and Nietzsche had a particularly complicated and contentious relationship toward many of his contemporaries, for instance Wagner. Discuss Nietzsche's various attitudes toward his contemporaries as stated in *Basic Writings,* and conversely the ideas, figures, and ways of thinking that Nietzsche seems to find most sympathetic to his own philosophy.

7. Nietzsche has been considered a nihilist, and also a philosopher who more than anything sought to transcend nihilism. Discuss the idea of nihilism in broad terms, and Nietzsche's use or development of this idea.

8. What, for Nietzsche, is the "will to power"?

9. Throughout Nietzsche's work is a call for a new philosophy, for radical breaks with various conventional ideas and methodologies, and for new philosophers. What are some of Nietzsche's hopes for the future of philosophy?

A Note on the Type

The principal text of this Modern Library edition
was set in Times Roman, designed by Stanley Morison
specifically for *The Times* of London. The typeface was
introduced in the newspaper in 1932. Times Roman
has had its greatest success in the United States
as a book and commercial typeface, rather
than one used in newspapers.